Middle School 2-2
학교시험 완벽대비

2학기 전과정

적중 100plus

영어 기출문제집

중2
천재 │ 정사열

Best Collection

구성과 특징

교과서의 주요 학습 내용을 중심으로 학습 영역별 특성에 맞춰 단계별로 다양한 학습 기회를 제공하여
단원별 학습능력 평가는 물론 중간 및 기말고사 시험 등에 완벽하게 대비할 수 있도록 내용을 구성

Words & Expressions

Step1　Key Words 단원별 핵심 단어 설명 및 풀이
　　　　Key Expression 단원별 핵심 숙어 및 관용어 설명
　　　　Word Power 반대 또는 비슷한 뜻 단어 배우기
　　　　English Dictionary 영어로 배우는 영어 단어

Step2　실력평가 단원별 수시평가 대비 주관식, 객관식 문제풀이

Step3　서술형 대비 학업성취도 및 수행능력평가 대비 서술형 문제풀이

Conversation

Step1　핵심 의사소통 소통에 필요한 주요 표현 방법 요약
　　　　핵심 Check 기본적인 표현 방법 및 활용능력 확인

Step2　대화문 익히기 교과서 대화문 심층 분석 및 확인

Step3　교과서 확인학습 빈칸 채우기를 통한 문장 완성 능력 확인

Step4　기본평가 시험대비 기초 학습 능력 평가

Step5　실력평가 단원별 수시평가 대비 주관식, 객관식 문제풀이

Step6　서술형 대비 학업성취도 및 수행능력평가 대비 서술형 문제풀이

Grammar

Step1　주요 문법 단원별 주요 문법 사항과 예문을 알기 쉽게 설명

　　　　핵심 Check 기본 문법사항에 대한 이해 여부 확인

Step2　기본평가 시험대비 기초 학습 능력 평가

Step3　실력평가 단원별 수시평가 대비 주관식, 객관식 문제풀이

Step4　서술형 대비 학업성취도 및 수행능력평가 대비 서술형 문제풀이

Reading

Step1　구문 분석 단원별로 제시된 문장에 대한 구문별 분석과 내용 설명
　　　　확인문제 문장에 대한 기본적인 이해와 인지능력 확인

Step2　확인학습A 빈칸 채우기를 통한 문장 완성 능력 확인

Step3　확인학습B 제시된 우리말을 영어로 완성하여 작문 능력 키우기

Step4　실력평가 단원별 수시평가 대비 주관식, 객관식 문제풀이

Step5　서술형 대비 학업성취도 및 수행능력평가 대비 서술형 문제풀이
　　　　교과시 구식구식 교과서에 나오는 기타 문장까지 완벽 학습

Composition

|영역별 핵심문제|

단어 및 어휘, 대화문, 문법, 독해 등 각 영역별 기출문제의
출제 유형을 분석하여 실전에 대비하고 연습할 수 있도록 문
제를 배열

|단원별 예상문제|

기출문제를 분석한 후 새로운 시험 출제 경향을 더하여 새롭
게 출제될 수 있는 문제를 포함하여 시험에 완벽하게 대비할
수 있도록 준비

|서술형 실전 및 창의사고력 문제|

학교 시험에서 점차 늘어나는 서술형 시험에 집중 대비하고
고득점을 취득하는데 만전을 기하기 위한 학습 코너

|단원별 모의고사|

영역별, 단계별 학습을 모두 마친 후 실전 연습을 위한
모의고사

on the textbook

교과서 파헤치기

- 단어Test1~3 영어 단어 우리말 쓰기, 우리말을 영어 단어로 쓰기, 영영풀이에 해당하는 단어와 우리말 쓰기
- 대화문Test1~2 대화문 빈칸 완성 및 전체 대화문 쓰기
- 본문Test1~5 빈칸 완성, 우리말 쓰기, 문장 배열연습, 영어 작문하기 복습 등 단계별 반복 학습을 통해 교
 과서 지문에 대한 완벽한 습득
- 구석구석지문Test1~2 지문 빈칸 완성 및 전문 영어로 쓰기

Lesson 5

Shapes Around Us

 의사소통 기능

- 능력 여부 묻기
 Do you know how to solve this puzzle?

- 열거하기
 First, draw a square. Then, draw a triangle.
 Finally, draw a circle.

언어 형식

- 의문사+to부정사
 I don't know **how to spin** this.

- 동사+목적어+형용사(목적격 보어) (5형식)
 Square decided to **make** the room **better**.

Words & Expressions

Key Words

- **boil** [bɔil] 동 끓이다
- **bookshelf** [búkʃelf] 명 책꽂이
- **carry** [kǽri] 동 옮기다
- **choose** [tʃuːz] 동 고르다, 선택하다
- **circle** [sɔ́ːrkl] 명 원
- **complain** [kəmpléin] 동 불평하다
- **control** [kəntróul] 동 통제하다, 조절하다
- **decide** [disáid] 동 결정하다
- **difficult** [dífikʌlt] 형 어려운
- **divide** [diváid] 동 나누다
- **dot** [dɑt] 명 점
- **draw** [drɔː] 동 (그림을) 그리다
- **dried fish** 마른 생선, 건어물
- **dried soup** 건조 수프
- **excited** [iksáitid] 형 흥분된
- **exercise** [éksərsàiz] 동 운동하다
- **face** [feis] 동 마주하다
- **finally** [fáinəli] 부 마지막으로
- **half** [hæf] 명 반, 절반
- **hanger** [hǽŋər] 명 옷걸이
- **hold** [hould] 동 잡고 있다, 지탱하다
- **hot pepper** (매운) 고추
- **hula hoop** 훌라후프
- **hurry** [hɔ́ːri] 동 서두르다
- **hurt** [həːrt] 동 다치게 하다
- **jacket** [dʒǽkit] 명 윗옷
- **mess** [mes] 명 혼잡, 혼란
- **move** [muːv] 명 움직임, 이동 동 움직이다

- **must** [məst] 조 ~임에 틀림없다
- **perfect** [pɔ́ːrfikt] 형 완벽한
- **plastic bag** 비닐봉지
- **pointy** [pɔ́inti] 형 끝이 뾰족한
- **press** [pres] 동 누르다
- **puzzle** [pʌ́zl] 명 퍼즐, 수수께끼
- **realize** [ríːəlàiz] 동 깨닫다, 알아차리다
- **reply** [riplái] 동 대답하다
- **roll** [roul] 동 구르다
- **round** [raund] 형 둥근
- **rush** [rʌʃ] 동 서두르다, 돌진하다
- **sauce** [sɔːs] 명 소스
- **shape** [ʃeip] 명 모양, 모습
- **share** [ʃɛər] 동 공유하다
- **shout** [ʃaut] 동 소리치다, 외치다
- **sick** [sik] 형 아픈
- **solve** [sɑlv] 동 풀다, 해결하다
- **spin** [spin] 동 돌리다, 회전시키다
- **spirit** [spírit] 명 영혼, 요정
- **square** [skwɛər] 명 사각형
- **stick** [stik] 명 막대기, 나뭇가지
- **tidy** [táidi] 형 잘 정돈된, 단정한, 깔끔한
- **triangle** [tráiæŋgl] 명 삼각형
- **used jeans** 낡은 청바지
- **vegetable** [védʒətəbl] 명 야채
- **water** [wɔ́ːtər] 동 물을 주다
- **wheel** [hwiːl] 명 바퀴
- **without** [wiðáut] 전 ~ 없이

Key Expressions

- **a bag of** 한 자루의, 한 봉지의
- **by oneself** 자기 혼자서
- **cut A into pieces** A를 조각으로 자르다
- **divide A into B** A를 B로 나누다
- **each other** 서로 (주로 둘 사이에 쓰임)
- **have to+동사원형** ~해야 한다
- **How about+동사원형-ing ~?** ~하는 게 어때?
- **how to+동사원형** ~하는 방법
- **in charge of ~** ~을 담당하여
- **in control** 담당하고 있는, 통제 중인
- **Let me see.** (= **Let's see.**) 어디 보자.
- **make a mess** 엉망으로 만들다

- **one another** (주로 셋 이상 사이에 쓰임) 서로
- **one by one** 하나씩, 차례대로
- **pick up ~** ~을 집다, ~을 들어올리다
- **press and hold** 길게 누르다
- **put A on B** A를 B에 놓다[두다, 뿌리다]
- **put on** 입다, 쓰다, 신다
- **take away** ~을 치우다
- **take out** 꺼내다, 끄집어내다, 가지고 나가다
- **the other side** 반대편
- **There lived+주어** ~가 살았다
- **what to+동사원형** 무엇을 ~할지
- **wrap up** 감싸다, 포장하다

Word Power

※ 서로 반대되는 뜻을 가진 어휘

☐ **together** (같이, 함께) ↔ **apart** (따로, 떨어져)

☐ **difficult** (어려운) ↔ **easy** (쉬운)

☐ **tidy** (잘 정돈된) ↔ **untidy** (어수선한)

☐ **divide** (분리하다) ↔ **join** (결합하다)

☐ **perfect** (완벽한) ↔ **imperfect** (불완전한)

☐ **without** (~ 없이) ↔ **with** (~이 있는, ~와 함께)

※ 서로 비슷한 뜻을 가진 어휘

☐ **solve : work out** (문제를 해결하다)

☐ **hurry : rush** (서두르다)

☐ **realize : be aware of** (~을 알게 되다)

☐ **decide : determine** (결정[결심]하다)

☐ **face : confront** (직면하다)

☐ **reply : respond** (대답하다)

☐ **mess : disorder** (혼잡, 혼란, 무질서)

☐ **choose : select** (고르다, 선택하다)

☐ **dot : spot** (점)

☐ **finally : lastly** (마지막으로)

English Dictionary

☐ **complain** 불평하다
→ to say that you are not satisfied with something
무언가에 만족하지 않다고 말하다

☐ **control** 조절하다, 통제하다
→ to have the power to make it work in the way you want
당신이 원하는 방식으로 작동하도록 하는 힘을 가지다

☐ **decide** 결정하다
→ to make a choice about what you are going to do
당신이 하려는 것에 대해 선택을 하다

☐ **excited** 흥분한
→ feeling very happy and enthusiastic
매우 행복하고 열광적으로 느끼는

☐ **hanger** 옷걸이
→ a curved piece of wire, wood or plastic on which clothes are hung while they are being stored
옷이 보관되는 동안 걸려 있는 철사, 나무 또는 플라스틱의 휘어진 부품

☐ **hold** 잡고 있다, 지탱하다
→ to have something in your hands or arms
손이나 팔로 무언가를 쥐고 있다

☐ **hula hoop** 훌라후프
→ a very large ring that you try to keep spinning round your body
몸 주위로 계속 돌리는 매우 큰 고리

☐ **jacket** 재킷, 윗옷
→ a short coat that covers the upper part of the body
몸의 윗부분을 덮는 짧은 코트

☐ **mess** 혼란, 혼잡
→ a situation in which a place is dirty or not neat
장소가 더럽거나 단정하지 못한 상황

☐ **perfect** 완벽한
→ complete and correct in every way
모든 면에서 완전하고 올바른

☐ **pointy** 끝이 뾰족한
→ having a point at the end
끝에 뾰족한 끝을 가지고 있는

☐ **realize** 깨닫다, 알아차리다
→ to gradually begin to understand something that you did not know or notice before
전에 알지 못하거나 알아차리지 못한 것을 서서히 이해하기 시작하다

☐ **reply** 대답하다
→ to answer someone by saying or writing something
무언가를 말하거나 씀으로써 누군가에게 답하다

☐ **roll** 구르다
→ to move forward while turning over and over
계속 회전하면서 앞으로 움직이다

☐ **rush** 서두르다, 돌진하다
→ to move quickly toward someone
누군가를 향해 빠르게 움직이다

☐ **spirit** 요정
→ an imaginary creature with magic powers
마법의 힘을 가진 상상의 생명체

☐ **wheel** 바퀴
→ a round object that turns around and around to make a car, bicycle, or other vehicle move
차, 자전거 또는 다른 차량이 움직이도록 계속 도는 둥근 물체

01 다음 문장의 빈칸에 들어갈 말로 알맞은 것은?

> This bookshelf can't stand alone. Do you know how to _____ this problem?

① divide ② move
③ draw ④ solve
⑤ complain

서답형

02 다음 글의 빈칸에 주어진 영영풀이에 해당하는 말을 세 단어로 쓰시오.

> • Triangle was _____ the hangers and the plants.
> <영영 풀이> responsible for something or someone

➡ _____

03 다음 중 밑줄 친 단어의 우리말 뜻이 잘못된 것은?

① Their pointy leaves will hurt someone! 끝이 뾰족한
② Mike waters the flowers every day. 물을 주다
③ He complained that you two always made a mess. 불평했다
④ I don't know how to spin this. 돌리다
⑤ I try to make this room tidy. 지저분한

서답형

04 다음 우리말에 맞게 세 단어로 쓰시오. (시제를 맞추시오.)

> Circle은 둥근 것들을 돌보았다.
> ➡ Circle _____ the round things.

➡ _____

[05~06] 다음 영영풀이에 해당하는 단어를 고르시오.

05

> an imaginary creature with magic powers

① wheel ② spirit
③ ghost ④ dot
⑤ puzzle

06

> to have the power to make something work in the way you want

① decide ② roll
③ control ④ hold
⑤ reply

07 다음 빈칸에 들어갈 말로 가장 알맞은 것은?

> Do you know how to _____ a bear with three dots?

① hurry ② remember
③ share ④ draw
⑤ shout

08 다음 빈칸에 들어갈 단어가 알맞게 짝지어진 것은?

> • Do you know how to divide this _____ four equal pieces?
> • He picked _____ the square hula-hoop to exercise.

① off – of ② as – as
③ for – to ④ into – up
⑤ of – for

01 대화의 빈칸에 들어갈 단어를 주어진 철자로 시작하여 쓰시오.

> A: Do you know how to draw a fish?
> B: Sure. (A)F_____, draw a large square. Then, draw a triangle. (B)F_____, draw a small circle in the square.

➡ (A) _____ (B) _____

02 다음 우리말과 같은 표현이 되도록 문장의 빈칸을 채우시오.

(1) Mike의 방에는 세 도형 요정이 살았다.
➡ _____ _____ three shape _____ in Mike's room.

(2) 이 훌라후프를 치워, 그렇지 않으면 굴러가서 뭔가를 부술 거야!
➡ _____ this hula-hoop _____, _____ it will _____ and break something!

(3) 난 이 방을 정돈하려고 애쓰고 있어.
➡ I _____ _____ make this room _____.

(4) Triangle과 Circle은 서로를 쳐다보았다.
➡ Triangle and Circle looked at _____ _____.

03 다음 빈칸에 밑줄 친 단어와 같은 뜻을 가진 단어를 쓰시오. (주어진 철자로 쓸 것)

> G: Do you know how to divide this cake into four e_____ pieces?
> B: Let me see. How about dividing it this way? Then the pieces will be the same size and shape.

➡ _____

04 각 문장에 들어갈 단어를 〈보기〉의 영영풀이를 보고 쓰시오.

> ┤ 보기 ├
> (1) to make a choice about what you are going to do
> (2) a situation in which a place is dirty or not neat
> (3) to say that you are not satisfied with something
> (4) complete and correct in every way

(1) I can't _____ which to choose.
(2) The kids made a _____ in the bathroom.
(3) They always _____ that they cannot find time to do what they want to do.
(4) She speaks _____ English.

05 〈보기〉에서 알맞은 단어를 골라 문장을 완성하시오. (필요하면 단어를 추가하거나 변형하여 쓰시오.)

> ┤ 보기 ├
> point / control / square / divide

(1) Triangle and Circle went out and Square was now _____. He made the hangers, plants, and all the round things _____.

(2) Take these plants away, or their _____ leaves will hurt someone!

Conversation

① **능력 여부 묻기**

> **Do you know how to solve this puzzle?** 이 퍼즐을 어떻게 푸는지 아니?

- 'how to+동사원형'은 '~하는 방법, 어떻게 ~하는지'라는 의미로, 상대방의 능력을 묻거나 무언가를 하는 방법을 물을 때 'Do you know how to+동사원형 ~?'의 표현을 사용하며, 'Can you+동사원형 ~?'으로 바꿔 쓸 수 있다. 'how to+동사원형'은 'how+주어+should+동사원형 ~'으로 바꾸어 쓸 수 있다.

 - Do you know how to take a picture? 너는 사진을 어떻게 찍는지 아니?
 = Do you know how you should take a picture?
 = Can you take a picture? 너는 사진을 찍을 수 있니?

- **능력 여부를 묻는 말에 대한 대답**

 (1) 할 수 있다고 말할 때

 - Sure. 물론. / Yes, I can. 응, 할 수 있어. / Of course. 물론이지.
 Yes, I'm good at 명사/동사ing. 응, 나는 ~을 잘해.

 (2) 할 수 없다고 말할 때

 - No, I can't. 아니, 못해.
 = No, I'm not good at 명사/동사ing. 아니, 나는 ~을 잘 못해.
 = No, I don't know how to 동사원형. 아니, 나는 ~하는 방법을 몰라.

핵심 Check

1. 다음 우리말에 맞도록 빈칸에 들어갈 알맞은 것은?

 너는 이 문제를 푸는 방법을 아니?

 Do you know _____ to solve this problem?

 ① when ② how ③ what ④ why ⑤ where

2. 다음 대화의 밑줄 친 부분과 바꿔 쓸 수 있는 것은?

 A: <u>Can you make paper airplanes?</u>

 B: Sure. I'll show you how.

 ① Will you make paper airplanes?
 ② When will you learn how to make paper airplanes?
 ③ Do you know how to make paper airplanes?
 ④ How did you make paper airplanes?
 ⑤ How long have you learned how to make paper airplanes?

② 열거하기

First, draw a square. Then, draw a triangle. Finally, draw a circle.
먼저 사각형을 그려. 그러고 나서 삼각형을 그려. 마지막으로 원을 그려.

■ 어떤 것을 열거하거나 절차나 순서에 대해 말할 때 주로 First, Second, Third …(첫째, 둘째, 셋째 …)를 사용해서 각 단계의 내용을 열거한다.
First of all[Above all/To begin with], Next, And then, Finally[Lastly](처음으로, 그 다음에, 그러고 나서, 마침내[마지막으로])를 사용할 수도 있다.

• A: Can you tell me how to use a microwave? 전자레인지 사용하는 법을 나한테 말해 주겠니?
 B: Sure. 물론이지.
 First, put the food in the microwave. Second, set the timer and push the start button. Finally, take the food out when the time is up. 먼저 전자레인지에 음식을 넣어. 둘째, 타이머를 정하고 시작 버튼을 눌러. 마지막으로, 시간이 다 되면 음식을 꺼내.

핵심 Check

3. 다음 대화의 빈칸에 알맞은 것은?

 A: First, write the number '5' between the two eyes.

 B: Okay, what's next?

 A: _____

 B: A circle? Okay.

 ① What do you mean?
 ② Next, write the number '6.'
 ③ Finally, draw the two eyes.
 ④ Second, draw a small circle under the number '5.'
 ⑤ First of all, draw a circle under the eyes.

4. 다음 대화의 빈칸에 알맞은 말은?

 A: Do you know how to cook *ramyeon*?

 B: Sure. First, boil some water. Then, put the *ramyeon* and dried soup mix. _____, boil for 4 more minutes.

 ① To begin with ② Above all ③ Finally
 ④ Second ⑤ First of all

Get Ready 2

(1) **G:** This bookshelf can't stand alone. Do you know ❶how to solve this problem?

B: ❷Put some legs on the bottom.

(2) **G:** Do you know how to ❸divide this cake into four equal pieces?

B: ❹Let me see. … ❺How about dividing it this way? Then the pieces will be the same size and shape.

(3) **G:** This car doesn't move. Do you know how to move it?

B: Sure. Put wheels under the car.

(1)
G: 이 책꽂이는 혼자서 서 있을 수 없어. 이 문제를 어떻게 해결할지 아니?
B: 바닥에 다리를 몇 개 붙여.
(2)
G: 이 케이크를 네 개의 같은 조각으로 어떻게 나눌 수 있는지 아니?
B: 글쎄. … 이 방법으로 그것을 나누는 것은 어때? 그럼 그 조각들은 같은 크기에 같은 모양이 될 거야.
(3)
G: 이 차는 움직이지 않아. 어떻게 움직이게 할 수 있는지 아니?
B: 물론이지. 차 아래에 바퀴들을 붙여.

❶ 'how to+동사원형'은 '~하는 방법, 어떻게 ~하는지'라는 의미로, 상대방의 능력을 묻거나 무언가를 하는 방법을 묻는 표현이다.
❷ put A on B: A를 B에 두다
❸ divide A into B: A를 B로 나누다
❹ 생각할 시간을 필요로 할 때 사용하는 표현으로 '글쎄, 어디 보자'의 의미로 사용된다.
❺ How about -ing ~?: '~하는 게 어때?'라는 뜻으로 'What about -ing ~?'와 같이 제안을 하는 표현이다.

Check(√) True or False

(1) This bookshelf can stand alone if you put some legs on the bottom.　　T ☐ F ☐

(2) The boy knows how to divide the cake into the same size and shape.　　T ☐ F ☐

(3) The girl knows how to move this car.　　T ☐ F ☐

Start Off Listen & Talk A-1

G: These twelve sticks make four squares. Do you know ❶how to make three squares of the same size with three moves?

B: Sure. ❷First, move this stick here.

G: 이 12개의 막대기들은 사각형 4개를 만들어. 세 번 움직여서 어떻게 같은 크기의 사각형 3개를 만드는지 아니?
B: 물론이지. 먼저, 이 막대기를 여기로 옮겨.

❶ 'how to+동사원형'은 '~하는 방법, 어떻게 ~하는지'라는 의미로, 상대방의 능력을 묻거나 무언가를 하는 방법을 묻는 표현이다. 'how+주어+should+동사원형 ~'으로 바꾸어 쓸 수 있다.
❷ 열거를 할 때 사용하는 표현이다.

Check(√) True or False

(4) The girl wants to make three squares of the same size.　　T ☐ F ☐

(5) They are solving puzzles.　　T ☐ F ☐

 Start Off Listen & Talk A-2

B: Here's a triangle with three pencils. Do you know ❶how to make three more triangles with three more pencils?

G: ❷Let me see. … It's too difficult for me. Can I break the pencils in half?

B: No, you can't.

❶ 'how to+동사원형'은 '~하는 방법, 어떻게 ~하는지'라는 의미로, 상대방의 능력을 묻거나 무언가를 하는 방법을 묻는 표현이다. 'how+주어+should+동사원형 ~'으로 바꾸어 쓸 수 있다.

❷ 생각할 시간을 필요로 할 때 사용하는 표현으로 '글쎄, 어디 보자'의 의미로 사용된다.

 Start Off Listen & Talk B

B: Do you know ❶how to divide this into four equal pieces?

G: Sure. ❷First, divide it into three equal squares. Then, divide each square into four smaller squares. Finally, color three small squares in the inside corner of the L.

B: Oh, I can see three other L shapes around it! You're great!

❶ 'how to+동사원형'은 '~하는 방법, 어떻게 ~하는지'라는 의미로, 상대방의 능력을 묻거나 무언가를 하는 방법을 묻는 표현이다.

❷ 어떤 일을 하는 절차나 방법을 단계적으로 설명할 때, "First, … Then, … Finally, …"를 사용하여 각 단계의 내용을 열거한다.

 Speak Up Look and talk.

A: Do you know ❶how to draw a fish with shapes?

B: Sure. First, draw a large square. Then, draw a triangle. Finally, draw a small circle in the square.

❶ 'how you should draw with shapes'로 바꿀 수 있다.

 Speak Up Mission

G: Do you know how to make paper airplanes?

B: Sure. I'll show you ❶how.

❶ 여기서 how는 명사로 '방법'이라는 의미다.

 Real-life Scene

B: Do you know ❶how to solve this puzzle?

G: What is it?

B: You must take a dog, a chicken, and a bag of rice across the river. The boat only carries you and one of the things at a time.

G: That's easy. I can ❷take them to the other side one by one.

B: But without you, the dog will kill the chicken, and the chicken will eat the rice.

G: Let me see. … ❸First, take the chicken and come back. Then, take the rice and come back with the chicken.

B: And?

G: After that, take the dog and come back. Finally, take the chicken.

B: You're great!

❶ 'how to+동사원형'은 '~하는 방법, 어떻게 ~하는지'라는 의미로, 'how you should solve this puzzle'로 바꾸어 쓸 수 있다.

❷ take A to B: A를 B로 데려가다

❸ 어떤 일을 하는 절차나 방법을 단계적으로 설명할 때, "First, … Then, … Finally, …"를 사용하여 각 단계의 내용을 열거한다.

 Express Yourself A

1. B: Do you know how to make this?
 G: Sure. First, ❶cut off the leg from used jeans.
2. B: This looks great.
 G: I think so, too. Do you know how to make it?
 B: It's easy. First, put some rice on *gim*. Then, add some dried fish and hot peppers. Finally, ❷wrap it up and make a triangle.
3. B: Do you know how to fly this?
 G: Yes. I'll show you how. It has to face the wind. Hold it up like this.

❶ cut off: ~을 자르다

❷ wrap ~ up: ~을 싸다

 Learning Diary Check Yourself

W: Excuse me. Do you know ❶how to draw a mouse with shapes?

M: Sure. First, draw a large triangle. Then, draw two dots and 6 lines. Finally, draw two small circles.

W: Thanks. I'll draw it ❷myself now.

❶ 'how you should draw a mouse with shapes'로 바꿀 수 있다.

❷ myself는 주어를 강조하는 재귀대명사이다.

• 다음 우리말과 일치하도록 빈칸에 알맞은 말을 쓰시오.

Get Ready 2

(1) G: This bookshelf can't stand _____. Do you know _____ _____ _____ this problem?

 B: _____ some legs _____ the _____.

(2) G: Do you know _____ _____ _____ _____ this cake _____ four equal pieces?

 B: _____ me _____. … How about _____ it this way? Then the pieces will be the same size and shape.

(3) G: This car doesn't move. Do you know _____ _____ _____ it?

 B: Sure. _____ wheels under the car.

Start Off Listen & Talk A

1. G: These twelve sticks make four squares. Do you know _____ _____ _____ three squares of the same size with three moves?

 B: Sure. _____, move this stick here.

2. B: Here's a triangle with three pencils. Do you know _____ _____ _____ three more triangles with three more pencils?

 G: Let me see. … It's too _____ for me. Can I break the pencils _____ _____?

 B: No, you can't.

Start Off Listen & Talk B

B: Do you know _____ _____ _____ this _____ four equal pieces?

G: Sure. _____, divide it into three _____ squares. _____, _____ each square _____ four smaller squares. _____, color three small squares in the inside corner of the L.

B: Oh, I can see three other L shapes around it! You're great!

Speak Up Look and talk.

A: Do you know _____ _____ _____ a fish with shapes?

B: Sure. _____, draw a large square. _____, draw a triangle. _____, draw a small circle in the square.

해석

(1) G: 이 책꽂이는 혼자서 서 있을 수 없어. 이 문제를 어떻게 해결할지 아니?
 B: 바닥에 다리를 몇 개 붙여.

(2) G: 이 케이크를 네 개의 같은 조각으로 어떻게 나눌 수 있는지 아니?
 B: 글쎄. … 이 방법으로 그것을 나누는 것은 어때? 그럼 그 조각들은 같은 크기에 같은 모양이 될 거야.

(3) G: 이 차는 움직이지 않아. 어떻게 움직이게 할 수 있는지 아니?
 B: 물론이지. 차 아래에 바퀴들을 붙여.

1. G: 이 12개 막대기들은 사각형 4개를 만들어. 세 번 움직여서 어떻게 같은 크기의 사각형 3개를 만드는지 아니?
 B: 물론이지. 먼저, 이 막대기를 여기로 옮겨.

2. B: 여기 연필 세 자루로 만든 삼각형이 하나 있어. 연필 세 자루를 더 추가해서 어떻게 삼각형 3개를 더 만드는지 아니?
 G: 글쎄.… 내게는 너무 어려워. 연필을 반으로 부러뜨려도 돼?
 B: 아니, 안 돼.

B: 이것을 4개의 같은 조각으로 나누는 방법을 아니?
G: 물론이지. 먼저, 그것을 3개의 같은 사각형으로 나눠. 그러고 나서, 각 사각형을 4개의 더 작은 사각형으로 나눠. 마지막으로, ㄴ자 모양의 안쪽 모서리에 있는 3개의 작은 사각형에 색칠해.
B: 오, 그 주변에 3개의 다른 ㄴ자 모양들이 보여! 너 대단하다!

A: 너는 도형들로 물고기를 그리는 방법을 알고 있니?
B: 물론. 먼저, 큰 사각형을 그려. 그러고 나서, 삼각형을 그려. 마지막으로, 사각형 안에 작은 원을 하나 그려.

Speak Up Mission

G: Do you know _____ _____ _____ paper airplanes?

B: Sure. I'll show you _____.

Real-life Scene

B: Do you know _____ _____ _____ this puzzle?

G: What is it?

B: You must _____ a dog, a chicken, and a bag of rice across the river. The boat only carries you and one of the things _____ _____ _____.

G: That's easy. I can _____ them _____ the other side _____ _____ _____.

B: But _____ you, the dog will kill the chicken, and the chicken will eat the rice.

G: Let me see. … _____, take the chicken and come back. _____, take the rice and come back with the chicken.

B: And?

G: After that, take the dog and come back. _____, take the chicken.

B: You're great!

Express Yourself A

1. B: Do you know _____ _____ _____ this?

 G: Sure. First, _____ _____ the leg from _____ jeans.

2. B: This looks great.

 G: I think so, too. Do you know _____ to make it?

 B: It's easy. _____, put some rice on *gim*. _____, add some _____ fish and hot peppers. _____, _____ it up and make a triangle.

3. B: Do you know _____ _____ fly this?

 G: Yes. I'll show you how. It has to _____ the wind. _____ it up like this.

Learning Diary Check Yourself

W: Excuse me. Do you know how _____ _____ a mouse with shapes?

M: Sure. _____, draw a large triangle. _____, draw two dots and 6 lines. _____, draw two small circles.

W: Thanks. I'll _____ it _____ now.

해석

G: 너는 종이 비행기를 어떻게 접는지 아니?

B: 물론이지. 내가 너에게 방법을 보여 줄게.

B: 이 퍼즐을 어떻게 푸는지 아니?

G: 그게 뭔데?

B: 너는 개, 닭, 쌀 한 자루를 강 건너로 옮겨야 해. 그 배는 한 번에 너와 그것들 중 하나만 옮길 수 있어.

G: 그것은 쉬워. 난 반대편으로 그것들을 하나씩 옮길 수 있어.

B: 하지만 네가 없으면, 개는 닭을 죽일 것이고, 닭은 쌀을 먹을 거야.

G: 어디 보자. … 먼저, 닭을 데려다 놓고 돌아와. 그러고 나서, 쌀을 가져다 놓고 닭을 데려와.

B: 그리고?

G: 그 후에, 개를 데려다 놓고 돌아와. 마지막으로, 닭을 데려가는 거야.

B: 너 대단하구나!

1. B: 이것을 어떻게 만드는지 아니?
 G: 물론이지. 먼저, 낡은 청바지에서 다리 부분을 잘라내.

2. B: 이것은 멋져 보여.
 G: 나도 그렇게 생각해. 그걸 어떻게 만드는지 아니?
 B: 그건 쉬워. 먼저, 김 위에 밥을 좀 얹어. 그러고 나서, 멸치와 매운 고추를 추가해. 마지막으로, 그것을 모두 싸서 삼각형을 만들어.

3. B: 이것을 어떻게 날리는지 아니?
 G: 그래. 내가 너에게 방법을 보여 줄게. 그것은 바람을 마주해야만 해. 이렇게 그것을 들고 있어.

W: 실례합니다. 도형으로 쥐를 어떻게 그리는지 아세요?

M: 물론이죠. 먼저, 큰 삼각형을 그려요. 그러고 나서, 점 두 개와 선 6개를 그려요. 마지막으로, 작은 원 두 개를 그려요.

W: 감사합니다. 이제 제가 그것을 직접 그려 볼게요.

01 다음 대화의 빈칸에 들어갈 말은?

> G: This bookshelf can't stand alone. Do you know _____ this problem?
> B: Put some legs on the bottom.

① how solving ② what to solve ③ how to solve
④ when to solve ⑤ where to solve

02 다음 대화의 빈칸에 들어갈 말로 알맞지 <u>않은</u> 것은?

> G: These twelve sticks make four squares. Do you know how to make three squares of the same size with three moves?
> B: Sure. _____, move this stick here.

① To begin with ② First of all ③ First
④ Above all ⑤ Finally

03 다음 대화의 우리말에 맞게 부정사를 이용하여 4단어의 영어로 쓰시오.

> B: This looks great.
> G: I think so, too. Do you know <u>그것을 어떻게 만드는지</u>?
> B: It's easy. First, put some rice on *gim*. Then, add some dried fish and hot peppers. Finally, wrap it up and make a triangle.

➡ _____

04 다음 대화의 밑줄 친 우리말에 맞게 주어진 단어를 알맞은 순서로 배열하시오.

> G: Do you know <u>이 케이크를 네 개의 같은 조각으로 어떻게 나눌 수 있는지</u>?
> B: Let me see. ... How about dividing it this way? Then the pieces will be the same size and shape.

(divide / how / this cake / into / to / four / pieces / equal)
➡ _____

[01~02] 다음 대화를 읽고 물음에 답하시오.

B: Here's a triangle with three pencils. Do you know _____(A)_____ with three more pencils?

G: Let me see. ... It's too difficult for me. Can I break the pencils (B)반으로?

B: No, you can't.

01 위 대화의 빈칸 (A)에 들어갈 말로 알맞은 것은?

① where to buy three more pencils
② how to draw a bear with a pencil
③ how to make three more triangles
④ how to make potato salad
⑤ how to use these triangles

서답형

02 위 대화의 밑줄 친 (B)의 우리말에 맞게 주어진 철자로 시작하여 쓰시오.

➡ i _____

[03~04] 다음 대화를 읽고 물음에 답하시오.

B: Do you know _____?

G: Yes. I'll show you how. It has to face the wind. Hold it up like this.

03 위 대화의 빈칸에 들어갈 말로 가장 적절한 것은?

① how to make it
② how to show this
③ when to fly this
④ how to fly this
⑤ where to fly this

서답형

04 위 문제의 답을 '주어+동사'가 있는 문장으로 바꾸어 쓰시오.

➡ _____

[05~06] 다음 대화를 읽고 물음에 답하시오.

B: Do you know _____(A)_____

G: Sure. ___(B)___, divide it into three equal squares. Then, divide each square into four smaller squares. ___(C)___, color three small squares in the inside corner of the L.

B: Oh, I can see three other L shapes around it! You're great!

05 위 대화의 빈칸 (A)에 들어갈 말로 가장 알맞은 것은?

① how to make three squares of the same size with three moves?
② how to make paper airplanes?
③ how to draw a mouse with shapes?
④ how to divide this into four equal pieces?
⑤ how to draw a fish with shapes?

06 위 대화의 (B)와 (C)에 들어갈 말로 알맞은 것은?

① First – Finally
② Then – Next
③ First of all – Second
④ Above all – Three
⑤ One – The other

[07~09] 다음 대화를 읽고 물음에 답하시오.

A: Do you know _____(A)_____?
B: What is it?
A: You must take a dog, a chicken, and a bag of rice across the river. (①) The boat only carries you and one of the things at a time.
B: That's easy. I can take them to the other side ___(B)___. (②)
A: But without you, the dog will kill the chicken, and the chicken will eat the rice.
B: Let me see. ⋯ First, take the chicken and come back. (③) Then, take the rice and come back with the chicken. (④)
A: And?
B: (⑤) Finally, take the chicken.
A: You're great!

07 위 대화의 빈칸 (A)에 들어갈 말로 알맞은 것은?

① how to make paper airplanes
② how to solve this puzzle
③ how to take a dog across the river
④ how to row a boat
⑤ how to come back with the chicken

08 위 대화의 빈칸 (B)에 들어갈 말로 알맞은 것은?

① each other ② together
③ one by one ④ one another
⑤ with me

09 위 대화의 (①)~(⑤)에서 다음 주어진 문장이 들어갈 위치로 알맞은 것은?

After that, take the dog and come back.

① ② ③ ④ ⑤

10 다음 중 짝지어진 대화가 <u>어색한</u> 것을 고르시오.

① A: Do you know how to cook *ramyeon*?
 B: Sure.
② A: Do you know how to make paper cranes?
 B: Sure. I'll show you how.
③ A: Do you know how to fix this?
 B: That's not right.
④ A: Do you know how to divide this cake into four equal pieces?
 B: Let me see.
⑤ A: Can I help you?
 B: Yes, can you tell me where to sit?

[11~12] 다음 대화를 읽고 물음에 답하시오.

G: Do you know how to draw a fish with ___(A)___s?
B: Sure. First, draw a large square. ___(B)___, draw a triangle. Finally, draw a small circle in the square.

11 위 대화의 빈칸 (A)의 단어에 대한 영어 설명을 읽고 알맞은 단어를 쓰시오.

an arrangement that is formed by joining lines together in a particular way or by the line or lines around its outer edge

➡ _____

12 위 대화의 빈칸 (B)에 들어갈 말로 알맞은 것을 <u>모두</u> 고르시오.

① Then ② Third
③ Two ④ Second
⑤ Next

[01~02] 다음 대화를 읽고 물음에 답하시오.

A: Do you know how to solve this puzzle?
B: What is it?
A: You must take a dog, a chicken, and a bag of rice ①across the river. The boat only carries you and one of the things ②at a time.
B: That's easy. I can take them to the other side ③one by one.
A: But ④with you, the dog will kill the chicken, and the chicken will eat the rice.
B: ___(A)___ ... First, take the chicken and come back. Then, take the rice and come back with the chicken.
A: And?
B: After that, ⑤take the dog and come back. Finally, take the chicken.
A: You're great!

01 위 대화의 밑줄 친 ①~⑤ 중 어휘의 쓰임이 어색한 것을 찾아 바르게 고치시오.

➡ 번호: _____.

➡ 고쳐 쓰기: _____.

02 위 대화의 빈칸 (A)에 들어갈 표현을 주어진 영영풀이를 참고하여 세 단어로 쓰시오. (3 words)

> used when you want to think carefully about something or are trying to remember

➡ _____

[03~04] 다음 대화를 읽고 물음에 답하시오.

A: 너는 도형들로 쥐를 그리는 방법을 알고 있니?
B: Sure. First, draw a large ___(a)___. Then, draw two small ___(b)___. Finally, draw ___(c)___ and six ___(d)___.

03 위 대화의 밑줄 친 우리말에 맞게 주어진 단어를 알맞은 순서로 배열하시오.

> you / how / to / know / do / draw / a mouse / shapes / with

➡ _____

04 위 대화의 빈칸 (a)~(d)에 들어갈 말을 다음 그림을 보고 완성하시오.

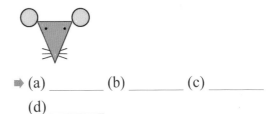

➡ (a) _____ (b) _____ (c) _____
(d) _____

05 다음 대화의 밑줄 친 우리말에 맞게 주어진 단어를 이용하여 4 단어의 영어로 쓰시오.

> (how / move)

G: This car doesn't move. Do you know 그것을 어떻게 움직이게 하는지?
B: Sure. Put wheels under the car.

➡ _____

Grammar

1 의문사+to부정사

> • Do you know **how to solve** this problem? 이 문제를 어떻게 해결할지 아니?
> • Will you tell me **where to meet**? 어디서 만날지 내게 말해 줄래?

■ '의문사+to부정사'는 'what/when/where/how/whom + to부정사'의 형태로 쓰이며, 문장 속에서 주어, 목적어, 보어 역할을 하는 명사구로 사용되며, '…할지'라는 뜻을 나타낸다. 주로 동사의 목적어로 사용된다. 'why + to부정사'는 쓰이지 않는다.

 • **How to spend** money is very important. 〈주어〉 돈을 어떻게 쓰는지가 매우 중요하다.

 • I don't know **how to spin** this. 〈know의 목적어〉 이걸 어떻게 돌리는지 모르겠어.

의문사	to부정사	의미
what	to do	무엇을 해야 할지
whom	to meet	누구를 만나야 할지
which	to buy	어느 것을 사야 할지
when	to start	언제 출발해야 할지
where	to go	어디로 가야 할지
how	to fix	어떻게 고치는지

■ '의문형용사 + 명사 + to부정사'나 '의문부사 + 형용사 + to부정사' 형태로도 사용된다.

 • Can you tell me **which bus to take**? 어느 버스를 타야 할지 말해줄 수 있어?

 • I don't know **how much to buy**. 얼마나 많이 사야 할지 모르겠다.

■ '의문사+to부정사'는 '의문사 + 주어 + should[can] + 동사원형'으로 바꿔 쓸 수 있다.

 • I don't know **when to start**. 언제 출발해야 할지 모르겠어.
 = I don't know when I should start.

 • Do you know **how to fix** this? 이걸 어떻게 고칠 수 있는지 아니?
 = Do you know how you can fix this?

핵심 Check

1. 다음 우리말에 맞게 빈칸에 알맞은 말을 쓰시오.

 (1) 그걸 어떻게 움직이는지 아니?

 ➡ Do you know _____ _____ _____ it?

 (2) 어디에 앉아야 할지 제게 말해 주시겠어요?

 ➡ Can you tell me _____ _____ _____?

② 동사+목적어+형용사(목적격 보어)

> • Square decided to **make** the room **better**. Square는 방을 더 낫게 만들기로 결심했다.
> • I **found** math **interesting**. 나는 수학이 재미있다는 것을 알았다.

■ '주어 + 동사 + 목적어 + 목적격 보어'의 형식을 취하는 문장을 5형식 문장이라고 하며, 목적격 보어 자리에는 명사, 형용사, to부정사, 현재분사, 과거분사, 동사원형 등 다양한 형태가 올 수 있다. 이때, 목적격 보어는 목적어의 특징이나 상태 등을 설명하는 역할을 한다. 형용사를 목적격 보어로 취하는 동사에는 make, keep, find, get, leave, paint, think 등이 있다.

 • His mom **made** him **a doctor**. 〈명사〉 그의 엄마는 그를 의사가 되도록 했다.

 • That **made** me **happy**. 〈형용사〉 그게 나를 행복하게 했다.

 • I **asked** him **to mail** the letter. 〈to부정사〉 나는 그에게 편지를 부쳐달라고 부탁했다.

 • I've never **seen** him **singing** in public. 〈현재분사〉 나는 그가 사람들 앞에서 노래 부르는 걸 본 적이 없어.

 • I **had** it **stolen** somewhere. 〈과거분사〉 어딘가에서 그것을 도난당했습니다.

 • Her father didn't **let** her **go** to the party. 〈동사원형〉 그녀의 아버지는 그녀를 파티에 못 가게 하셨어.

■ 목적격 보어를 형용사가 아닌 부사로 쓰지 않도록 주의해야 한다.

 • Everyone wonders if money can **make** us **happy**. 모든 사람들이 돈으로 행복해질 수 있는지 궁금해 한다.

 • In the winter, it **keeps** your head **warm**. 겨울에는, 그것이 너의 머리를 계속 따뜻하도록 해준다.

■ **5형식 문장과 4형식 문장 비교**

 5형식 문장: 주어+동사+목적어+목적격 보어

 • He **made** me **happy**. (me = happy) 그는 나를 행복하게 했다.

 4형식 문장: 주어+동사+간접목적어+직접목적어

 • He **made** me **a desk**. (me ≠ a desk) 그는 나에게 책상을 만들어 주었다.

핵심 Check

2. 다음 우리말에 맞게 빈칸에 알맞은 말을 쓰시오.

 (1) 난 이 방을 정돈하려고 애쓰지만, 너희 둘은 항상 엉망으로 만들어.

 ➡ I try to make this room _____, but you two always make _____

 _____.

 (2) 숙제는 나를 지치게 만든다.

 ➡ My homework makes me _____.

01 다음 빈칸에 들어갈 알맞은 것은?

• Do you know _____ to make paper airplanes?

① whom ② who ③ what
④ which ⑤ how

02 다음 문장에서 어법상 어색한 부분을 바르게 고쳐 쓰시오.

(1) Can you tell me how cook spaghetti?

_____ ➡ _____

(2) I don't know when I to start.

_____ ➡ _____

(3) The story made me sadly.

_____ ➡ _____

(4) She asked him wait outside.

_____ ➡ _____

03 다음 우리말에 맞게 괄호 안에 주어진 단어를 빈칸에 바르게 배열하시오. (필요하면 어형을 바꿀 것)

(1) 그것이 계속 나를 들뜨게 했다. (me / excite / kept)

➡ It _____ _____ _____.

(2) 무엇을 사야 할지 모르겠어. (buy / what / to)

➡ I don't know _____ _____ _____.

(3) 열쇠를 어디에 두면 좋을지 모르겠다. (put / where / the / key / to)

➡ I am not sure _____ _____ _____ _____ _____.

04 다음 괄호 안에 주어진 단어를 어법에 맞게 빈칸에 쓰시오.

(1) I did not know whom _____ for the gift. (thank)

(2) We found the test _____. (difficult)

중요

01 다음 중 어법상 바르지 <u>않은</u> 것은?

① Do you know how to divide this cake into four equal pieces?
② I couldn't know where to buy the shirt.
③ Can you tell me whom to meet tomorrow?
④ The boy will ask her what to do it next.
⑤ Elle told him where to meet her when he left for the day.

서답형

02 주어진 어휘를 이용하여 다음 우리말을 영어로 쓰시오.

나는 그 책이 재미있다는 것을 알게 되었다. (find, interesting.)

➡ _____

서답형

03 다음 괄호 안에서 알맞은 말을 고르시오.

(1) We asked her when (to start / starting) to paint the wall.
(2) We couldn't decide (what / why) to do, so we just waited.
(3) Christine didn't tell her husband (how / what) to use the washing machine.
(4) Regular exercising makes me (health / healthy).
(5) The bird's song made the man (happy / happily).
➡ (1) _____ (2) _____ (3) _____
 (4) _____ (5) _____

[04~05] 다음 빈칸에 알맞은 말을 고르시오.

04

My sister _____ the living room clean.

① made ② charged
③ asked ④ begged
⑤ ordered

05

Jenny doesn't know _____ to make a bookmark.

① what ② how
③ that ④ whom
⑤ why

중요

06 주어진 문장의 밑줄 친 부분과 용법이 <u>다른</u> 것은?

He <u>made</u> the hangers, the plants, and all the round things square.

① Jogging in the morning <u>made</u> her keep in shape.
② My dog <u>made</u> me happy.
③ The Olympic Games <u>made</u> a lot of people excited.
④ Linsey <u>made</u> him wait for her for more than two hours.
⑤ Mom <u>made</u> me delicious gimbap last night.

서답형

07 다음 빈칸에 알맞은 말을 쓰시오.

Do you know how _____ ride a bike?

➡ _____

서답형

08 두 문장의 의미가 같도록 빈칸에 알맞은 말을 쓰시오.

(1) Now, do you all understand how to play this game?

= Now, do you all understand _____ _____ _____ _____ t h i s game?

(2) Do you know how to make a bag out of used jeans?

= D o y o u k n o w _____ _____ _____ _____ a bag out of used jeans?

(3) Tell me what to do.

= Tell me _____ _____ _____ _____.

중요

09 다음 중 어법상 어색한 문장을 고르시오.

① Doing the same work again and again makes me tire.

② The 2002 World Cup games made Korean people excited.

③ I knew how to make a kite.

④ Watching TV before going to bed can keep you awake.

⑤ Listening to music always makes us comfortable.

[10~11] 다음 우리말에 맞게 영작한 것을 고르시오.

10

그것은 나를 전보다 더 똑똑하게 만들었어.

① It made me smart than before.

② It made me smarter than before.

③ It made me smartly than before.

④ It made me more smartly than before.

⑤ It made me smartlier than before.

11

그들은 그 북을 어디에 놓아야 할지 몰랐다.

① They didn't know how to put the drum.

② They didn't know what to put the drum.

③ They didn't know where to put the drum.

④ They didn't know when to put the drum.

⑤ They didn't know which to put the drum.

중요

12 다음 빈칸에 적절하지 않은 것을 모두 고르시오.

I'd like to know _____ to go.

① how ② where ③ when
④ what ⑤ why

서답형

13 다음 두 문장의 뜻이 같도록 빈칸에 알맞은 말을 쓰시오.

• I found the book interesting.
• I found that _____ _____ _____ _____.

서답형

14 우리말과 일치하도록 주어진 어휘를 이용하여 빈칸에 알맞은 말을 쓰시오.

(1) 그녀는 어느 옷을 사야 할지 알 수 없었다. (buy, dress)

➡ She didn't know _____ _____ _____ _____.

(2) 그 수학 시험이 모든 학생들을 불안하게 했다. (make, every, nervous)

➡ The math test _____ _____ _____ _____.

서답형

15 다음 문장에서 어법상 <u>어색한</u> 것을 바르게 고치시오.

(1) She couldn't decide where going to buy some bread.

_____ ➡ _____

(2) How to say greetings are important for Koreans.

_____ ➡ _____

(3) Harold didn't know what to help her at that time.

_____ ➡ _____

(4) Do you know how should draw a mouse with shapes?

_____ ➡ _____

(5) I found Stella very smartly.

_____ ➡ _____

(6) The baby made the mom happiness by smiling back.

_____ ➡ _____

(7) Doing a lot of homework makes me tiring.

_____ ➡ _____

중요

16 다음 밑줄 친 부분의 쓰임이 나머지 넷과 <u>다른</u> 것은?

① The teacher will tell Rick when <u>to begin</u>.

② Do you know how <u>to make</u> three squares of the same size with three moves?

③ Matilda asked Alex where <u>to get</u> those dresses.

④ He had no friends <u>to support</u> him.

⑤ Andrew couldn't decide what <u>to do</u> next for her.

서답형

17 다음 문장을 같은 뜻의 다른 문장으로 바꿔 쓸 때 빈칸을 두 단어로 채우시오.

I watched the movie and I felt sad.
→ The movie made _____.

➡ _____

서답형

18 주어진 어휘를 이용하여 다음 우리말을 두 가지로 영작하시오.

오늘 밤 파티를 위해 무엇을 사야 할지 내게 말해 줘. (tell, buy)

➡ _____

➡ _____

19 다음 중 어법상 <u>틀린</u> 것은?

① Watching a movie with a girl friend makes the movie more interested.

② Computer games make people around the world excited.

③ Playing soccer makes me happy.

④ Reading books for homework makes me bored.

⑤ Washing the dishes after dinner makes me tired.

20 다음 중 어법상 옳은 문장의 개수는?

ⓐ I can make this room better all by myself.

ⓑ Can you tell me where sit?

ⓒ I don't know what doing.

ⓓ Do you know how to fly this?

ⓔ This jacket will keep you warmly.

① 1개　② 2개　③ 3개　④ 4개　⑤ 5개

01 다음 문장에서 어법상 <u>어색한</u> 것을 바르게 고쳐 다시 쓰시오.

(1) He showed what to draw a triangle that has three sides of the same length.

➡ _____

(2) When we to go there is not decided yet.

➡ _____

(3) Do you know why to share photos on the Internet?

➡ _____

(4) The bird's song makes him happily.

➡ _____

(5) At first, Sophie thought Nicholas honesty.

➡ _____

(6) We found *Alita: Battle Angel* very interested.

➡ _____

02 다음 빈칸을 어법에 맞게 채우시오.

I'll tell you how to solve it.
= I'll tell you how _____ _____
_____ it.

03 다음 그림을 보고 괄호 안에 주어진 어휘를 이용하여 주어진 대화의 빈칸을 알맞게 채우시오.

(1)

A: Do you like sandwiches?
B: Yes, I do. Eating sandwiches makes _____ . (full)

➡ _____

(2)

A: Does Minsu know _____ *ramyeon*? (cook)
B: Sure. He is a good cook.

➡ _____

04 괄호 안에 주어진 어휘를 이용하여 영작하시오.

(1) 너 이 꽃을 어떻게 기르는지 아니? (know, grow, this flower, 8 단어)

➡ _____

(2) 과자를 얼마나 많이 사야 할지 나에게 말해 줘. (tell, cookies, buy, 7 단어)

➡ _____

(3) 그들은 어느 길을 택할 것인가 결정할 수가 없었다. (decide, which, take, 7 단어)

➡ _____

(4) 내 낮은 성적이 엄마를 실망하게 했다. (poor, grade, make, disappoint, 7 단어)

➡ _____

(5) 우리는 그가 어리석다고 생각했다. (stupid, 4 단어)

➡ _____

(6) 이 선풍기가 여러분을 이번 여름에 시원하게 해 줄 것이다. (this fan, keep, cool, 8 단어)

➡ _____

05 주어진 어휘와 to부정사를 이용하여 자신의 문장을 쓰시오.

(1) how, make

➡ _____

(2) what, write

➡ _____

(3) where, put

➡ _____

(4) which, tell, read, book

➡ _____

06 우리말에 맞게 다음 빈칸에 알맞은 말을 쓰시오.

(1) 그는 그 책이 매우 재미있다는 것을 알았다.

➡ He found the book very _____.

(2) 밖에 나가면 햇볕 때문에 따뜻해질 거예요.

➡ If you go out, the sun will keep you _____.

(3) Romeo는 Juliet이 친절하다고 믿었다.

➡ Romeo believed Juliet _____.

(4) 그녀가 아이를 혼자 내버려두었다.

➡ She left her child _____.

07 두 문장이 같은 뜻이 되도록 빈칸에 알맞은 것을 쓰시오.

(1) I can't decide what to eat for lunch.

= I can't decide _____ _____ _____ _____ for lunch.

(2) Which dress to buy is a difficult decision for her to make.

= _____ _____ _____ _____ _____ is a difficult decision for her to make.

08 다음 문장을 주어진 어휘로 시작하는 문장으로 바꿔 쓰시오.

(1) When she got the present, she felt happy.

➡ The present made _____.

(2) When I heard the news, I got excited.

➡ Hearing the news _____.

Reading

Three Shape Spirits

There lived three shape spirits in Mike's room. Square controlled the table, the bookshelf, and the window. Triangle was in charge of the hangers and the plants. Circle took care of the round things. They worked together to make a nice room for Mike.

One day Square decided to make the room better and shouted at the other spirits.

"Take these plants away, or their pointy leaves will hurt someone!" he said to Triangle.

"But Mike waters them every day," said Triangle.

"Take this hula hoop away, or it will roll and break something!" he said to Circle.

"But Mike exercises with it every day," said Circle.

"I try to make this room tidy, but you two always make a mess," he complained.

Triangle and Circle looked at each other.

"So you think you can do it without us?" Triangle asked Square.

"Sure. I can make this room better all by myself," replied Square.

"Great! Then we can get some rest," Circle said to Square.

spirit 영혼, 요정	
hanger 옷걸이	
hula hoop 훌라후프	
wheel 바퀴	
pointy 끝이 뾰족한	
control 통제하다, 조절하다	
in charge of …을 담당하여	
decide 결정하다	
roll 구르다, 굴러가다	
mess 혼란, 혼잡	
complain 불평하다	

● 다음 문장이 본문의 내용과 일치하면 T, 일치하지 않으면 F를 쓰시오.

1 Square controlled the table, the bookshelf, and the window. ☐

2 Circle took care of the hangers and the plants. ☐

3 Three shape spirits worked together to make a nice room for Mike. ☐

4 One day Triangle decided to make the room better. ☐

5 Mike exercises with the hula hoop every day. ☐

6 Square thinks he can do nothing without Triangle and Circle. ☐

Triangle and Circle went out and Square was now in control. He made the hangers, plants, and all the round things square. Then he looked around and smiled. "Much better!"

When Mike came home from school, he picked up a square hanger to hang his jacket on.

"What? This will not hold my clothes."

He went to water the plants and saw their square leaves.

"Poor things. ... They must be sick."

He picked up the square hula hoop to exercise.

"Hmm ... I don't know how to spin this."

He went to take out his bike and looked at the square wheels.

"Well, I can't ride this. I'll just have to walk." Then he hurried out of the house.

When the other spirits came back, Square rushed over to them. "Mike doesn't like his room. I don't know what to do," he said.

They looked at the hangers, the plants, and all the new square things. Then they looked at one another, and Square realized his problem.

"Let's make this room great again," he said to the others, and the three spirits worked together once again.

clothes 옷, 의복

pick up 집다, 집어 들다

out of ~에서, ~ 밖으로

spin 돌리다, 회전하다

rush 서두르다, 돌진하다

📎 **확인문제**

● 다음 문장이 본문의 내용과 일치하면 T, 일치하지 않으면 F를 쓰시오.

1 Square made the hangers, plants, and all the round things square. ☐

2 Mike picked up a triangular hanger to hang his jacket on. ☐

3 Mike doesn't know how to spin the square hula hoop. ☐

4 Mike went to take out his bike and looked at the round wheels. ☐

5 Square rushed over to the other spirits when they came back. ☐

6 Triangle and Circle said to Square, "Let's make this room great again." ☐

우리말을 참고하여 빈칸에 알맞은 말을 쓰시오.

1 Three Shape _____

2 _____ _____ three shape spirits in Mike's room.

3 Square _____ the table, the bookshelf, and the window.

4 Triangle _____ _____ _____ _____ the hangers and the plants.

5 Circle _____ _____ _____ the round things.

6 They _____ _____ to make a nice room for Mike.

7 One day Square decided _____ _____ _____ _____ _____ and shouted at the other spirits.

8 "_____ these plants _____, or their _____ leaves will hurt someone!" he said to Triangle.

9 "But Mike _____ _____ every day," said Triangle.

10 "_____ this hula hoop _____, or it will _____ _____ _____ something!" he said to Circle.

11 "But Mike _____ _____ _____ every day," said Circle.

12 "I try to make this room _____, but you two always _____ _____ _____," he complained.

13 Triangle and Circle _____ _____ each other.

14 "So you think you can do it _____ _____?" Triangle asked Square.

15 "Sure. I can make this room better _____ _____ _____," replied Square.

16 "Great! Then we can _____ _____ _____," Circle said to Square.

17 Triangle and Circle went out and Square was now _____ _____.

<table>
<tr><td>1</td><td>세 도형 요정들</td></tr>
<tr><td>2</td><td>Mike의 방에는 세 도형 요정이 살았다.</td></tr>
<tr><td>3</td><td>Square는 탁자, 책장, 그리고 창문을 담당했다.</td></tr>
<tr><td>4</td><td>Triangle은 옷걸이들과 식물들을 담당했다.</td></tr>
<tr><td>5</td><td>Circle은 둥근 것들을 돌보았다.</td></tr>
<tr><td>6</td><td>그들은 Mike에게 좋은 방을 만들어 주기 위해서 함께 일했다.</td></tr>
<tr><td>7</td><td>어느 날 Square는 방을 더 낫게 만들기로 결심하고 나머지 요정들에게 소리쳤다.</td></tr>
<tr><td>8</td><td>"이 식물들을 치워, 그렇지 않으면 그것들의 끝이 뾰족한 잎사귀들이 누군가를 다치게 할 거야!" 그가 Triangle에게 말했다.</td></tr>
<tr><td>9</td><td>"하지만 Mike가 매일 그들에게 물을 주는데." Triangle이 말했다.</td></tr>
<tr><td>10</td><td>"이 훌라후프를 치워, 그렇지 않으면 굴러가서 뭔가를 부술 거야!" 그가 Circle에게 말했다.</td></tr>
<tr><td>11</td><td>"하지만 Mike는 매일 그걸로 운동을 하는데." Circle이 말했다.</td></tr>
<tr><td>12</td><td>"난 이 방을 정돈하려고 애쓰지만, 너희 둘은 항상 엉망으로 만들어." 그가 불평했다.</td></tr>
<tr><td>13</td><td>Triangle과 Circle이 서로를 쳐다보았다.</td></tr>
<tr><td>14</td><td>"그래서 네 생각에는 네가 우리 없이 다 할 수 있다는 거야?" Triangle이 Square에게 물었다.</td></tr>
<tr><td>15</td><td>"물론이지. 난 완전히 혼자서 이 방을 더 낫게 만들 수 있어." Square가 대답했다.</td></tr>
<tr><td>16</td><td>"잘됐네! 그럼 우린 쉴 수 있겠어." Circle이 Square에게 말했다.</td></tr>
<tr><td>17</td><td>Triangle과 Circle이 밖으로 나갔고 이제 Square가 모든 것을 담당했다.</td></tr>
</table>

18 He made the hangers, plants, and all the round things _____.

19 Then he _____ _____ and smiled.

20 "_____ better!"

21 When Mike came home from school, he _____ _____ a square hanger _____ _____ his jacket _____.

22 "What? This will not _____ _____ _____."

23 He _____ _____ _____ the plants and saw their square leaves.

24 "Poor things. ... They _____ _____ sick."

25 He _____ _____ the square hula hoop _____ _____.

26 "Hmm ... I don't know _____ _____ _____ this."

27 He went _____ _____ _____ his bike and looked at the square wheels.

28 "Well, I can't ride this. I'll just _____ _____ walk."

29 Then he _____ _____ _____ the house.

30 When the other spirits came back, Square _____ _____ _____ them.

31 "Mike doesn't like his room. I don't know _____ _____," he said.

32 They looked at the hangers, the plants, and _____ _____ _____ _____ _____.

33 Then they looked at _____ _____, and Square _____ his problem.

34 "Let's make this room _____ again," he said to _____, and the three spirits worked together _____ _____.

18 그는 옷걸이들과 식물들과 모든 둥근 물건들을 사각형으로 만들었다.

19 그리고 나서 그는 주위를 둘러보고 미소 지었다.

20 "훨씬 좋군!"

21 Mike가 학교에서 집으로 왔을 때, 그는 재킷을 걸기 위해 사각형 옷걸이 하나를 집었다.

22 "뭐야? 이것은 내 옷을 걸고 있지 못할 거야."

23 그는 식물에 물을 주러 가서 그것들의 사각형 잎사귀들을 보았다.

24 "불쌍한 것들.… 그들은 병든 것이 틀림없어."

25 그는 운동을 하기 위해 사각형 홀라후프를 집어 들었다.

26 "흠… 이걸 어떻게 돌리는지 모르겠어."

27 그는 자전거를 꺼내러 가서 사각형 바퀴들을 보았다.

28 "음, 난 이걸 탈 수 없어. 그냥 걸어가야 할 것 같아."

29 그리고 나서 그는 서둘러 집을 나섰다.

30 다른 요정들이 돌아왔을 때, Square는 그들에게 달려갔다.

31 "Mike는 그의 방을 좋아하지 않아. 난 뭘 해야 할지 모르겠어." 그가 말했다.

32 그들은 옷걸이들, 식물들, 그리고 모든 새로 사각형이 된 물건들을 바라보았다.

33 그리고 나서 그들은 서로를 바라보았고, Square는 자신의 문제를 깨달았다.

34 "이 방을 다시 멋지게 만들자." 그가 나머지 요정들에게 말했고, 세 요정들은 다시 한 번 함께 일했다.

• 우리말을 참고하여 본문을 영작하시오.

1 세 도형 요정들

➡ _____

2 Mike의 방에는 세 도형 요정이 살았다.

➡ _____

3 Square는 탁자, 책장, 그리고 창문을 담당했다.

➡ _____

4 Triangle은 옷걸이들과 식물들을 담당했다.

➡ _____

5 Circle은 둥근 것들을 돌보았다.

➡ _____

6 그들은 Mike에게 좋은 방을 만들어 주기 위해서 함께 일했다.

➡ _____

7 어느 날 Square는 방을 더 낫게 만들기로 결심하고 나머지 요정들에게 소리쳤다.

➡ _____

8 "이 식물들을 치워, 그렇지 않으면 그것들의 끝이 뾰족한 잎사귀들이 누군가를 다치게 할 거야!" 그가 Triangle에게 말했다.

➡ _____

9 "하지만 Mike가 매일 그들에게 물을 주는데." Triangle이 말했다.

➡ _____

10 "이 훌라후프를 치워, 그렇지 않으면 굴러가서 뭔가를 부술 거야!" 그가 Circle에게 말했다.

➡ _____

11 "하지만 Mike는 매일 그걸로 운동을 하는데." Circle이 말했다.

➡ _____

12 "난 이 방을 정돈하려고 애쓰지만, 너희 둘은 항상 엉망으로 만들어." 그가 불평했다.

➡ _____

13 Triangle과 Circle이 서로를 쳐다보았다.

➡ _____

14 "그래서 네 생각에는 네가 우리 없이 다 할 수 있다는 거야?" Triangle이 Square에게 물었다.

➡ _____

15 "물론이지. 난 완전히 혼자서 이 방을 더 낫게 만들 수 있어." Square가 대답했다.

➡ _____

16 "잘됐네! 그럼 우린 쉴 수 있겠어." Circle이 Square에게 말했다.

➡ _____

17 Triangle과 Circle이 밖으로 나갔고 이제 Square가 모든 것을 담당했다.

➡ _____

18 그는 옷걸이들과 식물들과 모든 둥근 물건들을 사각형으로 만들었다.

➡ _____

19 그러고 나서 그는 주위를 둘러보고 미소 지었다.

➡ _____

20 "훨씬 좋군!"

➡ _____

21 Mike가 학교에서 집으로 왔을 때, 그는 재킷을 걸기 위해 사각형 옷걸이 하나를 집었다.

➡ _____

22 "뭐야? 이것은 내 옷을 걸고 있지 못할 거야."

➡ _____

23 그는 식물에 물을 주러 가서 그것들의 사각형 잎사귀들을 보았다.

➡ _____

24 "불쌍한 것들.… 그들은 병든 것이 틀림없어."

➡ _____

25 그는 운동을 하기 위해 사각형 훌라후프를 집어 들었다.

➡ _____

26 "흠… 이걸 어떻게 돌리는지 모르겠어."

➡ _____

27 그는 자전거를 꺼내러 가서 사각형 바퀴들을 보았다.

➡ _____

28 "음, 난 이걸 탈 수 없어. 그냥 걸어가야 할 것 같아."

➡ _____

29 그러고 나서 그는 서둘러 집을 나섰다.

➡ _____

30 다른 요정들이 돌아왔을 때, Square는 그들에게 달려갔다.

➡ _____

31 "Mike는 그의 방을 좋아하지 않아. 난 뭘 해야 할지 모르겠어." 그가 말했다.

➡ _____

32 그들은 옷걸이들, 식물들, 그리고 모든 새로 사각형이 된 물건들을 바라보았다.

➡ _____

33 그러고 나서 그들은 서로를 바라보았고, Square는 자신의 문제를 깨달았다.

➡ _____

34 "이 방을 다시 멋지게 만들자." 그가 나머지 요정들에게 말했고, 세 요정들은 다시 한 번 함께 일했다.

➡ _____

[01~03] 다음 글을 읽고 물음에 답하시오.

There lived three shape spirits in Mike's room. Square controlled the table, the bookshelf, and the window. Triangle was in ⓐcharge of the hangers and the plants. Circle took care of the round things. ⓑThey worked together to make a nice room for Mike.

01 위 글의 밑줄 친 ⓐcharge와 같은 의미로 쓰인 것을 고르시오.

① Delivery is free of charge.
② When did they charge at the enemy?
③ He took charge of the farm after his father's death.
④ Before use, charge the battery.
⑤ What did they charge for the repairs?

서답형

02 위 글의 밑줄 친 ⓑThey가 가리키는 것을 쓰시오.

➡ ＿＿＿＿＿＿＿＿＿＿ 또는

＿＿＿＿＿＿＿＿＿＿

중요

03 위 글의 내용과 어울리는 속담을 모두 고르시오.

① Too many cooks spoil the broth.
② Two heads are better than one.
③ A stitch in time saves nine stitches.
④ Every cloud has a silver lining.
⑤ Many hands make light work.

[04~06] 다음 글을 읽고 물음에 답하시오.

One day Square decided to make the room better and shouted at (A)[another / the other] spirits.

"Take these plants away, or their pointy leaves will hurt someone!" he said to Triangle.

"But Mike waters them every day," said Triangle.

"Take this hula hoop away, or it will roll and break something!" he said to Circle.

"But Mike exercises with it every day," said Circle.

"I try ⓐto make this room (B)[messy / tidy], but you two always make a mess," he complained.

Triangle and Circle looked at each other.

"So you think you can do it (C)[with / without] us?" Triangle asked Square.

"Sure. I can make this room better all by myself," replied Square.

"Great! Then we can get some rest," Circle said to Square.

서답형

04 위 글의 괄호 (A)~(C)에서 문맥이나 어법상 알맞은 것을 골라 쓰시오.

➡ (A) ＿＿＿ (B) ＿＿＿ (C) ＿＿＿

05 위 글의 밑줄 친 ⓐto make와 to부정사의 용법이 다른 것을 모두 고르시오.

① To help others makes me happy.
② I have no friend to help me.
③ I found it useless to meet her there.
④ To lose weight, he started jogging.
⑤ His fault is to talk too much.

06 위 글의 내용과 일치하지 <u>않는</u> 것은?

① Square는 방을 더 낫게 만들기로 결심했다.
② Mike는 매일 식물들에게 물을 준다.
③ 훌라후프가 굴러가서 뭔가를 부술 거라고 Circle이 말했다.
④ Square는 Triangle과 Circle이 방을 항상 엉망으로 만든다고 불평했다.
⑤ Square는 완전히 혼자서 이 방을 더 낫게 만들 수 있다고 대답했다.

[07~09] 다음 글을 읽고 물음에 답하시오.

Triangle and Circle went out and Square was now in control. ⓐ그는 옷걸이들과 식물들과 모든 둥근 물건들을 사각형으로 만들었다. Then he looked around and smiled. "Much better!"

When Mike came home from school, he picked up a square hanger to hang his jacket on.

"What? This will not hold my clothes."

He went to water the plants and saw their square leaves.

"Poor things. ... They ⓑ<u>must</u> be sick."

He picked up the square hula hoop to exercise.

"Hmm ... I don't know how to spin this."

He went to take out his bike and looked at the square wheels.

"Well, I can't ride this. I'll just have to walk." Then he hurried out of the house.

서답형

07 위 글의 밑줄 친 ⓐ의 우리말에 맞게 주어진 어휘를 이용하여 11 단어로 영작하시오.

| the hangers, all the round things |

➡ _____

08 위 글의 밑줄 친 ⓑ<u>must</u>와 같은 의미로 쓰인 것을 <u>모두</u> 고르시오.

① All visitors <u>must</u> report to reception.
② You <u>must</u> be hungry after all that walking.
③ I <u>must</u> be going now.
④ You <u>must</u> do as you are told.
⑤ He <u>must</u> be at home. I see his car in his garage.

중요

09 위 글을 읽고 대답할 수 <u>없는</u> 질문은?

① After Triangle and Circle went out, who was in control?
② In what shape did Square make all the things in the room?
③ When Mike came home, why did he go to the plants?
④ How many plants with the square leaves were there?
⑤ Why did Mike have to walk?

[10~12] 다음 글을 읽고 물음에 답하시오.

When the other spirits came back, Square rushed over to them.

"Mike doesn't like his room. ⓐ난 뭘 해야 할지 모르겠어," he said.

They looked at the hangers, the plants, and all the new square things. Then they looked at one another, and Square realized his problem.

ⓑ<u>"Let's make this room greatly again,"</u> <u>he said to the others, and the three spirits</u> <u>worked together once again.</u>

서답형

10 위 글의 밑줄 친 ⓐ의 우리말에 맞게 영작하시오.

➡ _____

서답형

11 위 글의 밑줄 친 ⓑ에서 어법상 틀린 부분을 찾아 고치시오.

_____ ➡ _____

중요

12 위 글의 종류로 알맞은 것을 고르시오.

① review ② article ③ fable

④ legend ⑤ poem

[13~15] 다음 글을 읽고 물음에 답하시오.

One day Square decided to make the room better and shouted ⓐ ①the other spirits.

"Take these plants away, or their pointy leaves will hurt someone!" he said to Triangle.

"But Mike waters ②them every day," said Triangle.

"Take this hula hoop away, or it will roll and break something!" he said to Circle.

"But Mike exercises ⓑ it every day," said Circle.

"I try to make this room tidy, but you two always make a mess," he complained.

Triangle and Circle looked at ③each other.

"So you think you can do it without ④us?" Triangle asked Square.

"Sure. I can make this room better all by myself," replied Square.

"Great! Then ⑤we can get some rest," Circle said to Square.

중요

13 밑줄 친 ①~⑤ 중에서 가리키는 대상이 나머지 넷과 다른 것은?

① ② ③ ④ ⑤

14 위 글의 빈칸 ⓐ와 ⓑ에 들어갈 전치사가 바르게 짝지어진 것은?

① at – with ② to – on

③ to – from ④ at – on

⑤ on – with

서답형

15 다음 문장에서 위 글의 내용과 다른 부분을 고쳐 문장을 다시 쓰시오.

Triangle and Circle thought that they could make the room better all by themselves without Square.

➡ _____

[16~18] 다음 글을 읽고 물음에 답하시오.

When the other spirits came back, Square rushed over to them.

"Mike doesn't like his room. I don't know what to do," he said.

They looked at the hangers, the plants, and all the new square things. Then they looked at one another, and Square realized his problem.

"Let's make this room great again," he said to ⓐ , and the three spirits worked together once again.

Adapted from *The Greedy Triangle*

(Marilyn Burns, 2008)

16 위 글에서 알 수 있는 Square의 심경 변화로 가장 알맞은 것을 고르시오.

① excited → disappointed
② worried → hopeful
③ confident → excited
④ satisfied → depressed
⑤ worried → upset

17 위 글의 빈칸 ⓐ에 들어갈 알맞은 말을 고르시오.

① others ② the others
③ another ④ some
⑤ the other

18 위 글을 읽고 답할 수 없는 질문은?

① When the other spirits came back, what did Square do?
② Does Mike like his room?
③ How many new square things are there in the room?
④ Did Square make the room great again by himself?
⑤ Why did the three spirits work together once again?

[19~21] 다음 글을 읽고 물음에 답하시오.

"I try to make this room tidy, but ⓐyou two always make a mess," he ⓑ .
Triangle and Circle looked at each other.
"So you think you can do it without us?" Triangle asked Square.
"Sure. ⓒ난 완전히 혼자서 이 방을 더 낫게 만들 수 있어," replied Square.
"Great! Then we can get some rest," Circle said to Square.

서답형

19 위 글의 밑줄 친 ⓐyou two가 가리키는 것을 본문에서 찾아 쓰시오.

➡ _____

20 위 글의 빈칸 ⓑ에 들어갈 알맞은 말을 고르시오.

① praised ② required
③ allowed ④ complained
⑤ prevented

서답형

21 위 글의 밑줄 친 ⓒ의 우리말에 맞게 한 단어를 보충하여, 주어진 어휘를 알맞게 배열하시오.

myself / this / all / make / room / can / I / by

➡ _____

[22~23] 다음 글을 읽고 물음에 답하시오.

Square for Mom
I made a square bag out of (A)[using / used] jeans.
My mom knew (B)[how / what] to wear with it.
ⓐ그것은 엄마를 들뜨게 했어.
That made me (C)[happy / happily].

22 위 글의 괄호 (A)~(C)에서 어법상 알맞은 낱말을 골라 쓰시오.

➡ (A) _____ (B) _____ (C) _____

23 위 글의 밑줄 친 ⓐ의 우리말에 맞게 주어진 어휘를 이용하여 영작하시오. (필요하면 변형할 것, 4 단어)

excite, her

➡ _____

[01~03] 다음 글을 읽고 물음에 답하시오.

There lived three (A)[shape / shapes] spirits in Mike's room. Square (B)[controled / controlled] the table, the bookshelf, and the window. Triangle was (C)[in / on] charge of the hangers and the plants. Circle took care of the round things. They worked together to make a nice room ___ⓐ___ Mike.

01 위 글의 괄호 (A)~(C)에서 문맥이나 어법상 알맞은 낱말을 골라 쓰시오.

➡ (A) _____ (B) _____ (C) _____

02 What did Square control? Answer in English in a full sentence.

➡ _____

03 위 글의 빈칸 ⓐ에 알맞은 전치사를 쓰시오.

➡ _____

[04~06] 다음 글을 읽고 물음에 답하시오.

Triangle and Circle went out and Square was now in control. He made the hangers, plants, and all the round things square. Then he looked around and smiled. "Much better!"

When Mike came home from school, he picked up a square hanger to hang his jacket on.

"What? This will not hold my (A)[cloths / clothes]."

He went to water the plants and saw their square leaves.

"Poor things. ... They (B)[must / have to] be sick."

He picked up the square hula hoop to exercise.

ⓐ"Hmm ... I don't know how to spin this."

He went to take out his bike and looked at the square wheels.

"Well, I can't ride this. I'll just (C)[must / have to] walk." Then he hurried out of the house.

04 위 글의 괄호 (A)~(C)에서 문맥이나 어법상 알맞은 낱말을 골라 쓰시오.

➡ (A) _____ (B) _____ (C) _____

05 물건들이 다음처럼 사각형으로 바뀐 것에 대한 Mike의 생각을 우리말로 쓰시오.

➡ 사각형 옷걸이:

사각형 잎사귀들을 가진 식물들:

06 위 글을 읽고 Mike가 밑줄 친 ⓐ처럼 말한 이유를 우리말로 쓰시오.

➡ _____

[07~09] 다음 글을 읽고 물음에 답하시오.

Triangle and Circle went out and Square was now in control. He made the hangers, plants, and all the round things square. Then he looked around and smiled. "Much better!"

When Mike came home from school, he picked up a square hanger to hang his jacket on.

"What? This will not hold my clothes."

He went to water the plants and saw their square leaves.

"Poor things. ... They must be sick."

He picked up the square hula hoop to exercise.

"Hmm ... ⓐI don't know how to spin this."

He went to take out his bike and looked at the square wheels.

"Well, I can't ride this. I'll just have to walk." Then he hurried out of the house.

07 위 글에서 Triangle이 담당하던 물건들을 Square가 어떻게 바꾸었는지 우리말로 쓰시오.

➡ (1) _____

(2) _____

08 위 글의 밑줄 친 ⓐ를 다음과 같이 바꿔 쓸 때 빈칸에 들어갈 알맞은 말을 쓰시오.

➡ I don't know how _____ spin this.

09 위 글에서 Square가 Circle이 담당하던 물건들을 바꾼 것 때문에, Mike가 할 수 없게 된 것 두 가지를 우리말로 쓰시오.

➡ (1) _____

(2) _____

[10~11] 다음 글을 읽고 물음에 답하시오.

One day Square decided to make the room better and shouted at the other spirits.

"Take these plants away, or their pointy leaves will hurt someone!" he said to Triangle.

"But Mike waters them every day," said Triangle.

"ⓐTake this hula hoop away, or it will roll and break something!" he said to Circle.

"But Mike exercises with it every day," said Circle.

"I try to make this room tidy, but you two always make a mess," he complained.

Triangle and Circle looked at each other.

ⓑ"So you think you can do it with us?" Triangle asked Square.

"Sure. I can make this room better all by myself," replied Square.

"Great! Then we can get some rest," Circle said to Square.

10 위 글의 밑줄 친 ⓐ를 (1) If, (2) Unless를 사용하여 고치시오.

➡ (1) _____

(2) _____

11 위 글의 밑줄 친 ⓑ에서 흐름상 어색한 부분을 찾아 고치시오.

_____ ➡ _____

해석

Your Turn

1. **A:** Do you know how to cook *ramyeon*?
 '어떻게 ~하는지' '~하는 방법'으로 해석, 상대방의 능력이나 하는 방법을 물을 때 사용
 B: Sure. First, boil some water. Then, put the *ramyeon* and dried soup mix.
 어떤 일을 하는 절차나 방법을 단계적으로 설명할 때, " First. …
 Finally, boil for 4 more minutes. Then. … Finally. …"를 사용하여 각 단계의 내용을 열거한다.

2. **A:** Do you know how to make potato salad?

 B: Sure. First, boil the potatoes. Then, cut them into pieces. Finally, put
 ~을 조각으로 자르다
 some sauce on them.

3. **A:** Do you know how to make sandwiches?

 B: Sure. First, put an egg on bread. Then, add some vegetables. Finally, put
 bread on top.
 맨 위에

구문해설 • **boil** 끓이다 • **dried** 건조된, 마른 • **potato** 감자
• **cut A into pieces** A를 조각으로 자르다 • **vegetable** 야채, 채소

Express Yourself

Square for Mom
 ~을 위한
I made a square bag out of used jeans.
 (재료를 나타내어) …에서, …으로 낡은
My mom knew what to wear with it.
 = she should = the bag
It made her excited.
 exciting(×)
That made me happy.
목적격보어 자리에 부사를 쓸 수 없고 형용사로 써야 한다.

구문해설 • **jeans:** 청바지 • **wear:** ~을 입다 • **excited:** 신이 난, 들뜬, 흥분한

Link to the World

Euclid taught math at the Library of Alexandria when Ptolemy I was the king
 접속사(~일 때)
of Egypt.

People call him "the father of math." He showed how to draw a triangle
call A B(A를 B라고 부르다) 의문사+to부정사(showed의 목적어)
that has three sides of the same length.
주격 관계대명사
He also showed how to find the center of the biggest circle in a triangle.
 의문사+to부정사(showed의 목적어)
One day, Ptolemy I asked, "Is there an easier way to study math?" Euclid
 부정사(형용사적 용법)
replied, "There is no royal road to learning."
 전치사 동명사

구문해설 • **royal road:** 쉬운 방법, 지름길, 왕도

1. A: 너 라면을 요리할 줄 아니?
 B: 물론이지. 먼저, 약간의 물을 끓여. 그러고 나서, 라면과 건조 수프를 넣어. 마지막으로, 4분을 더 끓여.

2. A: 너 감자 샐러드를 만들 줄 아니?
 B: 물론이지. 먼저, 감자를 삶아. 그러고 나서, 감자를 여러 조각으로 잘라. 마지막으로, 그 위에 소스를 좀 뿌려.

3. A: 너 샌드위치를 만들 줄 아니?
 B: 물론이지. 먼저, 빵 위에 계란을 올려. 그러고 나서, 채소를 약간 추가해. 마지막으로, 빵을 맨 위에 올려.

엄마를 위한 사각형
난 낡은 청바지로 사각형 가방을 만들었어.
엄마는 그걸 들 때 뭘 입어야 할지 아셔.
그것은 엄마를 들뜨게 했어.
그게 나를 행복하게 했어.

유클리드는 프톨레마이오스 1세(Ptolemy I)가 이집트의 왕이었을 때 알렉산드리아 도서관에서 수학을 가르쳤다.
사람들은 그를 '수학의 아버지'라고 부른다. 그는 같은 길이의 세 변을 가진 삼각형을 어떻게 그리는지를 보여 주었다.
그는 또한 한 개의 삼각형 안에서 가장 큰 원의 중심을 어떻게 찾는지도 보여 주었다.
어느 날, 프톨레마이오스 1세가 "수학을 공부하는 더 쉬운 방법은 없나요?"라고 물었다. 유클리드는 "배움에 왕도는 없습니다."라고 응답했다.

영역별 핵심문제

01 다음 주어진 두 단어의 관계가 같도록 빈칸에 알맞은 단어를 쓰시오.

> hurry : rush = lastly : _____

02 다음 대화의 빈칸에 공통으로 들어갈 단어로 알맞은 것은?

> G: Do you know _____ to divide this cake into four equal pieces?
> B: Let me see... _____ about dividing it this way? Then the pieces will be the same size and shape.

① what[What] ② why[Why]
③ when[When] ④ who[Who]
⑤ how[How]

03 다음 글의 빈칸 ⓐ와 ⓑ에 들어갈 단어로 알맞은 것은?

> One day Square decided to make the room better and ⓐ_____ at the other spirits.
> "Take these plants away, or their pointy leaves will ⓑ_____ someone!" he said to Triangle.

① whispered – save
② shouted – hurt
③ shouted – take
④ hurried – reply
⑤ divided – control

04 빈칸에 들어갈 말로 알맞은 것은?

> • _____ : to become separated into smaller parts
> e.g. I know how to _____ this cake into four equal pieces.

① take ② divide ③ hold
④ carry ⑤ move

05 다음 영영풀이에 해당하는 것을 고르시오.

> to gradually begin to understand something that you did not know or notice before

① roll ② hang ③ perform
④ realize ⑤ remember

06 다음 밑줄 친 부분의 의미가 바르지 <u>않은</u> 것은?

① The boat only carries you and one of the things <u>at a time</u>. 한 번에
② I can take them to the other side <u>one by one</u>. 하나씩
③ I can make this room better all <u>by myself</u>. 저절로
④ He picked up a hanger to <u>hang</u> his jacket on. 걸다
⑤ He went to take out his bike and looked at the <u>square wheels</u>. 사각형 바퀴

Conversation

07 주어진 그림을 참고하여 대화의 빈칸에 들어갈 말로 알맞은 것을 고르시오.

Ben: Do you know how to divide this into four equal pieces?

Jenny: Sure. First, divide it into three _____(A)_____ . Then, divide each square into four smaller squares. Finally, color three small squares in the inside corner of the L.

Ben: Oh, I can see ____(B)____ other L shapes around it! You're great!

① different triangles – two
② equal squares – four
③ equal circles – three
④ equal squares – three
⑤ different squares – four

08 대화의 빈칸에 들어갈 말의 순서로 알맞은 것은?

G: Do you know how to make this?
B: _____

(A) Finally, wrap it up and make a triangle.
(B) Then, add some dried fish and hot peppers.
(C) It's easy. First, put some rice on *gim*.

① (A) – (B) – (C) ② (B) – (A) – (C)
③ (B) – (C) – (A) ④ (C) – (A) – (B)
⑤ (C) – (B) – (A)

[09~10] 다음 대화를 읽고 물음에 답하시오.

(1)
W: Excuse me. Do you know ____(A)____ draw a mouse with shapes?
M: Sure. First, draw a large triangle. Then, draw two dots and 6 lines. Finally, draw two small circles.
W: Thanks. I'll draw it myself now.

(2)
A: Do you know ____(A)____ make potato salad?
B: Sure. (a)First, boil the potatoes. Then, cut them into pieces. Finally, put some sauce on them.

09 (1)과 (2)의 빈칸 (A)에 공통으로 들어갈 두 단어를 쓰시오.

➡ _____

10 위 대화의 밑줄 친 (a)의 의도로 알맞은 것은?

① 능력 묻기 ② 소개하기
③ 관심 묻기 ④ 열거하기
⑤ 동작 묘사

[11~12] 다음 대화의 빈칸에 들어갈 알맞은 표현은?

11
A: _____
B: Sure. First, put an egg on bread. Then, add some vegetables. Finally, put bread on top.

① Do you know how to make potato salad?
② Are you good at cooking?
③ Do you know how to cook *ramyeon*?
④ Why are you making sandwiches?
⑤ Do you know how to make sandwiches?

12

G: Do you know how to make paper airplanes?

B: _____

① No, you can't.

② Sure. I'll show you how.

③ Put some legs on the bottom.

④ Sure. Put wheels under the car.

⑤ Sure. Push the button here.

Grammar

13 다음 빈칸에 알맞은 말이 바르게 짝지어진 것은?

- Mildred _____ her room bright.
- It shows _____ to divide a square into seven pieces.

① made – how ② wanted – why

③ ordered – that ④ asked – what

⑤ forced – where

14 다음 중 어법상 어색한 문장은?

① I don't know what to do.

② I can't decide which car to buy.

③ She knew where to stop and where to pass.

④ Rose was wondering whom to meet that afternoon.

⑤ He wants to know when should begin the project.

15 다음 중 어법상 옳은 것은?

① Let's make her happily.

② Samantha looked very friendly.

③ The thick clothes keep me warmly.

④ Jogging early in the morning makes me health.

⑤ Rick painted his house greenly.

16 다음 주어진 단어를 이용하여 빈칸에 알맞은 말을 쓰시오.

어느 것을 먹어야 할지 결정하지 못하겠어.
= I can't decide _____. (eat)

➡ _____

17 괄호 안에서 알맞은 것을 고르시오.

(1) He also showed (how / what) to find the center of the biggest circle in a triangle.

(2) Can you tell me where (sitting / to sit)?

(3) Do you know (how / why) to solve the puzzle in another way?

(4) I'm not sure how (I should / I) draw a bear with shapes.

(5) Try to make the poem (special / specially) using your imagination and creativity.

(6) The boys (founded / found) the movie exciting.

18 다음 글에서 어법상 잘못 쓰인 것을 찾아 알맞게 고치시오. (2곳)

One day, Square wanted the other spirits to take the round or triangular things away to make the room better. Triangle and Circle left the room to get some rest and Square made the hangers, the plants, and the all round things square. However, Mike didn't like the newly changed things, and Square didn't know how to do. He realized his problem, and the three spirits worked together again.

➡ _____

➡ _____

Reading

[19~20] 다음 글을 읽고 물음에 답하시오.

There lived three shape spirits in Mike's room. Square controlled the table, the bookshelf, and the window. Triangle was in charge of the hangers and the plants. Circle took care of the round things. They worked together ⓐto make a nice room for Mike.

19 아래 〈보기〉에서 위 글의 밑줄 친 ⓐto make와 문법적 쓰임이 같은 것의 개수를 고르시오.

┌─── 보기 ───┐
① He was pleased to make such a beautiful garden.
② She went shopping to make me a delicious lunch.
③ Please tell me the way to make a wooden table.
④ He must be foolish to make such a big mistake.
⑤ I tried to make a model airplane.
└────────────┘

① 1개　② 2개　③ 3개　④ 4개　⑤ 5개

20 위 글의 내용과 일치하지 <u>않는</u> 것은?

① Mike의 방에는 세 도형 요정이 살았다.
② Square는 탁자, 옷장, 그리고 창문을 담당했다.
③ Triangle은 옷걸이들과 식물들을 담당했다.
④ Circle은 둥근 것들을 돌보았다.
⑤ 세 도형 요정들은 Mike에게 좋은 방을 만들기 위해서 함께 일했다.

[21~23] 다음 글을 읽고 물음에 답하시오.

One day Square decided to make the room better and shouted at the other spirits.
"Take these plants away, or their pointy leaves will hurt someone!" he said to Triangle.
"But Mike waters them every day," said Triangle.
"Take this hula hoop away, ___ⓐ___ it will roll and break something!" he said to Circle.
"But Mike exercises with it every day," said Circle.
"I try to make this room tidy, but you two always make a mess," he complained.
Triangle and Circle looked at each other.
"So you think you can do it without us?" Triangle asked Square.
"Sure. I can make this room better all ⓑby myself," replied Square.
"Great! Then we can get some rest," Circle said to Square.

21 주어진 영영풀이에 해당하는 단어를 본문에서 찾아 쓰시오.

neat and arranged in an organized way

➡ _____

22 위 글의 빈칸 ⓐ에 알맞은 말을 쓰시오.

➡ _____

23 위 글의 밑줄 친 ⓑby myself와 바꿔 쓸 수 있는 한 단어를 쓰시오.

➡ _____

[24~26] 다음 글을 읽고 물음에 답하시오.

Triangle and Circle went out and Square was now ____ⓐ____ control. He made the hangers, plants, and all the round things square. Then he looked around and smiled. "Much better!"

When Mike came home from school, he picked up a square hanger to hang his jacket ____ⓑ____.

"What? ①This will not hold my clothes."

He went to water the plants and saw ②their square leaves.

"Poor things. ... ③They must be sick."

He picked up the square hula-hoop to exercise.

"Hmm ... I don't know how to spin ④this."

He went to take out his bike and looked at the square wheels.

"Well, I can't ride ⑤this. I'll just have to walk." Then he hurried out of the house.

24 위 글의 빈칸 ⓐ와 ⓑ에 들어갈 전치사가 바르게 짝지어진 것은?

① in – on ② at – to
③ in – from ④ for – to
⑤ for – on

25 위 글의 밑줄 친 ①~⑤가 지칭하는 것이 옳지 않은 것은?

① a square hanger
② the plants
③ the plants
④ the square hula hoop
⑤ the square wheels

26 본문의 내용과 일치하도록 다음 빈칸 (A)와 (B)에 알맞은 단어를 쓰시오.

Mike couldn't do such things as hanging his jacket, spinning the hula hoop, and (A)_____ his bike because (B)_____ made the things square.

[27~28] 다음 글을 읽고 물음에 답하시오.

ⓐWhen the other spirits came back, Square rushed over to them.

"Mike doesn't like his room. I don't know what to do," he said.

They looked at the hangers, the plants, and all the new square things. Then they looked at one another, and Square realized ⓑhis problem.

"Let's make this room great again," he said to the others, and the three spirits worked together once again.

Adapted from *The Greedy Triangle*
(Marilyn Burns, 2008)

27 위 글의 밑줄 친 ⓐWhen과 같은 의미로 쓰인 것을 고르시오.

① I don't know <u>when</u> Mike went out.
② Do you remember <u>when</u> you saw it?
③ <u>When</u> did he promise to meet her?
④ He stays at home <u>when</u> it rains.
⑤ <u>When</u> can she come?

28 다음 빈칸에 알맞은 단어를 넣어 밑줄 친 ⓑhis problem에 대한 설명을 완성하시오.

Square made the hangers and the plants square, so Mike didn't _____ _____ _____.

출제율 95%

01 다음 짝지어진 단어의 관계가 같도록 빈칸에 알맞은 말을 쓰시오.

> perfect : imperfect = join : _____

출제율 90%

02 우리말에 맞게 빈칸에 알맞은 단어를 쓰시오.

> • 먼저, 낡은 청바지에서 다리 부분을 잘라내.
> (A) _____, _____ _____ the leg from used jeans.
> • 마지막으로, 그것을 싸서 삼각형을 만들어.
> (B) _____, _____ it _____ and make a triangle.

출제율 95%

03 다음 글의 괄호 안에 알맞은 말을 선택하시오.

> One day Square decided to make the room better and shouted at the other spirits.
> "Take these plants away, or their (A) [round / pointy] leaves will hurt someone!" he said to Triangle.
> "But Mike waters them every day," said Triangle.
> "Take this hula hoop away, or it will (B) [hang / roll] and break something!" he said to Circle.
> "But Mike exercises with it every day," said Circle.
> "I try to make this room tidy, but you two always make a mess," he (C)[complained / cheered].

	(A)	(B)	(C)
①	round	roll	complained
②	round	hang	cheered
③	pointy	roll	cheered
④	pointy	roll	complained
⑤	pointy	hang	complained

출제율 90%

04 다음 영영풀이에 해당하는 단어는?

> a short coat that covers the upper part of the body

① plant ② shirt ③ jacket
④ space ⑤ bottom

[05~06] 다음 대화를 읽고 물음에 답하시오.

Boy: Do you know how to solve this puzzle?
Girl: What is it?
Boy: You must take a dog, a chicken, and a bag of rice across the river. The boat only carries you and one of the things at a time.
Girl: That's easy. I can take them to the other side one by one.
Boy: But without you, the dog will kill the chicken, and the chicken will eat the rice.
Girl: Let me see. ... First, take the chicken and come back. Then, take the rice and come back with the chicken.
Boy: And?
Girl: After that, take the dog and come back. Finally, take the chicken.
Boy: You're great!

출제율 100%

05 다음 질문에 대한 답을 대화에서 찾아 영어로 쓰시오.

> Q: What's the problem if the girl takes the rice first?

➡ _____

06 위 대화를 읽고 답할 수 <u>없는</u> 질문은?

① Did the girl know the answer at first?

② What must be taken to the other side of the river?

③ Which must be taken across the river last?

④ When did the boy know the answer?

⑤ What will the chicken do if the girl takes the dog first?

[07~08] 다음 대화를 읽고 물음에 답하시오.

B: ⓐ<u>This</u> looks great.

G: I think so, too. Do you know how to make it?

B: It's easy. First, put some rice on *gim*. Then, add some dried fish and hot peppers. Finally, wrap it up and make a triangle.

07 위 대화의 밑줄 친 ⓐ<u>This</u>는 무엇을 가리키는가?

① a square kite

② a triangle *gimbap*

③ triangle sunglasses

④ a circle bookmark

⑤ a round bear

08 위 대화에서 언급된 것을 만들 때 재료로 언급되지 <u>않은</u> 것은?

① rice ② *gim*

③ dried fish ④ wrap

⑤ hot peppers

09 다음 두 사람의 대화가 <u>어색한</u> 것은?

① A: So you think you can do it without us?

 B: Sure!

② A: Do you know how to solve this puzzle?

 B: What is it?

③ A: Do you know how to cook *ramyeon*?

 B: Sure. First, put an egg on bread. Then, add some vegetables. Finally, put bread on top.

④ A: Do you know how to draw a bear with shapes?

 B: Sure. First, draw a large circle. Then, draw three small circles. Finally, draw three dots.

⑤ A: Do you know how to make three more triangles with three more pencils?

 B: Let me see. ... It's too difficult for me.

10 대화의 밑줄 친 우리말에 맞게 문장의 빈칸에 들어갈 알맞은 말을 고르시오.

B: Do you know how to fly this?

G: Yes. I'll show you how. <u>그것은 바람을 마주해야만 해</u>. Hold it up like this.

It has to _____ the wind.

① reply ② visit

③ face ④ move

⑤ control

✎ 출제율 95%

11 다음 중 어법상 <u>어색한</u> 것은?

① He made the tables square.

② Julia painted the table brown.

③ This thick jacket kept me warm last winter.

④ The boy found the ants very strongly.

⑤ Don't get me wrong.

✎ 출제율 85%

12 다음 그림을 보고 괄호 안에 주어진 어휘를 이용하여 빈칸에 알맞은 말을 쓰시오.

A: Do you know ＿＿＿＿＿＿＿ cookies? (bake)

B: Yes, I do. I like baking cookies.

✎ 출제율 100%

13 주어진 문장의 밑줄 친 부분과 용법이 <u>다른</u> 하나는?

> The pig <u>made</u> the tent dirty.

① The movie <u>made</u> me excited.

② The song <u>makes</u> me sad.

③ Her mom <u>made</u> her a dress.

④ Having regular exercise <u>makes</u> us healthy.

⑤ His joke <u>made</u> me laugh a lot.

✎ 출제율 90%

14 다음 괄호 안에 주어진 단어를 어법에 맞게 빈칸에 한 단어씩 쓰시오.

(1) I didn't know where to fish.

= I didn't know ＿＿＿＿ ＿＿＿＿ ＿＿＿＿ ＿＿＿＿. (fish)

(2) Will you tell me ＿＿＿＿ ＿＿＿＿ ＿＿＿＿ to the bus stop? (get)

= Will you tell me how I can get to the bus stop?

(3) Marie asked her mom ＿＿＿＿ ＿＿＿＿ ＿＿＿＿ after. (look)

= Marie asked her mom whom she should look after.

(4) Please tell me which apple to choose.

= Please tell me ＿＿＿＿ ＿＿＿＿ ＿＿＿＿ ＿＿＿＿ ＿＿＿＿. (choose)

[15~16] 다음 글을 읽고 물음에 답하시오.

ⓐThere lived three shape spirits in Mike's room. Square controlled the table, the bookshelf, and the window. Triangle was in charge of the hangers and the plants. Circle took care of the round things. They worked together to make a nice room for Mike.

✎ 출제율 95%

15 위 글의 밑줄 친 ⓐThere와 의미가 <u>다른</u> 것을 <u>모두</u> 고르시오.

① <u>There</u> are two people waiting outside.

② <u>There</u> seemed to be no doubt about it.

③ I hope we get <u>there</u> in time.

④ <u>There</u> is a book on the desk.

⑤ What were you doing <u>there</u>?

✎ 출제율 85%

16 Who took care of the round things? Answer in English in two words.

➡ ＿＿＿＿＿＿＿＿＿＿＿＿＿＿＿

[17~19] 다음 글을 읽고 물음에 답하시오.

Triangle and Circle went out and Square was now in control. He made the hangers, plants, and all the round things ____ⓐ____ . Then he looked around and smiled. "Much better!"

When Mike came home from school, he picked up a square hanger ①to hang his jacket on.

"What? This will not hold my clothes."

He went ②to water the plants and saw their square leaves.

"Poor things. ... They must be sick."

He picked up the square hula hoop ③to exercise.

"Hmm ... I don't know how ④to spin this."

He went ⑤to take out his bike and looked at the square wheels.

"Well, I can't ride this. I'll just have to walk." Then he hurried out of the house.

출제율 90%

17 위 글의 빈칸 ⓐ에 들어갈 알맞은 말을 고르시오.

① pointy ② triangle ③ tidy
④ circle ⑤ square

출제율 95%

18 밑줄 친 ①~⑤ 중에서 to부정사의 용법이 나머지 넷과 <u>다른</u> 것은?

① ② ③ ④ ⑤

출제율 95%

19 위 글의 내용과 일치하지 <u>않는</u> 것은?

① Triangle과 Circle이 밖으로 나갔고 이제 Square가 모든 것을 담당했다.
② Mike가 학교에서 집으로 왔을 때, 그는 옷걸이에 재킷을 걸었다.
③ Mike는 식물들이 병든 것이 틀림없다고 생각했다.
④ Mike는 사각형 훌라후프를 돌릴 수 없었다.
⑤ Mike는 자전거를 타는 대신 걸어가기로 했다.

[20~22] 다음 글을 읽고 물음에 답하시오.

Triangle Sunglasses

I made triangle sunglasses ⓐout of a paper box and a plastic bag.

My baby sister knew ⓑ언제 그걸 써야 할지.

They made her excited.

That made me happy.

출제율 95%

20 위 글의 밑줄 친 ⓐout of와 같은 의미로 쓰인 것을 고르시오.

① This robot was made <u>out of</u> an empty can.
② Two bears came <u>out of</u> the forest.
③ She did so <u>out of</u> curiosity.
④ He came <u>out of</u> a poor family.
⑤ Out of sight, <u>out of</u> mind.

출제율 95%

21 위 글의 밑줄 친 ⓑ의 우리말에 맞게 주어진 어휘를 이용하여 5 단어로 영작하시오.

> put, on

➡ _____

출제율 95%

22 위 글을 읽고 알 수 <u>없는</u> 것을 고르시오.

① 삼각형 선글라스를 만든 사람
② 삼각형 선글라스의 재료
③ 삼각형 선글라스를 쓸 사람
④ 삼각형 선글라스를 써야 할 때
⑤ 글쓴이의 기분

01 다음은 상대방의 능력 여부를 묻는 말이다. 주어진 단어를 이용하여 대화의 내용에 어울리는 질문을 완성하시오.

> B: Do you know _____?
> G: Sure. First, divide it into three equal squares. Then, divide each square into four smaller squares. Finally, color three small squares in the inside corner of the L.
> B: Oh, I can see three other L shapes around it! You're great!

> how / divide / this / equal pieces

➡ _____

02 다음은 연을 날리는 방법에 대한 글이다. 주어진 문장을 순서대로 배열하여 절차를 말하는 대화를 완성하시오.

> • hold it up until it catches the wind
> • let the line out
> • stand with your back to the wind

> A: Do you know how to fly this?
> B: _____
> _____
> _____

03 다음 대화의 밑줄 친 우리말에 맞게 주어진 어휘를 이용하여 영어로 쓰시오.

> ┌─ 보기 ─
> (A) (know / how / divide / this cake / pieces)
> (B) (how / divide / it / this)

> G: (A)이 케이크를 네 개의 같은 조각으로 어떻게 나눌 수 있는지 아니?
> B: Let me see. ... (B)이 방법으로 그것을 나누는 것은 어때? Then the pieces will be the same size and shape.

➡ (A) _____

(B) _____

04 다음 우리말을 주어진 어휘를 이용하여 영작하시오.

(1) 연필 세 자루를 더 추가해서 어떻게 삼각형 3개를 더 만드는지 아니? (make, more, with)
➡ _____

(2) 이 꽃들을 어디서 길러야 하는지 내게 알려 줘. (grow, let, these)
➡ _____

(3) 언제 출발해야 하는지 말해 줄 수 있어? (tell, can, start)
➡ _____

(4) 작은 검정색 원들이 그것을 완벽하게 만들었어. (perfect, make, the)
➡ _____

(5) 그것은 점심시간에 나를 배부르게 했지. (make, it, lunch time, full, at)
➡ _____

(6) 나의 아버지는 내가 정직하다고 믿는다. (father, believe)
➡ _____

One day Square decided (A)[to make / making] the room better and shouted at the other spirits.

"Take these plants away, ___ⓐ___ their (B)[pointing / pointy] leaves will hurt someone!" he said to Triangle.

"But Mike (C)[water / waters] them every day," said Triangle.

"Take this hula hoop away, or it will roll and break something!" he said to Circle.

"But Mike exercises with it every day," said Circle.

"I try to make this room tidy, but you two always make a mess," he complained.

Triangle and Circle looked at each other.

"So you think you can do it without us?" Triangle asked Square.

"Sure. I can make this room better all by myself," replied Square.

"Great! Then we can get some rest," Circle said to Square.

05 위 글의 빈칸 ⓐ에 들어갈 알맞은 말을 쓰시오.

➡ _____

06 위 글의 괄호 (A)~(C)에서 문맥이나 어법상 알맞은 낱말을 골라 쓰시오.

➡ (A) _____ (B) _____ (C) _____

07 다음 질문에 대한 알맞은 대답을 주어진 단어로 시작하여 쓰시오. (6 단어)

Q: Why does Square tell Circle to take the hula hoop away?

A: Because _____ if Circle doesn't take it away.

➡ _____

Triangle and Circle went out and Square was now in control. He made the hangers, plants, and all the round things square. Then he looked around and smiled. "Much better!"

When Mike came home from school, he picked up a square hanger to hang his jacket on.

"What? This will not hold my clothes."

He went to water the plants and saw their square leaves.

"Poor things. ... They must be sick."

He picked up the square hula hoop to exercise.

"Hmm ... I don't know how to spin this."

He went to take out his bike and looked at the square wheels.

ⓐ"Well, I can't ride this. I'll just have to walk." Then he hurried out of the house.

08 위 글에서 Circle이 담당하던 물건들을 Square가 어떻게 바꾸었는지 우리말로 쓰시오.

➡ (1) _____
 (2) _____

09 다음 문장에서 위 글의 내용과 다른 부분을 찾아서 모두 고치시오.

• When Mike came home from school, he hung jacket on a hanger, and rode his bike.

➡ _____

10 위 글을 읽고 Mike가 밑줄 친 ⓐ처럼 말한 이유를 우리말로 쓰시오.

➡ _____

창의사고력 서술형 문제

01 다음 주어진 어구를 이용하여 상대방의 능력을 묻는 질문과 그에 대한 절차를 설명하는 대화를 완성하시오.

〈능력 묻기〉

how to share a photo / how to make potato salad / how to make sandwiches

〈절차 열거하기〉

press and hold a photo, choose "Share.", choose an SNS /

boil the potatoes, cut them into pieces, put some sauce on them /

put an egg on bread, add some vegetables, put bread on top

(1) _____

(2) _____

(3) _____

02 주어진 어휘를 이용하여 3문장 이상을 쓰시오.

what	how	when	where	whom	eat	take	go	put	meet

(1) _____

(2) _____

(3) _____

(4) _____

(5) _____

03 빈칸에 알맞은 말을 써서 문장을 완성하시오.

Triangle Sunglasses

I made triangle sunglasses (A)_____ a paper box and a plastic bag.

My baby sister knew (B)_____ to put them on.

They made her (C)_____.

That made me (D)_____.

단원별 모의고사

01 다음 단어에 대한 영어 설명이 <u>어색한</u> 것은?

① square: a flat shape with four sides of equal length and four angles of 90°
② reply: to answer someone by saying or writing something
③ excited: feeling very happy and relaxed
④ hold: to have something in your hands or arms
⑤ hula hoop: a very large ring that you try to keep spinning round your body

02 다음 짝지어진 단어의 관계가 같도록 빈칸에 알맞은 말을 쓰시오.

dot : spot = choose : _____

03 다음 영영풀이에 해당하는 단어를 고르시오.

to turn around and around, especially fast

① spin ② move
③ hang ④ roll
⑤ rush

04 대화의 빈칸에 들어갈 단어를 주어진 철자로 시작하여 쓰시오.

G: Do you know how to divide this cake into four equal pieces?
B: Let me see. ... How about dividing it this way? Then the pieces will be the s_____ size and shape.

➡ _____

05 빈칸 (A)와 (B)에 들어갈 알맞은 단어는?

• Triangle was in (A)_____ of the hangers and the plants.
• The three spirits are looking at one (B)_____.

　　(A)　　　(B)
① care – other
② control – each
③ control – other
④ charge – the other
⑤ charge – another

06 대화의 빈칸에 들어갈 말로 알맞은 것은?

B: Here's a triangle with three pencils. Do you know how to make three more triangles with three more pencils?
G: Let me see... _____ Can I break the pencils in half?
B: No, you can't.

① Do you know how to do it?
② It's about how to make three more triangles.
③ It's too difficult for me.
④ I don't think you know the answer.
⑤ Sorry, I can't remember it.

07 다음 대화의 빈칸에 들어갈 말을 세 단어의 영어로 쓰시오.

A: Do you know _____ a fish with shapes?
B: Sure. First, draw a large square. Then, draw a triangle. Finally, draw a small circle in the square.

➡ _____

[08~09] 다음 대화를 읽고 물음에 답하시오.

> Boy: Do you know how to solve this puzzle?
> Girl: What is it?
> Boy: You must take a dog, a chicken, and a bag of rice across the river. The boat only carries you and one of the things __(a)__ a time.
> Girl: That's easy. I can take them to the other side one __(b)__ one.
> Boy: But without you, the dog will kill the chicken, and the chicken will eat the rice.
> Girl: Let me see. ... First, take the chicken and come back. Then, take the rice and come back with the chicken.
> Boy: And?
> Girl: After that, take the dog and come back. Finally, take the chicken.
> Boy: You're great!

08 위 대화의 (a)와 (b)에 알맞은 전치사로 짝지어진 것은?

① on – to
② at – by
③ for – in
④ from – with
⑤ with – for

09 위 대화의 내용과 일치하지 <u>않는</u> 것은?

① The boy and the girl are talking about a puzzle.
② Without the girl, the dog will kill the chicken.
③ Without the girl, the chicken will eat the rice.
④ The girl must carry a dog, rice, and a chicken together on the boat.
⑤ The girl finally solves the puzzle.

10 다음 대화에서 말한 퍼즐의 답으로 알맞은 것은?

> B: Do you know how to divide this into four equal pieces?
> G: Sure. First, divide it into three equal squares. Then, divide each square into four smaller squares. Finally, color three small squares in the inside corner of the L.
> B: Oh, I can see three other L shapes around it! You're great!

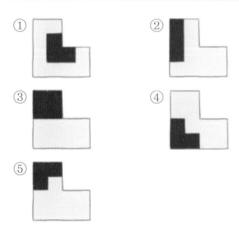

11 다음 두 사람의 대화가 <u>어색한</u> 것은?

① A: Do you know how to fly this kite?
　 B: Yes. I'll show you how.
② A: Excuse me. Do you know how to draw a mouse with shapes?
　 B: Sure.
③ A: Do you know how to solve this puzzle?
　 B: When is it?
④ A: Do you know how to solve the puzzle in another way?
　 B: Let me see.
⑤ A: Do you know how to cook *ramyeon*?
　 B: Sure. First, boil some water.

12 다음은 감자 샐러드를 만드는 방법에 관한 대화다. 빈칸에 어울리는 단어를 쓰시오.

> A: Do you know how to make potato salad?
> B: Sure. (A)_____, boil the potatoes. Then, cut them (B)_____ pieces. Finally, put some sauce (C)_____ them.

13 다음 그림을 보고 괄호 안에 주어진 어휘를 이용하여 빈칸에 알맞은 말을 쓰시오.

> A: Do you like cooking?
> B: Of course. Cooking makes _____.
> (excite)

14 다음 빈칸에 들어갈 말로 알맞지 <u>않은</u> 것을 <u>모두</u> 고르시오.

> I told him _____ to do it.

① what ② when ③ how
④ where ⑤ why

15 다음 빈칸에 공통으로 들어갈 말로 가장 알맞은 것은?

> • Refrigerators _____ food cool.
> • City workers _____ them clean and green.

① need ② require ③ ask
④ force ⑤ keep

16 다음 중 어법상 <u>어색한</u> 것을 고르시오.

① She painted the house bright.
② I taught him how could read English.
③ The bird kept the eggs warm.
④ I knew where to put the small four-leaf-clover.
⑤ I don't know what I should say to him.

17 다음 문장에서 어법상 <u>어색한</u> 것을 바르게 고쳐 다시 쓰시오.

(1) Do you know what make triangle sunglasses?

➡ _____

(2) When to finish the works were an important issue.

➡ _____

(3) Tell me whom I to meet.

➡ _____

(4) The news made them sadly.

➡ _____

(5) We found he honesty.

➡ _____

[18~19] 다음 글을 읽고 물음에 답하시오.

> There lived three shape spirits in Mike's room. Square controlled the table, the bookshelf, and the window. Triangle was in charge of the hangers and the plants. Circle ⓐ took care of the round things. They worked together to make a nice room for Mike.

18 Who was in charge of the plants? Answer in English.

➡ _____

19 위 글의 밑줄 친 ⓐtook care of와 바꿔 쓸 수 있는 것을 모두 고르시오.

① took after ② cared for
③ looked like ④ called for
⑤ looked after

[20~21] 다음 글을 읽고 물음에 답하시오.

One day Square decided to make the room better and shouted at the other spirits.

"Take these plants away, or their pointy leaves will hurt someone!" ①he said to Triangle.

"But Mike waters them every day," said Triangle.

ⓐ"Take this hula hoop away, and it will roll and break something!" he said to Circle.

"But Mike exercises with ②it every day," said Circle.

"③I try to make this room tidy, but you two always make a mess," he complained.

Triangle and Circle looked at each other.

"So ④you think you can do it without us?" Triangle asked Square.

"Sure. I can make this room better all by ⑤myself," replied Square.

"Great! Then we can get some rest," Circle said to Square.

20 밑줄 친 ①~⑤ 중에서 가리키는 대상이 나머지 넷과 다른 것은?

① ② ③ ④ ⑤

21 위 글의 밑줄 친 ⓐ에서 흐름상 어색한 부분을 찾아 고치시오.

_____ ➡ _____

[22~23] 다음 글을 읽고 물음에 답하시오.

Triangle and Circle went out and Square was now in control. He made the hangers, plants, and all the round things square. Then he looked around and smiled. "Much better!"

When Mike came home from school, he picked up a square hanger to hang his jacket on.

"What? This will not hold my clothes."

He went to water the plants and (A)[saw / to see] their square leaves.

"Poor things. ... They must be sick."

He picked up the square hula hoop (B)[exercising / to exercise].

"Hmm ... I don't know (C)[how / what] to spin this."

He went to take out his bike and looked at the square wheels.

"Well, I can't ride this. I'll just have to walk." Then he hurried out of the house.

22 위 글의 괄호 (A)~(C)에서 문맥이나 어법상 알맞은 낱말을 골라 쓰시오.

➡ (A) _____ (B) _____ (C) _____

23 위 글의 앞부분에서 알 수 있는 Square의 심경으로 가장 알맞은 것을 고르시오.

① bored ② disappointed
③ satisfied ④ ashamed
⑤ nervous

Lesson

6

Love the Earth

🎤 의사소통 기능

- 설명 요청하기
 What do you mean by that?

- 놀람 표현하기
 That's surprising!

🎤 언어 형식

- (a) few, (a) little
 Let's learn **a few** tips for living green.

- 수동태
 They **were** not **wrapped** at all.

Words & Expressions

Key Words

- **actually** [ǽktʃuəli] 부 사실, 실제로
- **agree** [əgríː] 동 동의하다
- **bin** [bin] 명 (쓰레기) 통
- **blender** [bléndər] 명 믹서기, 분쇄기
- **blue** [bluː] 형 우울한
- **bring**(–**brought**–**brought**) [briŋ] 동 가져오다
- **challenge** [tʃǽlindʒ] 명 도전
- **choose**(–**chose**–**chosen**) [tʃuːz] 동 선택하다
- **cloth** [klɔːθ] 명 천, 옷감
- **collect** [kəlékt] 동 모으다, 수집하다
- **cotton** [kátn] 명 무명, 면
- **cute** [kjuːt] 형 귀여운
- **empty** [émpti] 형 비어 있는
- **food waste** 음식 쓰레기
- **green energy** 친환경 에너지
- **happen** [hǽpən] 동 일어나다, 발생하다
- **instead** [instéd] 부 대신에
- **interesting** [íntərəstiŋ] 형 흥미로운
- **island** [áilənd] 명 섬
- **item** [áitəm] 명 품목, 항목
- **language** [lǽŋgwidʒ] 명 언어
- **machine** [məʃíːn] 명 기계
- **napkin** [nǽpkin] 명 냅킨
- **natural** [nǽtʃərəl] 형 자연의, 가공하지 않은
- **nothing** [nʌ́θiŋ] 대 아무것도 … 아님
- **ocean** [óuʃən] 명 대양, 바다
- **packaging** [pǽkidʒiŋ] 명 포장, 포장지
- **plate** [pleit] 명 접시
- **popped rice cake** 뻥튀기
- **problem** [prábləm] 명 문제
- **product** [prádʌkt] 명 제품, 상품
- **quite** [kwait] 부 매우, 꽤
- **recycle** [riːsáikl] 동 재활용하다
- **reduce** [ridjúːs] 동 줄이다, 축소하다
- **reusable** [riúːzəbəl] 형 재사용할 수 있는
- **reuse** [riːjúːz] 동 재사용하다
- **ride** [raid] 동 타다
- **save** [seiv] 동 절약하다, 아끼다
- **secret** [síːkrit] 명 비결, 비밀
- **serve** [səːrv] 동 제공하다, 나누어 주다
- **simple** [símpl] 형 단순한
- **skin** [skin] 명 피부
- **special** [spéʃəl] 형 특별한
- **spotless** [spátlis] 형 티끌 하나 없는
- **store** [stɔːr] 동 저장하다
- **street lamp** 가로등
- **surprising** [sərpráiziŋ] 형 놀라운
- **terrible** [térəbl] 형 끔찍한
- **thumb** [θʌm] 명 엄지손가락
- **tip** [tip] 명 비결, 조언
- **trash** [træʃ] 명 쓰레기
- **umbrella** [ʌmbrélə] 명 우산
- **wrap** [ræp] 동 포장하다
- **wrapping paper** 포장지

Key Expressions

- **a big fish** 중요한 사람
- **a few** 몇몇의, 몇 가지의
- **as busy as a bee** 매우 바쁜
- **be an early bird** 아침에 일찍 일어나다
- **be good for** ~에 좋다
- **be on cloud nine** 매우 행복하다
- **be powered** 동력을 공급받다
- **cut up** ~을 잘게 자르다
- **have a green thumb** 원예에 재능이 있다
- **have a heart of gold** 매우 친절하다
- **in the middle of** ~의 한가운데
- **kill two birds with one stone** 일석이조
- **leave** 목적어 **behind** ~을 남기다
- **live green** 친환경적으로 살다
- **out of** ~로부터
- 배수사 **as** 원급 **as** ~의 몇 배
- **take** 목적어 **back** ~을 다시 가져가다
- **throw a party** 파티를 열다
- **throw away** 버리다
- **You know what?** 그것 아세요?

Word Power

※ 명사에 -al을 붙여 형용사가 되는 어휘

☐ tradition(전통) – traditional(전통적인)

☐ nation(국가) – national(국가의)

☐ nature(자연) – natural(자연의, 가공하지 않은)

☐ culture (문화) – cultural (문화의)

※ 두 가지 품사를 가지는 어휘

☐ store 명 가게 동 저장하다

☐ empty 형 비어 있는 동 비우다

☐ produce 동 생산하다 명 농산물

☐ power 명 힘, 동력 동 동력을 공급하다

☐ challenge 명 도전 동 도전하다

☐ surprise 동 놀라게 하다 명 놀라움

※ Idioms

☐ answer the call of nature: go to the toilet (화장실에 가다)

☐ beat around the bush: say something indirectly (어떤 것을 간접적으로 말하다)

☐ can't see the forest for the trees: can't see the whole situation (전체 상황을 보지 못하다)

☐ under the weather: not feeling well (기분이 좋지 않은)

English Dictionary

☐ **agree** 동의하다
→ to have the same opinion
같은 의견을 갖다

☐ **challenge** 도전
→ something new and difficult that requires great effort
많은 노력을 요구하는 새롭고 어려운 일

☐ **cloth** 천, 옷감
→ fabric that is made by weaving a substance such as cotton, wool, silk, or nylon
면, 양털, 비단 또는 나일론과 같은 물질을 짬으로써 만들어진 천

☐ **cotton** 무명, 면
→ cloth or thread made from the white hair of the cotton plant 목화의 흰 털로 만들어진 천 또는 실

☐ **instead** 대신에
→ used to say what is not used, does not happen, etc, when something else is used, happens, etc.
다른 어떤 것이 사용되거나 발생했을 때 어떤 것이 사용되지 않거나 발생하지 않음을 말할 때 사용되는

☐ **leave** 남기다
→ to let something remain there when you go away
떠날 때 무언가를 그곳에 남아 있게 하다

☐ **napkin** 냅킨
→ a square of cloth or paper that you use to wipe your mouth or hands
입이나 손을 닦기 위해 사용하는 정사각형의 천이나 종이

☐ **recycle** 재활용하다
→ to change waste materials so that they can be used again 폐기물을 다시 사용할 수 있도록 바꾸다

☐ **reduce** 줄이다
→ to make smaller in size or number
규모나 숫자에서 더 적게 만들다

☐ **secret** 비결, 비밀
→ something that is known about by only a small number of people and is not told to anyone else
소수의 사람들만이 알고 있고 다른 사람들에게는 말하지 않는 어떤 것

☐ **skin** 피부
→ the natural outer layer of a person's or animal's body
사람이나 동물의 몸의 타고 난 외부막

☐ **tip** 조언
→ a useful piece of advice 유용한 충고

☐ **trash** 쓰레기
→ something worthless that you throw away
(= garbage, rubbish)
사람들이 버리는 가치 없는 어떤 것

☐ **wrap** 포장하다
→ to cover something with paper, cloth or other materials 종이, 천 또는 다른 재료로 무언가를 싸다

☐ **wrapping paper** 포장지
→ special paper that is used for wrapping presents
선물을 포장하기 위해 사용되는 특별한 종이

01 다음 문장의 빈칸에 들어갈 말로 알맞은 것은?

> It's hard to _____ one flavor at the ice cream store.

① divide　　② collect　　③ store
④ choose　　⑤ save

 서답형

02 다음 문장의 빈칸에 주어진 영영풀이에 해당하는 말을 쓰시오.

> • You have to drink a lot of water _____ of soda.
> <영영풀이> used to say what is not used, does not happen, etc, when something else is used, happens, etc.

➡ _____

중요

03 다음 중 밑줄 친 단어의 우리말 뜻이 잘못된 것은?

① English is a hard language to learn. (언어)
② Animals live peacefully in their natural environment. (자연의)
③ You can choose your own packaging. (포장)
④ This product is very popular now. (제품)
⑤ We can reduce waste by eating all our food. (재사용하다)

서답형

04 다음 우리말에 맞게 네 단어로 쓰시오.

> 바다 한가운데 있는 저것들은 뭐니?
> What are those _____ the ocean?

➡ _____

[05~06] 다음 영영풀이에 해당하는 단어를 고르시오.

05

> something worthless that you throw away

① blender　　② trash　　③ mess
④ nothing　　⑤ item

중요

06

> something new and difficult that requires great effort

① problem　　　　② control
③ challenge　　　④ packaging
⑤ spotless

07 다음 빈칸에 들어갈 말로 가장 알맞은 것은?

> Actually, we used popped rice cakes as plates, so we could eat them and leave _____ behind!

① something　　② anything
③ them　　　　④ nothing
⑤ everything

중요

08 다음 빈칸에 들어갈 말로 가장 알맞게 짝지어진 것은?

> • Please give us one simple _____ for reducing trash.
> • You threw a class birthday party, but didn't _____ a lot of trash.

① tip – produce
② secret – ride
③ product – store
④ machine – choose
⑤ challenge – reuse

01 대화의 빈칸에 들어갈 단어를 주어진 철자로 시작하여 쓰시오.

> G: Minji's classroom is s_____.
> B: What do you mean by that?
> G: Her classroom is really clean.

➡ _____

02 우리말에 맞게 주어진 단어를 이용하여 문장의 빈칸을 채우시오. (어형 변화 필수)

(1) 몇몇 포장지가 쉽게 재활용되지 않는다.
　➡ Some _____ paper is not easily _____. (wrap / recycle)

(2) 나는 재사용할 수 있는 물통을 매일 학교에 가져온다.
　➡ I bring a _____ water bottle to school every day. (reuse)

(3) 공장에는 많은 기계들이 있다.
　➡ There are many _____ in the factory. (machine)

(4) 친환경 버스는 쓰레기로부터 동력을 공급받아요.
　➡ The green bus is _____ by trash. (power)

03 글의 빈칸에 들어갈 단어를 영어 설명을 참고하여 쓰시오.

> • You can eat these spoons. They were made out of rice. They are 100% _____.
> <영어 설명> having no chemical substances added to food or drink and therefore thought to be healthy

➡ _____

04 우리말과 같은 뜻이 되도록 빈칸에 알맞은 단어를 쓰시오.

(1) 그 병을 재활용 통에 넣어라.
　➡ Put the bottle in the recycling _____.

(2) 그녀는 다음 도전을 할 준비가 되었다.
　➡ She is ready for the next _____.

(3) 나는 여름에 면 티셔츠를 입는 것을 좋아한다.
　➡ I like to wear _____ T-shirts in the summer.

(4) 극장에 비어 있는 자리들이 많다.
　➡ There are many _____ seats in the theater.

05 영영풀이에 해당하는 단어를 <보기>에서 찾아 첫 번째 칸에 쓰고, 두 번째 칸에는 우리말 뜻을 쓰시오.

> ┤ 보기 ├
> napkin / cloth / secret / reduce / recycle / collect / empty / item / ocean

(1) _____: fabric that is made by weaving a substance such as cotton, wool, silk, or nylon: _____

(2) _____: a square of cloth or paper that you use to wipe your mouth or hands: _____

(3) _____: to change waste materials so that they can be used again: _____

(4) _____: something that is known about by only a small number of people and is not told to anyone else: _____

Conversation

1 설명 요청하기

> **What do you mean by that?** 그게 무슨 뜻이야?

■ "What do you mean by ~?"는 상대방이 한 말에 대해 추가 설명을 요청할 때 쓰는 표현이다. 응답으로는 상대방이 이해하지 못한 내용을 쉽게 풀어서 설명해 준다.
여기서 that은 상대방이 말한 내용을 언급하는 지시대명사이고 by that은 '그 말로써, 그것으로'라는 뜻으로, 직역하면 '그 말로써 너는 무엇을 의미하니?'라는 뜻이다.

설명을 요청하는 다양한 표현

- What is that exactly?
- What is the meaning of ~?
- Can you give more of an explanation?
- Tell me more about it.
- I'd like to know what it means.
- Can you tell me what it means?
- Could you explain ~?
- Do you mind if I ask you to explain ~?

■ **설명할 때**

It means ~.

몰라서 설명을 하지 못하는 경우에는 "I'm sorry, but I don't know what it means." 또는 "I'm not sure what it means." 등으로 답한다.

- A: I'm watching a historic moment on TV. 나는 TV에서 역사적인 순간을 보고 있어.
 B: What do you mean by that? 그게 무슨 말이니?
 A: Our country will be launching a new satellite soon. 우리나라가 곧 새로운 위성을 발사할 거야.

핵심 Check

1. 다음 대화의 빈칸에 들어갈 말로 알맞은 것은?

 G: I feel blue today.

 B: What do you _____ by that?

 G: I mean I feel sad.

 ① mind ② mean ③ know
 ④ feel ⑤ give

② 놀람 표현하기

> **That's surprising!** 놀랍구나!

■ 'That's surprising!'은 상대방이 한 말에 대해 놀람을 표현할 때 쓴다. 놀람을 표현할 때는 'I'm surprised that ~.' 또는 'I'm amazed that ~.'라고 표현할 수 있다.

'How could that be possible?'은 '그것이 어떻게 가능하겠어요?'의 의미로 놀람을 나타내는 표현이다.

- A: I made no trash at all today. 난 오늘 쓰레기를 전혀 만들지 않았어.
 B: That's surprising! 놀랍구나!

- I'm surprised that you think so. 네가 그렇게 생각하니 놀랍다.

- I'm amazed that she did that. 그녀가 그것을 했다니 놀랍다.

놀람을 표현하는 여러 표현들

What a surprise! / That's unbelievable! / I can't believe it.

That's amazing! / I'm so surprised! / That can't be possible.

■ **놀랄만한 일을 알려 주는 표현**
놀랄만한 일을 알려 주거나 대화를 시작할 때 쓰는 표현으로 '있잖아, 어떻게 생각해?' 등의 뜻으로 사용된다.

- You know what? / Guess what?

핵심 Check

2. 다음 대화의 빈칸에 들어갈 말로 알맞지 <u>않은</u> 것은?

A: My friend, Youngmin, is so strong that he can lift a car.

B: Really? _____

① I can't believe it.
② That can't be possible.
③ I don't care.
④ What a surprise!
⑤ That's amazing!

Get Ready 2

(1) B: This shopping bag is so beautiful.

G: Thank you. We made it out of a broken umbrella.

B: ❶What a surprise!

(2) B: Why are you eating a cup?

G: Actually, this cup is a cookie. I can use it ❷as a cup and then eat it.

B: That's surprising!

(3) B: This bike blender kills two birds with one stone.

G: ❸What do you mean by that?

B: ❹When you ride this bike, you exercise and make juice.

G: Oh, I get it.

(1) B: 이 쇼핑백이 아주 아름다워요.

G: 고마워요. 우리는 망가진 우산으로 만들었어요.

B: 놀랍군요!

(2) B: 컵을 왜 먹고 있나요?

G: 사실, 이 컵은 쿠키예요. 나는 이걸 컵으로 사용하고 난 후에 먹을 수 있어요.

B: 놀랍군요!

(3) B: 이 자전거 믹서기는 일석이조예요.

G: 그게 무슨 뜻이에요?

B: 당신이 자전거를 탈 때, 당신은 운동도 하고 주스도 만들어요.

G: 아, 이제 알겠어요.

❶ "What a surprise!"는 상대방이 한 말에 대해 놀람을 표현할 때 쓴다.

❷ as는 전치사로 '~로써'의 의미이다.

❸ "What do you mean by ~?"는 상대방이 한 말에 대해 추가 설명을 요청할 때 쓰는 표현이다. 'Can you tell me what it means?'로 바꾸어 말할 수 있다.

❹ 부사절을 이끄는 when은 '~할 때'로 해석한다.

Check(√) True or False

(1) This shopping bag is made out of a broken umbrella.　　T ☐ F ☐

(2) B is surprised to see G eating a cup.　　T ☐ F ☐

(3) This bike blender can kill two birds at once.　　T ☐ F ☐

 Start Off Listen & Talk A

(1) G: I ❶feel blue today.

B: What do you mean by that?

G: ❷I mean I feel sad. We make too much trash.

B: Ah, I get it now. We should recycle and reuse more.

(2) G: Minji's classroom is spotless.

B: ❸What do you mean by that?

G: Her classroom is really clean. Look.

B: You're right. Let's learn some good tips from her.

(1) G: 난 오늘 우울해.

B: 그게 무슨 뜻이야?

G: 내가 슬프다는 뜻이야. 우리가 쓰레기를 너무 많이 만들어.

B: 아, 이제 알겠어. 우리가 재활용과 재사용을 더 많이 해야겠어.

(2) G: 민지네 교실은 티끌 하나 없어.

B: 그게 무슨 뜻이야?

G: 그녀의 교실은 정말 깨끗해. 봐.

B: 맞아. 그녀한테서 몇 가지 좋은 비결을 배우자.

❶ blue는 형용사로 '우울한'의 의미로 사용되었다.

❷ 'I mean ~'은 설명을 요청하는 말에 대해 설명을 해 줄 때 사용하는 표현이다.

❸ 상대방이 한 말에 대해 추가 설명을 요청할 때 쓰는 표현이다.

Check(√) True or False

(4) G feels sad because of much trash.　　T ☐ F ☐

(5) They want to learn some tips of cleaning the classroom.　　T ☐ F ☐

Start Off Listen & Talk B

B: Hey, Minji. What is one ❶tip for a clean classroom?
G: Well, we're doing a clean bin project today.
B: ❷What do you mean by that?
G: We don't throw away trash, so our trash can stays empty.
B: ❸That's surprising! Please tell me more about it.
G: Sure. No problem.

❶ 여기서 tip은 '비결'이란 뜻으로 사용되었다.
❷ "What do you mean by ~?"는 상대방이 한 말에 대해 추가 설명을 요청할 때 쓰는 표현이다.
❹ 상대방이 한 말에 대해 놀람을 표현할 때 쓴다.

Speak Up Look and talk

B: Plastic bottles are a big problem for the Earth.
G: ❶What do you mean by that?
B: ❷They take 450 years to break down.
G: That's surprising!

❶ "What do you mean by ~?"는 상대방이 한 말에 대해 추가 설명을 요청할 때 쓰는 표현이다.
❷ take 시간+to+동사원형: ~하는 데 시간이 걸리다

Speak Up Mission

A: My mom ❶has a green thumb.
B: What do you mean by that?
A: ❷She is good at growing plants.
B: I get it.

❶ have a green thumb: 원예에 재능이 있다
❷ be good at은 '~을 잘하다'라는 뜻이다.

Real-life Scene

A: What are those ❶in the middle of the ocean?
B: They are trash islands.
A: Trash islands? What do you mean by that?
B: ❷A lot of plastic trash goes into the ocean and becomes big islands like those.
A: That sounds terrible! How big are those islands?
B: The biggest one is ❸about 14 times as large as South Korea.
A: ❹That's surprising! I think we should not use plastic products.
B: I agree.

❶ in the middle of: ~의 중앙에
❷ a lot of는 '많은'의 뜻으로 셀 수 있는 명사와 셀 수 없는 명사를 둘 다 꾸며줄 수 있다. like는 전치사로 '~와 같은'의 뜻이다.
❸ about은 부사로 '대략'의 뜻이고, '배수사+as+원급+as ~' 구문은 '~의 몇 배'로 해석한다.
❹ 상대방이 한 말에 대해 놀람을 표현할 때 쓴다. 'That's unbelievable!', 'I can't believe it.', 'That's amazing!' 등으로 표현할 수 있다.

Fun Time

A: Minsu is ❶a big fish.
B: What do you mean by that?
A: ❷I mean, he is an important person.
B: Ah, I get it.

❶ a big fish: 중요한 사람
❷ 'I mean ~'은 설명을 요청하는 말에 대해 설명을 해 줄 때 사용하는 표현이다.

Express Yourself

(1) B: This is the energy tree.
　　G: What do you mean by that?
　　B: It produces energy from the sun. And ❶it is used as a street lamp at night.
　　G: That's surprising!
(2) B: What is this bus called?
　　G: It is called the green bus.
　　B: What is special about it?
　　G: The green bus ❷is powered by trash.
　　B: That's surprising!

❶ be used는 수동태로 '사용되다'는 뜻이다.
❷ is powered는 수동태로 '동력을 공급받다'는 의미이다.

Learning Diary Listen & Speak

B: Hey, Minji. Your classroom is spotless.
G: Thank you.
B: What's one tip for a clean classroom?
G: Well, we're doing a clean bin project this week.
B: What do you mean by that?
G: We don't ❶throw away trash, so our trash can stay empty.
B: Ah, ❷I get it now. Thanks for your tip.
G: My pleasure.

❶ throw away: 버리다
❷ '이해했다'는 의미로 'I understand.'로 말할 수 있다.

● 다음 우리말과 일치하도록 빈칸에 알맞은 말을 쓰시오.

Get Ready 2

(1) B: This shopping bag is so beautiful.
 G: Thank you. We made it _____ _____ a _____ umbrella.
 B: What a _____!

(2) B: _____ are you eating a cup?
 G: _____, this cup is a cookie. I can _____ it _____ a cup and then eat it.
 B: _____ _____!

(3) B: This bike blender _____ _____ _____ _____ _____ _____.
 G: _____ do you _____ _____ that?
 B: When you ride this bike, you _____ and _____ _____.
 G: Oh, I _____ it.

Start Off Listen & Talk A

(1) G: I feel _____ today.
 B: What do you _____ _____ _____?
 G: I _____ I feel _____. We make _____ _____ _____.
 B: Ah, I _____ it now. We _____ _____ and _____ more.

(2) G: Minji's classroom is _____.
 B: _____ _____ _____ _____ by that?
 G: Her classroom is really _____. Look.
 B: You're right. _____ _____ some good _____ from her.

Start Off Listen & Talk B

B: Hey, Minji. What is _____ _____ for a clean classroom?
G: Well, we're doing a clean bin project today.
B: _____ do you _____ _____ _____?
G: We don't _____ _____ trash, so our trash can _____ _____.
B: That's _____! Please tell me more about it.
G: Sure. No problem.

Speak Up Look and talk

B: Plastic _____ are a big problem _____ _____.
G: _____ do you _____ by that?
B: They _____ 450 years _____ _____ _____.
G: That's _____!

해석

(1) B: 이 쇼핑백이 아주 아름다워요.
 G: 고마워요. 우리는 망가진 우산으로 만들었어요.
 B: 놀랍군요!

(2) B: 컵을 왜 먹고 있나요?
 G: 사실, 이 컵은 쿠키예요. 나는 이걸 컵으로 사용하고 난 후에 먹을 수 있어요.
 B: 놀랍군요!

(3) B: 이 자전거 믹서기는 일석이조예요.
 G: 그게 무슨 뜻이에요?
 B: 당신이 자전거를 탈 때, 당신은 운동도 하고 주스도 만들어요.
 G: 아, 이제 알겠어요.

(1) G: 난 오늘 우울해.
 B: 그게 무슨 뜻이야?
 G: 내가 슬프다는 뜻이야. 우리가 쓰레기를 너무 많이 버려.
 B: 아, 이제 알겠어. 우리는 재활용과 재사용을 더 많이 해야겠어.

(2) G: 민지네 교실은 티끌 하나 없어.
 B: 그게 무슨 뜻이야?
 G: 그녀의 교실은 정말 깨끗해. 봐.
 B: 맞아. 그녀한테서 몇 가지 좋은 비결을 배우자.

B: 이봐, 민지야. 깨끗한 교실을 위한 한 가지 비결이 뭐니?
G: 음, 우리는 오늘 깨끗한 쓰레기통 프로젝트를 하고 있어.
B: 그게 무슨 뜻이야?
G: 우리가 쓰레기를 버리지 않아서 쓰레기통이 비어 있는 거지.
B: 놀랍구나! 나한테 그것에 대해 좀 더 이야기해 줘.
G: 물론이지. 문제없어.

B: 플라스틱병은 지구에 큰 문젯거리야.
G: 그게 무슨 뜻이야?
B: 그것들이 분해되는 데 450년이 걸려.
G: 놀랍구나!

Speak Up Mission

A: My mom has a _____ _____.
B: _____ do you mean _____ _____?
A: She _____ _____ _____ growing _____.
B: I get it.

Real-life Scene

G: What are those _____ _____ _____ _____ the ocean?
B: They are _____ _____.
G: Trash islands? What do you _____ _____ that?
B: _____ _____ _____ plastic trash goes into the _____ and becomes big _____ _____ those.
G: That _____ _____! _____ _____ are those islands?
B: The _____ one is about 14 times _____ _____ _____ South Korea.
G: That's _____! I think we _____ _____ use plastic products.
B: I _____.

Fun Time

A: I _____ to school every day.
B: That's _____!

A: Minsu is a _____ _____.
B: _____ do you _____ by that?
A: I mean, he is an _____ person.
B: Ah, I get it.

Express Yourself

(1) B: This is the _____ _____.
 G: What do you _____ by that?
 B: It _____ energy from the sun. And it _____ _____ as a _____ _____ at night.
 G: That's surprising!

(2) B: What is this bus _____?
 G: It _____ _____ the green bus.
 B: What is _____ about it?
 G: The green bus is _____ by trash.
 B: That's surprising!

Learning Diary Listen & Speak

B: Hey, Minji. Your classroom is _____.
G: Thank you.
B: What's _____ for a clean classroom?
G: Well, we're doing a clean _____ project this week.
B: _____ _____ _____ _____ _____ _____?
G: We don't _____ _____ trash, so our trash can _____ _____.
B: Ah, I get it now. Thanks for your tip.
G: My _____.

해석

A: 우리 엄마는 원예에 재능이 있으셔.
B: 그게 무슨 뜻이니?
A: 그녀는 식물을 잘 기르셔.
B: 알겠어.

G: 바다 한가운데 있는 저것들은 뭐니?
B: 그것들은 쓰레기 섬이야.
G: 쓰레기 섬? 그게 무슨 뜻이니?
B: 많은 플라스틱 쓰레기가 바다에 흘러 들어가서 저것들과 같은 큰 섬이 돼.
G: 끔찍하구나! 저 섬들은 얼마나 크니?
B: 가장 큰 것은 남한의 약 14배 정도 야.
G: 놀랍구나! 우리는 플라스틱 제품을 쓰지 말아야 해.
B: 맞아.

A: 나는 매일 학교에 스케이트보드를 타 고 가.
B: 그거 놀랍구나!

A: 민수는 큰 물고기야.
B: 그게 무슨 뜻이니?
A: 그가 정말 중요한 사람이라는 뜻이 야.
B: 아, 알겠어.

(1) B: 이것은 에너지 나무예요.
 G: 그게 무슨 뜻이에요?
 B: 그것은 태양으로부터 에너지를 생산해요. 그리고 밤에는 가로등 으로 사용돼요.
 G: 놀랍군요!

(2) B: 이 버스는 뭐라고 불리나요?
 G: 그것은 친환경 버스라고 불려요.
 B: 뭐가 특별한가요?
 G: 친환경 버스는 쓰레기로부터 동 력을 공급받아요.
 B: 놀랍군요!

B: 이봐, 민지야. 네 교실은 티끌 하나 없더라.
G: 고마워.
B: 깨끗한 교실을 위한 한 가지 조언이 뭐니?
G: 음, 우리는 이번 주에 깨끗한 휴지통 프로젝트를 하는 중이야.
B: 그게 무슨 뜻이니?
G: 우리가 쓰레기를 안 버려서 쓰레기 통이 비어 있어.
B: 아, 알겠어. 조언 고마워.
G: 천만에.

01 다음 대화의 빈칸에 들어갈 말로 알맞지 <u>않은</u> 것은?

> B: This shopping bag is so beautiful.
> G: Thank you. We made it out of a broken umbrella.
> B: _____

① That's unbelievable!　　② I can't believe it.
③ What a surprise!　　④ No wonder you're upset.
⑤ That's amazing!

02 다음 대화의 빈칸에 들어갈 말로 알맞은 것은?

> B: This bike blender kills two birds with one stone.
> G: _____
> B: When you ride this bike, you exercise and make juice.
> G: Oh, I get it.

① Can you tell me what it means?　　② What did you do?
③ What happened?　　④ What do you want to do?
⑤ I have no idea how to ride this bike.

03 다음 대화의 우리말에 맞게 주어진 단어를 이용하여 영어로 쓰시오.

> G: Minji's classroom is spotless.
> B: <u>그게 무슨 뜻이야?</u> (what / mean / by that)
> G: Her classroom is really clean. Look.
> B: You're right. Let's learn some good tips from her.

➡ _____

04 다음 대화를 알맞은 순서대로 배열하시오.

> (A) Why are you eating a cup?
> (B) That's surprising!
> (C) Actually, this cup is a cookie. I can use it as a cup and then eat it.

➡ _____

[01~02] 다음 대화를 읽고 물음에 답하시오.

B: This bike blender _____(A)_____.

G: (B)What do you mean by that?

B: When you ride this bike, you exercise and make juice.

G: Oh, I get it.

01 위 대화의 빈칸 (A)에 들어갈 말로 알맞은 것은?

① is on cloud nine

② has a heart of gold

③ kills two birds with one stone

④ is under the weather

⑤ has a green thumb

 위 대화의 밑줄 친 (B)의 의도로 알맞은 것은?

① 놀람 표현하기 ② 바람 표현하기

③ 허가 여부 묻기 ④ 능력 묻기

⑤ 설명 요청하기

서답형

03 다음 대화의 우리말 해석에 맞게 주어진 단어를 이용하여 영어로 쓰시오.

> B: Plastic bottles are a big problem for the Earth.
>
> G: What do you mean by that?
>
> B: 그것들이 분해되는 데 450년이 걸려.
>
> G: That's surprising!

(take / break down)

➡ _____

[04~06] 다음 대화를 읽고 물음에 답하시오.

B: Hey, Minji. What is one tip for a clean classroom?

G: Well, we're doing a clean bin project today.

B: _____(A)_____

G: We don't throw away trash, so our trash can stay empty.

B: _____(B)_____ Please tell me more about it.

G: Sure. No problem.

 위 대화의 빈칸 (A)에 들어갈 말로 가장 적절한 것은?

① Can you tell me how to make a clean bin?

② How could that be possible?

③ When are you going to hold a clean bin project?

④ What do you mean by that?

⑤ Where do you throw away trash?

05 위 대화의 빈칸 (B)에 들어갈 말로 알맞은 것은?

① I wonder if you like this idea.

② That's surprising!

③ Anything else?

④ I'd like to buy that trash bin.

⑤ I don't think it's right.

서답형

06 다음 영영풀이가 설명하는 단어를 위 대화에서 찾아 쓰시오.

a useful piece of advice

➡ _____

[07~08] 다음 대화를 읽고 물음에 답하시오.

A: What are those in the middle of the ocean?
B: They are trash islands.
A: Trash islands? ①What do you mean by that?
B: A lot of plastic trash goes into the ocean and ②becomes big islands like those.
A: That ③sounds great! How big are those islands?
B: The biggest one is about 14 times as ④large as South Korea.
A: That's surprising! I think we ⑤should not use plastic products.
B: I agree.

07 위 대화를 읽고 답할 수 없는 것은?

① What are the trash islands?
② What are the trash islands made of?
③ How big is the biggest trash island?
④ How much trash do they throw away?
⑤ What are they planning to do?

08 밑줄 친 ①~⑤ 중 위 대화의 흐름상 어색한 것은?

①　　　②　　　③　　　④　　　⑤

[09~10] 대화의 빈칸에 들어갈 말로 알맞은 것은?

09

A: Minsu is a big fish.
B: _____
A: I mean, he is an important person.
B: Ah, I get it.

① Why do you say so?
② How did he catch it?
③ What did you say?
④ What makes you think so?
⑤ What do you mean by that?

10

B: What is this bus called?
G: It is called the green bus.
B: _____
G: The green bus is powered by trash.
B: That's surprising!

① That sounds terrible!
② What is special about it?
③ Do you know how to fix it?
④ Can it be true?
⑤ I don't get it.

11 다음 중 짝지어진 대화가 어색한 것을 고르시오.

① A: What does ASAP mean?
　 B: It means "as soon as possible."
② A: I skateboard to school every day.
　 B: That's surprising!
③ A: I feel blue today.
　 B: Then, what color do you like?
④ A: I take a quick 5 minute shower every day.
　 B: That's surprising!
⑤ A: My brother is an early bird.
　 B: What do you mean by that?

12 대화의 빈칸에 들어갈 말은?

G: Minji's classroom is _____.
B: What do you mean by that?
G: Her classroom is really clean. Look.
B: You're right. Let's learn some good tips from her.

① on cloud nine　　② spotless
③ an early bird　　④ the trash island
⑤ a big problem

[01~02] 다음 대화를 읽고 물음에 답하시오.

A: What are those in the middle of the ocean?

B: They are trash islands.

A: Trash islands? _____(A)_____

B: A lot of plastic trash goes into the ocean and becomes big islands like those.

A: That sounds terrible! How big are those islands?

B: (B)가장 큰 것은 남한의 약 14 배 정도야.

A: That's surprising! I think we should not use plastic products.

B: I agree.

01 위 대화의 빈칸 (A)에 들어갈 표현을 주어진 조건에 맞게 쓰시오.

┤ 조건 ├
- 상대방이 한 말에 대해 추가 설명을 요청할 때 쓰는 표현을 쓸 것.
- 'mean'과 'by that'을 이용할 것.
- 6 단어의 문장을 쓸 것.

➡ _____

 02 위 대화의 밑줄 친 (B)의 우리말에 맞게 주어진 어구를 알맞은 순서로 배열하시오.

one / is / about / the / 14 times / biggest / as / as / South Korea / large

➡ _____

[03~04] 다음 대화를 읽고 물음에 답하시오.

B: Hey, Minji. What is one tip for a clean classroom?

G: Well, we're doing a clean bin project today.

B: What do you mean by that?

G: _____(A)_____

B: _____(B)_____ Please tell me more about it.

G: Sure. No problem.

03 빈칸 (A)에 그림과 주어진 어구를 이용하여 'clean bin project'의 내용이 무엇인지 주어진 단어로 시작하여 영어로 쓰시오.

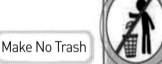

Make No Trash

trash can / throw away / stay / so / empty

➡ We _____ .

04 주어진 영어 질문을 참고하여 위 대화의 빈칸 (B)에 알맞은 표현을 쓰시오.

What would you say when you are very surprised at something?

➡ _____

 05 대화의 흐름상 빈칸에 들어갈 표현을 쓰시오.

B: This bike blender _____ .

G: What do you mean by that?

B: When you ride this bike, you exercise and make juice.

G: Oh, I get it.

┤ 조건 ├
- 6 단어로 쓸 것.
- bird와 stone을 사용할 것.

➡ _____

교과서
Grammar

① (a) few, (a) little

- Let's learn **a few** tips for living green. 친환경적으로 살기 위한 몇 가지 비결을 배웁시다.
- I need **a little** bread. 난 빵이 약간 필요해.

■ 'few' 뒤에는 셀 수 있는 명사(복수 명사), 'little' 뒤에는 셀 수 없는 명사(단수 명사)를 쓴다.

■ **a few / a little : 약간의**

a few와 a little은 some보다는 적지만 0보다는 많음을 의미하는 것으로, 약간은 있음을 강조할 때 쓰인다.

- I need **a few** apples. 난 사과가 약간 필요해.
- He drank **a little** water. 그는 약간의 물을 마셨다.

■ **few / little: 거의 없는**

few와 little은 사실상 거의 없거나 0에 가까운 수 또는 양을 의미한다.

- He has **few** friends. 그는 친구가 거의 없다.
- There is **little** time to spare. 꾸물거릴 시간이 없다.

핵심 Check

1. 다음 괄호 안에서 알맞은 말을 고르시오.

(1) There are (a few / a little) flowers in the garden.

(2) I will eat (a few / a little) milk.

(3) We need to buy (few / a few / little / a little) butter to make the cake.

② 수동태

> • He **built** the house. 〈능동태〉 그가 그 집을 지었다.
>
> • The house **was built** by him. 〈수동태〉 그 집은 그에 의해 지어졌다.

■ 수동태는 '주어+be동사+동사의 과거분사(+by 행위자)'의 형식을 가지며 '~해지다, …에 의해 ~되다[당하다]'라는 의미로 주어가 동사가 나타내는 행위를 당하거나 행동의 영향을 받는 것을 나타낸다. 수동태 문장의 주어 자리에는 능동태 문장의 목적어가 오고, by 다음에는 능동태 문장의 주어를 쓴다. 보통 누가 그 동작을 했는지가 중요하지 않거나 잘 모를 때 수동태 문장으로 표현한다. 수동태는 현재, 과거, 미래 시제로 쓸 수 있고, 'be동사+동사의 과거분사'에서 be동사로 시제를 표현한다.

　• A woman **took** the picture. 한 여성이 그 사진을 찍었습니다. → The picture **was taken** by a woman.

■ 4형식 문장의 수동태는 간접목적어와 직접목적어 각각을 주어로 하는 수동태가 가능하다. 직접목적어를 주어로 한 수동태에서는 간접목적어 앞에 특정한 전치사를 써야 한다.
전치사 to를 쓰는 동사는 'give, send, tell, teach, show, bring' 등이고, 전치사 for를 쓰는 동사는 'buy, make, choose, cook, get' 등이며, 전치사 of를 쓰는 동사는 'ask' 등이 있다. 또한 make, buy, read, write 등은 직접목적어를 주어로 하는 수동태만 가능하다.

　• His dad **made** him a desk.
　　→ A desk **was made** for him by his dad. 책상이 그의 아빠에 의해 그에게 만들어졌다.
　　→ He was made a desk by his dad. (×)

■ 조동사가 있는 문장의 수동태는 '조동사+be+p.p.' 형식을 갖는다.

　• She **will send** him a book. → A book **will be sent** to him by her. 책이 그녀에 의해 그에게 보내질 것이다.

■ 5형식 문장의 수동태는 목적격 보어 자리에 동사원형이 쓰이면 수동태 문장에서는 to부정사 형태로 바꾸어야 한다.

　• Mom **made** Tony **do** the dishes.
　　→ Tony **was made to do** the dishes by Mom. Tony는 엄마에 의해 설거지하도록 시켜졌다.

■ by 이외의 전치사를 사용하는 수동태에 유의한다.

• be interested in: ~에 흥미가 있다	be filled with: ~로 가득 차다
• be covered with: ~로 덮여 있다	be surprised at: ~에 놀라다
• be made of: ~로 만들어지다(물리적 변화)	be made from: ~로 만들어지다(화학적 변화)
• be satisfied with: ~에 만족하다	be pleased with: ~로 기뻐하다

핵심 Check

2. 다음 괄호 안에서 알맞은 말을 고르시오.

　(1) The bridge (built / was built) by Tom.

　(2) English was taught (for / to) us by James.

　(3) The mountain was covered (by / with) snow.

01 다음 빈칸에 알맞은 것은?

> • Leonardo da Vinci painted *the Mona Lisa.*
> → *The Mona Lisa* _____ by Leonardo da Vinci.

① paints ② painted ③ has painted
④ is painted ⑤ was painted

02 다음 빈칸에 들어갈 말로 적절한 것은?

> Let's learn _____ tips for living green.

① few ② a few ③ little
④ a little ⑤ any

03 다음 우리말에 맞게 빈칸에 알맞은 말을 쓰시오.

(1) 그 꽃병은 Bill에 의해 깨졌다.
➡ The vase _____ _____ by Bill.
(2) 'Harry Potter'는 J.K. Rowling에 의해 쓰여졌다.
➡ *Harry Potter* _____ _____ by J.K. Rowling.
(3) 나는 일주일에 몇 번쯤은 오후 시간을 한가로이 보낸다.
➡ I often have _____ _____ free afternoons a week.
(4) 성공할 가능성이 거의 없다.
➡ There is _____ hope for success.

04 다음 문장에서 어법상 어색한 부분을 바르게 고치시오.

(1) I need a few bread.

_____ ➡ _____

(2) His car washes every weekend by him.

_____ ➡ _____

01 다음 빈칸에 알맞은 것은?

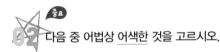

> This book _____ by Harper Lee.

① writes ② wrote

③ to write ④ was written

⑤ was writing

02 다음 중 어법상 <u>어색한</u> 것을 고르시오.

① Can I borrow a few books?

② This book has few mistakes.

③ There lived a little princess in the woods.

④ They have little interest on this topic.

⑤ I will have it for you in just a little minutes.

03 다음 중 태의 전환이 <u>어색한</u> 것은?

① You threw a class birthday party.
 → A class birthday party was thrown by you.

② The light bulb was invented by Thomas Edison.
 → Thomas Edison invented the light bulb.

③ Mom made me come early.
 → I was made come early by Mom.

④ Her mom chose her the largest cookies for her party.
 → The largest cookies were chosen for her for her party by her mom.

⑤ We served the ice cream on plates.
 → The ice cream was served on plates by us.

04 다음 중 어법상 옳은 것은?

① We have little money.

② Everyone was liked her cute napkins.

③ There are a little people in the hall.

④ The flowers will be bought to her by Murphy.

⑤ I'll be there in a few day.

05 다음 우리말을 바르게 영작한 것은?

> 좋은 선물이 그녀를 위해 그녀의 언니에 의해 골라졌다.

① A nice present was chosen to her by her sister.

② A nice present was chosen for her by her sister.

③ A nice present was chosen of her by her sister.

④ She was chosen for a nice present by her sister.

⑤ A nice present was chosen for her sister by her.

서답형

06 다음 괄호 안에서 알맞은 것을 고르시오.

(1) An interesting story was told (to / for) me by an old lady.

(2) A new suit was made (to / for) him last week.

(3) That was not the question which was asked (to / of) me.

07 다음 대화의 빈칸에 들어갈 말로 알맞은 것은?

> M: I'm thirsty. Could you buy me a can of coke?
> W: I'm sorry, but I can't. I have _____ money left.

① little ② a little ③ few
④ a few ⑤ a lot of

08 다음 중 태의 전환이 <u>잘못된</u> 것은?

① Melanie sent me a dress bought at the shop.
 → A dress sent to me was bought at the shop by Melanie.
② They made Benjamin do the dishes tonight after dinner.
 → Benjamin was made to do the dishes tonight after dinner.
③ The doctor advised him to drink a lot of water.
 → He was advised to drink a lot of water by the doctor.
④ My father planted this tree last year.
 → This tree was planted by my father last year.
⑤ Martha bought her son a new pen.
 → A new pen was bought for her son by Martha.

09 다음 빈칸에 공통으로 들어갈 알맞은 것은?

> • I saw _____ people riding the elevator.
> • If you're tired, rest for _____ days.

① few ② a few ③ little
④ a little ⑤ a deal of

10 다음 문장을 수동태로 바르게 바꾼 것은?

> You can throw away trash there.

① Trash can throw away there by you.
② Trash can thrown away there by you.
③ Trash can be thrown away there you.
④ Trash can be thrown there by you.
⑤ Trash can be thrown away there by you.

11 다음 빈칸에 공통으로 들어갈 말로 가장 적절한 것은?

> • Were you pleased _____ the result?
> • The forest was filled _____ the sound of running water.

① at ② with ③ in
④ by ⑤ of

서답형

12 다음 그림을 참고하여 주어진 문장의 빈칸을 알맞게 채우시오.

> There is _____ coffee left in the cup.

➡ _____

서답형

13 괄호 안에 주어진 어휘를 어법에 맞게 빈칸에 쓰시오. (현재 시제로 쓸 것.)

- The worm _____ by the early bird. (catch)
- Many smartphones _____ in Korea. (make)
- These days, he _____ writing. (interest)
- The highway _____ snow. (cover)

서답형

14 주어진 어구를 이용하여 다음 우리말을 영어로 쓰시오.

(1) 그녀는 파티에 초대받았다. (invite)

➡ _____

(2) 사용된 종이는 많은 사람에 의해 재활용된다. (used paper, recycle)

➡ _____

(3) 그의 상사는 그를 일찍 돌아오도록 했다. (수동 태로 쓸 것.) (his boss, make, return)

➡ _____

(4) 이렇게 해서 약간의 에너지가 생산됩니다. (energy, this way, produce)

➡ _____

(5) 100세까지 사는 사람은 거의 없다. (live, to be)

➡ _____

서답형

15 주어진 단어의 형태를 알맞게 바꿔 문장을 완성하시오.

That watch _____ me by him. (give)

서답형

16 다음 문장을 수동태로 바꿔 쓰시오.

(1) The green tower cleans the air.

➡ _____

(2) I need a little bread to make sandwiches.

➡ _____

(3) Who draw the picture *The Starry Night*?

➡ _____

(4) Ms. Brown cooked John some food.

➡ _____

(5) We saw Susan talking on the phone with her friend.

➡ _____

(6) Teachers can show the students their exam result.

➡ _____

서답형

17 다음 문장에서 어법상 어색한 부분을 찾아 바르게 고치시오.

(1) The accident was taken place last night.

_____ ➡ _____

(2) *Hamlet* wrote Shakespeare around 1601.

_____ ➡ _____

(3) Give me a little ideas about this project.

_____ ➡ _____

01 다음 문장을 수동태는 능동태로, 능동태는 수동태로 고치시오.

(1) Jane gave Brian some books.

　➡ _____

(2) This movie will be made next month by them.

　➡ _____

(3) Midori made her daughter a dress.

　➡ _____

(4) She never completely gave up hope.

　➡ _____

(5) Who invented the World Wide Web in 1991?

　➡ _____

02 다음 〈보기〉에 주어진 어휘를 이용하여 문맥에 맞게 문장을 완성하시오.

┌─── 보기 ───┐

few　a few　little　a little

└────────────┘

(1) Einstein's idea was very difficult to understand and so _____ people could understand it.

(2) He has _____ difficulty in reading and writing Greek as he lived in Greece for long.

(3) Yesterday I met _____ friends of mmine and enjoyed ourselves.

(4) It's hot. So I will have _____ ice cream.

03 다음 문장에서 어법상 <u>어색한</u> 부분을 찾아 바르게 고쳐 다시 쓰시오.

(1) They were given us one simple tip for reducing trash.

　➡ _____

(2) Today, this house is using by travelers.

　➡ _____

(3) The wooden table is made from wood.

　➡ _____

(4) Emily was never seen sing in public by us.

　➡ _____

(5) When a child, I was read a storybook every night by my mom.

　➡ _____

(6) A ring with an expensive stone will be sent for Kate.

　➡ _____

04 주어진 문장과 비슷한 의미의 문장을 빈칸을 채워 완성하시오.

┌────────────────────────────┐

• Almost all of the students didn't succeed in explaining what it was.

= _____ students explained what it was.

└────────────────────────────┘

➡ _____

05 다음 우리말을 괄호 안에 주어진 어휘를 이용하여 영작하시오.

(1) 많은 나무가 종이를 만들기 위해 잘린다. (a lot, cut down, make)

➡ _____

(2) 비 오는 날 밤에는 별이 보이지 않는다. (see, rainy night)

➡ _____

(3) 날이 어두워지고 있어서 가로등이 켜졌다. (getting dark, street lights, turn, as)

➡ _____

(4) 똑같은 질문이 그녀에게 물어졌다. (the same question, asked)

➡ _____

(5) 그들은 그녀가 너에게 편지를 쓰도록 시켰다. (make, write a letter) (수동태로 쓸 것.)

➡ _____

(6) 그 소식을 듣고 모두 다 놀랐다. (everybody, the news, surprise)

➡ _____

06 다음 문장에서 어법상 어색한 부분을 찾아 바르게 고치시오.

(1) Students were asked to bring their own cups, but only a little students did.

_____ ➡ _____

(2) Office jobs require few physical effort.

_____ ➡ _____

(3) Little of the soldiers were killed in the war.

_____ ➡ _____

(4) He drank the water in the bottle but a little water was left to satisfy his thirsty.

_____ ➡ _____

07 다음 문장을 수동태로 바꿔 쓰시오.

(1) Matilda gave me some chocolates yesterday. (두 가지로 쓸 것.)

➡ _____

(2) Jenny chose her friend a beautiful hair band.

➡ _____

(3) The stranger asked me the way to the bus stop.

➡ _____

08 다음 그림을 묘사하는 문장을 'few' 또는 'little'을 사용하여 완성하시오.

➡ _____ pencils were given to me by Juliet.

09 다음 글에서 어법상 어색한 것을 찾아 바르게 고치시오.

Last Saturday, I joined "Save Our Forest" program. I went up the mountain and picked up trash. I could find a little people around. There were a little cans on the bench. I picked up a little bottles, too. There was few water inside. I decided to join this program every month.

_____ ➡ _____

_____ ➡ _____

_____ ➡ _____

_____ ➡ _____

No Trash Challenge

We all had a "No Trash Challenge" day last month. The winner was
└→ 과거를 나타내는 시간의 부사구 'last month'가 쓰여, 동사도 과거시제로 쓰였다.
Grade 2 Class 3. Let's read the interview and learn a few tips for living
'Let's+동사원형': '~하자'(제안·권유) '몇몇의'(복수 명사를 꾸며 준다.)
green.

Do Not Use Wrapping Paper
동사원형으로 시작하는 명령문('~하라'), 명령문의 부정은 동사원형 앞에 'Don't[Do not]'을 붙임
Reporter: You threw a class birthday party, but didn't produce a lot
= much
of trash. What were your secrets?

Minsu: First, we agreed not to wrap our gifts, because some wrapping
to부정사의 부정: 'not+to부정사'
paper is not easily recycled. So we brought gifts such as teddy
(부정문의 수동태) 포장지가 재활용되지 않는다는 수동 의미로 해석 = like
bears, key rings, and hairpins that were not wrapped at all.
주격 관계대명사(선행사 gifts를 꾸며 준다.) not ... at all: 전혀 ~이 아니다

Buy the Largest Size

Jieun: Also, we chose the largest size when we bought ice cream
and cookies for the party. Larger sizes use less packaging and
'larger. less'는 각각 'large. little'의 비교급
make less trash.

Eat the Plates

Reporter: And how did you serve the ice cream?

Junha: We served it on plates. You know what? We ate even the plates
'그거 알아?': 재미있거나 놀라운 의견·소식 등을 말하려고 할 때 쓰는 말
after we used them.
= the plates

 확인문제

- 다음 문장이 본문의 내용과 일치하면 T, 일치하지 않으면 F를 쓰시오.

1 The winner of "No Trash Challenge" day was Grade 2 Class 3. ☐

2 Minsu's classmates agreed to wrap their gifts. ☐

3 Smaller sizes use less packaging and make less trash. ☐

4 Junha's classmates ate even the plates after they used them. ☐

trash: 쓰레기

challenge: 도전

wrap: 싸다. 포장하다

gift: 선물

recycle: 재활용하다

packaging: 포장. 포장지

serve: 제공하다

plate: 접시

reduce: 줄이다. 축소하다

Reporter: You ate the plates? What do you mean by that?

<small>평서문에 의문 부호를 붙이고 끝을 올려 말함으로써 상대방의 말을 되묻는 표현이 된다.</small>

Junha: Actually, we used popped rice cakes as plates, so we could

<small>조동사 could+동사원형: ~할 수 있었다</small>

eat them and leave nothing behind!

<small>등위접속사 'and'가 동사원형 'eat'과 'leave'를 연결</small>

Reporter: Ah, I get it. That's quite interesting.

<small>알겠어요. (이제야) 이해가 되는군요.　　　아주</small>

<small>actually: 사실</small>
<small>instead: 대신에</small>
<small>cotton: 무명, 면</small>
<small>food waste: 음식 쓰레기</small>

Bring Your Own Things

Reporter: What about cups and spoons?

<small>What about ~? = How about ~?: ~은 어떻습니까?</small>

Minsu: We didn't use paper cups or plastic spoons. Instead, we brought

<small>대신에</small>

our own cups and spoons from home and then took them back.

<small>'동사+부사'로 이루어진 이어동사: 목적어가 인칭대명사인 경우 목적어를 부사 앞에 써야 한다.</small>

Use Cloth Napkins

Reporter: What else did you do to make less trash?

<small>그밖에 무엇을　　　　부사적 용법의 to부정사(목적)</small>

Jieun: We used cloth napkins. You know, paper napkins are not

<small>알다시피</small>

good for your skin.

<small>~에 좋다</small>

Reporter: But where did you get the cloth napkins?

Jieun: They were made by Minji. She cut up her old cotton shirt to

<small>= the cloth napkins　수동태　　　　　~을 잘게 자르다</small>

make some for us. Everyone liked her cute napkins.

<small>to(×)　　　모두(단수 취급)</small>

Leave No Food Behind

Reporter: Please give us one simple tip for reducing trash.

<small>4형식: 간접목적어(us)+직접목적어(one simple tip ...).　　for+동명사 reducing</small>

Junha: Don't leave any food on your plate. Food waste really is a big

<small>부정문에서 '어떤 ~도 (아닌)'</small>

problem. But see? We ate everything, even our plates, ha-ha.

<small>~까지도</small>

확인문제

● 다음 문장이 본문의 내용과 일치하면 T, 일치하지 않으면 F를 쓰시오.

1　Junha's classmates used popped rice cakes as plates. ☐

2　After Junha's classmates ate the plates, they left some trash behind. ☐

3　Minsu's classmates used paper cups and plastic spoons. ☐

4　Jieun's classmates used cloth napkins instead of paper napkins. ☐

5　Minji cut up her old cotton shirt and made some cloth napkins. ☐

6　Junha doesn't think food waste is a big problem. ☐

● 우리말을 참고하여 빈칸에 알맞은 말을 쓰시오.

1 No Trash _____

2 We all had a "_____ _____ _____" day last month.

3 The winner was _____ _____ _____ .

4 Let's read the interview and learn _____ _____ _____ for _____ _____ .

5 Do Not Use _____ _____

6 Reporter: You threw a class birthday party, but _____ _____ a lot of trash.

7 What were _____ _____ ?

8 Minsu: First, we _____ _____ _____ _____ our gifts, because some wrapping paper _____ _____ _____ _____ .

9 So we brought gifts _____ _____ teddy bears, key rings, and hairpins that were _____ wrapped _____ _____ .

10 Buy the _____ Size

11 Jieun: Also, we _____ _____ _____ _____ when we bought ice cream and cookies for the party.

12 Larger sizes use _____ _____ and make _____ _____ .

13 _____ the Plates

14 Reporter: And _____ did you _____ the ice cream?

15 Junha: We served it _____ _____ .

16 _____ _____ _____ ?

17 We ate _____ _____ _____ after we used them.

18 Reporter: You _____ _____ _____ ?

19 What do you mean _____ _____ ?

1 쓰레기를 없애기 위한 도전

2 우리는 모두 지난달에 '쓰레기를 없애기 위한 도전'의 날을 가졌습니다.

3 우승자는 2학년 3반이었습니다.

4 인터뷰를 읽고, 친환경적으로 살기 위한 몇 가지 비결을 배웁시다.

5 포장지를 사용하지 마라

6 기자: 여러분은 학급 생일 파티를 열었지만, 쓰레기가 많이 나오지 않았어요.

7 비결이 무엇입니까?

8 민수: 우선, 우리는 몇몇 포장지가 쉽게 재활용되지 않기 때문에 선물을 포장하지 않는 것에 동의했습니다.

9 그래서 우리는 전혀 포장되어 있지 않은 곰 인형, 열쇠고리, 머리핀과 같은 선물을 가져왔습니다.

10 가장 큰 크기를 사라

11 지은: 또한, 우리는 파티를 위한 아이스크림과 쿠키를 살 때, 가장 큰 크기를 골랐습니다.

12 크기가 더 크면 포장을 더 적게 사용하고 쓰레기를 더 적게 배출하거든요.

13 접시를 먹어라

14 기자: 그리고 아이스크림은 어떻게 나누어 주었나요?

15 준하: 우리는 접시에 그것을 나누어 주었습니다.

16 아세요?

17 우리는 사용한 후에 접시까지도 먹었어요.

18 기자: 접시를 먹었다고요?

19 그게 무슨 뜻이죠?

20 Junha: Actually, we used popped rice cakes _____ _____, so we could eat them and _____ _____ _____!

21 Reporter: Ah, I _____ _____.

22 That's _____ interesting.

23 _____ Your Own Things

24 Reporter: _____ _____ cups and spoons?

25 Minsu: We _____ _____ paper cups or plastic spoons.

26 _____, we _____ our own cups and spoons _____ home and then _____ _____ _____.

27 Use _____ Napkins

28 Reporter: What else did you do to _____ _____ _____?

29 Jieun: We used _____ _____.

30 You know, paper napkins _____ _____ _____ _____ your skin.

31 Reporter: But _____ _____ _____ _____ the cloth napkins?

32 Jieun: They _____ _____ _____ Minji.

33 She _____ _____ her old cotton shirt to make some for us.

34 Everyone liked _____ _____ _____.

35 _____ No Food _____

36 Reporter: Please give us _____ _____ _____ for reducing trash.

37 Junha: _____ _____ any food on your plate.

38 _____ _____ really is a big problem.

39 But _____?

40 We _____ _____, even our plates, ha-ha.

20 준하: 사실, 우리는 뻥튀기를 접시로 사용해서, 그것들을 먹고 아무것도 남기지 않을 수 있었죠.

21 기자: 아, 알겠어요.

22 그거 꽤 흥미롭군요.

23 여러분 자신의 물건을 가져와라

24 기자: 컵과 숟가락은 어떻게 했나요?

25 민수: 우리는 종이컵이나 플라스틱 숟가락을 사용하지 않았습니다.

26 대신에, 우리 컵과 숟가락을 집에서 가져온 후, 다시 가져갔습니다.

27 천 냅킨을 사용해라

28 기자: 쓰레기를 더 줄이기 위해 그 외에 무엇을 했나요?

29 지은: 우리는 천 냅킨을 사용했어요.

30 아시다시피, 종이 냅킨은 여러분의 피부에 안 좋잖아요.

31 기자: 하지만 천 냅킨을 어디서 구했나요?

32 지은: 그것들은 민지가 만들었어요.

33 그녀가 우리에게 몇 개를 만들어 주기 위해 자신의 낡은 면 셔츠를 잘랐어요.

34 그녀의 귀여운 냅킨을 모두가 좋아했어요.

35 음식을 남기지 마라

36 기자: 우리에게 쓰레기를 줄이기 위한 간단한 조언을 하나만 해 주세요.

37 준하: 접시에 음식을 남기지 마세요.

38 음식 쓰레기는 정말 큰 문제입니다.

39 하지만 아시죠?

40 우리는 모두 다 먹었죠, 접시까지도요, 하하.

● 우리말을 참고하여 본문을 영작하시오.

1 쓰레기를 없애기 위한 도전
➡ _____

2 우리는 모두 지난달에 '쓰레기를 없애기 위한 도전'의 날을 가졌습니다.
➡ _____

3 우승자는 2학년 3반이었습니다.
➡ _____

4 인터뷰를 읽고, 친환경적으로 살기 위한 몇 가지 비결을 배웁시다.
➡ _____

5 포장지를 사용하지 마라
➡ _____

6 기자: 여러분은 학급 생일 파티를 열었지만, 쓰레기가 많이 나오지 않았어요.
➡ _____

7 비결이 무엇입니까?
➡ _____

8 민수: 우선, 우리는 몇몇 포장지가 쉽게 재활용되지 않기 때문에 선물을 포장하지 않는 것에 동의했습니다.
➡ _____

9 그래서 우리는 전혀 포장되어 있지 않은 곰 인형, 열쇠고리, 머리핀과 같은 선물을 가져왔습니다.
➡ _____

10 가장 큰 크기를 사라
➡ _____

11 지은: 또한, 우리는 파티를 위한 아이스크림과 쿠키를 살 때, 가장 큰 크기를 골랐습니다.
➡ _____

12 크기가 더 크면 포장을 더 적게 사용하고 쓰레기를 더 적게 배출하거든요.
➡ _____

13 접시를 먹어라
➡ _____

14 기자: 그리고 아이스크림은 어떻게 나누어 주었나요?
➡ _____

15 준하: 우리는 접시에 그것을 나누어 주었습니다.
➡ _____

16 아세요?
➡ _____

17 우리는 사용한 후에 접시까지도 먹었어요.
➡ _____

18 기자: 접시를 먹었다고요?
➡ _____

19 그게 무슨 뜻이죠?
➡ _____

20 준하: 사실, 우리는 뻥튀기를 접시로 사용해서, 그것들을 먹고 아무것도 남기지 않을 수 있었죠.

➡ _____

21 기자: 아, 알겠어요.

➡ _____

22 그거 꽤 흥미롭군요.

➡ _____

23 여러분 자신의 물건을 가져와라

➡ _____

24 기자: 컵과 숟가락은 어떻게 했나요?

➡ _____

25 민수: 우리는 종이컵이나 플라스틱 숟가락을 사용하지 않았습니다.

➡ _____

26 대신에, 우리 컵과 숟가락을 집에서 가져온 후, 다시 가져갔습니다.

➡ _____

27 천 냅킨을 사용해라

➡ _____

28 기자: 쓰레기를 더 줄이기 위해 그 외에 무엇을 했나요?

➡ _____

29 지은: 우리는 천 냅킨을 사용했어요.

➡ _____

30 아시다시피, 종이 냅킨은 여러분의 피부에 안 좋잖아요.

➡ _____

31 기자: 하지만 천 냅킨을 어디서 구했나요?

➡ _____

32 지은: 그것들은 민지가 만들었어요.

➡ _____

33 그녀가 우리에게 몇 개를 만들어 주기 위해 자신의 낡은 면 셔츠를 잘랐어요.

➡ _____

34 그녀의 귀여운 냅킨을 모두가 좋아했어요.

➡ _____

35 음식을 남기지 마라

➡ _____

36 기자: 우리에게 쓰레기를 줄이기 위한 간단한 조언을 하나만 해 주세요.

➡ _____

37 준하: 접시에 음식을 남기지 마세요.

➡ _____

38 음식 쓰레기는 정말 큰 문제입니다.

➡ _____

39 하지만 아시죠?

➡ _____

40 우리는 모두 다 먹었죠, 접시까지도요, 하하.

➡ _____

[01~03] 다음 글을 읽고 물음에 답하시오.

We all had a "No Trash Challenge" day last month. The winner was ⓐ2학년 3반. Let's read the interview and learn a few tips for ⓑ living green.

01 다음 빈칸에 위 글의 밑줄 친 ⓐ의 우리말을 영어로 쓰시오.

➡ _____ 2 _____ 3

02 위 글의 밑줄 친 ⓑliving과 문법적 쓰임이 같은 것을 모두 고르시오.

① He is the greatest living poet.
② How about living in the country?
③ She is living in the apartment with her family.
④ There is a TV in the living room.
⑤ There were no people living in western America at that time.

03 위 글의 뒤에 올 내용으로 가장 알맞은 것을 고르시오.

① 쓰레기 문제의 발생 원인에 관한 인터뷰
② 친환경적으로 살기 위한 비결에 관한 인터뷰
③ 과대 포장의 문제점들에 관한 인터뷰
④ 쓰레기를 없애기 위한 도전의 애로 사항
⑤ 학생들의 포장지 재활용 사례들 소개

[04~06] 다음 글을 읽고 물음에 답하시오.

Buy the Largest Size

Jieun: Also, we chose the largest size when we bought ice cream and cookies for the party. (A)[Larger / Smaller] sizes use less packaging and make less trash

Eat the Plates

Reporter: And how did you serve the ice cream?

Junha: We served it on plates. You know what? We ate even the plates after we used them.

Reporter: You ate the plates? What do you mean by that?

Junha: Actually, we used (B)[popping / popped] rice cakes ⓐas plates, so we could eat them and leave nothing behind!

Reporter: Ah, ⓑI get it. That's (C)[quiet / quite] interesting.

04 위 글의 괄호 (A)~(C)에서 문맥이나 어법상 알맞은 낱말을 골라 쓰시오.

➡ (A) _____ (B) _____ (C) _____

05 위 글의 밑줄 친 ⓐas와 같은 의미로 쓰인 것을 고르시오.

① As it was getting dark, we soon turned back.
② Take things as they are.
③ This box will serve as a table.
④ As spring comes, the birds move northward.
⑤ This is twice as large as that.

06 위 글의 밑줄 친 ⓑI get it.과 바꿔 쓸 수 없는 말을 고르시오.

① I know.　　② I understand.
③ I see.　　④ I got it.
⑤ I think I get it now.

[07~09] 다음 글을 읽고 물음에 답하시오.

Do Not Use Wrapping Paper

Reporter: You ___ⓐ___ a class birthday party, but didn't produce a lot of trash. What were your secrets?

Minsu: First, we agreed not ⓑto wrap our gifts, because some wrapping paper is not easily recycled. So we brought gifts such as teddy bears, key rings, and hairpins that were not wrapped at all.

07 위 글의 빈칸 ⓐ에 들어갈 수 없는 말을 고르시오.

① gave ② had ③ took
④ threw ⑤ hosted

08 아래 〈보기〉에서 위 글의 밑줄 친 ⓑto wrap과 문법적 쓰임이 다른 것의 개수를 고르시오.

> ┤ 보기 ├
>
> ① I think it wrong to tell a lie.
> ② My plan is to master English in a year.
> ③ I don't know what to do now.
> ④ This water is not good to drink.
> ⑤ It is necessary to use the dictionary.

① 1개 ② 2개 ③ 3개 ④ 4개 ⑤ 5개

09 위 글의 내용과 일치하지 않는 것은?

① There was a class birthday party at Minsu's class.
② After the party was over, Minsu's classroom was full of trash.
③ Minsu's class agreed not to wrap their gifts.
④ Some wrapping paper is not easy to recycle.
⑤ Minsu's class brought gifts that were not wrapped at all.

[10~12] 다음 글을 읽고 물음에 답하시오.

Bring Your Own Things

Reporter: What about cups and spoons?

Minsu: We didn't use paper cups or plastic spoons. ___ⓐ___, we brought our own cups and spoons from home and then took them back.

Use Cloth Napkins

Reporter: What else did you do to make less trash?

Jieun: We used ①cloth napkins. You know, paper napkins are not good for your skin.

Reporter: But where did you get the cloth napkins?

Jieun: ②They were made by Minji. She cut up her ③old cotton shirt to make ④some for us. Everyone liked ⑤her cute napkins.

10 위 글의 빈칸 ⓐ에 들어갈 알맞은 말을 고르시오.

① Therefore ② Instead
③ Similarly ④ In other words
⑤ In addition

11 밑줄 친 ①~⑤ 중에서 가리키는 대상이 나머지 넷과 다른 것은?

① ② ③ ④ ⑤

12 위 글을 읽고 cloth napkins에 대해 알 수 없는 것을 고르시오.

① 만든 이유 ② 만든 사람
③ 재료 ④ 제작에 걸린 시간
⑤ 천 냅킨에 대한 반응

[13~15] 다음 글을 읽고 물음에 답하시오.

ⓐ_____ **No Food Behind**

Reporter: Please give us one simple tip for _____ⓑ trash.

Junha: Don't leave any food on your plate. Food waste really is a big problem. But see? We ate everything, even our plates, ha-ha.

서답형

13 위 글의 빈칸 ⓐ에 들어갈 알맞은 단어를 본문에서 찾아 쓰시오.

➡ _____

서답형

14 위 글의 빈칸 ⓑ에 reduce를 알맞은 형태로 쓰시오.

➡ _____

서답형

15 다음 빈칸 (A)와 (B)에 알맞은 단어를 넣어 준하네 반이 쓰레기를 줄인 방법을 완성하시오.

> Junha's classmates reduced trash by leaving no (A)_____ on their plates. They didn't leave even their (B)_____ behind by eating them.

[16~18] 다음 친환경 도시 계획 아이디어를 읽고 물음에 답하시오.

Save energy

Trash powers the green bus.

GREEN BUS

- In this city, the green bus _____ⓐ by trash. Energy is saved ⓑthis way.
- In this city, the energy tree is used as a street lamp. ⓒA few energy is produced this way.

서답형

16 그림을 참조하여 위 글의 빈칸 ⓐ에 들어갈 알맞은 말을 쓰시오.

➡ _____

서답형

17 위 글의 밑줄 친 ⓑthis way가 가리키는 내용을 우리말로 쓰시오.

➡ _____

서답형

18 위 글의 밑줄 친 ⓒ에서 어법상 틀린 부분을 찾아 고치시오.

_____ ➡ _____

[19~21] 다음 글을 읽고 물음에 답하시오.

Buy the Largest Size

Jieun: Also, we chose the largest size when we bought ice cream and cookies for the party. Larger sizes use less packaging and make less trash.

Eat the Plates

Reporter: And how did you serve the ice cream?

Junha: We served it on plates. _____ⓐ We ate even the plates after we used them. (①)

Reporter: You ate the plates? (②)

Junha: Actually, we used popped rice cakes as plates, so we could eat them and leave nothing behind! (③)

Reporter: Ah, I get it. (④) That's quite interesting. (⑤)

19 위 글의 빈칸 ⓐ에 들어가기에 적절하지 <u>않은</u> 말을 고르시오.

① You know what?　　② Guess what!
③ I'll tell you what.　　④ Guess why!
⑤ You know something?

20 위 글의 흐름으로 보아, 주어진 문장이 들어가기에 가장 적절한 곳은?

> What do you mean by that?

①　　　②　　　③　　　④　　　⑤

21 위 글을 읽고 대답할 수 <u>없는</u> 질문은?

① What size did Jieun's class choose when they bought ice cream and cookies?
② Why did Jieun's class choose that size?
③ How did Junha's class serve the ice cream?
④ What were the plates that Junha's class used made of?
⑤ How did Jieun's class recycle the bags of cookies after eating the cookies?

[22~24] 다음 글을 읽고 물음에 답하시오.

Bring Your Own Things
Reporter: ⓐ<u>What about</u> cups and spoons?
Minsu: We didn't use paper cups or plastic spoons. ⓑ<u>Instead, we brought our own cups and spoons from home and then took back them.</u>

서답형
22 위 글의 밑줄 친 ⓐ<u>What about</u>과 바꿔 쓸 수 있는 말을 쓰시오.

➡ _____

서답형
23 위 글의 밑줄 친 ⓑ에서 어법상 <u>틀린</u> 부분을 찾아 고치시오.

_____ ➡ _____

서답형
24 본문의 내용과 일치하도록 다음 빈칸에 알맞은 단어를 쓰시오. (own을 사용할 것.)

> Minsu's friends used _____ _____ _____ _____ _____ instead of using disposable paper cups or plastic spoons.　　*disposable: 일회용의

[25~26] 다음 친환경 도시 계획안을 설명하는 보고서를 읽고 물음에 답하시오.

> **Green City Ideas**
> ⓐ<u>So many ideas were presented by the Earth Savers Club.</u>
> In the restaurants, ⓑ<u>food is served on small plates.</u> ⓒ<u>Food waste is reduced (A)this way.</u>
> At every house, ⓓ<u>rain water is stored in the tanks.</u> ⓔ<u>Water is saved (B)this way.</u>

서답형
25 다음 빈칸에 알맞은 단어를 넣어 위 글의 밑줄 친 ⓐ~ⓔ를 능동태로 각각 고치시오.

➡ ⓐ The Earth Savers Club _____ so many ideas. ⓑ they _____ _____ on small plates ⓒ They reduce _____ _____ ⓓ people _____ _____ in the tanks ⓔ People _____ water

서답형
26 위 글의 밑줄 친 (A)와 (B)의 <u>this way</u>가 가리키는 내용을 각각 우리말로 쓰시오.

➡ (A) _____
(B) _____

[01~03] 다음 글을 읽고 물음에 답하시오.

We all had a "No Trash Challenge" day last month. The winner was Grade 2 Class 3. Let's read the interview and learn (A)[a few / a little] tips for ⓐliving (_____).

Do Not Use Wrapping Paper

Reporter: You threw a class birthday party, but didn't produce a lot of trash. What were your secrets?

Minsu: First, we agreed not to wrap our gifts, because some wrapping paper is not easily (B)[recycling / recycled]. So we brought gifts such as teddy bears, key rings, and hairpins that (C)[was / were] not wrapped at all.

01 위 글의 밑줄 친 ⓐ의 뜻이 다음과 같도록 빈칸에 철자 g로 시작하는 단어를 쓰시오.

> living an eco-friendly life

➡ _____

02 위 글의 괄호 (A)~(C)에서 문맥이나 어법상 알맞은 낱말을 골라 쓰시오.

➡ (A) _____ (B) _____ (C) _____

03 Why did Minsu's class agree not to wrap their gifts? Fill in the blanks with the suitable words.

➡ Because there is some _____ _____ which is not easily _____.

[04~06] 다음 글을 읽고 물음에 답하시오.

Buy the Largest Size

Jieun: Also, we chose the largest size when we bought ice cream and cookies for the party. Larger sizes use less packaging and make less trash.

Eat the Plates

Reporter: And how did you serve the ice cream?

Junha: We served it on plates. You know what? We ate even the plates after we used them.

Reporter: ⓐYou ate the plates? What do you mean by that?

Junha: Actually, we used popped rice cakes as plates, so we could eat them and leave nothing ___(A)___!

Reporter: Ah, I get it. That's quite interesting.

04 위 글의 빈칸 (A)에 들어갈 알맞은 말을 쓰시오.

➡ _____

05 Why did Jieun's class choose the largest size when they bought ice cream and cookies for the party? Fill in the blanks with the suitable words.

➡ It's because smaller sizes use _____ packaging and make _____ trash.

06 위 글의 밑줄 친 ⓐ를 의문문의 형태로 바꾸시오.

➡ _____

[07~09] 다음 글을 읽고 물음에 답하시오.

Use Cloth Napkins

Reporter: What else did you do to make less trash?

Jieun: We used cloth napkins. You know, paper napkins are not good for your skin.

Reporter: But where did you get the cloth napkins?

Jieun: ⓐThey were made by Minji. She cut up her old cotton shirt ⓑto make some for us. Everyone liked her cute napkins.

07 위 글의 밑줄 친 ⓐ를 능동태로 고치시오.

➡ _____

08 위 글의 밑줄 친 ⓑ를 다음과 같이 바꿔 쓸 때 빈칸에 들어갈 알맞은 말을 쓰시오.

➡ (1) _____ some for us

(2) _____ some for us

(3) _____ she _____ make some for us

(4) _____ she _____ make some for us

09 본문의 내용과 일치하도록 다음 빈칸 (A)와 (B)에 알맞은 단어를 쓰시오.

Minji cut up her (A)_____ _____ _____ and made some cloth napkins for her classmates because paper napkins are not good for the (B)_____.

[10~12] 다음 글을 읽고 물음에 답하시오.

We all had a "No Trash Challenge" day last month. The winner was Grade 2 Class 3. ⓐ Let's read the interview and learn a few tips for living green.

Do Not Use Wrapping Paper

Reporter: You threw a class birthday party, but didn't produce a lot of trash. What were your secrets?

Minsu: First, ⓑ선물을 포장하지 않는 것에 동의했습니다, because some wrapping paper is not easily recycled. So we brought gifts such as teddy bears, key rings, and hairpins that were not wrapped at all.

10 위 글의 밑줄 친 ⓐ를 다음과 같이 바꿔 쓸 때 빈칸에 들어갈 알맞은 말을 쓰시오.

➡ = _____ don't we read the interview and learn a few tips for living green?

= _____ _____ reading the interview and learning a few tips for living green?

= _____ we read the interview and learn a few tips for living green?

11 위 글의 밑줄 친 ⓑ의 우리말에 맞게 한 단어를 보충하여, 주어진 어휘를 알맞게 배열하시오.

gifts / wrap / we / to / our / agreed

➡ _____

12 본문의 내용과 일치하도록 다음 빈칸 (A)와 (B)에 알맞은 단어를 쓰시오.

Though Minsu's class held a class birthday party, there was not much (A)_____ left because they brought gifts that were not (B)_____ at all.

Project Do it yourself

• This is a hand puppet. It is made of my old sock. It took only a little time to
　　　　　　　　　　～로 만들어지다　　　　　　'It takes+시간+to v' 구문으로 '～하는 데 시간이 걸리다'라는 뜻이다.

make this. Let's make a few more sock puppets and have a wonderful puppet
　　　　　　　　a few+복수 명사: 몇 개의

show together.

• This is a paper bag lamp. It is made out of a used paper shopping bag. Light
　　　　　　　　　　　　　　　　　　　　an(×)　과거분사로 '사용된' 의 의미

shines beautifully through the holes.

구문해설 • puppet: 인형　• be made of: ～로 만들어지다　• a little+셀 수 없는 명사(단수 명사): 약간의
• a few+셀 수 있는 복수 명사: 몇몇의　• only a little: 아주 적은, 거의 없는　• shine: 빛나다

Express Yourself C

Green City Ideas

So many ideas were presented by the Earth Savers Club.
　　└→ The Earth Savers Club presented so many ideas. (능동태)
In the restaurants, food is served on small plates. Food waste is reduced this
　　　　　　　　　└→ they serve food on small plates (능동태)　　　└→ They reduce food waste
way.　　　　　　　　　　　　　　　　　　　　　　　　　　　　　　this way. (능동태)

At every house, rain water is stored in the tanks. Water is saved this way.
　　　　　　　└→ people store rain water in the tanks (능동태)　└→ People save water this way. (능동태)

구문해설 • Green: 환경 보호의, 환경 친화적인　• present: (특정한 방식으로) 보여 주다[나타내다/묘사하다]
• serve: 제공하다　• reduce: 줄이다　• store: 저장하다
• save: 절약하다, 구하다, (돈을) 모으다, 저축하다

Link to The World

Spoons that You Can Eat
목적격 관계대명사(= which)

• You can eat these spoons. They were made out of rice. They are 100%
　　　　　　　　　　　　　　　　　수동태　　　　～으로

natural.

• We can use these green spoons and reduce plastic trash.
= These green spoons can be used and plastic trash can be reduced by us.
• We also can save water because we don't have to wash these spoons.
= Water can also be saved by us　　　　～할 필요가 없다

구문해설 • out of: (수단·재료) ～으로　• natural: 천연의, 자연의 [내추럴]

• 이것은 손 인형입니다. 그것은 제 오래된 양말로 만들어졌습니다. 이것을 만드는 데는 시간이 거의 안 걸렸습니다. 손 인형을 몇 개 더 만들어서 함께 멋진 인형극을 해 봅시다.

• 이것은 종이 가방 램프입니다. 그것은 사용한 종이 쇼핑 가방으로 만들었습니다. 빛이 구멍을 통해 아름답게 빛납니다.

친환경 도시 아이디어

아주 많은 의견이 '지구를 지키는 동호회'에 의해 제안되었습니다.

식당에서는 음식이 작은 접시에 제공됩니다. 이렇게 해서 음식 쓰레기가 줄어듭니다.

모든 집에서는 빗물이 탱크에 저장됩니다. 이렇게 해서 물이 절약됩니다.

먹을 수 있는 숟가락

• 당신은 이 숟가락을 먹을 수 있습니다. 그것들은 쌀로 만들어졌습니다. 그것들은 100% 천연 제품입니다.

• 우리는 이 친환경 숟가락을 사용하여 플라스틱 쓰레기를 줄일 수 있습니다.

• 우리는 이 숟가락들을 씻을 필요가 없기 때문에 물도 절약할 수 있습니다.

영역별 핵심문제

영역별 핵심문제

Words & Expressions

01 다음 주어진 두 단어의 관계가 같도록 빈칸에 알맞은 단어를 쓰시오.

> nation : national = culture : _____

02 다음 빈칸에 들어갈 말로 알맞은 것은?

> • You threw a class birthday party, but didn't produce a lot of _____.
> • Don't leave any food on your plate. _____ really is a big problem.

① challenge – Air pollution
② plates – Many plates
③ reusable items – Food waste
④ packaging – Wrapping paper
⑤ trash – Food waste

03 다음 영영 풀이에 해당하는 것을 고르시오.

> to make smaller in size or number

① leave ② increase ③ reduce
④ realize ⑤ agree

04 다음 빈칸에 들어갈 말로 알맞은 것은?

> • I had a _____ cold for two weeks.
> • Why don't you _____ the gift for your mother with a red ribbon?

① spotless – save
② terrible – wrap
③ terrible – save
④ spotless – wrap
⑤ natural – provide

05 다음 글의 빈칸 ⓐ와 ⓑ에 들어갈 말로 알맞은 것은?

> We didn't use paper cups or plastic spoons. Instead, we ____ⓐ____ our own cups and spoons from home and then ____ⓑ____ .

① brought – saved them
② saved – took them back
③ used – took back them
④ brought – took them back
⑤ got – saved them

06 다음 밑줄 친 부분의 의미가 바르지 않은 것은?

① There are many islands in the Pacific <u>Ocean</u>. (대양, 바다)
② I bring a <u>reusable</u> water bottle to school every day. (재활용할 수 있는)
③ I like clothing with <u>simple</u> designs. (단순한)
④ She still sucks her <u>thumb</u> when she's worried. (엄지손가락)
⑤ She also drinks a lot of water for her <u>skin</u>. (피부)

Conversation

07 대화의 빈칸에 들어갈 말로 알맞은 말을 고르시오.

> B: This shopping bag is so beautiful.
> G: Thank you. We made it out of a broken umbrella.
> B: _____

① What a pity!
② I don't think it's right.
③ I don't think so.
④ I can't believe it.
⑤ I don't agree with you.

08 자연스러운 대화가 되도록 알맞은 순서로 배열한 것은?

> (A) They take 4,000 years to break down.
> (B) What do you mean by that?
> (C) That's surprising!
> (D) Glass bottles are a big problem for the Earth.

① (A) – (B) – (C) – (D)
② (B) – (A) – (C) – (D)
③ (C) – (A) – (B) – (D)
④ (D) – (A) – (B) – (C)
⑤ (D) – (B) – (A) – (C)

[09~10] 다음 대화를 읽고 물음에 답하시오.

> G: I feel blue today.
> B: _____ (A) _____
> G: I mean I feel sad. We make too much trash.
> B: Ah, I get it now. _____ (B) _____

09 빈칸 (A)에 들어갈 추가적인 설명을 요구하는 표현을 쓰시오.

> ┌─ 조건 ┤
> • meaning of that을 이용할 것

➡ _____

10 위 대화의 빈칸 (B)에 들어갈 말로 알맞은 것은?

① You'd better not use trash.
② That's very surprising news.
③ We should recycle and reuse more.
④ What were your secrets?
⑤ Give me some water.

[11~12] 다음 대화의 빈칸에 들어갈 알맞은 표현은?

11
> B: Hey, Minji. What is one tip for a clean classroom?
> G: Well, _____.
> B: What do you mean by that?
> G: We don't throw away trash, so our trash can stay empty.

① I mean it's time to finish working and go home
② we're doing a clean bin project today
③ we make too much trash
④ we have five classes a day
⑤ your classroom is spotless

12
> A: Cans are a big problem for the Earth.
> B: What do you mean by that?
> A: _____

① Take a soda can and shake it well.
② They are not good for your health.
③ Put some cans in the bin.
④ They take 200 years to break down.
⑤ This example is just the tip of the iceberg.

13 다음 대화의 빈칸에 알맞은 표현은?

> A: Jiho _____.
> B: What do you mean by that?
> A: I mean, he works hard.
> B: Ah, I get it.

① can't see the forest for the trees
② is as busy as a bee
③ is under the weather
④ is an early bird
⑤ has a green thumb

Grammar

14 다음 주어진 문장과 같은 뜻이 되도록 빈칸을 채우시오.

(1) The boy gave me a box.

➡ I _____.

(2) We did not wrap the key rings and hairpins at all.

➡ The key rings and hairpins _____ _____ by us.

15 다음 중 어법상 올바른 것은?

① Each small plate has a few food on it.

② Let's read the interview and learn a little tips for living green.

③ I was made leave the city by Jim.

④ This book has few mistakes.

⑤ My car fixed by him last week.

16 다음 빈칸에 들어갈 말을 순서대로 바르게 짝지은 것을 고르시오.

> • To make orange juice, I need _____ oranges.
> • The glass _____ by Amy this morning.

① little – breaks

② a few – broke

③ a few – was broken

④ few – broke

⑤ few – was broken

17 다음 중 어법상 어색한 문장은?

① They were made of popped rice cakes.

② These boxes will sent to Ralph tomorrow by his brother.

③ By whom was the bridge built a few hundreds years ago?

④ The river is cleaned up by this machine.

⑤ This book is read by many people nowadays.

18 다음 빈칸에 a little을 쓸 수 없는 것은?

① There is _____ water left in the bottle.

② Will you give me _____ flour and butter?

③ We spent _____ money at the market.

④ They bought _____ honey to make a cake.

⑤ The little girl has _____ dolls to play with.

19 다음 문장에서 틀린 것을 고쳐 다시 쓰시오.

(1) I don't even know what was happened to Jim.

➡ _____

(2) A new smartphone was bought to Tom by his mom.

➡ _____

(3) He was made feel sick by the smell of the trash.

➡ _____

(4) Cutie is called the dog by my dad.

➡ _____

(5) He has few patience.

➡ _____

(6) I need few eggs to make some sandwiches.

➡ _____

20 다음 빈칸에 들어갈 전치사가 나머지와 다른 것은?

① We should be satisfied _____ what we have.

② The microwave oven was invented _____ Percy Spencer.

③ The song, *Yesterday*, was first sung _____ the *Beatles*.

④ This room was cleaned _____ him.

⑤ *King Lear* was written _____ Shakespeare.

Reading

[21~23] 다음 글을 읽고 물음에 답하시오.

ⓐ

Reporter: You threw a class birthday party, but didn't produce a lot of trash. What were your secrets?

Minsu: First, we agreed not to wrap our gifts, because some wrapping paper is not easily recycled. So we brought gifts such as teddy bears, key rings, and hairpins ⓑ_____ were not wrapped ⓒat all.

21 위 글의 빈칸 ⓐ에 들어갈 제목으로 알맞은 것을 고르시오.

① Leave No Food Behind

② Eat the Plates

③ Bring Your Own Things

④ Do Not Use Wrapping Paper

⑤ Buy the Largest Size

22 위 글의 빈칸 ⓑ에 들어갈 알맞은 말을 모두 고르시오.

① what ② that

③ these ④ those

⑤ which

23 위 글의 밑줄 친 ⓒat all과 바꿔 쓸 수 있는 말을 고르시오.

① in the least ② at last

③ hardly ④ seldom

⑤ at least

[24~26] 다음 글을 읽고 물음에 답하시오.

Buy the Largest Size

Jieun: Also, we chose the largest size when we bought ice cream and cookies for the party. Larger sizes use less packaging and make less trash.

Eat the Plates

Reporter: And how did you serve the ice cream?

Junha: We served ①it on plates. You know what? We ate even the plates after we used ②them.

Reporter: You ate the plates? What do you mean by ③that?

Junha: ⓐActually, we used popped rice cakes as plates, so we could eat ④them and leave nothing behind!

Reporter: Ah, I get it. ⑤That's quite interesting.

24 밑줄 친 ①~⑤ 중에서 가리키는 대상에 대한 설명이 옳지 않은 것을 고르시오.

① the ice cream

② the plates

③ You ate the plates

④ ice cream and cookies

⑤ we used popped rice cakes as plates, so we could eat them and leave nothing behind!

25 위 글의 밑줄 친 ⓐActually와 바꿔 쓸 수 있는 말을 고르시오. (2개)

① In fact
② Needless to say
③ On the contrary
④ At last
⑤ As a matter of fact

26 위 글의 내용과 일치하지 <u>않는</u> 것은?

① Jieun's class chose the largest size when they bought ice cream and cookies for the party.
② If we buy larger sizes, we can reduce packaging and produce less trash.
③ The reporter asked how Junha's class served the ice cream.
④ Junha's class served the ice cream on plates.
⑤ Junha's class washed the plates after they used them.

[27~28] 다음 글을 읽고 물음에 답하시오.

Bring Your Own Things

Reporter: What about cups and spoons?

Minsu: We didn't use paper cups or plastic spoons. Instead, we brought our own cups and spoons from home and then took them back.

Use Cloth Napkins

Reporter: What else did you do ⓐto make less trash?

Jieun: We used cloth napkins. You know, paper napkins are not good for your skin.

Reporter: But where did you get the cloth napkins?

Jieun: They were made by Minji. She cut up her old cotton shirt to make some for us. Everyone liked her cute napkins.

27 위 글의 밑줄 친 ⓐto make와 to부정사의 용법이 같은 것을 <u>모두</u> 고르시오.

① He awoke to find himself famous.
② He has many children to look after.
③ She decided to buy new shoes.
④ We eat to live, not live to eat.
⑤ It is difficult to know oneself.

28 위 글을 읽고 쓰레기를 줄이기 위해 학생들이 실천한 방법 두 가지를 우리말로 쓰시오.

➡ (1) _____

(2) _____

[29~30] 다음 글을 읽고 물음에 답하시오.

Leave No Food Behind

Reporter: Please give us one simple tip for reducing trash.

Junha: Don't leave any food on your plate. Food ⓐwaste really is a big problem. But see? ⓑWe ate everything, even our plates, ha-ha.

29 위 글의 밑줄 친 ⓐwaste와 바꿔 쓸 수 있는 말을 <u>모두</u> 고르시오.

① trash
② garbage
③ ash
④ rubbish
⑤ recycled product

30 위 글의 밑줄 친 ⓑ를 다음과 같이 바꿔 쓸 때 빈칸에 공통으로 들어갈 알맞은 단어를 쓰시오.

➡ We ate not only the food on our _____ but our _____ as well.

단원별 예상문제

출제율 90%

01 다음 문장의 빈칸에 적당한 말을 쓰시오.

> Turn off the tap to _____ water.

출제율 95%

02 우리말에 맞게 빈칸에 알맞은 단어를 쓰시오.

> (A) 우리는 몇몇 포장지가 쉽게 재활용되지 않기 때문에 선물을 포장하지 않는 것에 동의했습니다.
>
> We agreed not to _____ our gifts, because some wrapping paper is not easily _____.
>
> (B) 우리는 사용한 후에 접시까지도 먹었어요.
>
> We ate even the _____ after we used them.

출제율 100%

03 다음 대화의 빈칸에 알맞은 표현은?

> A: My mom _____.
> B: What do you mean by that?
> A: She is good at growing plants.
> B: I get it.

① feels blue ② is on cloud nine

③ is an early bird ④ has a green thumb

⑤ has a heart of gold

출제율 85%

04 다음 영영 풀이에 해당하는 단어는?

> a situation that is unsatisfactory and causes difficulties

① cotton ② shirt

③ problem ④ space

⑤ secret

[05~06] 다음 대화를 읽고 물음에 답하시오.

> A: What are those in the middle of the ocean?
> B: They are trash islands.
> A: Trash islands? What do you mean by that?
> B: A lot of plastic trash goes into the ocean and becomes big islands like those.
> A: That sounds terrible! How big are those islands?
> B: The biggest one is about 14 times as large as South Korea.
> A: That's surprising! I think we should not use plastic products.
> B: I agree.

출제율 90%

05 다음 질문에 대한 답을 대화에서 찾아 영어로 쓰시오.

> Q: How big is the biggest trash island?
>
> ➡ _____

출제율 90%

06 위 대화의 내용과 일치하지 <u>않는</u> 것은?

① They are talking about trash islands.

② Trash islands are in the middle of the ocean.

③ Trash islands are made of a lot of plastic trash.

④ South Korea is the biggest user of plastic products.

⑤ They decide not to use plastic products.

출제율 95%

07 대화의 빈칸에 들어갈 말로 <u>어색한</u> 것은?

> B: This is the energy tree.
> G: What do you mean by that?
> B: It produces energy from the sun. And it is used as a street lamp at night.
> G: _____

① What a surprise!　② I can't believe it.

③ That's amazing!　④ That's exhausting!

⑤ That can't be possible.

출제율 95%

08 다음 두 사람의 대화가 <u>어색한</u> 것은?

① A: Jieun has a heart of gold.

　B: What do you mean by that?

② A: Glass bottles take 4,000 years to break down.

　B: That's surprising!

③ A: Minji's classroom is spotless.

　B: That sounds terrible!

④ A: This elephant can paint pictures.

　B: That's surprising!

⑤ A: We don't throw away trash, so our trash can stays empty.

　B: That's surprising!

출제율 90%

09 대화의 밑줄 친 우리말에 맞게 문장의 빈칸에 들어갈 알맞은 말을 고르시오.

> B: What is this bus called?
>
> G: It is called the green bus.
>
> B: What is special about it?
>
> G: <u>친환경 버스는 쓰레기로부터 동력을 공급받아요.</u>
>
> B: That's surprising!

➡ The green bus ＿＿＿＿＿＿ by trash.

[10~11] 밑줄 친 부분의 형태가 <u>잘못된</u> 것은?

출제율 100%

10 ① A new camera <u>was given</u> to me by him.

② I <u>was</u> very <u>satisfied with</u> my student's answer.

③ Luckily a chair <u>was got for</u> Alice.

④ The old lady <u>was taken care</u> by one of the nurses.

⑤ She <u>was made to</u> repeat the whole story.

출제율 90%

11 ① He has few friends.

② He drank a little water.

③ The post office is a little blocks from your office, isn't it?

④ I need a little sugar.

⑤ There are a few cookies on the plate.

출제율 95%

12 두 문장의 전환이 <u>잘못된</u> 것은?

① Did Minji made the napkin?

　= Was the napkin made by Minji?

② I heard Susan open the window.

　= Susan was heard open the window by me.

③ Her friend will look after her pet while she is away.

　= Her pet will be looked after by her friend while she is away.

④ Edvard Munch painted *The Scream* in 1893.

　= *The Scream* was painted by Edvard Munch in 1893.

⑤ They sell tickets at the box office.

　= Tickets are sold at the box office.

출제율 90%

13 빈칸에 들어갈 수 <u>없는</u> 것을 고르시오.

> ＿＿＿＿ deer are living in this mountain.

① Much　　　　② Few

③ A few　　　　④ Lots of

⑤ A number of

14 few와 little을 활용하여 빈칸을 알맞게 채우시오.

출제율 90%

(1) To make apple juice, I need _____ apples and _____ sugar.

(2) I moved to this town yesterday, so I know _____ people here.

(3) Mike was thinking of his girl friend, so he paid _____ attention to the teacher.

15 우리말 의미에 맞도록 괄호 안의 단어를 이용하여 영작하시오.

출제율 85%

(1) 난 케첩이 약간 필요해. (little, ketchup)

➡ _____

(2) 나는 그 학급의 학생들 몇 명을 안다. (few, in the class)

➡ _____

(3) 오래된 책과 잡지는 재활용 쓰레기통에 수거된다. (the recycling bin, collect, in)

➡ _____

[16~18] 다음 글을 읽고 물음에 답하시오.

We all had a "No Trash Challenge" day last month. The winner was Grade 2 Class 3. Let's read the interview and learn a few tips for living green.

Do Not Use Wrapping Paper

Reporter: You threw a class birthday party, but didn't produce ⓐa lot of trash. What were your secrets?

Minsu: First, we agreed not to wrap our gifts, because some ⓑwrapping paper is not easily recycled. So we brought gifts such as teddy bears, key rings, and hairpins that were not wrapped at all.

16 위 글의 밑줄 친 ⓐa lot of와 바꿔 쓸 수 없는 말을 고르시오.

출제율 95%

① a good deal of　　② many

③ plenty of　　④ lots of

⑤ a great deal of

17 아래 〈보기〉에서 위 글의 밑줄 친 ⓑwrapping과 문법적 쓰임이 같은 것의 개수를 고르시오.

출제율 100%

┌─── 보기 ───┐

① I like a sleeping car.

② Look at the man who is smoking in the smoking room.

③ Did you fall in love with the dancing girl?

④ She is a walking dictionary.

⑤ I'm looking for my boxing gloves.

① 1개　② 2개　③ 3개　④ 4개　⑤ 5개

18 다음 문장에서 위 글의 내용과 다른 부분을 찾아서 고치시오.

출제율 90%

• Minsu's class brought gifts that were not wrapped at all because it was not easy to wrap them.

➡ _____

또는 _____

➡ _____

[19~21] 다음 글을 읽고 물음에 답하시오.

Buy the Largest Size

Jieun: Also, we chose the largest size when we bought ice cream and cookies for the party. Larger sizes use less packaging and make less trash.

Eat the Plates

Reporter: And how did you serve the ice cream?

Junha: We served it ___ⓐ___ plates. You know what? We ate even the plates after we used them.

Reporter: You ate the plates? What do you mean ___ⓑ___ that?

Junha: Actually, we used popped rice cakes as plates, so we could eat them and ⓒleave nothing behind!

Reporter: Ah, I get it. That's quite interesting.

출제율 100%

19 위 글의 빈칸 ⓐ와 ⓑ에 들어갈 전치사가 바르게 짝지어진 것은?

① on – from ② to – by
③ in – from ④ in – for
⑤ on – by

출제율 90%

20 위 글의 밑줄 친 ⓒleave와 같은 의미로 쓰인 것을 고르시오.

① They leave for Dallas at 7.
② How much annual leave do you get?
③ Leave the door open, please.
④ When people climb the mountains, they leave behind garbage.
⑤ Leave it to me; I'm sure I can do it.

출제율 85%

21 다음 빈칸 (A)와 (B)에 알맞은 단어를 넣어 준하네 반이 아이스크림을 먹고 쓰레기를 남기지 않은 방법을 완성하시오.

> When Junha's class served the ice cream, they used popped rice cakes instead of common (A)_____, so there was (B)_____ left behind when they finished eating.

[22~23] 다음 글을 읽고 물음에 답하시오.

Leave No Food Behind

Reporter: Please give us one simple tip for reducing trash.

Junha: ⓐDon't leave any food on your plate. Food waste really is a big problem. But see? We ___(A)___ everything, even our plates, ha-ha.

출제율 95%

22 위 글의 빈칸 (A)에 들어갈 알맞은 단어를 고르시오.

① left ② reused ③ ate
④ borrowed ⑤ shared

출제율 90%

23 위 글의 밑줄 친 ⓐ를 다음과 같이 바꿔 쓸 때 빈칸에 들어갈 알맞은 말을 쓰시오.

➡ You _____ _____ leave any food on your plate.

[24~25] 다음 글을 읽고 물음에 답하시오.

> This is a hand puppet. It is made (A)[of / from] my old sock. It took only (B)[a few / a little] time ___ⓐ___ this. Let's make (C)[a few / a little] more sock puppets and have a wonderful puppet show together.

출제율 90%

24 위 글의 빈칸 ⓐ에 make를 알맞은 형태로 쓰시오.

➡ _____

출제율 100%

25 위 글의 괄호 (A)~(C)에서 문맥이나 어법상 알맞은 낱말을 골라 쓰시오.

➡ (A) _____ (B) _____ (C) _____

 01 주어진 질문에 대한 답을 〈조건〉에 맞게 다음 대화의 빈칸에 쓰시오.

> B: Plastic bottles are a big problem for the Earth.
> G: What do you mean by that?
> B: _____
> G: That's surprising!

┌─── 조건 ───┐
• 주어는 They로 할 것
• 기간은 450 years로 할 것

Q: How long does it take for plastic bottles to break down?

➡ _____

02 다음 대화를 읽고 아래의 요약문을 완성하시오.

> A: What are those in the middle of the ocean?
> B: They are trash islands.
> A: Trash islands? What do you mean by that?
> B: A lot of plastic trash goes into the ocean and becomes big islands like those.
> A: That sounds terrible! How big are those islands?
> B: The biggest one is about 14 times as large as South Korea.
> A: That's surprising! I think we should not use plastic products.
> B: I agree.

⬇

> The students are talking about trash islands _____ the ocean. The islands are made of _____.
> The biggest island is about _____ South Korea. The students decide _____ plastic products.

03 다음 주어진 문장을 능동태는 수동태로, 수동태는 능동태로 바꾸시오.

(1) Do you recycle wrapping paper easily?

➡ _____

(2) A dog took away my shoes.

➡ _____

(3) An old lady told me this story. (2가지로 쓸 것.)

➡ _____

(4) The energy tree is used as a street lamp.

➡ _____

(5) This tower was made out of plastic water bottles.

➡ _____

04 다음 문장에서 틀린 것을 고쳐 다시 쓰시오.

(1) How did the ice cream serve?

➡ _____

(2) Princess is called me by my dad.

➡ _____

(3) They made little mistakes.

⇒ _____

(4) It took only a few time to make this.

⇒ _____

[05~07] 다음 글을 읽고 물음에 답하시오.

We all had a "No Trash Challenge" day last month. The winner was Grade 2 Class 3. Let's read the interview and ⓐlearn a few tips for living green.

Do Not Use Wrapping Paper

Reporter: You threw a class birthday party, but didn't produce a lot of trash. What were ⓑyour secrets?

Minsu: First, we agreed not to wrap our gifts, ⓒ몇몇 포장지가 쉽게 재활용되지 않기 때문에. So we brought gifts such as teddy bears, key rings, and hairpins that were not wrapped at all.

05 위 글의 밑줄 친 ⓐ를 다음과 같이 바꿔 쓸 때 빈칸에 들어갈 알맞은 말을 쓰시오.

⇒ learn a few _____ of advice for living green

06 위 글의 밑줄 친 ⓑyour secrets에 해당하는 것을 본문에서 찾아 쓰시오.

⇒ _____

07 위 글의 밑줄 친 ⓒ의 우리말에 맞게 주어진 어휘를 이용하여 8단어로 영작하시오.

| because, is, easily recycled |

⇒ _____

[08~10] 다음 글을 읽고 물음에 답하시오.

Buy the Largest Size

Jieun: Also, we chose the largest size when we bought ice cream and cookies for the party. ⓐLarger sizes use more packaging and make more trash.

Eat the Plates

Reporter: And (A)[how / why] did you serve the ice cream?

Junha: We served it on plates. You know what? We ate even the plates after we used them.

Reporter: You ate the plates? What do you mean by that?

Junha: Actually, we used popped rice cakes as plates, so we could eat them and leave (B)[nothing / something] behind!

Reporter: Ah, I get it. That's quite (C) [interesting / interested].

08 위 글의 밑줄 친 ⓐ에서 흐름상 어색한 부분을 찾아 고치시오.

⇒ _____,

09 위 글의 괄호 (A)~(C)에서 문맥이나 어법상 알맞은 낱말을 골라 쓰시오.

⇒ (A) _____ (B) _____ (C) _____

10 다음 빈칸 (A)와 (B)에 알맞은 단어를 넣어 준하네 반이 아이스크림을 먹은 방법을 소개하시오.

| Junha's class used popped rice cakes as (A)_____ and (B)_____ them together with the ice cream without leaving trash behind. |

창의사고력 서술형 문제

01 각 표현과 의미를 서로 연결하고, 각 표현의 의미에 대해 추가 설명을 요청하는 표현을 써서 〈보기〉와 같이 문장을 완성하시오.

〈표현〉 My mom has a green thumb. / Jieun has a heart of gold. / My brother is on cloud nine. / Junha is an early bird.

〈의미〉 be really happy / be a really kind person / get up early in the morning / be good at growing plants

〈보기〉 A: My mom has a green thumb. B: What do you mean by that? A: She is good at growing plants. B: I get it.

02 주어진 동사와 수동태를 사용하여 다양한 문장을 완성하시오.

build / pyramid,　sing / BTS,　turn off / the light,　make / wine

(1) _____

(2) _____

(3) _____

(4) _____

03 다음 내용을 바탕으로 재활용 작품을 소개하는 글을 쓰시오.

a hand puppet
재료: my old sock
제작에 걸린 시간: only a little time

a paper bag lamp
재료: a used paper shopping bag
특징: Light shines beautifully through the holes.

Do It Yourself
This is (A)_____. It is made of (B)_____. It took (C)_____ to make this. Let's make a few more sock puppets and have a wonderful puppet show together.

This is a paper bag lamp. It is made out of (D)_____. Light shines beautifully through (E)_____ .

단원별 모의고사

01 다음 단어에 대한 영어 설명이 <u>어색한</u> 것은?

① agree: to have the same opinion
② wrap: to cover something with paper, cloth or other materials
③ cotton: cloth or thread made from the white hair of the cotton plant
④ skin: the natural outer layer of a person's or animal's body
⑤ wrapping paper: a square of cloth or paper that you use to wipe your mouth or hands

02 다음 문장의 의미로 알맞은 것은?

> He can't see the forest for the trees.

① He says something indirectly.
② He can't see the whole situation.
③ He is feeling under the weather today.
④ He goes to the toilet.
⑤ He is really happy.

03 다음 영영풀이에 해당하는 단어를 고르시오.

> the boxes, bottles, plastic, etc. used for wrapping products

① packaging ② wrap ③ plate
④ cloth ⑤ napkin

04 대화의 빈칸에 주어진 단어를 이용하여 알맞게 쓰시오.

> G: I feel blue today.
> B: What do you mean by that?
> G: I mean I feel sad. We make too much trash.
> B: Ah, I get it now. We should _____ (cycle) and _____ (use) more.

05 빈칸에 들어갈 알맞은 단어는?

> You can eat these spoons. They were made out of rice. They are 100% __(A)__ . We can use these green spoons and __(B)__ plastic trash. We also can __(C)__ water because we don't have to wash these spoons.

(A) (B) (C)
① national – produce – waste
② cultural – reduce – waste
③ natural – reduce – save
④ natural – produce – save
⑤ cultural – reduce – save

06 다음 대화의 빈칸 ⓐ와 ⓑ에 들어갈 말로 알맞은 것은?

> (1) A: I skateboard to school every day.
> B: _____ ⓐ _____
> (2) A: Minsu is a big fish.
> B: _____ ⓑ _____
> A: I mean, he is an important person.

┤ 조건 ├
• ⓐ는 'what'을 이용하여 놀라움을 나타내는 표현을 세 단어로 쓸 것.
• ⓑ는 'what'과 'mean', 대명사 'that'을 사용하여 추가 설명을 요구하는 표현을 6 단어로 쓸 것.

➡ ⓐ _____
 ⓑ _____

07 대화의 빈칸에 들어갈 말로 알맞은 것은?

> G: Minji's classroom is spotless.
> B: What do you mean by that?
> G: _____ Look.
> B: You're right. Let's learn some good tips from her.

① That's very surprising news.
② Her classroom is really dark.
③ Minji is very honest.
④ Her classroom is really clean.
⑤ Sorry, I can't understand it.

[08~09] 다음 대화를 읽고 물음에 답하시오.

> A: What are ⓐthose in the middle of the ocean?
> B: They are trash islands.
> A: Trash islands? What do you ⓑmean by that?
> B: A lot of plastic trash goes into the ocean and ⓒbecomes big islands like those.
> A: That ⓓsounds terrible! How big are those islands?
> B: The biggest one is ⓔabout 14 times as larger as South Korea.
> A: That's surprising! _____ (A)
> B: I agree.

08 위 대화의 흐름상 빈칸 (A)에 들어갈 말로 알맞은 것은?

① I think a plastic bottle is very useful.
② Without any plastic, our life is difficult to live.
③ We need to use as many plastic products as possible.
④ I think we should not use plastic products.
⑤ We must not eat much meat for the environment of the Earth.

09 위 대화의 밑줄 친 ⓐ~ⓔ 중 어법상 어색한 것은?

① ⓐ ② ⓑ ③ ⓒ ④ ⓓ ⑤ ⓔ

10 대화의 빈칸에 들어갈 표현으로 알맞은 것은?

> A: Minsu is _____.
> B: What do you mean by that?
> A: I mean, he is an important person.
> B: Ah, I get it.

① a big fish ② a big ear
③ a big mouth ④ an early bird
⑤ on cloud nine

11 다음 대화의 빈칸에 적절한 말은?

> B: This is the energy tree.
> G: What do you mean by that?
> B: It produces energy from the sun. And it is used as a street lamp at night.
> G: _____

① That's too bad.
② That sounds terrible!
③ That's surprising!
④ I agree.
⑤ You're right.

12 대화의 밑줄 친 우리말에 맞게 주어진 단어를 이용하여 영어로 쓰시오.

> A: Glass bottles are a big problem for the Earth.
> B: What do you mean by that?
> A: 그것들이 분해되는 데 4000년이 걸려. (take / break)
> B: That's surprising!

➡ _____

13 어법상 어색한 것을 찾아 바르게 고치시오.

> This is a hand puppet. It makes of my old sock. It took only a few time to make this. Let's make a little more sock puppets and have a wonderful puppet show together.

➡ _____, _____, _____,

14 밑줄 친 부분 중 생략할 수 있는 것은?

① So many ideas were presented <u>by the Earth Savers Club</u>.
② *The Old Man And the Sea* was written <u>by Hemingway</u>.
③ The air is cleaned <u>by the green tower</u>.
④ Is English spoken in Canada <u>by them</u>?
⑤ Your car was washed by <u>a man</u>.

15 빈칸에 들어갈 말이 바르게 짝지어진 것은?

> Each small plate has _____ food on it. Food _____ on small plates.

① a few – is served
② a few – serves
③ a little – is served
④ a little – serves
⑤ little – serve

16 밑줄 친 부분의 쓰임이 다른 하나는?

① Plastic trash is <u>reduced</u> this way.
② My child's health <u>put</u> me under a lot of stress.
③ In this city, the green bus is <u>powered</u> by trash.
④ Solar panels are <u>attached</u> to a tree.
⑤ The tower is <u>built</u> of small stones.

17 다음 우리말을 괄호 안에 주어진 어휘를 이용하여 영작하시오.

(1) 빗물이 탱크에 저장됩니다. (rain water, the tanks, store)

➡ _____

(2) 이렇게 해서 약간의 에너지가 생산됩니다. (energy, produce, this way)

➡ _____

[18~20] 다음 글을 읽고 물음에 답하시오.

> **Reporter:** You threw a class birthday party, but didn't produce a lot of trash. What were your secrets?
> **Minsu:** First, we agreed not ___(A)___ our gifts, because some ___(B)___ paper is not easily recycled. So we brought gifts ⓐsuch as teddy bears, key rings, and hairpins ⓑthat were not ___(C)___ at all.

18 위 글의 빈칸 (A)~(C)에 wrap을 알맞은 형태로 쓰시오.

➡ (A) _____ (B) _____ (C) _____

19 위 글의 밑줄 친 ⓐsuch as와 바꿔 쓸 수 있는 한 단어를 쓰시오.

➡ _____

20 밑줄 친 ⓑthat과 쓰임이 다른 것을 모두 고르면?

① It's impossible <u>that</u> she has not received it yet.
② He said <u>that</u> the story was true.
③ This is the very book <u>that</u> he was reading.
④ He was the first man <u>that</u> came here.
⑤ There was no hope <u>that</u> he would recover his health.

[21~22] 다음 글을 읽고 물음에 답하시오.

ⓐ

Jieun: Also, we chose the largest size when we bought ice cream and cookies for the party. Larger sizes use less packaging and make less trash.

ⓑ

Reporter: And how did you serve the ice cream?

Junha: We served it on plates. You know what? We ate even the plates after we used them.

Reporter: You ate the plates? ⓒ그게 무슨 뜻이죠?

Junha: Actually, we used popped rice cakes as plates, so we could eat them and leave nothing behind!

Reporter: Ah, I get it. That's quite interesting.

21 위 글의 ⓐ와 ⓑ에 들어갈 제목으로 알맞은 것을 아래 〈보기〉에서 각각 고르시오.

┌── 보기 ├──
① Use Cloth Napkins
② Eat the Plates
③ Bring Your Own Things
④ Do Not Use Wrapping Paper
⑤ Buy the Largest Size
└─────────────┘

➡ ⓐ _____ 번, ⓑ _____ 번

22 위 글의 밑줄 친 ⓒ의 우리말에 맞게 주어진 어휘를 이용하여 6 단어로 영작하시오.

┌─────────────────┐
│　　　　mean, that　　　　│
└─────────────────┘

➡ _____

[23~24] 다음 글을 읽고 물음에 답하시오.

Bring Your Own Things

Reporter: (A)[What about / Why don't you] cups and spoons?

Minsu: We didn't use paper cups or plastic spoons. (B)[Instead / Instead of], we brought our own cups and spoons from home and then took them back.

Use Cloth Napkins

Reporter: What else did you do to make less trash?

Jieun: We used cloth napkins. You know, paper napkins are not good (C)[at / for] your skin.

Reporter: But where did you get the cloth napkins?

Jieun: They were made by Minji. She cut up her old cotton shirt to make some for us. Everyone liked her cute napkins.

23 위 글의 괄호 (A)~(C)에서 문맥이나 어법상 알맞은 낱말을 골라 쓰시오.

➡ (A) _____ (B) _____ (C) _____

24 위 글의 내용을 잘못 이해한 사람은?

① 지희: 민수의 반 친구들은 종이컵이나 플라스틱 숟가락을 사용하지 않았다.

② 혜민: 민수의 반 친구들은 사용한 종이컵이나 플라스틱 숟가락을 집에 가져가서 버렸다.

③ 나영: 지은이의 반 친구들은 쓰레기를 더 줄이기 위해 천 냅킨을 사용했다.

④ 호진: 민지가 자신의 낡은 면 셔츠를 잘라서 천 냅킨을 만들었다.

⑤ 채린: 지은이의 반 친구들은 민지가 만든 귀여운 냅킨을 모두 좋아했다.

Lesson

7

A Step Inside the Culture

🎙 의사소통 기능

- 관심에 대해 묻기
 Are you interested in taking pictures?

- 칭찬하기
 Good job!

🎙 언어 형식

- 현재분사
 It looks like a happy woman **walking** down a road with autumn leaves.

- It ... to부정사
 It is not easy **to write** by hand well at first.

Words & Expressions

Key Words

☐ **actually** [ǽktʃuəli] 부 실제로, 사실
☐ **artistic** [ɑːrtístik] 형 예술의, 예술적인
☐ **autumn** [ɔ́ːtəm] 명 가을
☐ **awesome** [ɔ́ːsəm] 형 멋있는, 대단한, 굉장한
☐ **beatbox** [bíːtbɑks] 동 비트 박스를 하다
☐ **below** [bilóu] 전 …의 아래에
☐ **between** [bitwíːn] 전 …의 사이에
☐ **both** [bouθ] 대 둘 다
☐ **calligraphy** [kəlígrəfi] 명 캘리그래피
☐ **character** [kǽriktər] 명 글자, 성격
☐ **classical** [klǽsikəl] 형 고전의
☐ **craft** [kræft] 명 공예
☐ **creative** [kriéitiv] 형 창의적인
☐ **collect** [kəlékt] 동 모으다
☐ **culture** [kʌ́ltʃər] 명 문화
☐ **detective** [ditéktiv] 명 탐정 형 탐정의
☐ **difference** [dífərəns] 명 차이
☐ **dish** [diʃ] 명 음식, 접시
☐ **draw** [drɔː] 동 그리다
☐ **dynasty** [dáinəsti] 명 왕조, 왕가
☐ **enjoy** [indʒɔ́i] 동 즐기다
☐ **example** [igzǽmpl] 명 예, 사례
☐ **excellent** [éksələnt] 형 훌륭한, 뛰어난
☐ **express** [iksprés] 동 표현하다
☐ **fantasy** [fǽntəsi] 명 판타지, 환상, 공상
☐ **figure** [fígjər] 명 (사람, 동물의) 상, 모형
☐ **foreign** [fɔ́ːrən] 형 외국의
☐ **handwriting** [hǽndraitiŋ] 명 손 글씨, 필적
☐ **hold** [hould] 동 잡다

☐ **horror** [hɔ́ːrər] 명 공포
☐ **imagine** [imǽdʒin] 동 상상하다
☐ **include** [inklúːd] 동 포함하다
☐ **inside** [insáid] 전 …의 안에, …의 안으로
☐ **learn** [ləːrn] 동 배우다
☐ **lightning** [láitniŋ] 명 번개
☐ **monster** [mɑ́nstər] 명 괴물
☐ **nowadays** [náuədèiz] 부 요즘에는, 오늘날에는
☐ **online** [ɔ́nlain] 형 온라인의, 인터넷의
☐ **period** [píːriəd] 명 시대, 기간
☐ **perfect** [pə́rfikt] 형 완벽한
☐ **performance** [pərfɔ́ːrməns] 명 공연
☐ **person** [pə́ːrsn] 명 사람
☐ **poem** [póuəm] 명 시
☐ **popular** [pɑ́pjulər] 형 인기 있는
☐ **practice** [prǽktis] 동 연습하다 명 연습
☐ **season** [síːzn] 명 계절
☐ **selfie** [sélfi] 명 셀피, 자신의 사진 찍기
☐ **sharp** [ʃɑːrp] 형 날카로운
☐ **step** [step] 명 (발)걸음
☐ **tail** [teil] 명 꼬리
☐ **tale** [teil] 명 이야기
☐ **title** [táitl] 명 제목
☐ **try** [trai] 동 시도하다, 노력하다
☐ **tool** [tuːl] 명 도구, 수단
☐ **unique** [juːníːk] 형 독특한, 특별한
☐ **widely** [wáidli] 부 널리
☐ **wizard** [wízərd] 명 마법사
☐ **work of art** 예술 작품, 미술품

Key Expressions

☐ **at first** 처음에(= **at the beginning**)
☐ **be interested in** …에 관심이 있다
☐ **be made of** …로 만들어지다
☐ **build up** 만들다(= **develop**)
☐ **dance to** …에 맞춰 춤추다
☐ **do taekwondo** 태권도를 하다
☐ **for free** 무료로
☐ **go shopping** 쇼핑하러 가다
☐ **keep -ing** …을 계속하다(= **continue**)

☐ **lead to** …로 이끌다, …로 이어지다
☐ **look like**+명사 …처럼 보이다
☐ **ride a bike** 자전거를 타다
☐ **take**+시간+**to V** …하는 데 시간이 걸리다
☐ **take a class** 수업을 듣다
☐ **take a picture** 사진을 찍다
☐ **What do you think?** 너는 어떻게 생각하니?
☐ **You got it.** 바로 그거야.

Word Power

※ 서로 반대되는 뜻을 가진 어휘

- □ **include**(포함하다) ↔ **exclude**(제외하다)
- □ **difference**(차이) ↔ **similarity**(유사, 비슷함)
- □ **popular**(인기 있는) ↔ **unpopular**(인기 없는)

- □ **outside** (밖에) ↔ **inside** (안에)
- □ **perfect**(완벽한) ↔ **imperfect**(불완전한)
- □ **foreign**(외국의) ↔ **domestic**(국내의)

※ 서로 비슷한 뜻을 가진 어휘

- □ **autumn** : **fall** (가을)
- □ **awesome** : **amazing** (굉장한)
- □ **wizard** : **sorcerer** (마법사)
- □ **at first** : **at the beginning** (처음에)

- □ **sharp** : **keen** (날카로운)
- □ **unique** : **distinct** (독특한)
- □ **excellent** : **outstanding** (우수한)
- □ **tool** : **implement** (도구)

English Dictionary

□ **artistic** 예술의
→ relating to any form of art 어떤 예술의 형태와 관련된

□ **autumn** 가을
→ the season between summer and winter
여름과 겨울 사이의 계절

□ **below** …의 아래에
→ in a lower place or position 더 낮은 장소나 위치에

□ **calligraphy** 캘리그래피
→ the art of producing beautiful handwriting using a brush or a special pen
브러시나 특수 펜을 이용한 아름다운 필체를 제작하는 기술

□ **dynasty** 왕조
→ a series of rulers of a country who all belong to the same family
모두 같은 가문에 속한 한 나라의 일련의 통치자들

□ **express** 표현하다
→ to show feeling or opinion 감정이나 의견을 나타내다

□ **include** 포함하다
→ to make someone or something part of a group
누군가나 어떤 것을 그룹의 일부로 만들다

□ **lightning** 번개
→ the bright flashes of light that you see in the sky during a storm
폭풍우가 몰아치는 동안 하늘에서 보이는 밝은 빛의 섬광

□ **nowadays** 요즘에는, 오늘날
→ at the present time
현재의 시간에

□ **period** 시기
→ a particular time in history 역사에서의 특별한 시기

□ **poem** 시
→ a piece of writing using beautiful or unusual language arranged in fixed lines that have a particular beat and often rhyme
특정한 박자와 종종 운율을 가진 고정된 행으로 배열된 아름답거나 독특한 언어를 사용하는 한편의 글

□ **popular** 인기 있는
→ liked by most people
대부분의 사람들이 좋아하는

□ **season** 계절
→ one of four periods of year that is based on the earth's position toward the sun
태양을 향한 지구의 위치를 바탕으로 한 1년의 네 시기 중 하나

□ **tale** 이야기
→ a story about imaginary events or people
상상의 사건이나 사람들에 관한 이야기

□ **title** 제목
→ the name of a book, poem, movie, play, or other work of art
책, 시, 영화, 연극 또는 다른 예술 작품의 이름

□ **tool** 도구
→ a piece of equipment, usually one you hold in your hand, that is designed to do a particular type of work
특정한 유형의 일을 하기 위해 고안된 보통 손에 드는 장비

□ **unique** 독특한
→ not the same as anything or anyone else
다른 어떤 것 또는 누구와도 같지 않은

□ **wizard** 마법사
→ a man in stories who has magic powers
마법의 힘을 가지고 있는 이야기 속의 남자

중요

01 다음 문장의 빈칸에 들어갈 말로 알맞은 것은?

> How do you _____ your feelings? Do you sing or dance?

① divide
② include
③ express
④ imagine
⑤ save

서답형

02 다음 빈칸에 영영풀이에 해당하는 말을 주어진 철자로 쓰시오.

> • Nowadays, it is p_____ to express feelings through handwriting.
> <영영풀이> liked by most people

➡ _____

03 다음 중 밑줄 친 단어의 우리말 뜻이 <u>잘못된</u> 것은?

① Are you <u>interested</u> in Korean culture? (관심 있는)
② The <u>wizard</u> waved his magic stick back and forth. (마법사)
③ Computers are <u>widely</u> used these days. (널리)
④ Every person has a <u>unique</u> fingerprint. (독특한)
⑤ He told a <u>tale</u> about magical animals. (꼬리)

서답형

04 우리말에 맞게 빈칸에 알맞은 말을 두 단어로 쓰시오.

> 사실, 나는 무료로 온라인 강좌를 듣고 있어.
> ➡ Actually, I'm taking an online class _____.

➡ _____

[05~06] 다음 영영풀이에 해당하는 단어를 고르시오.

05
> to make someone or something part of a group

① mix
② imagine
③ ride
④ include
⑤ collect

중요

06
> in a lower place or position

① beyond
② below
③ among
④ above
⑤ between

서답형

[07~08] 다음 빈칸에 공통으로 들어갈 단어를 쓰시오.

07
> • *Hangeul* is a lot easier to learn than Chinese _____s.
> • In Korea, the green dinosaur Dooly is a beloved _____.
> • Generosity is part of the Korean _____.
>
> *generosity 관대함

➡ _____

08
> • All calligraphers had to _____ hard to make their unique styles.
> • It's not easy to write by hand well at first, but _____ makes perfect.

➡ _____

01 대화의 빈칸에 들어갈 단어를 주어진 철자로 시작하여 쓰시오.

> A: I enjoyed your p_____. You did a good job.
> B: Thank you. Are you interested in playing the ukulele?
> A: Sure.

02 다음 빈칸에 영어 설명을 참고하여 주어진 철자로 시작하여 쓰시오.

> • It looks like a happy woman walking down a road with a _____ leaves.
> <영어 설명> the season between summer and winter

03 우리말과 같은 뜻이 되도록 빈칸에 알맞은 단어를 쓰시오.

(1) 아래에 있는 한국과 영국의 두 사례를 보아라.
 ➡ Look at the two _____ from Korea and the UK _____.

(2) 여러분은 그 차이를 구별할 수 있는가?
 ➡ Can you tell the _____?

(3) 여러분은 영화 포스터, 책 표지, 음악 CD, 그리고 의류에서 디자이너들의 예술적인 손길을 발견할 수 있다.
 ➡ You can find designers' _____ _____es on movie posters, book covers, music CDs, and clothes.

(4) 괴물의 커다란 입, 날카로운 이빨, 그리고 추하고 긴 꼬리를 상상할 수 있는가?
 ➡ Can you _____ the _____'s big mouth, sharp teeth, and ugly, long tail?

04 영영풀이에 해당하는 단어를 <보기>에서 찾아 첫 번째 칸에 쓰고, 두 번째 칸에는 우리말 뜻을 쓰시오.

> ─┤ 보기 ├─
> monster / vegetable / dynasty / traditional / fantasy

(1) _____: a pleasant, exciting, or unusual experience that you imagine is happening to you: _____

(2) _____: an imaginary creature that is large and frightening: _____

(3) _____: a series of rulers of a country who all belong to the same family: _____

05 우리말에 맞게 주어진 단어를 이용하여 문장의 빈칸을 채우시오. (어형 변화 필수)

(1) 캘리그래피는 요즈음 우리 주변에서 널리 쓰이고 있다.
 ➡ Today calligraphy is _____ used around us. (wide)

(2) Harry의 번개와 마술사 모자가 보이는가?
 ➡ Do you see Harry's _____ and the wizard hat? (light)

(3) 요즈음에는 손 글씨를 통해 감정을 표현하는 것이 인기다.
 ➡ Nowadays, it is popular _____ feelings through handwriting. (expression)

(4) 오래 전의 다양한 종류의 많은 캘리그래피 작품들이 세계 곳곳에서 발견되고 있다.
 ➡ Many _____ kinds of calligraphy _____ from long ago can be _____ all around the world. (differ / work / find)

교과서 Conversation

1 관심에 대해 묻기

Are you interested in taking pictures? 사진 찍는 것에 관심이 있니?

■ "Are you interested in ...?"은 상대방에게 무언가에 관심이 있는지 묻는 표현이다. 'in' 다음에는 명사 또는 동명사 형태가 온다. 이에 대한 대답은 "Yes, I am." 혹은 "No, I'm not. I'm interested in ..."으로 한다.

 e.g. A: Are you interested in cooking?
 B: Yes, I am. / No, I'm not. I'm interested in swimming.

관심에 대해 묻는 표현

- What are you interested in?
- Do you find something interesting?
- Are you interested in science?
- Are you interested in taking pictures?
- What are you into?
- What are your main interests?

■ **관심 표현과 관련된 유사한 표현**

I am interested in ~., I have an interest in ~., I am fascinated by ~. 등이 있다.

 ex) I am interested in K-pop.
 = I have an interest in K-pop.
 = I am fascinated by K-pop. 저는 K-pop에 관심 있습니다.

핵심 Check

1. 다음 대화의 빈칸에 들어갈 말로 알맞은 것은?

 A: _____

 B: I'm interested in musicals.

 ① Do you find musicals interesting?
 ② What are you going to do?
 ③ Do you want to learn a musical?
 ④ What makes you think so?
 ⑤ What are you interested in?

② 칭찬하기

> Good job! 잘했어!

■ "You did a good job." 혹은 "Good job."은 상대방의 어떤 행동에 대해 칭찬하는 표현이다.

　e.g. A: I got a good grade on the math exam.
　　　B: Good job!

칭찬하기

- (Very) Good!
- Great! / Excellent!
- What a nice dress!
- (You did a) Good job!
- Good work!
- Well done!
- Good for you!
- How kind she is!

칭찬에 답하기

- Thanks. / Thank you (very much).
- I'm glad you like(d) ~.

핵심 Check

2. 다음 대화의 빈칸에 들어갈 말로 알맞지 <u>않은</u> 것은?

B: _____ Someone is holding a cloud? How creative!

G: Thank you.

① Good work!
② How nice!
③ Good job!
④ Don't get stressed.
⑤ Excellent!

Get Ready 2

(1) **B:** Do you like K-pop?

G: Yes. ❶I enjoy listening to SJ's songs. I can ❷dance to his songs.

B: ❸Great!

(2) **B:** ❹Are you interested in cooking Korean dishes?

W: Yes. I sometimes cook *bulgogi* for my family and they love it.

(3) **B:** ❺Are you interested in learning *Hangeul*?

G: Yes. Actually, I'm learning it in my calligraphy class. Look! This is my work.

B: Excellent!

(1) **B:** 너는 K-pop을 좋아하니?
G: 응. 나는 SJ의 노래를 듣는 것을 즐겨. 그의 노래에 맞춰 춤을 출 수 있어.
B: 멋지다!
(2) **B:** 당신은 한국 음식을 요리하는 것에 관심이 있나요?
W: 네. 때때로 저는 가족을 위해 불고기를 요리하고 그들은 그것을 좋아해요.
(3) **B:** 너는 한글 배우는 것에 관심이 있니?
G: 응. 실제로, 나는 캘리그래피 수업에서 한글을 배우고 있어. 봐! 이게 나의 작품이야.
B: 훌륭하다!

❶ enjoy는 동명사를 목적어로 취하면서 '~을 즐기다'는 의미로 사용된다.
❷ 'dance to ...'는 '…에 맞춰 춤추다'는 의미로 여기서 to는 전치사이다.
❸ 상대방을 칭찬할 때 사용하는 표현이다.
❹, ❺ 상대방이 어느 것에 관심을 가지고 있는지 물어볼 때 사용하는 표현으로 'be interested in ...'은 '…에 관심이 있다'는 뜻이다.

Check(√) True or False

(1) G can dance to SJ's songs.　　　　　　　　　　　　　　　T ☐ F ☐

(2) W isn't interested in cooking Korean dishes, but sometimes cook *bulgogi*.　T ☐ F ☐

(3) G is learning *Hangeul* in her calligraphy class.　　　　　　　T ☐ F ☐

Start Off Listen & Talk A

(1) **B:** ❶Good job! Someone is holding a cloud? How creative!

G: Thank you. Are you interested in taking pictures?

B: Yes, I am. Actually, ❷I'm taking an online class for free.

G: Oh, ❸good for you.

(2) **G:** ❹Good work! I think your painting expresses the feeling of autumn well.

B: Thank you. ❺Are you interested in painting?

G: Yes, I am. I started taking a class on weekends.

B: Oh, I didn't know that.

(1) **B:** 잘했다! 누군가 구름을 잡고 있는 거야? 정말 창의적이구나!
G: 고마워. 너는 사진 찍는 것에 관심이 있니?
B: 응, 그래. 사실, 나는 무료로 온라인 강좌를 듣고 있어.
G: 오, 잘됐구나.
(2) **G:** 잘했다! 네 그림은 가을의 느낌을 잘 표현하고 있는 것 같아.
B: 고마워. 너는 그림에 관심이 있니?
G: 응, 그래. 나는 주말마다 수업을 듣기 시작했어.
B: 오, 몰랐어.

❶, ❸, ❹ 상대방을 칭찬할 때 사용하는 표현으로 'Excellent!, Well done!' 등으로 바꾸어 쓸 수 있다.
❷ 'take a class'는 '수업을 듣다'는 뜻이고, 'for free'는 '무료로'의 뜻이다.
❺ 상대방이 관심을 가지고 있는지 물어볼 때 사용하는 표현이다.

Check(√) True or False

(4) G is interested in taking pictures.　　　　　　　　　　　　T ☐ F ☐

(5) We can guess both G and B are interested in painting.　　　　T ☐ F ☐

 Start Off Listen & Talk B

B: ❶You did a good job! It's awesome.
G: Thanks.
B: What is it made of? Glass?
G: Yes, it is. ❷Are you interested in glass art?
B: Yes, very much. ❸How long did it take to make it?
G: It took one month.

❶ 상대방을 칭찬할 때 사용하는 표현으로 'Excellent!, Well done!' 등으로 바꾸어 쓸 수 있다.
❷ 상대방이 어디에 관심을 가지고 있는지 물어볼 때 사용하는 표현이다.
❸ 시간이 얼마나 걸리는지 물어볼 때 사용하는 표현이다..

 Speak Up Look and talk

B: I enjoyed your performance. You did a good job.
G: Thank you. Are you interested in playing the ukulele?
B: Sure. Can you teach me?
G: ❶No problem.

❶ 상대방의 부탁에 승낙하는 표현이다.

 Speak Up Mission

A: Are you interested in watching horror movies?
B: ❶Yes, I am. I watch horror movies very often. / ❷No, I'm not. I'm interested in reading detective stories.

❶ 관심이 있는지 묻는 말에 대한 긍정의 답이다.
❷ 관심이 있는지 묻는 말에 대한 부정의 답이다.

 Real-life Scene

James: What are you doing, Mina?
Mina: I'm practicing calligraphy.
James: You're writing with a brush. ❶It looks fun.
Mina: Are you interested in calligraphy?
James: Yes, very much.
Mina: Look at this! I just wrote it. ❷What do you think?
James: It ❸looks like a person dancing with open arms.

Mina: You got it. This Korean word means "dance."
James: ❹You did a good job! Can I try it?
Mina: ❺Why not? Take this brush.

❶ 'look+형용사'로 '재미있어 보인다'라는 의미이다.
❷ 상대방의 의견을 구하는 표현으로 '어떻게 생각하니?'의 뜻이다.
❸ 'look like+명사'는 '…처럼 보이다'라는 뜻이다.
❹ 상대방을 칭찬할 때 사용하는 표현이다.
❺ 'Why not?'은 '왜 안 되겠니?'의 뜻으로 상대방의 제안에 승낙하는 표현이다.

 Your Turn

A: You're writing something. What's this?
B: It's my art homework. Do you like it?
A: Sure. ❶I think you did a good job!

❶ 상대방을 칭찬할 때 사용하는 표현으로 'Good for you., Excellent!, Well done.' 등으로 바꾸어 쓸 수 있다.

 Express Yourself

(1) B: Look! Two girls are learning *Hangeul*.
 G: Are you interested in *Hangeul*, Kevin?
 B: Yes, very much. I want to join them and learn it.
(2) B: Julie, are you interested in *hanbok*?
 G: ❶Not really.
 B: Then, what are you interested in?
 G: Well, I'm interested in *taekwondo*. It is a traditional Korean sport. It's awesome.
(3) G: ❷Look at the two men learning *pansori*.
 B: Are you interested in *pansori*, Nancy?
 G: Sure. I like the sound of it. I want to learn it.

❶ 관심이 있는지 묻는 말에 '별로 관심없어.'라는 부정의 뜻이다.
❷ learning=who are learning

 Learning Diary Listen & Speak

B: Minji, are you interested in animals?
G: Yes, I am. ❶I'm good at taking care of them.
B: ❷How about plants? Are you interested in them, too?
G: No, I'm not. I can't grow them well.

❶ 'be good at ~'은 '~을 잘하다'라는 의미이다.
❷ How about ~?: ~은 어때?

• 다음 우리말과 일치하도록 빈칸에 알맞은 말을 쓰시오.

Get Ready 2

(1) B: Do you like K-pop?
 G: Yes. I _____ _____ to SJ's songs. I can _____ _____ his songs.
 B: _____!

(2) B: Are you _____ _____ _____ Korean dishes?
 W: Yes. I _____ cook *bulgogi* _____ my family and they love it.

(3) B: _____ _____ _____ in learning *Hangeul*?
 G: Yes. _____, I'm learning it in my _____ class. Look! This is my work.
 B: _____!

Start Off Listen & Talk A

(1) B: _____ _____! Someone is _____ a cloud? _____ _____!
 G: Thank you. Are you interested _____ _____ _____?
 B: Yes, I am. Actually, I'm _____ an online class _____ _____.
 G: Oh, _____ _____ you.

(2) G: _____ work! I think your painting _____ the _____ of _____ well.
 B: Thank you. _____ you _____ in painting?
 G: Yes, I am. I started _____ a class on weekends.
 B: Oh, I didn't know _____.

Start Off Listen & Talk B

B: You _____ a good job! It's _____.
G: Thanks.
B: What is it _____ _____? Glass?
G: Yes, it is. _____ you _____ _____ glass art?
B: Yes, very much. _____ _____ did it _____ _____ _____ it?
G: _____ _____ one month.

Speak Up Look and talk

B: I _____ your _____. You did _____ _____ _____.
G: Thank you. Are you _____ in _____ ukulele?
B: Sure. _____ _____ teach me?
G: No problem.

(1) B: 너는 K-pop을 좋아하니?
 G: 응. 나는 SJ의 노래를 듣는 것을 즐겨. 그의 노래에 맞춰 춤을 출 수 있어.
 B: 멋지다!

(2) B: 당신은 한국 음식을 요리하는 것에 관심이 있나요?
 W: 네. 때때로 저는 가족을 위해 불고기를 요리하고 그들은 그것을 좋아해요.

(3) B: 너는 한글 배우는 것에 관심이 있니?
 G: 응. 실제로, 나는 캘리그래피 수업에서 한글을 배우고 있어. 봐! 이게 나의 작품이야.
 B: 훌륭하다!

(1) B: 잘했다! 누군가 구름을 잡고 있는 거야? 정말 창의적이구나!
 G: 고마워. 너는 사진 찍는 것에 관심이 있니?
 B: 응, 그래. 사실, 나는 무료 온라인 강좌를 듣고 있어.
 G: 오, 잘됐구나.

(2) G: 잘했다! 네 그림은 가을 느낌을 잘 표현하고 있는 것 같아.
 B: 고마워. 너는 그림에 관심이 있니?
 G: 응, 그래. 나는 주말마다 수업을 듣기 시작했어.
 B: 오, 몰랐어.

B: 너 정말 잘했구나! 정말 멋져.
G: 고마워.
B: 무엇으로 만든 거니? 유리?
G: 응, 그래. 너는 유리 공예에 관심이 있니?
B: 응, 많이 관심 있어. 그거 만드는 데 시간이 얼마나 걸렸니?
G: 한 달 걸렸어.

B: 너의 공연 즐거웠어. 정말 잘했어.
G: 고마워. 너는 우쿨렐레 연주하는 것에 관심이 있니?
B: 물론이야. 날 가르쳐 줄 수 있니?
G: 그럼.

Speak Up Mission

A: Are you _____ in watching _____ movies?
B: Yes, I _____. I watch horror movies very often. / No, _____ _____. I'm _____ _____ reading _____ stories.

Real-life Scene

James: What are you doing, Mina?
Mina: I'm _____ _____.
James: You're _____ with a brush. It _____ _____.
Mina: Are you _____ in _____?
James: Yes, very much.
Mina: Look at this! I just wrote it. _____ do you _____?
James: It _____ _____ a person _____ with _____ arms.
Mina: You _____ it. This Korean word _____ "dance."
James: You _____ a good _____! Can I _____ it?
Mina: _____ _____? Take this brush.

Your Turn

A: You're writing _____. What's this?
B: It's my art homework. Do you like it?
A: Sure. I think you _____ a _____ job!

Express Yourself

(1) B: Look! Two girls are _____ *Hangeul*.
 G: Are you _____ _____ *Hangeul*, Kevin?
 B: Yes, very much. I want to _____ them and _____ it.

(2) B: Julie, are you interested _____ *hanbok*?
 G: _____ really.
 B: Then, _____ are you _____ in?
 G: Well, I'm _____ in *taekwondo*. It is a _____ Korean sport. It's _____.

(3) G: Look at the two men _____ *pansori*.
 B: Are you _____ in *pansori*, Nancy?
 G: Sure. I like the _____ of it. I _____ _____ _____ it.

Learning Diary Listen & Speak

B: Minji, are you _____ in animals?
G: Yes, I am. I'm _____ _____ _____ _____ _____ them.
B: _____ _____ plants? Are you _____ in them, too?
G: No, I'm not. I can't _____ them well.

해석

A: 너는 공포 영화 보는 것에 관심이 있니?
B: 응, 그래. 나는 공포 영화를 아주 자주 봐. / 아니, 그렇지 않아. 나는 탐정 소설 읽는 것에 관심이 있어.

James: 미나야, 뭐 하고 있니?
미나: 캘리그래피를 연습하고 있어.
James: 너는 붓으로 쓰고 있구나. 재미있어 보인다.
미나: 너는 캘리그래피에 관심이 있니?
James: 응, 무척.
미나: 이것 봐! 내가 방금 썼어. 어떻게 생각해?
James: 두 팔을 벌리고 춤을 추는 사람처럼 보여.
미나: 바로 그거야. 이 한글 단어가 '춤'이라는 뜻이거든.
James: 잘했다! 내가 해 봐도 되니?
미나: 물론이야. 이 붓을 잡아.

A: 너 뭔가 쓰고 있구나. 이게 뭐야?
B: 내 미술 숙제야. 마음에 드니?
A: 물론이야. 잘한 것 같아!

(1) B: 봐! 두 여자아이가 한글을 배우고 있어.
 G: 너는 한글에 관심이 있니, Kevin?
 B: 응, 무척. 나는 그들과 합류해서 그것을 배우고 싶어.

(2) B: Julie, 너 한복에 관심이 있니?
 G: 사실은 관심이 없어.
 B: 그럼, 너는 무엇에 관심이 있니?
 G: 음, 나는 태권도에 관심이 있어. 그것은 한국 전통 스포츠야. 아주 멋져.

(3) G: 판소리를 배우고 있는 두 남자 좀 봐.
 B: 너는 판소리에 관심이 있니, Nancy?
 G: 물론이야. 나는 그 소리가 좋아. 그것을 배우고 싶어.

B: 민지야, 너는 동물에 관심이 있니?
G: 응, 그래. 나는 동물을 돌보는 것을 잘해.
B: 식물은 어떠니? 식물에도 관심이 있니?
G: 아니, 없어. 식물은 잘 못 키워.

Conversation 시험대비 기본평가

01 다음 대화의 빈칸에 들어갈 말로 알맞은 것은?

> A: Are you interested in *Hangeul*?
> B: Yes, I am. _____

① I want to wear it.
② I want to play it.
③ I'm not interested in learning it.
④ I want to learn it.
⑤ I want to eat it.

02 다음 대화의 빈칸에 들어갈 말로 알맞은 것은?

> G: Look at the two men learning *pansori*.
> B: _____, Nancy?
> G: Sure. I like the sound of it. I want to learn it.

① Are you interested in *pansori*
② Are you good at *pansori*
③ What happened
④ Do you learn *pansori*
⑤ What are you interested in

03 다음 대화의 우리말에 맞게 주어진 단어를 이용하여 영어로 쓰시오.

> A: You're writing something. What's this?
> B: It's my art homework. Do you like it?
> A: Sure. 잘한 것 같아! (think / do / good job)

➡ _____

04 다음 대화를 알맞은 순서대로 배열하시오.

> (A) No problem.
> (B) I enjoyed your performance. Good job!
> (C) Thanks. Are you interested in *taekwondo*?
> (D) Sure. Can you teach me?

➡ _____

[01~02] 다음 대화를 읽고 물음에 답하시오.

> B: Do you like K-pop?
> G: Yes. I enjoy listening to SJ's songs. I can dance ___(A)___ his songs.
> B: ___(B)___

01 위 대화의 빈칸 (A)에 들어갈 말로 알맞은 것은?

① with ② of ③ to ④ in ⑤ for

02 위 대화의 빈칸 (B)에 들어갈 말로 나머지와 성격이 다른 하나는?

① Great! ② Excellent!
③ Good job! ④ Well done!
⑤ I'm into K-pop, too.

서답형

03 다음 대화에서 빈칸에 주어진 단어를 활용하여 관심을 묻는 말을 완성하시오.

> A: _____ (be / interest / ride)
> B: Yes, I am. I ride a bike very often.

➡ _____

[04~06] 다음 대화를 읽고 물음에 답하시오.

> B: You did a good job! It's awesome.
> G: Thanks.
> B: What is it made of? Glass?
> G: Yes, it is. ___(A)___
> B: Yes, very much. ___(B)___
> G: It took one month.

04 위 대화의 빈칸 (A)에 들어갈 말로 가장 적절한 것은?

① Are you interested in cooking?
② Are you interested in glass art?

③ I enjoyed your performance.
④ Can you teach me?
⑤ Are you interested in music?

05 위 대화의 빈칸 (B)에 들어갈 말로 알맞은 것은?

① How often did you make it?
② How far is it?
③ What date is it today?
④ How long did it take to make it?
⑤ How old is it?

서답형

06 다음 영영풀이가 설명하는 단어를 위 대화에서 찾아 쓰시오.

> • extremely impressive, serious, or difficult so that you feel great respect, worry, or fear
> • very good

➡ _____

[07~08] 다음 대화를 읽고 물음에 답하시오.

> James: What are you doing, Mina?
> Mina: I'm ①practicing calligraphy.
> James: You're writing with a brush. It ②looks fun.
> Mina: ③Are you interested in calligraphy?
> James: Yes, very much.
> Mina: Look at this! I just wrote it. What do you think?
> James: It ④looks a person dancing with open arms.
> Mina: You got it. This Korean word means "dance."
> James: You ⑤did a good job! Can I try it?
> Mina: Why not? Take this brush.

07 위 대화를 읽고 답할 수 없는 것은?

① What is Mina doing?

② Is Mina writing with a pen?

③ Is James interested in calligraphy?

④ Is it easy to start writing calligraphy?

⑤ What does James think of Mina's work?

08 위 대화의 밑줄 친 ①~⑤ 중 어법상 어색한 것은?

① ② ③ ④ ⑤

[09~10] 다음 대화의 빈칸에 들어갈 말로 알맞은 것은?

09

> G: Good work! I think your painting expresses the feeling of autumn well.
> B: Thank you. _____
> G: Yes, I am. I started taking a class on weekends.
> B: Oh, I didn't know that.

① What are you interested in?

② What is special about it?

③ Are you interested in painting?

④ Are you interested in Korean culture?

⑤ What do you think?

10

> B: Julie, are you interested in *hanbok*?
> G: _____
> B: Then, what are you interested in?
> G: Well, I'm interested in *taekwondo*. It is a traditional Korean sport. It's awesome.

① Not really. ② I like *hanbok*.

③ Why not? ④ Yes, I am.

⑤ How about you?

11 다음 중 짝지어진 대화가 어색한 것을 고르시오.

① A: Are you interested in taking pictures?
 B: Good job!

② A: Who is the man playing the piano?
 B: He's Jake.

③ A: Are you interested in music?
 B: Yes, I am.

④ A: Are you interested in cartoons?
 B: No, I'm not. I'm interested in sports.

⑤ A: I enjoyed your performance. You did a good job.
 B: Thank you.

[12~13] 다음 대화를 읽고 물음에 답하시오.

> B: Minji, are you interested in animals? (①)
> G: Yes, I am. _____
> B: (②) Are you interested in them, too? (③)
> G: No, I'm not. (④) I can't grow them well. (⑤)

12 대화의 빈칸에 들어갈 말은?

① I'm interested in collecting insects.

② I'm good at taking care of them.

③ I play soccer very often.

④ I'm interested in Chinese culture.

⑤ You aren't interested in animals.

13 다음 주어진 문장이 들어갈 위치로 알맞은 것은?

> How about plants?

① ② ③ ④ ⑤

[01~03] 다음 대화를 읽고 물음에 답하시오.

James: What are you doing, Mina?

Mina: I'm practicing calligraphy.

James: You're writing with a brush. It looks fun.

Mina: _____(A)

James: Yes, very much.

Mina: Look at this! I just wrote it. (a)어떻게 생각해?

James: It looks like a person dancing with open arms.

Mina: You got it. _____(B)

James: You did a good job! Can I try it?

Mina: Why not? Take this brush.

01 위 대화의 빈칸 (A)에 들어갈 표현을 주어진 〈조건〉에 맞게 쓰시오.

┌─ 조건 ┐
• 상대방이 캘리그래피에 관심이 있는지 묻는 표현을 쓸 것.
• 'interest'와 'calligraphy'를 활용할 것.
• 5단어의 문장을 사용할 것.

➡ _____

02 다음 그림을 참고하여 Mina가 만든 캘리그래피가 무엇을 나타내는지 빈칸 (B)를 완성하시오. (주어진 단어를 이용할 것)

(this / Korean word / mean)

➡ _____

03 위 대화의 밑줄 친 (a)의 우리말에 맞게 'what'으로 시작하는 4단어로 영작하시오.

➡ _____

04 다음 그림을 보고 상대방이 무엇에 관심이 있는지 묻고 답하는 대화문을 완성하시오.

take selfies
(not interested)

cook
(interested)

A: Are you _____(A)_____?
B: No, I'm not. _____(B)

➡ (A) _____
(B) _____

05 대화의 흐름상 빈칸에 들어갈 표현을 주어진 〈조건〉에 맞게 쓰시오.

B: You did a good job! It's awesome.

G: Thanks.

B: What is it made of? Glass?

G: Yes, it is. Are you interested in glass art?

B: Yes, very much. _____

G: It took one month.

┌─ 조건 ┐
• 시간이 얼마나 걸리는 지 묻는 표현을 쓸 것.
• 대명사 'it'을 2번 사용할 것.
• 과거시제를 사용할 것.

➡ _____

교과서 Grammar

① 현재분사

> • It looks like a happy woman **walking** down a road with autumn leaves.
> 그것은 마치 단풍잎이 깔린 길을 따라 걷고 있는 행복한 여인처럼 보인다.

■ **형태와 의미**

형태: '동사원형+-ing'이며, 동명사의 형태와 같다.

의미: '…하고 있는, …하는'의 의미이다.

■ **쓰임:** 분사는 동사와 형용사의 성질을 나누어 가지고 있다고 해서 붙여진 이름으로, 현재분사가 동사의 역할을 할 때는 주로 진행형인 'be동사+현재분사'의 형태로 쓰이고, 형용사의 역할을 할 때는 명사를 수식하거나 보충 설명할 때 쓰인다.

■ **현재분사의 위치**

형용사 역할을 하는 현재분사는 일반적으로 명사 앞에 와서 명사를 수식하는데, 대개 분사가 단독으로 쓰일 경우이다. 반면, 분사가 목적어나 어구를 수반할 때에는 명사 뒤에 와서 앞의 명사를 수식한다. 이를 현재분사의 '후치 수식'이라고 한다.

■ **'관계대명사+be동사'의 생략**

현재분사가 뒤에서 명사를 수식하는 경우, 명사와 현재분사 사이에 보통 '관계대명사+be동사'가 생략되어 있다고 볼 수 있다.

• The boy **playing** soccer is my brother. 축구를 하고 있는 저 소년은 나의 동생이다.
　= The boy **who is playing** soccer is my brother.

■ **현재분사 vs. 과거분사**

현재분사는 '능동이나 진행'을 나타내는 반면 과거분사는 '수동이나 완료'를 나타낸다.

• The man **playing** the piano is Jake. 피아노를 치고 있는 남자는 Jake이다.

• Look at the **broken** window. 깨어진 창문을 보아라.

■ **현재분사와 동명사**

현재분사와 동명사는 같은 형태를 갖지만 현재분사는 형용사처럼 명사를 수식하거나 진행 시제를 나타내며 동명사는 '…하는 것, …하기'의 의미로 명사처럼 '주어, (동사나 전치사의) 목적어 및 보어 역할'을 한다.

• Look at the **sleeping** baby. 잠자고 있는 아기를 보아라. 〈현재분사〉

• **Sleeping** is important. 잠자는 것은 중요하다. 〈동명사〉

핵심 Check

1. 주어진 어휘를 빈칸에 어법에 맞게 쓰시오.

(1) Look at the two men _____ *pansori*. (learn)

(2) I was awakened by a _____ bell. (ring)

② It ... to부정사

> • **It** is not easy **to write** by hand well at first. 처음부터 손으로 글씨를 잘 쓰기는 쉽지 않다.

■ **형태와 의미**

형태: It is+형용사+to+동사원형 ….

의미: …하는 것은 ~하다

■ **쓰임**: 비교적 긴 to부정사 부분이 문장의 주어로 쓰일 때 대부분 주어 자리에 형식상의 주어(가주어) 'it'을 쓰고 원래 주어(진주어)인 to부정사(구)는 문장의 끝으로 보낸다. 가주어 'It'은 아무 의미 없이 자리만 주어 자리에 있을 뿐이므로 해석하지 않고 진주어부터 해석한다.

• **It** is popular **to express** feelings through handwriting.

= **To express** feelings through handwriting is popular. 손 글씨를 통해 감정을 표현하는 것이 인기다.

■ **'It ... to부정사'의 의미상 주어**

to부정사의 동작을 실제로 하는 사람을 to부정사의 의미상 주어라고 한다. to부정사의 의미상 주어는 to부정사 바로 앞에 'for+명사의 목적격'의 형태로 쓴다. 문장에 쓰인 형용사가 nice, kind, smart, wise 등과 같이 사람의 성향, 성격을 나타내는 말일 때는 'of+목적격'을 쓴다. to부정사의 의미상 주어가 없는 경우는 특별한 사람이 아니라 일반적인 사람이기 때문이다. 또한 to부정사의 부정은 to부정사 앞에 not[never]을 써서 'not[never]+to V'로 나타내고 '…하지 않는 것은 ~하다'로 해석한다.

• Doctors say **it** is good **for** children **to wear** sunglasses.
의사들은 아이들이 선글라스를 쓰는 것이 좋다고 말한다.

• **It** was wise **of** you **to say** so. 당신이 그렇게 말한 것은 현명했습니다.

■ **it의 여러 가지 쓰임**

• Jane bought a hairpin. **It** was very cute. 〈인칭대명사〉

• **It**'s Sunday today. 〈비인칭 주어(요일)〉

• **It** is snowing. 〈비인칭 주어(날씨)〉

• **It**'s difficult to master English. 〈가주어〉

• I found **it** easy to solve the puzzle. 〈가목적어〉

핵심 Check

2. 다음 우리말과 일치하도록 빈칸에 알맞은 말을 쓰시오.

(1) 기억을 하는 것이 왜 중요할까요?

➡ Why _____ _____ _____ _____ remember?

(2) 외국어를 배우는 것은 쉽지 않다.

➡ _____ is not easy _____ _____ a foreign language.

01 다음 빈칸에 알맞은 것을 고르시오.

> A: Do you like to play *yunnori*?
> B: Yes. It is exciting _____ *yunnori*.

① play ② plays ③ to play
④ to playing ⑤ of you to play

02 다음 문장에서 어법상 어색한 부분을 바르게 고쳐 쓰시오.

(1) I know the boy kick a ball.

_____ ➡ _____

(2) Who is the playing the piano man?

_____ ➡ _____

(3) There were lots of stars shining.

_____ ➡ _____

(4) It is exciting live in Korea.

_____ ➡ _____

(5) That is hard to make *gimchi*.

_____ ➡ _____

(6) It is difficult to not think of her.

_____ ➡ _____

03 주어진 어휘를 바르게 배열하여 우리말을 영어로 쓰시오. (필요할 경우 단어를 추가하거나 변형할 것.)

(1) 거리에서 노래를 부르고 있는 소녀들은 나의 학생들이다. (my students, the girls, on the street, sing, are)

➡ _____

(2) 다양한 프로그램을 제공하는 것은 좋은 아이디어이다. (a good idea, various programs, provide, is, to)

➡ _____

(3) 자고 있는 아기를 보아라. (sleep, look, the, baby, at)

➡ _____

01 다음 중 어법상 바르지 않은 것은?

① There was a man running on the playground.

② He is taking a picture in front of an old palace.

③ The river running through Seoul is the Han River.

④ The sleeping baby in the bed is really cute.

⑤ They are enjoying looking at some works of art.

02 다음 중 어법상 바른 것은?

① It is common knowledge what swimming is a good exercise.

② It's kind of you ask me some questions.

③ It is important to stay healthy.

④ It's good owns your own business.

⑤ That's necessary to say no.

03 다음 빈칸에 알맞은 말이 바르게 짝지어진 것은?

| • Who is the girl _____ beside the piano? |
| • It is silly _____ a needless question. |

① singing – asked

② singing – to ask

③ sang – asked

④ sang – to ask

⑤ sings – asking

04 다음 문장의 빈칸에 들어갈 알맞은 것은?

| _____ is hard to communicate with foreigners. |

① It
② One
③ That
④ This
⑤ What

05 밑줄 친 단어의 쓰임이 다른 하나는?

① The girl walking in the park is my sister.

② Do you know the woman talking to Tom?

③ The alarm clocks ringing noisily are Jason's.

④ The boy singing on the stage is my best friend.

⑤ I started taking a music class on weekends.

06 다음 괄호 안에서 알맞은 말을 고르시오.

(1) Who is the girl (carried / carrying) a basket?

(2) I got an e-mail (written / writing) in Chinese.

(3) The (cat sleeping / sleeping cat) is mine.

(4) It is important (to listen / listen) to others carefully.

(5) (It / That) is not easy to dance *talchum*.

07 다음 중 어법상 옳은 것은?

① The person runs fastest in our class is Angie.
② Look at the singing *pansori* men.
③ His dream is help the poor.
④ The bus taking us to the airport broke down.
⑤ The boy is washed the dog.

08 다음 중 밑줄 친 부분의 쓰임이 <u>다른</u> 하나는?

① <u>It</u> is impossible for them to do it.
② <u>It</u> was windy and rainy.
③ <u>It</u>'s important to keep traffic rules.
④ <u>It</u> is a good habit to keep a diary every day.
⑤ <u>It</u> is exciting to kick a *jegi*.

09 밑줄 친 부분 중 생략할 수 있는 것을 고르시오.

①Who ②is the woman ③that is ④sitting between Tom ⑤and Mike?

① ② ③ ④ ⑤

10 주어진 어휘를 바르게 배열하여 다음 우리말을 영작하시오.

외국어를 배우는 것은 중요하다.
(language, it, a, learn, is, foreign, important, to)

➡ _____

11 다음 두 문장을 한 문장으로 바르게 연결한 것은?

• There were many people.
• They were waiting for the train.

① There were many people wait for the train.
② There were many people waited for the train.
③ There were many people to wait for the train.
④ There were many people were waiting for the train.
⑤ There were many people waiting for the train.

12 다음 우리말과 일치하도록 빈칸에 알맞은 것으로 묶은 것은?

• 매일 한 문장이라도 읽는 것이 좋다.
= _____ is good _____ even a sentence every day.

① It – to read
② It – read
③ That – to read
④ That – read
⑤ This – reading

13 다음 밑줄 친 부분이 어법상 <u>어색한</u> 것을 고르시오.

① The boy <u>played</u> soccer on the ground is my brother.
② The man <u>driving</u> the red car almost hit the person.
③ He bought a cell phone <u>made</u> in Korea.
④ Who is the boy <u>drinking</u> milk at the table?
⑤ This is the picture <u>painted</u> by Gogh.

14 다음 문장에서 어법상 <u>어색한</u> 것을 바르게 고쳐 다시 쓰시오.

(1) For me do this work would be really stupid.

➡ _____

(2) That is easy to solve the puzzle.

➡ _____

(3) It was amazing see such an old house there.

➡ _____

(4) There was an eating ice cream girl.

➡ _____

(5) A boy carried a box got on the bus.

➡ _____

(6) Last week I read *Harry Potter* writing by JK Rowling.

➡ _____

15 주어진 어휘를 어법에 맞게 빈칸에 쓰시오.

(1) The name of a fruit _____ with "m" is melon. (begin)

(2) It looks like a person _____ with open arms. (dance)

(3) The woman _____ at the news started to cry. (frighten)

(4) They are the photos _____ there. (take)

[16~17] 다음 우리말에 맞게 영작한 것을 고르시오.

16

나는 태권도를 배우고 있는 여자아이를 안다.

① I know the girl learn *taekwondo*.
② I know the girl learns *taekwondo*.
③ I know the girl to learn *taekwondo*.
④ I know the girl learning *taekwondo*.
⑤ I know the girl to learning *taekwondo*.

17

패스트푸드를 자주 먹는 것은 너의 건강에 좋지 않다.

① It is not good for your health eat fast food often.
② It is not good for your health eats fast food often.
③ It is not good for your health to eat fast food often.
④ That is not good for your health to eat fast food often.
⑤ That is not good for your health eating fast food often.

18 다음 중 어법상 <u>어색한</u> 것을 고르시오. (2개)

① It seemed necessary for me to attend the meeting.
② It's quite nice for her to say "Thank you."
③ It is not easy to exercise regularly.
④ The little girl singing on the stage is very cute.
⑤ I know the wearing a red cap girl.

01 다음 우리말에 맞게 주어진 어구를 바르게 배열하시오.

(1) Jack은 그의 아내에게 진주로 만든 목걸이를 주었다. (Jack, pearls, his wife, made, gave, a, necklace, of)

➡ _____

(2) 칼로 소고기 샌드위치를 자르고 있는 남자는 누구니? (the beef sandwiches, knife, the man, a, who, cutting, is, with)

➡ _____

(3) 좋은 책을 발견하는 것은 멋진 일이다. (it, is, awesome, to, find, a, good book)

➡ _____

(4) 캘리그래피 쓰기를 시작하는 것은 쉽다. (calligraphy, start, is, writing, easy, it, to)

➡ _____

(5) 태양을 직접 보는 것은 위험합니까? (sun, it, dangerous, directly, is, look, the, to, at)

➡ _____

02 다음 우리말을 (1) to부정사 주어를 써서, (2) 가주어를 써서 영작하시오.

• 제기를 차는 것은 재미있다.
➡ (1) _____
(2) _____

• 패러글라이딩을 하는 것은 위험해 보인다.
➡ (1) _____
(2) _____

03 그림을 보고, 주어진 어휘를 이용하여 빈칸에 알맞은 말을 쓰시오.

(1) (enjoy, do)

➡ Who is the man _____ B-boying? _____ is fun _____ B-boying.

(2) (play)

➡ The men are _____ *nongak*. _____ is exciting _____ *nongak*.

04 다음 두 문장을 같은 뜻을 갖는 한 문장으로 고쳐 쓰시오.

(1) • The business woman is Sophie.
• The woman is running a big company.
➡ _____

(2) • The bridge was built long time ago.
• It is a connection to the past.
➡ _____

05 다음 문장을 It으로 시작하여 다시 쓰시오.

(1) To meet trouble halfway is silly.

➡ _____

(2) To get your e-mail this morning was great.

➡ _____

(3) To wear a helmet while riding a bike is safe.

➡ _____

(4) For the police to calm down the angry crowd was difficult.

➡ _____

(5) That blood is thicker than water is quite true.

➡ _____

06 다음 우리말을 괄호 안에 주어진 어휘를 이용하여 영작하시오.

(1) 한복을 입고 있는 두 여자아이는 나의 친구들이다. (the, wear, *hanbok*, 8 단어)

➡ _____

(2) 그 남자는 그의 집 지붕을 파랗게 칠했다. (man, roof, have, paint, 10 단어)

➡ _____

(3) 과거에 대해 이야기하는 것은 재미있다. (it, the past, talk, interesting, 8 단어)

➡ _____

(4) 당신이 친절한 이웃을 갖고 있는 것은 운이 좋은 것이다. (lucky, to have, neighbor, 9 단어)

➡ _____

07 다음 문장에서 어법상 <u>어색한</u> 것을 바르게 고치시오.

(1) Timothy got an email sending by a stranger this morning.

_____ ➡ _____

(2) Who are the boys played soccer on the ground?

_____ ➡ _____

(3) This calligraphy shows two laughing out loud people.

➡ _____

(4) Buy a ticket at the subway station is not so hard.

_____ ➡ _____,

➡ _____

(5) This is not fun to stay in the hospital all alone.

_____ ➡ _____

(6) It is important for her eats very small amounts of food.

_____ ➡ _____

08 두 문장이 같은 뜻이 되도록 to부정사를 이용하여 문장을 완성하시오.

(1) I have difficulty in writing letters in English.

➡ It is difficult _____

_____.

(2) Watching the horror movie was terrible for her.

➡ It was terrible _____

_____.

Write Your Feelings

How do you express your feelings? Do you sing or dance? Do you write a poem or draw a picture? Nowadays, it is popular to express
　　　　　　　　　　　　　　　　　　　가주어(해석하지 않음)　　　　진주어
feelings through handwriting. Let's look at some works of art.

In the work of art on the right, the word includes an image of a delicious fruit, *hongsi*. It shows that autumn is a season of fruit. The
콤마 앞뒤의 'a delicious fruit'와 'hongsi'는 동격　접속사('shows'의 목적어 역할을 하는 명사절을 이끎)　소유의 의미
work of art on the left shows a Korean word and a Chinese character.

It looks like a happy woman walking down a road with autumn leaves.
　～처럼 보인다　　　　　현재분사의 후치 수식(앞의 명사 'woman'을 뒤에서 수식)　～이 있는
Both of these works express the feeling of autumn through beautiful handwriting. This kind of art is called calligraphy.
　　　　　　　　　　　　　　　　　　　　수동태(~라고 불린다)
Calligraphy is not new. Many different kinds of calligraphy works
　　　　　　　　　　　　　문장의 주부: 'Many … from long ago'
from long ago can be found all around the world. Look at the two
　　　　　　조동사 'can'이 포함된 수동태 (can+be동사의 원형+과거분사)
examples from Korea and the UK below. Can you tell the difference?
　　　　　　　　　　　　　　　　　　　　　　　　= distinguish
The left one was created by Chusa in the period of the Joseon Dynasty.
　　　　=example　수동태 과거
The characters were painted with a soft brush.
주어가 복수형이므로 동사는 'were+과거분사' 형의 수동태　'with': 도구를 나타내는 전치사

Vocabulary (right column):
express: 표현하다
poem: 시
nowadays: 요즘에는, 오늘날에는
popular: 인기 있는
handwriting: 손 글씨, 필적
include: 포함하다
autumn: 가을
season: 계절
both: 둘 다
calligraphy: 캘리그래피
below: ~의 아래에
period: 시대, 기간
dynasty: 왕조, 왕가

 확인문제

● 다음 문장이 본문의 내용과 일치하면 T, 일치하지 않으면 F를 쓰시오.

1　Nowadays, to express feelings through handwriting is popular. ☐

2　In the work of art on the right, the word excludes an image of a delicious fruit, *hongsi*. ☐

3　Both of the works express the feeling of autumn through beautiful drawing. ☐

4　Both of the works are called calligraphy. ☐

The right one, *The Canterbury Tales*, was created by Chaucer in
'The right one'과 'The Canterbury Tales'는 동격 과거 수동태

England in the late 1400s. It was written with a pen. Different writing
'1400년대 후반에' cf. in the early 1400s (1400년대 초반에)

tools led to different styles of calligraphy. Of course, all calligraphers

had to practice hard to make their unique styles.
to부정사의 부사적 용법(목적)

Today calligraphy is widely used around us. You can find designers'
수동태('쓰인다, 사용된다'). 부사 'widely'가 수식하는 과거분사 'used' 앞에 위치

artistic touches on movie posters, book covers, music CDs, and clothes.

Below are some examples. Look at the title on the movie poster. How
부사 'below'가 맨 앞에 오면서 '부사+동사+주어'의 어순으로 도치

do you feel? Can you imagine the monster's big mouth, sharp teeth,

and ugly, long tail? How about the title on the fantasy novel? Do you
= What about

see Harry's lightning and the wizard hats?
(남자) 마법사. witch: 마녀

Anyone can start writing calligraphy. It's not easy to write by
긍정문에서 '누구든지' = to write(일반적으로 '~하기를 시작하다'는 뜻일 때 동명사가 더 자주 쓰임) 가주어 진주어

hand well at first, but practice makes perfect. Keep trying and make
꾸준한 연습을 강조하는 속담. 'perfect'는 원래 형용사지만 여기서는 명사처럼 쓰였음. 계속 ~하다

it part of your everyday life. Write with your feelings on birthday
= calligraphy 'make+목적어+목적격보어'의 5형식 문장으로 이루어졌음

cards, bookmarks, or gifts. Soon you will build up your own world of
만들다, 세우다

calligraphy.

tale: 이야기

tool: 도구, 수단

lead to: ~로 이끌다, ~로 이어지다

unique: 독특한, 특별한

widely: 널리

artistic: 예술의, 예술적인

imagine: 상상하다

monster: 괴물

sharp: 날카로운

tail: 꼬리

fantasy: 판타지, 환상, 공상

lightning: 번개

wizard: 마법사

at first: 처음에는

keep -ing: ~을 계속하다

build up: 만들다

확인문제

● 다음 문장이 본문의 내용과 일치하면 T, 일치하지 않으면 F를 쓰시오.

1 Chaucer created *The Canterbury Tales*. ☐

2 *The Canterbury Tales* was written with a brush. ☐

3 Different styles of calligraphy resulted from different writing tools. ☐

4 Today it is difficult to find calligraphy used around us. ☐

5 We see Harry's lightning and the wizard hats from the title on the fantasy
 novel. ☐

6 It's easy to write by hand well at first. ☐

● 우리말을 참고하여 빈칸에 알맞은 말을 쓰시오.

1 _____ Your Feelings

2 _____ do you express your _____?

3 Do you _____ or _____?

4 Do you write a poem or _____ _____ _____?

5 _____, it is popular to express feelings _____ _____.

6 Let's look at some _____ _____ _____.

7 In the work of art on the right, the word _____ _____ _____ of a delicious fruit, *hongsi*.

8 It shows that autumn is _____ _____ _____.

9 The work of art on the left shows a _____ _____ and a _____ _____.

10 It _____ _____ a happy woman _____ down a road with autumn leaves.

11 Both of these works _____ _____ _____ of autumn _____ beautiful handwriting.

12 This kind of art is called _____.

13 Calligraphy is _____ _____.

14 Many different kinds of calligraphy works from long ago _____ _____ _____ all around the world.

15 Look at the two examples _____ Korea and the UK _____.

16 Can you _____ _____ _____?

17 The left one _____ _____ _____ Chusa in the period of the Joseon Dynasty.

18 The characters _____ _____ _____ a soft brush.

1	여러분의 느낌을 써라
2	여러분은 자신의 느낌을 어떻게 표현하는가?
3	노래를 부르거나 춤을 추는가?
4	시를 쓰거나 그림을 그리는가?
5	요즈음에는 손 글씨를 통해 감정을 표현하는 것이 인기다.
6	몇몇 작품을 살펴보자.
7	오른쪽 예술 작품에서는 단어가 맛있는 과일인 홍시의 이미지를 포함하고 있다.
8	그것은 가을이 결실의 계절임을 보여 준다.
9	왼쪽에 있는 예술 작품은 한글 단어와 한자를 보여 주고 있다.
10	그것은 마치 단풍잎이 깔린 길을 따라 걷고 있는 행복한 여인처럼 보인다.
11	이 두 작품은 아름다운 손 글씨를 통해 가을의 느낌을 표현한다.
12	이런 종류의 예술은 '캘리그래피'라고 불린다.
13	캘리그래피는 새로운 것이 아니다.
14	오래전의 다양한 종류의 많은 캘리그래피 작품들이 세계 곳곳에서 발견되고 있다.
15	아래에 있는 한국과 영국의 두 사례를 보라.
16	여러분은 그 차이를 구별할 수 있는가?
17	왼쪽 작품은 조선 왕조 시대에 추사에 의해 창작되었다.
18	그 글자들은 부드러운 붓으로 그려졌다.

19 The right one, *The Canterbury Tales*, was created by Chaucer in England ＿＿＿＿＿ ＿＿＿＿＿ ＿＿＿＿＿ ＿＿＿＿＿.

20 It ＿＿＿＿＿ ＿＿＿＿＿ ＿＿＿＿＿ a pen.

21 ＿＿＿＿＿ ＿＿＿＿＿ ＿＿＿＿＿ led to ＿＿＿＿＿ ＿＿＿＿＿ of calligraphy.

22 Of course, all calligraphers had to ＿＿＿＿＿ ＿＿＿＿＿ to make their ＿＿＿＿＿ ＿＿＿＿＿.

23 Today calligraphy ＿＿＿＿＿ ＿＿＿＿＿ ＿＿＿＿＿ around us.

24 You can find ＿＿＿＿＿ ＿＿＿＿＿ ＿＿＿＿＿ on movie posters, book covers, music CDs, and clothes.

25 Below ＿＿＿＿＿ ＿＿＿＿＿ ＿＿＿＿＿.

26 Look at ＿＿＿＿＿ ＿＿＿＿＿ on the movie poster.

27 ＿＿＿＿＿ do you feel?

28 Can you imagine the monster's big mouth, ＿＿＿＿＿ ＿＿＿＿＿, and ＿＿＿＿＿, long tail?

29 ＿＿＿＿＿ ＿＿＿＿＿ the title on the fantasy novel?

30 Do you see Harry's ＿＿＿＿＿ and the ＿＿＿＿＿ ＿＿＿＿＿?

31 ＿＿＿＿＿ can start ＿＿＿＿＿ calligraphy.

32 It's not easy to write ＿＿＿＿＿ ＿＿＿＿＿ well at first, but ＿＿＿＿＿ ＿＿＿＿＿ ＿＿＿＿＿.

33 ＿＿＿＿＿ ＿＿＿＿＿ and make it ＿＿＿＿＿ of your ＿＿＿＿＿ life.

34 Write ＿＿＿＿＿ ＿＿＿＿＿ on birthday cards, bookmarks, or gifts.

35 Soon you will ＿＿＿＿＿ ＿＿＿＿＿ your own world of calligraphy.

19 오른쪽의 '캔터베리 이야기' 는 1400년대 후반 영국에서 Chaucer에 의해 창작되었다.

20 그것은 펜으로 쓰였다.

21 각기 다른 필기구가 각기 다른 캘리그래피의 스타일을 이끌었다.

22 물론, 모든 캘리그래피 작가들은 자신의 독특한 스타일을 만들어 내기 위해 열심히 연습해야 했다.

23 캘리그래피는 요즈음 우리 주변에서 널리 쓰이고 있다.

24 여러분은 영화 포스터, 책 표지, 음악 CD, 그리고 의류에서 디자이너들의 예술적인 손길을 발견할 수 있다.

25 아래에 몇 가지 예가 있다.

26 영화 포스터의 제목을 보라.

27 어떤 느낌이 드는가?

28 괴물의 커다란 입, 날카로운 이빨, 그리고 추하고 긴 꼬리를 상상할 수 있는가?

29 공상 소설의 제목은 어떠한가?

30 Harry의 번개와 마술사 모자가 보이는가?

31 누구든지 캘리그래피를 쓰기 시작할 수 있다.

32 처음부터 손으로 글씨를 잘 쓰기는 쉽지 않지만, 연습하면 완벽해진다.

33 계속해서 노력하고 자신의 일상의 한 부분이 되게 하라.

34 생일 카드, 책갈피, 또는 선물에 느낌을 담아 써 보라.

35 곧 자신만의 캘리그래피 세계를 만들게 될 것이다.

● 우리말을 참고하여 본문을 영작하시오.

1 여러분의 느낌을 써라
➡ _____

2 여러분은 자신의 느낌을 어떻게 표현하는가?
➡ _____

3 노래를 부르거나 춤을 추는가?
➡ _____

4 시를 쓰거나 그림을 그리는가?
➡ _____

5 요즈음에는 손 글씨를 통해 감정을 표현하는 것이 인기다.
➡ _____

6 몇몇 작품을 살펴보자.
➡ _____

7 오른쪽 예술 작품에서는 단어가 맛있는 과일인 홍시의 이미지를 포함하고 있다.
➡ _____

8 그것은 가을이 결실의 계절임을 보여 준다.
➡ _____

9 왼쪽에 있는 예술 작품은 한글 단어와 한자를 보여 주고 있다.
➡ _____

10 그것은 마치 단풍잎이 깔린 길을 따라 걷고 있는 행복한 여인처럼 보인다.
➡ _____

11 이 두 작품은 아름다운 손 글씨를 통해 가을의 느낌을 표현한다.
➡ _____

12 이런 종류의 예술은 '캘리그래피'라고 불린다.
➡ _____

13 캘리그래피는 새로운 것이 아니다.
➡ _____

14 오래전의 다양한 종류의 많은 캘리그래피 작품들이 세계 곳곳에서 발견되고 있다.
➡ _____

15 아래에 있는 한국과 영국의 두 사례를 보라.
➡ _____

16 여러분은 그 차이를 구별할 수 있는가?
➡ _____

17 왼쪽 작품은 조선 왕조 시대에 추사에 의해 창작되었다.
➡ _____

18 그 글자들은 부드러운 붓으로 그려졌다.

➡ _____

19 오른쪽의 '캔터베리 이야기'는 1400년대 후반 영국에서 Chaucer에 의해 창작되었다.

➡ _____

20 그것은 펜으로 쓰였다.

➡ _____

21 각기 다른 필기구가 각기 다른 캘리그래피의 스타일을 이끌었다.

➡ _____

22 물론, 모든 캘리그래피 작가들은 자신의 독특한 스타일을 만들어 내기 위해 열심히 연습해야 했다.

➡ _____

23 캘리그래피는 요즈음 우리 주변에서 널리 쓰이고 있다.

➡ _____

24 여러분은 영화 포스터, 책 표지, 음악 CD, 그리고 의류에서 디자이너들의 예술적인 손길을 발견할 수 있다.

➡ _____

25 아래에 몇 가지 예가 있다.

➡ _____

26 영화 포스터의 제목을 보라.

➡ _____

27 어떤 느낌이 드는가?

➡ _____

28 괴물의 커다란 입, 날카로운 이빨, 그리고 추하고 긴 꼬리를 상상할 수 있는가?

➡ _____

29 공상 소설의 제목은 어떠한가?

➡ _____

30 Harry의 번개와 마술사 모자가 보이는가?

➡ _____

31 누구든지 캘리그래피를 쓰기 시작할 수 있다.

➡ _____

32 처음부터 손으로 글씨를 잘 쓰기는 쉽지 않지만, 연습하면 완벽해진다.

➡ _____

33 계속해서 노력하고 자신의 일상의 한 부분이 되게 하라.

➡ _____

34 생일 카드, 책갈피, 또는 선물에 느낌을 담아 써 보라.

➡ _____

35 곧 자신만의 캘리그래피 세계를 만들게 될 것이다.

➡ _____

[01~03] 다음 글을 읽고 물음에 답하시오.

How do you express your feelings? Do you sing or dance? Do you write a poem or draw a picture? Nowadays, it is popular to express feelings through handwriting. Let's look at some works of art.

In the work of art on the right, the word includes a/an ⓐ＿＿＿ of a delicious fruit, *hongsi*. It shows that autumn is a season of fruit. The work of art on the left shows a Korean word and a Chinese character. It looks like a happy woman ⓑwalking down a road with autumn leaves. Both of these works express the feeling of autumn through beautiful handwriting. This kind of art is called calligraphy.

01 위 글의 빈칸 ⓐ에 들어갈 가장 알맞은 말을 고르시오.

① scene
② image
③ imagination
④ figure
⑤ scenery

02 위 글의 밑줄 친 ⓑwalking과 문법적 쓰임이 다른 것을 모두 고르시오.

① Who is the boy underlined dancing on the street?
② My hobby is drawing cartoons.
③ Who is the man talking with Sumi?
④ I'm interested in playing the piano.
⑤ The girl crying over there is Mary.

03 위 글의 내용과 일치하지 않는 것은?

① These days, to express feelings through handwriting is popular.
② The work of art on the right shows that autumn is a season of fruit.
③ We can see a Korean word and a Chinese character in the work of art on the left.
④ The work of art on the left expresses the feeling of autumn through beautiful painting.
⑤ The works of art on the right and on the left are called calligraphy.

[04~06] 다음 글을 읽고 물음에 답하시오.

Today calligraphy is widely used around us. You can find designers' artistic ⓐtouches on movie posters, book covers, music CDs, and clothes. ⓑBelow some examples are. Look at ⓒthe title on the movie poster. How do you feel? Can you imagine the monster's big mouth, sharp teeth, and ugly, long tail? How about the title on the fantasy novel? Do you see Harry's lightning and the wizard hats?

04 위 글의 밑줄 친 ⓐtouches와 같은 의미로 쓰인 것을 고르시오.

① I spent the morning putting the finishing touches to the report.
② Her story touches us all deeply.
③ The gentle touches of his hand on her shoulder made her jump.
④ He touches me on the shoulder.
⑤ He never touches alcoholic drinks.

05 위 글의 밑줄 친 ⓑ에서 어법상 <u>틀린</u> 부분을 찾아 고치시오.

_____ ➡ _____

06 위 글의 ⓒthe title on the movie poster에서 상상할 수 <u>없</u>는 것을 <u>모두</u> 고르시오.

① the monster's big mouth
② Harry's lightning
③ the monster's sharp teeth
④ the monster's ugly, long tail
⑤ the wizard hats

[07~08] 다음 글을 읽고 물음에 답하시오.

Look at the two girls learning *taekwondo*. *Taekwondo* is a traditional Korean sport, and we wear *dobok* to do it. It is exciting to learn *taekwondo*. ⓐAre you interesting? Please come and try.

07 위 글의 종류로 알맞은 것을 고르시오.

① summary ② PR leaflet
③ review ④ article
⑤ essay

08 위 글의 밑줄 친 ⓐ에서 어법상 <u>틀린</u> 부분을 찾아 고치시오.

_____ ➡ _____

[09~11] 다음 글을 읽고 물음에 답하시오.

Calligraphy is not new. Many different kinds of calligraphy works from long ago can be found all around the world. Look at the two examples from Korea and the UK below.

Can you tell the difference? ⓐThe left one was created by Chusa in the period of the Joseon Dynasty. The characters were painted with a soft brush.

The right one, *The Canterbury Tales*, was created by Chaucer in England in the late 1400s. It was written with a pen. ⓑ각기 다른 필기구가 각기 다른 캘리그래피의 스타일을 이끌었다. Of course, all calligraphers had to practice hard to make their unique styles.

09 다음 빈칸 (A)~(C)에 알맞은 단어를 넣어 위 글의 밑줄 친 ⓐ에 대한 소개를 완성하시오.

It is an example of the calligraphy works from long ago. (A)_____ created it in the period of the (B)_____ _____ by painting the characters with a (C)_____ _____.

10 위 글의 밑줄 친 ⓑ의 우리말에 맞게 주어진 어휘를 이용하여 9 단어로 영작하시오.

led to, different

➡ _____

11 위 글을 읽고 *The Canterbury Tales*에 대해 알 수 <u>없</u>는 것을 고르시오.

① 작가 ② 작가의 국적
③ 줄거리 ④ 집필된 시기
⑤ 집필할 때 사용한 필기구

[12~15] 다음 글을 읽고 물음에 답하시오.

Anyone can start writing calligraphy. ⓐ It's not easy to write by hand well at first, but practice makes perfect. Keep trying and make ⓑit part of your everyday life. Write ⓒ느낌을 담아 on birthday cards, bookmarks, or gifts. ⓓSoon you will build up your own world of calligraphy.

12 위 글의 밑줄 친 ⓐ를 바꿔 쓴 문장으로 옳지 <u>않은</u> 것을 모두 고르시오.

① To write by hand well at first is not easy

② That's not easy to write by hand well at first

③ It's difficult to write by hand well at first

④ Writing by hand well at first is not easy

⑤ To write by the hand well at first is not easy

서답형

13 위 글의 밑줄 친 ⓑit가 가리키는 것을 본문에서 찾아 쓰시오.

➡ _____

서답형

14 위 글의 밑줄 친 ⓒ의 우리말을 세 단어로 쓰시오.

➡ _____

서답형

15 위 글의 밑줄 친 ⓓ를 다음과 같이 바꿔 쓸 때 빈칸에 공통으로 들어갈 알맞은 단어를 쓰시오. (대·소문자 무시)

➡ = It will not be long _____ you build up your own world of calligraphy.

= _____ long you will build up your own world of calligraphy.

[16~17] 다음 한국 문화 체험 홍보문을 읽고 물음에 답하시오.

Look at the two boys playing *yunnori*. *Yunnori* is a traditional Korean (A)[board /

broad] game, and we use *yuts* and *mals* (B)[to play / playing] it. It is exciting to play *yunnori*. Are you (C)[interesting / interested]? Please come and try.

서답형

16 What do we use to play *yunnori*? Answer in English in a full sentence. (5 words)

➡ _____

서답형

17 위 글의 괄호 (A)~(C)에서 문맥이나 어법상 알맞은 낱말을 골라 쓰시오.

➡ (A) _____ (B) _____ (C) _____

[18~20] 다음 글을 읽고 물음에 답하시오.

Calligraphy is not new. (①) Many different kinds of calligraphy works from long ago can be found all around the world. (②) Look at the two examples from Korea and the UK below. (③) The left one was created by Chusa in the period of the Joseon Dynasty. (④) The characters were painted with a soft brush. (⑤)

The right one, *The Canterbury Tales*, was created by Chaucer in England in the late 1400s. It was written with a pen. ⓐDifferent writing tools led to different styles of calligraphy. Of course, all calligraphers had to practice hard to make their unique styles.

중요

18 위 글의 흐름으로 보아, 주어진 문장이 들어가기에 가장 적절한 곳은?

Can you tell the difference?

① ② ③ ④ ⑤

서답형

19 위 글의 밑줄 친 ⓐDifferent writing tools가 가리키는 것을 본문에서 찾아 쓰시오.

➡ _____

중요

20 위 글의 주제로 알맞은 것을 고르시오.

① Calligraphy was present in the East.

② Calligraphy was present in the West.

③ Calligraphy is not new.

④ There are various tools for writing calligraphy.

⑤ All calligraphers had to practice hard.

[21~23] 다음 글을 읽고 물음에 답하시오.

How do you express your feelings? Do you sing or dance? Do you write a poem or draw a picture? Nowadays, ⓐit is popular to express feelings through handwriting. Let's look at some works of art.

In the work of art ___(A)___ the right, the word includes an image of a delicious fruit, *hongsi*. It shows that autumn is a season of fruit. The work of art ___(A)___ the left shows a Korean word and a Chinese character. ⓑIt looks a happy woman walking down a road with autumn leaves. Both of these works express the feeling of autumn ___(B)___ beautiful handwriting. This kind of art is called calligraphy.

21 위 글의 빈칸 (A)와 (B)에 들어갈 전치사가 바르게 짝지어진 것은?

① to – through ② in – from

③ on – from ④ to – by

⑤ on – through

22 아래 〈보기〉에서 위 글의 밑줄 친 ⓐit과 문법적 쓰임이 같은 것의 개수를 고르시오.

┌─ 보기 ─┐

① Did you see it?

② I make it a rule to get up early.

③ It's impossible to get there in time.

④ It's two miles from here to the beach.

⑤ It is important to choose good friends.

└──────┘

① 1개 ② 2개 ③ 3개 ④ 4개 ⑤ 5개

서답형

23 위 글의 밑줄 친 ⓑ에서 어법상 틀린 부분을 찾아 고치시오.

_____ ➡ _____

[24~25] 다음 글을 읽고 물음에 답하시오.

Look at the boy ⓐkicking a *jegi*. ⓑKicking a *jegi* is a traditional Korean game, and we kick it with one of our feet. It is exciting to kick a *jegi*. Are you interested? Please come and try.

중요

24 위 글의 목적으로 알맞은 것을 고르시오.

① to promote ② to compare

③ to survey ④ to report

⑤ to communicate

서답형

25 다음 〈보기〉에서 위 글의 밑줄 친 ⓐkicking, ⓑKicking과 문법적 쓰임이 같은 것을 각각 골라 번호를 쓰시오.

┌─ 보기 ─┐

① Kicking a *jegi* is interesting.

② The men kicking a *jegi* are my brothers.

③ I'm good at kicking a *jegi*.

④ We enjoyed kicking a *jegi*.

⑤ I don't like the boys kicking a *jegi* there.

└──────┘

➡ ⓐ와 같은 것: _____ ,

　 ⓑ와 같은 것: _____

[01~03] 다음 글을 읽고 물음에 답하시오.

How do you express your feelings? Do you sing or dance? Do you write a poem or draw a picture? Nowadays, it is popular to express feelings through handwriting. Let's look at some works of art.

In the work of art on the right, the word includes an image of a delicious fruit, *hongsi*. It shows that autumn is a season of fruit. The work of art on the left shows a Korean word and a Chinese character. ⓐ그것은 마치 단풍잎이 깔린 길을 따라 걷고 있는 행복한 여인처럼 보인다. Both of these works express the feeling of autumn through beautiful handwriting. This kind of art is called calligraphy.

01 위 글에서 자신의 느낌을 표현하는 방법으로 소개된 것을 우리말로 모두 쓰시오.

➡ (1) _____ (2) _____
　 (3) _____ (4) _____
　 (5) _____

02 위 글의 밑줄 친 ⓐ의 우리말에 맞게 주어진 어휘를 알맞게 배열하시오.

> walking down / autumn leaves / like / with / a road / looks / a happy woman / it

➡ _____

03 본문의 내용과 일치하도록 다음 빈칸 (A)와 (B)에 알맞은 단어를 쓰시오.

> At the present time, expressing feelings through (A)_____ is popular and we call this kind of art (B)_____.

[04~07] 다음 글을 읽고 물음에 답하시오.

Calligraphy is not new. Many different kinds of calligraphy works from long ago can ____ⓐ____ all around the world. Look at the two examples from Korea and the UK below. Can you tell the difference? The left one was created by Chusa in the period of the Joseon Dynasty. The characters were painted with a soft brush.

The right one, *The Canterbury Tales*, was created by Chaucer in England in the late ⓑ 1400s. It was written with a pen. Different writing tools led to different styles of calligraphy. Of course, all calligraphers had to practice hard to make their unique styles.

04 위 글의 빈칸 ⓐ에 find를 알맞은 형태로 쓰시오.

➡ _____

05 위 글을 읽고 다음 빈칸 (1)~(4)에 들어갈 알맞은 말을 〈보기〉에서 골라 쓰시오.

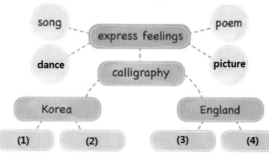

> ┤ 보기 ├
> • *The Canterbury Tales*　• brush
> • pen　　　　　　　　　• Chusa's work

➡ (1) _____ (2) _____
　 (3) _____ (4) _____

06 위 글의 밑줄 친 ⓑ1400s를 읽는 법을 영어로 쓰시오.

➡ _____

07 What did all calligraphers have to do to make their unique styles? Answer in English in a full sentence. (5 words)

➡ _____

[08~09] 다음 글을 읽고 물음에 답하시오.

Today calligraphy is widely used around us. You can find designers' artistic touches on movie posters, book covers, music CDs, and clothes. Below are ⓐsome examples. Look at the title on the movie poster. How do you feel? Can you imagine the monster's big mouth, sharp teeth, and ugly, long tail? How about the title on the fantasy novel? Do you see Harry's lightning and the wizard hats?

08 다음 빈칸에 알맞은 단어를 넣어 위 글의 밑줄 친 ⓐsome examples가 가리키는 내용을 완성하시오.

They are some examples of movie posters, book covers, music CDs, and clothes using calligraphy, on which you can find designers' _____ _____.

09 본문의 내용과 일치하도록 다음 빈칸 (A)와 (B)에 알맞은 단어를 쓰시오.

There are two commercial products including calligraphy titles. One is the title on the (A)_____ _____ and the other is the title on the (B)_____ _____.

[10~12] 다음 글을 읽고 물음에 답하시오.

(A)[How / What] do you express your feelings? Do you sing or dance? Do you write a poem or draw a picture? Nowadays, it is popular ⓐto express feelings through handwriting. Let's look at some works of art.

In the work of art on the right, the word (B)[excludes / includes] an image of a delicious fruit, *hongsi*. It shows that autumn is a season of fruit. The work of art on the left shows a Korean word and a Chinese character. It looks like a happy woman walking down a road with autumn leaves. Both of these works express the feeling of autumn through beautiful (C)[drawing / handwriting]. ⓑThis kind of art is called calligraphy.

10 위 글의 괄호 (A)~(C)에서 문맥이나 어법상 알맞은 낱말을 골라 쓰시오.

➡ (A) _____ (B) _____ (C) _____

11 다음 빈칸 (A)와 (B)에 알맞은 단어를 넣어 위 글의 밑줄 친 ⓐ의 예를 완성하시오.

(1) The word including an image of a delicious fruit, *hongsi*, shows that autumn is a season of (A)_____.
(2) The beautiful handwriting which is made up of a Korean word and a Chinese character expresses the feeling of (B)_____, and it looks like a (C)_____ woman walking down a road with autumn leaves.

12 위 글의 밑줄 친 ⓑ를 능동태로 고치시오.

➡ _____

해석

After You Read B

These Korean characters mean "Let's laugh." This calligraphy shows two

people laughing out loud.
앞의 명사 'two people'을 뒤에서 수식하는 현재분사의 후치 수식

These Korean characters mean "tree." This calligraphy shows a tree growing
앞의 명사 'tree'를 뒤에서 수식하는 현재분사의 후치 수식

in a pot.

구문해설 • character: 글자 • mean: 의미하다 • pot: 항아리, 화분

이 한글 글자는 "웃읍시다"를 의미합니다. 이 캘리그래피는 큰 소리로 웃고 있는 두 사람을 나타냅니다.

이 한글 글자는 "나무"를 의미합니다. 이 캘리그래피는 화분에서 자라는 나무를 나타냅니다.

Express Yourself C

Look at the two girls learning[doing] *taekwondo*. *Taekwondo* is a traditional

Korean sport, and we wear *dobok* to do it. It is exciting to learn *taekwondo*.
 to부정사의 부사적 용법(목적) 가주어 진주어
Are you interested? Please come and try.

Look at the two boys playing *yunnori*. *Yunnori* is a traditional Korean board

game, and we use *yuts* and *mals* to play it. It is exciting to play *yunnori*.
 to부정사의 부사적 용법(목적) 가주어
Are you interested? Please come and try.
be interested: 관심이 있다

구문해설 • traditional: 전통적인 • use: 사용하다 • wear: 입다, 신다, 착용하다

태권도를 배우고[하고] 있는 두 여자아이를 보세요. 태권도는 한국의 전통 스포츠이고, 우리는 그것을 하기 위해 도복을 입습니다. 태권도를 배우는 것은 흥미진진합니다. 관심이 있나요? 와서 한번 해 보세요.

윷놀이를 하는 두 남자아이를 보세요. 윷놀이는 한국의 전통적인 말판 놀이고, 우리는 그것을 하기 위해 윷과 말을 사용합니다. 윷놀이를 하는 것은 흥미진진합니다. 관심이 있나요? 와서 한번 해 보세요.

Link to the World

1 This is a set of Russian dolls. It is called matryoshka.
 ~라고 불린다

2 When you open it, smaller dolls keep coming out of it. It is interesting
 접속사 '~할 때' 계속해서 나온다 ~에서 가주어
 to see a smaller doll inside each doll.
 진주어 each+단수 명사

3 The first set of matryoshka dolls was a mother doll with six children.
 주어 동사 ~이 있는

4 Today, many new styles of matryoshkas are created and loved by many
 수동태 '만들어지다' created와 병렬 관계
 people.

구문해설 • Russian: 러시아의 • is called: ~라 불린다 • keep -ing: 계속 ~하다
 • interesting: 흥미로운 • inside: ~ 안의

1. 이것은 한 세트의 러시아 인형이다. 그것은 '마트료시카'라고 불린다.

2. 그것을 열면, 더 작은 인형들이 계속해서 나온다. 각각의 인형 안에서 더 작은 인형을 보는 것은 재미있다.

3. 최초의 '마트료시카' 인형 세트는 여섯 아이를 둔 어머니 인형이었다.

4. 오늘날에는, 많은 새로운 스타일의 '마트료시카'가 제작되어 많은 사람에게 사랑을 받고 있다.

Words & Expressions

01 다음 주어진 두 단어의 관계가 같도록 빈칸에 주어진 철자로 단어를 쓰시오.

> include : exclude = terrible : e_____

02 다음 빈칸에 들어갈 단어로 알맞은 것은?

> • You need _____ skills to draw and paint well.
> • When _____ comes, the leaves will change colors.
> • The tour _____ a visit to the Louvre Museum.

① handwriting – autumn – expressed
② handwriting – autumn – included
③ artistic – autumn – included
④ artistic – winter – expressed
⑤ artistic – winter – imagined

03 다음 영영풀이에 해당하는 것을 고르시오.

> not the same as anything or anyone else

① artistic ② huge ③ similar
④ foreign ⑤ unique

04 다음 빈칸에 들어갈 말로 알맞은 것은?

> • Learning a _____ language is not easy.
> • I can't recognize his _____ written in this letter.

① native – face
② foreign – handwriting
③ native – handwriting
④ foreign – dynasty
⑤ natural – face

05 다음 글의 빈칸 ⓐ와 ⓑ에 들어갈 단어로 알맞은 것은?

> This is a set of Russian dolls. It is called matryoshka. When you open it, smaller dolls ⓐ_____ coming out of it. It is interesting to see a smaller doll ⓑ_____ each doll. The first set of matryoshka dolls was a mother doll with six children.

① take – inside ② leave – behind
③ bring – between ④ keep – inside
⑤ keep – between

06 다음 밑줄 친 부분의 의미가 바르지 않은 것은?

① She read the beautiful <u>poem</u> aloud. (시)
② This restaurant is very <u>popular</u> with tourists. (인기 있는)
③ The knife looks very <u>sharp</u>. (무딘)
④ The cute puppy barked and wagged its <u>tail</u>. (꼬리)
⑤ <u>Nowadays</u>, most teenagers have their own cell phones. (요즈음)

Conversation

07 대화의 밑줄 친 우리말에 맞게 주어진 단어를 알맞은 순서로 배열하시오.

> **G:** 판소리를 배우고 있는 두 남자 좀 봐.
> **B:** Are you interested in pansori, Nancy?
> **G:** Sure. I like the sound of it.

(the / men / look / learning / at / two / *pansori*)

➡ _____

08 자연스러운 대화가 되도록 알맞은 순서로 배열한 것은?

> (A) Thank you. Are you interested in dancing *talchum*?
> (B) Sure. Can you teach me?
> (C) No problem.
> (D) I enjoyed your performance. You did a good job.

① (A) – (B) – (C) – (D)
② (B) – (A) – (C) – (D)
③ (C) – (A) – (B) – (D)
④ (D) – (A) – (B) – (C)
⑤ (D) – (B) – (A) – (C)

[09~10] 다음 대화를 읽고 물음에 답하시오.

> B: _____(A)_____
> G: Yes. Actually, I'm learning it in my calligraphy class. Look! This is my work.
> B: _____(B)_____

09 빈칸 (A)에 알맞은 표현을 주어진 조건에 맞게 쓰시오.

> ┤ 조건 ├
> • *Hangeul*을 배우는 데 관심이 있는지 묻는 표현을 쓸 것.
> • 'have'와 'interest'를 사용할 것.

➡ _____

10 위 대화의 빈칸 (B)에 들어갈 말로 알맞은 것은?

① So what?
② You know what?
③ What are you into?
④ I'm interested in musicals.
⑤ Excellent!

[11~12] 다음 대화의 빈칸에 들어갈 알맞은 표현은?

11

> A: Are you interested in going shopping?
> B: No, I'm not. _____

① I mean it's time to go shopping.
② I'm interested in riding a bike.
③ What do you want to do?
④ I'm interested in going shopping.
⑤ I feel like going shopping.

12

> *(At an art exhibition)*
> B: Good job! Someone is holding a cloud? How creative!
> G: Thank you. _____
> B: Yes, I am. Actually, I'm taking an online class for free.
> G: Oh, good for you.

① You did a good job! It's awesome.
② Are you interested in doing *taekwondo*?
③ Are you interested in taking pictures?
④ Are you interested in beatboxing?
⑤ Are you interested in cooking?

Grammar

13 다음 빈칸에 들어갈 표현이 순서대로 바르게 짝지어진 것을 고르시오.

> _____ is getting popular for students _____ themselves through selfies.

① It – to express
② It – express
③ That – to express
④ That – express
⑤ This – expressing

14 밑줄 친 부분의 쓰임이 나머지 넷과 다른 것은?

① The man driving the bus is my father.
② Did you notice her cooking food in the kitchen?
③ Look at the two boys playing *yunnori*.
④ Mary is making a call in a public phone booth.
⑤ Are you interested in watching horror movies?

15 다음 빈칸에 들어갈 말이 나머지와 다른 하나는?

① It is dangerous _____ children to walk home alone.
② It's fun _____ me to do different things.
③ It was foolish _____ him to waste his money on such trifles.
④ Wasn't it exciting _____ you to see lots of dolphins at one time?
⑤ It will be awesome _____ me to be a member of the club.

16 다음 중 밑줄 친 부분의 쓰임이 다른 하나는?

① It was not easy to go up the hill on our bicycles.
② They thought it was a good idea to make them do the work.
③ It was hard to decide which room was the largest.
④ It was behind the chair in the living room.
⑤ It was nice of you to take me to the airport.

[17~18] 다음 빈칸에 들어갈 알맞은 것은?

17

> Everyone _____ in this town knows little about him.

① live
② lives
③ lived
④ living
⑤ to live

18

> It is interesting for me _____ a smaller doll inside each doll.

① see
② sees
③ saw
④ seeing
⑤ to see

19 괄호 안에 주어진 어휘를 사용해 다음을 영작하시오.

(1) Kate는 눈으로 덮인 산을 올라갔다. (climb, cover)

➡ _____

(2) 언제 깨진 창문을 고칠 거예요? (going, fix, break)

➡ _____

(3) Mariko는 공원에서 놀고 있는 그녀의 딸을 보았다. (look, play)

➡ _____

(4) 헬멧 없이 자전거를 타는 것은 위험하다. (a bike, a helmet, dangerous, to)

➡ _____

(5) Laura가 중국어 말하기를 배운 것은 아주 현명했다. (learn, wise, how to speak, it)

➡ _____

Reading

[20~22] 다음 글을 읽고 물음에 답하시오.

How do you express your feelings? Do you sing or dance? Do you write a poem or draw a picture? Nowadays, it is popular ⓐto express feelings through handwriting. Let's look at some works of art.

In the work of art on the right, the word includes an image of a delicious fruit, *hongsi*. It shows that autumn is a season of fruit. The work of art on the left shows a Korean word and a Chinese character. It looks like a happy woman walking down a road with autumn leaves. Both of these works express the feeling of autumn through beautiful handwriting. This kind of art is called ___(A)___.

20 주어진 영영풀이를 참고하여 빈칸 (A)에 철자 c로 시작하는 단어를 쓰시오.

the art of producing beautiful handwriting using a brush or a special pen

➡ _____

21 다음 문장에서 위 글의 내용과 <u>다른</u> 부분을 찾아서 고치시오.

Both the works of art mentioned in the text express the traditional culture of autumn through beautiful handwriting.

_____ ➡ _____

22 위 글의 밑줄 친 ⓐto express와 to부정사의 용법이 같은 것을 <u>모두</u> 고르시오.

① Do you want to express feelings through handwriting?

② The best way to express feelings is using various facial expressions.

③ He danced on the stage to express feelings.

④ She was too shy to express feelings.

⑤ I decided to express feelings through handwriting.

[23~25] 다음 글을 읽고 물음에 답하시오.

Calligraphy is not new. Many different kinds of calligraphy works from long ago can be found all around the world. Look at the two examples from Korea and the UK below. Can you ⓐtell the difference? The left one was created by Chusa in the period of the Joseon Dynasty. The characters were painted with a soft brush.

The right one, *The Canterbury Tales*, was created by Chaucer in England in the late 1400s. It was written with a pen. ___(A)___ led to different styles of calligraphy. Of course, all calligraphers had to practice hard to make their unique styles.

23 위 글의 빈칸 (A)에 들어갈 알맞은 말을 고르시오.

① Difference between the subjects of the works

② Difference between the East and the West

③ Difference between the periods of creation

④ Different writing tools

⑤ Various writing styles

24 위 글의 밑줄 친 ⓐtell the difference와 바꿔 쓸 수 있는 단어를 고르시오.

① differ ② insist ③ distinguish

④ vary ⑤ persuade

25 위 글의 내용과 일치하지 <u>않는</u> 것은?

① Many different kinds of calligraphy works can be found all around the world.
② The left calligraphy work was created in the late 1400s.
③ The characters of the left calligraphy work were painted with a soft brush.
④ *The Canterbury Tales* was created by Chaucer in England.
⑤ *The Canterbury Tales* was written with a pen.

[26~27] 다음 글을 읽고 물음에 답하시오.

Today calligraphy is widely used around us. (①) You can find designers' artistic touches on movie posters, book covers, music CDs, and clothes. (②) Look at the title on the movie poster. (③) How do you feel? (④) Can you imagine the monster's big mouth, sharp teeth, and ugly, long tail? (⑤) How about the title on the fantasy novel? Do you see Harry's lightning and the wizard hats?

26 위 글의 흐름으로 보아, 주어진 문장이 들어가기에 가장 적절한 곳은?

> Below are some examples.

①　　②　　③　　④　　⑤

27 위 글을 읽고 대답할 수 <u>없는</u> 질문은?

① Nowadays, is calligraphy widely used around us?
② Where is calligraphy used?
③ How do designers add artistic touches to calligraphy titles?
④ What can you imagine from the title on the movie poster?
⑤ What do you see from the title on the fantasy novel?

[28~29] 다음 글을 읽고 물음에 답하시오.

(A)[Anyone / Someone] can start writing calligraphy. It's not easy to write (B)[by hand / on a keyboard] well at first, but practice makes perfect. ⓐ계속해서 노력하고 자신의 일상의 한 부분이 되게 하라. Write with your feelings on birthday cards, bookmarks, or gifts. (C)[Long before / Soon] you will build up your own world of calligraphy.

28 위 글의 괄호 (A)~(C)에서 문맥상 알맞은 낱말을 골라 쓰시오.

➡ (A) _____ (B) _____ (C) _____

29 위 글의 밑줄 친 ⓐ의 우리말에 맞게 한 단어를 보충하여, 주어진 어휘를 알맞게 배열하시오.

> it / life / trying / and / of / keep / part / make / your

➡ _____

출제율 90%

01 다음 문장의 빈칸에 알맞은 말을 쓰시오.

> Hammers and saws are a carpenter's
> _____ .

출제율 95%

02 다음 우리말에 맞게 빈칸에 알맞은 단어를 쓰시오.

> (A) 왼쪽 작품은 조선 왕조 시대에 추사에 의해
> 창작되었다.
> The left work was created by Chusa
> in the _____ of the Joseon Dynasty.
> (B) 공상 소설의 제목은 어떠한가?
> How about the _____ on the
> fantasy novel?

출제율 95%

03 다음 대화의 빈칸에 알맞은 표현은?

> B: You did a good job! It's awesome.
> G: Thanks.
> B: What is it made of? Glass?
> G: Yes, it is. Are you interested in glass
> art?
> B: Yes, very much. How long did it take
> to make it?
> G: _____

① It was not easy.

② It was 5 feet long.

③ It was 10 feet high.

④ It took one month.

⑤ It was made of glass.

출제율 95%

04 다음 영영풀이에 해당하는 단어는?

> a story about imaginary events or people

① monster ② tool ③ tale

④ tail ⑤ tooth

[05~07] 다음 대화를 읽고 물음에 답하시오.

> James: What are you doing, Mina?
> Mina: I'm practicing calligraphy.
> James: You're writing with a brush. It looks
> fun.
> Mina: Are you interested in calligraphy?
> James: Yes, very much.
> Mina: Look at this! I just wrote it. What do you
> think?
> James: It looks like a person dancing with
> open arms.
> Mina: You got it. This Korean word means
> "dance."
> James: You did a good job! Can I try it?
> Mina: Why not? Take this brush.

출제율 85%

05 다음 질문에 대한 답을 대화에서 찾아 영어로 쓰시오.

> Q: What is Mina doing?
>
> ➡ _____

출제율 100%

06 위 대화의 제목으로 알맞은 것은?

① How to Write Calligraphy

② The Way to Write Calligraphy Well

③ The Meaning of Dance in Korea

④ The Importance of Practice

⑤ Fun with Calligraphy

출제율 95%

07 위 대화의 내용과 일치하지 않는 것은?

① They are talking about calligraphy.

② Mina is practicing calligraphy.

③ James is interested in calligraphy.

④ Mina's work is a person dancing with
open arms.

⑤ James is going to try writing calligraphy.

08 다음 대화의 빈칸에 알맞은 표현은?

> A: _____
>
> B: Yes, I am. I want to eat it.

① Are you interested in *pansori*?
② Are you interested in *bibimbap*?
③ Are you interested in *taekwondo*?
④ Are you interested in *yunnori*?
⑤ Are you interested in *hanbok*?

09 다음 대화의 빈칸에 들어갈 말로 어색한 것은?

> B: Minji, _____?
>
> G: Yes. I'm good at taking care of them.
>
> B: How about plants? Are you interested in them, too?
>
> G: No, I'm not. I can't grow them well.

① are you interested in animals
② do you have an interest in animals
③ are you into animals
④ what are you interested in
⑤ do you find raising animals interesting

10 다음 두 사람의 대화가 어색한 것은?

① A: Are you interested in *yunnori*?
　 B: Yes, I am. I want to play it.
② A: Are you interested in *taekwondo*?
　 B: Yes, I am. I want to learn it.
③ A: Do you like reading books?
　 B: Yes, I do. It is boring to read books.
④ A: Are you interested in *Hangeul*, Kevin?
　 B: Yes, very much. I want to learn it.
⑤ A: Who is the woman sitting between Tom and Mike?
　 B: She's Natalie.

11 다음 ⓐ~ⓗ 중 옳은 것을 모두 고르면?

> ⓐ It is fun reads books.
> ⓑ Look at the boy enjoying *tuho*.
> ⓒ This calligraphy shows a tree to grow in a pot.
> ⓓ Isn't it exciting to see a singing contest?
> ⓔ Who was the man played the piano on the stage?
> ⓕ It's no use crying over spilt milk.
> ⓖ We live in a house built in 1906.
> ⓗ It is a lot of fun to dancing *talchum*.

① ⓐ, ⓒ, ⓕ
② ⓑ, ⓒ, ⓓ, ⓔ
③ ⓑ, ⓓ, ⓕ, ⓖ
④ ⓒ, ⓑ, ⓔ, ⓗ
⑤ ⓒ, ⓓ, ⓔ, ⓖ

12 다음 밑줄 친 부분의 쓰임이 나머지와 다른 것을 고르시오.

① It looks like a happy woman <u>walking</u> down a road with autumn leaves.
② Do you know the boy <u>wearing</u> a mask?
③ Jenny loves <u>going</u> hiking.
④ My brother is <u>washing</u> the dishes.
⑤ The girls <u>dancing</u> to the music are my friends.

13 다음 중 어법상 적절한 문장은?

① It is important keeps your teeth clean.
② It was boring wait for her.
③ It was impossible to estimating the flood damage this year.
④ It is a nice idea to have cold noodles in summer.
⑤ It is nice for you to help that old man.

14 다음 우리말을 주어진 어휘를 이용하여 6단어로 영작하시오. 출제율 90%

건강을 유지하는 것은 중요하다. (to stay, important, healthy)

➡ _____

[15~17] 다음 글을 읽고 물음에 답하시오.

How do you express your feelings? Do you sing or dance? Do you write a poem or draw a picture? Nowadays, it is popular to express feelings through handwriting. Let's look at some works of art.

(①) In the work of art on the right, the word includes an image of a delicious fruit, *hongsi*. (②) The work of art on the left shows a Korean word and a Chinese ⓐcharacter. (③) It looks like a happy woman walking down a road with autumn leaves. (④) Both of these works express the feeling of autumn through beautiful handwriting. (⑤) This kind of art is called calligraphy.

15 위 글의 흐름으로 보아, 주어진 문장이 들어가기에 가장 적절한 곳은? 출제율 100%

It shows that autumn is a season of fruit.

① ② ③ ④ ⑤

16 위 글의 밑줄 친 ⓐcharacter와 같은 의미로 쓰인 것을 고르시오. 출제율 95%

① He has a strong character.
② She has a face without any character.
③ Who is the major character in this book?
④ Please write in a large character.
⑤ My father is a man of fine character.

17 위 글을 읽고 대답할 수 없는 질문은? 출제율 95%

① What is the best way to express your feelings?
② What image does the work of art on the right include?
③ What does the work of art on the left show?
④ What does the work of art on the left look like?
⑤ What is this kind of art called?

[18~20] 다음 글을 읽고 물음에 답하시오.

Calligraphy is not new. Many different kinds of calligraphy works from long ago can be found all around the world. Look at the two examples from Korea and the UK below. Can you tell the difference? The left ___(A)___ was created by Chusa in the period of the Joseon Dynasty. The characters were painted with a soft brush.

The right ___(B)___ , *The Canterbury Tales*, was created by Chaucer in England in the late 1400s. It was written with a pen. Different writing tools led to different styles of calligraphy. Of course, all calligraphers had to practice hard to make their unique styles.

18 위 글의 빈칸 (A)와 (B)에 공통으로 들어갈 알맞은 대명사를 쓰시오. 출제율 90%

➡ _____

19 다음 영영풀이에 해당하는 단어를 본문에서 찾아 쓰시오. _{출제율 90%}

> a series of rulers of a country who all belong to the same family

➡ _____

20 위 글의 왼쪽 그림에 대해 알 수 없는 것을 고르시오. _{출제율 100%}

① 작가 ② 제작된 국가
③ 제작된 시기 ④ 사용한 필기구
⑤ 시를 인용한 이유

[21~23] 다음 글을 읽고 물음에 답하시오.

Today calligraphy is widely used around us. You can find designers' (A)[artistic / awkward] touches on movie posters, book covers, music CDs, and clothes. Below are some examples. Look at the title on the movie poster. How do you feel? Can you imagine the monster's big mouth, sharp teeth, and ugly, long (B)[tail / tale]? How about ⓐthe title on the fantasy novel? Do you see Harry's (C)[lightning / lightening] and the wizard hats?

21 위 글의 제목으로 알맞은 것을 고르시오. _{출제율 95%}

① How to Find Designers' Artistic Touches
② What Can You Find on the Movie Poster?
③ Examples of Calligraphy Used around Us
④ Let's Find Calligraphy Used on the Movie Poster
⑤ Let's Find Calligraphy Used on the Fantasy Novel

22 위 글의 괄호 (A)~(C)에서 문맥상 알맞은 낱말을 골라 쓰시오. _{출제율 90%}

➡ (A) _____ (B) _____ (C) _____

23 위 글을 읽고 밑줄 친 ⓐthe title on the fantasy novel에서 볼 수 있는 것 두 가지를 우리말로 쓰시오. _{출제율 90%}

➡ (1) _____ (2) _____

[24~25] 다음 글을 읽고 물음에 답하시오.

Anyone can start writing calligraphy. ⓐ It's easy to write by hand well at first, but _____(A)_____. Keep trying and make it part of your everyday life. Write with your feelings on birthday cards, bookmarks, or gifts. Soon you will build up your own world of calligraphy.

24 위 글의 빈칸 (A)에 들어갈 알맞은 말을 고르시오. _{출제율 90%}

① look before you leap
② practice makes perfect
③ two heads are better than one
④ make hay while the sun shines
⑤ haste makes waste

25 위 글의 밑줄 친 ⓐ에서 흐름상 어색한 부분을 찾아 고치시오. _{출제율 85%}

_____ ➡ _____

01 다음 대화의 빈칸에 들어갈 표현을 주어진 〈조건〉에 맞게 완성하시오.

> B: Good job! Someone is holding a cloud? How creative!
> G: Thank you. _____
> B: Yes, I am. Actually, I'm taking an online class for free.
> G: Oh, good for you.

┌─── 조건 ───┐
• 관심이 있는지 묻는 표현을 쓸 것.
• 'take pictures'를 활용할 것.
• 'interested'를 사용할 것.
└─────────┘

➡ _____

 다음 대화의 밑줄 친 우리말에 맞게 주어진 단어를 이용하여 쓰시오.

> B: You did a good job! It's awesome.
> G: Thanks.
> B: What is it made of? Glass?
> G: Yes, it is. Are you interested in glass art?
> B: Yes, very much. 그거 만드는 데 시간이 얼마나 걸렸니?
> G: It took one month.

(long / take / make / it)

➡ _____

03 다음 대화를 읽고 아래의 요약문을 완성하시오.

> James: What are you doing, Mina?
> Mina: I'm practicing calligraphy.
> James: You're writing with a brush. It looks fun.
> Mina: Are you interested in calligraphy?

James: Yes, very much.
Mina: Look at this! I just wrote it. What do you think?
James: It looks like a person dancing with open arms.
Mina: You got it. This Korean word means "dance."
James: You did a good job! Can I try it?
Mina: Why not? Take this brush.

⬇

Mina and James are talking about Mina's _____ work. Mina is _____ calligraphy with a _____. She writes a Korean word meaning "_____." James thinks she did a _____ job. He is going to try _____ calligraphy.

04 다음 문장을 주어진 말로 시작하여 다시 쓰시오.

(1) Dick must be sent to hospital because of his illness.
➡ It is necessary _____
_____.

(2) Jane thinks she should eat lots of vegetables.
➡ Jane thinks it is necessary _____
_____.

05 다음 두 문장을 관계대명사를 사용하지 않고 하나의 문장으로 고쳐 쓰시오.

> • She bought a smartphone.
> • The smartphone was made in Korea.

➡ _____

How do you express your feelings? Do you sing or dance? Do you write a poem or draw a picture? Nowadays, ⓐ손 글씨를 통해 감정을 표현하는 것이 인기다. Let's look at some works of art.

In the work of art on the right, the word includes an image of a delicious fruit, *hongsi*. It shows that autumn is a season of fruit. ⓑ The work of art on the left shows a Korean word and a Chinese character. It looks like a happy woman walking down a road with autumn leaves. Both of these works express the feeling of autumn through beautiful handwriting. This kind of art is called calligraphy.

06 위 글의 밑줄 친 ⓐ의 우리말에 맞게 주어진 어휘를 이용하여 8단어로 영작하시오.

> it, through

➡ _____

07 다음 빈칸 (A)와 (B)에 알맞은 단어를 넣어 위 글의 밑줄 친 ⓑ에 대한 소개를 완성하시오.

> It is the calligraphy expressing the (A)_____ of autumn, and it shows a (B)_____ _____ and a (C)_____ _____. It looks like a happy woman walking down a road with autumn leaves.

08 본문의 내용과 일치하도록 다음 빈칸 (A)와 (B)에 알맞은 단어를 쓰시오.

> Calligraphy is the (A)_____ through which we can express (B)_____.

[09~11] 다음 글을 읽고 물음에 답하시오.

Calligraphy is not (A)[new / old]. Many different kinds of calligraphy works from long ago can be found all around the world. Look at the two examples from Korea and the UK below. Can you tell the difference? ⓐThe left one was created by Chusa in the period of the Joseon Dynasty. The characters were painted with a soft brush.

The right one, *The Canterbury Tales*, was created by Chaucer in England in the late 1400s. It was written with a pen. Different writing tools led to different styles of calligraphy. Of course, all calligraphers had to practice (B)[hard / hardly] to make their (C)[common / unique] styles.

09 위 글의 괄호 (A)~(C)에서 문맥이나 어법상 알맞은 낱말을 골라 쓰시오.

➡ (A) _____ (B) _____ (C) _____

10 위 글의 밑줄 친 ⓐ를 능동태로 고치시오.

➡ _____

11 다음 빈칸 (A)와 (B)에 알맞은 단어를 넣어 위 글의 *The Canterbury Tales*에 대한 소개를 완성하시오.

> (A)_____ created it in England in the late 1400s. He wrote it with (B)_____ _____.

창의사고력 서술형 문제

01 주어진 십대의 취미 중 하나를 선택하여, 관심이 있는지 묻고 그에 대한 긍정의 답과 부정의 답을 〈보기〉의 문장과 같이 쓰시오. (부정의 답에는 관심 있는 취미를 쓰시오.)

〈Teens Hobbies〉

go shopping / watch horror movies / take selfies / listen to music / play soccer / ride a bike / collect figures / read detective stories

〈보기〉

A: Are you interested in watching horror movies?

B: Yes, I am. I watch horror movies very often. / No, I'm not. I'm interested in reading detective stories.

02 주어진 어휘와 가주어를 이용하여 3 문장 이상을 쓰시오.

learn English	play *yunnori*	keep promises
study history	swim in this river	see his art collection

(1) _____

(2) _____

(3) _____

(4) _____

(5) _____

(6) _____

03 다음 내용을 바탕으로 한국 문화 체험을 홍보하는 글을 쓰시오.

- 전통적인 한국의 문화 활동: kicking a *jegi*, a traditional Korean game
- 하는 방법: kick a *jegi* with one of our feet
- 기타: It is exciting to kick a *jegi*

Look at the boy (A)_____ a *jegi*. Kicking a *jegi* is a (B)_____, and we kick it with (C)_____. It is (D)_____ to kick a *jegi*. Are you interested? Please come and try.

단원별 모의고사

01 다음 단어에 대한 영어 설명이 <u>어색한</u> 것은?

① wildly: by a lot of people or in a lot of places

② imagine: to think about something and form a picture or idea of it

③ sharp: pointed

④ include: to make someone or something part of a group

⑤ tool: a piece of equipment, usually one you hold in your hand, that is designed to do a particular type of work

02 우리말에 맞게 문장의 빈칸에 알맞은 단어를 쓰시오.

> 각기 다른 필기구가 각기 다른 캘리그래피의 스타일을 이끌었다.
>
> ➡ Different writing tools _____ different styles of calligraphy.

03 다음 영영풀이에 해당하는 단어를 고르시오.

> beautiful writing, often created with a special pen or brush

① handwriting
② character
③ calligraphy
④ painting
⑤ selfie

04 대화의 빈칸 (A)와 (B)에 들어갈 말을 쓰시오.

> B: Minji, are you (A)_____ in animals?
> G: Yes, I am. I'm good at (B)_____ care of them.
> B: How about plants? Are you interested in them, too?
> G: No, I'm not. I can't grow them well.

05 그림을 보고 빈칸에 들어갈 알맞은 단어를 쓰시오.

> The work of art above shows a Korean word and a Chinese _____. It looks like a happy woman walking down a road with autumn leaves.

① painting
② culture
③ handwriting
④ character
⑤ tale

06 대화의 빈칸에 들어갈 말로 알맞은 것은?

> B: Look! Two girls are learning *Hangeul*.
> G: Are you interested in *Hangeul*, Kevin?
> B: _____ I want to join them and learn it.

① Good for you.
② No, I'm not.
③ Minji is interested in *Hangeul*.
④ Of course not.
⑤ Yes, very much

07 다음 대화의 빈칸 ⓐ와 ⓑ에 들어갈 알맞은 말을 쓰시오.

> B: _____ ⓐ _____! It's awesome.
> G: Thanks.
> B: What is it made of? Glass?
> G: Yes, it is. _____?
> B: Yes, very much. How long did it take to make it?
> G: It took one month.

ⓐ • 상대방을 칭찬하는 표현을 쓸 것.
 • 'do', 'job'을 활용하여 5단어로 쓸 것.
ⓑ • glass art에 관심이 있는지 묻는 표현을
 쓸 것.
 • 'be'동사 의문문으로 쓸 것.

➡ ⓐ _____
 ⓑ _____

10 대화의 빈칸에 들어갈 표현으로 알맞은 것은?

A: You're writing something. What's this?
B: It's my art homework. Do you like it?
A: Sure. _____

① I think you did a good job!
② Anyone can start painting.
③ You have to practice more.
④ I don't like it.
⑤ I want to learn it.

[08~09] 다음 대화를 읽고 물음에 답하시오.

James: What are you doing, Mina?
Mina: I'm practicing calligraphy. (①)
James: You're writing with a brush. It looks fun. (②)
Mina: Are you interested in calligraphy?
James: Yes, very much.
Mina: Look at this! I just wrote it. (③)
James: It looks like a person dancing with open arms. (④)
Mina: You got it. This Korean word means "dance." (⑤)
James: You did a good job! Can I try it?
Mina: _____(A)_____ Take this brush.

11 다음 대화의 빈칸에 적절한 말은?

B: Julie, are you interested in *hanbok*?
G: Not really.
B: Then, _____
G: Well, I'm interested in *taekwondo*. It is a traditional Korean sport. It's awesome.

① are you interested in *bibimbap*?
② what are you going to do?
③ I think you did a good job!
④ are you interested in cooking?
⑤ what are you interested in?

08 주어진 문장이 들어갈 위치로 알맞은 것은?

What do you think?

① ② ③ ④ ⑤

12 대화의 밑줄 친 우리말에 맞게 주어진 단어를 활용하여 영어로 쓰시오.

Mina: Look at this! I just wrote it. What do you think?
James: 두 팔을 벌리고 춤을 추는 사람처럼 보여. (look like / dance / with open arms)
Mina: You got it. This Korean word means "dance."
James: You did a good job!

09 위 대화의 흐름상 빈칸 (A)에 들어갈 말로 알맞은 것은?

① Are you interested in calligraphy?
② I'm afraid not.
③ How kind you are!
④ Why not?
⑤ Well done!

➡ _____

13 빈칸에 괄호 안에 주어진 동사를 알맞게 쓰시오.

> The boy _____ on the grass is my son.
> (sit)

14 가주어를 사용하여 주어진 문장과 같은 의미가 되도록 쓰시오.

(1) Knives and forks are easy to use.

➡ _____

(2) To read books is important.

➡ _____

15 다음 문장에서 어법상 어색한 것을 바르게 고치시오.

(1) There is a sign said "No smoking."

_____ ➡ _____

(2) That's fun to watch basketball games.

_____ ➡ _____

16 다음 중 어법상 어색한 것을 고르시오.

① It is exciting to learn *taekwondo*.

② It is not wise for you to put all your eggs in one basket.

③ It is important to save energy.

④ Look at the man cooking *bibimbap*.

⑤ There was a fence painted green.

[17~19] 다음 글을 읽고 물음에 답하시오.

How do you express your feelings? Do you sing or dance? Do you write a poem or draw a picture? Nowadays, it is popular to express feelings through handwriting. Let's look at some ⓐworks of art.

In ⓑthe work of art on the right, the word includes an image of a delicious fruit, *hongsi*. It shows that autumn is a season of fruit. The work of art on the left shows a Korean word and a Chinese character. It looks like a happy woman walking down a road with autumn leaves. Both of these works express the feeling of autumn through beautiful handwriting. This kind of art is called calligraphy.

17 위 글의 주제로 알맞은 것을 고르시오.

① There are many ways to express your feelings.

② The word can include an image of a delicious fruit.

③ It is possible to express feelings through handwriting.

④ A Korean word and a Chinese character can be used together in calligraphy.

⑤ There are many kinds of calligraphy.

18 위 글의 밑줄 친 ⓐworks와 같은 의미로 쓰인 것을 고르시오.

① She works for an engineering company.

② This machine works by electricity.

③ The engineering works are closed today.

④ This pill works on me.

⑤ Kate bought the complete works of Shakespeare.

19 다음 빈칸 (A)와 (B)에 알맞은 단어를 넣어 위 글의 밑줄 친 ⓑ에 대한 소개를 완성하시오.

> It is the calligraphy including an (A)_____ of a delicious fruit, *hongsi*, which shows that (B)_____ is a season of fruit.

[20~22] 다음 글을 읽고 물음에 답하시오.

ⓐThe right one, *The Canterbury Tales,* was created by Chaucer in England in the late 1400s. ⓑIt was written with a pen. Different writing tools ⓒled to different styles of calligraphy. Of course, all calligraphers had to practice hard ⓓto make their unique styles.

20 위 글의 밑줄 친 ⓐ와 ⓑ를 능동태로 고치시오.

➡ ⓐ _____

ⓑ _____

21 위 글의 밑줄 친 ⓒled to와 바꿔 쓸 수 없는 말을 모두 고르시오.

① resulted from　　② caused
③ came about　　　④ resulted in
⑤ brought about

22 아래 〈보기〉에서 위 글의 밑줄 친 ⓓto make와 문법적 쓰임이 같은 것의 개수를 고르시오.

┌─── 보기 ───┐
① They thought it difficult to make their unique styles.
② They were happy to make their unique styles.
③ They studied many other styles to make their unique styles.
④ They explained the plan to make their unique styles to me.
⑤ They were creative enough to make their unique styles.
└─────────────┘

① 1개　② 2개　③ 3개　④ 4개　⑤ 5개

[23~24] 다음 글을 읽고 물음에 답하시오.

ⓐ캘리그래피는 요즈음 우리 주변에서 널리 쓰이고 있다. You can find designers' artistic touches on movie posters, book covers, music CDs, and clothes. Below are some examples. Look at the title on the movie poster. How do you feel? Can you imagine the monster's big mouth, sharp teeth, and ugly, long tail? How about the title on the fantasy novel? Do you see Harry's lightning and the wizard hats?

23 위 글의 밑줄 친 ⓐ의 우리말에 맞게 주어진 어휘를 이용하여 7 단어로 영작하시오.

┌─────────────────────────┐
　　　　　Today, is, around
└─────────────────────────┘

➡ _____

24 위 글의 내용과 일치하지 않는 것은?

① It's possible to find designers' artistic touches on movie posters.
② We use calligraphy in movie posters, book covers, music CDs, and clothes.
③ We can imagine the monster's big mouth, sharp teeth, and ugly, long tail from the title on the movie poster.
④ We see Harry's lightning and the wizard hats from the title on the fantasy novel.
⑤ The title on the fantasy novel is a good example of drawing used around us.

Lesson 8

Design for All

 의사소통 기능

- 불평하기
 I'm not happy about the desk.
- 의도 표현하기
 I'm thinking of putting some pads on it.

 언어 형식

- so ~ that ... can't
 The shoes were **so** uncomfortable **that** she **couldn't** walk well.
- 사역동사
 What **made** her **do** all this?

Words & Expressions

Key Words

- **add** [æd] 동 더하다, 추가하다
- **almost** [ɔ́:lmoust] 부 거의
- **another** [ənʌ́ðər] 형 또 하나의, 또 다른
- **bath** [bæθ] 명 목욕
- **bathtub** [bǽθtəb] 명 욕조
- **below** [bilóu] 전 (위치가 …보다) 아래에
- **blind** [blaind] 형 눈이 먼
- **bookshelf** [búkʃelf] 명 책꽂이
- **Braille** [breil] 명 점자
- **cold answer** 냉담한 대답
- **company** [kʌ́mpəni] 명 회사
- **cotton** [kátn] 명 솜
- **cross** [krɔːs] 동 건너다
- **crowded** [kráudid] 형 붐비는
- **cushion** [kúʃən] 명 쿠션, 방석
- **decide** [disáid] 동 결심하다
- **decorate** [dékərèit] 동 장식하다
- **difficulty** [dífikʌlti] 명 어려움
- **dirty** [də́:rti] 형 더러운
- **easily** [íːzili] 부 쉽게
- **either** [íːðər] 부 (부정문에서) …도 또한[역시]
- **finally** [fáinəli] 부 마침내
- **flat** [flæt] 형 평평한
- **fountain** [fáuntən] 명 분수, 원천
- **handle** [hǽndl] 명 손잡이
- **hang** [hæŋ] 동 매달다, 걸다
- **hearing** [híəriŋ] 명 청력
- **however** [hauévər] 부 그러나, 하지만
- **journey** [dʒə́:rni] 명 여행, 여정

- **jump rope** 줄넘기를 하다
- **locker** [lákər] 명 사물함
- **low(–lower–lowest)** [lou] 형 낮은
- **moment** [móumənt] 명 순간
- **pad** [pæd] 명 패드, 깔개
- **point of view** 관점
- **product** [prádʌkt] 명 상품, 제품
- **reach** [riːtʃ] 동 …에 닿다
- **seat** [siːt] 명 자리, 좌석
- **sign** [sain] 명 표지판
- **solution** [səlúːʃən] 명 해결책
- **station** [stéiʃən] 명 역, 정류장
- **step** [step] 명 계단
- **step box** 디딤대
- **stick** [stik] 명 지팡이, 막대기
- **swing** [swiŋ] 명 그네
- **switch** [switʃ] 명 스위치
- **thick** [θik] 형 두꺼운
- **tight** [tait] 형 꽉 조이는, 딱 붙는
- **together** [təgéðər] 부 함께
- **traffic** [trǽfik] 명 교통
- **traffic light** 신호등
- **uncomfortable** [ənkʌ́mfərtəbəl] 형 불편한
- **universal** [jùːnəvə́:rsəl] 형 보편적인
- **view** [vjuː] 명 견해, 관점
- **way** [wei] 명 방법
- **wheelchair** [hwíːltʃɛ̀ər] 명 휠체어
- **wiper** [wáipər] 명 닦개, 와이퍼

Key Expressions

- **be planning to+동사원형** …할 계획이다
- **be thinking of** …할 것을 고려[생각] 중이다
- **by oneself** 혼자서
- **get hurt** 다치다
- **get in** …에 들어가다 (= enter)
- **get on** …을 타다
- **go through** …을 겪다
- **How about –ing?** …하는 게 어때?
- **in danger** 위험에 처한
- **lots of** (= a lot of) 많은

- **more and more** 점점 더 많은
- **put A on B** A를 B에 놓다[두다]
- **put on** …을 입다
- **so+형용사/부사+that+주어+can't …**
 너무 ~해서 …할 수 없다
- **such a(n)+형용사+명사+that+주어+can …**
 아주 ~해서 …할 수 있다
- **tired of** …에 지친, …에 싫증 난
- **turn on** …을 켜다
- **watch out** 조심하다

Word Power

※ 형용사 뒤에 -ly를 붙여 부사로 만들기

☐ **easy**(쉬운) – **easily**(쉽게)

☐ **difficult**(어려운) – **difficultly**(어렵게)

☐ **final**(마지막의) – **finally**(마침내)

☐ **safe**(안전한) – **safely**(안전하게)

☐ **comfortable**(편안한) – **comfortably**(편안하게)

☐ **thick**(두꺼운) – **thickly**(두껍게)

※ 서로 반대되는 뜻을 가진 어휘

☐ **difficulty** (어려움) ↔ **ease** (쉬움)

☐ **thick** (두꺼운) ↔ **thin** (마른, 야윈)

☐ **dirty** (더러운) ↔ **clean** (깨끗한)

☐ **low** (낮은) ↔ **high** (높은)

☐ **comfortable** (편안한) ↔ **uncomfortable** (불편한)

☐ **tight** (꽉 조이는) ↔ **loose** (느슨한)

English Dictionary

☐ **below** …의 아래에
→ in a lower place or position 더 낮은 장소나 위치에

☐ **blind** 눈이 먼
→ unable to see 볼 수 없는

☐ **company** 회사
→ a business organization that makes money by producing or selling goods or services
물건이나 서비스를 생산하거나 팔아서 돈을 버는 사업 조직

☐ **cross** 건너다
→ to go across from one side of something to the other
어떤 것의 한쪽 편에서 반대편으로 가로질러 가다

☐ **crowded** 붐비는
→ having a lot of people or too many people
많은 사람들 또는 너무 많은 사람들이 있는

☐ **decorate** 장식하다
→ to add something to an object or place, especially in order to make it more attractive
특히 더 매력적으로 만들기 위해 물건이나 장소에 어떤 것을 더하다

☐ **flat** 평평한
→ not having a part that is higher or lower than another
다른 부분보다 더 높거나 더 낮은 부분을 가지지 않은

☐ **handle** 손잡이
→ a part that is designed especially to be held by the hand 특히 손에 쥐어지게 설계된 부분

☐ **journey** 여행, 여정
→ an act of traveling from one place to another
한 장소에서 또 다른 장소로 여행하는 행위

☐ **locker** 사물함
→ a cupboard, often tall and made of metal, in which you can keep your possessions, and leave them for a period of time 소유물을 보관할 수 있고 일정 기간 동안 남겨둘 수 있는 금속으로 만들어진 종종 큰 벽장

☐ **low** 낮은
→ small in height or smaller than the usual height
높이가 작은 또는 일반적인 높이보다 더 작은

☐ **product** 제품
→ something that is made or grown for selling
팔기 위해 만들어지거나 재배되는 것

☐ **solution** 해결책
→ the answer to a problem
문제에 대한 해답

☐ **station** 역, 정류장
→ a building or place where buses or trains stop so that people can get on or off
사람들이 타고 내릴 수 있도록 버스나 기차가 멈춰서는 건물이나 장소

☐ **stick** 지팡이
→ a long, thin wooden pole that especially old or injured people use to walk
노인들이나 부상당한 사람들이 걷기 위해 사용하는 길고 가는 나무로 된 막대

☐ **switch** 스위치
→ a button or key that controls the light or machine
전구나 기계를 통제하는 버튼이나 키

☐ **uncomfortable** 불편한
→ not feeling comfortable and pleasant
편안하거나 유쾌하게 느끼지 않는

☐ **universal** 보편적인
→ related to everyone in the world
세상의 모든 사람과 관련된

☐ **view** 관점, 견해
→ a personal opinion or belief about a situation or subject
어떤 상황이나 주제에 관한 개인적인 의견이나 믿음

01 다음 빈칸에 들어갈 말로 알맞은 것은?

> She couldn't see or hear well. She couldn't walk well without a stick. With all these _____, the woman had to climb stairs in subway stations and get on crowded buses.

① difference ② products ③ steps
④ difficulties ⑤ journeys

서답형

02 다음 문장의 빈칸에 주어진 영영풀이에 해당하는 말을 쓰시오.

> • One example of her _____ design ideas is low-floor buses.
> <영영풀이> related to everyone in the world

➡ _____

서답형

03 다음 우리말에 맞게 두 단어로 쓰시오.

> 그녀는 혼자서 전등을 켤 수 없어요.
> ➡ She can't turn on the light _____.

➡ _____

04 다음 중 밑줄 친 단어의 우리말 뜻이 잘못된 것은?

① Sometimes she got hurt or found herself in danger. (위험에 처한)
② She became tired of the same cold answer. (싫증 난)
③ She put on her grandmother's clothes, uncomfortable shoes, and thick glasses. (불편한)
④ During her journey, Patricia felt the difficulties old people go through. (겪다)
⑤ Every moment was very difficult for her. (다른)

[05~06] 다음 영영풀이에 해당하는 단어를 고르시오.

05

> a long, thin wooden pole that especially old or injured people use to walk

① stroller ② stick
③ wheelchair ④ seat
⑤ handle

중요

06

> in a lower place or position

① on ② below
③ beyond ④ above
⑤ between

서답형

07 다음 빈칸에 공통으로 들어갈 단어를 쓰시오.

> • Which _____ do I press to turn it off?
> • I can't work next weekend. Will you _____ with me?

➡ _____

서답형

08 다음 우리말에 맞게 빈칸에 주어진 철자로 시작하는 단어를 쓰시오.

> 그녀와 나는 내일 분수에서 만날 것이다.
> • She and I will meet at the f_____ tomorrow.

01 빈칸에 들어갈 단어를 주어진 철자로 시작하여 쓰시오.

> In 1979, a woman started a j_____ to cities in the U.S. and Canada. Every moment was very difficult for her, but she visited more than 115 cities and ended her trip in 1982.

02 우리말에 맞게 주어진 단어를 이용하여 문장의 빈칸을 채우시오. (어형 변화 필수)

(1) 그 여인은 지하철역에서 계단을 올라가거나 붐비는 버스에 올라타야 했다.

➡ The woman had to climb stairs in subway stations and get on _____ buses. (crowd)

(2) 그녀는 똑같은 냉담한 대답에 지쳤다.

➡ She became _____ _____ the same cold answer. (tire)

(3) 그녀는 자신의 할머니 옷을 입고, 불편한 신발을 신고, 두꺼운 안경을 썼다.

➡ She put on her grandmother's clothes, _____ shoes, and thick glasses. (comfortable)

03 다음 빈칸에 영영풀이에 해당하는 단어를 주어진 철자로 시작하여 쓰시오.

> • Products like big f_____ light switches are helping people live better lives.
> <영영풀이> not having a part that is higher or lower than another

04 우리말과 같은 뜻이 되도록 빈칸에 알맞은 단어를 쓰시오.

(1) 나는 그의 견해에 동의하지 않는다.

➡ I don't agree with his _____.

(2) 이 재킷은 내겐 너무 꽉 조인다.

➡ This jacket is too _____ for me.

(3) 그녀의 유니버설 디자인 아이디어의 한 가지 예는 저상 버스이다. 그것은 계단이 없고 낮은 바닥을 가지고 있어서 휠체어를 탄 사람조차 아무 도움 없이 이용할 수 있다.

➡ One _____ of her universal design ideas is low-floor buses. They have no steps and have such a low floor that even a person in a _____ can use them _____ any help.

(4) 1970년대 동안, 그녀는 큰 디자인 회사에서 일했다.

➡ _____ the 1970's, she worked for a big design _____.

05 영영풀이에 해당하는 단어를 <보기>에서 찾아 첫 번째 칸에 쓰고, 두 번째 칸에는 우리말 뜻을 쓰시오.

> ┤ 보기 ├
> view / cross / product / low

(1) _____ : something that is made or grown for selling: _____

(2) _____ : small in height or smaller than the usual height: _____

(3) _____ : a personal opinion or belief about a situation or subject: _____

(4) _____ : to go across from one side of something to the other: _____

Conversation

① 불평하기

I'm not happy about the desk. 나는 책상이 마음에 들지 않아.

- "I'm not happy about …"은 '나는 …이 마음에 들지 않는다'라는 의미로, 만족스럽지 못한 것에 대해 불평하는 표현이다.

 e.g. A: I'm not happy about this restaurant.
 B: Is there anything wrong?

불평하는 표현

- It's not fair.
- I don't like ….
- I'm not satisfied with ….
- I'm not content with ….
- I want to complain about ….
- … is not satisfactory to me.
- … is not good enough for me.

핵심 Check

1. 다음 대화의 빈칸에 들어갈 말로 알맞지 <u>않은</u> 것은?

 A: _____

 B: What's the problem?

 A: The power button doesn't work.

 ① I want to complain about this computer.
 ② I'd like to complain about this computer.
 ③ I'm not happy with this computer.
 ④ I'm not satisfied with this computer.
 ⑤ This computer is good enough for me.

2 의도 표현하기

> I'm thinking of putting some pads on it. 나는 그 위에 몇 장의 패드를 놓을까 생각 중이야.

■ "I'm thinking of …"는 '나는 …할까 생각 중이다'라는 뜻으로, 의도나 계획을 나타낼 때 쓰는 표현이다. 'of'는 전치사이므로 뒤에 명사나 동명사(-ing)가 와야 한다.

 e.g. A: I'm thinking of inviting Ms. Kim to the party.
 B: That's a good idea.

"I'm thinking of …"는 "I'm considering -ing …" 또는 "I intend to ～."와 바꿔 쓸 수 있다. 의지를 조금 더 강하게 표현할 때는 "I will ～"로 나타낼 수 있으며, 전치사 of 대신 about을 사용하여 "I'm thinking about ～"으로도 표현한다.

의도 표현하기

- • I will ….
- • I'm going to ….
- • I'm planning to ….
- • I'm considering -ing ….
- • I intend to ….

- • I'm thinking of buying a car. 나는 차를 살까 생각 중이다.
 = I'm considering buying a car.
 = I intend to buy a car.

핵심 Check

2. 다음 문장과 바꿔 쓸 수 있는 것은?

 I'm thinking of putting some pads on it.

 ① I will putting some pads on it.
 ② I intend putting some pads on it.
 ③ I'm intend to put some pads on it.
 ④ I'm considering putting some pads on it.
 ⑤ I'm considering to putting some pads on it.

3. 다음 우리말에 맞게 대화의 빈칸에 알맞은 말을 쓰시오.

 A: Are you _____ of buying a used car? (너는 중고차를 살 생각이니?)

 B: No, I'm _____ to buy a new one. (아니, 난 새 차를 살 계획이야.)

Get Ready 2

(1) B: ❶I'm not happy about this fountain. It's too high for some kids.

　　G: Well, ❷I'm planning to put lower fountains together with it.

　　B: That's a good idea.

(2) G: ❸I don't like the high steps here. People in wheelchairs can't get in.

　　B: Right. ❹I'm thinking of building a new way with no steps.

(3) G: I'm not happy about this swing. People in wheelchairs can't get on it easily.

　　B: Right. I'm planning to hang a bigger and safer seat for them.

　　G: Good idea.

(1) B: 나는 이 음수대가 마음에 들지 않아. 몇몇 아이들에게는 너무 높아.
　　G: 음, 나는 그것과 함께 더 낮은 음수대들을 놓으려고 계획 중이야.
　　B: 좋은 생각이야.

(2) G: 나는 여기 높은 계단이 마음에 들지 않아. 휠체어를 탄 사람들은 들어설 수가 없잖아.
　　B: 맞아. 나는 계단 없는 새 길을 짓는 것을 생각 중이야.

(3) G: 나는 이 그네가 마음에 들지 않아. 휠체어를 탄 사람들은 그것을 쉽게 탈 수 없어.
　　B: 맞아. 나는 그들을 위해 더 크고 더 안전한 자리를 매달려고 계획 중이야.
　　G: 좋은 생각이야.

❶ '나는 …이 마음에 들지 않는다.'라는 의미로, 만족스럽지 못한 것에 대해 불평하는 표현이다.

❷ 'be planning to+동사원형' 형태로 '나는 …할까 생각 중이다'라는 뜻으로, 의도나 계획을 나타낼 때 쓰는 표현이다.

❸ 'I don't like …'는 만족스럽지 못한 것에 대해 불평하는 표현이다.

❹ "I'm thinking of …"는 '나는 …할까 생각 중이다'라는 뜻으로, 의도나 계획을 나타낼 때 쓰는 표현이다. 'of'는 전치사이므로 뒤에 명사나 동명사(동사-ing)가 와야 한다.

Check(√) True or False

(1) B doesn't like this fountain because it is too high for some kids.　　T ☐ F ☐

(2) B isn't satisfied with the steps, so he is planning to build a new way with low steps.　　T ☐ F ☐

(3) B intends to hang a bigger and safer seat for those in wheelchairs.　　T ☐ F ☐

Start Off Listen & Talk A

(1) G: I'm not happy about the button.

　　B: Why? ❶What's wrong with it?

　　G: It's too high. Children or people in wheelchairs can't reach it. I'm thinking of putting ❷another switch for them.

(2) G: I'm not happy about the sign. There are some people ❸who can't see.

　　B: Right. Do you have any ideas?

　　G: Well, I'm thinking of adding Braille on the sign.

　　B: That's a good idea.

(1) G: 나는 그 버튼이 마음에 들지 않아.
　　B: 왜? 뭐가 잘못됐니?
　　G: 그것은 너무 높아. 아이들이나 휠체어를 탄 사람들은 거기까지 닿을 수가 없어. 나는 그들을 위해 또 다른 스위치를 달까 생각 중이야.

(2) G: 나는 표지판이 마음에 들지 않아. 볼 수 없는 사람들도 좀 있잖아.
　　B: 맞아. 너는 어떤 아이디어라도 있니?
　　G: 음, 나는 표지판 위에 점자를 추가할까 생각 중이야.
　　B: 그거 좋은 생각이다.

❶ What's the matter with it?과 같은 표현이다.

❷ another+단수명사

❸ 관계대명사절로 선행사 people을 꾸며주는 역할을 한다.

Check(√) True or False

(4) G isn't satisfied with the button, so she's planning to fix it.　　T ☐ F ☐

(5) G is thinking of adding Braille on the sign for blind people.　　T ☐ F ☐

 Start Off Listen & draw

B: I'm not happy about the lights.
G: ❶What's wrong with them?
B: The traffic lights look the same to some people ❷who are blind to colors.
G: Oh, I see. How about putting an image on each light?
B: A walking man on the green light and a standing man on the red light? Good idea!

❶ 무엇이 문제인지 물어보는 표현이다.
❷ 관계대명사절로 선행사 people을 수식하고, 'be blind to …'는 '…을 못보다'라는 뜻이다.

 Speak Up Look and talk

A: I'm not happy about the desk. It's too low.
B: ❶Right. I'm thinking of putting some pads on it.
A: ❷Good idea.

❶ 상대방의 말에 동의하는 말로 You're right.이라고 해도 좋다.
❷ 상대방의 말에 동의하는 표현이다.

 Speak Up Mission

A: I'm not happy about the bookshelf. It's too small.
B: ❶I think so, too. Do you have any ideas?
A: I'm thinking of putting another bookshelf on it.
B: That's a good idea.

❶ 상대방의 말에 동의하는 표현이다.

 Step Up Real-life Scene

Dad: What are you doing here?
Son: I'm thinking of ways ❶to help Miso.
Dad: What's wrong?
Son: She can't turn on the light ❷by herself. This switch is too high for her.
Dad: That's right. I'm not happy about it, ❸ either. Do you have any good ideas about that?
Son: I'm thinking of putting a step box here below the switch.

Dad: Good idea. And I'll change the switch to a bigger ❹one.
Son: Great. Grandma will like it, too. She can turn on the light more easily.

❶ ways를 수식하는 형용사적 용법이다.
❷ by oneself: 혼자서
❸ either: 부정문에서 '～도 역시'의 뜻이다.
❹ one은 부정대명사로 'switch'를 가리킨다.

 Express Yourself A

(1) G: I'm not happy about my brother's chair. It's too low and too hard.
 B: Right. I'm thinking of buying ❶this one. What do you think?
 G: Looks great. I think he can use it ❷for so long, even after he grows taller.
(2) B: I'm not happy about the door handles in my house. They are not easy ❸to use for my grandma.
 G: How about this one? She will pull it and open the door easily.
 B: That's good.
(3) G: I'm thinking of buying this spoon. It will help my grandma eat soup easily.
 B: Right. ❹She doesn't have to hold it with her fingers.

❶ this one = this chair
❷ for so long: 아주 오랫동안
❸ 형용사 easy를 꾸며주는 부정사의 부사 용법이다.
❹ doesn't have to+동사원형: …할 필요가 없다

 Learning Diary Check Yourself

G: I'm not happy about this light switch.
B: Why? What's wrong?
G: It's too small. Grandma can't use it easily.
B: ❶Do you have any ideas?
G: I'm thinking of changing it with ❷a bigger one. That'll help her turn on the light easily.
B: Good idea.

❶ 무슨 아이디어가 있느냐고 묻는 표현이다.
❷ a bigger one = a bigger switch

● 다음 우리말과 일치하도록 빈칸에 알맞은 말을 쓰시오.

Get Ready 2

(1) B: I'm _____ _____ _____ this _____. It's _____ _____ for some kids.
G: Well, I'_____ _____ _____ _____ lower fountains together with it.
B: That's a _____ _____.

(2) G: I _____ _____ the high steps here. People _____ _____ can't _____ _____.
B: Right. I'm _____ _____ _____ a new way _____ no _____.

(3) G: I'm not _____ about this swing. People in wheelchairs can't _____ _____ it _____.
B: Right. I'm _____ _____ _____ a bigger and safer seat for them.
G: Good idea.

Start Off Listen & Talk A

(1) G: I'm _____ _____ _____ the button.
B: Why? What's _____ with it?
G: It's too high. Children or people in wheelchairs can't _____ it. _____ _____ _____ putting _____ switch for them.

(2) G: I'm not _____ _____ the sign. There are some people _____ can't see.
B: Right. Do you have _____ ideas?
G: Well, I'm _____ of _____ Braille on the sign.
B: That's a _____ _____.

Start Off Listen & draw

B: _____ _____ _____ _____ the lights.
G: _____ _____ _____ them?
B: The traffic lights look _____ _____ to some people _____ are _____ _____ _____.
G: Oh, I see. _____ _____ _____ an image on each light?
B: A _____ man on the green light and a _____ man on the red light? Good idea!

Speak Up Look and talk

B: _____ _____ _____ _____ the desk. It's _____ _____.
G: Right. I'm _____ _____ _____ some pads on it.
B: Good idea.

(1) B: 나는 이 음수대가 마음에 들지 않아. 몇몇 아이들에게는 너무 높아.
G: 음, 나는 그것과 함께 더 낮은 음수대들을 놓으려고 계획 중이야.
B: 좋은 생각이야.
(2) G: 나는 여기 높은 계단이 마음에 들지 않아. 휠체어를 탄 사람들은 들어설 수가 없잖아.
B: 맞아. 나는 계단 없는 새 길을 짓는 것을 생각 중이야.
(3) G: 나는 이 그네가 마음에 들지 않아. 휠체어를 탄 사람들은 그것을 쉽게 탈 수 없어.
B: 맞아. 나는 그들을 위해 더 크고 더 안전한 자리를 매달려고 계획 중이야.
G: 좋은 생각이야.

(1) G: 나는 그 버튼이 마음에 들지 않아.
B: 왜? 뭐가 잘못됐니?
G: 그것은 너무 높아. 아이들이나 휠체어를 탄 사람들은 거기까지 닿을 수가 없어. 나는 그들을 위해 또 다른 스위치를 달까 생각 중이야.
(2) G: 나는 표지판이 마음에 들지 않아. 볼 수 없는 사람들도 좀 있잖아.
B: 맞아. 너는 어떤 아이디어라도 있니?
G: 음, 나는 표지판 위에 점자를 추가할까 생각 중이야.
B: 그거 좋은 생각이다.

B: 나는 불빛이 마음에 들지 않아.
G: 뭐가 잘못됐니?
B: 색맹인 사람들에게는 신호등이 똑같이 보일 거야.
G: 오, 알겠어. 각 불빛에 그림을 넣는 게 어떨까?
B: 파란불에는 걷는 사람을, 그리고 빨간불에는 서 있는 사람을? 좋은 생각이야!

B: 나는 책상이 마음에 들지 않아. 그것은 너무 낮아.
G: 맞아. 나는 그 위에 몇 장의 패드를 놓을까 생각 중이야.
B: 좋은 생각이야.

Speak Up Mission

A: I'm _____ _____ _____ the _____. It's too small.
B: I think so, too. Do you have _____ _____?
A: I'm _____ _____ _____ another bookshelf on it.
B: That's a good idea.

Speak Up Real-life Scene

Dad: What are you _____ here?
Son: I'm _____ of _____ to help Miso.
Dad: What's _____?
Son: She can't _____ _____ the light _____ _____. This switch is _____ _____ for her.
Dad: That's right. I'm not _____ _____ it, _____. Do you have any good ideas _____ _____?
Son: I'm _____ of putting a _____ _____ here _____ the switch.
Dad: Good idea. And I'll _____ the switch to a _____ _____.
Son: Great. Grandma will like it, too. She can _____ _____ the light more _____.

Express Yourself A

(1) G: _____ _____ _____ _____ my brother's chair. It's _____ _____ and _____ _____.
B: Right. _____ _____ _____ _____ this one. _____ do you _____?
G: _____ _____. I think he can use it for _____ _____, even after he _____ _____.

(2) B: I'm _____ _____ _____ the door _____ in my house. They are not _____ _____ _____ for my grandma.
G: _____ _____ this one? She will pull it and open the door easily.
B: That's good.

(3) G: _____ _____ _____ buying this spoon. It will help my grandma eat soup easily.
B: Right. She _____ _____ _____ hold it with her fingers.

Learning Diary Check Yourself

G: I'm _____ _____ about this _____ _____.
B: Why? What's _____?
G: It's _____ _____. Grandma can't use it easily.
B: Do you have _____ _____?
G: _____ _____ _____ _____ _____ it _____ a bigger one. That'll help her _____ _____ the light easily.
B: Good idea.

해석

A: 나는 책꽂이가 마음에 들지 않아. 그것은 너무 작아.
B: 나도 그렇게 생각해. 어떤 아이디어라도 있니?
A: 나는 그 위에 또 다른 책꽂이를 놓을까 생각 중이야.
B: 그거 좋은 생각이다.

아빠: 너는 여기서 무엇을 하고 있니?
아들: 저는 미소를 도울 방법을 생각하고 있어요.
아빠: 뭐가 잘못됐니?
아들: 그녀는 혼자서 전등을 켤 수 없어요. 이 스위치는 그녀에게 너무 높아요.
아빠: 그렇구나. 나도 그것이 마음에 들지 않는구나. 그것에 대한 어떤 아이디어라도 있니?
아들: 저는 여기 스위치 아래에 디딤대를 놓을까 생각하고 있어요.
아빠: 좋은 생각이구나. 그럼 나는 스위치를 더 큰 것으로 바꾸마.
아들: 좋아요. 할머니께서도 그것을 좋아하실 거예요. 할머니께서는 전등을 더 쉽게 켜실 수 있어요.

(1) G: 나는 내 남동생의 의자가 마음에 안 들어. 그것은 너무 낮고 딱딱해.
B: 맞아. 나는 이것을 살까 생각 중이야. 너는 어때?
G: 좋아 보이네. 나는 그가 키가 더 자란 후에도 그것을 오랫동안 사용할 수 있을 거라고 생각해.
(2) B: 나는 우리 집의 문손잡이가 마음에 안 들어. 그것들은 우리 할머니께서 사용하시기에 쉽지 않아.
G: 이것은 어때? 그녀는 그것을 당겨서 문을 쉽게 여실 거야.
B: 그것 좋네.
(3) G: 나는 이 숟가락을 살까 생각 중이야. 그것은 우리 할머니께서 국을 쉽게 드실 수 있도록 도와줄 거야.
B: 맞아. 그녀는 그것을 손가락으로 잡으실 필요가 없어.

G: 나는 이 조명 스위치가 마음에 들지 않아.
B: 왜? 뭐가 잘못됐니?
G: 그것은 너무 작아. 할머니께서 그것을 쉽게 사용하실 수가 없어.
B: 어떤 아이디어라도 있니?
G: 나는 그것을 좀 더 큰 것으로 바꿀까 생각 중이야. 그것은 할머니께서 조명을 쉽게 켜실 수 있도록 도와줄 거야.
B: 좋은 생각이다.

01 다음 대화의 빈칸에 들어갈 말로 알맞은 것은?

> B: _____ It's too high for some kids.
>
> G: Well, I'm planning to put lower fountains together with it.
>
> B: That's a good idea.

① I want this fountain.

② I'm satisfied with this fountain.

③ I'm not interested in this fountain.

④ I like this fountain.

⑤ I'm not happy about this fountain.

02 다음 대화의 빈칸에 들어갈 말로 적절한 것은?

> G: I don't like the high steps here. People in wheelchairs can't get in.
>
> B: Right. _____ building a new way with no steps.

① I intend to ② I'm thinking of

③ I'm planning to ④ I'm going to

⑤ I will

03 다음 대화의 우리말에 맞게 주어진 단어를 이용하여 영어로 쓰시오.

> B: 나는 셔츠가 마음에 들지 않아. (happy / the shirt)
>
> G: What's wrong with it?
>
> B: It's too tight for me.

➡ _____

04 다음 대화를 알맞은 순서대로 배열하시오.

> (A) That's a good idea.
>
> (B) I'm thinking of putting another bookshelf on it.
>
> (C) I'm not happy about the bookshelf. It's too small.
>
> (D) I think so, too. Do you have any ideas?

➡ _____

[01~02] 다음 대화를 읽고 물음에 답하시오.

G: _____(A)_____ this swing. People in wheelchairs can't get on it easily.

B: Right. (B)I'm planning to hang a bigger and safer seat for them.

G: Good idea.

01 위 대화의 빈칸 (A)에 들어갈 말로 어색한 것은?

① I'm not happy about
② I'm not satisfied with
③ I'm not content with
④ I don't like
⑤ I don't complain about

위 대화의 밑줄 친 (B)의 의도로 알맞은 것은?

① 금지하기 ② 계획 표현하기
③ 부탁하기 ④ 허용 여부 묻기
⑤ 불평하기

서답형

03 다음 대화의 빈칸에 관심을 묻는 말을 주어진 조건에 따라 완성하시오.

> G: I'm not happy about the button.
> B: Why? _____
> G: It's too high. Children or people in wheelchairs can't reach it. I'm thinking of putting another switch for them.

┌── 조건 ──┐
• 상대방이 문제를 제기할 때, '무슨 일이야?'라고 묻는 표현
• 'wrong'과 'with'를 사용할 것

[04~05] 다음 대화를 읽고 물음에 답하시오.

B: I'm not ⓐhappy about the lights.

G: What's ⓑwrong with them?

B: The traffic lights look ⓒdifferent to some people who are ⓓblind to colors.

G: Oh, I see. (A)How about putting an ⓔ image on each light?

B: A walking man on the green light and a standing man on the red light? Good idea!

04 위 대화의 밑줄 친 ⓐ~ⓔ 중 어휘의 쓰임이 어색한 것은?

① ⓐ ② ⓑ ③ ⓒ ④ ⓓ ⑤ ⓔ

05 위 대화의 밑줄 (A)와 같은 의미가 아닌 것은?

① What about putting
② Why don't we put
③ Shall we put
④ Why are you putting
⑤ What do you say to putting

[06~07] 다음 대화를 읽고 물음에 답하시오.

G: _____(A)_____ It will help my grandma eat soup easily.

B: Right. (B)그녀는 그것을 손가락으로 잡으실 필요가 없어.

06 위 대화의 빈칸 (A)에 들어갈 말로 어색한 것은?

① I'm thinking of buying this spoon.
② I'm considering buying this spoon.
③ I intend to buy this spoon.
④ I'm planning to buy this spoon.
⑤ I want to complain about buying this spoon.

서답형

07 위 대화의 밑줄 친 (B)의 우리말에 맞게 주어진 단어를 활용하여 영어로 쓰시오.

(have to / hold / her fingers)

➡ _____

[08~09] 다음 대화를 읽고 물음에 답하시오.

G: I'm not happy about this light switch.

B: Why? What's wrong?

G: (A)_____ Grandma can't use it easily.

B: Do you have any ideas?

G: I'm thinking of changing it with a bigger one. (B)That'll help her turning on the light easily.

B: Good idea.

08 위 대화의 빈칸 (A)에 들어갈 말로 적절한 것은?

① This switch is too bright.

② This switch is too big.

③ This switch is too high for her.

④ This switch is too small.

⑤ This switch is too low.

서답형

09 위 대화의 밑줄 친 (B)에서 어법상 틀린 부분을 찾아 바르게 고쳐 완전한 문장으로 쓰시오.

➡ _____

 중요

10 다음 중 짝지어진 대화가 어색한 것을 고르시오.

① A: I'm happy with the lights.

 B: Why? What's wrong?

② A: What's wrong?

 B: I lost my ticket.

③ A: I'm not happy about the desk. It's too low.

 B: Right.

④ A: I'm thinking of putting another bookshelf on it.

 B: That's a good idea.

⑤ A: I want to complain about this spaghetti.

 B: Me, too. It tastes bad.

중요

11 대화의 밑줄 친 부분의 의도로 알맞은 것은?

A: I'm not happy about the bookshelf. It's too small.

B: I think so, too.

① 부탁하기 ② 제안하기 ③ 불평하기

④ 선호 묻기 ⑤ 관심 표현하기

[12~13] 다음 대화를 읽고 물음에 답하시오.

B: (A)I'm not happy about the shirt.

G: What's wrong with it?

B: _____

12 위 대화의 빈칸에 들어갈 말은?

① I'm interested in this shirt.

② I'm thinking of buying this shirt.

③ It's too tight for me.

④ This shirt is so comfortable.

⑤ I want to buy some shirts.

서답형

13 위 대화의 밑줄 친 (A)와 같은 의미가 되도록 동사 'want'와 'complain'을 사용하여 문장을 쓰시오.

➡ _____

다음 제시된 물건의 문제점과 해결책을 보고, 주어진 단어를 이용하여 대화의 빈칸을 완성하시오.

locker

• problem – old
• solution – decorate its door

A: (1)_____(happy) the locker. It's too old.
B: I think so, too. Do you have any ideas?
A: (2)_____(think of) its door.
B: That's a good idea.

02 대화의 흐름상 빈칸에 들어갈 표현을 주어진 〈조건〉에 맞게 쓰시오.

A: _____
B: Why? What's wrong?
A: They are too bright.

┤ 조건 ├
• 전등에 대해 불만을 나타내는 표현을 쓸 것.
• 동사 'like'를 이용할 것.

➡ _____

[03~05] 다음 대화를 읽고 물음에 답하시오.

Dad: What are you doing here?
Son: I'm thinking of ways to help Miso.
Dad: What's wrong?

Son: (a)그녀는 혼자서 전등을 켤 수 없어요. This switch is too high for her.
Dad: That's right. _____(A)_____ Do you have any good ideas about that?
Son: I'm thinking of putting a step box here below the switch.
Dad: Good idea. And I'll change the switch to a bigger one.
Son: Great. Grandma will like it, too. She can turn on the light more easily.

03 위 대화의 빈칸 (A)에 들어갈 표현을 주어진 〈조건〉에 맞게 영어로 쓰시오.

┤ 조건 ├
• 아들이 말한 불평에 동의하는 표현을 쓸 것.
• 'happy, about'을 사용할 것.

➡ _____

04 위 대화의 밑줄 친 (a)의 우리말을 주어진 〈조건〉에 맞게 영어로 쓰시오.

┤ 조건 ├
• 재귀대명사를 사용할 것.
• 조동사 can을 활용할 것.
• 8 단어의 문장으로 쓸 것.

➡ _____

05 위 대화를 읽고 다음 물음에 영어로 답하시오.

Q: What will Dad do for Miso and Grandma?

➡ _____

Grammar

1 so+형용사/부사+that+주어+can't ...

> • The shoes were **so** uncomfortable **that** she **couldn't** walk well.
> 신발이 너무 불편해서 그녀는 잘 걸을 수 없었다.

■ so+형용사[부사]+that+주어+can't ...'
 • 의미: 너무 ~해서 …할 수 없다(결과)
 • 형태: so+형용사/부사+that+주어+can't ...

■ 'so+형용사[부사]+that+주어+동사' 구문은 '너무 ~해서 …하다'라는 뜻으로 so 다음에는 형용사나 부사가 나오고 that 다음에는 주어와 동사가 있는 절이 온다. so 다음에 나오는 말이 '원인', that 다음에 나오는 절이 그에 따른 '결과'를 나타낸다.

■ 'so+형용사[부사]+that+주어+can't ...' 구문은 'too+형용사[부사]+to ...' 구문으로 바꿔 쓸 수 있으며, 'so+형용사[부사]+that+주어+can ...' 구문은 '형용사[부사]+enough+to ...' 구문으로 바꿔 쓸 수 있다.

 • It's **so** cold **that** I **can't** go outside. 너무 추워서 나는 밖에 나갈 수 없다.
 = It's **too** cold for me **to** go outside.

 • My sister was **so** smart **that** she **could** solve the problem.
 = My sister was smart **enough to** solve the problem. 내 여동생은 너무 똑똑해서 그 문제를 풀 수 있었다.

■ 'so ... that' 구문에서 that 앞에 형용사나 부사 대신 명사가 오면 so 대신 such를 쓴다.

 • The buses have **such** a low floor **that** even a person in a wheelchair can use them without any help. 그 버스들은 아주 낮은 바닥을 가지고 있어서 휠체어를 탄 사람조차도 아무 도움 없이 이용할 수 있다.

■ 'so that+주어+동사'는 목적을 나타내어 '~하기 위해서' 혹은 '~하도록'이라는 의미로 쓰인다. 'so ~ that ...'과 혼동하지 않도록 유의한다.

 • Amy swims every day **so that** she can stay healthy. Amy는 건강을 유지하기 위해 매일 수영한다.

핵심 Check

1. 다음 괄호 안에서 알맞은 말을 고르시오.
 (1) She was (so / very) tired that she couldn't exercise.
 (2) The dress was so beautiful (that / what) Ann wanted to buy it.
 (3) The box was (too / very) heavy to carry.

② 사역동사

> • What **made** her **do** all this? 무엇이 그녀로 하여금 이 모든 것을 하게 만들었을까?
>
> • I **had** him **wash** my car. 나는 그에게 내 차를 닦게 시켰다.

■ **사역동사**

• 의미: ~하게 하다, ~시키다

• 종류: make, have, let 등

• 형태: 5형식 문장에서 '주어+동사+목적어+동사원형'

(5형식 문장: '주어+동사+목적어+목적격보어'의 어순으로 이루어진 문장을 말한다.)

■ 사역동사는 '사역동사+목적어+목적격보어'의 형태로 '~하게 하다(하라고 시키다)'의 뜻을 가지며 사역동사에는 make, have, let 등이 있다.

• He can **make** us **laugh** all day long. 그는 하루 종일 우리를 웃게 할 수도 있어.

• **Let** your body **relax**. 몸의 긴장을 풀어라.

■ 목적격보어로 동사원형이 오면 능동의 의미로 '~(목적어)가 …(목적격보어)을 하게 하다'의 뜻을 가지며 과거분사가 오면 수동의 의미로 '~(목적어)가 …(목적격보어)을 당하게[되게] 하다'의 뜻을 갖는다.

• I **had** him **write** the letter. 〈능동〉 나는 그에게 그 편지를 쓰게 하였다. (그가 편지를 쓰는 것으로 능동)

• I want to **have** my car **repaired**. 〈수동〉 제 차를 수리하려고 합니다. (차가 수리되는 것으로 수동)

■ 'help'와 'get'의 쓰임

– help는 목적격보어로 동사원형이나 to부정사가 나오며 뜻의 차이는 없다.

• Of course, this **helps** other people **get** on the bus more comfortably, too.
 = Of course, this **helps** other people **to get** on the bus more comfortably, too.
 물론, 이것은 다른 사람들도 버스를 더 편안하게 탈 수 있도록 도와준다.

– get이 '~하게 하다'라는 사역동사의 뜻으로 쓰일 때 목적격보어로 to부정사를 쓴다.

• Mom **got** me **to clean** the room. 〈능동〉 엄마는 내게 방청소를 시키셨다.

• I **got** my car **repaired**. 〈수동〉 나는 내 차가 수리되도록 했다.

핵심 Check

2. 다음 괄호 안에서 알맞은 말을 고르시오.

(1) Mom had my sister (clean / to clean) her room.

(2) My brother helped me (to do / doing) my science project.

(3) The doctor got him (quit / to quit) smoking.

01 다음 문장에서 어법상 <u>어색한</u> 부분을 바르게 고쳐 쓰시오.

(1) Dad made me to wash the car.

_____ ➡ _____

(2) I had him swimming across the river.

_____ ➡ _____

(3) Linda was very sick that she could not go out.

_____ ➡ _____

(4) Eugine was so busy to take a rest.

_____ ➡ _____

02 주어진 단어를 어법에 맞게 빈칸에 쓰시오.

(1) Ms. Kim had the boy _____ a line. (draw)
(2) Mom had the trash _____ away. (throw)
(3) Jessy got her dad _____ her off at her school. (drop)
(4) Courage helped him _____ the game. (win)

03 다음 우리말을 영어로 바르게 옮긴 것은?

> • 창문이 너무 더러워서 밖을 볼 수가 없어.

① The window is very dirty that I can't see through it.
② The window is so dirty that I can't see through it.
③ The window is dirty so that I can't see through it.
④ The window is dirty enough that I can't see through it.
⑤ The window is too dirty that I can't see through it.

04 주어진 단어를 바르게 배열하여 다음 우리말을 영어로 쓰시오. 필요하다면 단어를 변형하시오.

> • 그는 아무도 자신을 찾을 수 없도록 숨었다.
> (he / him / himself / one / find / so / hid / can / no / that)

➡ _____

 다음 빈칸에 알맞은 말이 순서대로 바르게 짝지어진 것은?

• Mr. Kim let the students _____ the classroom.
• This soup is _____ hot that I can't eat it.

① to leave – too
② leaving – very
③ leaving – so
④ leave – very
⑤ leave – so

02 다음 빈칸에 들어갈 말로 적절한 것을 모두 고르시오.

He helped me _____ the chair.

① makes
② making
③ made
④ make
⑤ to make

03 다음 빈칸에 알맞은 말이 바르게 짝지어진 것을 고르시오.

The seat is _____ high _____ I can't sit on it.

① so – that
② that – so
③ very – that
④ too – that
⑤ too – to

서답형

04 주어진 단어를 이용하여 다음 우리말을 영어로 쓰시오. (9 단어)

당신이 너무 빨리 말해서 이해할 수가 없어요.
(I, speak, fast, get)

➡ _____

다음 중 어법상 바르지 않은 것은?

① The teacher let her students listen to the music.
② She got her two boys to divide a cake exactly in half.
③ She will have her son to close the window.
④ He says television helped him to learn English.
⑤ Mom made me go to bed.

서답형

06 괄호 안에서 알맞은 것을 고르시오.

(1) Kate had her son (do / to do) the dishes.
(2) I finished my homework, so Mom let me (watch / watching) TV.
(3) Abigail got her chair (to paint / painted).
(4) Did you (make / help) your kid to take a bath?
(5) Mike got up so late (that / which) he was late for school.
(6) Bill was (so / very) tired that he couldn't take a walk.
(7) The ice cream was (too / very) sweet for me to eat.
(8) He is (too smart / smart enough) to understand this book.

07 다음 중 어법상 바르지 <u>않은</u> 것은?

> Annabell ①had ②some water ③boil ④ to prepare ⑤for dinner.

① ② ③ ④ ⑤

서답형

08 다음 문장에서 어법상 <u>틀린</u> 부분을 찾아 바르게 고쳐 쓰시오.

> He was tall so that he could hardly find any pants that fitted him.

➡ _____ ➡ _____

[09~10] 다음 우리말을 영어로 바르게 옮긴 것을 <u>모두</u> 고르시오.

09

> 그녀는 내가 숙제를 끝낼 수 있도록 도와주었다.

① She helped me finishes my homework.
② She helped me finished my homework.
③ She helped me finish my homework.
④ She helped me to finish my homework.
⑤ She helped me finishing my homework.

10

> 나는 부주의하게도 그 사람을 신용했다.

① I was very careless that I trusted the man.
② I was careless so that I trusted the man.
③ I was so careless that I trusted the man.
④ I was too careless to trust the man.
⑤ I was careless enough to trust the man.

11 다음 문장의 빈칸에 알맞지 <u>않은</u> 말은?

> Merriam _____ him go jogging every morning.

① wanted ② helped
③ let ④ had
⑤ made

12 다음 중 어법상 올바른 문장을 <u>모두</u> 고르시오.

① Emily had her daughters to take care of her dogs.
② I helped my brother to do his homework.
③ This rock is heavy so that I can't lift it.
④ The room was so dark that I turned on the light.
⑤ It was so a nice concert that the $15 for the ticket seemed cheap.

13 다음 중 (A)~(C)에서 어법상 옳은 것끼리 바르게 짝지은 것은?

> • Eddy made Sharon (A)(take / taking) some pictures of him.
> • He got Alexander (B)(teach / to teach) his daughter everything.
> • Andrew had his car (C)(drive / driven) by his son.

	(A)	(B)	(C)
①	taking	teach	driven
②	taking	to teach	drive
③	taking	teach	drive
④	take	to teach	drive
⑤	take	to teach	driven

서답형

14 다음 괄호 안에 주어진 단어를 이용하여 우리말을 영어로 옮기시오.

(1) 창문이 너무 무거워서 나는 그것을 열 수가 없어. (the window, open, heavy, so)

➡ _____

(2) 나의 형의 의자는 너무 낮아서 그가 편안하게 앉을 수 없다. (my brother, sit, low, comfortably, too, on)

➡ _____

(3) 이 벽들은 충분히 두꺼워서 외부의 소리를 차단해 주고 있다. (these walls, shut out, thick, outside, to)

➡ _____

(4) 숙제를 끝마쳐서 엄마는 내가 TV를 보도록 했다. (Mom, TV, watch, finish, let, so)

➡ _____

(5) 체육 선생님은 그 남자아이가 그 공을 가져오게 했다. (the P.E. teacher, the boy, bring, have)

➡ _____

서답형

15 다음 문장에서 어법상 <u>어색한</u> 부분을 바르게 고치시오.

(1) I got the man repairing my car.

_____ ➡ _____

(2) The school makes all the students to wear uniforms.

_____ ➡ _____

(3) The girl was too strong to solve the difficulties.

_____ ➡ _____

중요

16 다음 두 문장을 한 문장으로 바르게 연결한 것은?

• The dress was very expensive.
• So I didn't buy it.

① The dress was very expensive that I didn't buy it.
② The dress was expensive so that I didn't buy it.
③ The dress was so expensive that I didn't buy it.
④ The dress was expensive enough that I didn't buy it.
⑤ The dress was too expensive that I didn't buy it.

17 다음 중 밑줄 친 단어의 쓰임이 〈보기〉 같은 것은?

┤ 보기 ├

Susan <u>makes</u> her daughter clean her room.

① Melanie will <u>make</u> a wise mother.
② He went into the kitchen and <u>made</u> me a sandwich.
③ Everyone wonders if money can <u>make</u> us happy.
④ Our doubts about the weather <u>made</u> us cancel the picnic.
⑤ A cool slice of melon <u>makes</u> an excellent dessert in hot weather.

서답형

18 다음 문장을 주어진 어휘를 이용하여 바꿔 쓰시오.

The box is too heavy for me to move.

(1) so

➡ The box is _____.

(2) because

➡ I can't move the box _____

_____.

01 다음 문장에서 어법상 어색한 부분을 바르게 고쳐 다시 쓰시오.

(1) They made the students to wear school uniforms.

➡ _____

(2) She doesn't let her kids watching TV late at night.

➡ _____

(3) I had my puppy gets me the ball.

➡ _____

(4) My sister asked me to have her computer repair.

➡ _____

(5) I helped my cousin baked some cookies.

➡ _____

(6) He got his sister help him with his homework.

➡ _____

02 다음 두 문장을 〈보기〉와 같이 사역동사를 이용하여 한 문장으로 완성하시오.

┌─ 보기 ┤

• Nick was busy.

• So, he asked his brother to wash his car.

→ Nick had his brother wash his car.

• Patricia had a broken computer.

• So, she asked Benjamin to repair it.

➡ _____

03 다음 문장을 to부정사를 이용하여 바꿔 쓰시오.

(1) My brother is so young that he can't understand the words.

➡ _____

(2) Sam was so smart that he could understand what the scientist said.

➡ _____

(3) This coffee is so hot that I can't drink it.

➡ _____

(4) The bookshelf is so low that my little brother can reach it.

➡ _____

04 〈보기〉에서 의미상 적절한 단어를 골라 빈칸에 알맞은 형태로 쓰시오.

┌─ 보기 ┤

repair carry do wait

(1) She had me _____ the box for her.

(2) My dad had his car _____ by the man.

(3) His girl friend got him _____ for her on the street.

(4) I helped my brother _____ his homework.

05 다음 두 문장을 〈보기〉와 같이 한 문장으로 쓰시오.

> 보기
> The food was very hot. I couldn't eat it.
> → The food was so hot that I couldn't eat it.

(1) • The storm was really strong.
 • We couldn't go out.
 ➡ _____

(2) • I was very tired.
 • I didn't go there.
 ➡ _____

(3) • I can't hear the music.
 • It's because the bus is very noisy.
 ➡ _____

(4) • The fog was very thick.
 • So, driving became really dangerous.
 ➡ _____

06 그림을 보고 괄호 안에 주어진 어구들을 바르게 배열하여 문장을 완성하시오.

(the button, it, people, reach, is, that, in wheelchairs, high, can't, so)

➡ _____

07 다음 문장을 〈보기〉와 같이 주어진 동사를 이용하여 바꿔 쓰시오.

> 보기
> Mr. Kim got Jack to open the window. (have)
> → Mr. Kim had Jack open the window.

(1) Eve let him use her pen. (allow)
 ➡ _____

(2) She forced Dan to follow her advice. (make)
 ➡ _____

08 빈칸을 알맞게 채워 다음 문장과 같은 의미의 문장을 쓰시오.

> The button is very high, so the boy can't push the button.

= The boy can't push the button _____
_____.

= The button is _____
_____.

= The button is _____
_____.

09 다음 그림을 참고하여 단어 take의 알맞은 형태를 빈칸에 채우시오.

➡ The man let the girl _____ a rest under the tree.

Reading

Patricia Moore – Mother of Universal Design

In 1979, a woman started a journey to cities in the U.S. and Canada. She looked over 80. She couldn't see or hear well. She couldn't walk well without a stick.

With all these difficulties, the woman had to climb stairs in subway stations and get on crowded buses. She had to open heavy doors and use can openers with her weak hands. Sometimes she got hurt or found herself in danger. Every moment was very difficult for her, but she visited more than 115 cities and ended her trip in 1982.

Who was the woman and what made her do all this? She was Patricia Moore, a 26-year-old designer. During the 1970's, she worked for a big design company. She often asked at meetings, "How about designing for old or weak people?" The other designers always answered, "We don't design for those people."

She became tired of the same cold answer. Finally, she decided to become one of "those people" and travel around many cities to understand their difficulties better. For this, she put on her grandmother's clothes, uncomfortable shoes, and thick glasses. The shoes were so uncomfortable that she couldn't walk well without a stick. The glasses were so thick that she couldn't see well with them. She also put lots of cotton in her ears to make her hearing bad.

universal: 보편적인
journey: 여행, 여정
station: 역, 정류장
get on: ~을 타다
crowded: 붐비는, 복잡한
company: 회사
tired of: ~에 지친, 싫증 난
uncomfortable: 불편한(↔
comfortable 편한)

 확인문제

● 다음 문장이 본문의 내용과 일치하면 T, 일치하지 않으면 F를 쓰시오.

1 In 1979, a woman who looked over 80 started a journey to cities in the U.S. and Canada. ☐

2 Every moment was very difficult, so she gave up her trip. ☐

3 Patricia's glasses were so thick that she couldn't see well without them. ☐

4 Patricia put lots of cotton in her ears to make her hearing bad. ☐

During her journey, Patricia felt the difficulties old people go
<small>old 앞에 관계대명사 which[that]가 생략</small>

through. From this experience, she designed products anybody could
<small>anybody 앞에 관계대명사 which[that]가 생략</small>

use safely and easily. This was the beginning of "universal design,"

or "design for all."
<small>즉, 다시 말해서: 동격 어구를 연결</small>

One example of her universal design ideas is low-floor buses.
<small>주어 / 동사, are(×)</small>

They have no steps and have such a low floor that even a person
<small>such ~ that 주어 can …: 아주 ~해서 …할 수 있다 such+a[an]+형용사+명사</small>

in a wheelchair can use them without any help. Of course, this

helps other people get on the bus more comfortably, too.
<small>준사역동사 help의 목적격보어: 동사원형 또는 to부정사 (5형식 문장)</small>

Today more and more designers are following Patricia's way.
<small>점점 더 많은 / 현재진행형(be동사+동사-ing)</small>

Products like big flat light switches, doors with easy handles, and
<small>주어 / ~ 같은(전치사)</small>

phones with touch buttons are helping people live better lives.
<small>준사역동사 help의 목적격보어: 동사원형 또는 to부정사 (5형식 문장) / 동족목적어</small>

Look around you, feel the difficulties of people who are older or
<small>동사원형 'Look. feel. try'가 and로 이어진 명령문. / old의 비교급</small>

weaker, and try to find solutions from their point of view. You could
<small>weak의 비교급</small>

be the next Patricia Moore and make the world a better place for
<small>5형식 문장</small>

everybody.

go through: ~을 겪다

product: 상품, 제품

low: 낮은

flat: 평평한

switch: 스위치

handle: 손잡이

view: 견해, 관점

📎 **확인문제**

● 다음 문장이 본문의 내용과 일치하면 T, 일치하지 않으면 F를 쓰시오.

1 During her journey, Patricia felt the difficulties old people go through. ☐

2 One example of Patricia's universal design ideas is low-floor buses. ☐

3 Low-floor buses have no steps and have such a low floor that even a person in a
wheelchair can use them with some help. ☐

4 Low-floor buses are uncomfortable for people who are healthy. ☐

5 Today, there are few designers who are following Patricia's way. ☐

6 Products such as big flat light switches, doors with easy handles, and phones with
touch buttons are helping people live better lives. ☐

우리말을 참고하여 빈칸에 알맞은 말을 쓰시오.

1 Patricia Moore – Mother of _____ _____

2 In 1979, a woman _____ _____ _____ to cities in the U.S. and Canada.

3 She _____ _____ _____.

4 She _____ _____ _____ _____ well.

5 She couldn't walk well _____ _____ _____.

6 _____ _____ _____ _____, the woman had to climb stairs in subway stations and get on crowded buses.

7 She had to open heavy doors and use can openers _____ _____ _____ _____.

8 Sometimes she got hurt or _____ _____ _____ _____.

9 Every moment was _____ _____ _____ _____, but she visited _____ _____ 115 cities and ended her trip in 1982.

10 Who was the woman and _____ _____ _____ _____ all this?

11 She was Patricia Moore, _____ _____ _____.

12 _____ _____ _____, she worked for a big design company.

13 She often asked at meetings, "_____ _____ _____ for old or weak people?"

14 The other designers always answered, "We don't design _____ _____ _____."

15 She _____ _____ _____ the same cold answer.

16 _____, she decided to become one of "those people" and travel around many cities _____ _____ _____ _____ better.

1	Patricia Moore – 유니버설 디자인의 어머니
2	1979년에, 한 여성이 미국과 캐나다의 도시로 여행을 시작했다.
3	그녀는 80세가 넘어 보였다.
4	그녀는 잘 보거나 잘 들을 수 없었다.
5	그녀는 지팡이가 없이는 잘 걸을 수 없었다.
6	이 모든 어려움을 가진 채, 그 여성은 지하철역에서 계단을 올라가거나 붐비는 버스에 올라타야 했다.
7	그녀는 무거운 문을 열거나 그녀의 약한 손으로 깡통 따개를 사용해야 했다.
8	때때로 그녀는 다치거나 위험에 처하기도 했다.
9	모든 순간이 그녀에게 매우 어려웠으나, 그녀는 115개 이상의 도시를 방문하였으며 1982년에 여행을 끝마쳤다.
10	그 여성은 누구였고 무엇이 그녀로 하여금 이 모든 것을 하게 만들었을까?
11	그녀는 26살의 디자이너인 Patricia Moore였다.
12	1970년대 동안, 그녀는 큰 디자인 회사에서 일했다.
13	그녀는 종종 회의에서 물었다. "나이 들거나 약한 사람들을 위해 디자인하는 게 어떨까요?"
14	다른 디자이너들은 항상 대답했다. "우리는 그런 사람들을 위해 디자인하지 않습니다."
15	그녀는 똑같은 냉담한 대답에 지쳤다.
16	마침내, 그녀는 '그런 사람들' 중의 하나가 되어 그들의 어려움을 더 잘 이해하기 위해 많은 도시를 여행하기로 결심했다.

17 _____ _____, she put on her grandmother's clothes, _____ shoes, and _____ _____.

18 The shoes were _____ uncomfortable _____ she _____ walk well _____ _____ _____.

19 The glasses were _____ thick _____ she _____ see well _____ _____.

20 She also put lots of cotton in her ears _____ _____ _____ _____ _____.

21 _____ her journey, Patricia felt the difficulties old people _____ _____.

22 _____ this experience, she designed products anybody could use _____ and _____.

23 This was the beginning of "_____ _____," or "_____ _____."

24 _____ _____ of her universal design ideas is low-floor _____.

25 They have _____ _____ and have _____ _____ _____ _____ that even a person _____ _____ _____ can use them _____ _____ _____.

26 Of course, this helps other people get on the bus _____ _____, too.

27 Today more and more designers are _____.

28 Products _____ big flat light switches, doors with easy handles, and phones with touch buttons are helping people _____ _____.

29 Look around you, feel the difficulties of people who are older or weaker, and try to find solutions _____ _____ _____.

30 You could be the _____ Patricia Moore and make the world _____ _____ _____ _____ _____.

17 이를 위해, 그녀는 자신의 할머니 옷을 입고, 불편한 신발을 신고, 두꺼운 안경을 썼다.

18 신발은 너무 불편해서 그녀는 지팡이가 없이는 잘 걸을 수 없었다.

19 안경은 너무 두꺼워서 그녀는 안경을 쓰고는 잘 볼 수 없었다.

20 그녀는 또한 그녀의 청력을 나쁘게 하려고 귀에 많은 솜을 넣었다.

21 여행 동안, Patricia는 나이 든 사람들이 겪는 어려움을 느꼈다.

22 이 경험으로부터, 그녀는 누구나 안전하고 쉽게 사용할 수 있는 제품들을 고안했다.

23 이것이 '유니버설 디자인' 또는 '모두를 위한 디자인'의 시작이었다.

24 그녀의 유니버설 디자인 아이디어의 한 가지 예는 저상 버스이다.

25 그것은 계단이 없고 낮은 바닥을 가지고 있어서 휠체어를 탄 사람조차 아무 도움 없이 이용할 수 있다.

26 물론, 이것은 다른 사람들도 버스를 더 편안하게 탈 수 있도록 도와준다.

27 오늘날 점점 더 많은 디자이너가 Patricia의 방식을 따르고 있다.

28 크고 평평한 조명 스위치, 편한 손잡이를 가진 문, 터치 버튼을 가진 전화기와 같은 제품들은 사람들이 더 나은 삶을 살도록 도와주고 있다.

29 여러분의 주위를 둘러보고, 더 나이 들거나 더 약한 사람들의 어려움을 느껴 보고, 그들의 관점에서 해결책을 찾으려고 노력해 봐라.

30 여러분은 다음의 Patricia Moore가 되어 세상을 모두에게 더 나은 곳으로 만들 수 있을 것이다.

● 우리말을 참고하여 본문을 영작하시오.

1 Patricia Moore – 유니버설 디자인의 어머니

➡ _____

2 1979년에, 한 여성이 미국과 캐나다의 도시로 여행을 시작했다.

➡ _____

3 그녀는 80세가 넘어 보였다.

➡ _____

4 그녀는 잘 보거나 잘 들을 수 없었다.

➡ _____

5 그녀는 지팡이 없이는 잘 걸을 수 없었다.

➡ _____

6 이 모든 어려움을 가진 채, 그 여성은 지하철역에서 계단을 올라가거나 붐비는 버스에 올라타야 했다.

➡ _____

7 그녀는 무거운 문을 열거나 그녀의 약한 손으로 깡통 따개를 사용해야 했다.

➡ _____

8 때때로 그녀는 다치거나 위험에 처하기도 했다.

➡ _____

9 모든 순간이 그녀에게 매우 어려웠으나, 그녀는 115개 이상의 도시를 방문하였으며 1982년에 여행을 끝마쳤다.

➡ _____

10 그 여성은 누구였고 무엇이 그녀로 하여금 이 모든 것을 하게 만들었을까?

➡ _____

11 그녀는 26살의 디자이너인 Patricia Moore였다.

➡ _____

12 1970년대 동안, 그녀는 큰 디자인 회사에서 일했다.

➡ _____

13 그녀는 종종 회의에서 물었다. "나이 들거나 약한 사람들을 위해 디자인하는 게 어떨까요?"

➡ _____

14 다른 디자이너들은 항상 대답했다. "우리는 그런 사람들을 위해 디자인하지 않습니다."

➡ _____

15 그녀는 똑같은 냉담한 대답에 지쳤다.

➡ _____

16 마침내, 그녀는 '그런 사람들' 중의 하나가 되어 그들의 어려움을 더 잘 이해하기 위해 많은 도시를 여행하기로 결심했다.

➡ _____

17 이를 위해, 그녀는 자신의 할머니 옷을 입고, 불편한 신발을 신고, 두꺼운 안경을 썼다.

➡ _____

18 신발은 너무 불편해서 그녀는 지팡이 없이는 잘 걸을 수 없었다.

➡ _____

19 안경은 너무 두꺼워서 그녀는 안경을 쓰고는 잘 볼 수 없었다.

➡ _____

20 그녀는 또한 그녀의 청력을 나쁘게 하려고 귀에 많은 솜을 넣었다.

➡ _____

21 여행 동안, Patricia는 나이 든 사람들이 겪는 어려움을 느꼈다.

➡ _____

22 이 경험으로부터, 그녀는 누구나 안전하고 쉽게 사용할 수 있는 제품들을 고안했다.

➡ _____

23 이것이 '유니버설 디자인' 또는 '모두를 위한 디자인'의 시작이었다.

➡ _____

24 그녀의 유니버설 디자인 아이디어의 한 가지 예는 저상 버스이다.

➡ _____

25 그것은 계단이 없고 낮은 바닥을 가지고 있어서 휠체어를 탄 사람조차 아무 도움 없이 이용할 수 있다.

➡ _____

26 물론, 이것은 다른 사람들도 버스를 더 편안하게 탈 수 있도록 도와준다.

➡ _____

27 오늘날 점점 더 많은 디자이너가 Patricia의 방식을 따르고 있다.

➡ _____

28 크고 평평한 조명 스위치, 편한 손잡이를 가진 문, 터치 버튼을 가진 전화기와 같은 제품들은 사람들이 더 나은 삶을 살도록 도와주고 있다.

➡ _____

29 여러분의 주위를 둘러보고, 더 나이 들거나 더 약한 사람들의 어려움을 느껴 보고, 그들의 관점에서 해결책을 찾으려고 노력해 봐라.

➡ _____

30 여러분은 다음의 Patricia Moore가 되어 세상을 모두에게 더 나은 곳으로 만들 수 있을 것이다.

➡ _____

[01~04] 다음 글을 읽고 물음에 답하시오.

Who was the woman and what made her do all this? She was Patricia Moore, a (A)[26-year-old / 26-years-old] designer. During the 1970's, she worked for a big design company. She often asked at meetings, "How about designing for ①old or weak people?" (B)[Another / The other] designers always answered, "②We don't design for ③those people."

She became tired of ⓐthe same cold answer. Finally, she decided to become one of "④those people" and travel around many cities to understand ⑤their difficulties better. For this, she put on her grandmother's clothes, uncomfortable shoes, and thick glasses. The shoes were so uncomfortable that she couldn't walk well without a stick. The glasses were so thick that she couldn't see well with (C)[it / them]. She also put lots of cotton in her ears to make her hearing bad.

서답형

01 위 글의 괄호 (A)~(C)에서 문맥이나 어법상 알맞은 낱말을 골라 쓰시오.

➡ (A) _____ (B) _____ (C) _____

중요

02 위 글의 밑줄 친 ①~⑤ 중에서 가리키는 대상이 나머지 넷과 다른 것은?

① ② ③ ④ ⑤

서답형

03 위 글의 밑줄 친 ⓐthe same cold answer가 가리키는 것을 본문에서 찾아 쓰시오.

➡ _____

중요

04 위 글의 제목으로 알맞은 것을 고르시오.

① Patricia's Real Age
② Designers Refused Patricia's Proposal
③ Patricia Tried to Understand the Old in Person
④ Patricia Looked Old for Her Age
⑤ The Difficulties the Old Experience

[05~07] 다음 글을 읽고 물음에 답하시오.

In 1979, a woman started a journey to cities in the U.S. and Canada. She looked over 80. She couldn't see or hear well. She couldn't walk well without a stick.

With all these _____ⓐ_____, the woman had to climb stairs in subway stations and get on crowded buses. She had to open heavy doors and use can openers with her weak hands. ⓑSometimes she got hurt or found herself in danger. Every moment was very difficult for her, but she visited more than 115 cities and ended her trip in 1982.

서답형

05 본문의 한 단어를 변형하여 위 글의 빈칸 ⓐ에 들어갈 알맞은 단어를 쓰시오.

➡ _____

06 위 글의 밑줄 친 ⓑSometimes와 바꿔 쓸 수 없는 말을 고르시오.

① Once in a while ② Rarely
③ Now and then ④ At times
⑤ From time to time

서답형

07 본문의 내용과 일치하도록 다음 빈칸 (A)와 (B)에 알맞은 단어를 쓰시오.

> She started a (A)_____ to cities in the U.S. and Canada in 1979, and after visiting over (B)_____ _____, she ended it in 1982.

➡ (A) _____ (B) _____

[08~10] 다음 글을 읽고 물음에 답하시오.

During her journey, Patricia felt the difficulties old people go through. From this experience, she designed products anybody could use (A)[safe and easy / safely and easily]. This was the beginning of "universal design," or "design for all."

One example of her universal design ideas is low-floor buses. They have no steps and have (B)[so / such] a low floor that even a person in a wheelchair can use ⓐthem without any help. Of course, this helps other people ___(a)___ on the bus more (C)[comfortable / comfortably], too.

08 위 글의 빈칸 (a)에 들어갈 알맞은 말을 모두 고르시오.

① to get ② got
③ having got ④ get
⑤ getting

서답형

09 위 글의 괄호 (A)~(C)에서 어법상 알맞은 낱말을 골라 쓰시오.

➡ (A) _____ (B) _____
(C) _____

10 위 글의 밑줄 친 ⓐthem이 가리키는 것을 본문에서 찾아 쓰시오.

➡ _____

[11~13] 다음 글을 읽고 물음에 답하시오.

Today more and more designers are following Patricia's way. Products ⓐlike big flat light switches, doors with easy handles, and phones with touch buttons are helping people live better lives. Look around you, feel the difficulties of people ___(A)___ are older or weaker, and try to find solutions from their ⓑpoint of view. You could be ⓒ the next Patricia Moore and make the world a better place for everybody.

11 위 글의 빈칸 (A)에 들어갈 알맞은 말을 모두 고르시오.

① what ② who ③ whom
④ which ⑤ that

서답형

12 위 글의 밑줄 친 ⓐlike, ⓑpoint of view와 바꿔 쓸 수 있는 단어들을 각각 쓰시오.

➡ ⓐ _____ ⓑ _____

서답형

13 위 글의 밑줄 친 ⓒthe next Patricia Moore가 되기 위해 해야 할 일을 우리말로 쓰시오.

➡ _____

[14~16] 전시 중인 제품에 대한 다음 글을 읽고 물음에 답하시오.

ⓐThe washing machine door in my house is so high that my little brother can't put clothes easily into it.　(A)　, this machine has a side door. It'll help my brother put clothes in more easily.

중요

14 위 글의 빈칸 (A)에 들어갈 알맞은 말을 고르시오.

① Therefore　　② For example
③ In addition　　④ However
⑤ In other words

서답형

15 위 글의 밑줄 친 ⓐ를 다음과 같이 바꿔 쓸 때 빈칸에 들어갈 알맞은 말을 쓰시오.

➡ The washing machine door in my house is _____ high _____ my little brother _____ put clothes easily into it.

서답형

16 현재 집에 있는 세탁기의 단점과 전시 중인 제품에서 개선된 점을 우리말로 쓰시오.

➡ 현재 집에 있는 세탁기의 단점: _____

전시 중인 제품에서 개선된 점: : _____

[17~19] 다음 글을 읽고 물음에 답하시오.

In 1979, a woman started a journey to cities ___ⓐ___ the U.S. and Canada. She looked over 80. She couldn't see or hear well. She couldn't walk well without a stick.

With all these difficulties, the woman had to climb stairs ___ⓑ___ subway stations and get on crowded buses. She had to open heavy doors and use can openers with her weak hands. Sometimes she got hurt or found herself ___ⓒ___ danger. Every moment was very difficult ___ⓓ___ her, but she visited (a)more than 115 cities and ended her trip ___ⓔ___ 1982.

서답형

17 위 글의 빈칸 ⓐ~ⓔ에 들어갈 전치사가 나머지와 다른 것을 고르시오.

➡ _____

서답형

18 위 글의 밑줄 친 (a)more than과 바꿔 쓸 수 있는 단어를 본문에서 찾아 쓰시오.

➡ _____

중요

19 위 글의 내용과 일치하지 않는 것은?

① A woman started a trip to cities in the U.S. and Canada in 1979.
② It was difficult for her to see or hear well.
③ Her eyesight and hearing were not good.
④ From time to time, she got hurt.
⑤ Because of so many difficulties, she gave up her journey.

[20~22] 다음 글을 읽고 물음에 답하시오.

During her journey, Patricia felt the difficulties old people ⓐgo through.　(A)　 this experience, ⓑ그녀는 누구나 안전하고 쉽게 사용할 수 있는 제품들을 고안했다. This was the beginning of "universal design," or "design for all."

One example of her universal design ideas is low-floor buses. They have no steps and have such a low floor that even a person ___(B)___ a wheelchair can use them without any help. Of course, this helps other people get on the bus more comfortably, too.

20 위 글의 빈칸 (A)와 (B)에 들어갈 전치사가 바르게 짝지어진 것은?

① For – by
② From – in
③ With – in
④ For – to
⑤ From – by

서답형

21 위 글의 밑줄 친 ⓐgo through와 바꿔 쓸 수 있는 한 단어를 본문에서 찾아 쓰시오.

➡ _____

서답형

22 위 글의 밑줄 친 ⓑ의 우리말에 맞게 주어진 어휘를 이용하여 9 단어로 영작하시오.

> products, anybody, safely, easily

➡ _____

[23~25] 다음 글을 읽고 물음에 답하시오.

She became tired of the same cold answer. (①) For this, she put on her grandmother's clothes, uncomfortable shoes, and thick glasses. (②) ⓐThe shoes were so uncomfortable that she couldn't walk well without a stick. (③) The glasses were so thick that she couldn't see well with ⓑthem. (④) She also put lots of cotton in her ears to make her hearing bad. (⑤)

중요

23 위 글의 흐름으로 보아, 주어진 문장이 들어가기에 가장 적절한 곳은?

> Finally, she decided to become one of "those people" and travel around many cities to understand their difficulties better.

① ② ③ ④ ⑤

24 위 글의 밑줄 친 ⓐ와 같은 의미의 문장을 모두 고르시오.

① The shoes were such uncomfortable that she couldn't walk well without a stick.
② The shoes were too uncomfortable for her to walk well without a stick.
③ The shoes were very uncomfortable, so she couldn't walk well without a stick.
④ The shoes were uncomfortable enough for her to walk well without a stick.
⑤ The shoes were uncomfortable in order that she couldn't walk well without a stick.

서답형

25 위 글의 밑줄 친 ⓑthem이 가리키는 것을 본문에서 찾아 쓰시오.

➡ _____

[26~28] 전시 중인 제품에 대한 다음 글을 읽고 물음에 답하시오.

The desk in my house is so high that my little sister can't use it ___ⓐ___ . However, this desk has special legs. ⓑIt'll help my sister read books more comfortably.

서답형

26 위 글의 빈칸 ⓐ에 with ease와 같은 뜻의 한 단어를 쓰시오.

➡ _____

서답형

27 다음 빈칸에 알맞은 단어를 넣어 밑줄 친 ⓑIt에 대한 설명을 완성하시오.

> this desk with _____

28 Why is it difficult for the little sister to use her desk in her house? Fill in the blanks with the suitable words.

➡ It's because it is _____ for her _____ with ease.

[01~03] 다음 글을 읽고 물음에 답하시오.

In ⓐ1979, a woman started a journey to cities in the U.S. and Canada. She (A)[looked / looked like] over 80. She couldn't see or hear well. ⓑShe couldn't walk well with a stick.

ⓒWithout all these difficulties, the woman had to climb stairs in subway stations and get on (B)[crowding / crowded] buses. She had to open heavy doors and use can openers with her weak hands. Sometimes she got hurt or found (C)[her / herself] in danger. Every moment was very difficult for her, but she visited more than ⓓ115 cities and ended her trip in ⓔ1982.

중요

01 위 글의 괄호 (A)~(C)에서 어법상 알맞은 낱말을 골라 쓰시오.

➡ (A) _____ (B) _____ (C) _____

02 위 글의 밑줄 친 ⓐ1979, ⓓ115, ⓔ1982를 영어로 읽는 법을 쓰시오.

➡ ⓐ _____ ⓓ _____

ⓔ _____

03 위 글의 밑줄 친 ⓑ와 ⓒ에서 흐름상 어색한 부분을 찾아 고치시오.

➡ ⓑ _____ ⓒ _____

[04~06] 다음 글을 읽고 물음에 답하시오.

Who was the woman and what made her do all this? She was Patricia Moore, a 26-year-old designer. During the 1970's, she worked for a big design company. She often asked at meetings, "How about designing for old or weak people?" The other designers always answered, "We don't design for those people."

She became tired of the same cold answer. Finally, she decided ⓐto become one of "those people" and travel around many cities to understand their difficulties better. For this, she put on her grandmother's clothes, uncomfortable shoes, and thick glasses. The shoes were so uncomfortable that she couldn't walk well without a stick. ⓑThe glasses were so thick that she couldn't see well with them. She also put lots of cotton in her ears to make her hearing bad.

04 위 글에서 Patricia가 밑줄 친 ⓐ의 결심을 실천하기 위해 했던 일을 우리말로 쓰시오.

➡ (1) _____

(2) _____

중요

05 위 글의 밑줄 친 ⓑ를 다음과 같이 바꿔 쓸 때 빈칸에 들어갈 알맞은 말을 쓰시오.

➡ The glasses were _____ thick _____ her _____ see well with them.

06 본문의 내용과 일치하도록 다음 빈칸 (A)와 (B)에 알맞은 단어를 쓰시오.

Patricia tried to understand the difficulties of (A)_____ _____ _____ people better by becoming one of "(B)_____ _____" and traveling around many cities.

[07~08] 다음 글을 읽고 물음에 답하시오.

During her journey, Patricia felt the difficulties old people go through. ⓐFrom this experience, she designed products anybody could use them safely and easily. This was the beginning of "universal design," or "design for all."

One example of her universal design ideas is low-floor buses. They have no steps and have such a low floor that even a person in a wheelchair can use them without any help. Of course, this helps other people get on the bus more ⓑcomfort, too.

07 위 글의 밑줄 친 ⓐ에서 어법상 틀린 부분을 찾아 고치시오.

_____ ➡ _____

08 위 글의 밑줄 친 ⓑ를 알맞은 형으로 바꿔 쓰시오.

➡ _____

[09~11] 다음 글을 읽고 물음에 답하시오.

Today more and more designers are following Patricia's way. Products like big flat light switches, doors with easy handles, and ⓐphones with touch buttons are helping people living better lives. Look around you, feel the difficulties of people who are older or weaker, and try to find solutions ⓑfrom their point of view. You could be the next Patricia Moore and make the world a better place for everybody.

09 위 글에서 Patricia의 방식을 따라 디자이너들이 만든 제품의 예를 우리말로 쓰시오. (세 가지)

➡ (1) _____ (2) _____
 (2) _____

10 위 글의 밑줄 친 ⓐ에서 어법상 틀린 부분을 찾아 고치시오.

_____ ➡ _____

11 위 글의 밑줄 친 ⓑ를 다음과 같이 바꿔 쓸 때 빈칸에 들어갈 알맞은 말을 쓰시오.

➡ from the point of view of _____ or _____ people

[12~13] 다음 글을 읽고 물음에 답하시오.

ⓐThe hole cover was so dangerous that I couldn't ride my bike on it. So I want to change the cover like this. The new cover will help people ride a bike __(A)__.

12 위 글의 빈칸 (A)에 in safety와 바꿔 쓸 수 있는 한 단어를 쓰시오.

➡ _____

13 위 글의 밑줄 친 ⓐ를 다음과 같이 바꿔 쓸 때 빈칸에 들어갈 알맞은 말을 쓰시오.

➡ The hole cover was _____ dangerous, _____ I couldn't ride my bike on it.

해석

Express Yourself C1

The washing machine door in my house is so high that my little brother can't
　　　　　　　　　　　　　　　　　　　so+형용사/부사+that+주어+can't … = too ~ to … = very ~. so+주어+can't …

put clothes easily into it. However, this machine has a side door. It'll help my
　　　　　　　put을 수식하는 부사

brother put clothes in more easily.
　　　= to put　　　　　　easily의 비교급

구문해설 ・ washing machine: 세탁기 ・ however: 그러나 ・ side door: 옆문 ・ clothes: 옷

우리 집에 있는 세탁기 문은 너무 높아서 나의 남동생은 그 안에 옷을 쉽게 넣을 수 없다. 그러나, 이 기계는 옆문을 가지고 있다. 그것은 내 남동생 옷을 더 쉽게 넣을 수 있도록 도와줄 것이다.

Project Step 3

The hole cover was so dangerous that I couldn't ride my bike on it. So I want
　　　　　　　　　　　　so+형용사+that+주어+can't … = too ~ to …　　　　　= the hole cover

to change the cover like this. The new cover will help people ride a bike
　　　　　　　　　　　　전치사　　　　　　　　　　　　　　준사역동사　　목적격보어(= to ride)

safely.

구문해설 ・ hole cover: 맨홀 덮개

맨홀 덮개가 너무 위험해서 나는 그 위에서 자전거를 탈 수 없었다. 그래서 나는 덮개를 이렇게 바꾸고 싶다. 새로운 덮개는 사람들이 자전거를 안전하게 타도록 도와줄 것이다.

Link to the World

・ Kim Mandeok was born to a poor family in Jeju. She worked hard and
　　　　　　　　　　…에서 태어났다

become rich.

・ In 1794, lots of people in Jeju were dying of hunger because of bad weather.
　　　　　　　　　　　　　　　　　…로 죽어가고 있었다　　　'~ 때문에' 뒤에 명사가 나온다.

・ She spent almost all she had and saved a lot of people.
　　　　　　　　　　목적격 관계대명사절로 선행사 'all'을 수식

・ King Jeongjo let her take a trip to Mountain Geumgang.
　　　　　　　　let+목적어+동사원형: …가 ~하도록 허락하다

구문해설 ・ lots of: 많은 ・ hunger: 굶주림 ・ because of+명사(구): … 때문에 ・ save: 구하다
・ take a trip: 여행하다

・ 김만덕은 제주의 가난한 가정에서 태어났다. 그녀는 열심히 일해서 부자가 되었다.

・ 1794년에 제주의 많은 사람이 나쁜 날씨로 인해 굶주림으로 죽어가고 있었다.

・ 그녀는 자신이 가진 거의 모든 것을 써서 많은 사람을 구했다.

・ 정조 임금은 그녀가 금강산으로 여행을 하도록 허락했다.

영역별 핵심문제

01 다음 주어진 두 단어의 관계가 같도록 빈칸에 주어진 철자로 단어를 쓰시오.

> comfortable : uncomfortable
> = loose : _____

02 다음 빈칸에 들어갈 말이 바르게 짝지어진 것은?

> Look around you, feel the _____ of people who are older or weaker, and try to find _____ from their point of _____.

① difficulties – solutions – place
② difficulties – help – place
③ difficulties – solutions – view
④ experience – help – design
⑤ experience – solutions – view

03 다음 영영풀이에 해당하는 것을 고르시오.

> having a lot of people or too many people

① station ② huge
③ vacant ④ crowded
⑤ company

04 다음 빈칸에 들어갈 말이 바르게 짝지어진 것은?

> • I have _____ finished my homework.
> • The dog helps the _____ man.
> • Be careful when you _____ the street.

① almost – old – across
② almost – blind – cross
③ almost – old – reach
④ most – blind – cross
⑤ most – old – across

05 다음 그림을 보고, 빈칸에 알맞은 단어를 쓰시오.

➡ Ted _____ _____ with his dog every day.

06 다음 밑줄 친 부분의 의미가 바르지 <u>않은</u> 것은?

① She designed <u>products</u> anybody could use safely and easily. (생산적인)
② One <u>example</u> of her universal design ideas is low-floor buses. (예, 사례)
③ This helps other people get on the bus more <u>comfortably</u>. (편안하게)
④ This room has a <u>low</u> ceiling. (낮은)
⑤ Laughter is a <u>universal</u> language. (보편적인)

07 대화의 밑줄 친 우리말에 맞게 주어진 단어를 알맞은 순서로 배열하시오.

> G: I'm not happy about the sign. <u>볼 수 없는 사람들도 좀 있잖아.</u>
> B: Right.

(are / can't / people / who / there / some / see)

➡ _____

08 자연스러운 대화가 되도록 알맞은 순서로 배열한 것은?

> (A) They are too bright.
> (B) Why? What's wrong?
> (C) I'm not happy about the lights.
> (D) I see. Let's switch to other lights.

① (A) – (B) – (C) – (D)
② (B) – (A) – (C) – (D)
③ (C) – (A) – (B) – (D)
④ (C) – (B) – (A) – (D)
⑤ (D) – (B) – (A) – (C)

09 주어진 문장이 들어갈 위치로 알맞은 것은?

> G: I'm not happy about my brother's chair. (①) It's too low and too hard.
> B: Right. (②) I'm thinking of buying this one. (③)
> G: Looks great. (④) I think he can use it for so long, even after he grows taller. (⑤)

> What do you think?

① ② ③ ④ ⑤

[10~12] 다음 대화를 읽고 물음에 답하시오.

> Dad: What are you doing here?
> Son: _____(A)_____ ways to help Miso.
> Dad: What's wrong?
> Son: She can't turn on the light ⓐby herself. This switch is ⓑtoo high for her.
> Dad: That's right. I'm not happy about it, ⓒtoo. Do you have any good ideas about that?
> Son: _____(B)_____ putting a step box here below the switch.
> Dad: Good idea. And I'll change the switch to a ⓓbigger one.

> Son: Great. Grandma will like it, too. She can turn on the light ⓔmore easily.

10 위 대화의 빈칸 (A)와 (B)에 공통으로 들어갈 말로 알맞은 것은?

① I know
② I'm going to
③ I'm not satisfied with
④ I'm interested in
⑤ I'm thinking of

11 위 대화의 밑줄 친 ⓐ~ⓔ 중, 어법상 어색한 것은?

① ⓐ ② ⓑ ③ ⓒ ④ ⓓ ⑤ ⓔ

12 위 대화를 읽고 답할 수 없는 질문은?

① Can Miso turn on the light by herself?
② What will Dad do for Miso and Grandma?
③ What will the boy do to help Miso?
④ What's wrong with the step box?
⑤ Who came up with the idea of a bigger switch?

Grammar

13 다음 중 어법상 바르지 않은 것은?

① The river is too deep for you to swim in.
② He is rich enough to buy the car.
③ The food was so salty that I couldn't eat it.
④ It was such a fine day that we took a walk to the park.
⑤ I was very thirsty that I drank a bottle of water.

14 주어진 어휘를 이용하여 다음 우리말을 영어로 옮길 때 두 번째와 다섯 번째로 오는 단어를 쓰시오.

> 그것은 나의 할머니께서 문을 더 편안하게 여실 수 있도록 도와줄 것이다.
> (It'll, my grandma, comfortably)

➡ _____

15 다음 문장을 so와 that을 이용하여 바꾸어 쓰시오.

(1) This question is too difficult for me to solve.

➡ _____

(2) The big panel was light enough to float on the water.

➡ _____

(3) He held her by the sleeve very tightly, so she couldn't ran away.

➡ _____

(4) I can't hear the music because the bus is very noisy.

➡ _____

(5) He took a taxi not to be late.

➡ _____

[16~17] 다음 빈칸에 알맞은 것을 고르시오.

16
> Mike's room is a mess. I'll have it _____.

① clean ② cleans

③ cleaned ④ cleaning

⑤ to clean

17
> My grandma is _____ sick that she can't go out.

① too ② enough

③ so ④ such

⑤ very

18 다음 그림을 보고 괄호 안에 주어진 어휘를 이용하여 빈칸에 알맞은 말을 쓰시오.

> My friend got hurt. I should have him _____ to the hospital. (take)

19 다음 빈칸에 알맞은 말이 순서대로 짝지어진 것은?

> • The princess got her maid _____ her hair smoothly.
> • Olivia helped me _____ a birthday cake.

① brushing – make

② to brush – making

③ to brush – to make

④ brush – made

⑤ brush – make

20 다음 중 어법상 올바른 것은?

① He is enough tall to touch the ceiling.

② Nobody could catch up with her so that she ran fast.

③ Ron asked me to have his computer repair.

④ The teacher let the students play outside.

⑤ I'll have him copied all the files for the meeting.

21 다음 중 어법상 올바른 문장의 개수는?

ⓐ Ella had her pictures taken.

ⓑ The teacher let Joseph play the guitar singing a song.

ⓒ Sarah always lets me to use her laptop computer.

ⓓ It'll help my grandma eating food more comfortably.

ⓔ My dad got the robot to do a lot of house work.

ⓕ He had his bicycle repaired yesterday.

ⓖ Charlotte did her best to have the project finish on time.

① 1개　② 2개　③ 3개　④ 4개　⑤ 5개

Reading

[22~24] 다음 글을 읽고 물음에 답하시오.

(A)[During / For] her journey, ⓐPatricia felt the difficulties old people go through. (①) From this experience, she designed products (B)[anybody / somebody] could use safely and easily. (②)

One example of her universal design ideas (C)[is / are] low-floor buses. (③) They have no steps and have such a low floor that even a person in a wheelchair can use them without any help. (④) Of course, this helps other people get on the bus more comfortably, too. (⑤)

22 위 글의 괄호 (A)~(C)에서 문맥이나 어법상 알맞은 낱말을 골라 쓰시오.

➡ (A) _____ (B) _____ (C) _____

23 위 글의 밑줄 친 문장 ⓐ에 생략된 말을 넣어 문장을 다시 쓰시오.

➡ _____

24 위 글의 흐름으로 보아, 주어진 문장이 들어가기에 가장 적절한 곳은?

This was the beginning of "universal design," or "design for all."

①　　②　　③　　④　　⑤

[25~26] 다음 글을 읽고 물음에 답하시오.

In 1979, a woman started a journey to cities in the U.S. and Canada. She looked over 80. She couldn't see or hear well. She couldn't walk well without a stick.

With ⓐall these difficulties, the woman had to climb stairs in subway stations and get on crowded buses. ⓑShe had to open heavy doors and used can openers with her weak hands. Sometimes she got hurt or found herself in danger. Every moment was very difficult for her, but she visited more than 115 cities and ended her trip in 1982.

25 위 글의 밑줄 친 ⓐall these difficulties가 가리키는 내용을 우리말로 쓰시오.

➡ (1) _____

 (2) _____

26 위 글의 밑줄 친 ⓑ에서 어법상 틀린 부분을 찾아 고치시오.

_____ ➡ _____

[27~29] 다음 글을 읽고 물음에 답하시오.

 She became ⓐtired of the same cold answer. Finally, she decided to become one of "those people" and travel around many cities to understand their difficulties better. For this, she put on her grandmother's clothes, uncomfortable shoes, and thick glasses. The shoes were so uncomfortable that she couldn't walk well without a stick. The glasses were so thick that she couldn't see well with them. She also put lots of cotton in her ears to ⓑmake her hearing bad.

27 위 글의 밑줄 친 ⓐtired of와 바꿔 쓸 수 있는 말을 모두 고르시오.

① sick of ② tired with

③ worn out ④ bored with

⑤ tired from

28 위 글의 밑줄 친 ⓑ와 문장의 형식이 같은 것을 모두 고르시오.

① make me a dress

② make him play the piano

③ make him very happy

④ make toward home

⑤ make a fortune

29 다음 중 Patricia에 대한 설명으로 옳지 않은 것은?

① 많은 도시를 여행하기로 결심했다.

② 자신의 할머니 옷을 입었다.

③ 자신의 할머니의 불편한 신발을 신었다.

④ 자신의 할머니의 두꺼운 안경을 썼다.

⑤ 청력이 나쁜 사람이었다.

[30~31] 다음 글을 읽고 물음에 답하시오.

 Today more and more designers are following Patricia's way. Products like big flat light switches, doors with easy handles, and phones with touch buttons are helping people live better lives. Look around you, feel the difficulties of people who are older or weaker, and try ⓐto find solutions from their point of view. You could be the next Patricia Moore and make the world a better place for everybody.

30 아래 〈보기〉에서 위 글의 밑줄 친 ⓐto find와 문법적 쓰임이 다른 것의 개수를 고르시오.

┤ 보기 ├
① It's not easy to find solutions to this.

② He decided to find solutions to this.

③ I was so happy to find solutions to this.

④ She wants to find solutions to this.

⑤ Show me the way to find solutions to this.

① 1개 ② 2개 ③ 3개 ④ 4개 ⑤ 5개

31 위 글의 제목으로 알맞은 것을 고르시오.

① How to Follow Patricia's Way

② Produce Big Flat Light Switches

③ Popular Phones with Touch Buttons

④ Find Solutions from Others' Viewpoint

⑤ The Invention of Eco-friendly Products

출제율 90%

01 다음 문장의 빈칸에 적당한 말을 쓰시오.

> She couldn't walk well without a
> _____.

출제율 95%

02 우리말에 맞게 빈칸에 알맞은 단어를 쓰시오.

> (A) 과거에 사람들은 지구가 평평하다고 믿었다.
> ➡ In the past, people believed the Earth
> was _____.
> (B) 문을 열고 싶다면 문손잡이를 돌리세요.
> ➡ Turn the door _____ if you want to
> open the door.

출제율 95%

03 다음 대화의 빈칸에 알맞은 표현은?

> G: I'm not happy about the button.
> B: Why? What's wrong with it?
> G: _____ Children or people in
> wheelchairs can't reach it. I'm thinking
> of putting another switch for them.

① It's too small.　② It's too tight.
③ It's too high.　④ It takes long time.
⑤ It's too bright.

출제율 85%

04 다음 영영풀이에 해당하는 단어는?

> a cupboard, often tall and made of metal,
> in which you can keep your possessions,
> and leave them for a period of time

① backpack　② tool
③ pad　④ swing
⑤ locker

[05~07] 다음 대화를 읽고 물음에 답하시오.

Dad: What are you doing here?
Son: I'm thinking of ways to help Miso.
Dad: What's wrong? (①)
Son: She can't turn on the light by herself. This
switch is too high for her.
Dad: That's right. (②) Do you have any good
ideas about that?
Son: (③) I'm thinking of putting a step box
here below the switch.
Dad: (④) Good idea. And I'll change the
switch to a bigger one.
Son: Great. (⑤) Grandma will like it, too. She
can turn on the light more easily.

출제율 95%

05 위 대화의 ①~⑤ 중, 주어진 문장이 들어갈 위치로 알맞은
것은?

> I'm not happy about it, either.

①　②　③　④　⑤

출제율 95%

06 위 대화의 제목으로 알맞은 것은?

① Importance of Helping Others
② Difficulty of Doing the Housework
③ How to Install the Switch
④ Good Ideas for Family
⑤ Being Good to Grandma

출제율 100%

07 위 대화의 내용과 일치하지 <u>않는</u> 것은?

① The switch is too high for Miso.
② The boy will put a step box below the
switch.
③ Both the boy and his dad aren't happy
with the switch.
④ The boy's grandma can't turn on the
switch by herself.
⑤ The boy's grandma will like the new switch.

[08~09] 다음 대화를 읽고 물음에 답하시오.

G: _____(A)_____
B: Why? What's wrong?
G: It's too small. Grandma can't use it easily.
B: Do you have any ideas?
G: _____(B)_____ That'll help her turn on the light easily.
B: Good idea.

08 위 대화의 빈칸 (A)에 알맞은 표현은?
출제율 90%

① I'm not happy about the locker.
② I'm not happy about the TV.
③ I'm not happy about this light switch.
④ I'm not happy about the board.
⑤ I'm not happy about the mirror.

09 위 대화의 빈칸 (B)에 알맞은 표현은?
출제율 95%

① I'm thinking of putting a cushion on it.
② I'm thinking of hanging a wiper on it.
③ I'm thinking of putting a step box below it.
④ I'm thinking of hanging a bigger and safer seat.
⑤ I'm thinking of changing it with a bigger one.

10 다음 대화의 빈칸에 문제의 해결책을 주어진 〈조건〉에 맞게 쓰시오.
출제율 85%

G: I'm not happy about the sign. There are some people who can't see.
B: Right. Do you have any ideas?
G: Well, _____
B: That's a good idea.

┌─ 조건 ─┐
- '나는 …할까 생각 중이다'라는 뜻으로, 의도나 계획을 나타내는 표현을 쓸 것.
- 'be / think of / add / Braille / the sign'을 이용할 것.
└────────┘

➡ _____

11 다음 우리말을 주어진 표현을 이용하여 영작하시오.
출제율 90%

그녀는 매우 친절해서 나에게 역으로 가는 길을 말해 주었다. (so ~ that)

➡ _____

12 다음 글에서 어법상 틀린 부분을 모두 찾아 바르게 고쳐 쓰시오.
출제율 90%

The hole cover was very dangerous that I couldn't ride my bike on it. So I want to change the cover like this. The new cover will help people riding a bike safely.

➡ _____, _____

[13~14] 어법상 올바른 문장을 모두 고르시오.

13
출제율 100%

① It'll help my grandma take a bath more comfortably.
② Ms. Han made her son to go to bed immediately.
③ It gave him so a shock that he couldn't say a word.
④ I am such tired that I can't walk any more.
⑤ The car is so expensive that I can't buy it.

14
① I'm so tired to go there.

② The man is rich enough that he can buy the big house.

③ This problem is too difficult to solve.

④ King Jeongjo let her take a trip to Mountain Geumgang.

⑤ Mom made me cleaning my room.

[15~16] 다음 글을 읽고 물음에 답하시오.

Who was the woman and what made her _____ⓐ_____ all this? She was Patricia Moore, a 26-year-old designer. During the 1970's, she worked for a big design company. She often asked at meetings, "How about designing for old or weak people?" The other designers always answered, "We don't design for those people."

She became tired of the same cold answer. Finally, she decided ⓑto become one of "those people" and travel around many cities ⓒto understand their difficulties better. For this, she put on her grandmother's clothes, uncomfortable shoes, and thick glasses. The shoes were so uncomfortable that she couldn't walk well without a stick. The glasses were so thick that she couldn't see well with them. She also put lots of cotton in her ears to make her hearing bad.

15 위 글의 빈칸 ⓐ에 들어갈 알맞은 말을 고르시오.

① to do　　② do　　③ done

④ doing　　⑤ to have done

16 다음 〈보기〉에서 위 글의 밑줄 친 ⓑto become, ⓒto understand와 to부정사의 용법이 같은 것을 각각 고르시오.

┌── 보기 ──┐

① It was not easy to understand their difficulties.

② She was very happy to become one of "those people."

③ I tried to understand their difficulties.

④ He wanted to understand their difficulties.

⑤ Tom went to New York to become one of "those people."

└────────┘

➡ ⓑ와 용법이 같은 것: _____

　ⓒ와 용법이 같은 것: _____

[17~19] 다음 글을 읽고 물음에 답하시오.

During her journey, Patricia felt the difficulties old people go through. From this experience, she designed products anybody could use safely and easily. This was the beginning of "universal design," or "design for all."

One example of her universal design ideas is low-floor buses. ⓐ그것들은 계단이 없고 낮은 바닥을 가지고 있어서 that even a person in a wheelchair can use them without any help. Of course, this helps other people get on the bus more comfortably, too.

17 위 글의 밑줄 친 ⓐ의 우리말에 맞게 주어진 어휘를 알맞게 배열하시오.

such / steps / have / floor / and / no / a / have / low / they

18 위 글의 주제로 알맞은 것을 고르시오.

① the difficulties old people go through

② how to design safely and easily

③ the beginning of "universal design"

④ the strong points of low floor buses

⑤ people who can help other people

19 본문의 내용과 일치하도록 다음 빈칸 (A)와 (B)에 알맞은 단어를 쓰시오.

> Patricia created "(A)_____ _____"
> from the experience she went through
> in person, and it could be "(B)_____
> _____ _____" as you can see in the
> case of low floor buses.

[20~22] 다음 글을 읽고 물음에 답하시오.

> In 1979, a woman started a ⓐjourney to
> cities in the U.S. and Canada. (①) She looked
> over 80. (②) She couldn't see or hear well.
> She couldn't walk well without a stick.
> (③) She had to open heavy doors and use can
> openers with her weak hands. (④) Sometimes
> she got hurt or found herself in danger. (⑤)
> Every moment was very difficult for her, but
> she visited more than 115 cities and ended her
> trip in 1982.

20 위 글의 흐름으로 보아, 주어진 문장이 들어가기에 가장 적절한 곳은?

> With all these difficulties, the woman
> had to climb stairs in subway stations
> and get on crowded buses.

① ② ③ ④ ⑤

21 위 글의 밑줄 친 ⓐjourney와 바꿔 쓸 수 있는 단어를 쓰시오.

➡ _____

22 본문의 내용과 일치하도록 다음 빈칸 (A)와 (B)에 알맞은 단어를 쓰시오.

> Though there were many (A)_____,
> the woman visited more than (B)_____
> _____ in the U.S. and Canada and
> ended her trip in 1982.

[23~24] 다음 글을 읽고 물음에 답하시오.

> Today more and more designers are
> following Patricia's way. Products like big
> ___ⓐ___ light switches, doors with easy
> ___ⓑ___, and phones with ___ⓒ___ buttons are
> helping people live better lives. Look around
> you, feel the difficulties of people who are
> older or weaker, and try to find solutions from
> their point of view. You could be the next
> Patricia Moore and make the world a better
> place for everybody.

23 다음 그림을 참조하여 위 글의 빈칸 ⓐ~ⓒ에 들어갈 알맞은 말을 쓰시오.

➡ ⓐ _____ ⓑ _____ ⓒ _____

24 다음 문장에서 위 글의 내용과 <u>다른</u> 부분을 찾아서 고치시오.

> To be the next Patricia Moore and make
> the world a better place for everybody,
> you should feel the difficulties of people
> who are older or weaker, and try to find
> solutions from your viewpoint.

_____ ➡ _____

01 대화의 우리말 해석에 맞게 주어진 어구를 알맞은 순서로 배열하시오.

> B: I'm not happy about the lights.
> G: What's wrong with them?
> B: 색맹인 사람들에게는 신호등이 똑같아 보일 거야.
> G: Oh, I see. How about putting an image on each light?
> B: A walking man on the green light and a standing man on the red light? Good idea!

> (the traffic / the same / who / to / lights / look / blind to / some people / colors / are)

➡ _____

02 주어진 그림과 글을 보고 대화의 빈칸을 완성하시오.

My brother's chair is so low that he can't sit on it comfortably. However, this chair has special pads. They'll help my brother read books more comfortably.

> G: _____ my brother's chair. It's _____ and too hard.
> B: Right. _____ buying this one. What do you think?
> G: Looks great. I think he can read books more _____.

03 다음 대화를 읽고 아래의 요약문을 완성하시오.

> Dad: What are you doing here?
> Son: I'm thinking of ways to help Miso.
> Dad: What's wrong?
> Son: She can't turn on the light by herself. This switch is too high for her.
> Dad: That's right. I'm not happy about it, either. Do you have any good ideas about that?
> Son: I'm thinking of putting a step box here below the switch.
> Dad: Good idea. And I'll change the switch to a bigger one.
> Son: Great. Grandma will like it, too. She can turn on the light more easily.

> Miso can't turn on the light _____ because the switch is too _____ for her. So, her brother decides to put _____ _____ the switch to help her. Dad also will _____ the switch to a _____ one for Miso and Grandma so that they can turn it on _____.

04 다음 문장을 make를 이용하여 비슷한 의미의 문장으로 바꿔 쓰시오.

(1) Mom told me to throw away the trash.

➡ _____

(2) The teacher ordered the students to do homework.

➡ _____

(3) Anna asked her daughter to come home early at night.

➡ _____

05 다음 문장을 to부정사를 이용하여 다시 쓰시오.

(1) Betty was so busy that she couldn't come to the party.

➡ _____

(2) This food is so delicious that I can eat it all.

➡ _____

(3) This problem is so easy that anyone can solve it.

➡ _____

06 다음 두 문장을 to부정사를 이용하여 하나의 문장으로 쓰시오.

(1) • This ice cream is very cold.
 • I can't eat it.

➡ _____

(2) • It rained really hard.
 • We couldn't play soccer.

➡ _____

[07~09] 다음 글을 읽고 물음에 답하시오.

Who was the woman and ⓐwhat made her do all this? She was Patricia Moore, a 26-year-old designer. During the 1970's, she worked for a big design company. She often asked at meetings, "ⓑHow about designing for ⓒold or weak people?" The other designers always answered, "We don't design for those people."

07 위 글의 밑줄 친 ⓐ를 다음과 같이 바꿔 쓸 때 빈칸에 들어갈 알맞은 말을 쓰시오.

➡ _____ did she do all this?

08 위 글의 밑줄 친 ⓑ를 다음과 같이 바꿔 쓸 때 빈칸에 들어갈 알맞은 말을 쓰시오.

➡ (1) _____ about designing
 (2) _____ don't we design
 (3) _____ we design

09 위 글의 밑줄 친 ⓒ와 같은 뜻이 되도록 다음 빈칸에 알맞은 단어를 쓰시오.

➡ _____ old or _____ weak

[10~12] 다음 글을 읽고 물음에 답하시오.

During her journey, Patricia felt the difficulties old people go through. From ⓐthis experience, she designed products anybody could use safely and easily. This was the beginning of "ⓑuniversal design," or "design for all."

One example of her universal design ideas is low-floor buses. ⓒThey have no steps and have such a low floor that even a person in a wheelchair can use them without any help. Of course, this helps other people get on the bus more comfortably, too.

10 위 글의 밑줄 친 ⓐthis experience가 가리키는 내용을 우리말로 쓰시오.

➡ _____

11 위 글에서 ⓑuniversal design의 예를 찾아 영어로 쓰시오.

➡ _____

12 위 글의 밑줄 친 ⓒ를 다음과 같이 바꿔 쓸 때 빈칸에 들어갈 알맞은 말을 쓰시오.

➡ They have no steps and their floor is _____ low

01 각 물건의 문제점과 그에 대한 해결책을 제시하는 대화를 〈보기〉와 같이 쓰시오.

〈물건의 문제점〉

locker – too old / bookshelf – too small

〈해결책〉

decorate its door / put another bookshelf on it

〈보기〉

A: I'm not happy about the bookshelf. It's too small.

B: I think so, too. Do you have any ideas?

A: I'm thinking of putting another bookshelf on it.

B: That's a good idea.

02 〈보기〉에 주어진 표현과 사역동사나 so와 that을 이용하여 4 문장 이상 쓰시오.

보기

clean his room fix her computer go to the K-pop concert

cried very loudly / covered my ears spoke very fast / could not understand him

(1) _____

(2) _____

(3) _____

(4) _____

03 다음 내용을 바탕으로, 불편한 점을 개선하여 디자인한 작품의 안내문을 쓰시오.

• 불편한 점: The desk is too high for my little sister to use easily.

• 개선한 점: This desk has special legs.

The desk in my house is (A)_____ high (B)_____ my little sister (C)_____ use it easily. However, this desk has (D)_____. It'll help my sister read books more comfortably.

단원별 모의고사

01 다음 단어에 대한 영어 설명이 <u>어색한</u> 것은?

① company: a business organization that makes money by producing or selling goods or services

② pad: a button or key that controls the light or machine

③ handle: a part that is designed especially to be held by the hand

④ solution: the answer to a problem

⑤ uncomfortable: not feeling comfortable and pleasant

02 우리말에 맞게 문장의 빈칸에 세 단어를 쓰시오.

> 여러분의 주위를 둘러보고, 더 나이 들거나 더 약한 사람들의 어려움을 느껴 보고, 그들의 관점에서 해결책을 찾으려고 노력해 봐.
>
> ➡ Look around you, feel the difficulties of people who are older or weaker, and try to find solutions from their _____.

03 다음 영영풀이에 해당하는 단어를 고르시오.

> a building or place where buses or trains stop so that people can get on or off

① company　　　② bathtub

③ cushion　　　④ station

⑤ seat

04 그림을 보고 대화의 빈칸 (A)와 (B)에 들어갈 말을 쓰시오.

G: I'm (A)_____ of buying this spoon. It will help my grandma eat soup easily.

B: Right. She (B)_____ it with her fingers.

05 다음 대화의 빈칸에 들어갈 말로 <u>어색한</u> 것은?

A: _____

B: Why? What's wrong?

A: There are not enough chairs here. I'm thinking of telling the guide to give us more chairs.

① I'm not happy about this place.

② I'm not satisfied with this place.

③ This place is not satisfactory to me.

④ I'm not content with this place.

⑤ I don't want to complain about this place.

06 대화의 빈칸에 들어갈 말로 알맞은 것은?

G: I'm not happy about the button.

B: Why? What's wrong with it?

G: It's too high. Children or people in wheelchairs can't _____ it. I'm thinking of putting another switch for them.

① reach　　　② take　　　③ bring

④ distinguish　　　⑤ add

07 다음 대화의 빈칸에 들어갈 말로 알맞은 것은?

> B: I'm not happy about the desk. It's too low.
> G: Right. _____
> B: Good idea.

> ┤ 조건 ├
> • 계획이나 의도를 말하는 표현을 쓸 것.
> • B가 한 불만에 대한 해결책으로 'put some pads'를 사용할 것.
> • 'intend to'를 사용할 것.

➡ _____

[08~09] 다음 대화를 읽고 물음에 답하시오.

Dad: What are you doing here?
Son: I'm thinking of ways to help Miso.
Dad: What's wrong?
Son: She can't turn on the light by herself. This switch is too high for her.
Dad: That's right. 나도 그것이 마음에 들지 않는구나. Do you have any good ideas about that?
Son: _____ (A)
Dad: Good idea. And I'll change the switch to a bigger one.
Son: Great. Grandma will like it, too. She can turn on the light more easily.

08 위 대화의 흐름상 빈칸 (A)에 들어갈 말로 알맞은 것은?

① I'm thinking of buying this spoon.
② I'm not happy about my brother's chair.
③ I'm thinking of hanging a wiper on it.
④ I'm thinking of putting a step box here below the switch.
⑤ I'm thinking of putting another bookshelf on it.

09 밑줄 친 우리말에 맞게 'happy'를 사용하여 영어로 쓰시오.

➡ _____

10 대화의 빈칸에 들어갈 말로 가장 알맞은 것은?

> G: I don't like the high steps here.
> _____
> B: Right. I'm thinking of building a new way with no steps.

① The music is too loud.
② It's too low and too hard.
③ People in wheelchairs can't get in.
④ There are some people who are blind to colors.
⑤ There are some people who can't see.

11 다음 대화의 빈칸에 적절한 말은?

> G: I'm not happy about the sign.
> _____
> B: Right. Do you have any ideas?
> G: Well, I'm thinking of adding Braille on the sign.
> B: That's a good idea.

① People in wheelchairs can't get on it easily.
② There are some people who are blind to colors.
③ There are some people who can't see.
④ It's too low and too hard.
⑤ There are not enough signs here.

12 대화의 밑줄 친 우리말에 맞게 주어진 단어를 활용하여 영어로 쓰시오.

> G: I'm not happy about this light switch.
> B: Why? What's wrong?
> G: It's too small. Grandma can't use it easily.
> B: Do you have any ideas?
> G: 나는 그것을 더 큰 것으로 바꿀까 생각 중이야. That'll help her turn on the light easily.
> B: Good idea.

> (think of / change / with / one)

➡ _____

13 다음 두 문장을 'so ~ that' 구문을 사용하여 한 문장으로 연결하여 쓰시오.

(1) • The noise was very loud.
 • So, I couldn't sleep.

 ➡ _____

(2) • I can't get on the bus.
 • Because the steps are so high.

 ➡ _____

14 다음 중 어법상 올바르지 않은 것은?

① The teacher had his students to follow the rules.
② Minsu helped his friend walk to the school nurse.
③ Mr. Yi let the girl get some rest under the tree.
④ This chair was so uncomfortable that nobody could sit on it for a long time.
⑤ The bus handle is so high that I can't hold it.

15 다음 문장에서 어법상 어색한 부분을 바르게 고치시오.

(1) The bathtub in my house is too high for my grandma to get in it easily.

 _____ ➡ _____

(2) The man had me to carry his luggage.

 _____ ➡ _____

[16~17] 다음 글을 읽고 물음에 답하시오.

Today more and more designers are following ⓐPatricia's way. Products like big flat light switches, doors with easy handles, and phones with touch buttons are helping people live better lives. Look around you, feel the difficulties of people who are older or weaker, and try to find solutions ⓑfrom their point of view. You could be the next Patricia Moore and make the world a better place for everybody.

16 다음 빈칸 (A)와 (B)에 알맞은 단어를 넣어 ⓐPatricia's way 에 대한 설명을 완성하시오.

> It's the way to help people live (A)_____ _____ by feeling the difficulties of people who are older or weaker, and trying to find (B)_____ from their viewpoint.

17 위 글의 밑줄 친 ⓑ를 다음과 같이 바꿔 쓸 때 빈칸에 들어갈 알맞은 말을 쓰시오.

➡ by putting yourself in _____ shoes

[18~19] 다음 글을 읽고 물음에 답하시오.

During her journey, Patricia felt the difficulties old people go through. From this experience, she designed products anybody could use safely and easily. This was the beginning of "universal design," or "design for all."

One example of her universal design ideas is low-floor buses. They have no steps and have such a low floor that even a person in a wheelchair can use them without any help. Of course, ⓐthis helps other people get on the bus more comfortably, too.

18 위 글의 밑줄 친 ⓐthis가 가리키는 것을 본문에서 찾아 쓰시오.

➡ _____

19 위 글의 내용과 일치하지 <u>않는</u> 것은?

① Patricia는 여행 동안 나이 든 사람들이 겪는 어려움을 느꼈다.

② 이 경험으로부터, 그녀는 누구나 안전하고 쉽게 사용할 수 있는 제품들을 고안했다.

③ Patricia가 자신의 여행 경험으로부터 제품들을 고안한 것이 '유니버설 디자인'의 시작이었다.

④ 유니버설 디자인 아이디어의 한 가지 예는 저상 버스이다.

⑤ 휠체어를 타지 않은 사람들은 저상 버스를 탈 때 불편함을 느낀다.

[20~21] 다음 글을 읽고 물음에 답하시오.

She became tired of the same cold answer. ⓐFinally, she decided to become one of "those people" and travel around many cities to understand their difficulties better. For this, she put on her grandmother's clothes,

uncomfortable shoes, and thick glasses. ⓑThe shoes were so uncomfortable that she couldn't walk well with a stick. ⓒThe glasses were so thick that she couldn't see well without them. She also put lots of cotton in her ears to make her hearing bad.

20 위 글의 밑줄 친 ⓐFinally와 바꿔 쓸 수 <u>없는</u> 말을 <u>모두</u> 고르시오.

① In the end ② Actually

③ Especially ④ At last

⑤ In the long run

21 위 글의 밑줄 친 ⓑ와 ⓒ에서 흐름상 <u>어색한</u> 부분을 찾아 고치시오.

➡ ⓑ _____ ⓒ _____

[22~23] 다음 글을 읽고 물음에 답하시오.

With all these difficulties, the woman had to climb stairs in subway stations and get _____ⓐ_____ crowded buses. She had to open heavy doors and use can openers with her weak hands. ⓑSometimes she got hurt or found her in danger. Every moment was very difficult _____ⓒ_____ her, but she visited more than 115 cities and ended her trip in 1982.

22 위 글의 빈칸 ⓐ와 ⓒ에 알맞은 전치사로 짝지어진 것은?

① on – for ② in – with

③ on – from ④ to – for

⑤ in – from

23 위 글의 밑줄 친 ⓑ에서 어법상 어색한 것을 고쳐 쓰시오.

_____ ➡ _____

Special

Teens' Magazine

Words & Expressions

Key Words

- **activity** [əktívəti] 명 활동
- **bread** [bred] 명 빵
- **break time** 쉬는 시간
- **bright** [brait] 형 밝은, 똑똑한
- **brrr** 감 부르르, 부들부들
- **can** [kæn] 명 캔, 깡통
- **change** [tʃeindʒ] 동 갈아입다, 바꾸다
- **choose** [tʃu:z] 동 고르다
- **circle** [sə́rkl] 명 동그라미, 원
- **close** 부 [klous] 가까이 동 [klouz] 닫다
- **clothes** [klouz] 명 옷
- **cute** [kju:t] 형 귀여운
- **delicious** [dilíʃəs] 형 맛있는
- **dessert** [dizə́rt] 명 후식, 디저트
- **enjoy** [indʒɔ́i] 동 즐기다
- **exactly** [igzǽktli] 부 정확하게
- **favorite** [féivərit] 형 가장 좋아하는
- **finish** [fíniʃ] 동 끝나다, 끝내다
- **friendly** [fréndli] 형 친근한, 다정한
- **grade** [greid] 명 성적
- **handwriting** [hǽndraitiŋ] 명 손 글씨
- **hopeful** [hóupful] 형 희망적인
- **like** [laik] 전 ~처럼, ~와 같이
- **mirror** [mírər] 명 거울

- **most** [moust] 형 대부분의
- **never** [névər] 부 결코 ~ 하지 않다
- **ocean** [óuʃən] 명 바다, 대양
- **outside** [áutsàid] 부 밖에
- **P.E. class** 체육 수업
- **place** [place] 명 장소 동 놓다, 두다
- **recycle bin** 재활용 수거함
- **save** [seiv] 동 절약하다
- **second** [sékənd] 명 초, 짧은 시간, 두 번째
- **slow** [slou] 형 느린
- **shape** [ʃeip] 명 모양, 도형
- **sky** [skai] 명 하늘
- **special** [spéʃəl] 형 특별한
- **sweet** [swi:t] 명 단것, 단 음식
- **though** [ðou] 접 비록 ~일지라도
- **trash can** 쓰레기 통
- **umbrella** [ʌmbrélə] 명 우산
- **visit** [vízit] 동 방문하다
- **wave** [weiv] 동 파도치다, 손을 흔들다
- **wet** [wet] 형 젖은
- **wheel** [hwi:l] 명 바퀴
- **winner** [wínər] 명 승자
- **youth** [ju:θ] 명 젊음, 청춘

Key Expressions

- **add A to B** A를 B에 더하다
- **a lot of** 많은
- **be full of** ~로 가득 차다
- **break down into** ~로 부서지다
- **cover A up with B** B로 A를 덮다
- **cut A into B** A를 B로 자르다
- **don't need to** ~할 필요가 없다
- **in such a way that ~** ~하게 되는 방식으로
- **in the middle of** ~의 한가운데에

- **make a presentation** 발표하다
- **wait a second** 잠깐 기다리다
- **such as** ~와 같은
- **take a break** 휴식을 취하다
- **take a test** 시험을 치다
- **take A to B** A를 B로 데려가다
- **up and down** 위아래로
- **up to** ~까지
- **walk back** 물러서다

Word Power

※ 서로 반대되는 뜻을 가진 어휘

- □ **fun** (재미있는) ↔ **boring** (지루한)
- □ **handsome** (잘생긴) ↔ **ugly** (못생긴)
- □ **push** (누르다) ↔ **pull** (당기다)
- □ **hungry** (배고픈) ↔ **full** (배부른)
- □ **close** (닫다) ↔ **open** (열다)

- □ **wet** (젖은) ↔ **dry** (마른)
- □ **slow** (느린) ↔ **fast** (빠른)
- □ **outside** (밖에) ↔ **inside** (안에)
- □ **same** (같은) ↔ **different** (다른)
- □ **close** (가까이) ↔ **far** (멀리)

※ 서로 비슷한 뜻을 가진 어휘

- □ **a lot of** : **lots of** (많은)
- □ **delicious** : **tasty** (맛있는)
- □ **sleepy** : **drowsy** (졸린)
- □ **finish** : **end** (끝내다)
- □ **choose** : **pick** (고르다)
- □ **exactly** : **accurately** (정확하게)

- □ **handsome** : **good-looking** (잘생긴)
- □ **though** : **although** (비록 ~일지라도)
- □ **be full of** : **be filled with** (~으로 가득 차다)
- □ **such as** : **like** (~와 같은)
- □ **shape** : **figure** (도형)
- □ **bright** : **clever** (똑똑한)

English Dictionary

- □ **bread** 빵
 → a food made from flour, water, and usually yeast, mixed together and baked
 밀가루, 물 및 보통 효모로 만들어지고 함께 섞어서 구워진 음식

- □ **choose** 고르다
 → to decide what you want from two or more things or possibilities
 둘 또는 그 이상의 것이나 가능성으로부터 원하는 것을 결정하다

- □ **circle** 원
 → a continuous curved line, the points of which are always the same distance away from a fixed central point
 고정된 중심점으로부터 항상 동일한 거리인 점들의 연속된 곡선

- □ **friendly** 친절한
 → behaving in a pleasant, kind way towards someone
 누군가를 향해 유쾌하고 친절하게 행동하는

- □ **grade** 성적
 → a number or letter that shows how good someone's work or performance is
 누군가의 일이나 수행이 얼마나 좋은지 보여주는 숫자나 글자

- □ **save** 절약하다
 → to keep something, especially money, for use in the future
 미래에 사용하기 위해 어떤 것, 특히 돈을 간직하다

- □ **wave** 손을 흔들다
 → to raise your hand and move it from side to side as a way of greeting someone
 누군가에게 인사하는 방식으로써 손을 들어올려 옆으로 흔들다

- □ **wheel** 바퀴
 → a circular object connected at the centre to a bar, used for making vehicles or parts of machines move
 중심에서 막대기에 연결되어 차량 또는 기계 부품을 이동시키기 위해 사용되는 원형 물체

- □ **youth** 젊음
 → the period of your life when you are young, or the state of being young
 당신이 젊을 때의 인생 시기, 혹은 젊은 상태

Reading

Teens' Magazine

Works of Art in Shapes

Like a Circle

I love you like a circle because a circle never ends.
전치사(~처럼, ~와 같이)

Snowman

It's cold outside.
밖에(는)
I don't want to go out and play.
But Mom says I have to.
It's starting to snow and I'm going to be cold.
I don't like playing outside on days like these.
=like to play
But wait a second, I have the most wonderful idea!
I'll cover myself up with snow and I'll hide here! brrr... brrr...

Looking Back with Your Handwriting

Life is art. Live yours in COLOR.
=your life
IT ISN'T OVER UNTIL IT'S OVER.
be over: 끝나다
I am a slow walker, but I never walk back.
빈도부사로, be동사 뒤에, 일반동사 앞에 위치
I love the little things you do.
'you' 앞에 목적격 관계대명사 'that'이 생략
Follow your dream.

My Bike

Two wheels take me / To any place / To school / Back home / To the
take ~ to ...: ~을 ...로 데려가다
mountain / To the river / I love my bike / I enjoy riding it every day
'enjoy'는 동명사를 목적어로 취하는 동사

Giving Tree

Out there – wet
In here – dry
Pretty big umbrella
형용사 앞에서: (부사) '꽤, 상당히'
Between me and the sky

circle: 동그라미, 원
second: 초, 짧은 시간, 두 번째
wait a second: 잠깐만
cover ~ up with ...: ~의 위까지 ...로 덮다
brrr: 부르르, 부들부들
slow: 느린 ↔ fast 빠른
never: 결코 ...하지 않다
walk back: 물러서다
wheel: 바퀴
wet: 젖은, 축축한
dry 마른
sky: 하늘

 확인문제

● 다음 문장이 본문의 내용과 일치하면 T, 일치하지 않으면 F를 쓰시오.

1 The bike takes the writer to any place. ☐

2 The giving tree is like an umbrella between the writer and the sky. ☐

Selfies of This Year

Though we lost the game, we had a lot of fun.
양보의 뜻을 지닌 접속사(비록 …이지만)

Look at the robots we made. Aren't they cute?
'we made' 앞에는 목적격 관계대명사 that[which]이 생략

We made a big cake for Mr. Han. It made him happy.
5형식. him은 목적어이고 happy는 목적격 보어로 형용사

Have you ever seen a handsome Peter Pan like me?
'경험'을 묻는 현재완료의 의문문 전치사(…와 같이)

What Do You Think of Your School Life?

The most uncomfortable moment
↔ comfortable

1. When I take tests

2. When I am really hungry and have nothing to eat
to부정사의 형용사적 용법

3. When I change clothes before and after P.E. class
cloth: 옷감 clothes: 옷

4. others: When I am sleepy in class

When the teacher doesn't finish classes after the bell rings

The most lovely time

1. Lunch time

2. Class with my favorite teacher

3. The last class on Friday

4. others: When I am sleeping during break time

When I see myself in the mirror
재귀대명사(주어와 목적어가 동일인)

The most awesome news

1. I got better grades than before

2. School finishes earlier today
early의 비교급

3. I don't go to school because it rains or snows a lot

4. others: We eat delicious sweets for dessert

My best friend and I are in the same class

cute: 귀여운

break time: 쉬는 시간

grade: 등급. 성적

choose: 고르다

sweet: 단것

확인문제

● 다음 문장이 본문의 내용과 일치하면 T, 일치하지 않으면 F를 쓰시오.

1 Thanks to the cake that Mr. Han made, we felt happy. ☐

2 To students, taking tests is the most uncomfortable. ☐

3 The students don't like the last class on Friday. ☐

The most difficult work to do
형용사적 용법의 to부정사
1. Washing trash cans

2. Studying

3. Making a presentation in front of friends
~ 앞에(서)
4. others: Being on time every day
동명사
Group work

make a presentation 발표하다

youth: 젊음, 청춘

such as: …와 같은

take a break: 휴식을 취하다

cut ~ into …: ~을 …로 자르다

place: 놓다, 두다; 장소, 곳

in such a way that …: …하게 되는 방식으로

exactly: 정확하게

Places We Love in Our Village

Daehan Traditional Market - 10 Likes

If you want to eat something delicious, visit Daehan Market. You can buy "*yeopjeon*" and use it to make your lunch box full. You can
목적을 나타내는 to부정사의 부사적 용법
choose many kinds of food and add them to your lunch box.

Saebom Youth Center - 12 Likes

This is Saebom Youth Center in the middle of our town. We like this place because we can learn many things, such as dance and
~와 같은
music. We can also play board games and take a break here.

Mr. Kim's Bakery - 12 Likes

This is a small bakery near the school. We like to go there after school because we're always hungry! It is good to enjoy delicious
가주어 진주어
bread with friends.

Let's Have Fun with Puzzles!

Shape Puzzles

If you cut the shape A into two same pieces, you can then make all the other shapes(B, C, D, E, F, G) from those two pieces.

Ten Balls in Five Lines

Place 10 balls in 5 lines in such a way that each line has exactly 4
a way를 수식하는 관계대명사절
balls on it.

확인문제

● 다음 문장이 본문의 내용과 일치하면 T, 일치하지 <u>않으면</u> F를 쓰시오.

1 To students, the most difficult work to do is doing their homework. ☐

2 At Saebom Youth Center, students can learn many things. ☐

You Are Eating Plastic Spoons!

1. A lot of plastic spoons are thrown away every year.
_{'be동사+과거분사' 형태의 수동태이다. thrown은 throw의 과거분사}

2. Most plastic breaks down into smaller pieces in the ocean.
_{대부분의}

3. Very small pieces of plastic go into fish.

4. If you eat the fish, you eat the plastic, too. Up to 11,000 pieces each year!
_{up to: ~까지}

Let's Make a Dream School!

We had a universal design contest for our school last month. Here are the winners' works.

1. When your hands come close, water comes out. When you pull your hands away, the water stops. You don't need to turn or touch any parts. We can save lots of water with this. – by O Juyeon(1-3)

2. This is our school park between two buildings. Anybody can go up and down easily here. Also we can sit and get some rest here. – by Gim Jimin(3-5)
_{anybody가 긍정문에 쓰여 '어떤 누구라도'의 의미}

3. These are special desks and chairs for the classroom. For group activities, you can get them together and make a wonderful group table for three, four, or five students. – by Choi Yumi(2-1)

LET'S LAUGH

Funny Earth Day Jokes Ha! Ha! Ha!

Why are recycle bins hopeful?

- Because they're full of cans.
_{be full of: ~으로 가득 차다}

How can you tell the ocean is friendly?
_{'the ocean' 앞에 접속사 that이 생략된 문장. that절은 tell의 목적어}

- It waves.

Why did the sun go to school?

- To get brighter.
_{get+형용사: ~해지다}

Sidebar:
break down into: …로 부서지다
winner: 승자
close: 가까이
don't need to: …할 필요가 없다
up and down: 위아래로
recycle bin: 재활용 수거함
can: 캔, 깡통
friendly: 친근한, 다정한
wave: 파도치다, 손을 흔들다
bright: 밝은, 똑똑한

 확인문제

● 다음 문장이 본문의 내용과 일치하면 T, 일치하지 않으면 F를 쓰시오.

1 Many plastic spoons are thrown away every year. ☐

2 The fish eat the plastic up to 11,000 pieces each year. ☐

3 The sun goes to school to get brighter. ☐

우리말을 참고하여 빈칸에 알맞은 말을 쓰시오.

1 _____ Magazine

2 Works of Art _____ _____

3 _____ a Circle

4 I love you _____ a circle _____ a circle never ends.

5 _____

6 It's cold _____.

7 I don't want to _____ _____ and _____.

8 But Mom says I _____ _____.

9 It's starting _____ _____ and I'm going to _____
_____.

10 I don't like playing outside _____ _____ _____ _____.

11 But wait _____ _____, I have _____
idea!

12 I'll _____ _____ _____ with snow and I'll _____
_____!

13 _____ _____ with Your Handwriting

14 Life is _____.

15 Live _____ in COLOR.

16 IT ISN'T OVER _____ IT'S _____.

17 I am a _____ _____, but I never walk back.

18 I love the _____ _____ you do.

19 _____ your dream.

20 _____ _____

21 Two wheels _____ me / _____ _____ _____ / To
school / Back _____ / To the mountain / To the river / I love my
bike / I _____ _____ it every day

22 _____ Tree

23 Out _____ – wet

24 In _____ – dry

25 Pretty big _____

1	십대들의 잡지
2	모양으로 표현된 예술 작품
3	동그라미처럼
4	나는 동그라미처럼 너를 사랑해. 왜냐하면 동그라미는 절대 끝나지 않기에.
5	눈사람
6	바깥은 추워.
7	나는 밖으로 나가 놀고 싶지 않네.
8	하지만 엄마는 그래야 한다고 하시네.
9	눈이 오기 시작하고 나는 추워질 거야.
10	나는 이런 날에는 나가서 놀고 싶지 않아.
11	하지만 잠깐만, 나는 최고로 멋진 생각이 났어!
12	나는 눈으로 내 몸을 덮고 여기에 숨어야지!
13	손 글씨로 돌아보기
14	인생은 예술이다.
15	다양한 색깔로 살아라.
16	끝날 때까지 끝난 게 아니다.
17	나는 느리게 걷는 사람이지만 절대 물러서지는 않는다.
18	나는 네가 하는 작은 일들을 사랑해.
19	네 꿈을 좇으라.
20	나의 자전거
21	바퀴 두 개가 나를 데려가네 / 어느 곳으로든지 / 학교로 / 다시 집으로 / 산으로 / 강으로 / 나는 내 자전거가 아주 좋아 / 나는 그걸 매일 즐겨 타네
22	아낌없이 주는 나무
23	저곳 바깥은 – 젖어 있고
24	이곳 안쪽은 – 말라 있네
25	엄청 큰 우산이네

26 _____ me and the sky

27 _____ of This Year

28 _____ we lost the game, we had a lot of fun.

29 Look at the _____ we made.

30 Aren't they _____?

31 We made _____ _____ _____ for Mr. Han.

32 It _____ _____ _____.

33 _____ _____ _____ _____ a handsome Peter Pan like me?

34 _____ Do You Think of Your School _____?

35 The most uncomfortable _____

36 1. When I _____ _____

37 2. When I am really hungry and _____ _____ to eat

38 3. When I change clothes _____ and _____ P.E. class

39 4. others: When I am _____ in class

40 When the teacher doesn't finish classes _____ the bell _____

41 The most _____ _____

42 1. _____ time

43 2. class with my _____ teacher

44 3. the _____ _____ on Friday

45 4. others: when I am sleeping _____ _____ _____

46 when I see _____ in the mirror

47 The most _____ news

48 1. I got better grades _____ _____

49 2. School _____ _____ today

50 3. I don't go to school _____ it _____ or _____ a lot

51 4. others: We eat delicious sweets _____ _____

52 My best friend and I are in the _____ _____

53 The _____ _____ work to do

54 1. Washing _____ cans

26 나와 하늘 사이에 있는

27 올해의 셀피들

28 우리는 게임에 졌지만, 아주 즐거웠다.

29 우리가 만든 로봇들을 봐.

30 귀엽지 않니?

31 우리는 한 씨 할아버지께 드릴 큰 케이크를 만들었다.

32 그것은 할아버지를 행복하게 해 주었다.

33 나처럼 잘생긴 피터 팬을 본 적이 있니?

34 학교생활에 대해 어떻게 생각하니?

35 가장 불편한 순간

36 1. 시험을 칠 때

37 2. 정말 배가 고픈데 먹을 것이 없을 때

38 3. 체육 시간 전후에 옷을 갈아입을 때

39 4. 기타: 수업 중에 졸릴 때

40 종이 울렸는데 선생님이 수업을 끝내지 않을 때

41 가장 사랑스러운 시간

42 1. 점심시간

43 2. 가장 좋아하는 선생님의 수업 시간

44 3. 금요일의 마지막 수업 시간

45 4. 기타: 쉬는 시간에 잠잘 때

46 거울 속의 나를 볼 때

47 가장 멋진 뉴스

48 1. 전보다 좋은 성적을 받았다

49 2. 오늘 수업이 일찍 끝난다

50 3. 비나 눈이 많이 와서 학교에 가지 않는다

51 4. 기타: 후식으로 맛있는 단것을 먹는다

52 가장 친한 친구와 내가 같은 반이 되었다

53 가장 하기 힘든 일

54 1. 쓰레기통 씻기

55 2. _____

56 3. _____ _____ in front of friends

57 4. others: Being _____ _____ every day

58 Group work

59 _____ We Love in Our _____

60 Daehan _____ Market

61 If you want to eat _____ _____, visit Daehan Market.

62 You can buy "*yeopjeon*" and use it to _____ your lunch box _____.

63 You can _____ many kinds of food and _____ them _____ your lunch box.

64 Saebom _____ Center

65 This is Saebom Youth Center _____ _____ _____ _____ our town.

66 We like this place because we can learn many things, _____ _____ dance and music.

67 We can also play board games and _____ _____ _____ here.

68 Mr. Kim's Bakery

69 This is a small bakery _____ the school.

70 We like to go there _____ school _____ we're always hungry!

71 It is good _____ _____ delicious bread with friends.

72 Let's _____ _____ with Puzzles!

73 _____ Puzzles

74 If you _____ the shape A _____ two same pieces, you can then make all the other shapes(B, C, D, E, F, G) _____ those two pieces.

75 Ten Balls in _____ _____

76 Place 10 balls in 5 lines _____ _____ _____ that each line has exactly 4 balls on it.

55 2. 공부하기

56 3. 친구들 앞에서 발표하기

57 4. 기타: 매일 제시간에 등교하기

58 모둠 활동

59 우리 마을에서 우리가 좋아하는 곳

60 대한 전통 시장

61 맛있는 것이 먹고 싶으면, 대한 시장을 방문하세요.

62 엽전을 사면 여러분의 점심 도시락을 가득 채우는 데 그걸 쓸 수 있어요.

63 많은 종류의 음식을 골라서 점심 도시락에 담을 수 있답니다.

64 새봄 청소년 센터

65 이곳은 우리 마을 한가운데에 있는 새봄 청소년 센터입니다.

66 춤과 음악 같은 많은 것을 배울 수 있어서 우리는 이곳을 좋아한답니다.

67 우리는 또한 이곳에서 보드게임도 하고 휴식도 취할 수 있어요.

68 김 씨네 빵집

69 이곳은 학교 근처의 작은 빵집입니다.

70 우리는 항상 배가 고파서 방과 후에 거기에 가는 것을 좋아해요!

71 친구들과 맛있는 빵을 즐기는 것이 좋아요.

72 퍼즐로 즐거운 시간을 보내자!

73 도형 퍼즐

74 A를 똑같은 두 개의 조각으로 자르면, 그 두 조각으로 다른 모든 형태(B, C, D, E, F, G)를 만들 수 있다.

75 5개의 선에 놓인 10개의 공

76 각각의 선 위에 정확하게 4개의 공이 놓이도록 10개의 공을 5개의 선에 놓아라.

77 You Are _____ Plastic Spoons!

78 1. A lot of plastic spoons _____ _____ _____ every year.

79 2. Most plastic _____ _____ _____ smaller pieces in the ocean.

80 3. Very small pieces of plastic _____ into _____.

81 4. If you eat the fish, you eat the plastic, too. _____ _____ 11,000 pieces each year!

82 _____ Make a Dream School!

83 We had a _____ _____ contest for our school last month.

84 Here are the _____ _____.

85 1. When your hands _____ _____, water comes out.

86 When you _____ your hands _____, the water stops.

87 You don't _____ _____ turn or touch any parts.

88 We can _____ _____ _____ _____ with this. – by O Juyeon(1-3)

89 2. This is our school park _____ two buildings.

90 Anybody can go _____ and _____ _____ here.

91 Also we can sit and _____ _____ _____ here. – by Gim Jimin(3-5)

92 3. These are _____ desks and chairs for the classroom.

93 For group activities, you can get them _____ and make a wonderful group table _____ three, four, or five students. – by Choi Yumi(2-1)

94 LET'S _____

95 Funny Earth Day _____ Ha! Ha! Ha!

96 Why are recycle bins _____?

97 Because they're _____ _____ cans.

98 _____ can you tell the ocean is _____?

99 It waves.

100 _____ did the sun go to school?

101 _____ _____ brighter.

● 우리말을 참고하여 본문을 영작하시오.

1 십대들의 잡지
➡

2 모양으로 표현된 예술 작품
➡

3 동그라미처럼
➡

4 나는 동그라미처럼 너를 사랑해. 왜냐하면 동그라미는 절대 끝나지 않기에.
➡

5 눈사람
➡

6 바깥은 추워.
➡

7 나는 밖으로 나가 놀고 싶지 않네.
➡

8 하지만 엄마는 그래야 한다고 하시네.
➡

9 눈이 오기 시작하고 나는 추워질 거야.
➡

10 나는 이런 날에는 나가서 놀고 싶지 않아.
➡

11 하지만 잠깐만, 나는 최고로 멋진 생각이 났어!
➡

12 나는 눈으로 내 몸을 완전히 덮고 여기에 숨어야지!
➡

13 손 글씨로 돌아보기
➡

14 인생은 예술이다.
➡

15 다양한 색깔로 살아라.
➡

16 끝날 때까지 끝난 게 아니다.
➡

17 나는 느리게 걷는 사람이지만 절대 물러서지는 않는다.
➡

18 나는 네가 하는 작은 일들을 사랑해.
➡

19 네 꿈을 좇으라.
➡

20 나의 자전거
➡

21 바퀴 두 개가 나를 데려가네 / 어느 곳으로든지 / 학교로 / 다시 집으로 / 산으로 / 강으로 / 나는 내 자전거가 아주 좋아 / 나는 그걸 매일 즐겨 타네
➡

22 아낌없이 주는 나무
➡

23 저곳 바깥은 – 젖어 있고
➡

24 이곳 안쪽은 – 말라 있네
➡ _____

25 엄청 큰 우산이네
➡ _____

26 나와 하늘 사이에 있는
➡ _____

27 올해의 셀피들
➡ _____

28 우리는 게임에 졌지만, 아주 즐거웠다.
➡ _____

29 우리가 만든 로봇들을 봐.
➡ _____

30 귀엽지 않니?
➡ _____

31 우리는 한 씨 할아버지께 드릴 큰 케이크를 만들었다.
➡ _____

32 그것은 할아버지를 행복하게 해 주었다.
➡ _____

33 나처럼 잘생긴 피터 팬을 본 적이 있니?
➡ _____

34 학교생활에 대해 어떻게 생각하니?
➡ _____

35 가장 불편한 순간
➡ _____

36 1. 시험을 칠 때
➡ _____

37 2. 정말 배가 고픈데 먹을 것이 없을 때
➡ _____

38 3. 체육 시간 전후에 옷을 갈아입을 때
➡ _____

39 4. 기타: 수업 중에 졸릴 때
➡ _____

40 종이 울렸는데 선생님이 수업을 끝내지 않을 때
➡ _____

41 가장 사랑스러운 시간
➡ _____

42 1. 점심시간
➡ _____

43 2. 가장 좋아하는 선생님의 수업 시간
➡ _____

44 3. 금요일의 마지막 수업 시간
➡ _____

45 4. 기타: 쉬는 시간에 잠잘 때
➡ _____

46 거울 속의 나를 볼 때
➡ _____

47 가장 멋진 뉴스
➡ _____

48 1. 전보다 좋은 성적을 받았다
➡ _____

49 2. 오늘 수업이 일찍 끝난다
➡ _____

50 3. 비나 눈이 많이 와서 학교에 가지 않는다
➡ _____

51 4. 기타: 후식으로 맛있는 단것을 먹는다
➡ _____

52 가장 친한 친구와 내가 같은 반이 되었다
➡ _____

53 가장 하기 힘든 일
➡ _____

54 1. 쓰레기통 씻기
➡ _____

55 2. 공부하기
➡ _____

56 3. 친구들 앞에서 발표하기
➡ _____

57 4. 기타: 매일 제시간에 등교하기
➡ _____

58 모둠 활동
➡ _____

59 우리 마을에서 우리가 좋아하는 곳
➡ _____

60 대한 전통 시장
➡ _____

61 맛있는 것이 먹고 싶으면, 대한 시장을 방문하세요.
➡ _____

62 엽전을 사면 여러분의 점심 도시락을 가득 채우는 데 그걸 쓸 수 있어요.
➡ _____

63 많은 종류의 음식을 골라서 점심 도시락에 담을 수 있답니다.
➡ _____

64 새봄 청소년 센터
➡ _____

65 이곳은 우리 마을 한가운데에 있는 새봄 청소년 센터입니다.
➡ _____

66 춤과 음악 같은 많은 것을 배울 수 있어서 우리는 이곳을 좋아한답니다.
➡ _____

67 우리는 또한 이곳에서 보드게임도 하고 휴식도 취할 수 있어요.
➡ _____

68 김 씨네 빵집
➡ _____

69 이곳은 학교 근처의 작은 빵집입니다.
➡ _____

70 우리는 항상 배가 고파서 방과 후에 거기에 가는 것을 좋아해요!
➡ _____

71 친구들과 맛있는 빵을 즐기는 것이 좋아요.
➡ _____

72 퍼즐로 즐거운 시간을 보내자!
➡ _____

73 도형 퍼즐
➡ _____

74 A를 똑같은 두 개의 조각으로 자르면, 그 두 조각으로 다른 모든 형태(B, C, D, E, F, G)를 만들 수 있다.
➡ _____

75 5개의 선에 놓인 10개의 공
➡ _____

76 각각의 선 위에 정확하게 4개의 공이 놓이도록 10개의 공을 5개의 선에 놓아라.
➡ _____

77 너는 플라스틱 숟가락을 먹고 있다!
➡ _____

78 1. 해마다 많은 플라스틱 숟가락이 버려진다.
➡ _____

79 2. 대부분의 플라스틱 숟가락은 바닷속에서 더 작은 조각으로 부서진다.
➡ _____

80 3. 아주 작은 플라스틱 조각들이 물고기의 몸속으로 들어간다.
➡ _____

81 4. 여러분이 그 물고기를 먹으면 여러분도 플라스틱을 먹게 되는 것이다. 해마다 11,000개의 조각까지!
➡ _____

82 꿈의 학교를 만들어 보자!
➡ _____

83 지난달에 우리는 우리 학교를 위한 유니버설 디자인 경시대회를 열었습니다.
➡ _____

84 여기 우승자들의 작품이 있습니다.
➡ _____

85 1. 손을 가까이 가져가면 물이 나옵니다.
➡ _____

86 손을 멀리 떨어뜨리면 물이 멈춥니다.
➡ _____

87 어떤 부분도 돌리거나 만질 필요가 없습니다.
➡ _____

88 우리는 이것으로 많은 물을 절약할 수 있답니다. — 오주연(1-3)
➡ _____

89 2. 이것은 두 개의 건물 사이에 있는 학교 정원입니다.
➡ _____

90 여기서는 누구라도 쉽게 위아래로 이동할 수 있습니다.
➡ _____

91 또한, 우리는 이곳에 앉아 휴식을 취할 수 있습니다. — 김지민(3-5)
➡ _____

92 3. 교실용의 특별한 책상과 의자가 있습니다.
➡ _____

93 모둠 활동을 하기 위해 그것들을 함께 모아 3명, 4명, 또는 5명이 활동할 훌륭한 모둠 책상을 만들 수 있습니다. — 최유미(2-1)
➡ _____

94 웃읍시다
➡ _____

95 재미있는 지구의 날 농담들 하! 하! 하!
➡ _____

96 재활용 통은 왜 희망적인가?
➡ _____

97 왜냐면 '깡통[할 수 있다]'으로 가득 차 있기 때문이지.
➡ _____

98 바다가 다정하다는 것을 어떻게 알 수 있는가?
➡ _____

99 그것이 일렁이기[손을 흔들기] 때문이지.
➡ _____

100 태양은 왜 학교에 가는가?
➡ _____

101 더 밝아지기[똑똑해지기] 위해서지.
➡ _____

01 다음 문장에 공통으로 들어갈 말을 쓰시오.

> (1) _____ we lost the game, we had a lot of fun.
> (2) _____ Tim often annoyed Anne, she was fond of him.

➡ _____

02 다음 빈칸에 들어갈 말을 〈보기〉에서 찾아 쓰시오. (필요하면 변형하여 쓰시오.)

> ┌ 보기 ┐
> throw away / such as / friend

(1) We like this place because we can learn many things, _____ dance and music.

(2) A lot of plastic spoons _____ every year.

(3) How can you tell that the ocean is _____?

03 영영풀이에 해당하는 단어를 〈보기〉에서 찾아 첫 번째 칸에 쓰고, 두 번째 칸에는 우리말 뜻을 쓰시오.

> ┌ 보기 ┐
> grade / wheel / bread / circle

(1) _____ : a circular object connected at the centre to a bar, used for making vehicles or parts of machines move: _____

(2) _____ : a continuous curved line, the points of which are always the same distance away from a fixed central point: _____

(3) _____ : a number or letter that shows how good someone's work or performance is: _____

(4) _____ : a food made from flour, water, and usually yeast, mixed together and baked: _____

04 우리말과 같은 뜻이 되도록 빈칸을 채우시오.

(1) 여기에 우승자들의 작품이 있습니다.
➡ Here are the winners' _____.

(2) 교실용의 특별한 책상과 의자가 있습니다.
➡ There are _____ desks and chairs for the classroom.

05 어법상 어색한 것을 고쳐 바르게 쓰시오.

(1) I'll cover up myself with snow and I'll hide here!
➡ _____

(2) Her daughter was made for a cloth doll by her.
➡ _____

(3) When have you gone to Seoul?
➡ _____

06 주어진 어휘를 이용하여 영작하시오.

(1) 그는 젊지만 새치가 많다. (though, gray hair, 9 단어) (though로 시작할 것)
➡ _____

(2) 친구들이 있는 것은 좋다. (it, good, have, to)
➡ _____

Snowman

It's cold outside.

I don't want to go out and play.

But Mom says I ⓐhave to.

It's starting to snow and I'm going to be cold.

I don't ____(A)____ playing outside on days __(B)__ these.

But wait a second, I have ⓑthe most wonderful idea!

I'll cover myself up with snow and I'll hide here!

brrr...

07 위 글의 빈칸 (A)와 (B)에 공통으로 들어갈 알맞은 말을 쓰시오.

➡ _____

중요

08 위 글의 밑줄 친 ⓐhave to 뒤에 생략된 말을 쓰시오.

➡ _____

09 위 글의 밑줄 친 ⓑ가 가리키는 것을 본문에서 찾아 쓰시오.

➡ _____

[10~12] 다음 글을 읽고 물음에 답하시오.

You Are Eating Plastic Spoons!

1. ⓐA lot of plastic spoons are thrown away every year.

2. Most plastic breaks down into smaller pieces in the ocean.

3. Very small pieces of plastic go into fish.

4. ⓑIf you eat the fish, you eat the plastic, too. Up to ⓒ11,000 pieces each year!

중요

10 위 글의 밑줄 친 ⓐ를 능동태로 고치시오.

➡ _____

11 다음 빈칸에 알맞은 단어를 넣어, 위 글에서 밑줄 친 ⓑ처럼 말한 이유를 완성하시오.

That's because when you eat the fish, you eat not only the fish _____ _____ the very small pieces of plastic that the fish ate.

12 위 글의 밑줄 친 ⓒ를 읽는 법을 영어로 쓰시오.

➡ _____

고난이도

[13~15] 다음 글을 읽고 물음에 답하시오.

LET'S LAUGH

Funny Earth Day Jokes Ha! Ha! Ha!

Why are recycle bins hopeful?

- Because they're full of ⓐcans.

How can you tell the ocean is friendly?

- It ⓑwaves.

Why did the sun go to school?

- To get ⓒbrighter.

13 위 글의 밑줄 친 ⓐcan의 중의적인 뜻을 우리말로 쓰시오.

➡ 본래의 뜻: _____ 숨어 있는 뜻: _____

14 위 글의 밑줄 친 ⓑwaves의 중의적인 뜻을 우리말로 쓰시오.

➡ 본래의 뜻: _____ 숨어 있는 뜻: _____

15 위 글의 밑줄 친 ⓒbrighter의 중의적인 뜻을 우리말로 쓰시오.

➡ 본래의 뜻: _____ 숨어 있는 뜻: _____

01 다음 단어에 대한 영어 설명이 <u>어색한</u> 것은?

① choose: to decide what you want from two or more things or possibilities

② youth: the period of your life when you are young, or the state of being young

③ shake hands: to raise your hand and move it from side to side as a way of greeting someone

④ friendly: behaving in a pleasant, kind way towards someone

⑤ save: to keep something, especially money, for use in the future

02 다음 짝지어진 단어의 관계가 같도록 빈칸에 알맞은 말을 쓰시오.

exactly : accurately = such as : _____

03 다음 주어진 글의 제목을 쓰고자 할 때 빈칸에 들어갈 단어로 알맞은 것은?

The most _____ moment
1. When I take tests
2. When I am really hungry and have nothing to eat
3. When I change clothes before and after P.E. class

① exciting ② amazing
③ uncomfortable ④ lovely
⑤ friendly

04 다음 〈보기〉의 단어를 활용하여 빈칸에 두 단어로 쓰시오.

| 보기 |
break / up / lot

(1) Most plastic _____ into smaller pieces in the ocean.

(2) If you eat the fish, you eat the plastic, too. _____ 11,000 pieces each year!

(3) We can save _____ water with this invention.

05 다음 우리말에 맞게 주어진 문장의 빈칸에 들어갈 말을 쓰시오.

(1) A를 똑같은 두 개의 조각으로 자르면, 그 두 조각으로 다른 모든 형태(B, C, D, E, F, G)를 만들 수 있다.
➡ If you _____ the shape A _____ two same pieces, you can then make all the other _____ (B, C, D, E, F, G) from those two pieces.

(2) 바퀴 두 개가 어느 곳으로든지 나를 데려간다.
➡ Two wheels _____ me _____ any place.

06 다음 영영풀이에 해당하는 단어는?

sweet food eaten at the end of a meal

① dessert ② batter
③ recipe ④ desert
⑤ cooker

07 다음 중 짝지어진 단어의 관계가 <u>다른</u> 것은?

① push : pull ② handsome : ugly
③ outside : inside ④ sleepy : drowsy
⑤ close : far

출제율 90%

08 다음 문장의 빈칸에 공통으로 들어갈 말을 쓰시오.

> • I'll cover myself _____ with snow and I'll hide here!
> • Anybody can go _____ and down easily here.

출제율 85%

09 다음 중 어법상 적절한 것은?

① Place 10 balls in 5 lines in a such way that each line has exactly 4 balls on it.
② How can you tell is the ocean friendly?
③ Many kinds of food can be chosen for you.
④ If you eat the fish, you eat the plastic, either.
⑤ A little of plastic spoons are thrown away every year.

출제율 95%

10 다음 중 밑줄 친 부분의 쓰임이 나머지 넷과 다른 것은?

① It is fun to play *tuho*.
② How long does it take from here to the station?
③ Was it interesting to play the game?
④ It's now safe to unplug your USB Disk.
⑤ It's no use shouting.

출제율 90%

11 다음 문장을 주어진 문장의 빈칸을 채워 같은 뜻의 문장으로 바꿔 쓰시오.

> We like this place because we can learn many things.

➡ We can learn many things, _____ _____.

출제율 95%

12 다음 문장에서 어법상 어색한 것을 바르게 고쳐 쓰시오.

(1) We have had a universal design contest for our school last month.

➡ _____

(2) That is good to enjoy delicious bread with friends.

➡ _____

[13~15] 다음 글을 읽고 물음에 답하시오.

> **Snowman**
> It's cold outside.
> I don't want to go out and play.
> But Mom says I have to.
> It's ⓐstarting to snow and I'm going to be cold.
> I don't like ⓑplaying outside on ⓒdays like these.
> But wait a second, I have the most wonderful idea!
> ⓓI'll cover me up with snow and I'll hide here!
> brrr...
> brrr...

출제율 90%

13 다음 〈보기〉에서 위 글의 밑줄 친 ⓐstarting, ⓑplaying과 문법적 쓰임이 같은 것을 각각 고르시오.

> ① Getting up early in the morning is hard.
> ② Look at the flying bird.
> ③ She stopped smoking for the health.
> ④ Learning Japanese is very interesting.
> ⑤ She is walking to the park.

➡ ⓐ _____ ⓑ _____

✏️ 출제율 95%

14 위 글의 밑줄 친 ⓒdays like these는 어떤 날을 의미하는지 우리말로 쓰시오.

➡ _____

✏️ 출제율 90%

15 위 글의 밑줄 친 ⓓ에서 어법상 틀린 부분을 찾아 고치시오.

_____ ➡ _____

[16~18] 다음 글을 읽고 물음에 답하시오.

Selfies of This Year

____ⓐ____ we lost the game, we had a lot of fun.
Look at the robots ⓑwe made. Aren't they cute?

We made a big cake for Mr. Han. It made him happy.

ⓒHave you ever seen a handsome Peter Pan like me?

✏️ 출제율 95%

16 위 글의 빈칸 ⓐ에 들어갈 알맞은 말을 고르시오.

① Because ② If ③ As
④ Though ⑤ While

✏️ 출제율 95%

17 위 글의 밑줄 친 ⓑwe made 앞에 생략된 말을 쓰시오.

➡ _____

✏️ 출제율 95%

18 아래 〈보기〉에서 위 글의 밑줄 친 ⓒ와 현재완료의 용법이 같은 것의 개수를 고르시오.

┌─ 보기 ─┐

① How many times have you seen a monkey?
② He has gone to America.
③ I have just finished my work.
④ I have never met her before.
⑤ How long have you known Mrs. Green?

└────────┘

① 1개 ② 2개 ③ 3개 ④ 4개 ⑤ 5개

[19~21] 다음 글을 읽고 물음에 답하시오.

Looking Back with Your ⓐHandwriting
Life is art. Live ⓑyours in COLOR.
IT ISN'T OVER UNTIL IT'S OVER.
I am a slow walker, but I never walk back.
I love the ⓒlittle things you do.
Follow your dream.

✏️ 출제율 95%

19 위 글의 밑줄 친 ⓐHandwriting과 바꿔 쓸 수 있는 말을 고르시오.

① Printout ② Calligraphy
③ Advertisement ④ Product
⑤ Catalog

✏️ 출제율 90%

20 위 글의 밑줄 친 ⓑyours가 가리키는 것을 영어로 쓰시오. (두 단어)

➡ _____

✏️ 출제율 85%

21 위 글의 밑줄 친 ⓒlittle과 같은 의미로 쓰인 것을 모두 고르시오.

① You still have a little time left.
② Look at the little bird.
③ I can speak English a little.
④ He lived in a little village.
⑤ She visited a little island last year.

[22~24] 다음 글을 읽고 물음에 답하시오.

The most lovely time

1. lunch time
2. class with my favorite teacher
3. the (A)[last / latest] class on Friday
4. others: when I am sleeping (B)[during / for] break time
 when I see (C)[me / myself] in the mirror

✎ 출제율 90%

22 위 글의 괄호 (A)~(C)에서 문맥이나 어법상 알맞은 낱말을 골라 쓰시오.

➡ (A) _____ (B) _____ (C) _____

✎ 출제율 95%

23 위 글의 종류로 알맞은 것을 고르시오.

① review ② summary ③ essay
④ article ⑤ survey

✎ 출제율 95%

24 위 글의 내용과 일치하지 <u>않는</u> 것은?

① The students like lunch time best.
② The students like class with their favorite teacher better than the last class on Friday.
③ The students like sleeping during break time better than eating lunch.
④ The students prefer lunch time to the last class on Friday.
⑤ The students prefer studying with their favorite teacher to sleeping during break time.

[25~27] 다음 글을 읽고 물음에 답하시오.

Places We Love in Our Village
Daehan Traditional Market -10 Likes

If you want to eat something delicious, visit Daehan Market. You can buy "*yeopjeon*" and use ⓐit ⓑto make your lunch box full. You can choose many kinds of food and add ⓒthem to your lunch box.

✎ 출제율 90%

25 위 글의 밑줄 친 ⓐit과 ⓒthem이 가리키는 것을 본문에서 찾아 각각 쓰시오.

➡ ⓐ _____ ⓒ _____

✎ 출제율 95%

26 위 글의 밑줄 친 ⓑto make와 to부정사의 용법이 다른 것을 <u>모두</u> 고르시오. (3개)

① To use the dictionary is necessary.
② I got up early to catch the train.
③ He grew up to be a doctor.
④ I am sorry to give you trouble.
⑤ There is no water to drink.

✎ 출제율 85%

27 위 글의 내용과 일치하도록 다음 빈칸에 알맞은 단어를 쓰시오.

If you want to make your lunch box full at Daehan Traditional Market, you can use "_____."

[28~30] 다음 글을 읽고 물음에 답하시오.

Selfies of This Year

Though we lost the game, we ⓐhad a lot of fun.

Look at the robots we made. Aren't ⓑthey cute?

We made a big cake for Mr. Han. ⓒIt made him happily.

Have you ever seen a handsome Peter Pan like me?

✎ 출제율 95%

28 위 글의 밑줄 친 ⓐ를 다음과 같이 바꿔 쓸 때 빈칸에 들어갈 알맞은 말을 쓰시오.

➡ had a great _____ = enjoyed _____ very much

✎ 출제율 85%

29 위 글의 밑줄 친 ⓑthey가 가리키는 것을 본문에서 찾아 쓰시오.

➡ _____

✎ 출제율 90%

30 위 글의 밑줄 친 ⓒ에서 어법상 틀린 부분을 찾아 고치시오.

_____ ➡ _____

[31~33] 다음 글을 읽고 물음에 답하시오.

The most (A)[awesome / awful] news

2 3 4

1

1. I got better grades than before
2. School finishes earlier today
3. I don't go to school ⓐbecause it rains or snows a lot
4. others: We eat delicious sweets for (B) [desert / dessert]
 My best friend and I are in (C) [different / the same] class

✎ 출제율 95%

31 위 글의 괄호 (A)~(C)에서 문맥상 알맞은 낱말을 골라 쓰시오.

➡ (A) _____ (B) _____ (C) _____

✎ 출제율 90%

32 위 글의 밑줄 친 ⓐ를 다음과 같이 바꿔 쓸 때 빈칸에 들어갈 알맞은 말을 쓰시오. (of를 이용할 것)

➡ _____ the heavy rain or snow

✎ 출제율 90%

33 다음 문장에서 위 글의 내용과 <u>다른</u> 부분을 찾아서 고치시오.

> To the students, the news that school finishes earlier than usual is the most wonderful news.

➡ _____

[34~36] 다음 글을 읽고 물음에 답하시오.

ⓐ _____

Saebom Youth Center - 12 Likes

 This is Saebom Youth Center in the middle of our town. We like this place because we can learn many things, ⓑsuch as dance and music. We can also play board games and take a break here.

✎ 출제율 100%

34 위 글의 빈칸 ⓐ에 들어갈 제목으로 알맞은 것을 고르시오.

① What Do You Think of Your School Life?
② Places We Love in Our Village
③ Let's Have Fun with Puzzles!
④ Let's Make a Dream School!
⑤ Funny Earth Day Jokes Ha! Ha! Ha!

✎ 출제율 90%

35 위 글의 밑줄 친 ⓑsuch as와 바꿔 쓸 수 있는 한 단어를 쓰시오.

➡ _____

✎ 출제율 95%

36 위 글의 새봄 청소년 센터에서 할 수 있는 일로 언급되지 않은 것을 고르시오.

① 춤을 배울 수 있다.
② 음악을 배울 수 있다.
③ 보드 게임을 할 수 있다.
④ 하이킹을 갈 수 있다.
⑤ 휴식을 취할 수 있다.

MEMO

MEMO

Middle School 2-2
2학기 전과정

중간 + 기말

plus

영어 기출문제집

영어 중 2

천재 | 정사열

Best Collection

내용문의 중등영어발전소 적중100 편집부 TEL 070-7707-0457

INSIGHT
on the textbook

교과서 파헤치기

영어 기출 문제집

2학기 전과정
적중 100 plus

영어 중 2

천재 | 정사열

INSIGHT
on the textbook

교과서 파헤치기

※ 다음 영어를 우리말로 쓰시오.

01 circle	22 difficult
02 shape	23 complain
03 roll	24 square
04 excited	25 control
05 boil	26 hurt
06 pointy	27 shout
07 share	28 spirit
08 press	29 spin
09 bookshelf	30 realize
10 perfect	31 finally
11 exercise	32 water
12 solve	33 rush
13 hurry	34 tidy
14 plastic bag	35 one another
15 divide	36 wrap up
16 choose	37 take away
17 stick	38 in charge of ~
18 hanger	39 by oneself
19 mess	40 divide A into B
20 round	41 in control
21 triangle	42 cut A into pieces
	43 the other side

※ 다음 우리말을 영어로 쓰시오.

01 끓이다

02 통제하다, 조절하다

03 다치게 하다

04 모양, 모습

05 마주하다

06 마지막으로

07 고르다, 선택하다

08 막대기, 나뭇가지

09 불평하다

10 옷걸이

11 삼각형

12 풀다, 해결하다

13 소리치다, 외치다

14 끝이 뾰족한

15 옮기다

16 공유하다

17 구르다

18 책꽂이

19 완벽한

20 둥근

21 잘 정돈된, 단정한

22 나누다

23 서두르다

24 회전시키다

25 영혼, 요정

26 대답하다

27 혼잡, 혼란

28 깨닫다, 알아차리다

29 물을 주다

30 서두르다, 돌진하다

31 ~ 없이

32 퍼즐, 수수께끼

33 사각형

34 움직임, 이동

35 A를 B로 나누다

36 하나씩, 차례대로

37 ~을 집다

38 ~을 치우다

39 A를 B에 놓다[두다]

40 감싸다, 포장하다

41 ~을 담당하여

42 (주로 셋 이상 사이에 쓰임) 서로

43 자기 혼자서

※ 다음 영영풀이에 알맞은 단어를 <보기>에서 골라 쓴 후, 우리말 뜻을 쓰시오.

1 _____ : having a point at the end: _____

2 _____ : an imaginary creature with magic powers: _____

3 _____ : to move forward while turning over and over: _____

4 _____ : complete and correct in every way: _____

5 _____ : feeling very happy and enthusiastic: _____

6 _____ : to make a choice about what you are going to do: _____

7 _____ : a situation in which a place is dirty or not neat: _____

8 _____ : to say that you are not satisfied with something: _____

9 _____ : to answer someone by saying or writing something: _____

10 _____ : to have something in your hands or arms: _____

11 _____ : to move quickly toward someone: _____

12 _____ : a very large ring that you try to keep spinning round your body:

13 _____ : to have the power to make it work in the way you want: _____

14 _____ : to gradually begin to understand something that you did not know or

notice before: _____

15 _____ : a curved piece of wire, wood or plastic on which clothes are hung while

they are being stored: _____

16 _____ : a round object that turns around and around to make a car, bicycle, or

other vehicle move: _____

보기			
complain	roll	mess	control
hanger	hold	realize	perfect
spirit	decide	hula hoop	pointy
rush	wheel	reply	excited

※ 다음 우리말과 일치하도록 빈칸에 알맞은 말을 쓰시오.

Get Ready 2

(1) G: This bookshelf _____ _____ _____. Do you know _____ _____ _____ this problem?

B: _____ some legs _____ the _____.

(2) G: Do you know _____ _____ _____ this cake _____ four _____ _____?

B: _____ me _____. … How about _____ it this way? Then the pieces will be _____ _____ _____ _____ and _____.

(3) G: This car _____ _____. Do you know _____ _____ _____ it?

B: Sure. _____ _____ under the car.

Start Off Listen & Talk A

1. G: These twelve sticks make four squares. Do you know _____ _____ _____ _____ _____ of the same size _____ _____ _____?

B: Sure. _____, _____ _____ _____ here.

2. B: Here's a triangle _____ three pencils. Do you know _____ _____ _____ three more triangles with three more pencils?

G: Let me see. … It's _____ _____ _____ me. _____ I _____ the pencils _____ _____?

B: No, _____ _____.

Start Off Listen & Talk B

B: Do you know _____ _____ _____ this _____ four equal _____?

G: Sure. _____, _____ it _____ three _____ squares. _____, _____ each square _____ four smaller squares. _____, color three small squares in the inside corner of the L.

B: Oh, I can see three _____ L shapes _____ it! You're great!

Speak Up Look and talk.

A: Do you know _____ _____ _____ a fish with shapes?

B: Sure. _____, draw a large square. _____, draw a triangle. _____, draw a small circle _____ _____ _____.

(1) G: 이 책꽂이는 혼자서 서 있을 수 없어. 이 문제를 어떻게 해결할지 아니?
B: 바닥에 다리를 몇 개 붙여.

(2) G: 이 케이크를 네 개의 같은 조각으로 어떻게 나눌 수 있는지 아니?
B: 글쎄. … 이 방법으로 그것을 나누는 것은 어때? 그럼 그 조각들은 같은 크기에 같은 모양이 될 거야.

(3) G: 이 차는 움직이지 않아. 어떻게 움직이게 할 수 있는지 아니?
B: 물론이지. 차 아래에 바퀴들을 붙여.

1. G: 이 12개 막대기들은 사각형 4개를 만들어. 세 번 움직여서 어떻게 같은 크기의 사각형 3개를 만드는지 아니?
B: 물론이지. 먼저, 이 막대기를 여기로 옮겨.

2. B: 여기 연필 세 자루로 만든 삼각형이 하나 있어. 연필 세 자루를 더 추가해서 어떻게 삼각형 3개를 더 만드는지 아니?
G: 글쎄. … 내게는 너무 어려워. 연필을 반으로 부러뜨려도 돼?
B: 아니, 안 돼.

B: 이것을 4개의 같은 조각으로 나누는 방법을 아니?
G: 물론이지. 먼저, 그것을 3개의 같은 사각형으로 나눠. 그러고 나서, 각 사각형을 4개의 더 작은 사각형으로 나눠. 마지막으로, L자 모양의 안쪽 모서리에 있는 3개의 작은 사각형에 색칠해.
B: 오, 그 주변에 3개의 다른 L자 모양이 보여! 너 대단하다!

A: 너는 도형들로 물고기를 그리는 방법을 알고 있니?
B: 물론. 먼저, 큰 사각형을 그려. 그러고 나서, 삼각형을 그려. 마지막으로, 사각형 안에 작은 원을 그려.

Speak Up Mission

G: Do you know _____ _____ _____ paper airplanes?

B: Sure. I'll _____ _____ _____.

Real-life Scene

B: Do you know _____ _____ _____ this puzzle?

G: What is it?

B: You must _____ a dog, a chicken, and a bag of rice _____ _____ _____. The boat _____ _____ you and one of the things _____ _____ _____.

G: That's easy. I can _____ them _____ the _____ _____ _____ _____ _____.

B: But _____ you, the dog will kill the chicken, and the chicken will _____ _____ _____.

G: Let me see. … _____, take the chicken and come back. _____, take the rice and _____ _____ _____ the chicken.

B: And?

G: After that, take the dog and come back. _____, take the chicken.

B: You're great!

Express Yourself A

1. **B:** Do you know _____ _____ _____ this?

 G: Sure. First, _____ _____ the leg from _____ _____.

2. **B:** This _____ _____.

 G: I think so, too. Do you know _____ _____ _____ it?

 B: It's easy. _____, put some rice on *gim*. _____, add some _____ fish and hot peppers. _____, _____ _____ _____ and _____ _____ _____ _____.

3. **B:** Do you know _____ _____ _____ this?

 G: Yes. I'll show you how. It _____ _____ _____ the wind. _____ it _____ like this.

Learning Diary Check Yourself

W: Excuse me. Do you know _____ _____ _____ a mouse _____ _____?

M: Sure. _____, draw a large _____. _____, draw two _____ and 6 lines. _____, draw two _____.

W: Thanks. I'll _____ it _____ now.

G: 너는 종이 비행기를 어떻게 접는지 아니?

B: 물론이지. 내가 너에게 방법을 보여 줄게.

B: 이 퍼즐을 어떻게 푸는지 아니?

G: 그게 뭔데?

B: 너는 개, 닭, 쌀 한 자루를 강 건너로 옮겨야 해. 그 배는 한 번에 너와 그것들 중 하나만 옮길 수 있어.

G: 그것은 쉬워. 난 반대편으로 그것들을 하나씩 옮길 수 있어.

B: 하지만 네가 없으면, 개는 닭을 죽일 것이고, 닭은 쌀을 먹을 거야.

G: 어디 보자. … 먼저, 닭을 데려다 놓고 돌아와. 그러고 나서, 쌀을 가져다 놓고 닭을 데려와.

B: 그리고?

G: 그 후에, 개를 데려다 놓고 돌아와. 마지막으로, 닭을 데려가는 거야.

B: 너 대단하구나!

1. **B:** 이것을 어떻게 만드는지 아니?
 G: 물론이지. 먼저, 낡은 청바지에서 다리 부분을 잘라내.

2. **B:** 이것은 멋져 보여.
 G: 나도 그렇게 생각해. 그걸 어떻게 만드는지 아니?
 B: 그건 쉬워. 먼저, 김 위에 밥을 좀 얹어. 그러고 나서, 멸치와 매운 고추를 추가해. 마지막으로, 그것을 모두 싸서 삼각형을 만들어.

3. **B:** 이것을 어떻게 날리는지 아니?
 G: 그래. 내가 너에게 방법을 보여 줄게. 그것은 바람을 마주해야만 해. 이렇게 그것을 들고 있어.

W: 실례합니다. 도형으로 쥐를 어떻게 그리는지 아세요?

M: 물론이죠. 먼저, 큰 삼각형을 그려요. 그러고 나서, 점 두 개와 선 6개를 그려요. 마지막으로, 작은 원 두 개를 그려요.

W: 감사합니다. 이제 제가 그것을 직접 그려 볼게요.

※ 다음 우리말에 맞도록 대화를 영어로 쓰시오.

Get Ready 2

(1) G: _____

 B: _____

(2) G: _____

 B: _____

(3) G: _____

 B: _____

(1) G: 이 책꽂이는 혼자서 서 있을 수 없어. 이 문제를 어떻게 해결할지 아니?
 B: 바닥에 다리를 몇 개 붙여.

(2) G: 이 케이크를 네 개의 같은 조각으로 어떻게 나눌 수 있는지 아니?
 B: 글쎄. … 이 방법으로 그것을 나누는 것은 어때? 그럼 그 조각들은 같은 크기에 같은 모양이 될 거야.

(3) G: 이 차는 움직이지 않아. 어떻게 움직이게 할 수 있는지 아니?
 B: 물론이지. 차 아래에 바퀴들을 붙여.

Start Off Listen & Talk A

1. G: _____

 B: _____

2. B: _____

 G: _____

 B: _____

1. G: 이 12개 막대기들은 사각형 4개를 만들어. 세 번 움직여서 어떻게 같은 크기의 사각형 3개를 만드는지 아니?
 B: 물론이지. 먼저, 이 막대기를 여기로 옮겨.

2. B: 여기 연필 세 자루로 만든 삼각형이 하나 있어. 연필 세 자루를 더 추가해서 어떻게 삼각형 3개를 더 만드는지 아니?
 G: 글쎄. … 내게는 너무 어려워. 연필을 반으로 부러뜨려도 돼?
 B: 아니, 안 돼.

Start Off Listen & Talk B

B: _____

G: _____

B: _____

B: 이것을 4개의 같은 조각으로 나누는 방법을 아니?
G: 물론이지. 먼저, 그것을 3개의 같은 사각형으로 나눠. 그리고 나서, 각 사각형을 4개의 더 작은 사각형으로 나눠. 마지막으로, L자 모양의 안쪽 모서리에 있는 3개의 작은 사각형에 색칠해.
B: 오, 그 주변에 3개의 다른 L자 모양들이 보여! 너 대단하다!

Speak Up Look and talk.

A: _____

B: _____

A: 너는 도형들로 물고기를 그리는 방법을 알고 있니?
B: 물론. 먼저, 큰 사각형을 그려. 그리고 나서, 삼각형을 그려. 마지막으로, 사각형 안에 작은 원을 그려.

Speak Up Mission

G: _____

B: _____

Real-life Scene

B: _____

G: _____

B: _____

G: _____

B: _____

G: _____

B: _____

G: _____

B: _____

Express Yourself A

1. B: _____

 G: _____

2. B: _____

 G: _____

 B: _____

3. B: _____

 G: _____

Learning Diary Check Yourself

W: _____

M: _____

W. _____

G: 너는 종이 비행기를 어떻게 접는지 아니?

B: 물론이지. 내가 너에게 방법을 보여 줄게.

B: 이 퍼즐을 어떻게 푸는지 아니?

G: 그게 뭔데?

B: 너는 개, 닭, 쌀 한 자루를 강 건너로 옮겨야 해. 그 배는 한 번에 너와 그것들 중 하나만 옮길 수 있어.

G: 그것은 쉬워. 난 반대편으로 그것들을 하나씩 옮길 수 있어.

B: 하지만 네가 없으면, 개는 닭을 죽일 것이고, 닭은 쌀을 먹을 거야.

G: 어디 보자. … 먼저, 닭을 데려다 놓고 돌아와. 그러고 나서, 쌀을 가져다 놓고 닭을 데려와.

B: 그리고?

G: 그 후에, 개를 데려다 놓고 돌아와. 마지막으로, 닭을 데려가는 거야.

B: 너 대단하구나!

1. B: 이것을 어떻게 만드는지 아니?
 G: 물론이지. 먼저, 낡은 청바지에서 다리 부분을 잘라내.

2. B: 이것은 멋져 보여.
 G: 나도 그렇게 생각해. 그걸 어떻게 만드는지 아니?
 B: 그건 쉬워. 먼저, 김 위에 밥을 좀 얹어. 그러고 나서, 멸치와 매운 고추를 추가해. 마지막으로, 그것을 모두 싸서 삼각형을 만들어.

3. B: 이것을 어떻게 날리는지 아니?
 G: 그래. 내가 너에게 방법을 보여 줄게. 그것은 바람을 마주해야만 해. 이렇게 그것을 들고 있어.

W: 실례합니다. 도형으로 쥐를 어떻게 그리는지 아세요?

M: 물론이죠. 먼저, 큰 삼각형을 그려요. 그러고 나서, 점 두 개와 선 6개를 그려요. 마지막으로, 작은 원 두 개를 그려요.

W. 감사합니다. 이제 제가 그것을 직접 그려 볼게요.

※ 다음 우리말과 일치하도록 빈칸에 알맞은 것을 골라 쓰시오.

1 Three _____ _____
 A. Spirits B. Shape

2 _____ _____ three shape _____ in Mike's room.
 A. spirits B. lived C. there

3 Square _____ the table, the _____, and the _____.
 A. bookshelf B. controlled C. window

4 Triangle was in _____ of the _____ and the _____.
 A. hangers B. charge C. plants

5 Circle _____ _____ of the _____ things.
 A. care B. round C. took

6 They _____ _____ to make a nice room _____ Mike.
 A. together B. for C. worked

7 One day Square _____ to make the room _____ and _____ at the other spirits.
 A. better B. shouted C. decided

8 "_____ these plants _____, or their _____ leaves will hurt someone!" he said to Triangle.
 A. away B. take C. pointy

9 "But Mike _____ them _____ _____," said Triangle.
 A. every B. waters C. day

10 "_____ this hula hoop _____, or it will _____ and _____ something!" he said to Circle.
 A. away B. break C. take D. roll

11 "But Mike _____ it _____ day," said Circle.
 A. with B. every C. exercises

12 "I try to make this room _____, but you two always make a _____," he _____.
 A. complained B. tidy C. mess

13 Triangle and Circle _____ _____ each _____.
 A. other B. at C. looked

14 "So you _____ you can do it _____ us?" Triangle _____ Square.
 A. without B. think C. asked

15 "Sure. I can make this room _____ all _____ _____," replied Square.
 A. better B. myself C. by

16 "Great! Then we can _____ some _____," Circle _____ to Square.
 A. get B. said C. rest

17 Triangle and Circle _____ _____ and Square was now _____ _____.
 A. out B. control C. went D. in

1 세 도형 요정들

2 Mike의 방에는 세 도형 요정이 살았다.

3 Square는 탁자, 책장, 그리고 창문을 담당했다.

4 Triangle은 옷걸이들과 식물들을 담당했다.

5 Circle은 둥근 것들을 돌보았다.

6 그들은 Mike에게 좋은 방을 만들어 주기 위해서 함께 일했다.

7 어느 날 Square는 방을 더 낫게 만들기로 결심하고 나머지 요정들에게 소리쳤다.

8 "이 식물들을 치워, 그렇지 않으면 그것들의 끝이 뾰족한 잎사귀들이 누군가를 다치게 할 거야!" 그가 Triangle에게 말했다.

9 "하지만 Mike가 매일 그들에게 물을 주는데." Triangle이 말했다.

10 "이 훌라후프를 치워, 그렇지 않으면 굴러가서 뭔가를 부술 거야!" 그가 Circle에게 말했다.

11 "하지만 Mike는 매일 그걸로 운동을 하는데." Circle이 말했다.

12 "난 이 방을 정돈하려고 애쓰지만, 너희 둘은 항상 엉망으로 만들어." 그가 불평했다.

13 Triangle과 Circle이 서로를 쳐다보았다.

14 "그래서 네 생각에는 네가 우리 없이 다 할 수 있다는 거야?" Triangle이 Square에게 물었다.

15 "물론이지. 난 완전히 혼자서 이 방을 더 낫게 만들 수 있어." Square가 대답했다.

16 "잘됐네! 그럼 우린 쉴 수 있겠어." Circle이 Square에게 말했다.

17 Triangle과 Circle이 밖으로 나갔고 이제 Square가 모든 것을 담당했다.

18 He made the _____, plants, and all the _____ things _____.

 A. square B. hangers C. round

19 Then he _____ _____ and _____.

 A. around B. looked C. smiled

20 "_____ _____!"

 A. better B. much

21 When Mike came home from school, he _____ _____ a square hanger to _____ his jacket _____.

 A. hang B. up C. on D. picked

22 "What? This will not _____ my _____."

 A. clothes B. hold

23 He _____ to _____ the plants and saw their square _____.

 A. leaves B. water C. went

24 "_____ things. ... They _____ _____ sick."

 A. be B. poor C. must

25 He _____ _____ the square hula hoop _____ _____.

 A. to B. picked C. exercise D. up

26 "Hmm ... I don't know _____ _____ _____ this."

 A. to B. how C. spin

27 He went to _____ _____ his bike and _____ _____ the square wheels.

 A. out B. at C. looked D. take

28 "Well, I can't _____ this. I'll just _____ _____ walk."

 A. have B. ride C. to

29 Then he _____ _____ _____ the house.

 A. out B. hurried C. of

30 When the _____ spirits came _____, Square rushed _____ to them.

 A. back B. over C. other

31 "Mike _____ like his room. I don't know _____ _____," he said.

 A. what B. doesn't C. do D. to

32 They looked at the _____, the plants, and _____ the new _____ things.

 A. square B. all C. hangers

33 Then they looked at _____ _____, and Square _____ his problem.

 A. realized B. another C. one

34 "Let's make this room _____ again," he said to the _____, and the three spirits worked together _____ _____.

 A. once B. others C. great D. again

18 그는 옷걸이들과 식물들과 모든 둥근 물건들을 사각형으로 만들었다.

19 그리고 나서 그는 주위를 둘러보고 미소 지었다.

20 "훨씬 좋군!"

21 Mike가 학교에서 집으로 왔을 때, 그는 재킷을 걸기 위해 사각형 옷걸이가 하나를 집었다.

22 "뭐야? 이것은 내 옷을 걸고 있지 못할 거야."

23 그는 식물에 물을 주러 가서 그것들의 사각형 잎사귀들을 보았다.

24 "불쌍한 것들.… 그들은 병든 것이 틀림없어."

25 그는 운동을 하기 위해 사각형 훌라후프를 집어 들었다.

26 "흠… 이걸 어떻게 돌리는지 모르겠어."

27 그는 자전거를 꺼내러 가서 사각형 바퀴들을 보았다.

28 "음. 난 이걸 탈 수 없어. 그냥 걸어가야 할 것 같아."

29 그리고 나서 그는 서둘러 집을 나섰다.

30 다른 요정들이 돌아왔을 때, Square는 그들에게 달려갔다.

31 "Mike는 그의 방을 좋아하지 않아. 난 뭘 해야 할지 모르겠어." 그가 말했다.

32 그들은 옷걸이들, 식물들, 그리고 모든 새로 사각형이 된 물건들을 바라보았다.

33 그리고 나서 그들은 서로를 바라보았고, Square는 자신의 문제를 깨달았다.

34 "이 방을 다시 멋지게 만들자." 그가 나머지 요정들에게 말했고, 세 요정들은 다시 한 번 함께 일했다.

※ 다음 우리말과 일치하도록 빈칸에 알맞은 말을 쓰시오.

1 Three _____ _____

2 _____ _____ three _____ _____ in Mike's room.

3 Square _____ the table, the _____ , and the window.

4 Triangle _____ _____ _____ _____ the hangers and the plants.

5 Circle _____ _____ _____ the _____ _____ .

6 They _____ _____ _____ a nice room for Mike.

7 One day Square decided _____ _____ _____ _____ _____ and _____ _____ the other spirits.

8 " _____ these plants _____ , or their _____ _____ will hurt someone!" he said to Triangle.

9 "But Mike _____ _____ _____ _____ ," said Triangle.

10 " _____ this hula hoop _____ , or it will _____ _____ _____ something!" he said to Circle.

11 "But Mike _____ _____ every day," said Circle.

12 "I _____ _____ make this room _____ , but you two always _____ _____ _____ ," he _____ .

13 Triangle and Circle _____ _____ _____ .

14 "So you think you can do it _____ _____ ?" Triangle asked Square.

15 "Sure. I can _____ this room _____ _____ _____ _____ ," replied Square.

16 "Great! Then we can _____ _____ _____ ," Circle said to Square.

17 Triangle and Circle _____ _____ and Square was now _____ _____ .

1 세 도형 요정들

2 Mike의 방에는 세 도형 요정이 살았다.

3 Square는 탁자, 책장, 그리고 창문을 담당했다.

4 Triangle은 옷걸이들과 식물들을 담당했다.

5 Circle은 둥근 것들을 돌보았다.

6 그들은 Mike에게 좋은 방을 만들어 주기 위해서 함께 일했다.

7 어느 날 Square는 방을 더 낫게 만들기로 결심하고 나머지 요정들에게 소리쳤다.

8 "이 식물들을 치워, 그렇지 않으면 그것들의 끝이 뾰족한 잎사귀들이 누군가를 다치게 할 거야!" 그가 Triangle에게 말했다.

9 "하지만 Mike가 매일 그들에게 물을 주는데." Triangle이 말했다.

10 "이 훌라후프를 치워, 그렇지 않으면 굴러가서 뭔가를 부술 거야!" 그가 Circle에게 말했다.

11 "하지만 Mike는 매일 그걸로 운동을 하는데." Circle이 말했다.

12 "난 이 방을 정돈하려고 애쓰지만, 너희 둘은 항상 엉망으로 만들어." 그가 불평했다.

13 Triangle과 Circle이 서로를 쳐다보았다.

14 "그래서 네 생각에는 네가 우리 없이 다 할 수 있다는 거야?" Triangle이 Square에게 물었다.

15 "물론이지. 난 완전히 혼자서 이 방을 더 낫게 만들 수 있어." Square가 대답했다.

16 "잘됐네! 그럼 우린 쉴 수 있겠어." Circle이 Square에게 말했다.

17 Triangle과 Circle이 밖으로 나갔고 이제 Square가 모든 것을 담당했다.

18 He _____ the hangers, plants, and all the round things _____ .

19 Then he _____ _____ and _____ .

20 "_____ _____ !"

21 When Mike _____ _____ from school, he _____ _____ a square hanger _____ _____ his jacket _____ .

22 "What? This will not _____ _____ _____ ."

23 He _____ _____ _____ the plants and saw their square leaves.

24 "Poor things. ... They _____ _____ sick."

25 He _____ _____ the square hula hoop _____ _____ .

26 "Hmm ... I don't know _____ _____ _____ this."

27 He went _____ _____ _____ his bike and _____ _____ the square wheels.

28 "Well, I _____ _____ this. I'll just _____ _____ walk."

29 Then he _____ _____ _____ the house.

30 When the _____ spirits _____ _____ , Square _____ _____ _____ them.

31 "Mike doesn't like his room. I don't know _____ _____ _____ ," he said.

32 They _____ _____ the hangers, the plants, and _____ _____ _____ _____ _____ .

33 Then they looked at _____ _____ , and Square _____ his problem.

34 "Let's make this room _____ again," he said to _____ _____ , and the three spirits worked together _____ _____ .

18 그는 옷걸이들과 식물들과 모든 둥근 물건들을 사각형으로 만들었다.

19 그러고 나서 그는 주위를 둘러보고 미소 지었다.

20 "훨씬 좋군!"

21 Mike가 학교에서 집으로 왔을 때, 그는 재킷을 걸기 위해 사각형 옷걸이 하나를 집었다.

22 "뭐야? 이것은 내 옷을 걸고 있지 못할 거야."

23 그는 식물에 물을 주러 가서 그것들의 사각형 잎사귀들을 보았다.

24 "불쌍한 것들.… 그들은 병든 것이 틀림없어."

25 그는 운동을 하기 위해 사각형 훌라후프를 집어 들었다.

26 "흠… 이걸 어떻게 돌리는지 모르겠어."

27 그는 자전거를 꺼내러 가서 사각형 바퀴들을 보았다.

28 "음, 난 이걸 탈 수 없어. 그냥 걸어가야 할 것 같아."

29 그러고 나서 그는 서둘러 집을 나섰다.

30 다른 요정들이 돌아왔을 때, Square는 그들에게 달려갔다.

31 "Mike는 그의 방을 좋아하지 않아. 난 뭘 해야 할지 모르겠어." 그가 말했다.

32 그들은 옷걸이들, 식물들, 그리고 모든 새로 사각형이 된 물건들을 바라보았다.

33 그러고 나서 그들은 서로를 바라보았고, Square는 자신의 문제를 깨달았다.

34 "이 방을 다시 멋지게 만들자." 그가 나머지 요정들에게 말했고, 세 요정들은 다시 한 번 함께 일했다.

※ 다음 문장을 우리말로 쓰시오.

1 ▶ Three Shape Spirits

 ➡ _____

2 ▶ There lived three shape spirits in Mike's room.

 ➡ _____

3 ▶ Square controlled the table, the bookshelf, and the window.

 ➡ _____

4 ▶ Triangle was in charge of the hangers and the plants.

 ➡ _____

5 ▶ Circle took care of the round things.

 ➡ _____

6 ▶ They worked together to make a nice room for Mike.

 ➡ _____

7 ▶ One day Square decided to make the room better and shouted at the other spirits.

 ➡ _____

8 ▶ "Take these plants away, or their pointy leaves will hurt someone!" he said to Triangle.

 ➡ _____

9 ▶ "But Mike waters them every day," said Triangle.

 ➡ _____

10 ▶ "Take this hula hoop away, or it will roll and break something!" he said to Circle.

 ➡ _____

11 ▶ "But Mike exercises with it every day," said Circle.

 ➡ _____

12 ▶ "I try to make this room tidy, but you two always make a mess," he complained.

 ➡ _____

13 ▶ Triangle and Circle looked at each other.

 ➡ _____

14 ▶ "So you think you can do it without us?" Triangle asked Square.

 ➡ _____

15 ▶ "Sure. I can make this room better all by myself," replied Square.

 ➡ _____

16 ▶ "Great! Then we can get some rest," Circle said to Square.

 ➡ _____

17 Triangle and Circle went out and Square was now in control.

➡ _____

18 He made the hangers, plants, and all the round things square.

➡ _____

19 Then he looked around and smiled.

➡ _____

20 "Much better!"

➡ _____

21 When Mike came home from school, he picked up a square hanger to hang his jacket on.

➡ _____

22 "What? This will not hold my clothes."

➡ _____

23 He went to water the plants and saw their square leaves.

➡ _____

24 "Poor things. ... They must be sick."

➡ _____

25 He picked up the square hula hoop to exercise.

➡ _____

26 "Hmm ... I don't know how to spin this."

➡ _____

27 He went to take out his bike and looked at the square wheels.

➡ _____

28 "Well, I can't ride this. I'll just have to walk."

➡ _____

29 Then he hurried out of the house.

➡ _____

30 When the other spirits came back, Square rushed over to them.

➡ _____

31 "Mike doesn't like his room. I don't know what to do," he said.

➡ _____

32 They looked at the hangers, the plants, and all the new square things.

➡ _____

33 Then they looked at one another, and Square realized his problem.

➡ _____

34 "Let's make this room great again," he said to the others, and the three spirits worked together once again.

➡ _____

※ 다음 괄호 안의 단어들을 우리말에 맞도록 바르게 배열하시오.

1 (Shape / Three / Spirits)
➡ _____

2 (lived / there / shape / three / in / spirits / room. / Mike's)
➡ _____

3 (controlled / the / Square / table, / bookshelf, / the / and / window. / the)
➡ _____

4 (was / Triangle / charge / in / of / hangers / the / plants. / the / and)
➡ _____

5 (took / Circle / of / care / the / things. / round)
➡ _____

6 (worked / they / to / together / make / nice / a / Mike. / for / room)
➡ _____

7 (day / one / decided / Square / make / to / room / the / and / better / shouted / the / at / spirits. / other)
➡ _____

8 (these / "take / away, / plants / or / pointy / their / will / leaves / someone!" / hurt / said / he / Triangle. / to)
➡ _____

9 (Mike / "but / them / waters / day," / every / Triangle. / said)
➡ _____

10 (this / "take / away, / hula hoop / it / or / roll / will / break / and / something!" / said / he / Circle. / to)
➡ _____

11 (Mike / "but / with / exercises / it / day," / every / Circle. / said)
➡ _____

12 (try / "I / to / this / make / tidy, / room / but / two / you / make / always / mess," / a / complained. / he)
➡ _____

13 (Circle / and / Triangle / at / looked / other. / each)
➡ _____

14 (you / "so / think / can / you / do / without / it / us?" / Square. / asked / Triangle)
➡ _____

15 ("sure. // can / I / this / make / better / room / by / all / myself," / Square. / replied)
➡ _____

16 ("great! // we / then / get / can / rest," / some / to / Circle / Square. / said)
➡ _____

17 (Circle / and / Triangle / out / went / and / was / Square / control. / in / now)
➡ _____

1 세 도형 요정들

2 Mike의 방에는 세 도형 요정이 살았다.

3 Square는 탁자, 책장, 그리고 창문을 담당했다.

4 Triangle은 옷걸이들과 식물들을 담당했다.

5 Circle은 둥근 것들을 돌보았다.

6 그들은 Mike에게 좋은 방을 만들어 주기 위해서 함께 일했다.

7 어느 날 Square는 방을 더 낫게 만들기로 결심하고 나머지 요정들에게 소리쳤다.

8 "이 식물들을 치워. 그렇지 않으면 그것들의 끝이 뾰족한 잎사귀들이 누군가를 다치게 할 거야!" 그가 Triangle에게 말했다.

9 "하지만 Mike가 매일 그들에게 물을 주는데." Triangle이 말했다.

10 "이 훌라후프를 치워. 그렇지 않으면 굴러가서 뭔가를 부술 거야!" 그가 Circle에게 말했다.

11 "하지만 Mike는 매일 그걸로 운동을 하는데." Circle이 말했다.

12 "난 이 방을 정돈하려고 애쓰지만, 너희 둘은 항상 엉망으로 만들어." 그가 불평했다.

13 Triangle과 Circle이 서로를 쳐다보았다.

14 "그래서 네 생각에는 네가 우리 없이 다 할 수 있다는 거야?" Triangle이 Square에게 물었다.

15 "물론이지. 난 완전히 혼자서 이 방을 더 낫게 만들 수 있어." Square가 대답했다.

16 "잘됐네! 그럼 우린 쉴 수 있겠어." Circle이 Square에게 말했다.

17 Triangle과 Circle이 밖으로 나갔고 이제 Square가 모든 것을 담당했다.

18 (made / he / hangers, / the / and / plants, / all / round / the / square. / things)

➡ _____

19 (he / then / around / looked / smiled. / and)

➡ _____

20 (better!" / "much)

➡ _____

21 (Mike / when / home / came / school, / from / picked / up / he / hanger / square / a / hang / to / on. / jacket / his)

➡ _____

22 ("what? // will / this / hold / clothes." / my / not)

➡ _____

23 (went / he / water / to / plants / the / and / their / leaves. / saw / square)

➡ _____

24 (things. / "poor // ... / must / they / sick." / be)

➡ _____

25 (picked / he / up / square / the / to / hula hoop / exercise.)

➡ _____

26 ("hmm / ... / don't / I / know / to / how / this." / spin)

➡ _____

27 (went / he / take / to / his / out / bike / and / at / looked / wheels. / square / the)

➡ _____

28 (I / "well, / can't / this. / ride // just / I'll / walk." / to / have)

➡ _____

29 (he / then / out / hurried / of / house. / the)

➡ _____

30 (the / when / spirits / other / back, / came / rushed / Square / them. / to / over)

➡ _____

31 (doesn't / "Mike / his / like / room. // don't / I / know / to / what / do," / said. / he)

➡ _____

32 (looked / they / at / hangers, / the / plants, / and / all / new / the / things. / square)

➡ _____

33 (they / then / at / looked / another, / one / and / realized / Square / problem. / his)

➡ _____

34 (make / "let's / room / this / again," / great / said / he / the / to / others, / and / three / the / worked / spirits / again. / once / together)

➡ _____

18 그는 옷걸이들과 식물들과 모든 둥근 물건들을 사각형으로 만들었다.

19 그리고 나서 그는 주위를 둘러보고 미소 지었다.

20 "훨씬 좋군!"

21 Mike가 학교에서 집으로 왔을 때, 그는 재킷을 걸기 위해 사각형 옷걸이 하나를 집었다.

22 "뭐야? 이것은 내 옷을 걸고 있지 못할 거야."

23 그는 식물에 물을 주러 가서 그것들의 사각형 잎사귀들을 보았다.

24 "불쌍한 것들.… 그들은 병든 것이 틀림없어."

25 그는 운동을 하기 위해 사각형 훌라후프를 집어 들었다.

26 "흠… 이걸 어떻게 돌리는지 모르겠어."

27 그는 자전거를 꺼내러 가서 사각형 바퀴들을 보았다.

28 "음, 난 이걸 탈 수 없어. 그냥 걸어가야 할 것 같아."

29 그리고 나서 그는 서둘러 집을 나섰다.

30 다른 요정들이 돌아왔을 때, Square는 그들에게 달려갔다.

31 "Mike는 그의 방을 좋아하지 않아. 난 뭘 해야 할지 모르겠어." 그가 말했다.

32 그들은 옷걸이들, 식물들, 그리고 모든 새로 사각형이 된 물건들을 바라보았다.

33 그리고 나서 그들은 서로를 바라보았고, Square는 자신의 문제를 깨달았다.

34 "이 방을 다시 멋지게 만들자." 그가 나머지 요정들에게 말했고, 세 요정들은 다시 한 번 함께 일했다.

※ 다음 우리말을 영어로 쓰시오.

1 세 도형 요정들

➡ _____

2 Mike의 방에는 세 도형 요정이 살았다.

➡ _____

3 Square는 탁자, 책장, 그리고 창문을 담당했다.

➡ _____

4 Triangle은 옷걸이들과 식물들을 담당했다.

➡ _____

5 Circle은 둥근 것들을 돌보았다.

➡ _____

6 그들은 Mike에게 좋은 방을 만들어 주기 위해서 함께 일했다.

➡ _____

7 어느 날 Square는 방을 더 낮게 만들기로 결심하고 나머지 요정들에게 소리쳤다.

➡ _____

8 "이 식물들을 치워, 그렇지 않으면 그것들의 끝이 뾰족한 잎사귀들이 누군가를 다치게 할 거야!" 그가 Triangle에게 말했다.

➡ _____

9 "하지만 Mike가 매일 그들에게 물을 주는데." Triangle이 말했다.

➡ _____

10 "이 훌라후프를 치워, 그렇지 않으면 굴러가서 뭔가를 부술 거야!" 그가 Circle에게 말했다.

➡ _____

11 "하지만 Mike는 매일 그걸로 운동을 하는데." Circle이 말했다.

➡ _____

12 "난 이 방을 정돈하려고 애쓰지만, 너희 둘은 항상 엉망으로 만들어." 그가 불평했다.

➡ _____

13 Triangle과 Circle이 서로를 쳐다보았다.

➡ _____

14 "그래서 네 생각에는 네가 우리 없이 다 할 수 있다는 거야?" Triangle이 Square에게 물었다.

➡ _____

15 "물론이지. 난 완전히 혼자서 이 방을 더 낮게 만들 수 있어." Square가 대답했다.

➡ _____

16 "잘됐네! 그럼 우린 쉴 수 있겠어." Circle이 Square에게 말했다.

➡ _____

17 Triangle과 Circle이 밖으로 나갔고 이제 Square가 모든 것을 담당했다.

➡ _____

18 그는 옷걸이들과 식물들과 모든 둥근 물건들을 사각형으로 만들었다.

➡ _____

19 그러고 나서 그는 주위를 둘러보고 미소 지었다.

➡ _____

20 "훨씬 좋군!"

➡ _____

21 Mike가 학교에서 집으로 왔을 때, 그는 재킷을 걸기 위해 사각형 옷걸이 하나를 집었다.

➡ _____

22 "뭐야? 이것은 내 옷을 걸고 있지 못할 거야."

➡ _____

23 그는 식물에 물을 주러 가서 그것들의 사각형 잎사귀들을 보았다.

➡ _____

24 "불쌍한 것들.… 그들은 병든 것이 틀림없어."

➡ _____

25 그는 운동을 하기 위해 사각형 훌라후프를 집어 들었다.

➡ _____

26 "흠… 이걸 어떻게 돌리는지 모르겠어."

➡ _____

27 그는 자전거를 꺼내러 가서 사각형 바퀴들을 보았다.

➡ _____

28 "음, 난 이걸 탈 수 없어. 그냥 걸어가야 할 것 같아."

➡ _____

29 그러고 나서 그는 서둘러 집을 나섰다.

➡ _____

30 다른 요정들이 돌아왔을 때, Square는 그들에게 달려갔다.

➡ _____

31 "Mike는 그의 방을 좋아하지 않아. 난 뭘 해야 할지 모르겠어." 그가 말했다.

➡ _____

32 그들은 옷걸이들, 식물들, 그리고 모든 새로 사각형이 된 물건들을 바라보았다.

➡ _____

33 그러고 나서 그들은 서로를 바라보았고, Square는 자신의 문제를 깨달았다.

➡ _____

34 "이 방을 다시 멋지게 만들자." 그가 나머지 요정들에게 말했고, 세 요정들은 다시 한 번 함께 일했다.

➡ _____

※ 다음 우리말과 일치하도록 빈칸에 알맞은 말을 쓰시오.

Your Turn

1. A: Do you know _____ _____ _____ *ramyeon*?

 B: Sure. _____, boil some water. _____, put the *ramyeon* and dried soup mix. _____, boil for 4 _____ _____.

2. A: Do you know _____ _____ _____ potato salad?

 B: Sure. First, _____ the potatoes. Then, _____ them _____ pieces. Finally, _____ some sauce _____ them.

3. A: Do you know _____ _____ _____ _____?

 B: Sure. First, _____ an egg _____ _____. Then, _____ some vegetables. Finally, _____ bread _____ _____.

Express Yourself

1. _____ for Mom

2. I made a square bag _____ _____ _____ _____ _____.

3. My mom knew _____ _____ _____ _____ it.

4. It _____ her _____. That _____ me _____.

Link to the World

1. Euclid _____ math _____ the Library of Alexandria _____ Ptolemy 1 was the king of Egypt.

2. People _____ him "the _____ of _____."

3. He showed _____ _____ _____ a triangle that has _____ _____ of the _____ _____.

4. He also showed _____ _____ _____ the center of _____ _____ _____ in a triangle.

5. _____ _____, Ptolemy 1 asked, "Is there _____ _____ _____ _____ _____ math?"

6. Euclid replied, "There is no _____ _____ _____ _____."

1. A: 너 라면을 요리할 줄 아니?
 B: 물론이지. 먼저, 약간의 물을 끓여. 그러고 나서, 라면과 건조 수프를 넣어. 마지막으로, 4분을 더 끓여.
2. A: 너 감자 샐러드를 만들 줄 아니?
 B: 물론이지. 먼저, 감자를 삶아. 그러고 나서, 감자를 여러 조각으로 잘라. 마지막으로, 그 위에 소스를 좀 뿌려.
3. A: 너 샌드위치를 만들 줄 아니?
 B: 물론이지. 먼저, 빵 위에 계란을 올려. 그러고 나서, 채소를 약간 추가해. 마지막으로, 빵을 맨 위에 올려.

1. 엄마를 위한 사각형
2. 난 낡은 청바지로 사각형 가방을 만들었어.
3. 엄마는 그걸 걸칠 때 뭘 입어야 할지 아셔.
4. 그것은 엄마를 들뜨게 했어. 그게 나를 행복하게 했어.

1. 유클리드는 프톨레마이오스 1세(Ptolemy I)가 이집트의 왕이었을 때 알렉산드리아 도서관에서 수학을 가르쳤다.
2. 사람들은 그를 '수학의 아버지'라고 부른다.
3. 그는 같은 길이의 세 변을 가진 삼각형을 어떻게 그리는지를 보여 주었다.
4. 그는 또한 한 삼각형 안에서 가장 큰 원의 중심을 어떻게 찾는지도 보여 주었다.
5. 어느 날, 프톨레마이오스 1세가 "수학을 공부하는 더 쉬운 방법은 없나요?" 하고 물었다.
6. 유클리드는 "배움에 왕도는 없습니다."라고 응답했다.

※ 다음 우리말을 영어로 쓰시오.

Your Turn

1. A: 너 라면을 요리할 줄 아니?
 ➡ _____

 B: 물론이지. 먼저, 약간의 물을 끓여. 그리고 나서, 라면과 건조 수프를 넣어. 마지막으로, 4분을 더 끓여.
 ➡ _____

2. A: 너 감자 샐러드를 만들 줄 아니?
 ➡ _____

 B: 물론이지. 먼저, 감자를 삶아. 그리고 나서, 감자를 여러 조각으로 잘라. 마지막으로, 그 위에 소스를 좀 뿌려.
 ➡ _____

3. A: 너 샌드위치를 만들 줄 아니?
 ➡ _____

 B: 물론이지. 먼저, 빵 위에 계란을 올려. 그리고 나서, 채소를 약간 추가해. 마지막으로, 빵을 맨 위에 올려.
 ➡ _____

Express Yourself

1. 엄마를 위한 사각형
 ➡ _____

2. 난 낡은 청바지로 사각형 가방을 만들었어.
 ➡ _____

3. 엄마는 그걸 걸칠 때 뭘 입어야 할지 아셔.
 ➡ _____

4. 그것은 엄마를 들뜨게 했어. 그게 나를 행복하게 했어.
 ➡ _____

Link to the World

1. 유클리드는 프톨레마이오스 1세(Ptolemy I)가 이집트의 왕이었을 때 알렉산드리아 도서관에서 수학을 가르쳤다.
 ➡ _____

2. 사람들은 그를 '수학의 아버지'라고 부른다.
 ➡ _____

3. 그는 같은 길이의 세 변을 가진 삼각형을 어떻게 그리는지를 보여 주었다.
 ➡ _____

4. 그는 또한 한 삼각형 안에서 가장 큰 원의 중심을 어떻게 찾는지도 보여 주었다.
 ➡ _____

5. 어느 날, 프톨레마이오스 1세가 "수학을 공부하는 더 쉬운 방법은 없나요?" 하고 물었다.
 ➡ _____

6. 유클리드는 "배움에 왕도는 없습니다."라고 응답했다.
 ➡ _____

※ 다음 영어를 우리말로 쓰시오.

01 packaging	22 terrible
02 challenge	23 store
03 secret	24 save
04 empty	25 natural
05 serve	26 recycle
06 spotless	27 simple
07 choose	28 food waste
08 actually	29 cotton
09 cloth	30 bin
10 reuse	31 skin
11 reusable	32 blender
12 reduce	33 machine
13 happen	34 language
14 wrapping paper	35 be good for
15 instead	36 throw away
16 thumb	37 as busy as a bee
17 wrap	38 in the middle of
18 plate	39 a big fish
19 collect	40 배수사 as 원급 as
20 trash	41 be on cloud nine
21 product	42 have a green thumb
	43 have a heart of gold

※ 다음 우리말을 영어로 쓰시오.

01 포장, 포장지 _____

02 저장하다 _____

03 도전 _____

04 피부 _____

05 비어 있는 _____

06 자연의, 가공하지 않은 _____

07 재사용하다 _____

08 절약하다, 아끼다 _____

09 음식 쓰레기 _____

10 일어나다, 발생하다 _____

11 모으다, 수집하다 _____

12 제공하다, 나누어 주다 _____

13 섬 _____

14 재사용할 수 있는 _____

15 티끌 하나 없는 _____

16 품목, 항목 _____

17 선택하다 _____

18 특별한 _____

19 끔찍한 _____

20 엄지손가락 _____

21 사실, 실제로 _____

22 줄이다, 축소하다 _____

23 (쓰레기) 통 _____

24 포장하다 _____

25 언어 _____

26 기계 _____

27 단순한 _____

28 대신에 _____

29 대양, 바다 _____

30 쓰레기 _____

31 제품, 상품 _____

32 재활용하다 _____

33 무명, 면 _____

34 비결, 비밀 _____

35 ～을 잘게 자르다 _____

36 ～의 한가운데 _____

37 파티를 열다 _____

38 ～에 좋다 _____

39 버리다 _____

40 동력을 공급받다 _____

41 매우 바쁜 _____

42 ～을 다시 가져가다 _____

43 ～의 몇 배 _____

※ 다음 영영풀이에 알맞은 단어를 <보기>에서 골라 쓴 후, 우리말 뜻을 쓰시오.

1 _____ : a useful piece of advice: _____

2 _____ : the natural outer layer of a person's or animal's body: _____

3 _____ : to have the same opinion: _____

4 _____ : to make smaller in size or number: _____

5 _____ : the short, thick finger on the side of your hand: _____

6 _____ : something new and difficult that requires great effort: _____

7 _____ : special paper that is used for wrapping presents: _____

8 _____ : to let something remain there when you go away: _____

9 _____ : something worthless that you throw away(= garbage, rubbish):

10 _____ : cloth or thread made from the white hair of the cotton plant: _____

11 _____ : to cover something with paper, cloth or other materials: _____

12 _____ : to change waste materials so that they can be used again: _____

13 _____ : something that is known about by only a small number of people and is
 not told to anyone else: _____

14 _____ : used to say what is not used, does not happen, etc, when something else
 is used, happens, etc.: _____

15 _____ : a square of cloth or paper that you use to wipe your mouth or hands:

16 _____ : fabric that is made by weaving a substance such as cotton, wool, silk, or
 nylon: _____

보기			
cloth	skin	tip	wrapping paper
agree	instead	challenge	cotton
napkin	reduce	wrap	trash
recycle	secret	leave	thumb

※ 다음 우리말과 일치하도록 빈칸에 알맞은 말을 쓰시오.

Get Ready 2

(1) B: This shopping bag is so _____.
G: Thank you. We made it _____ _____ a _____ umbrella.
B: What a _____!

(2) B: _____ are you _____ a cup?
G: _____, this cup is a cookie. I can _____ it _____ a cup and then eat it.
B: _____ _____!

(3) B: This bike blender _____ _____ _____ _____ _____.
G: _____ do you _____ _____ that?
B: When you ride this bike, you _____ and _____.
G: Oh, I _____ it.

Start Off Listen & Talk A

(1) G: I _____ _____ today.
B: What do you _____ _____ _____ _____?
G: I _____ I feel _____. We make _____ _____ _____.
B: Ah, I _____ it now. We _____ _____ and _____ more.

(2) G: Minji's classroom is _____.
B: _____ _____ _____ _____ _____ by that?
G: Her classroom is really _____. Look.
B: You're right. _____ _____ some good _____ from her.

Start Off Listen & Talk B

B: Hey, Minji. What is _____ _____ for a _____ classroom?
G: Well, we're doing a _____ bin project today.
B: _____ do you _____ _____ _____ _____?
G: We don't _____ _____, so our trash can _____ _____.
B: That's _____! Please _____ _____ _____ about it.
G: Sure. No _____.

Speak Up Look and talk

B: Plastic _____ are a big problem _____ _____ _____.
G: _____ do you _____ _____ that?
B: They _____ 450 years _____ _____ _____.
G: That's _____!

(1) B: 이 쇼핑백이 아주 아름다워요.
G: 고마워요. 우리는 망가진 우산으로 만들었어요.
B: 놀랍군요!

(2) B: 컵을 왜 먹고 있나요?
G: 사실, 이 컵은 쿠키예요. 나는 이걸 컵으로 사용하고 난 후에 먹을 수 있어요.
B: 놀랍군요!

(3) B: 이 자전거 믹서기는 일석이조예요.
G: 그게 무슨 뜻이에요?
B: 당신이 자전거를 탈 때, 당신은 운동도 하고 주스도 만들어요.
G: 아, 이제 알겠어요.

(1) G: 난 오늘 우울해.
B: 그게 무슨 뜻이야?
G: 내가 슬프다는 뜻이야. 우리가 쓰레기를 너무 많이 버려.
B: 아, 이제 알겠어. 우리는 재활용과 재사용을 더 많이 해야겠어.

(2) G: 민지네 교실은 티끌 하나 없어.
B: 그게 무슨 뜻이야?
G: 그녀의 교실은 정말 깨끗해. 봐.
B: 맞아. 그녀한테서 몇 가지 좋은 비결을 배우자.

B: 이봐, 민지야. 깨끗한 교실을 위한 한 가지 비결이 뭐니?
G: 음, 우리는 오늘 깨끗한 쓰레기통 프로젝트를 하고 있어.
B: 그게 무슨 뜻이야?
G: 우리가 쓰레기를 버리지 않아서 쓰레기통이 비어 있는 거지.
B: 놀랍구나! 나한테 그것에 대해 좀 더 이야기해 줘.
G: 물론이지. 문제없어.

B: 플라스틱병은 지구에 큰 문젯거리야.
G: 그게 무슨 뜻이야?
B: 그것들이 분해되는 데 450년이 걸려.
G: 놀랍구나!

Speak Up Mission

A: My mom has a _____ _____.
B: _____ do you mean _____ _____?
A: She _____ _____ _____ growing _____.
B: I _____ it.

Real-life Scene

G: What are those _____ _____ _____ _____ the ocean?
B: They are _____ _____.
G: Trash islands? What do you _____ _____ that?
B: _____ _____ _____ plastic trash goes into the _____ and _____ _____ _____ _____ _____ those.
G: That _____ _____! _____ _____ are those islands?
B: The _____ one is about 14 times _____ _____ _____ South Korea.
G: That's _____! I think we _____ _____ use plastic products.
B: I _____.

Fun Time

A: I _____ to school _____ _____.
B: That's _____!

A: Minsu is a _____ _____.
B: _____ do you _____ _____ _____?
A: I mean, he is an _____ person.
B: Ah, I get it.

Express Yourself

(1) B: This is the _____ _____.
 G: What do you _____ by that?
 B: It _____ energy from the sun. And it _____ _____ as a _____ _____ at night.
 G: That's _____!

(2) B: What _____ this bus _____?
 G: It _____ _____ the green bus.
 B: What is _____ about it?
 G: The green bus is _____ _____ _____.
 B: That's _____!

Learning Diary Listen & Speak

B: Hey, Minji. Your classroom is _____.
G: Thank you.
B: What's _____ _____ for a clean classroom?
G: Well, we're doing a _____ _____ project this week.
B: _____ _____ _____ _____ _____ _____ _____ _____?
G: We don't _____ _____ trash, so our trash can _____ _____ _____.
B: Ah, I get it now. _____ _____ your tip.
G: My _____.

A: 우리 엄마는 원예에 재능이 있으셔.
B: 그게 무슨 뜻이니?
A: 그녀는 식물을 잘 기르셔.
B: 알겠어.

G: 바다 한가운데 있는 저것들은 뭐니?
B: 그것들은 쓰레기 섬이야.
G: 쓰레기 섬? 그게 무슨 뜻이니?
B: 많은 플라스틱 쓰레기가 바다에 흘러 들어가서 저것들과 같은 큰 섬이 돼.
G: 끔찍하구나! 저 섬들은 얼마나 크니?
B: 가장 큰 것은 남한의 약 14배 정도야.
G: 놀랍구나! 우리는 플라스틱 제품을 쓰지 말아야 해.
B: 맞아.

A: 나는 매일 학교에 스케이트보드를 타고 가.
B: 그거 놀랍구나!

A: 민수는 큰 물고기야.
B: 그게 무슨 뜻이니?
A: 그가 정말 중요한 사람이라는 뜻이야.
B: 아, 알겠어.

(1) B: 이것은 에너지 나무예요.
 G: 그게 무슨 뜻이에요?
 B: 그것은 태양으로부터 에너지를 생산해요. 그리고 밤에는 가로등으로 사용돼요.
 G: 놀랍군요!

(2) B: 이 버스는 뭐라고 불리나요?
 G: 그것은 친환경 버스라고 불려요.
 B: 뭐가 특별한가요?
 G: 친환경 버스는 쓰레기로부터 동력을 공급받아요.
 B: 놀랍군요!

B: 이봐, 민지야. 네 교실은 티끌 하나 없더라.
G: 고마워.
B: 깨끗한 교실을 위한 한 가지 조언이 뭐니?
G: 음, 우리는 이번 주에 깨끗한 휴지통 프로젝트를 하는 중이야.
B: 그게 무슨 뜻이니?
G: 우리가 쓰레기를 안 버려서 쓰레기통이 비어 있어.
B: 아, 알겠어. 조언 고마워.
G: 천만에.

※ 다음 우리말에 맞도록 대화를 영어로 쓰시오.

Get Ready 2

(1) B: _____

　　G: _____

　　B: _____

(2) B: _____

　　G: _____

　　B: _____

(3) B: _____

　　G: _____

　　B: _____

　　G: _____

Start Off Listen & Talk A

(1) G: _____

　　B: _____

　　G: _____

　　B: _____

(2) G: _____

　　B: _____

　　G: _____

　　B: _____

Start Off Listen & Talk B

B: _____

G: _____

B: _____

G: _____

B: _____

G: _____

Speak Up Look and talk

B: _____

G: _____

B: _____

G: _____

(1) B: 이 쇼핑백이 아주 아름다워요.
　　G: 고마워요. 우리는 망가진 우산으로 만들었어요.
　　B: 놀랍군요!

(2) B: 컵을 왜 먹고 있나요?
　　G: 사실, 이 컵은 쿠키예요. 나는 이걸 컵으로 사용하고 난 후에 먹을 수 있어요.
　　B: 놀랍군요!

(3) B: 이 자전거 믹서기는 일석이조예요.
　　G: 그게 무슨 뜻이에요?
　　B: 당신이 자전거를 탈 때, 당신은 운동도 하고 주스도 만들어요.
　　G: 아, 이제 알겠어요.

(1) G: 난 오늘 우울해.
　　B: 그게 무슨 뜻이야?
　　G: 내가 슬프다는 뜻이야. 우리가 쓰레기를 너무 많이 버려.
　　B: 아, 이제 알겠어. 우리는 재활용과 재사용을 더 많이 해야겠어.

(2) G: 민지네 교실은 티끌 하나 없어.
　　B: 그게 무슨 뜻이야?
　　G: 그녀의 교실은 정말 깨끗해. 봐.
　　B: 맞아. 그녀한테서 몇 가지 좋은 비결을 배우자.

B: 이봐, 민지야. 깨끗한 교실을 위한 한 가지 비결이 뭐니?
G: 음, 우리는 오늘 깨끗한 쓰레기통 프로젝트를 하고 있어.
B: 그게 무슨 뜻이야?
G: 우리가 쓰레기를 버리지 않아서 쓰레기통이 비어 있는 거지.
B: 놀랍구나! 나한테 그것에 대해 좀 더 이야기해 줘.
G: 물론이지. 문제없어.

B: 플라스틱병은 지구에 큰 문젯거리야.
G: 그게 무슨 뜻이야?
B: 그것들이 분해되는 데 450년이 걸려.
G: 놀랍구나!

Speak Up Mission

A: _____

B: _____

A: _____

B: _____

Real-life Scene

G: _____

B: _____

G: _____

B: _____

G: _____

B: _____

G: _____

B: _____

Fun Time

A: _____

B: _____

A: _____

B: _____

A: _____

B: _____

Express Yourself

(1) B: _____

G: _____

B: _____

G: _____

(2) B: _____

G: _____

B: _____

G: _____

B: _____

Learning Diary Listen & Speak

B: _____

G: _____

B: _____

G: _____

B: _____

G: _____

B: _____

G: _____

A: 우리 엄마는 원예에 재능이 있으셔.
B: 그게 무슨 뜻이니?
A: 그녀는 식물을 잘 기르셔.
B: 알겠어.

G: 바다 한가운데 있는 저것들은 뭐니?
B: 그것들은 쓰레기 섬이야.
G: 쓰레기 섬? 그게 무슨 뜻이니?
B: 많은 플라스틱 쓰레기가 바다에 흘러 들어가서 저것들과 같은 큰 섬이 돼.
G: 끔찍하구나! 저 섬들은 얼마나 크니?
B: 가장 큰 것은 남한의 약 14배 정도야.
G: 놀랍구나! 우리는 플라스틱 제품을 쓰지 말아야 해.
B: 맞아.

A: 나는 매일 학교에 스케이트보드를 타고 가.
B: 그거 놀랍구나!

A: 민수는 큰 물고기야.
B: 그게 무슨 뜻이니?
A: 그가 정말 중요한 사람이라는 뜻이야.
B: 아, 알겠어.

(1) B: 이것은 에너지 나무예요.
 G: 그게 무슨 뜻이에요?
 B: 그것은 태양으로부터 에너지를 생산해요. 그리고 밤에는 가로등으로 사용돼요.
 G: 놀랍군요!

(2) B: 이 버스는 뭐라고 불리나요?
 G: 그것은 친환경 버스라고 불려요.
 B: 뭐가 특별한가요?
 G: 친환경 버스는 쓰레기로부터 동력을 공급받아요.
 B: 놀랍군요!

B: 이봐, 민지야. 네 교실은 티끌 하나 없더라.
G: 고마워.
B: 깨끗한 교실을 위한 한 가지 조언이 뭐니?
G: 음, 우리는 이번 주에 깨끗한 휴지통 프로젝트를 하는 중이야.
B: 그게 무슨 뜻이니?
G: 우리가 쓰레기를 안 버려서 쓰레기통이 비어 있어.
B: 아, 알겠어. 조언 고마워.
G: 천만에.

※ 다음 우리말과 일치하도록 빈칸에 알맞은 것을 골라 쓰시오.

1 _____ Trash _____
A. Challenge B. No

2 We all _____ a "No _____ Challenge" day _____ month.
A. Trash B. last C. had

3 The _____ was _____ 2 _____ 3.
A. Class B. winner C. Grade

4 _____ read the interview and learn a _____ _____ for living _____.
A. green B. let's C. tips D. few

5 _____ Not Use _____ _____
A. Paper B. Do C. Wrapping

6 Reporter: You _____ a class birthday party, but didn't _____ a lot of _____.
A. produce B. threw C. trash

7 What were _____ _____?
A. secrets B. your

8 Minsu: First, we _____ not to _____ our gifts, _____ some wrapping paper is not easily _____.
A. recycled B. wrap C. because D. agreed

9 So we _____ gifts such _____ teddy bears, key rings, and hairpins that were not _____ at _____.
A. as B. all C. wrapped D. brought

10 _____ the _____ Size
A. Largest B. Buy

11 Jieun: Also, we _____ the _____ size when we _____ ice cream and cookies for the party.
A. largest B. bought C. chose

12 Larger sizes use _____ _____ and make less _____.
A. packaging B. trash C. less

13 _____ the _____
A. Plates B. Eat

14 Reporter: And _____ did you _____ the ice cream?
A. serve B. how

15 Junha: We _____ it _____ _____.
A. on B. served C. plates

16 You _____ _____?
A. what B. know

17 We ate _____ the plates _____ we _____ them.
A. used B. even C. after

18 Reporter: You _____ the _____?
A. plates B. ate

19 What do you _____ _____ _____?
A. by B. mean C. that

1 쓰레기를 없애기 위한 도전

2 우리는 모두 지난달에 '쓰레기를 없애기 위한 도전'의 날을 가졌습니다.

3 우승자는 2학년 3반이었습니다.

4 인터뷰를 읽고, 친환경적으로 살기 위한 몇 가지 비결을 배웁시다.

5 포장지를 사용하지 마라

6 기자: 여러분은 학급 생일 파티를 열었지만, 쓰레기가 많이 나오지 않았어요.

7 비결이 무엇입니까?

8 민수: 우선, 우리는 몇몇 포장지가 쉽게 재활용되지 않기 때문에 선물을 포장하지 않는 것에 동의했습니다.

9 그래서 우리는 전혀 포장되어 있지 않은 곰 인형, 열쇠고리, 머리핀과 같은 선물을 가져왔습니다.

10 가장 큰 크기를 사라

11 지은: 또한, 우리는 파티를 위한 아이스크림과 쿠키를 살 때, 가장 큰 크기를 골랐습니다.

12 크기가 더 크면 포장을 더 적게 사용하고 쓰레기를 더 적게 배출하거든요.

13 접시를 먹어라

14 기자: 그리고 아이스크림은 어떻게 나누어 주었나요?

15 준하: 우리는 접시에 그것을 나누어 주었습니다.

16 아세요?

17 우리는 사용한 후에 접시까지도 먹었어요.

18 기자: 접시를 먹었다고요?

19 그게 무슨 뜻이죠?

20 Junha: Actually, we used popped rice cakes _____ _____, so we could eat them and _____ nothing _____!
A. behind B. leave C. plates D. as

21 Reporter: Ah, I _____ _____.
A. it B. get

22 That's _____ _____.
A. interesting B. quite

23 _____ Your _____ Things
A. Own B. Bring

24 Reporter: _____ _____ cups and spoons?
A. about B. what

25 Minsu: We _____ _____ paper cups or _____ spoons.
A. plastic B. use C. didn't

26 _____, we _____ our own cups and spoons from home and then _____ them _____.
A. took B. brought C. instead D. back

27 _____ _____ Napkins
A. Cloth B. Use

28 Reporter: What _____ did you do to make _____ _____?
A. else B. trash C. less

29 Jieun: We _____ _____ napkins.
A. used B. cloth

30 You know, paper napkins are not _____ _____ your _____.
A. good B. skin C. for

31 Reporter: But _____ did you _____ the _____ napkins?
A. cloth B. get C. where

32 Jieun: They _____ _____ _____ Minji.
A. were B. by C. made

33 She _____ _____ her old cotton shirt to _____ some for us.
A. make B. up C. cut

34 _____ liked _____ _____ napkins.
A. cute B. everyone C. her

35 _____ No Food _____
A. Behind B. Leave

36 Reporter: Please give us one _____ _____ for _____ _____.
A. simple B. reducing C. tip D. trash

37 Junha: _____ _____ any food on your _____.
A. leave B. plate C. don't

38 _____ really is a _____ problem.
A. waste B. big C. food

39 _____ _____?
A. see B. but

40 We _____ _____, _____ our plates, ha-ha.
A. ate B. even C. everything

20 준하: 사실, 우리는 뻥튀기를 접시로 사용해서, 그것들을 먹고 아무것도 남기지 않을 수 있었죠.

21 기자: 아, 알겠어요.

22 그거 꽤 흥미롭군요.

23 여러분 자신의 물건을 가져와라

24 기자: 컵과 숟가락은 어떻게 했나요?

25 민수: 우리는 종이컵이나 플라스틱 숟가락을 사용하지 않았습니다.

26 대신에, 우리 컵과 숟가락을 집에서 가져온 후, 다시 가져갔습니다.

27 천 냅킨을 사용해라

28 기자: 쓰레기를 더 줄이기 위해 그 외에 무엇을 했나요?

29 지은: 우리는 천 냅킨을 사용했어요.

30 아시다시피, 종이 냅킨은 여러분의 피부에 안 좋잖아요.

31 기자: 하지만 천 냅킨을 어디서 구했나요?

32 지은: 그것들은 민지가 만들었어요.

33 그녀가 우리에게 몇 개를 만들어 주기 위해 자신의 낡은 면 셔츠를 잘랐어요.

34 그녀의 귀여운 냅킨을 모두가 좋아했어요.

35 음식을 남기지 마라

36 기자: 우리에게 쓰레기를 줄이기 위한 간단한 조언을 하나만 해 주세요.

37 준하: 접시에 음식을 남기지 마세요.

38 음식 쓰레기는 정말 큰 문제입니다.

39 하지만 아시죠?

40 우리는 모두 다 먹었죠, 접시까지도요, 하하.

※ 다음 우리말과 일치하도록 빈칸에 알맞은 말을 쓰시오.

1 No _____ _____

2 We all had a "_____ _____ _____" day last month.

3 The winner was _____ _____ _____ _____ .

4 _____ _____ the interview and learn _____ _____
_____ for _____ _____ .

5 _____ _____ Use _____ _____

6 Reporter: You _____ a class birthday party, but _____
_____ a _____ of trash.

7 What were _____ _____ ?

8 Minsu: First, we _____ _____ _____ _____ our gifts,
_____ some wrapping paper _____ _____ _____
_____ .

9 So we brought gifts _____ _____ teddy bears, key rings, and
hairpins that were _____ _____ _____ _____ .

10 _____ the _____ Size

11 Jieun: Also, we _____ _____ _____ _____ _____ when we
_____ ice cream and cookies for the party.

12 Larger sizes use _____ _____ and make _____ _____ .

13 _____ the _____

14 Reporter: And _____ did you _____ the ice cream?

15 Junha: We _____ it _____ _____ .

16 _____ _____ _____ ?

17 We ate _____ _____ _____ after we _____ them.

18 Reporter: You _____ _____ _____ ?

19 What do you _____ _____ _____ ?

1 쓰레기를 없애기 위한 도전

2 우리는 모두 지난달에 '쓰레기를 없애기 위한 도전'의 날을 가졌습니다.

3 우승자는 2학년 3반이었습니다.

4 인터뷰를 읽고, 친환경적으로 살기 위한 몇 가지 비결을 배웁시다.

5 포장지를 사용하지 마라

6 기자: 여러분은 학급 생일 파티를 열었지만, 쓰레기가 많이 나오지 않았어요.

7 비결이 무엇입니까?

8 민수: 우선, 우리는 몇몇 포장지가 쉽게 재활용되지 않기 때문에 선물을 포장하지 않는 것에 동의했습니다.

9 그래서 우리는 전혀 포장되어 있지 않은 곰 인형, 열쇠고리, 머리핀과 같은 선물을 가져왔습니다.

10 가장 큰 크기를 사라

11 지은: 또한, 우리는 파티를 위한 아이스크림과 쿠키를 살 때, 가장 큰 크기를 골랐습니다.

12 크기가 더 크면 포장을 더 적게 사용하고 쓰레기를 더 적게 배출하거든요.

13 접시를 먹어라

14 기자: 그리고 아이스크림은 어떻게 나누어 주었나요?

15 준하: 우리는 접시에 그것을 나누어 주었습니다.

16 아세요?

17 우리는 사용한 후에 접시까지도 먹었어요.

18 기자: 접시를 먹었다고요?

19 그게 무슨 뜻이죠?

20 Junha: Actually, we used _____ rice cakes _____ _____ , so we could eat them and _____ _____ _____ !

21 Reporter: Ah, I _____ _____ .

22 That's _____ _____ .

23 _____ Your _____ Things

24 Reporter: _____ _____ cups and spoons?

25 Minsu: We _____ _____ paper cups or plastic spoons.

26 _____ , we _____ our own cups and spoons _____ home and then _____ _____ _____ .

27 Use _____ Napkins

28 Reporter: What else did you do to _____ _____ _____ ?

29 Jieun: We _____ _____ _____ .

30 You know, paper napkins _____ _____ _____ _____ _____ .

31 Reporter: But _____ _____ _____ _____ the cloth napkins?

32 Jieun: They _____ _____ _____ Minji.

33 She _____ _____ her old cotton shirt to make some for us.

34 _____ liked _____ _____ _____ .

35 _____ No Food _____

36 Reporter: Please give us _____ _____ _____ for _____ _____ .

37 Junha: _____ _____ any food on your _____ .

38 _____ _____ really is a big problem.

39 But _____ ?

40 We _____ _____ , _____ our plates, ha-ha.

20 준하: 사실. 우리는 뻥튀기를 접시로 사용해서, 그것들을 먹고 아무것도 남기지 않을 수 있었죠.

21 기자: 아, 알겠어요.

22 그거 꽤 흥미롭군요.

23 여러분 자신의 물건을 가져와라

24 기자: 컵과 숟가락은 어떻게 했나요?

25 민수: 우리는 종이컵이나 플라스틱 숟가락을 사용하지 않았습니다.

26 대신에, 우리 컵과 숟가락을 집에서 가져온 후, 다시 가져갔습니다.

27 천 냅킨을 사용해라

28 기자: 쓰레기를 더 줄이기 위해 그 외에 무엇을 했나요?

29 지은: 우리는 천 냅킨을 사용했어요.

30 아시다시피. 종이 냅킨은 여러분의 피부에 안 좋잖아요.

31 기자: 하지만 천 냅킨을 어디서 구했나요?

32 지은: 그것들은 민지가 만들었어요.

33 그녀가 우리에게 몇 개를 만들어 주기 위해 자신의 낡은 면 셔츠를 잘랐어요.

34 그녀의 귀여운 냅킨을 모두가 좋아했어요.

35 음식을 남기지 마라

36 기자: 우리에게 쓰레기를 줄이기 위한 간단한 조언을 하나만 해 주세요.

37 준하: 접시에 음식을 남기지 마세요.

38 음식 쓰레기는 정말 큰 문제입니다.

39 하지만 아시죠?

40 우리는 모두 다 먹었죠, 접시까지도요, 하하.

※ 다음 문장을 우리말로 쓰시오.

1 ▸ No Trash Challenge
➡ _____

2 ▸ We all had a "No Trash Challenge" day last month.
➡ _____

3 ▸ The winner was Grade 2 Class 3.
➡ _____

4 ▸ Let's read the interview and learn a few tips for living green.
➡ _____

5 ▸ Do Not Use Wrapping Paper
➡ _____

6 ▸ Reporter: You threw a class birthday party, but didn't produce a lot of trash.
➡ _____

7 ▸ What were your secrets?
➡ _____

8 ▸ Minsu: First, we agreed not to wrap our gifts, because some wrapping paper is not easily recycled.
➡ _____

9 ▸ So we brought gifts such as teddy bears, key rings, and hairpins that were not wrapped at all.
➡ _____

10 ▸ Buy the Largest Size
➡ _____

11 ▸ Jieun: Also, we chose the largest size when we bought ice cream and cookies for the party.
➡ _____

12 ▸ Larger sizes use less packaging and make less trash.
➡ _____

13 ▸ Eat the Plates
➡ _____

14 ▸ Reporter: And how did you serve the ice cream?
➡ _____

15 ▸ Junha: We served it on plates.
➡ _____

16 ▸ You know what?
➡ _____

17 ▸ We ate even the plates after we used them.
➡ _____

18 ▸ Reporter: You ate the plates?
➡ _____

19 ▸ What do you mean by that?
➡ _____

20 Junha: Actually, we used popped rice cakes as plates, so we could eat them and leave nothing behind!
➡ _____

21 Reporter: Ah, I get it.
➡ _____

22 That's quite interesting.
➡ _____

23 Bring Your Own Things
➡ _____

24 Reporter: What about cups and spoons?
➡ _____

25 Minsu: We didn't use paper cups or plastic spoons.
➡ _____

26 Instead, we brought our own cups and spoons from home and then took them back.
➡ _____

27 Use Cloth Napkins
➡ _____

28 Reporter: What else did you do to make less trash?
➡ _____

29 Jieun: We used cloth napkins.
➡ _____

30 You know, paper napkins are not good for your skin.
➡ _____

31 Reporter: But where did you get the cloth napkins?
➡ _____

32 Jieun: They were made by Minji.
➡ _____

33 She cut up her old cotton shirt to make some for us.
➡ _____

34 Everyone liked her cute napkins.
➡ _____

35 Leave No Food Behind
➡ _____

36 Reporter: Please give us one simple tip for reducing trash.
➡ _____

37 Junha: Don't leave any food on your plate.
➡ _____

38 Food waste really is a big problem.
➡ _____

39 But see?
➡ _____

40 We ate everything, even our plates, ha-ha.
➡ _____

※ 다음 괄호 안의 단어들을 우리말에 맞도록 바르게 배열하시오.

1 (Trash / No / Challenge)
➡ _____

2 (all / we / a / had / Trash / "No / Challenge" / day / month. / last)
➡ _____

3 (winner / the / Grade / was / 3. / Class / 2)
➡ _____

4 (read / let's / interview / the / and / a / learn / few / for / tips / green. / living)
➡ _____

5 (Not / Do / Wrapping / Use / Paper)
➡ _____

6 (Reporter: / threw / you / class / a / party, / birthday / didn't / but / a / produce / lot / trash. / of)
➡ _____

7 (were / what / secrets? / your)
➡ _____

8 (Minsu: / we / first, / agreed / to / not / wrap / gifts, / our / some / because / paper / wrapping / not / is / recycled. / easily)
➡ _____

9 (we / so / gifts / brought / as / such / bears, / teddy / rings, / key / and / that / hairpins / not / were / all. / at / wrapped)
➡ _____

10 (the / Buy / Size / Largest)
➡ _____

11 (Jieun: / we / also, / chose / largest / the / size / when / bought / we / cream / ice / and / for / cookies / party. / the)
➡ _____

12 (sizes / larger / less / use / packaging / and / make / trash. / less)
➡ _____

13 (Plates / the / Eat)
➡ _____

14 (Reporter: / how / and / you / did / serve / cream? / ice / the)
➡ _____

15 (Junha: / served / we / it / plates. / on)
➡ _____

16 (know / what? / you)
➡ _____

17 (ate / we / the / even / plates / after / we / them. / used)
➡ _____

18 (Reporter: / ate / you / plates? / the)
➡ _____

19 (do / what / mean / you / that? / by)
➡ _____

1 쓰레기를 없애기 위한 도전

2 우리는 모두 지난달에 '쓰레기를 없애기 위한 도전'의 날을 가졌습니다.

3 우승자는 2학년 3반이었습니다.

4 인터뷰를 읽고, 친환경적으로 살기 위한 몇 가지 비결을 배웁시다.

5 포장지를 사용하지 마라

6 기자: 여러분은 학급 생일 파티를 열었지만, 쓰레기가 많이 나오지 않았어요.

7 비결이 무엇입니까?

8 민수: 우선, 우리는 몇몇 포장지가 쉽게 재활용되지 않기 때문에 선물을 포장하지 않는 것에 동의했습니다.

9 그래서 우리는 전혀 포장되어 있지 않은 곰 인형, 열쇠고리, 머리핀과 같은 선물을 가져왔습니다.

10 가장 큰 크기를 사라

11 지은: 또한, 우리는 파티를 위한 아이스크림과 쿠키를 살 때, 가장 큰 크기를 골랐습니다.

12 크기가 더 크면 포장을 더 적게 사용하고 쓰레기를 더 적게 배출하거든요.

13 접시를 먹어라

14 기자: 그리고 아이스크림은 어떻게 나누어 주었나요?

15 준하: 우리는 접시에 그것을 나누어 주었습니다.

16 아세요?

17 우리는 사용한 후에 접시까지도 먹었어요.

18 기자: 접시를 먹었다고요?

19 그게 무슨 뜻이죠?

20 (Junha: / we / actually, / used / rice / popped / cakes / plates, / as / so / could / we / them / eat / and / leave / behind! / nothing)
➡ _____

21 (Reporter: / I / ah, / it. / get)
➡ _____

22 (quite / that's / interesting.)
➡ _____

23 (Your / Bring / Things / Own)
➡ _____

24 (Reporter: / about / what / cups / spoons? / and)
➡ _____

25 (Minsu: / didn't / we / paper / use / cups / plastic / or / spoons.)
➡ _____

26 (we / instead, / brought / own / our / and / cups / from / spoons / home / and / took / then / back. / them)
➡ _____

27 (Cloth / Use / Napkins)
➡ _____

28 (Reporter: / else / what / you / did / to / do / make / trash? / less)
➡ _____

29 (Jieun: / used / we / napkins. / cloth)
➡ _____

30 (know, / you / napkins / paper / not / are / for / good / skin. / your)
➡ _____

31 (Reporter: / where / but / you / did / get / the / napkins? / cloth)
➡ _____

32 (Jieun: / were / they / by / made / Minji.)
➡ _____

33 (cut / she / up / old / her / shirt / cotton / make / to / us. / for / some)
➡ _____

34 (liked / everyone / her / napkins. / cute)
➡ _____

35 (No / Behind / Leave / Food)
➡ _____

36 (Reporter: / give / please / us / simple / one / for / tip / trash. / reducing)
➡ _____

37 (Junha: / leave / don't / food / any / on / plate. / your)
➡ _____

38 (waste / food / is / really / big / a / problem.)
➡ _____

39 (see? / but)
➡ _____

40 (ate / we / everythiing, / our / even / ha-ha. / plates,)
➡ _____

20 준하: 사실, 우리는 뻥튀기를 접시로 사용해서, 그것들을 먹고 아무것도 남기지 않을 수 있었죠.

21 기자: 아, 알겠어요.

22 그거 꽤 흥미롭군요.

23 여러분 자신의 물건을 가져와라

24 기자: 컵과 숟가락은 어떻게 했나요?

25 민수: 우리는 종이컵이나 플라스틱 숟가락을 사용하지 않았습니다.

26 대신에, 우리 컵과 숟가락을 집에서 가져온 후, 다시 가져갔습니다.

27 천 냅킨을 사용해라

28 기자: 쓰레기를 더 줄이기 위해 그 외에 무엇을 했나요?

29 지은: 우리는 천 냅킨을 사용했어요.

30 아시다시피, 종이 냅킨은 여러분의 피부에 안 좋잖아요.

31 기자: 하지만 천 냅킨을 어디서 구했나요?

32 지은: 그것들은 민지가 만들었어요.

33 그녀가 우리에게 몇 개를 만들어 주기 위해 자신의 낡은 면 셔츠를 잘랐어요.

34 그녀의 귀여운 냅킨을 모두가 좋아했어요.

35 음식을 남기지 마라

36 기자: 우리에게 쓰레기를 줄이기 위한 간단한 조언을 하나만 해 주세요.

37 준하: 접시에 음식을 남기지 마세요.

38 음식 쓰레기는 정말 큰 문제입니다.

39 하지만 아시죠?

40 우리는 모두 다 먹었죠, 접시까지도요, 하하.

※ 다음 우리말을 영어로 쓰시오.

1 쓰레기를 없애기 위한 도전
➡ _____

2 우리는 모두 지난달에 '쓰레기를 없애기 위한 도전'의 날을 가졌습니다.
➡ _____

3 우승자는 2학년 3반이었습니다.
➡ _____

4 인터뷰를 읽고, 친환경적으로 살기 위한 몇 가지 비결을 배웁시다.
➡ _____

5 포장지를 사용하지 마라
➡ _____

6 기자: 여러분은 학급 생일 파티를 열었지만, 쓰레기가 많이 나오지 않았어요.
➡ _____

7 비결이 무엇입니까?
➡ _____

8 민수: 우선, 우리는 몇몇 포장지가 쉽게 재활용되지 않기 때문에 선물을 포장하지 않는 것에 동의했습니다.
➡ _____

9 그래서 우리는 전혀 포장되어 있지 않은 곰 인형, 열쇠고리, 머리핀과 같은 선물을 가져왔습니다.
➡ _____

10 가장 큰 크기를 사라
➡ _____

11 지은: 또한, 우리는 파티를 위한 아이스크림과 쿠키를 살 때, 가장 큰 크기를 골랐습니다.
➡ _____

12 크기가 더 크면 포장을 더 적게 사용하고 쓰레기를 더 적게 배출하거든요.
➡ _____

13 접시를 먹어라
➡ _____

14 기자: 그리고 아이스크림은 어떻게 나누어 주었나요?
➡ _____

15 준하: 우리는 접시에 그것을 나누어 주었습니다.
➡ _____

16 아세요?
➡ _____

17 우리는 사용한 후에 접시까지도 먹었어요.
➡ _____

18 기자: 접시를 먹었다고요?
➡ _____

19 그게 무슨 뜻이죠?
➡ _____

20 준하: 사실, 우리는 뻥튀기를 접시로 사용해서, 그것들을 먹고 아무것도 남기지 않을 수 있었죠.
➡ _____

21 기자: 아, 알겠어요.
➡ _____

22 그거 꽤 흥미롭군요.
➡ _____

23 여러분 자신의 물건을 가져와라
➡ _____

24 기자: 컵과 숟가락은 어떻게 했나요?
➡ _____

25 민수: 우리는 종이컵이나 플라스틱 숟가락을 사용하지 않았습니다.
➡ _____

26 대신에, 우리 컵과 숟가락을 집에서 가져온 후, 다시 가져갔습니다.
➡ _____

27 천 냅킨을 사용해라
➡ _____

28 기자: 쓰레기를 더 줄이기 위해 그 외에 무엇을 했나요?
➡ _____

29 지은: 우리는 천 냅킨을 사용했어요.
➡ _____

30 아시다시피, 종이 냅킨은 여러분의 피부에 안 좋잖아요.
➡ _____

31 기자: 하지만 천 냅킨을 어디서 구했나요?
➡ _____

32 지은: 그것들은 민지가 만들었어요.
➡ _____

33 그녀가 우리에게 몇 개를 만들어 주기 위해 자신의 낡은 면 셔츠를 잘랐어요.
➡ _____

34 그녀의 귀여운 냅킨을 모두가 좋아했어요.
➡ _____

35 음식을 남기지 마라
➡ _____

36 기자: 우리에게 쓰레기를 줄이기 위한 간단한 조언을 하나만 해 주세요.
➡ _____

37 준하: 접시에 음식을 남기지 마세요.
➡ _____

38 음식 쓰레기는 정말 큰 문제입니다.
➡ _____

39 하지만 아시죠?
➡ _____

40 우리는 모두 다 먹었죠, 접시까지도요, 하하.
➡ _____

※ 다음 우리말과 일치하도록 빈칸에 알맞은 말을 쓰시오.

Project Do it yourself

1. This is a hand puppet. It _____ _____ _____ my old sock.

2. It took only _____ _____ _____ _____ _____ this.

3. _____ _____ _____ _____ more sock puppets and have a wonderful _____ _____ together.

4. This is a paper bag lamp. It _____ _____ _____ _____ a _____ paper shopping bag.

5. Light _____ _____ _____ the holes.

1. 이것은 손 인형입니다. 그것은 제 오래된 양말로 만들어졌습니다.
2. 이것을 만드는 데는 시간이 거의 안 걸렸습니다.
3. 손 인형을 몇 개 더 만들어서 함께 멋진 인형극을 해 봅시다.
4. 이것은 종이 가방 램프입니다. 그것은 사용한 종이 쇼핑 가방으로 만들었습니다.
5. 빛이 구멍을 통해 아름답게 빛납니다.

Express Yourself C

1. _____ City _____

2. So many ideas _____ _____ _____ the Earth Savers Club.

3. In the restaurants, food _____ _____ _____ _____ _____.

4. _____ _____ is _____ this way.

5. At every house, _____ _____ _____ _____ in the tanks.

6. _____ _____ _____ this way.

1. 친환경 도시 아이디어
2. 아주 많은 의견이 '지구를 지키는 동호회'에 의해 제안되었습니다.
3. 식당에서는 음식이 작은 접시에 제공됩니다.
4. 이렇게 해서 음식 쓰레기가 줄어듭니다.
5. 모든 집에서는 빗물이 탱크에 저장됩니다.
6. 이렇게 해서 물이 절약됩니다.

Link to The World

1. Spoons _____ You _____ _____ _____

2. You _____ _____ _____ _____.

3. They _____ _____ _____ _____ rice.

4. They are 100% _____.

5. We can _____ these _____ spoons and _____ plastic _____.

6. We also _____ _____ water _____ we _____ _____ _____ wash these spoons.

1. 먹을 수 있는 숟가락
2. 당신은 이 숟가락을 먹을 수 있습니다.
3. 그것들은 쌀로 만들어졌습니다.
4. 그것들은 100% 천연 제품입니다.
5. 우리는 이 친환경 숟가락을 사용하여 플라스틱 쓰레기를 줄일 수 있습니다.
6. 우리는 이 숟가락들을 씻을 필요 없기 때문에 물도 절약할 수 있습니다.

※ 다음 우리말을 영어로 쓰시오.

Project Do it yourself

1. 이것은 손 인형입니다. 그것은 제 오래된 양말로 만들어졌습니다.
 ➡ _____

2. 이것을 만드는 데는 시간이 거의 안 걸렸습니다.
 ➡ _____

3. 손 인형을 몇 개 더 만들어서 함께 멋진 인형극을 해 봅시다.
 ➡ _____

4. 이것은 종이 가방 램프입니다. 그것은 사용한 종이 쇼핑 가방으로 만들었습니다.
 ➡ _____

5. 빛이 구멍을 통해 아름답게 빛납니다.
 ➡ _____

Express Yourself C

1. 친환경 도시 아이디어
 ➡ _____

2. 아주 많은 의견이 '지구를 지키는 동호회'에 의해 제안되었습니다.
 ➡ _____

3. 식당에서는 음식이 작은 접시에 제공됩니다.
 ➡ _____

4. 이렇게 해서 음식 쓰레기가 줄어듭니다.
 ➡ _____

5. 모든 집에서는 빗물이 탱크에 저장됩니다.
 ➡ _____

6. 이렇게 해서 물이 절약됩니다.
 ➡ _____

Link to The World

1. 먹을 수 있는 숟가락
 ➡ _____

2. 당신은 이 숟가락을 먹을 수 있습니다.
 ➡ _____

3. 그것들은 쌀로 만들어졌습니다.
 ➡ _____

4. 그것들은 100% 천연 제품입니다.
 ➡ _____

5. 우리는 이 친환경 숟가락을 사용하여 플라스틱 쓰레기를 줄일 수 있습니다.
 ➡ _____

6. 우리는 이 숟가락들을 씻을 필요가 없기 때문에 물도 절약할 수 있습니다.
 ➡ _____

※ 다음 영어를 우리말로 쓰시오.

01 awesome		22 poem	
02 below		23 foreign	
03 classical		24 creative	
04 actually		25 popular	
05 example		26 monster	
06 season		27 both	
07 unique		28 perfect	
08 widely		29 tool	
09 excellent		30 imagine	
10 difference		31 handwriting	
11 express		32 lightning	
12 fantasy		33 collect	
13 include		34 sharp	
14 dynasty		35 be made of	
15 wizard		36 lead to	
16 tale		37 build up	
17 detective		38 look like+명사	
18 craft		39 take a class	
19 figure		40 take+시간+to V	
20 artistic		41 for free	
21 performance		42 dance to	
		43 at first	

Step2

※ 다음 우리말을 영어로 쓰시오.

01 ~의 아래에 _____

02 탐정; 탐정의 _____

03 공예 _____

04 실제로 _____

05 완벽한 _____

06 글자, 성격 _____

07 공연 _____

08 판타지, 환상, 공상 _____

09 창의적인 _____

10 멋있는, 대단한, 굉장한 _____

11 손 글씨, 필적 _____

12 잡다 _____

13 훌륭한, 뛰어난 _____

14 (사람, 동물의) 상, 모형 _____

15 시 _____

16 왕조, 왕가 _____

17 차이 _____

18 예술의, 예술적인 _____

19 이야기 _____

20 공포 _____

21 널리 _____

22 인기 있는 _____

23 꼬리 _____

24 외국의 _____

25 배우다 _____

26 번개 _____

27 예, 사례 _____

28 ~의 사이에 _____

29 모으다 _____

30 괴물 _____

31 마법사 _____

32 날카로운 _____

33 표현하다 _____

34 독특한, 특별한 _____

35 ~에 맞춰 춤추다 _____

36 처음에 _____

37 만들다 _____

38 무료로 _____

39 ~에 관심이 있다 _____

40 ~로 이끌다, ~로 이어지다 _____

41 ~로 만들어지다 _____

42 수업을 듣다 _____

43 ~처럼 보이다 _____

※ 다음 영영풀이에 알맞은 단어를 <보기>에서 골라 쓴 후, 우리말 뜻을 쓰시오.

1 _____ : relating to any form of art: _____

2 _____ : in a lower place or position: _____

3 _____ : not the same as anything or anyone else: _____

4 _____ : a man in stories who has magic powers: _____

5 _____ : a series of rulers of a country who all belong to the same family: _____

6 _____ : to show feeling or opinion: _____

7 _____ : to make someone or something part of a group: _____

8 _____ : the bright flashes of light that you see in the sky during a storm: _____

9 _____ : at the present time: _____

10 _____ : the season between summer and winter: _____

11 _____ : liked by most people: _____

12 _____ : a story about imaginary events or people: _____

13 _____ : one of four periods of year that is based on the earth's position toward the sun: _____

14 _____ : the name of a book, poem, movie, play, or other work of art: _____

15 _____ : a piece of equipment, usually one you hold in your hand, that is designed to do a particular type of work: _____

16 _____ : a piece of writing using beautiful or unusual language arranged in fixed lines that have a particular beat and often rhyme: _____

보기			
tale	title	unique	below
poem	autumn	season	express
wizard	artistic	dynasty	lightning
nowadays	tool	popular	include

※ 다음 우리말과 일치하도록 빈칸에 알맞은 말을 쓰시오.

Get Ready 2

(1) B: Do you like K-pop?

 G: Yes. I _____ _____ to SJ's songs. I can _____ _____ his songs.

 B: _____!

(2) B: _____ you _____ _____ _____ _____ Korean dishes?

 W: Yes. I _____ cook *bulgogi* _____ my family and they love it.

(3) B: _____ _____ _____ _____ _____ _____ _____ *Hangeul*?

 G: Yes. _____, I'm learning it in my _____ _____. Look! This is my _____.

 B: _____!

Start Off Listen & Talk A

(1) B: _____ _____! Someone is _____ a cloud? _____ _____!

 G: Thank you. Are you _____ _____ _____ _____ _____?

 B: Yes, I am. Actually, I'm _____ an _____ _____ _____ _____.

 G: Oh, _____ _____ you.

(2) G: _____ work! I think your painting _____ the _____ of _____ well.

 B: Thank you. _____ you _____ in painting?

 G: Yes, I am. I started _____ a class _____ _____.

 B: Oh, I _____ know _____.

Start Off Listen & Talk B

B: You _____ a good _____! It's _____.

G: Thanks.

B: What is it _____ _____? Glass?

G: Yes, it is. _____ you _____ _____ _____ _____ _____?

B: Yes, very much. _____ _____ did it _____ _____ _____ it?

G: _____ _____ one month.

Speak Up Look and talk

B: I _____ your _____. You did _____ _____ _____.

G: Thank you. Are you _____ in _____ _____ ukulele?

B: Sure. _____ _____ teach me?

G: No _____.

(1) B: 너는 K-pop을 좋아하니?
 G: 응. 나는 SJ의 노래를 듣는 것을 즐겨. 그의 노래에 맞춰 춤을 출 수 있어.
 B: 멋지다!

(2) B: 당신은 한국 음식을 요리하는 것에 관심이 있나요?
 W: 네. 때때로 저는 가족을 위해 불고기를 요리하고 그들은 그것을 좋아해요.

(3) B: 너는 한글 배우는 것에 관심이 있니?
 G: 응. 실제로, 나는 캘리그래피 수업에서 한글을 배우고 있어. 봐! 이게 나의 작품이야.
 B: 훌륭하다!

(1) B: 잘했다! 누군가 구름을 잡고 있는 거야? 정말 창의적이구나!
 G: 고마워. 너는 사진 찍는 것에 관심이 있니?
 B: 응, 그래. 사실, 나는 무료 온라인 강좌를 듣고 있어.
 G: 오, 잘됐구나.

(2) G: 잘했다! 네 그림은 가을 느낌을 잘 표현하고 있는 것 같아.
 B: 고마워. 너는 그림에 관심이 있니?
 G: 응, 그래. 나는 주말마다 수업을 듣기 시작했어.
 B: 오, 몰랐어.

B: 너 정말 잘했구나! 정말 멋져.
G: 고마워.
B: 무엇으로 만든 거니? 유리?
G: 응, 그래. 너는 유리 공예에 관심이 있니?
B: 응, 많이 관심 있어. 그거 만드는 데 시간이 얼마나 걸렸니?
G: 한 달 걸렸어.

B: 너의 공연 즐거웠어. 정말 잘했어.
G: 고마워. 너는 우쿨렐레 연주하는 것에 관심이 있니?
B: 물론이야. 날 가르쳐 줄 수 있니?
G: 그럼.

Speak Up Mission

A: Are you _____ _____ _____ _____ movies?
B: Yes, I _____ . I watch horror movies very often. / No, _____ _____ . I'm _____ _____ _____ _____ stories.

Real-life Scene

James: What _____ you _____ , Mina?
Mina: I'm _____ _____ .
James: You're _____ with a brush. It _____ _____ .
Mina: Are you _____ in _____ ?
James: Yes, very much.
Mina: Look at this! I just wrote it. _____ do you _____ ?
James: It _____ _____ a person _____ with _____ arms.
Mina: You _____ it. This Korean word _____ "dance."
James: You _____ a good _____ ! Can I _____ it?
Mina: _____ _____ ? Take this _____ .

James: 미나야, 뭐 하고 있니?
미나: 캘리그래피를 연습하고 있어.
James: 너는 붓으로 쓰고 있구나. 재미
있어 보인다.
미나: 너는 캘리그래피에 관심이 있니?
James: 응, 무척.
미나: 이것 봐! 내가 방금 썼어. 어떻게
생각해?
James: 두 팔을 벌리고 춤을 추는 사
람처럼 보여.
미나: 바로 그거야. 이 한글 단어가 '춤'
이라는 뜻이거든.
James: 잘했다! 내가 해 봐도 되니?
미나: 물론이야. 이 붓을 잡아.

Your Turn

A: You're _____ _____ . What's this?
B: It's my _____ _____ . Do you like it?
A: Sure. I think you _____ a _____ job!

Express Yourself

(1) B: Look! Two girls are _____ Hangeul.
G: Are you _____ _____ Hangeul, Kevin?
B: Yes, very much. I want to _____ them and _____ it.

(2) B: Julie, are you _____ _____ hanbok?
G: _____ really.
B: Then, _____ are you _____ in?
G: Well, I'm _____ in taekwondo. It is a _____ Korean sport. It's _____ .

(3) G: _____ _____ the two men _____ pansori.
B: Are you _____ in pansori, Nancy?
G: Sure. I like the _____ of it. I _____ _____ _____ it.

(1) B: 봐! 두 여자아이가 한글을 배우고
있어.
G: 너는 한글에 관심이 있니,
Kevin?
B: 응, 무척. 나는 그들과 합류해서
그것을 배우고 싶어.

(2) B: Julie, 너 한복에 관심이 있니?
G: 사실은 관심이 없어.
B: 그럼, 너는 무엇에 관심이 있니?
G: 음, 나는 태권도에 관심이 있어.
그것은 한국 전통 스포츠야. 아주
멋져.

(3) G: 판소리를 배우고 있는 두 남자 좀
봐.
B: 너는 판소리에 관심이 있니,
Nancy?
G: 물론이야. 나는 그 소리가 좋아.
그것을 배우고 싶어.

Learning Diary Listen & Speak

B: Minji, are you _____ in animals?
G: Yes, I am. I'm _____ _____ _____ _____ them.
B: _____ _____ plants? Are you _____ in them, _____ ?
G: No, I'm not. I _____ _____ them well.

Step2

※ 다음 우리말에 맞도록 대화를 영어로 쓰시오.

Get Ready 2

(1) B: _____
G: _____
B: _____

(2) B: _____
W: _____

(3) B: _____
G: _____
B: _____

Start Off Listen & Talk A

(1) B: _____
G: _____
B: _____
G: _____

(2) G: _____
B: _____
G: _____
B: _____

Start Off Listen & Talk B

B: _____
G: _____
B: _____
G: _____
B: _____
G: _____

Speak Up Look and talk

B: _____
G: _____
B: _____
G: _____

(1) B: 너는 K-pop을 좋아하니?
G: 응. 나는 SJ의 노래를 듣는 것을 즐겨. 그의 노래에 맞춰 춤을 출 수 있어.
B: 멋지다!

(2) B: 당신은 한국 음식을 요리하는 것에 관심이 있나요?
W: 네. 때때로 저는 가족을 위해 불고기를 요리하고 그들은 그것을 좋아해요.

(3) B: 너는 한글 배우는 것에 관심이 있니?
G: 응. 실제로, 나는 캘리그래피 수업에서 한글을 배우고 있어. 봐! 이게 나의 작품이야.
B: 훌륭하다!

(1) B: 잘했다! 누군가 구름을 잡고 있는 거야? 정말 창의적이구나!
G: 고마워. 너는 사진 찍는 것에 관심이 있니?
B: 응, 그래. 사실, 나는 무료 온라인 강좌를 듣고 있어.
G: 오, 잘됐구나.

(2) G: 잘했다! 네 그림은 가을 느낌을 잘 표현하고 있는 것 같아.
B: 고마워. 너는 그림에 관심이 있니?
G: 응, 그래. 나는 주말마다 수업을 듣기 시작했어.
B: 오, 몰랐어.

B: 너 정말 잘했구나! 정말 멋져.
G: 고마워.
B: 무엇으로 만든 거니? 유리?
G: 응, 그래. 너는 유리 공예에 관심이 있니?
B: 응, 많이 관심 있어. 그거 만드는 데 시간이 얼마나 걸렸니?
G: 한 달 걸렸어.

B: 너의 공연 즐거웠어. 정말 잘했어.
G: 고마워. 너는 우쿨렐레 연주하는 것에 관심이 있니?
B: 물론이야. 날 가르쳐 줄 수 있니?
G: 그럼.

Speak Up Mission

A: _____

B: _____

A: 너는 공포 영화 보는 것에 관심이 있니?
B: 응, 그래. 나는 공포 영화를 아주 자주 봐. / 아니, 그렇지 않아. 나는 탐정 소설 읽는 것에 관심이 있어.

Real-life Scene

James: _____

Mina: _____

James: _____

Mina: _____

James: _____

Mina: _____

James: _____

Mina: _____

James: _____

Mina: _____

James: 미나야, 뭐 하고 있니?
미나: 캘리그래피를 연습하고 있어.
James: 너는 붓으로 쓰고 있구나. 재미있어 보인다.
미나: 너는 캘리그래피에 관심이 있니?
James: 응, 무척.
미나: 이것 봐! 내가 방금 썼어. 어떻게 생각해?
James: 두 팔을 벌리고 춤을 추는 사람처럼 보여.
미나: 바로 그거야. 이 한글 단어가 '춤'이라는 뜻이거든.
James: 잘했다! 내가 해 봐도 되니?
미나: 물론이야. 이 붓을 잡아.

Your Turn

A: _____

B: _____

A: _____

A: 너 뭔가 쓰고 있구나. 이게 뭐야?
B: 내 미술 숙제야. 마음에 드니?
A: 물론이야. 잘한 것 같아!

Express Yourself

(1) B: _____

G: _____

B: _____

(2) B: _____

G: _____

B: _____

G: _____

(3) G: _____

B: _____

G: _____

(1) B: 봐! 두 여자아이가 한글을 배우고 있어.
G: 너는 한글에 관심이 있니, Kevin?
B: 응, 무척. 나는 그들과 합류해서 그것을 배우고 싶어.

(2) B: Julie, 너 한복에 관심이 있니?
G: 사실은 관심이 없어.
B: 그럼, 너는 무엇에 관심이 있니?
G: 음, 나는 태권도에 관심이 있어. 그것은 한국 전통 스포츠야. 아주 멋져.

(3) G: 판소리를 배우고 있는 두 남자 좀 봐.
B: 너는 판소리에 관심이 있니, Nancy?
G: 물론이야. 나는 그 소리가 좋아. 그것을 배우고 싶어.

Learning Diary Listen & Speak

B: _____

G: _____

B: _____

G: _____

B: 민지야, 너는 동물에 관심이 있니?
G: 응, 그래. 나는 동물을 돌보는 것을 잘해.
B: 식물은 어떠니? 식물에도 관심이 있니?
G: 아니, 없어. 식물은 잘 못 키워.

※ 다음 우리말과 일치하도록 빈칸에 알맞은 것을 골라 쓰시오.

1 _____ Your _____
A. Feelings B. Write

2 _____ do you _____ your _____ ?
A. express B. feelings C. how

3 Do you _____ or _____ ?
A. dance B. sing

4 Do you _____ a _____ or _____ a picture?
A. poem B. write C. draw

5 _____, it is popular to _____ feelings _____ handwriting.
A. express B. nowadays C. through

6 Let's look _____ some _____ of _____ .
A. works B. at C. art

7 In the work of art on the right, the word _____ an _____ of a _____ fruit, *hongsi*.
A. image B. delicious C. includes

8 It shows that _____ is a _____ of _____ .
A. season B. autumn C. fruit

9 The _____ of art on the left shows a Korean _____ and a _____ _____ .
A. character B. word C. work D. Chinese

10 It _____ _____ a happy woman _____ _____ a road with autumn leaves.
A. like B. walking C. looks D. down

11 _____ of these works _____ the _____ of autumn _____ beautiful handwriting.
A. express B. through C. feeling D. both

12 This _____ of art is _____ _____ .
A. kind B. calligraphy C. called

13 Calligraphy is _____ _____ .
A. new B. not

14 Many different _____ of calligraphy _____ from long ago can _____ _____ all around the world.
A. found B. works C. kinds D. be

15 Look _____ the two _____ from Korea and the UK _____ .
A. below B. examples C. at

16 Can you _____ the _____ ?
A. difference B. tell

17 The left one was _____ _____ Chusa in the _____ of the Joseon Dynasty.
A. period B. created C. by

18 The characters were _____ _____ a soft _____ .
A. with B. painted C. brush

1 여러분의 느낌을 써라

2 여러분은 자신의 느낌을 어떻게 표현하는가?

3 노래를 부르거나 춤을 추는가?

4 시를 쓰거나 그림을 그리는가?

5 요즈음에는 손 글씨를 통해 감정을 표현하는 것이 인기다.

6 몇몇 작품을 살펴보자.

7 오른쪽 예술 작품에서는 단어가 맛있는 과일인 홍시의 이미지를 포함하고 있다.

8 그것은 가을이 결실의 계절임을 보여 준다.

9 왼쪽에 있는 예술 작품은 한글 단어와 한자를 보여 주고 있다.

10 그것은 마치 단풍잎이 깔린 길을 따라 걷고 있는 행복한 여인처럼 보인다.

11 이 두 작품은 아름다운 손 글씨를 통해 가을의 느낌을 표현한다.

12 이런 종류의 예술은 '캘리그래피'라고 불린다.

13 캘리그래피는 새로운 것이 아니다.

14 오래전의 다양한 종류의 많은 캘리그래피 작품들이 세계 곳곳에서 발견되고 있다.

15 아래에 있는 한국과 영국의 두 사례를 보라.

16 여러분은 그 차이를 구별할 수 있는가?

17 왼쪽 작품은 조선 왕조 시대에 추사에 의해 창작되었다.

18 그 글자들은 부드러운 붓으로 그려졌다.

19 The right one, *The Canterbury Tales*, was _____ _____ Chaucer in England _____ the _____ 1400s.

 A. late B. created C. in D. by

20 It _____ _____ _____ a pen.

 A. written B. with C. was

21 _____ writing _____ led to different _____ of calligraphy.

 A. styles B. tools C. different

22 _____ course, all calligraphers had to _____ _____ to make their _____ styles.

 A. hard B. of C. unique D. practice

23 Today calligraphy is _____ _____ _____ us.

 A. around B. widely C. used

24 You can find designers' _____ _____ on movie posters, book covers, music CDs, and _____.

 A. clothes B. touches C. artistic

25 _____ are some _____.

 A. examples B. below

26 Look _____ the _____ on the movie _____.

 A. title B. at C. poster

27 _____ do you _____?

 A. feel B. how

28 Can you _____ the monster's big mouth, _____ teeth, and _____, long _____?

 A. sharp B. imagine C. tail D. ugly

29 _____ the title on the _____ novel?

 A. fantasy B. about C. how

30 Do you see Harry's _____ and the _____ _____?

 A. wizard B. lightning C. hats

31 _____ can start _____ calligraphy.

 A. writing B. anyone

32 It's not easy to write _____ _____ well at first, but _____ makes _____.

 A. perfect B. hand C. practice D. by

33 _____ _____ and make it _____ of your _____ life.

 A. part B. trying C. everyday D. keep

34 Write _____ your _____ on birthday cards, bookmarks, or _____.

 A. feelings B. with C. gifts

35 Soon you will _____ _____ your _____ world of calligraphy.

 A. up B. own C. build

19 오른쪽의 '캔터베리 이야기'는 1400년대 후반 영국에서 Chaucer에 의해 창작되었다.

20 그것은 펜으로 쓰였다.

21 각기 다른 필기구가 각기 다른 캘리그래피의 스타일을 이끌었다.

22 물론, 모든 캘리그래피 작가들은 자신의 독특한 스타일을 만들어 내기 위해 열심히 연습해야 했다.

23 캘리그래피는 요즈음 우리 주변에서 널리 쓰이고 있다.

24 여러분은 영화 포스터, 책 표지, 음악 CD, 그리고 의류에서 디자이너들의 예술적인 손길을 발견할 수 있다.

25 아래에 몇 가지 예가 있다.

26 영화 포스터의 제목을 보라.

27 어떤 느낌이 드는가?

28 괴물의 커다란 입, 날카로운 이빨, 그리고 추하고 긴 꼬리를 상상할 수 있는가?

29 공상 소설의 제목은 어떠한가?

30 Harry의 번개와 마술사 모자가 보이는가?

31 누구든지 캘리그래피를 쓰기 시작할 수 있다.

32 처음부터 손으로 글씨를 잘 쓰기는 쉽지 않지만, 연습하면 완벽해진다.

33 계속해서 노력하고 자신의 일상의 한 부분이 되게 하라.

34 생일 카드, 책갈피, 또는 선물에 느낌을 담아 써 보라.

35 곧 자신만의 캘리그래피 세계를 만들게 될 것이다.

※ 다음 우리말과 일치하도록 빈칸에 알맞은 말을 쓰시오.

1 _____ Your _____

2 _____ do you _____ your _____ ?

3 Do you _____ or _____ ?

4 Do you write a _____ or _____ _____ _____ ?

5 _____ , it is _____ to express feelings _____ _____ .

6 _____ _____ _____ some _____ _____ _____ _____ .

7 In the _____ _____ _____ on the right, the word _____ _____ _____ of a delicious fruit, *hongsi*.

8 It shows that autumn is _____ _____ _____ _____ .

9 The work of art on the left shows a _____ _____ and a _____ _____ .

10 It _____ _____ a happy woman _____ down a road with _____ _____ .

11 Both of these works _____ _____ _____ of autumn _____ _____ _____ .

12 This kind of art is _____ _____ .

13 Calligraphy is _____ _____ .

14 Many different kinds of calligraphy works from long ago _____ _____ _____ all _____ _____ _____ .

15 Look at the two _____ _____ Korea and the UK _____ .

16 Can you _____ _____ _____ ?

17 The left one _____ _____ _____ Chusa in the _____ of the Joseon Dynasty.

18 The characters _____ _____ _____ a soft brush.

1 여러분의 느낌을 써라

2 여러분은 자신의 느낌을 어떻게 표현하는가?

3 노래를 부르거나 춤을 추는가?

4 시를 쓰거나 그림을 그리는가?

5 요즈음에는 손 글씨를 통해 감정을 표현하는 것이 인기다.

6 몇몇 작품을 살펴보자.

7 오른쪽 예술 작품에서는 단어가 맛있는 과일인 홍시의 이미지를 포함하고 있다.

8 그것은 가을이 결실의 계절임을 보여 준다.

9 왼쪽에 있는 예술 작품은 한글 단어와 한자를 보여 주고 있다.

10 그것은 마치 단풍잎이 깔린 길을 따라 걷고 있는 행복한 여인처럼 보인다.

11 이 두 작품은 아름다운 손 글씨를 통해 가을의 느낌을 표현한다.

12 이런 종류의 예술은 '캘리그래피'라고 불린다.

13 캘리그래피는 새로운 것이 아니다.

14 오래전의 다양한 종류의 많은 캘리그래피 작품들이 세계 곳곳에서 발견되고 있다.

15 아래에 있는 한국과 영국의 두 사례를 보라.

16 여러분은 그 차이를 구별할 수 있는가?

17 왼쪽 작품은 조선 왕조 시대에 추사에 의해 창작되었다.

18 그 글자들은 부드러운 붓으로 그려졌다.

19 The right one, *The Canterbury Tales*, _____ _____ _____ Chaucer in England _____ _____ _____ _____.

20 It _____ _____ _____ a pen.

21 _____ _____ _____ led to _____ _____ of calligraphy.

22 _____ _____, all calligraphers had to _____ _____ to make their _____ _____.

23 Today calligraphy _____ _____ _____ _____ us.

24 You can find _____ _____ _____ on movie posters, book covers, music CDs, and _____.

25 Below _____ _____ _____.

26 Look at _____ _____ on the movie poster.

27 _____ do you _____?

28 Can you imagine the monster's big mouth, _____ _____, and _____, _____ _____?

29 _____ _____ the title on the _____ _____?

30 Do you see Harry's _____ and the _____ _____?

31 _____ can start _____ _____.

32 It's not easy _____ _____ _____ _____ well at first, but _____ _____ _____.

33 _____ _____ and make it _____ of your _____ life.

34 Write _____ _____ _____ on birthday cards, _____, or _____.

35 Soon you will _____ _____ your own world of calligraphy.

19 오른쪽의 '캔터베리 이야기' 는 1400년대 후반 영국에서 Chaucer에 의해 창작되었다.

20 그것은 펜으로 쓰였다.

21 각기 다른 필기구가 각기 다른 캘리그래피의 스타일을 이끌었 다.

22 물론, 모든 캘리그래피 작가들 은 자신의 독특한 스타일을 만 들어 내기 위해 열심히 연습해 야 했다.

23 캘리그래피는 요즈음 우리 주변 에서 널리 쓰이고 있다.

24 여러분은 영화 포스터, 책 표지, 음악 CD, 그리고 의류에서 디자 이너들의 예술적인 손길을 발견 할 수 있다.

25 아래에 몇 가지 예가 있다.

26 영화 포스터의 제목을 보라.

27 어떤 느낌이 드는가?

28 괴물의 커다란 입, 날카로운 이 빨, 그리고 추하고 긴 꼬리를 상 상할 수 있는가?

29 공상 소설의 제목은 어떠한가?

30 Harry의 번개와 마술사 모자가 보이는가?

31 누구든지 캘리그래피를 쓰기 시 작할 수 있다.

32 처음부터 손으로 글씨를 잘 쓰 기는 쉽지 않지만, 연습하면 완 벽해진다.

33 계속해서 노력하고 자신의 일상 의 한 부분이 되게 하라.

34 생일 카드, 책갈피, 또는 선물에 느낌을 담아 써 보라.

35 곧 자신만의 캘리그래피 세계를 만들게 될 것이다.

※ 다음 문장을 우리말로 쓰시오.

1 Write Your Feelings

➡ _____

2 How do you express your feelings?

➡ _____

3 Do you sing or dance?

➡ _____

4 Do you write a poem or draw a picture?

➡ _____

5 Nowadays, it is popular to express feelings through handwriting.

➡ _____

6 Let's look at some works of art.

➡ _____

7 In the work of art on the right, the word includes an image of a delicious fruit, *hongsi*.

➡ _____

8 It shows that autumn is a season of fruit.

➡ _____

9 The work of art on the left shows a Korean word and a Chinese character.

➡ _____

10 It looks like a happy woman walking down a road with autumn leaves.

➡ _____

11 Both of these works express the feeling of autumn through beautiful handwriting.

➡ _____

12 This kind of art is called calligraphy.

➡ _____

13 Calligraphy is not new.

➡ _____

14 Many different kinds of calligraphy works from long ago can be found all around the world.

➡ _____

15 Look at the two examples from Korea and the UK below.

➡ _____

16 Can you tell the difference?

➡ _____

17 The left one was created by Chusa in the period of the Joseon Dynasty.

➡ _____

18 The characters were painted with a soft brush.

➡ _____

19 The right one, *The Canterbury Tales*, was created by Chaucer in England in the late 1400s.

➡ _____

20 It was written with a pen.

➡ _____

21 Different writing tools led to different styles of calligraphy.

➡ _____

22 Of course, all calligraphers had to practice hard to make their unique styles.

➡ _____

23 Today calligraphy is widely used around us.

➡ _____

24 You can find designers' artistic touches on movie posters, book covers, music CDs, and clothes.

➡ _____

25 Below are some examples.

➡ _____

26 Look at the title on the movie poster.

➡ _____

27 How do you feel?

➡ _____

28 Can you imagine the monster's big mouth, sharp teeth, and ugly, long tail?

➡ _____

29 How about the title on the fantasy novel?

➡ _____

30 Do you see Harry's lightning and the wizard hats?

➡ _____

31 Anyone can start writing calligraphy.

➡ _____

32 It's not easy to write by hand well at first, but practice makes perfect.

➡ _____

33 Keep trying and make it part of your everyday life.

➡ _____

34 Write with your feelings on birthday cards, bookmarks, or gifts.

➡ _____

35 Soon you will build up your own world of calligraphy.

➡ _____

Step4

※ 다음 괄호 안의 단어들을 우리말에 맞도록 바르게 배열하시오.

1 (Your / Feelings / Write)
➡ _____

2 (do / how / express / you / feelings? / your)
➡ _____

3 (you / do / dance? / or / sing)
➡ _____

4 (you / do / a / write / poem / or / a / draw / picture?)
➡ _____

5 (nowadays, / is / it / to / popular / feelings / express / handwriting. / through)
➡ _____

6 (look / let's / some / at / art. / or / works)
➡ _____

7 (the / in / of / work / art / the / on / right, / word / the / an / includes / image / of / delicious / *hongsi.* / a / fruit,)
➡ _____

8 (shows / it / autumn / that / a / is / fruit. / of / season)
➡ _____

9 (work / the / art / of / the / on / shows / left / Korean / a / word / and / a / character. / Chinese)
➡ _____

10 (looks / it / a / like / happy / walking / woman / down / road / a / with / leaves. / autumn)
➡ _____

11 (of / both / works / these / express / feeling / the / autumn / of / through / handwriting. / beautiful)
➡ _____

12 (kind / this / art / of / is / calligraphy. / called)
➡ _____

13 (is / calligraphy / new. / not)
➡ _____

14 (different / many / of / kinds / calligraphy / from / works / ago / long / be / can / all / found / world. / the / around)
➡ _____

15 (at / look / two / the / examples / Korea / from / and / below. / UK / the)
➡ _____

16 (you / can / the / tell / difference?)
➡ _____

17 (left / the / was / one / by / created / Chusa / the / in / period / the / of / Dynasty. / Joseon)
➡ _____

18 (character / the / painted / were / with / brush. / soft / a)
➡ _____

1 여러분의 느낌을 써라

2 여러분은 자신의 느낌을 어떻게 표현하는가?

3 노래를 부르거나 춤을 추는가?

4 시를 쓰거나 그림을 그리는가?

5 요즈음에는 손 글씨를 통해 감정을 표현하는 것이 인기다.

6 몇몇 작품을 살펴보자.

7 오른쪽 예술 작품에서는 단어가 맛있는 과일인 홍시의 이미지를 포함하고 있다.

8 그것은 가을이 결실의 계절임을 보여 준다.

9 왼쪽에 있는 예술 작품은 한글 단어와 한자를 보여 주고 있다.

10 그것은 마치 단풍잎이 깔린 길을 따라 걷고 있는 행복한 여인처럼 보인다.

11 이 두 작품은 아름다운 손 글씨를 통해 가을의 느낌을 표현한다.

12 이런 종류의 예술은 '캘리그래피'라고 불린다.

13 캘리그래피는 새로운 것이 아니다.

14 오래전의 다양한 종류의 많은 캘리그래피 작품들이 세계 곳곳에서 발견되고 있다.

15 아래에 있는 한국과 영국의 두 사례를 보라.

16 여러분은 그 차이를 구별할 수 있는가?

17 왼쪽 작품은 조선 왕조 시대에 추사에 의해 창작되었다.

18 그 글자들은 부드러운 붓으로 그려졌다.

19 (right / the / one, / *Canterbury* / *The* / *Tales*, / created / was / Chaucer / by / England / in / the / in / 1400s. / late)
➡ _____

20 (was / it / with / written / pen / a)
➡ _____

21 (writing / different / led / tools / to / styles / different / calligraphy. / of)
➡ _____

22 (course, / of / calligraphers / all / to / had / hard / practice / make / to / unique / their / styles.)
➡ _____

23 (calligraphy / today / widely / is / around / us. / used)
➡ _____

24 (can / you / designers' / find / touches / artistic / movie / on / book / posters, / covers, / CDs, / music / clothes. / and)
➡ _____

25 (are / examples. / below / some)
➡ _____

26 (at / look / title / the / the / on / poster. / movie)
➡ _____

27 (do / how / feel? / you)
➡ _____

28 (you / can / the / imagine / monster's / mouth, / big / teeth, / sharp / and / long / tail? / ugly,)
➡ _____

29 (about / how / title / the / the / on / novel? / fantasy)
➡ _____

30 (you / see / do / lightning / Harry's / and / hats? / wizard / the)
➡ _____

31 (can / anyone / start / calligraphy. / writing)
➡ _____

32 (not / it's / to / easy / by / write / hand / at / well / first, / but / makes / perfect. / practice)
➡ _____

33 (trying / keep / and / it / make / of / part / everyday / your / life.)
➡ _____

34 (with / write / feelings / your / birthday / on / cards, / gifts. / or / bookmarks,)
➡ _____

35 (you / soon / build / will / your / up / world / own / calligraphy. / of)
➡ _____

19 오른쪽의 '캔터베리 이야기' 는 1400년대 후반 영국에서 Chaucer에 의해 창작되었다.

20 그것은 펜으로 쓰였다.

21 각기 다른 필기구가 각기 다른 캘리그래피의 스타일을 이끌었다.

22 물론, 모든 캘리그래피 작가들은 자신의 독특한 스타일을 만들어 내기 위해 열심히 연습해야 했다.

23 캘리그래피는 요즈음 우리 주변에서 널리 쓰이고 있다.

24 여러분은 영화 포스터, 책 표지, 음악 CD, 그리고 의류에서 디자이너들의 예술적인 손길을 발견할 수 있다.

25 아래에 몇 가지 예가 있다.

26 영화 포스터의 제목을 보라.

27 어떤 느낌이 드는가?

28 괴물의 커다란 입, 날카로운 이빨, 그리고 추하고 긴 꼬리를 상상할 수 있는가?

29 공상 소설의 제목은 어떠한가?

30 Harry의 번개와 마술사 모자가 보이는가?

31 누구든지 캘리그래피를 쓰기 시작할 수 있다.

32 처음부터 손으로 글씨를 잘 쓰기는 쉽지 않지만, 연습하면 완벽해진다.

33 계속해서 노력하고 자신의 일상의 한 부분이 되게 하라.

34 생일 카드, 책갈피, 또는 선물에 느낌을 담아 써 보라.

35 곧 자신만의 캘리그래피 세계를 만들게 될 것이다.

Step5

※ 다음 우리말을 영어로 쓰시오.

1 여러분의 느낌을 써라

➡ _____

2 여러분은 자신의 느낌을 어떻게 표현하는가?

➡ _____

3 노래를 부르거나 춤을 추는가?

➡ _____

4 시를 쓰거나 그림을 그리는가?

➡ _____

5 요즈음에는 손 글씨를 통해 감정을 표현하는 것이 인기다.

➡ _____

6 몇몇 작품을 살펴보자.

➡ _____

7 오른쪽 예술 작품에서는 단어가 맛있는 과일인 홍시의 이미지를 포함하고 있다.

➡ _____

8 그것은 가을이 결실의 계절임을 보여 준다.

➡ _____

9 왼쪽에 있는 예술 작품은 한글 단어와 한자를 보여 주고 있다.

➡ _____

10 그것은 마치 단풍잎이 깔린 길을 따라 걷고 있는 행복한 여인처럼 보인다.

➡ _____

11 이 두 작품은 아름다운 손 글씨를 통해 가을의 느낌을 표현한다.

➡ _____

12 이런 종류의 예술은 '캘리그래피'라고 불린다.

➡ _____

13 캘리그래피는 새로운 것이 아니다.

➡ _____

14 오래전의 다양한 종류의 많은 캘리그래피 작품들이 세계 곳곳에서 발견되고 있다.

➡ _____

15 아래에 있는 한국과 영국의 두 사례를 보라.

➡ _____

16 여러분은 그 차이를 구별할 수 있는가?

➡ _____

17 왼쪽 작품은 조선 왕조 시대에 추사에 의해 창작되었다.

➡ _____

18 그 글자들은 부드러운 붓으로 그려졌다.

➡ _____

19 오른쪽의 '캔터베리 이야기'는 1400년대 후반 영국에서 Chaucer에 의해 창작되었다.

➡ _____

20 그것은 펜으로 쓰였다.

➡ _____

21 각기 다른 필기구가 각기 다른 캘리그래피의 스타일을 이끌었다.

➡ _____

22 물론, 모든 캘리그래피 작가들은 자신의 독특한 스타일을 만들어 내기 위해 열심히 연습해야 했다.

➡ _____

23 캘리그래피는 요즈음 우리 주변에서 널리 쓰이고 있다.

➡ _____

24 여러분은 영화 포스터, 책 표지, 음악 CD, 그리고 의류에서 디자이너들의 예술적인 손길을 발견할 수 있다.

➡ _____

25 아래에 몇 가지 예가 있다.

➡ _____

26 영화 포스터의 제목을 보라.

➡ _____

27 어떤 느낌이 드는가?

➡ _____

28 괴물의 커다란 입, 날카로운 이빨, 그리고 추하고 긴 꼬리를 상상할 수 있는가?

➡ _____

29 공상 소설의 제목은 어떠한가?

➡ _____

30 Harry의 번개와 마술사 모자가 보이는가?

➡ _____

31 누구든지 캘리그래피를 쓰기 시작할 수 있다.

➡ _____

32 처음부터 손으로 글씨를 잘 쓰기는 쉽지 않지만, 연습하면 완벽해진다.

➡ _____

33 계속해서 노력하고 자신의 일상의 한 부분이 되게 하라.

➡ _____

34 생일 카드, 책갈피, 또는 선물에 느낌을 담아 써 보라.

➡ _____

35 곧 자신만의 캘리그래피 세계를 만들게 될 것이다.

➡ _____

※ 다음 우리말과 일치하도록 빈칸에 알맞은 말을 쓰시오.

After You Read B

1. These _____ _____ mean "Let's laugh."

2. This calligraphy shows two people _____ _____ _____.

3. These Korean _____ _____ "tree."

4. This calligraphy shows a tree _____ _____ _____ _____.

1. 이 한글 문자는 '웃자.'라는 뜻이다.
2. 이 캘리그래피는 큰 소리로 웃고 있는 두 사람을 보여 준다.
3. 이 한글 문자는 '나무'를 의미한다.
4. 이 캘리그래피는 화분에서 자라고 있는 나무를 보여 준다.

Express Yourself C

1. _____ _____ the two girls _____ taekwondo.

2. Taekwondo is a _____ _____ sport, and we _____ dobok _____ _____ it.

3. _____ is exciting _____ _____ taekwondo.

4. _____ you _____?

5. Please _____ and _____.

6. _____ _____ the two boys _____ yunnori.

7. Yunnori is a _____ _____ board game, and we use yuts and mals _____ _____ it.

8. _____ is exciting _____ _____ yunnori.

9. _____ you _____?

10. Please _____ and _____.

1. 태권도를 배우고[하고] 있는 두 여자아이를 보세요.
2. 태권도는 한국의 전통 스포츠이고, 우리는 그것을 하기 위해 도복을 입습니다.
3. 태권도를 배우는 것은 흥미진진합니다.
4. 관심이 있나요?
5. 와서 한번 해 보세요.
6. 윷놀이를 하는 두 남자아이를 보세요.
7. 윷놀이는 한국의 전통적인 말판 놀이고, 우리는 그것을 하기 위해 윷과 말을 사용합니다.
8. 윷놀이를 하는 것은 흥미진진합니다.
9. 관심이 있나요?
10. 와서 한번 해 보세요.

Link to the World

1. This is a set of _____ _____. It _____ _____ matryoshka.

2. _____ you open it, smaller dolls _____ _____ out of it.

3. _____ is interesting _____ _____ a smaller doll _____ _____ _____.

4. _____ _____ _____ of matryoshka dolls was a mother doll _____ _____ _____ _____.

5. Today, _____ _____ _____ of matryoshkas _____ _____ and _____ by many people.

1. 이것은 한 세트의 러시아 인형이다. 그것은 '마트료시카'라고 불린다.
2. 그것을 열면, 더 작은 인형들이 계속해서 나온다.
3. 각각의 인형 안에서 더 작은 인형을 보는 것은 재미있다.
4. 최초의 '마트료시카' 인형 세트는 여섯 아이를 둔 어머니 인형이었다.
5. 오늘날에는, 많은 새로운 스타일의 '마트료시카'가 제작되어 많은 사람에게 사랑을 받고 있다.

※ **다음 우리말을 영어로 쓰시오.**

After You Read B

1. 이 한글 문자는 '웃자.'라는 뜻이다.
 ➡ _____

2. 이 캘리그래피는 큰 소리로 웃고 있는 두 사람을 보여 준다.
 ➡ _____

3. 이 한글 문자는 '나무'를 의미한다.
 ➡ _____

4. 이 캘리그래피는 화분에서 자라고 있는 나무를 보여 준다.
 ➡ _____

Express Yourself C

1. 태권도를 배우고[하고] 있는 두 여자아이를 보세요.
 ➡ _____

2. 태권도는 한국의 전통 스포츠이고, 우리는 그것을 하기 위해 도복을 입습니다.
 ➡ _____

3. 태권도를 배우는 것은 흥미진진합니다.
 ➡ _____

4. 관심이 있나요?
 ➡ _____

5. 와서 한번 해 보세요.
 ➡ _____

6. 윷놀이를 하는 두 남자아이를 보세요.
 ➡ _____

7. 윷놀이는 한국의 전통적인 말판 놀이고, 우리는 그것을 하기 위해 윷과 말을 사용합니다.
 ➡ _____

8. 윷놀이를 하는 것은 흥미진진합니다.
 ➡ _____

9. 관심이 있나요?
 ➡ _____

10. 와서 한번 해 보세요.
 ➡ _____

Link to the World

1. 이것은 한 세트의 러시아 인형이다. 그것은 '마트료시카'라고 불린다.
 ➡ _____

2. 그것을 열면, 더 작은 인형들이 계속해서 나온다.
 ➡ _____

3. 각각의 인형 안에서 더 작은 인형을 보는 것은 재미있다.
 ➡ _____

4. 최초의 '마트료시카' 인형 세트는 여섯 아이를 둔 어머니 인형이었다.
 ➡ _____

5. 오늘날에는, 많은 새로운 스타일의 '마트료시카'가 제작되어 많은 사람에게 사랑을 받고 있다.
 ➡ _____

※ 다음 영어를 우리말로 쓰시오.

01	bookshelf	
02	another	
03	uncomfortable	
04	dirty	
05	universal	
06	blind	
07	cotton	
08	tight	
09	hearing	
10	solution	
11	decide	
12	easily	
13	decorate	
14	add	
15	difficulty	
16	seat	
17	finally	
18	almost	
19	fountain	
20	handle	
21	product	
22	low	
23	crowded	
24	hang	
25	journey	
26	company	
27	bathtub	
28	moment	
29	locker	
30	thick	
31	view	
32	traffic	
33	flat	
34	bath	
35	go through	
36	put on	
37	watch out	
38	by oneself	
39	in danger	
40	tired of	
41	so+형용사/부사+that+주어+can't …	
42	get in	
43	more and more	

※ 다음 우리말을 영어로 쓰시오.

01 거의

02 매달다, 걸다

03 더러운

04 지팡이

05 해결책

06 쿠션, 방석

07 결심하다

08 청력

09 장식하다

10 어려움

11 쉽게

12 평평한

13 목욕

14 욕조

15 분수, 원천

16 손잡이

17 여행, 여정

18 건너다

19 붐비는

20 방법

21 눈이 먼

22 책꽂이

23 사물함

24 견해, 관점

25 불편한

26 낮은

27 두꺼운

28 상품, 제품

29 자리, 좌석

30 회사

31 꽉 조이는, 딱 붙는

32 보편적인

33 교통

34 또 하나의

35 ~을 타다

36 위험에 처한

37 혼자서

38 점점 더 많은

39 ~을 겪다

40 ~을 입다

41 ~에 지친, ~에 싫증 난

42 ~할 것을 고려[생각] 중이다

43 조심하다

※ 다음 영영풀이에 알맞은 단어를 <보기>에서 골라 쓴 후, 우리말 뜻을 쓰시오.

1 _____ : unable to see: _____

2 _____ : having a lot of people or too many people: _____

3 _____ : in a lower place or position: _____

4 _____ : the answer to a problem: _____

5 _____ : to go across from one side of something to the other: _____

6 _____ : a long, thin wooden pole that especially old or injured people use to walk: _____

7 _____ : not having a part that is higher or lower than another: _____

8 _____ : a part that is designed especially to be held by the hand: _____

9 _____ : an act of traveling from one place to another: _____

10 _____ : small in height or smaller than the usual height: _____

11 _____ : something that is made or grown for selling: _____

12 _____ : not feeling comfortable and pleasant: _____

13 _____ : a personal opinion or belief about a situation or subject: _____

14 _____ : to add something to an object or place, especially in order to make it more attractive: _____

15 _____ : a business organization that makes money by producing or selling goods or services: _____

16 _____ : a cupboard, often tall and made of metal, in which you can keep your possessions, and leave them for a period of time: _____

보기			
solution	low	crowded	cross
blind	handle	locker	stick
view	company	decorate	flat
journey	product	below	uncomfortable

※ 다음 우리말과 일치하도록 빈칸에 알맞은 말을 쓰시오.

Get Ready 2

(1) B: I'm _____ _____ _____ this _____. It's _____ _____ for some kids.

G: Well, I'_____ _____ _____ _____ _____ fountains together with it.

B: That's a _____ _____.

(2) G: I _____ _____ the high steps here. People _____ _____ can't _____ _____.

B: Right. I'm _____ _____ _____ a new way _____ no _____.

(3) G: I'm not _____ about this swing. People _____ _____ can't _____ _____ it _____.

B: Right. I'm _____ _____ _____ a bigger and _____ _____ for them.

G: Good idea.

(1) B: 나는 이 음수대가 마음에 들지 않아. 몇몇 아이들에게는 너무 높아.

G: 음, 나는 그것과 함께 더 낮은 음수대들을 놓으려고 계획 중이야.

B: 좋은 생각이야.

(2) G: 나는 여기 높은 계단이 마음에 들지 않아. 휠체어를 탄 사람들은 들어설 수가 없잖아.

B: 맞아. 나는 계단 없는 새 길을 짓는 것을 생각 중이야.

(3) G: 나는 이 그네가 마음에 들지 않아. 휠체어를 탄 사람들은 그것을 쉽게 탈 수 없어.

B: 맞아. 나는 그들을 위해 더 크고 더 안전한 자리를 매달려고 계획 중이야.

G: 좋은 생각이야.

Start Off Listen & Talk A

(1) G: I'm _____ _____ _____ the button.

B: Why? What's _____ _____ it?

G: It's too high. Children or people in wheelchairs can't _____ it. _____ _____ _____ putting _____ switch for them.

(2) G: I'm not _____ _____ the sign. _____ _____ some people _____ can't see.

B: Right. Do you have _____ ideas?

G: Well, I'm _____ of _____ _____ on the sign.

B: That's a _____ _____.

(1) G: 나는 그 버튼이 마음에 들지 않아.

B: 왜? 뭐가 잘못됐니?

G: 그것은 너무 높아. 아이들이나 휠체어를 탄 사람들은 거기까지 닿을 수가 없어. 나는 그들을 위해 또 다른 스위치를 달까 생각 중이야.

(2) G: 나는 표지판이 마음에 들지 않아. 볼 수 없는 사람들도 좀 있잖아.

B: 맞아. 너는 어떤 아이디어라도 있니?

G: 음, 나는 표지판 위에 점자를 추가할까 생각 중이야.

B: 그거 좋은 생각이다.

Start Off Listen & draw

B: _____ _____ _____ _____ _____ the lights.

G: _____ _____ _____ _____ them?

B: The _____ _____ look _____ _____ to some people _____ are _____ _____ _____.

G: Oh, I see. _____ _____ _____ _____ an image on each light?

B: A _____ man on the green light and a _____ man on the red light? Good idea!

B: 나는 불빛이 마음에 들지 않아.

G: 뭐가 잘못됐니?

B: 색맹인 사람들에게는 신호등이 똑같이 보일 거야.

G: 오, 알겠어. 각 불빛에 그림을 넣는 게 어떨까?

B: 파란불에는 걷는 사람을, 그리고 빨간불에는 서 있는 사람을? 좋은 생각이야!

Speak Up Look and talk

B: _____ _____ _____ _____ _____ the desk. It's _____ _____.

G: Right. I'm _____ _____ _____ some pads on it.

B: Good idea.

B: 나는 책상이 마음에 들지 않아. 그것은 너무 낮아.

G: 맞아. 나는 그 위에 몇 장의 패드를 놓을까 생각 중이야.

B: 좋은 생각이야.

Speak Up Mission

A: I'm _____ _____ _____ the _____. It's too small.
B: I think so, _____. Do you have _____ _____?
A: I'm _____ _____ _____ _____ _____ on it.
B: That's a _____ _____.

Speak Up Real-life Scene

Dad: What _____ you _____ here?
Son: I'm _____ of _____ to _____ Miso.
Dad: What's _____?
Son: She can't _____ _____ the light _____ _____. This switch is _____ _____ for her.
Dad: That's right. I'm not _____ _____ it, _____. Do you have any good ideas _____ _____?
Son: I'm _____ _____ _____ a _____ _____ here _____ the switch.
Dad: Good idea. And I'll _____ the switch to a _____ _____.
Son: Great. Grandma will like it, too. She can _____ _____ the light _____ _____.

Express Yourself A

(1) G: _____ _____ _____ _____ my brother's chair. It's _____ _____ and _____ _____.
B: Right. _____ _____ _____ _____ this one. _____ do you _____?
G: _____ _____. I think he can use it _____ _____ _____, even _____ he _____.

(2) B: I'm _____ _____ _____ the door _____ in my house. They are not _____ _____ _____ for my grandma.
G: _____ _____ this one? She will pull it and open the door _____.
B: That's good.

(3) G: _____ _____ _____ buying this spoon. It will _____ my grandma _____ soup easily.
B: Right. She _____ _____ _____ hold it with her fingers.

Learning Diary Check Yourself

G: I'm _____ _____ about this _____ _____.
B: Why? What's _____?
G: It's _____ _____. Grandma can't use it easily.
B: Do you have _____ _____?
G: _____ _____ _____ it _____ a _____ one. That'll help her _____ _____ the light easily.
B: Good idea.

A: 나는 책꽂이가 마음에 들지 않아. 그것은 너무 작아.
B: 나도 그렇게 생각해. 어떤 아이디어라도 있니?
A: 나는 그 위에 또 다른 책꽂이를 놓을까 생각 중이야.
B: 그거 좋은 생각이다.

아빠: 너는 여기서 무엇을 하고 있니?
아들: 저는 미소를 도울 방법을 생각하고 있어요.
아빠: 뭐가 잘못됐니?
아들: 그녀는 혼자서 전등을 켤 수 없어요. 이 스위치는 그녀에게 너무 높아요.
아빠: 그렇구나. 나도 그것이 마음에 들지 않는구나. 그것에 대한 어떤 아이디어라도 있니?
아들: 저는 여기 스위치 아래에 디딤대를 놓을까 생각하고 있어요.
아빠: 좋은 생각이구나. 그럼 나는 스위치를 더 큰 것으로 바꾸마.
아들: 좋아요. 할머니께서도 그것을 좋아하실 거예요. 할머니께서는 전등을 더 쉽게 켜실 수 있어요.

(1) G: 나는 내 남동생의 의자가 마음에 안 들어. 그것은 너무 낮고 딱딱해.
B: 맞아. 나는 이것을 살까 생각 중이야. 너는 어때?
G: 좋아 보이네. 나는 그가 키가 더 자란 후에도 그것을 오랫동안 사용할 수 있을 거라고 생각해.
(2) B: 나는 우리 집의 문손잡이가 마음에 안 들어. 그것들은 우리 할머니께서 사용하시기에 쉽지 않아.
G: 이것은 어때? 그녀는 그것을 당겨서 문을 쉽게 여실 거야.
B: 그것 좋네.
(3) G: 나는 이 숟가락을 살까 생각 중이야. 그것은 우리 할머니께서 국을 쉽게 드실 수 있도록 도와줄 거야.
B: 맞아. 그녀는 그것을 손가락으로 잡으실 필요가 없어.

G: 나는 이 조명 스위치가 마음에 들지 않아.
B: 왜? 뭐가 잘못됐니?
G: 그것은 너무 작아. 할머니께서 그것을 쉽게 사용하실 수가 없어.
B: 어떤 아이디어라도 있니?
G: 나는 그것을 좀 더 큰 것으로 바꿀까 생각 중이야. 그것은 할머니께서 조명을 쉽게 켜실 수 있도록 도와줄 거야.
B: 좋은 생각이다.

※ 다음 우리말에 맞도록 대화를 영어로 쓰시오.

Get Ready 2

(1) B: _____

 G: _____

 B: _____

(2) G: _____

 B: _____

(3) G: _____

 B: _____

 G: _____

Start Off Listen & Talk A

(1) G: _____

 B: _____

 G: _____

(2) G: _____

 B: _____

 G: _____

 B: _____

Start Off Listen & draw

B: _____

G: _____

B: _____

G: _____

B: _____

Speak Up Look and talk

B: _____

G: _____

B: _____

(1) B: 나는 이 음수대가 마음에 들지 않아. 몇몇 아이들에게는 너무 높아.

 G: 음, 나는 그것과 함께 더 낮은 음수대들을 놓으려고 계획 중이야.

 B: 좋은 생각이야.

(2) G: 나는 여기 높은 계단이 마음에 들지 않아. 휠체어를 탄 사람들은 들어설 수가 없잖아.

 B: 맞아. 나는 계단 없는 새 길을 짓는 것을 생각 중이야.

(3) G: 나는 이 그네가 마음에 들지 않아. 휠체어를 탄 사람들은 그것을 쉽게 탈 수 없어.

 B: 맞아. 나는 그들을 위해 더 크고 더 안전한 자리를 매달려고 계획 중이야.

 G: 좋은 생각이야.

(1) G: 나는 그 버튼이 마음에 들지 않아.

 B: 왜? 뭐가 잘못됐니?

 G: 그것은 너무 높아. 아이들이나 휠체어를 탄 사람들은 거기까지 닿을 수가 없어. 나는 그들을 위해 또 다른 스위치를 달까 생각 중이야.

(2) G: 나는 표지판이 마음에 들지 않아. 볼 수 없는 사람들도 좀 있잖아.

 B: 맞아. 너는 어떤 아이디어라도 있니?

 G: 음, 나는 표지판 위에 점자를 추가할까 생각 중이야.

 B: 그거 좋은 생각이다.

B: 나는 불빛이 마음에 들지 않아.

G: 뭐가 잘못됐니?

B: 색맹인 사람들에게는 신호등이 똑같이 보일 거야.

G: 오, 알겠어. 각 불빛에 그림을 넣는 게 어떨까?

B: 파란불에는 걷는 사람을, 그리고 빨간불에는 서 있는 사람을? 좋은 생각이야!

B: 나는 책상이 마음에 들지 않아. 그것은 너무 낮아.

G: 맞아. 나는 그 위에 몇 장의 패드를 놓을까 생각 중이야.

B: 좋은 생각이야.

Speak Up Mission

A: _____

B: _____

A: _____

B: _____

A: 나는 책꽂이가 마음에 들지 않아. 그것은 너무 작아.
B: 나도 그렇게 생각해. 어떤 아이디어라도 있니?
A: 나는 그 위에 또 다른 책꽂이를 놓을까 생각 중이야.
B: 그거 좋은 생각이다.

Speak Up Real-life Scene

Dad: _____

Son: _____

Dad: _____

Son: _____

Dad: _____

Son: _____

Dad: _____

Son: _____

아빠: 너는 여기서 무엇을 하고 있니?
아들: 저는 미소를 도울 방법을 생각하고 있어요.
아빠: 뭐가 잘못됐니?
아들: 그녀는 혼자서 전등을 켤 수 없어요. 이 스위치는 그녀에게 너무 높아요.
아빠: 그렇구나. 나도 그것이 마음에 들지 않는구나. 그것에 대한 어떤 아이디어라도 있니?
아들: 저는 여기 스위치 아래에 디딤대를 놓을까 생각하고 있어요.
아빠: 좋은 생각이구나. 그럼 나는 스위치를 더 큰 것으로 바꾸마.
아들: 좋아요. 할머니께서도 그것을 좋아하실 거예요. 할머니께서는 전등을 더 쉽게 켜실 수 있어요.

Express Yourself A

(1) G: _____

B: _____

G: _____

(2) B: _____

G: _____

B: _____

(3) G: _____

B: _____

(1) G: 나는 내 남동생의 의자가 마음에 안 들어. 그것은 너무 낮고 딱딱해.
B: 맞아. 나는 이것을 살까 생각 중이야. 너는 어때?
G: 좋아 보이네. 나는 그가 키가 더 자란 후에도 그것을 오랫동안 사용할 수 있을 거라고 생각해.
(2) B: 나는 우리 집의 문손잡이가 마음에 안 들어. 그것들은 우리 할머니께서 사용하시기에 쉽지 않아.
G: 이것은 어때? 그녀는 그것을 당겨서 문을 쉽게 여실 거야.
B: 그것 좋네.
(3) G: 나는 이 숟가락을 살까 생각 중이야. 그것은 우리 할머니께서 국을 쉽게 드실 수 있도록 도와줄 거야.
B: 맞아. 그녀는 그것을 손가락으로 잡으실 필요가 없어.

Learning Diary Check Yourself

G: _____

B: _____

G: _____

B: _____

G: _____

B: _____

G: 나는 이 조명 스위치가 마음에 들지 않아.
B: 왜? 뭐가 잘못됐니?
G: 그것은 너무 작아. 할머니께서 그것을 쉽게 사용하실 수가 없어.
B: 어떤 아이디어라도 있니?
G: 나는 그것을 좀 더 큰 것으로 바꿀까 생각 중이야. 그것은 할머니께서 조명을 쉽게 켜실 수 있도록 도와줄 거야.
B: 좋은 생각이다.

※ 다음 우리말과 일치하도록 빈칸에 알맞은 것을 골라 쓰시오.

1 Patricia Moore – _____ of _____ _____

 A. Universal B. Mother C. Design

2 In 1979, a _____ started a _____ to _____ in the U.S. and Canada.

 A. cities B. journey C. woman

3 She _____ _____ 80.

 A. over B. looked

4 She _____ _____ or _____ well.

 A. see B. couldn't C. hear

5 She couldn't _____ well _____ a _____.

 A. without B. walk C. stick

6 _____ all these _____, the woman had to _____ stairs in subway stations and get on _____ buses.

 A. climb B. difficulties C. crowded D. with

7 She had to open _____ doors and use can openers _____ her _____ hands.

 A. with B. heavy C. weak

8 Sometimes she _____ hurt or _____ herself _____ _____.

 A. found B. danger C. got D. in

9 Every _____ was very _____ for her, but she visited more _____ 115 cities and ended her _____ in 1982.

 A. difficult B. trip C. moment D. than

10 _____ was the woman and _____ made her _____ all this?

 A. what B. do C. who

11 She was Patricia Moore, _____ _____ _____.

 A. designer B. 26-year-old C. a

12 _____ the 1970's, she _____ for a big design _____.

 A. worked B. during C. company

13 She often asked at _____, "How about _____ for old or _____ people?"

 A. designing B. meetings C. weak

14 The _____ designers always answered, "We don't _____ for _____ people."

 A. other B. those C. design

15 She _____ _____ of the _____ cold answer.

 A. tired B. same C. became

16 _____, she decided to become one of "those people" and travel _____ many cities to _____ their _____ better.

 A. around B. difficulties C. understand D. finally

1 Patricia Moore – 유니버설 디자인의 어머니

2 1979년에, 한 여성이 미국과 캐나다의 도시로 여행을 시작했다.

3 그녀는 80세가 넘어 보였다.

4 그녀는 잘 보거나 잘 들을 수 없었다.

5 그녀는 지팡이 없이는 잘 걸을 수 없었다.

6 이 모든 어려움을 가진 채, 그 여성은 지하철역에서 계단을 올라가거나 붐비는 버스에 올라타야 했다.

7 그녀는 무거운 문을 열거나 그녀의 약한 손으로 깡통 따개를 사용해야 했다.

8 때때로 그녀는 다치거나 위험에 처하기도 했다.

9 모든 순간이 그녀에게 매우 어려웠으나, 그녀는 115개 이상의 도시를 방문하였으며 1982년에 여행을 끝마쳤다.

10 그 여성은 누구였고 무엇이 그녀로 하여금 이 모든 것을 하게 만들었을까?

11 그녀는 26살의 디자이너인 Patricia Moore였다.

12 1970년대 동안, 그녀는 큰 디자인 회사에서 일했다.

13 그녀는 종종 회의에서 물었다. "나이 들거나 약한 사람들을 위해 디자인하는 게 어떨까요?"

14 다른 디자이너들은 항상 대답했다. "우리는 그런 사람들을 위해 디자인하지 않습니다."

15 그녀는 똑같은 냉담한 대답에 지쳤다.

16 마침내, 그녀는 '그런 사람들' 중의 하나가 되어 그들의 어려움을 더 잘 이해하기 위해 많은 도시를 여행하기로 결심했다.

17 For this, she put on her grandmother's _____, _____ shoes, and _____ _____.

 A. uncomfortable B. glasses C. thick D. clothes

18 The shoes were _____ uncomfortable _____ she _____ walk well _____ a sick.

 A. that B. without C. couldn't D. so

19 The glasses were so _____ that she _____ see well _____ them.

 A. with B. couldn't C. thick

20 She also _____ lots _____ cotton in her ears to _____ her _____ bad.

 A. hearing B. make C. put D. of

21 _____ her journey, Patricia _____ the difficulties old people _____ _____.

 A. through B. during C. go D. felt

22 _____ this experience, she designed _____ anybody could use _____ and _____.

 A. safely B. products C. easily D. from

23 This was the _____ of " _____ _____," or "design for all."

 A. universal B. design C. beginning

24 One _____ of her _____ design ideas is _____ buses.

 A. low-floor B. example C. universal

25 They have no _____ and have _____ a low floor that even a person in a wheelchair can use them _____ any _____.

 A. without B. steps C. help D. such

26 Of _____, this helps _____ people _____ on the bus more _____, too.

 A. other B. comfortably C. course D. get

27 Today _____ and more designers are _____ Patricia's _____.

 A. way B. following C. more

28 Products like big _____ light switches, doors with _____ handles, and phones with _____ buttons are helping people live better _____.

 A. touch B. lives C. easy D. flat

29 Look _____ you, feel the difficulties of people who are older or _____, and try to find solutions from their _____ of _____.

 A. view B. around C. weaker D. point

30 You could be the _____ Patricia Moore and make the world a _____ for _____.

 A. place B. next C. everybody D. better

17 이를 위해, 그녀는 자신의 할머니 옷을 입고, 불편한 신발을 신고, 두꺼운 안경을 썼다.

18 신발은 너무 불편해서 그녀는 지팡이 없이는 잘 걸을 수 없었다.

19 안경은 너무 두꺼워서 그녀는 안경을 쓰고는 잘 볼 수 없었다.

20 그녀는 또한 그녀의 청력을 나쁘게 하려고 귀에 많은 솜을 넣었다.

21 여행 동안, Patricia는 나이 든 사람들이 겪는 어려움을 느꼈다.

22 이 경험으로부터, 그녀는 누구나 안전하고 쉽게 사용할 수 있는 제품들을 고안했다.

23 이것이 '유니버설 디자인' 또는 '모두를 위한 디자인'의 시작이었다.

24 그녀의 유니버설 디자인 아이디어의 한 가지 예는 저상 버스이다.

25 그것은 계단이 없고 낮은 바닥을 가지고 있어서 휠체어를 탄 사람조차 아무 도움 없이 이용할 수 있다.

26 물론, 이것은 다른 사람들도 버스를 더 편안하게 탈 수 있도록 도와준다.

27 오늘날 점점 더 많은 디자이너가 Patricia의 방식을 따르고 있다.

28 크고 평평한 조명 스위치, 편한 손잡이를 가진 문, 터치 버튼을 가진 전화기와 같은 제품들은 사람들이 더 나은 삶을 살도록 도와주고 있다.

29 여러분의 주위를 둘러보고, 더 나이 들거나 더 약한 사람들의 어려움을 느껴 보고, 그들의 관점에서 해결책을 찾으려고 노력해 봐라.

30 여러분은 다음의 Patricia Moore가 되어 세상을 모두에게 더 나은 곳으로 만들 수 있을 것이다.

※ 다음 우리말과 일치하도록 빈칸에 알맞은 말을 쓰시오.

1 Patricia Moore – Mother of _____ _____

2 In 1979, a woman _____ _____ _____ _____ in the U.S. and Canada.

3 She _____ _____ _____.

4 She _____ _____ _____ _____ well.

5 She _____ _____ well _____ _____ _____.

6 _____ _____ _____ _____, the woman had to climb stairs in subway stations and _____ _____ _____ buses.

7 She had to open _____ _____ and use can openers _____ _____ _____ _____.

8 Sometimes she got hurt or _____ _____ _____ _____.

9 Every moment was _____ _____ _____ _____, but she visited _____ _____ 115 cities and ended her trip in 1982.

10 Who was the woman and _____ _____ _____ _____ all this?

11 She was Patricia Moore, _____ _____ _____.

12 _____ _____ _____, she _____ _____ a big design company.

13 She often asked at meetings, "_____ _____ _____ for old or _____ _____?"

14 The other designers always answered, "We don't design _____ _____ _____."

15 She _____ _____ _____ the same _____ _____.

16 _____, she decided to become one of "those people" and travel around many cities _____ _____ _____ _____ better.

1 Patricia Moore – 유니버설 디자인의 어머니

2 1979년에, 한 여성이 미국과 캐나다의 도시로 여행을 시작했다.

3 그녀는 80세가 넘어 보였다.

4 그녀는 잘 보거나 잘 들을 수 없었다.

5 그녀는 지팡이가 없이는 잘 걸을 수 없었다.

6 이 모든 어려움을 가진 채, 그 여성은 지하철역에서 계단을 올라가거나 붐비는 버스에 올라타야 했다.

7 그녀는 무거운 문을 열거나 그녀의 약한 손으로 깡통 따개를 사용해야 했다.

8 때때로 그녀는 다치거나 위험에 처하기도 했다.

9 모든 순간이 그녀에게 매우 어려웠으나, 그녀는 115개 이상의 도시를 방문하였으며 1982년에 여행을 끝마쳤다.

10 그 여성은 누구였고 무엇이 그녀로 하여금 이 모든 것을 하게 만들었을까?

11 그녀는 26살의 디자이너인 Patricia Moore였다.

12 1970년대 동안, 그녀는 큰 디자인 회사에서 일했다.

13 그녀는 종종 회의에서 물었다. "나이 들거나 약한 사람들을 위해 디자인하는 게 어떨까요?"

14 다른 디자이너들은 항상 대답했다. "우리는 그런 사람들을 위해 디자인하지 않습니다."

15 그녀는 똑같은 냉담한 대답에 지쳤다.

16 마침내, 그녀는 '그런 사람들' 중의 하나가 되어 그들의 어려움을 더 잘 이해하기 위해 많은 도시를 여행하기로 결심했다.

17 _____ _____, she _____ _____ her grandmother's clothes, _____ shoes, and _____ _____.

18 The shoes were _____ uncomfortable _____ she _____ walk well _____ _____ _____.

19 The glasses were _____ thick _____ she _____ see well _____ _____.

20 She also put _____ _____ _____ in her ears _____ _____ _____ _____.

21 _____ her journey, Patricia _____ the _____ old people _____ _____.

22 _____ _____ _____, she designed products anybody could use _____ and _____.

23 This was the _____ of "_____ _____," or "_____ _____."

24 _____ _____ of her universal design ideas is _____ _____.

25 They have _____ _____ and have _____ _____ _____ _____ that even a person _____ _____ _____ can use them _____ _____ _____.

26 Of course, this _____ other people _____ _____ the bus _____ _____, too.

27 Today more and more designers are _____ _____ _____.

28 Products _____ big flat light switches, doors _____ easy handles, and phones _____ touch buttons are helping people _____ _____ _____.

29 _____ _____ you, feel the difficulties of people who are older or weaker, and try to find solutions _____ _____ _____.

30 You could be the _____ Patricia Moore and make the world _____ _____ _____ _____.

17 이를 위해, 그녀는 자신의 할머니 옷을 입고, 불편한 신발을 신고, 두꺼운 안경을 썼다.

18 신발은 너무 불편해서 그녀는 지팡이 없이는 잘 걸을 수 없었다.

19 안경은 너무 두꺼워서 그녀는 안경을 쓰고는 잘 볼 수 없었다.

20 그녀는 또한 그녀의 청력을 나쁘게 하려고 귀에 많은 솜을 넣었다.

21 여행 동안, Patricia는 나이 든 사람들이 겪는 어려움을 느꼈다.

22 이 경험으로부터, 그녀는 누구나 안전하고 쉽게 사용할 수 있는 제품들을 고안했다.

23 이것이 '유니버설 디자인' 또는 '모두를 위한 디자인'의 시작이었다.

24 그녀의 유니버설 디자인 아이디어의 한 가지 예는 저상 버스이다.

25 그것은 계단이 없고 낮은 바닥을 가지고 있어서 휠체어를 탄 사람조차 아무 도움 없이 이용할 수 있다.

26 물론, 이것은 다른 사람들도 버스를 더 편안하게 탈 수 있도록 도와준다.

27 오늘날 점점 더 많은 디자이너가 Patricia의 방식을 따르고 있다.

28 크고 평평한 조명 스위치, 편한 손잡이를 가진 문, 터치 버튼을 가진 전화기와 같은 제품들은 사람들이 더 나은 삶을 살도록 도와주고 있다.

29 여러분의 주위를 둘러보고, 더 나이 들거나 더 약한 사람들의 어려움을 느껴 보고, 그들의 관점에서 해결책을 찾으려고 노력해 봐라.

30 여러분은 다음의 Patricia Moore가 되어 세상을 모두에게 더 나은 곳으로 만들 수 있을 것이다.

※ 다음 문장을 우리말로 쓰시오.

1 Patricia Moore – Mother of Universal Design

➡ _____

2 In 1979, a woman started a journey to cities in the U.S. and Canada.

➡ _____

3 She looked over 80.

➡ _____

4 She couldn't see or hear well.

➡ _____

5 She couldn't walk well without a stick.

➡ _____

6 With all these difficulties, the woman had to climb stairs in subway stations and get on crowded buses.

➡ _____

7 She had to open heavy doors and use can openers with her weak hands.

➡ _____

8 Sometimes she got hurt or found herself in danger.

➡ _____

9 Every moment was very difficult for her, but she visited more than 115 cities and ended her trip in 1982.

➡ _____

10 Who was the woman and what made her do all this?

➡ _____

11 She was Patricia Moore, a 26-year-old designer.

➡ _____

12 During the 1970's, she worked for a big design company.

➡ _____

13 She often asked at meetings, "How about designing for old or weak people?"

➡ _____

14 The other designers always answered, "We don't design for those people."

➡ _____

15 She became tired of the same cold answer.

➡ _____

16 Finally, she decided to become one of "those people" and travel around many cities to understand their difficulties better.

➡ _____

17 For this, she put on her grandmother's clothes, uncomfortable shoes, and thick glasses.

➡ _____

18 The shoes were so uncomfortable that she couldn't walk well without a stick.

➡ _____

19 The glasses were so thick that she couldn't see well with them.

➡ _____

20 She also put lots of cotton in her ears to make her hearing bad.

➡ _____

21 During her journey, Patricia felt the difficulties old people go through.

➡ _____

22 From this experience, she designed products anybody could use safely and easily.

➡ _____

23 This was the beginning of "universal design," or "design for all."

➡ _____

24 One example of her universal design ideas is low-floor buses.

➡ _____

25 They have no steps and have such a low floor that even a person in a wheelchair can use them without any help.

➡ _____

26 Of course, this helps other people get on the bus more comfortably, too.

➡ _____

27 Today more and more designers are following Patricia's way.

➡ _____

28 Products like big flat light switches, doors with easy handles, and phones with touch buttons are helping people live better lives.

➡ _____

29 Look around you, feel the difficulties of people who are older or weaker, and try to find solutions from their point of view.

➡ _____

30 You could be the next Patricia Moore and make the world a better place for everybody.

➡ _____

본문 Test

※ 다음 괄호 안의 단어들을 우리말에 맞도록 바르게 배열하시오.

1 (Moore / Patricia / — / Universal / of / Mother / Design)
➡ _____

2 (1979, / in / woman / a / started / journey / a / cities / to / the / in / Canada. / and / U.S.)
➡ _____

3 (she / over / looked / 80.)
➡ _____

4 (couldn't / she / hear / or / see / well.)
➡ _____

5 (she / walk / couldn't / well / a / stick. / without)
➡ _____

6 (all / with / difficulties, / these / woman / the / had / climb / to / stairs / subway / in / stations / and / on / get / buses. / crowded)
➡ _____

7 (had / she / open / to / doors / heavy / and / can / use / openers / her / with / hands. / weak)
➡ _____

8 (she / sometimes / got / or / hurt / found / in / herself / danger.)
➡ _____

9 (moment / every / very / was / for / difficult / her, / but / visited / she / than / more / cities / 115 / and / her / ended / in / trip / 1982.)
➡ _____

10 (was / who / woman / the / and / made / what / her / all / do / this?)
➡ _____

11 (was / she / Moore, / Patricia / 26-year-old / a / designer.)
➡ _____

12 (the / during / 1970's, / worked / she / a / for / design / big / company.)
➡ _____

13 (she / asked / often / meetings, / at / "how / designing / about / old / for / or / people?" / weak)
➡ _____

14 (other / the / always / designers / answered, / "we / design / don't / those / people." / for)
➡ _____

15 (became / she / of / tired / same / the / answer. / cold)
➡ _____

16 (she / finally, / decided / become / to / of / one / "those / and / people" / travel / many / around / to / cities / understand / difficulties / their / better.)
➡ _____

1 Patricia Moore – 유니버설 디자인의 어머니

2 1979년에, 한 여성이 미국과 캐나다의 도시로 여행을 시작했다.

3 그녀는 80세가 넘어 보였다.

4 그녀는 잘 보거나 잘 들을 수 없었다.

5 그녀는 지팡이가 없이는 잘 걸을 수 없었다.

6 이 모든 어려움을 가진 채, 그 여성은 지하철역에서 계단을 올라가거나 붐비는 버스에 올라타야 했다.

7 그녀는 무거운 문을 열거나 그녀의 약한 손으로 깡통 따개를 사용해야 했다.

8 때때로 그녀는 다치거나 위험에 처하기도 했다.

9 모든 순간이 그녀에게 매우 어려웠으나, 그녀는 115개 이상의 도시를 방문하였으며 1982년에 여행을 끝마쳤다.

10 그 여성은 누구였고 무엇이 그녀로 하여금 이 모든 것을 하게 만들었을까?

11 그녀는 26살의 디자이너인 Patricia Moore였다.

12 1970년대 동안, 그녀는 큰 디자인 회사에서 일했다.

13 그녀는 종종 회의에서 물었다. "나이 들거나 약한 사람들을 위해 디자인하는 게 어떨까요?"

14 다른 디자이너들은 항상 대답했다. "우리는 그런 사람들을 위해 디자인하지 않습니다."

15 그녀는 똑같은 냉담한 대답에 지쳤다.

16 마침내, 그녀는 '그런 사람들' 중의 하나가 되어 그들의 어려움을 더 잘 이해하기 위해 많은 도시를 여행하기로 결심했다.

72 Lesson 8. Design for All

17 (this, / for / she / on / put / her / clothes, / grandmother's / shoes, / uncomfortable / and / glasses. / thick)
➡ _____

18 (shoes / the / so / were / uncomfortable / she / that / couldn't / well / walk / a / without / stick.)
➡ _____

19 (glasses / the / so / were / thick / she / that / couldn't / well / see / them. / with)
➡ _____

20 (she / put / also / of / lots / cotton / her / in / ears / make / to / hearing / her / bad.)
➡ _____

21 (her / during / journery, / felt / Particia / difficulties / the / people / old / through. / go)
➡ _____

22 (this / from / experience, / designed / she / anybody / products / use / could / easily. / and / safely)
➡ _____

23 (was / this / beginning / the / "universal / of / design," / or / all." / for / "design)
➡ _____

24 (example / one / her / of / universal / ideas / design / low-floor / is / buses.)
➡ _____

25 (have / they / steps / no / and / such / have / low / a / floor / that / a / even / person / a / in / wheelchair / use / can / them / any / help. / without)
➡ _____

26 (course, / of / helps / this / people / other / on / get / bus / the / more / too. / comfortably)
➡ _____

27 (more / today / more / and / designers / following / are / way. / Patricia's)
➡ _____

28 (like / products / big / light / flat / switches, / with / doors / handlers, / easy / and / with / phones / touch / buttons / helping / are / live / people / lives. / better)
➡ _____

29 (around / look / you, / the / feel / difficulties / people / of / are / who / older / weaker, / or / try / and / to / solutions / find / their / from / view. / of / point)
➡ _____

30 (could / you / the / be / next / Moore / Patricia / and / the / make / world / better / a / place / everybody. / for)
➡ _____

17 이를 위해, 그녀는 자신의 할머니 옷을 입고, 불편한 신발을 신고, 두꺼운 안경을 썼다.

18 신발은 너무 불편해서 그녀는 지팡이가 없이는 잘 걸을 수 없었다.

19 안경은 너무 두꺼워서 그녀는 안경을 쓰고는 잘 볼 수 없었다.

20 그녀는 또한 그녀의 청력을 나쁘게 하려고 귀에 많은 솜을 넣었다.

21 여행 동안, Patricia는 나이 든 사람들이 겪는 어려움을 느꼈다.

22 이 경험으로부터, 그녀는 누구나 안전하고 쉽게 사용할 수 있는 제품들을 고안했다.

23 이것이 '유니버설 디자인' 또는 '모두를 위한 디자인'의 시작이었다.

24 그녀의 유니버설 디자인 아이디어의 한 가지 예는 저상 버스이다.

25 그것은 계단이 없고 낮은 바닥을 가지고 있어서 휠체어를 탄 사람조차 아무 도움 없이 이용할 수 있다.

26 물론, 이것은 다른 사람들도 버스를 더 편안하게 탈 수 있도록 도와준다.

27 오늘날 점점 더 많은 디자이너가 Patricia의 방식을 따르고 있다.

28 크고 평평한 조명 스위치, 편한 손잡이를 가진 문, 터치 버튼을 가진 전화기와 같은 제품들은 사람들이 더 나은 삶을 살도록 도와주고 있다.

29 여러분의 주위를 둘러보고, 더 나이 들거나 더 약한 사람들의 어려움을 느껴 보고, 그들의 관점에서 해결책을 찾으려고 노력해 봐라.

30 여러분은 다음의 Patricia Moore가 되어 세상을 모두에게 더 나은 곳으로 만들 수 있을 것이다.

※ 다음 우리말을 영어로 쓰시오.

1 Patricia Moore – 유니버설 디자인의 어머니

➡ _____

2 1979년에, 한 여성이 미국과 캐나다의 도시로 여행을 시작했다.

➡ _____

3 그녀는 80세가 넘어 보였다.

➡ _____

4 그녀는 잘 보거나 잘 들을 수 없었다.

➡ _____

5 그녀는 지팡이 없이는 잘 걸을 수 없었다.

➡ _____

6 이 모든 어려움을 가진 채, 그 여성은 지하철역에서 계단을 올라가거나 붐비는 버스에 올라타야 했다.

➡ _____

7 그녀는 무거운 문을 열거나 그녀의 약한 손으로 깡통 따개를 사용해야 했다.

➡ _____

8 때때로 그녀는 다치거나 위험에 처하기도 했다.

➡ _____

9 모든 순간이 그녀에게 매우 어려웠으나, 그녀는 115개 이상의 도시를 방문하였으며 1982년에 여행을 끝마쳤다.

➡ _____

10 그 여성은 누구였고 무엇이 그녀로 하여금 이 모든 것을 하게 만들었을까?

➡ _____

11 그녀는 26살의 디자이너인 Patricia Moore였다.

➡ _____

12 1970년대 동안, 그녀는 큰 디자인 회사에서 일했다.

➡ _____

13 그녀는 종종 회의에서 물었다. "나이 들거나 약한 사람들을 위해 디자인하는 게 어떨까요?"

➡ _____

14 다른 디자이너들은 항상 대답했다. "우리는 그런 사람들을 위해 디자인하지 않습니다."

➡ _____

15 그녀는 똑같은 냉담한 대답에 지쳤다.

➡ _____

16 마침내, 그녀는 '그런 사람들' 중의 하나가 되어 그들의 어려움을 더 잘 이해하기 위해 많은 도시를 여행하기로 결심했다.

➡ _____

17 이를 위해, 그녀는 자신의 할머니 옷을 입고, 불편한 신발을 신고, 두꺼운 안경을 썼다.

➡ _____

18 신발은 너무 불편해서 그녀는 지팡이 없이는 잘 걸을 수 없었다.

➡ _____

19 안경은 너무 두꺼워서 그녀는 안경을 쓰고는 잘 볼 수 없었다.

➡ _____

20 그녀는 또한 그녀의 청력을 나쁘게 하려고 귀에 많은 솜을 넣었다.

➡ _____

21 여행 동안, Patricia는 나이 든 사람들이 겪는 어려움을 느꼈다.

➡ _____

22 이 경험으로부터, 그녀는 누구나 안전하고 쉽게 사용할 수 있는 제품들을 고안했다.

➡ _____

23 이것이 '유니버설 디자인' 또는 '모두를 위한 디자인'의 시작이었다.

➡ _____

24 그녀의 유니버설 디자인 아이디어의 한 가지 예는 저상 버스이다.

➡ _____

25 그것은 계단이 없고 낮은 바닥을 가지고 있어서 휠체어를 탄 사람조차 아무 도움 없이 이용할 수 있다.

➡ _____

26 물론, 이것은 다른 사람들도 버스를 더 편안하게 탈 수 있도록 도와준다.

➡ _____

27 오늘날 점점 더 많은 디자이너가 Patricia의 방식을 따르고 있다.

➡ _____

28 크고 평평한 조명 스위치, 편한 손잡이를 가진 문, 터치 버튼을 가진 전화기와 같은 제품들은 사람들이 더 나은 삶을 살도록 도와주고 있다.

➡ _____

29 여러분의 주위를 둘러보고, 더 나이 들거나 더 약한 사람들의 어려움을 느껴 보고, 그들의 관점에서 해결책을 찾으려고 노력해 봐라.

➡ _____

30 여러분은 다음의 Patricia Moore가 되어 세상을 모두에게 더 나은 곳으로 만들 수 있을 것이다.

➡ _____

※ 다음 우리말과 일치하도록 빈칸에 알맞은 말을 쓰시오.

Express Yourself C1

1. The _____ _____ door in my house is _____ high _____ my little brother _____ _____ clothes _____ into it.

2. _____, this machine has a _____ _____.

3. It'll _____ my brother _____ clothes in _____ _____.

1. 우리 집에 있는 세탁기 문은 너무 높아서 나의 남동생은 그 안에 옷을 쉽게 넣을 수 없다.
2. 그러나, 이 기계는 옆문을 가지고 있다.
3. 그것은 내 남동생이 옷을 더 쉽게 넣을 수 있도록 도와줄 것이다.

Project Step 3

1. The hole cover was _____ _____ _____ I _____ ride my bike on it.

2. So I want _____ _____ the cover _____ this.

3. The new cover will _____ people _____ a bike _____.

1. 맨홀 덮개가 너무 위험해서 나는 그 위에서 자전거를 탈 수 없었다.
2. 그래서 나는 덮개를 이처럼 바꾸고 싶다.
3. 새로운 덮개는 사람들이 자전거를 안전하게 타도록 도와줄 것이다.

Link to the World

1. Kim Mandeok _____ _____ _____ a poor family in Jeju.

2. She _____ _____ and _____ _____.

3. In 1794, lots of people in Jeju _____ _____ _____ hunger _____ _____ bad weather.

4. She _____ _____ _____ she had and _____ a lot of people.

5. King Jeongjo _____ _____ _____ _____ _____ to Mountain Geumgang.

1. 김만덕은 제주의 가난한 가정에서 태어났다.
2. 그녀는 열심히 일해서 부자가 되었다.
3. 1794년에 제주의 많은 사람이 나쁜 날씨로 인한 굶주림으로 죽어가고 있었다.
4. 그녀는 자신이 가진 거의 모든 것을 써서 많은 사람을 구했다.
5. 정조 임금은 그녀가 금강산으로 여행을 하도록 허락했다.

※ 다음 우리말을 영어로 쓰시오.

Express Yourself C1

1. 우리 집에 있는 세탁기 문은 너무 높아서 나의 남동생은 그 안에 옷을 쉽게 넣을 수 없다.

 ➡ _____

2. 그러나, 이 기계는 옆문을 가지고 있다.

 ➡ _____

3. 그것은 내 남동생이 옷을 더 쉽게 넣을 수 있도록 도와줄 것이다.

 ➡ _____

Project Step 3

1. 맨홀 덮개가 너무 위험해서 나는 그 위에서 자전거를 탈 수 없었다.

 ➡ _____

2. 그래서 나는 덮개를 이처럼 바꾸고 싶다.

 ➡ _____

3. 새로운 덮개는 사람들이 자전거를 안전하게 타도록 도와줄 것이다.

 ➡ _____

Link to the World

1. 김만덕은 제주의 가난한 가정에서 태어났다.

 ➡ _____

2. 그녀는 열심히 일해서 부자가 되었다.

 ➡ _____

3. 1794년에 제주의 많은 사람이 나쁜 날씨로 인한 굶주림으로 죽어가고 있었다.

 ➡ _____

4. 그녀는 자신이 가진 거의 모든 것을 써서 많은 사람을 구했다.

 ➡ _____

5. 정조 임금은 그녀가 금강산으로 여행을 하도록 허락했다.

 ➡ _____

Step1

※ 다음 영어를 우리말로 쓰시오.

01	activity	_____
02	slow	_____
03	winner	_____
04	delicious	_____
05	second	_____
06	wheel	_____
07	youth	_____
08	exactly	_____
09	finish	_____
10	break time	_____
11	bright	_____
12	sweet	_____
13	friendly	_____
14	though	_____
15	clothes	_____
16	special	_____
17	grade	_____
18	handwriting	_____
19	hopeful	_____
20	trash can	_____
21	wave	_____
22	outside	_____
23	wet	_____
24	choose	_____
25	ocean	_____
26	close	_____
27	place	_____
28	save	_____
29	never	_____
30	change	_____
31	circle	_____
32	cute	_____
33	mirror	_____
34	P.E. class	_____
35	cut A into B	_____
36	wait a second	_____
37	cover A up with B	_____
38	don't need to	_____
39	up and down	_____
40	take a break	_____
41	such as	_____
42	add A to B	_____
43	be full of	_____

※ 다음 우리말을 영어로 쓰시오.

01 느린 _____

02 대부분의 _____

03 결코 ~하지 않다 _____

04 활동 _____

05 동그라미, 원 _____

06 끝나다 _____

07 친근한, 다정한 _____

08 가까이; 닫다 _____

09 밖에 _____

10 절약하다 _____

11 맛있는 _____

12 젖은 _____

13 도형, 모양 _____

14 갈아입다, 바꾸다 _____

15 성적 _____

16 손 글씨 _____

17 희망적인 _____

18 초, 짧은 시간, 두 번째 _____

19 쉬는 시간 _____

20 승자 _____

21 고르다 _____

22 정확하게 _____

23 바다, 대양 _____

24 밝은, 똑똑한 _____

25 쓰레기 통 _____

26 특별한 _____

27 체육 수업 _____

28 장소; 놓다, 두다 _____

29 바퀴 _____

30 옷 _____

31 비록 ~일지라도 _____

32 파도치다, 손을 흔들다 _____

33 단것, 단 음식 _____

34 젊음, 청춘 _____

35 휴식을 취하다 _____

36 ~까지 _____

37 ~할 필요가 없다 _____

38 A를 B로 자르다 _____

39 물러서다 _____

40 A를 B에 더하다 _____

41 B로 A를 덮다 _____

42 ~로 가득 차다 _____

43 잠깐 기다리다 _____

※ 다음 영영풀이에 알맞은 단어를 <보기>에서 골라 쓴 후, 우리말 뜻을 쓰시오.

1 _____ : containing, or tasting as if it contains, a lot of sugar: _____

2 _____ : behaving in a pleasant, kind way towards someone: _____

3 _____ : a food made from flour, water, and usually yeast, mixed together and baked: _____

4 _____ : to decide what you want from two or more things or possibilities: _____

5 _____ : the mass of salt water that covers most of the earth's surface: _____

6 _____ : writing that is done with a pen or pencil, not printed or typed: _____

7 _____ : covered with or containing liquid, especially water: _____

8 _____ : to keep something, especially money, for use in the future: _____

9 _____ : a person, a team, an animal, etc. that wins something: _____

10 _____ : a number or letter that shows how good someone's work or performance is: _____

11 _____ : to raise your hand and move it from side to side as a way of greeting someone: _____

12 _____ : the period of your life when you are young, or the state of being young: _____

13 _____ : a particular position, point or area: _____

14 _____ : a piece of special flat glass that reflects images, so that you can see yourself when you look in it: _____

15 _____ : a continuous curved line, the points of which are always the same distance away from a fixed central point: _____

16 _____ : a circular object connected at the centre to a bar, used for making vehicles or parts of machines move: _____

보기			
sweet	ocean	circle	grade
choose	friendly	wave	youth
place	wet	save	handwriting
bread	mirror	winner	wheel

※ 다음 우리말과 일치하도록 빈칸에 알맞은 것을 골라 쓰시오.

1 _____ _____
A. Magazine B. Teens'

2 _____ of _____ in _____
A. Art B. Works C. Shapes

3 _____ a _____
A. Circle B. Like

4 I love you _____ a circle _____ a circle never _____.
A. because B. ends C. like

5 Snowman

6 It's _____ _____.
A. outside B. cold

7 I don't _____ to go _____ and _____.
A. out B. play C. want

8 But Mom _____ I _____ _____.
A. to B. says C. have

9 It's _____ to snow and I'm _____ to be _____.
A. going B. starting C. cold

10 I don't like playing _____ on _____ _____ these.
A. like B. outside C. days

11 But _____ a _____, I have the _____ wonderful idea!
A. wait B. most C. second

12 I'll _____ myself _____ with snow and I'll _____ here!
A. up B. hide C. cover

13 _____ _____ _____ Your Handwriting
A. with B. Back C. Looking

14 _____ is _____.
A. art B. life

15 _____ _____ in COLOR.
A. yours B. live

16 IT ISN'T OVER _____ IT'S _____.
A. OVER B. UNTIL

17 I am a _____ walker, but I _____ walk _____.
A. slow B. back C. never

18 I love the _____ _____ you _____.
A. little B. do C. things

19 _____ your _____.
A. dream B. follow

20 _____ _____
A. Bike B. My

1	십대들의 잡지
2	모양으로 표현된 예술 작품
3	동그라미처럼
4	나는 동그라미처럼 너를 사랑해. 왜냐하면 동그라미는 절대 끝나지 않기에.
5	눈사람
6	바깥은 추워.
7	나는 밖으로 나가 놀고 싶지 않네.
8	하지만 엄마는 그래야 한다고 하시네.
9	눈이 오기 시작하고 나는 추워질 거야.
10	나는 이런 날에는 나가서 놀고 싶지 않아.
11	하지만 잠깐만, 나는 최고로 멋진 생각이 났어!
12	나는 눈으로 내 몸을 덮고 여기에 숨어야지!
13	손 글씨로 돌아보기
14	인생은 예술이다.
15	다양한 색깔로 살아라.
16	끝날 때까지 끝난 게 아니다.
17	나는 느리게 걷는 사람이지만 절대 물러서지는 않는다.
18	나는 네가 하는 작은 일들을 사랑해.
19	네 꿈을 좇아라.
20	나의 자전거

21 Two wheels _____ me / To any _____ / To school / _____ home / To the mountain / To the river / I love my bike / I enjoy _____ it every day

 A. place B. riding C. take D. back

22 _____ _____

 A. Tree B. Giving

23 _____ there – _____

 A. wet B. out

24 _____ here – _____

 A. dry B. in

25 _____ _____ umbrella

 A. big B. pretty

26 _____ me _____ the sky

 A. and B. between

27 _____ of This _____

 A. Year B. Selfies

28 _____ we _____ the game, we had a _____ of fun.

 A. lot B. lost C. though

29 _____ _____ the robots we _____.

 A. at B. made C. look

30 _____ they _____?

 A. cute B. aren't

31 We _____ a _____ cake _____ Mr. Han.

 A. for B. big C. made

32 It _____ _____ _____.

 A. him B. made C. happy

33 _____ you ever _____ a handsome Peter Pan _____ me?

 A. seen B. like C. have

34 _____ Do You _____ of Your School _____?

 A. Think B. What C. Life

35 The _____ uncomfortable _____

 A. moment B. most

36 1. When I _____ _____

 A. tests B. take

37 2. _____ I am really _____ and have _____ to eat

 A. nothing B. when C. hungry

21 바퀴 두 개가 나를 데려가네 / 어느 곳으로든지 / 학교로 / 다시 집으로 / 산으로 / 강으로 / 나는 내 자전거가 아주 좋아 / 나는 그걸 매일 즐겨 타네

22 아낌없이 주는 나무

23 저곳 바깥은 – 젖어 있고

24 이곳 안쪽은 – 말라 있네

25 엄청 큰 우산이네

26 나와 하늘 사이에 있는

27 올해의 셀피들

28 우리는 게임에 졌지만, 아주 즐거웠다.

29 우리가 만든 로봇들을 봐.

30 귀엽지 않니?

31 우리는 한 씨 할아버지께 드릴 큰 케이크를 만들었다.

32 그것은 할아버지를 행복하게 해 주었다.

33 나처럼 잘생긴 피터 팬을 본 적이 있니?

34 학교생활에 대해 어떻게 생각하니?

35 가장 불편한 순간

36 1. 시험을 칠 때

37 2. 정말 배가 고픈데 먹을 것이 없을 때

38 3. When I _____ clothes _____ and after P.E. _____
 A. class B. before C. change

39 4. others: _____ I am _____ in _____
 A. sleepy B. class C. when

40 _____ the teacher doesn't finish _____ after the bell _____
 A. rings B. when C. classes

41 The most _____ _____
 A. lovely B. most

42 1. _____ _____
 A. time B. lunch

43 2. _____ _____ my _____ teacher
 A. favorite B. with C. class

44 3. the _____ _____ on Friday
 A. class B. last

45 4. others: _____ I am sleeping _____ _____ time
 A. during B. when C. break

46 _____ I see _____ in the _____
 A. mirror B. myself C. when

47 The _____ _____ news
 A. awesome B. most

48 1. I _____ better _____ than _____
 A. grades B.before C. got

49 2. School _____ _____ today
 A. earlier B. finishes

50 3. I don't go to school _____ _____ rains or snows a _____
 A. because B. lot C. it

51 4. others: We eat _____ sweets _____ dessert
 A. for B. delicious

52 My _____ friend and I are _____ the _____ class
 A. same B. best C. in

53 The _____ _____ work to _____
 A. difficult B. do C. most

54 1. _____ trash _____
 A. cans B. washing

55 2. Studying

38 3. 체육 시간 전후에 옷을 갈아입을 때

39 4. 기타: 수업 중에 졸릴 때

40 3. 종이 울렸는데 선생님이 수업을 끝내지 않을 때

41 가장 사랑스러운 시간

42 1. 점심시간

43 2. 가장 좋아하는 선생님의 수업 시간

44 3. 금요일의 마지막 수업 시간

45 4. 기타: 쉬는 시간에 잠잘 때

46 거울 속의 나를 볼 때

47 가장 멋진 뉴스

48 1. 전보다 좋은 성적을 받았다

49 2. 오늘 수업이 일찍 끝난다

50 3. 비나 눈이 많이 와서 학교에 가지 않는다

51 4. 기타: 후식으로 맛있는 단것을 먹는다

52 가장 친한 친구와 내가 같은 반이 되었다

53 가장 하기 힘든 일

54 1. 쓰레기통 씻기

55 2. 공부하기

56 3. _____ a _____ in _____ of friends

A. making B. front C. presentation

57 4. others: Being _____ time _____ day

A. on B. every

58 _____ _____

A. work B. group

59 _____ We _____ in Our _____

A. Village B. Love C. Places

60 Daehan _____ _____

A. Market B. Traditional

61 If you want to eat _____ _____, _____ Daehan Market.

A. delicious B. something C. visit

62 You can _____ "*yeopjeon*" and _____ it to _____ your lunch box _____.

A. full B. use C. make D. buy

63 You can _____ many kinds of food and _____ them _____ your lunch box.

A. add B. choose C. to

64 Saebom _____ _____

A. Center B. Youth

65 This is Saebom Youth Center in the _____ _____ our _____.

A. of B. town C. middle

66 We like this place _____ we can _____ many things, _____ _____ dance and music.

A. as B. because C. such D. learn

67 We can also _____ board games and _____ a _____ here.

A. take B. play C. break

68 _____ Kim's _____

A. Bakery B. Mr.

69 This is a _____ _____ _____ the school.

A. near B. bakery C. small

56 3. 친구들 앞에서 발표하기

57 4. 기타: 매일 제시간에 등교하기

58 모둠 활동

59 우리 마을에서 우리가 좋아하는 곳

60 대한 전통 시장

61 맛있는 것이 먹고 싶으면, 대한 시장을 방문하세요.

62 엽전을 사면 여러분의 점심 도시락을 가득 채우는 데 그걸 쓸 수 있어요.

63 많은 종류의 음식을 골라서 점심 도시락에 담을 수 있답니다.

64 새봄 청소년 센터

65 이곳은 우리 마을 한가운데에 있는 새봄 청소년 센터입니다.

66 춤과 음악 같은 많은 것을 배울 수 있어서 우리는 이곳을 좋아한답니다.

67 우리는 또한 이곳에서 보드게임도 하고 휴식도 취할 수 있어요.

68 김 씨네 빵집

69 이곳은 학교 근처의 작은 빵집입니다.

70 We like to go there _____ school _____ we're always _____ !

 A. because B. hungry C. after

71 _____ is good _____ enjoy delicious bread _____ friends.

 A. to B. with C. it

72 _____ _____ _____ with Puzzles!

 A. Have B. Let's C. Fun

73 _____ _____

 A. Puzzles B. Shape

74 If you _____ the shape A _____ two same pieces, you can then make all the other _____ (B, C, D, E, F, G) _____ those two pieces.

 A. into B. from C. cut D. shapes

75 Ten _____ in Five _____

 A. Lines B. Balls

76 Place 10 balls in 5 lines in _____ a _____ that each line has _____ 4 balls on it.

 A. way B. exactly C. such

77 You Are _____ _____ _____ !

 A. Eating B. Spoons C. Plastic

78 1. A _____ of plastic spoons are _____ _____ every year.

 A. away B. lot C. thrown

79 2. Most plastic _____ _____ into smaller _____ in the ocean.

 A. pieces B. down C. breaks

80 3. Very small _____ of plastic _____ _____ fish.

 A. into B. pieces C. go

81 4. _____ you eat the fish, you eat the plastic, _____ . Up _____ 11,000 pieces _____ year!

 A. each B. too C. to D. if

82 _____ _____ a Dream School!

 A. Make B. Let's

83 We had a _____ design _____ for our school _____ month.

 A. last B. universal C. contest

84 Here are the _____ _____ .

 A. works B. winners'

85 1. When your hands _____ _____ , water comes _____ .

 A. close B. out C. come

70 우리는 항상 배가 고파서 방과 후에 거기에 가는 것을 좋아해요!

71 친구들과 맛있는 빵을 즐기는 것이 좋아요.

72 퍼즐로 즐거운 시간을 보내자!

73 도형 퍼즐

74 A를 똑같은 두 개의 조각으로 자르면, 그 두 조각으로 다른 모든 형태(B, C, D, E, F, G)를 만들 수 있다.

75 5개의 선에 놓인 10개의 공

76 각각의 선 위에 정확하게 4개의 공이 놓이도록 10개의 공을 5개의 선에 놓아라.

77 너는 플라스틱 숟가락을 먹고 있다!

78 1. 해마다 많은 플라스틱 숟가락이 버려진다.

79 2. 대부분의 플라스틱 숟가락은 바닷속에서 더 작은 조각으로 부서진다.

80 3. 아주 작은 플라스틱 조각들이 물고기의 몸속으로 들어간다.

81 4. 여러분이 그 물고기를 먹으면 여러분도 플라스틱을 먹게 되는 것이다. 해마다 11,000개의 조각까지!

82 꿈의 학교를 만들어 보자!

83 지난달에 우리는 우리 학교를 위한 유니버설 디자인 경시대회를 열었습니다.

84 여기 우승자들의 작품이 있습니다.

85 1. 손을 가까이 가져가면 물이 나옵니다.

86 When you _____ your hands _____, the water _____.
A. away B. pull C. stops

87 You don't _____ to _____ or _____ any parts.
A. need B. touch C. turn

88 We can _____ _____ of water _____ this. – by O Juyeon(1-3)
A. lots B. with C. save

89 2. This is _____ school park _____ two _____.
A. between B. our C. buildings

90 _____ can go _____ and down _____ here.
A. easily B. anybody C. up

91 Also we _____ sit and _____ some _____ here. – by Gim Jimin(3-5)
A. rest B. get C. can

92 3. These are _____ desks and _____ for the _____.
A. special B. classroom C. chairs

93 For group _____, you can get them _____ and make a _____ group table for three, four, or five students. – by Choi Yumi(2-1)
A. together B. activities C. wonderful

94 _____ _____
A. LAUGH B. LET'S

95 _____ Earth Day _____ Ha! Ha! Ha!
A. Jokes B. Funny

96 Why are _____ bins _____?
A. hopeful B. recycle

97 _____ they're _____ _____ cans.
A. full B. because C. of

98 _____ can you _____ the ocean is _____?
A. tell B. how C. friendly

99 _____ _____.
A. waves B. it

100 _____ did the _____ go _____ school?
A. to B. why C. sun

101 To _____ _____.
A. brighter B. get

86 손을 멀리 떨어뜨리면 물이 멈춥니다.

87 어떤 부분도 돌리거나 만질 필요가 없습니다.

88 우리는 이것으로 많은 물을 절약할 수 있답니다. — 오주연(1-3)

89 2. 이것은 두 개의 건물 사이에 있는 학교 정원입니다.

90 여기서는 누구라도 쉽게 위아래로 이동할 수 있습니다.

91 또한, 우리는 이곳에 앉아 휴식을 취할 수 있습니다. — 김지민 (3-5)

92 3. 교실용의 특별한 책상과 의자가 있습니다.

93 모둠 활동을 하기 위해 그것들을 함께 모아 3명, 4명, 또는 5명이 활동할 훌륭한 모둠 책상을 만들 수 있습니다. — 최유미 (2-1)

94 웃읍시다

95 재미있는 지구의 날 농담들 하! 하! 하!

96 재활용 통은 왜 희망적인가?

97 왜냐하면 '깡통[할 수 있다]'으로 가득 차 있기 때문이지.

98 바다가 다정하다는 것을 어떻게 알 수 있는가?

99 그것이 일렁이기[손을 흔들기] 때문이지.

100 태양은 왜 학교에 가는가?

101 더 밝아지기[똑똑해지기] 위해 서지.

※ 다음 우리말과 일치하도록 빈칸에 알맞은 말을 쓰시오.

1 _____ _____

2 _____ of Art _____ _____

3 _____ a _____

4 I love you _____ a circle _____ a circle _____ _____.

5 _____

6 It's _____ _____.

7 I don't want to _____ _____ and _____.

8 But Mom says I _____ _____.

9 It's starting _____ _____ and I'm _____ _____ _____ _____.

10 I don't like playing outside _____ _____ _____ _____.

11 But _____ _____ _____, I have _____ _____ _____ idea!

12 I'll _____ _____ _____ with snow and I'll _____ _____!

13 _____ _____ _____ Your _____

14 _____ is _____.

15 Live _____ in COLOR.

16 IT ISN'T OVER _____ IT'S _____.

17 I am a _____ _____, but I never _____ _____.

18 I love the _____ _____ you do.

19 _____ your dream.

20 _____ _____

21 Two wheels _____ me / _____ _____ _____ / To school / Back _____ / To the mountain / To the river / I love my bike / I _____ _____ it _____ _____.

22 _____ Tree

23 Out _____ – _____

24 In _____ – _____

25 Pretty big _____

1 십대들의 잡지

2 모양으로 표현된 예술 작품

3 동그라미처럼

4 나는 동그라미처럼 너를 사랑해. 왜냐하면 동그라미는 절대 끝나지 않기에.

5 눈사람

6 바깥은 추워.

7 나는 밖으로 나가 놀고 싶지 않네.

8 하지만 엄마는 그래야 한다고 하시네.

9 눈이 오기 시작하고 나는 추워질 거야.

10 나는 이런 날에는 나가서 놀고 싶지 않아.

11 하지만 잠깐만. 나는 최고로 멋진 생각이 났어!

12 나는 눈으로 내 몸을 덮고 여기에 숨어야지!

13 손 글씨로 돌아보기

14 인생은 예술이다.

15 다양한 색깔로 살아라.

16 끝날 때까지 끝난 게 아니다.

17 나는 느리게 걷는 사람이지만 절대 물러서지는 않는다.

18 나는 네가 하는 작은 일들을 사랑해.

19 네 꿈을 좇으라.

20 나의 자전거

21 바퀴 두 개가 나를 데려가네 / 어느 곳으로든지 / 학교로 / 다시 집으로 / 산으로 / 강으로 / 나는 내 자전거가 아주 좋아 / 나는 그걸 매일 즐겨 타네

22 아낌없이 주는 나무

23 저곳 바깥은 – 젖어 있고

24 이곳 안쪽은 – 말라 있네

25 엄청 큰 우산이네

26 _____ me _____ the sky

27 _____ of _____ Year

28 _____ we _____ the game, we had a _____ of fun.

29 _____ _____ the _____ we made.

30 _____ they _____?

31 We made _____ _____ _____ for Mr. Han.

32 It _____ _____ _____ .

33 _____ _____ _____ _____ a handsome Peter Pan like me?

34 _____ Do You _____ Your School _____?

35 The most _____ _____

36 1. When I _____ _____

37 2. When I am really hungry and _____ _____ to eat

38 3. When I _____ clothes _____ and _____ P.E. class

39 4. others: When I am _____ _____ _____

40 When the teacher doesn't finish classes _____ the bell _____

41 The _____ _____ _____

42 1. _____ time

43 2. _____ with my _____ teacher

44 3. the _____ _____ on Friday

45 4. others: when I am _____ _____ _____ _____

46 when I see _____ in the _____

47 The _____ news

48 1. I got _____ _____ _____ _____

49 2. School _____ _____ today

50 3. I don't go to school _____ it _____ or _____ a lot

51 4. others: We eat _____ sweets _____

52 My best friend and I are _____ _____

53 The _____ _____ work _____ _____

54 1. Washing _____ _____

26 나와 하늘 사이에 있는

27 올해의 셀피들

28 우리는 게임에 졌지만, 아주 즐거웠다.

29 우리가 만든 로봇들을 봐.

30 귀엽지 않니?

31 우리는 한 씨 할아버지께 드릴 큰 케이크를 만들었다.

32 그것은 할아버지를 행복하게 해 주었다.

33 나처럼 잘생긴 피터 팬을 본 적이 있니?

34 학교생활에 대해 어떻게 생각하니?

35 가장 불편한 순간

36 1. 시험을 칠 때

37 2. 정말 배가 고픈데 먹을 것이 없을 때

38 3. 체육 시간 전후에 옷을 갈아입을 때

39 4. 기타: 수업 중에 졸릴 때

40 종이 울렸는데 선생님이 수업을 끝내지 않을 때

41 가장 사랑스러운 시간

42 1. 점심시간

43 2. 가장 좋아하는 선생님의 수업 시간

44 3. 금요일의 마지막 수업 시간

45 4. 기타: 쉬는 시간에 잠잘 때

46 거울 속의 나를 볼 때

47 가장 멋진 뉴스

48 1. 전보다 좋은 성적을 받았다

49 2. 오늘 수업이 일찍 끝난다

50 3. 비나 눈이 많이 와서 학교에 가지 않는다

51 4. 기타: 후식으로 맛있는 단것을 먹는다

52 가장 친한 친구와 내가 같은 반이 되었다

53 가장 하기 힘든 일

54 1. 쓰레기통 씻기

55 2. _____

56 3. _____ _____ _____ in _____ of friends

57 4. others: Being _____ _____ every day

58 _____ _____

59 _____ We Love in Our _____

60 Daehan _____ _____

61 If you want to eat _____ _____, visit Daehan Market.

62 You can buy "*yeopjeon*" and use it _____ _____ your lunch box _____.

63 You can _____ many _____ _____ food and _____ them _____ your lunch box.

64 Saebom _____ _____

65 This is Saebom Youth Center _____ _____ _____ _____ our town.

66 We like this place _____ we can learn many things, _____ _____ dance and music.

67 We can also play board games and _____ _____ here.

68 Mr. Kim's _____

69 This is a small bakery _____ the school.

70 We like to go there _____ school _____ we're _____ _____!

71 _____ is good _____ _____ delicious bread with friends.

72 _____ _____ _____ with Puzzles!

73 _____ _____

74 If you _____ the shape A _____ two same pieces, you can then make all the _____ _____(B, C, D, E, F, G) _____ those two pieces.

75 Ten Balls in _____ _____

76 Place 10 balls in 5 lines _____ _____ _____ _____ that _____ _____ has exactly 4 balls on it.

55 2. 공부하기

56 3. 친구들 앞에서 발표하기

57 4. 기타: 매일 제시간에 등교하기

58 모둠 활동

59 우리 마을에서 우리가 좋아하는 곳

60 대한 전통 시장

61 맛있는 것이 먹고 싶으면, 대한 시장을 방문하세요.

62 엽전을 사면 여러분의 점심 도시락을 가득 채우는 데 그걸 쓸 수 있어요.

63 많은 종류의 음식을 골라서 점심 도시락에 담을 수 있답니다.

64 새봄 청소년 센터

65 이곳은 우리 마을 한가운데에 있는 새봄 청소년 센터입니다.

66 춤과 음악 같은 많은 것을 배울 수 있어서 우리는 이곳을 좋아한답니다.

67 우리는 또한 이곳에서 보드게임도 하고 휴식도 취할 수 있어요.

68 김 씨네 빵집

69 이곳은 학교 근처의 작은 빵집입니다.

70 우리는 항상 배가 고파서 방과 후에 거기에 가는 것을 좋아해요!

71 친구들과 맛있는 빵을 즐기는 것이 좋아요.

72 퍼즐로 즐거운 시간을 보내자!

73 도형 퍼즐

74 A를 똑같은 두 개의 조각으로 자르면, 그 두 조각으로 다른 모든 형태(B, C, D, E, F, G)를 만들 수 있다.

75 5개의 선에 놓인 10개의 공

76 각각의 선 위에 정확하게 4개의 공이 놓이도록 10개의 공을 5개의 선에 놓아라.

77 You _____ _____ Plastic Spoons!

78 1. A lot of plastic spoons _____ _____ _____ every year.

79 2. Most plastic _____ _____ _____ smaller _____ in the ocean.

80 3. Very small pieces of plastic _____ _____ _____ .

81 4. If you eat the fish, you eat the plastic, too. _____ _____ 11,000 pieces _____ _____ !

82 _____ _____ a Dream School!

83 We had a _____ _____ contest for our school last month.

84 Here are the _____ _____ .

85 1. When your hands _____ _____ , water comes _____ .

86 When you _____ your hands _____ , the water stops.

87 You _____ _____ _____ turn or touch any parts.

88 We can _____ _____ _____ _____ with this. – by O Juyeon(1-3)

89 2. This is our school park _____ two _____ .

90 Anybody can go _____ and _____ here.

91 Also we can sit and _____ _____ _____ here. – by Gim Jimin(3-5)

92 3. These are _____ desks and chairs _____ the classroom.

93 For _____ _____ , you can get them _____ and make a wonderful group table _____ three, four, or five students. – by Choi Yumi(2-1)

94 _____ _____

95 Funny Earth Day _____ Ha! Ha! Ha!

96 _____ are _____ bins _____ ?

97 _____ they're _____ _____ cans.

98 _____ can you _____ the ocean is _____ ?

99 It _____ .

100 _____ did the sun go to school?

101 _____ _____ brighter.

77 너는 플라스틱 숟가락을 먹고 있다!

78 1. 해마다 많은 플라스틱 숟가락이 버려진다.

79 2. 대부분의 플라스틱 숟가락은 바닷속에서 더 작은 조각으로 부서진다.

80 3. 아주 작은 플라스틱 조각들이 물고기의 몸속으로 들어간다.

81 4. 여러분이 그 물고기를 먹으면 여러분도 플라스틱을 먹게 되는 것이다. 해마다 11,000개의 조각까지!

82 꿈의 학교를 만들어 보자!

83 지난달에 우리는 우리 학교를 위한 유니버설 디자인 경시대회를 열었습니다.

84 여기 우승자들의 작품이 있습니다.

85 1. 손을 가까이 가져가면 물이 나옵니다.

86 손을 멀리 떨어뜨리면 물이 멈춥니다.

87 어떤 부분도 돌리거나 만질 필요가 없습니다.

88 우리는 이것으로 많은 물을 절약할 수 있답니다. — 오주연(1-3)

89 2. 이것은 두 개의 건물 사이에 있는 학교 정원입니다.

90 여기서는 누구라도 쉽게 위아래로 이동할 수 있습니다.

91 또한, 우리는 이곳에 앉아 휴식을 취할 수 있습니다. — 김지민(3-5)

92 3. 교실용의 특별한 책상과 의자가 있습니다.

93 모둠 활동을 하기 위해 그것들을 함께 모아 3명, 4명, 또는 5명이 활동할 훌륭한 모둠 책상을 만들 수 있습니다. — 최유미(2-1)

94 웃읍시다

95 재미있는 지구의 날 농담들 하! 하! 하!

96 재활용 통은 왜 희망적인가?

97 왜냐하면 '깡통[할 수 있다]'으로 가득 차 있기 때문이지.

98 바다가 다정하다는 것을 어떻게 알 수 있는가?

99 그것이 일렁이기[손을 흔들기] 때문이지.

100 태양은 왜 학교에 가는가?

101 더 밝아지기[똑똑해지기] 위해서지.

※ 다음 문장을 우리말로 쓰시오.

1 Teens' Magazine
➡ _____

2 Works of Art in Shapes
➡ _____

3 Like a Circle
➡ _____

4 I love you like a circle because a circle never ends.
➡ _____

5 Snowman
➡ _____

6 It's cold outside.
➡ _____

7 I don't want to go out and play.
➡ _____

8 But Mom says I have to.
➡ _____

9 It's starting to snow and I'm going to be cold.
➡ _____

10 I don't like playing outside on days like these.
➡ _____

11 But wait a second, I have the most wonderful idea!
➡ _____

12 I'll cover myself up with snow and I'll hide here!
➡ _____

13 Looking Back with Your Handwriting
➡ _____

14 Life is art.
➡ _____

15 Live yours in COLOR.
➡ _____

16 IT ISN'T OVER UNTIL IT'S OVER.
➡ _____

17 I am a slow walker, but I never walk back.
➡ _____

18 I love the little things you do.
➡ _____

19 Follow your dream.
➡ _____

20 My Bike
➡ _____

21 Two wheels take me / To any place / To school / Back home / To the mountain / To the river / I love my bike / I enjoy riding it every day
➡ _____

22 Giving Tree
➡ _____

23 Out there – wet
➡ _____

24 In here – dry
➡

25 Pretty big umbrella
➡

26 Between me and the sky
➡

27 Selfies of This Year
➡

28 Though we lost the game, we had a lot of fun.
➡

29 Look at the robots we made.
➡

30 Aren't they cute?
➡

31 We made a big cake for Mr. Han.
➡

32 It made him happy.
➡

33 Have you ever seen a handsome Peter Pan like me?
➡

34 What Do You Think of Your School Life?
➡

35 The most uncomfortable moment
➡

36 1. When I take tests
➡

37 2. When I am really hungry and have nothing to eat
➡

38 3. When I change clothes before and after P.E. class
➡

39 4. others: When I am sleepy in class
➡

40 When the teacher doesn't finish classes after the bell rings
➡

41 The most lovely time
➡

42 1. lunch time
➡

43 2. class with my favorite teacher
➡

44 3. the last class on Friday
➡

45 4. others: when I am sleeping during break time
➡

46 when I see myself in the mirror
➡

47 The most awesome news
➡

48 1. I got better grades than before
➡

49 2. School finishes earlier today
➡

50 3. I don't go to school because it rains or snows a lot
➡

51 4. others: We eat delicious sweets for dessert
➡

52 My best friend and I are in the same class
➡

53 The most difficult work to do
➡

54 1. Washing trash cans
➡

55 2. Studying
➡

56 3. Making a presentation in front of friends
➡

57 4. others: Being on time every day
➡

58 Group work
➡

59 Places We Love in Our Village
➡

60 Daehan Traditional Market
➡

61 If you want to eat something delicious, visit Daehan Market.
➡

62 You can buy "*yeopjeon*" and use it to make your lunch box full.
➡

63 You can choose many kinds of food and add them to your lunch box.
➡

64 Saebom Youth Center
➡

65 This is Saebom Youth Center in the middle of our town
➡

66 We like this place because we can learn many things, such as dance and music.
➡

67 We can also play board games and take a break here.
➡

68 Mr. Kim's Bakery
➡

69 This is a small bakery near the school.
➡

70 We like to go there after school because we're always hungry!
➡

71 It is good to enjoy delicious bread with friends.
➡

72 Let's Have Fun with Puzzles!
➡

73 Shape Puzzles
➡

74 If you cut the shape A into two same pieces, you can then make all the other shapes(B, C, D, E, F, G) from those two pieces.
➡

75 Ten Balls in Five Lines
➡

76 Place 10 balls in 5 lines in such a way that each line has exactly 4 balls on it.
➡

77 You Are Eating Plastic Spoons!
➡ _____

78 1. A lot of plastic spoons are thrown away every year.
➡ _____

79 2. Most plastic breaks down into smaller pieces in the ocean.
➡ _____

80 3. Very small pieces of plastic go into fish.
➡ _____

81 4. If you eat the fish, you eat the plastic, too. Up to 11,000 pieces each year!
➡ _____

82 Let's Make a Dream School!
➡ _____

83 We had a universal design contest for our school last month.
➡ _____

84 Here are the winners' works.
➡ _____

85 1. When your hands come close, water comes out.
➡ _____

86 When you pull your hands away, the water stops.
➡ _____

87 You don't need to turn or touch any parts.
➡ _____

88 We can save lots of water with this. — by O Juyeon(1-3)
➡ _____

89 2. This is our school park between two buildings.
➡ _____

90 Anybody can go up and down easily here.
➡ _____

91 Also we can sit and get some rest here. by Gim Jimin(3-5)
➡ _____

92 3. These are special desks and chairs for the classroom.
➡ _____

93 For group activities, you can get them together and make a wonderful group table for three, four, or five students. — by Choi Yumi(2-1)
➡ _____

94 LET'S LAUGH
➡ _____

95 Funny Earth Day Jokes Ha! Ha! Ha!
➡ _____

96 Why are recycle bins hopeful?
➡ _____

97 Because they're full of cans.
➡ _____

98 How can you tell the ocean is friendly?
➡ _____

99 It waves.
➡ _____

100 Why did the sun go to school?
➡ _____

101 To get brighter.
➡ _____

※ 다음 괄호 안의 단어들을 우리말에 맞도록 바르게 배열하시오.

1 (Magazine / Teens')
➡ _____

2 (Art / of / Works / Shapes / in)
➡ _____

3 (Circle / a / Like)
➡ _____

4 (you / love / I / like / circle / a / because / circle / a / ends. / never)
➡ _____

5 (snowman)
➡ _____

6 (cold / it's / outside.)
➡ _____

7 (don't / I / want / go / to / out / play. / and)
➡ _____

8 (Mom / but / I / says / to. / have)
➡ _____

9 (starting / it's / snow / to / and / going / I'm / cold. / be / to)
➡ _____

10 (I / like / don't / outside / playing / days / these. / like / on)
➡ _____

11 (wait / but / second, / a / have / I / most / the / idea! / wonderful)
➡ _____

12 (I'll / myself / cover / with / up / snow / and / hide / here! / I'll)
➡ _____

13 (Back / with / Looking / Handwriting / Your)
➡ _____

14 (art. / is / life)
➡ _____

15 (yours / live / COLOR / in)
➡ _____

16 (IT / OVER / ISN'T / IT'S / UNTIL / OVER)
➡ _____

17 (am / I / slow / a / walker, / I / but / walk / never / back.)
➡ _____

18 (love / I / little / the / you / things / do.)
➡ _____

19 (your / follow / dream)
➡ _____

20 (Bike / My)
➡ _____

21 (wheels / me / take / two // any / to / place // school / to // home / back // the / mountain / to // the / to / river // love / I / bike / my // enjoy / I / riding / day / it / every)
➡ _____

22 (Tree / Giving)
➡ _____

23 (there / out / — / wet)
➡ _____

24 (here / in / — / dry)
➡ _____

25 (big / pretty / umbrella)
➡ _____

1 십대들의 잡지

2 모양으로 표현된 예술 작품

3 동그라미처럼

4 나는 동그라미처럼 너를 사랑해. 왜냐하면 동그라미는 절대 끝나지 않기에.

5 눈사람

6 바깥은 추워.

7 나는 밖으로 나가 놀고 싶지 않네.

8 하지만 엄마는 그래야 한다고 하시네.

9 눈이 오기 시작하고 나는 추워질 거야.

10 나는 이런 날에는 나가서 놀고 싶지 않아.

11 하지만 잠깐만, 나는 최고로 멋진 생각이 났어!

12 나는 눈으로 내 몸을 덮고 여기에 숨어야지!

13 손 글씨로 돌아보기

14 인생은 예술이다.

15 다양한 색깔로 살아라.

16 끝날 때까지 끝난 게 아니다.

17 나는 느리게 걷는 사람이지만 절대 물러서지는 않는다.

18 나는 네가 하는 작은 일들을 사랑해.

19 네 꿈을 좇으라.

20 나의 자전거

21 바퀴 두 개가 나를 데려가네 / 어느 곳으로든지 / 학교로 / 다시 집으로 / 산으로 / 강으로 / 나는 내 자전거가 아주 좋아 / 나는 그걸 매일 즐겨 타네

22 아낌없이 주는 나무

23 저곳 바깥은 – 젖어 있고

24 이곳 안쪽은 – 말라 있네

25 엄청 큰 우산이네

26 ▶ (me / between / the / and / sky)
→ _____

27 ▶ (of / Selfies / Year / This)
→ _____

28 ▶ (we / though / lost / game, / the / had / we / lot / a / fun. / of)
→ _____

29 ▶ (at / look / robots / the / made. / we)
→ _____

30 ▶ (they / cute? / aren't)
→ _____

31 ▶ (made / we / big / a / cake / Mr. / for / Han.)
→ _____

32 ▶ (made / it / happy. / him)
→ _____

33 ▶ (you / have / seen / ever / handsome / a / Pan / Peter / me? / like)
→ _____

34 ▶ (Do / What / Think / You / of / School / Your / Life?)
→ _____

35 ▶ (most / the / moment / uncomfortable)
→ _____

36 ▶ (1. / I / tests / take / when)
→ _____

37 ▶ (2. / I / when / really / am / and / hungry / nothing / have / eat / to)
→ _____

38 ▶ (3. / I / when / clothes / change / before / and / P.E. / after / class)
→ _____

39 ▶ (4. / others: / I / when / sleepy / am / class / in)
→ _____

40 ▶ (the / when / doesn't / teacher / classes / finish / after / rings / bell / the)
→ _____

41 ▶ (most / the / time / lovely)
→ _____

42 ▶ (1. / time / lunch)
→ _____

43 ▶ (2. / with / class / favorite / my / teacher)
→ _____

44 ▶ (3. / last / the / class / Friday / on)
→ _____

45 ▶ (4. / others: / I / when / am / sleeping / break / time / during)
→ _____

46 ▶ (I / when / myself / see / the / mirror / in)
→ _____

47 ▶ (most / the / news / awesome)
→ _____

48 ▶ (1. / got / I / better / than / grades / before)
→ _____

49 ▶ (2. / finishes / school / today / earlier)
→ _____

50 ▶ (3. / don't / I / go / school / to / because / rains / it / snows / or / lot / a)
→ _____

51 ▶ (4. / others: / eat / we / sweets / delicious / dessert / for)
→ _____

52 ▶ (best / my / friend / and / are / I / the / in / class / same)
→ _____

53 ▶ (the / difficult / most / do / to / work)
→ _____

54 ▶ (1. / trash / washing / cans)
→ _____

55 (2. / studying)
➡ _____

56 (3. / a / making / presentation / of / front / in / friends)
➡ _____

57 (4. / others: / on / being / every / time / day)
➡ _____

58 (work / group)
➡ _____

59 (We / Places / in / Love / Village / Our)
➡ _____

60 (Traditional / Daehan / Market)
➡ _____

61 (you / if / to / want / something / eat / delicious, / Daehan / visit / Market.)
➡ _____

62 (can / you / buy / and / "yeopjeon" / use / to / it / make / your / box / full. / lunch)
➡ _____

63 (can / you / many / choose / kinds / food / of / and / them / to / add / your / box. / lunch)
➡ _____

64 (Youth / Saebom / Center)
➡ _____

65 (is / this / Youth / Saebom / Center / the / in / middle / our / town. / of)
➡ _____

66 (like / we / place / this / because / can / we / many / learn / things, / as / such / music. / and / dance)
➡ _____

67 (can / we / play / also / games / board / and / a / take / here. / break)
➡ _____

68 (Kim's / Mr. / Bakery)
➡ _____

69 (is / this / small / a / bakery / the / near / school.)
➡ _____

70 (like / we / go / to / there / school / after / because / always / we're / hungry!)
➡ _____

71 (is / it / to / good / delicious / enjoy / with / friends. / bread)
➡ _____

72 (Have / Let's / with / Fun / Puzzles!)
➡ _____

73 (Puzzles / Shape)
➡ _____

74 (you / if / the / cut / shape / A / two / into / pieces, / same / can / you / then / all / make / other / shapes(B, C, D, E, F, G) / those / from / pieces. / two)
➡ _____

75 (Balls / Ten / Five / in / Lines)
➡ _____

76 (10 / place / balls / 5 / in / lines / such / in / way / a / each / that / has / line / 4 / exactly / balls / it. / on)
➡ _____

55 2. 공부하기

56 3. 친구들 앞에서 발표하기

57 4. 기타: 매일 제시간에 등교하기

58 모둠 활동

59 우리 마을에서 우리가 좋아하는 곳

60 대한 전통 시장

61 맛있는 것이 먹고 싶으면, 대한 시장을 방문하세요.

62 엽전을 사면 여러분의 점심 도시락을 가득 채우는 데 그걸 쓸 수 있어요.

63 많은 종류의 음식을 골라서 점심 도시락에 담을 수 있답니다.

64 새봄 청소년 센터

65 이곳은 우리 마을 한가운데에 있는 새봄 청소년 센터입니다.

66 춤과 음악 같은 많은 것을 배울 수 있어서 우리는 이곳을 좋아한답니다.

67 우리는 또한 이곳에서 보드게임도 하고 휴식도 취할 수 있어요.

68 김 씨네 빵집

69 이곳은 학교 근처의 작은 빵집입니다.

70 우리는 항상 배가 고파서 방과 후에 거기에 가는 것을 좋아해요!

71 친구들과 맛있는 빵을 즐기는 것이 좋아요.

72 퍼즐로 즐거운 시간을 보내자!

73 도형 퍼즐

74 A를 똑같은 두 개의 조각으로 자르면, 그 두 조각으로 다른 모든 형태(B, C, D, E, F, G)를 만들 수 있다.

75 5개의 선에 놓인 10개의 공

76 각각의 선 위에 정확하게 4개의 공이 놓이도록 10개의 공을 5개의 선에 놓아라.

77 (Are / You / Plastic / Eating / Spoons!)
➡ _____

78 (1. / lot / a / plastic / of / are / spoons / away / thrown / year. / every)
➡ _____

79 (2. / plastic / most / down / breaks / smaller / into / in / pieces / ocean. / the)
➡ _____

80 (3. / small / very / of / pieces / go / plastic / fish. / into)
➡ _____

81 (4. / you / if / eat / fish, / the / eat / you / plastic, / the / too. // to / up / pieces / 11,000 / year! / each)
➡ _____

82 (Make / Let's / Dream / a / School!)
➡ _____

83 (had / we / universal / a / design / for / our / contest / school / month. / last)
➡ _____

84 (are / here / winner's / the / works.)
➡ _____

85 (your / when / come / hands / close, / comes / water / out.)
➡ _____

86 (you / when / your / pull / away, / hands / water / the / stops.)
➡ _____

87 (don't / you / to / need / turn / to / or / any / parts. / touch)
➡ _____

88 (can / we / lots / save / water / of / this. / with / — / O / by / Juyeon(1-3))
➡ _____

89 (is / this / school / our / between / park / buildings. / two)
➡ _____

90 (can / anybody / up / go / and / here. / easily / down)
➡ _____

91 (we / also / sit / can / and / some / get / here. / rest / — / Jimin(3-5) / Gim / by)
➡ _____

92 (are / these / desks / special / and / for / chairs / the / classroom.)
➡ _____

93 (group / for / activities, / can / you / get / together / them / and / a / make / group / wonderful / for / table / three, / or / four, / students. / five / — / Choi / Yumi(2-1) / by)
➡ _____

94 (LAUGH / LET'S)
➡ _____

95 (Earth / Funny / Jokes / Day / Ha! / Ha! / Ha!)
➡ _____

96 (are / recycle / why / hopeful? / bins)
➡ _____

97 (they're / because / cans. / of / full)
➡ _____

98 (can / how / tell / you / ocean / the / friendly? / is)
➡ _____

99 (waves. / it)
➡ _____

100 (did / why / sun / the / school? / to / go)
➡ _____

101 (get / to / brighter.)
➡ _____

77 너는 플라스틱 숟가락을 먹고 있다!

78 1. 해마다 많은 플라스틱 숟가락이 버려진다.

79 2. 대부분의 플라스틱 숟가락은 바닷속에서 더 작은 조각으로 부서진다.

80 3. 아주 작은 플라스틱 조각들이 물고기의 몸속으로 들어간다.

81 4. 여러분이 그 물고기를 먹으면 여러분도 플라스틱을 먹게 되는 것이다. 해마다 11,000개의 조각까지!

82 꿈의 학교를 만들어 보자!

83 지난달에 우리는 우리 학교를 위한 유니버설 디자인 경시대회를 열었습니다.

84 여기 우승자들의 작품이 있습니다.

85 1. 손을 가까이 가져가면 물이 나옵니다.

86 손을 멀리 떨어뜨리면 물이 멈춥니다.

87 어떤 부분도 돌리거나 만질 필요가 없습니다.

88 우리는 이것으로 많은 물을 절약할 수 있답니다. — 오주연(1-3)

89 2. 이것은 두 개의 건물 사이에 있는 학교 정원입니다.

90 여기서는 누구라도 쉽게 위아래로 이동할 수 있습니다.

91 또한, 우리는 이곳에 앉아 휴식을 취할 수 있습니다. — 김지민 (3-5)

92 3. 교실용의 특별한 책상과 의자가 있습니다.

93 모둠 활동을 하기 위해 그것들을 함께 모아 3명, 4명, 또는 5명이 활동할 훌륭한 모둠 책상을 만들 수 있습니다. — 최유미 (2-1)

94 웃읍시다

95 재미있는 지구의 날 농담들 하! 하! 하!

96 재활용 통은 왜 희망적인가?

97 왜냐하면 '깡통[할 수 있다]'으로 가득 차 있기 때문이지.

98 바다가 다정하다는 것을 어떻게 알 수 있는가?

99 그것이 일렁이기[손을 흔들기] 때문이지.

100 태양은 왜 학교에 가는가?

101 더 밝아지기[똑똑해지기] 위해서지.

※ 다음 우리말을 영어로 쓰시오.

1 십대들의 잡지
➡ _____

2 모양으로 표현된 예술 작품
➡ _____

3 동그라미처럼
➡ _____

4 나는 동그라미처럼 너를 사랑해. 왜냐하면 동그라미는 절대 끝나지 않기에.
➡ _____

5 눈사람
➡ _____

6 바깥은 추워.
➡ _____

7 나는 밖으로 나가 놀고 싶지 않네.
➡ _____

8 하지만 엄마는 그래야 한다고 하시네.
➡ _____

9 눈이 오기 시작하고 나는 추워질 거야.
➡ _____

10 나는 이런 날에는 나가서 놀고 싶지 않아.
➡ _____

11 하지만 잠깐만, 나는 최고로 멋진 생각이 났어!
➡ _____

12 나는 눈으로 내 몸을 완전히 덮고 여기에 숨어야지!
➡ _____

13 손 글씨로 돌아보기
➡ _____

14 인생은 예술이다.
➡ _____

15 다양한 색깔로 살아라.
➡ _____

16 끝날 때까지 끝난 게 아니다.
➡ _____

17 나는 느리게 걷는 사람이지만 절대 물러서지는 않는다.
➡ _____

18 나는 네가 하는 작은 일들을 사랑해.
➡ _____

19 네 꿈을 좇으라.
➡ _____

20 나의 자전거
➡ _____

21 바퀴 두 개가 나를 데려가네 / 어느 곳으로든지 / 학교로 / 다시 집으로 / 산으로 / 강으로 / 나는 내 자전거가 아주 좋아 / 나는 그걸 매일 즐겨 타네
➡ _____

22 아낌없이 주는 나무
➡ _____

23 저곳 바깥은 – 젖어 있고
➡ _____

24 이곳 안쪽은 – 말라 있네
➡ _____

25 엄청 큰 우산이네
➡ _____

26 나와 하늘 사이에 있는
➡ _____

27 올해의 셀피들
➡ _____

28 우리는 게임에 졌지만, 아주 즐거웠다.
➡ _____

29 우리가 만든 로봇들을 봐.
➡ _____

30 귀엽지 않니?
➡ _____

31 우리는 한 씨 할아버지께 드릴 큰 케이크를 만들었다.
➡ _____

32 그것은 할아버지를 행복하게 해 주었다.
➡ _____

33 나처럼 잘생긴 피터 팬을 본 적이 있니?
➡ _____

34 학교생활에 대해 어떻게 생각하니?
➡ _____

35 가장 불편한 순간
➡ _____

36 1. 시험을 칠 때
➡ _____

37 2. 정말 배가 고픈데 먹을 것이 없을 때
➡ _____

38 3. 체육 시간 전후에 옷을 갈아입을 때
➡ _____

39 4. 기타: 수업 중에 졸릴 때
➡ _____

40 종이 울렸는데 선생님이 수업을 끝내지 않을 때
➡ _____

41 가장 사랑스러운 시간
➡ _____

42 1. 점심시간
➡ _____

43 2. 가장 좋아하는 선생님의 수업 시간
➡ _____

44 3. 금요일의 마지막 수업 시간
➡ _____

45 4. 기타: 쉬는 시간에 잠잘 때
➡ _____

46 거울 속의 나를 볼 때
➡ _____

47 가장 멋진 뉴스
➡ _____

48 1. 전보다 좋은 성적을 받았다
➡ _____

49 2. 오늘 수업이 일찍 끝난다
➡ _____

50 3. 비나 눈이 많이 와서 학교에 가지 않는다
➡ _____

51 4. 기타: 후식으로 맛있는 단것을 먹는다
➡

52 가장 친한 친구와 내가 같은 반이 되었다
➡

53 가장 하기 힘든 일
➡

54 1. 쓰레기통 씻기
➡

55 2. 공부하기
➡

56 3. 친구들 앞에서 발표하기
➡

57 4. 기타: 매일 제시간에 등교하기
➡

58 모둠 활동
➡

59 우리 마을에서 우리가 좋아하는 곳
➡

60 대한 전통 시장
➡

61 맛있는 것이 먹고 싶으면, 대한 시장을 방문하세요.
➡

62 엽전을 사면 여러분의 점심 도시락을 가득 채우는 데 그걸 쓸 수 있어요.
➡

63 많은 종류의 음식을 골라서 점심 도시락에 담을 수 있답니다.
➡

64 새봄 청소년 센터
➡

65 이곳은 우리 마을 한가운데에 있는 새봄 청소년 센터입니다.
➡

66 춤과 음악 같은 많은 것을 배울 수 있어서 우리는 이곳을 좋아한답니다.
➡

67 우리는 또한 이곳에서 보드게임도 하고 휴식도 취할 수 있어요.
➡

68 김 씨네 빵집
➡

69 이곳은 학교 근처의 작은 빵집입니다.
➡

70 우리는 항상 배가 고파서 방과 후에 거기에 가는 것을 좋아해요!
➡

71 친구들과 맛있는 빵을 즐기는 것이 좋아요.
➡

72 퍼즐로 즐거운 시간을 보내자!
➡

73 도형 퍼즐
➡

74 A를 똑같은 두 개의 조각으로 자르면, 그 두 조각으로 다른 모든 형태(B, C, D, E, F, G)를 만들 수 있다.
➡

75 5개의 선에 놓인 10개의 공
➡

76 각각의 선 위에 정확하게 4개의 공이 놓이도록 10개의 공을 5개의 선에 놓아라.
➡

77 너는 플라스틱 숟가락을 먹고 있다!
➡ _____

78 1. 해마다 많은 플라스틱 숟가락이 버려진다.
➡ _____

79 2. 대부분의 플라스틱 숟가락은 바닷속에서 더 작은 조각으로 부서진다.
➡ _____

80 3. 아주 작은 플라스틱 조각들이 물고기의 몸속으로 들어간다.
➡ _____

81 4. 여러분이 그 물고기를 먹으면 여러분도 플라스틱을 먹게 되는 것이다. 해마다 11,000개의 조각까지!

82 꿈의 학교를 만들어 보자!
➡ _____

83 지난달에 우리는 우리 학교를 위한 유니버설 디자인 경시대회를 열었습니다.

84 여기 우승자들의 작품이 있습니다.
➡ _____

85 1. 손을 가까이 가져가면 물이 나옵니다.
➡ _____

86 손을 멀리 떨어뜨리면 물이 멈춥니다.
➡ _____

87 어떤 부분도 돌리거나 만질 필요가 없습니다.
➡ _____

88 우리는 이것으로 많은 물을 절약할 수 있답니다. — 오주연(1-3)
➡ _____

89 2. 이것은 두 개의 건물 사이에 있는 학교 정원입니다.
➡ _____

90 여기서는 누구라도 쉽게 위아래로 이동할 수 있습니다.
➡ _____

91 또한, 우리는 이곳에 앉아 휴식을 취할 수 있습니다. — 김지민(3-5)
➡ _____

92 3. 교실용의 특별한 책상과 의자가 있습니다.
➡ _____

93 모둠 활동을 하기 위해 그것들을 함께 모아 3명, 4명, 또는 5명이 활동할 훌륭한 모둠 책상을 만들 수 있습니다. — 최유미(2-1)
➡ _____

94 웃읍시다
➡ _____

95 재미있는 지구의 날 농담들 하! 하! 하!
➡ _____

96 재활용 통은 왜 희망적인가?

97 왜냐하면 '깡통[할 수 있다]'으로 가득 차 있기 때문이지.
➡ _____

98 바다가 다정하다는 것을 어떻게 알 수 있는가?

99 그것이 일렁이기[손을 흔들기] 때문이지.
➡ _____

100 태양은 왜 학교에 가는가?
➡ _____

101 더 밝아지기[똑똑해지기] 위해서지.
➡ _____

MEMO

MEMO

영어 기출 문제집

2학기 전과정

적중100 plus

2학기

정답 및 해설

천재 | 정사열

중 2

영어 기출 문제집

적중100

2학기

정답 및 해설

천재 | 정사열

중 2

Lesson 5

Shapes Around Us

시험대비 실력평가
p.08

01 ④　　　　02 in charge of　　　　03 ⑤
04 took care of　　　　05 ②　　　　06 ③
07 ④　　　　08 ④

01 '이 책꽂이는 혼자 서 있을 수 없어. 이 문제를 어떻게 해결할지 아니?'

02 Triangle은 옷걸이와 식물들을 담당했다. / 어떤 것 또는 누군가를 책임지는

03 tidy는 형용사로 '단정한, 깔끔한'의 의미다.

04 '~을 돌보다'는 take care of를 사용하고, 돌보았다는 과거시제로 took을 사용한다.

05 마법의 힘을 가진 상상의 생명체

06 어떤 것이 당신이 원하는 방식으로 작동하도록 하는 힘을 가지다

07 '세 개의 점으로 어떻게 곰을 그릴 수 있는지 아니?'

08 divide A into B: A를 B로 나누다, pick up: ~을 들어 올리다

서술형 시험대비
p.09

01 (A) First　(B) Finally
02 (1) There lived, spirits　(2) Take, away, or, roll
　(3) try to, tidy　(4) each other　　03 equal
04 (1) decide　(2) mess　(3) complain　(4) perfect
05 (1) in control　(2) square　(3) pointy

01 물고기를 그리는 순서를 열거하는 표현이다.

02 (1) There lived+주어: ~가 살았다, spirit: 요정, 영혼 (2) take away: ~을 치우다, 명령문 ~, or ...: '~해라, 그렇지 않으면 …할 것이다', roll: 구르다 (3) try to+동사원형: ~하려고 애쓰다. tidy: 단정한, 정돈된 (4) each other: 서로

03 케이크를 똑같은 조각으로 나누는 방법에 대해 이야기하고 있다.

04 (1) 나는 어느 것을 고를지 결정할 수 없어. (2) 아이들이 목욕탕을 엉망으로 만들어 놓았다. (3) 그들은 하고 싶은 일을 할 시간이 없다고 늘 불평한다. (4) 그녀는 완벽한 영어를 말한다.

05 (1) 글의 흐름상 Triangle과 Circle이 나가고 Square가 모든 것을 담당했고(in control) 모든 것을 사각형으로 만들었다가 적절하다. (2) 사람을 다치게 하는 건 '뾰족한' 잎들이므로 형용사 pointy가 적절하다.

교과서 Conversation

핵심 Check
p.10~11

1 ②　　　　2 ③　　　　3 ④　　　　4 ③

교과서 대화문 익히기

Check(√) True or False
p.12

1 T　2 T　3 F　4 T　5 T

교과서 확인학습
p.14~15

Get Ready 2
(1) alone, how to solve / Put, on, bottom
(2) how to divide, into / Let, see, dividing
(3) how to move / Put

Start Off Listen & Talk A
1 how to make / First
2 how to make / difficult, in half

Start Off Listen & Talk B
how to divide, into / First, equal, Then, divide, into, Finally

Speak Up Look and talk.
how to draw / First, Then, Finally

Speak Up Mission
how to make / how

Real-life Scene
how to solve / take, at a time / take, to, one by one / without / First, Then / Finally

Express Yourself A
1 how to make / cut off, used
2 how / First, Then, dried, Finally, wrap
3 how to / face, Hold

Learning Diary Check Yourself
to draw / First, Then, Finally / draw, myself

시험대비 기본평가
p.16

01 ③　　　　02 ⑤　　　　03 how to make it
04 how to divide this cake into four equal pieces

01 '~하는 방법'이란 의미로 '의문사 how+to부정사'를 사용한다.

02 어떤 일을 하는 절차나 방법을 단계적으로 설명할 때 먼저 First로 시작한다. Finally는 열거할 때 마지막으로 내용을 언급하는 표현이다.

03 '~하는 방법'이란 의미로 'how+to부정사'를 사용한다.

04 '의문사+to부정사'를 이용하고, A를 B로 나눈다는 표현으로 'divide A into B' 구문을 이용하여 문장을 완성한다. 형용사 equal은 명사 pieces를 앞에서 꾸며준다.

01 ③	02 (i)n half	03 ④	
04 how you should[can] fly this		05 ④	
06 ①	07 ②	08 ③	09 ⑤
10 ③	11 shape	12 ①, ④, ⑤	

01 대화에서 G가 '연필을 반으로 부러뜨려도 돼?'라고 말하고 있기 때문에 더 많은 삼각형을 만드는 방법을 묻고 있음을 알 수 있다.

02 in half가 '반으로'라는 표현이다.

03 '바람을 마주하면서 이와 같이 들고 있어라'는 G의 대답으로 보아 무언가를 날리는 방법을 묻고 있다는 것을 알 수 있다.

04 '의문사+to부정사'는 '의문사+주어+should[can]+동사원형'으로 바꾸어 쓸 수 있다.

05 대화의 내용상 '이것을 4개의 같은 조각으로 나누는 방법을 아니?'라고 묻는 것이 가장 적절하다.

06 어떤 일을 하는 절차나 방법을 단계적으로 설명할 때 먼저 First로 시작한다. 그리고 열거할 때 마지막으로 내용을 언급하는 표현으로 Finally를 사용한다.

07 위 대화에서 A는 동물들을 강 반대편으로 모두 데려갈 수 있는 문제를 푸는 방법을 아는지 묻고 있다.

08 A는 '그 배는 한 번에 너와 셋 중 하나만 옮길 수 있어.'라고 했고, B가 '그건 쉬워.'라고 말한 것으로 보아 하나씩 옮긴다고 말하는 것이 자연스럽다.

09 After that(그 후에)은 '쌀을 가져다 놓고 닭을 데려온 후를 말하므로. 그 다음 개를 데려다 놓고 돌아온다는 내용이 오는 것이 적절하다.

10 ③은 '이것을 어떻게 고치는지 알고 있니?'라는 물음에 '그것은 틀렸어.'라고 말하는 것은 자연스럽지 못하다.

11 '선을 특정 방식으로 결합하거나 바깥쪽 가장자리 주변의 선 또는 선들로 결합하여 형성되는 배열'을 의미하는 '도형(shape)'이 적절하다.

12 도형으로 물고기를 그리는 방법에 대해 단계적으로 설명하는 글이다. 두 번째로 해야 할 일을 말할 때 사용하는 표현으로 Then, Next, Second 등을 사용한다. ③번의 Two는 순서를 나타낼 때 사용하는 표현이 아니다.

01 ④, with → without 02 Let me see.

03 Do you know how to draw a mouse with shapes?

04 (a) triangle (b) circles (c) two dots (d) lines

05 how to move it

01 '너와 함께 있으면 개는 닭을 잡아먹고, 닭은 쌀을 먹을 거야.'라는 말은 어색하다. 그래서 with를 without으로 고치면, '하지만 네가 없으면, 개는 닭을 죽일 것이고, 닭은 쌀을 먹을 거야.'라는 뜻이 되어 B가 퍼즐을 푸는 방법을 생각하게 된다.

02 어떤 일에 대해 주의 깊게 생각하고 싶거나 기억하려고 애쓸 때 사용하는 표현

03 일반동사 의문문으로 Do you know로 문장을 시작한다. 그리고 know의 목적어로 'how to+동사원형(draw)'이 오고 마지막으로 draw의 목적어로 a mouse와 부사구 with shapes를 쓴다.

04 그림과 같이 쥐를 그리는 방법은 먼저 큰 삼각형(triangle)을 하나 그리고, 그 다음 두 개의 작은 원(circles)을 그린다. 마지막으로 눈이 되는 두 개의 작은 점(dots)과 수염을 나타내는 6개의 선(lines)을 그린다.

05 '의문사+to부정사'를 이용하여 '어떻게 ~하는지'를 나타낸다. 우리말의 '그것'은 인칭대명사 it을 사용한다.

Grammar

1 (1) how to move (2) where to sit

2 (1) tidy, a mess (2) tired

01 ⑤

02 (1) how cook → how to cook (2) to start → should start (3) sadly → sad (4) wait → to wait

03 (1) kept me excited (2) what to buy (3) where to put the key

04 (1) to thank (2) difficult

01 paper airplanes라는 목적어가 있으므로 how가 적절하다.

02 (1) '의문사+to부정사'가 tell의 직접목적어가 되도록 해야 한다. (2) '의문사+to부정사'는 '의문사+주어+should 동사원형'과 같다. 두 번째 나오는 I를 생략하고 when to start로 쓸 수도 있다. (3) 목적격 보어로 부사가 아닌 형용사가 나와야 한다. (4) ask는 목적격 보어로 to부정사가 나온다.

03 (1) '주어+동사+목적어+목적격 보어'의 형식이 적절하다. (2) '의문사+to부정사'의 어순이 적절하다. (3) '의문사+to부정사'의 어순에서 the key가 put의 목적어이므로 put the key의 어순으로 쓴다.

04 (1) '의문사+to부정사'가 know의 목적어가 되도록 한다. (2) 목적격 보어로 형용사가 나와야 한다.

시험대비 실력평가　　　　　　　　　　　p.23~25

01 ④　　　　02 I found the book interesting.
03 (1) to start　(2) what　(3) how　(4) healthy
(5) happy　　04 ①　　　05 ②　　　06 ⑤
07 to　　　　08 (1) how you should play
(2) how you can[should] make　(3) what I should do
09 ①　　　10 ②　　　11 ③　　　12 ④, ⑤
13 the book was interesting
14 (1) which dress to buy　(2) made every student
nervous
15 (1) going → to go　(2) are → is　(3) what → how
(4) should draw → to draw 또는 you should draw
(5) smartly → smart　(6) happiness → happy
(7) tiring → tired
16 ④　　　17 me sad　　18 Tell me what to buy for
the party tonight. / Tell me what I should buy for the
party tonight.　　　　　19 ①　　　20 ②

01 ④ 목적어 it이 있으므로 what이 아니라 how 정도가 나와야 한다. leave for the day: 퇴근하다

02 '주어+동사+목적어+목적격 보어'의 형식으로 쓴다.

03 (1) '의문사+to부정사'가 ask의 직접목적어가 되도록 한다. (2) 'why+to부정사'는 쓰지 않는다. (3) the washing machine이 목적어로 나와 있으므로 how가 적절하다. (4), (5) 목적격 보어로 형용사가 나와야 한다.

04 5형식을 만들 수 있는 동사로 형용사를 목적격 보어로 받을 수 있는 동사가 나와야 한다. charge, ask, beg, order 등은 목적격 보어로 to부정사가 나온다.

05 a bookmark가 목적어로 나와 있으므로 how가 적절하며 'why to부정사'는 쓰지 않는다.

06 ⑤번은 4형식 동사로 쓰였고 주어진 문장과 나머지는 5형식 동사로 쓰였다. keep in shape: 건강을 유지하다

07 '의문사+to부정사'가 know의 목적어가 되도록 한다.

08 '의문사+to부정사'는 '의문사+주어+should/can+동사원형'으로 바꾸어 쓸 수 있다.

09 ① make가 사역동사(~시키다)로 쓰인 것이 아니므로 tire를 tired로 바꾸어야 한다.

10 '주어+동사+목적어+목적격 보어'의 형식을 이용하여 나타내며 목적격 보어로 형용사를 쓰는 것에 주의한다.

11 where to put: 어디에 놓아야 할지

12 go는 자동사이므로 목적어가 필요 없으므로 what은 적절하지 않고 'why+to부정사'는 쓰지 않는다.

13 '주어+동사+목적어+목적격 보어'의 5형식 문장을 '주어+동사+목적어'의 3형식 문장으로 바꿀 수 있는 경우이다.

14 (1) '의문형용사+명사+to부정사' 형태로 사용된 경우이다. (2) '주어+동사+목적어+목적격 보어'의 형식을 이용한다.

15 (1) '의문사+to부정사'가 decide의 목적어가 되도록 해야 한다. (2) '의문사+to부정사'가 주어로 쓰이면 단수 취급한다. (3) help의 목적어로 her가 나와 있으므로 how 정도로 바꾸는 것이 적절하다. (4) '의문사+to부정사' 또는 '의문사+주어+should 동사원형'이 적절하다. (5) 형용사가 '~하게'라는 뜻의 부사처럼 해석되더라도 보어 자리에는 형용사를 사용한다는 것에 주의한다. (6) make 동사 다음에 목적격 보어로 명사가 나오면 '목적어를 목적격 보어로 만들다'라는 뜻이 되므로 어색하다. 형용사로 고쳐야 한다. (7) '내가 피곤하게 되는' 것이므로 tiring이 아니라 tired가 적절하다.

16 ④번은 to부정사의 형용사적 용법이지만 나머지는 명사적 용법으로 '의문사+to부정사'로 쓰였다.

17 '영화를 보고 슬펐다'는 것을 make 동사를 이용하여 '주어+동사+목적어+목적격 보어'의 형식으로 쓴다.

18 '의문사+to부정사' = '의문사+주어+should+동사원형', what to buy: 무엇을 사야 할지

19 ① the movie가 우리를 재미있게 해주는 것이므로 interested가 아니라 interesting이 적절하다.

20 ⓑ where to sit, ⓒ what to do, ⓔ keep you warm으로 써야 한다.

서술형 시험대비　　　　　　　　　　　p.26~27

01 (1) He showed how to draw a triangle that has three sides of the same length.
(2) When to go there is not decided yet. 또는 When we should go there is not decided yet.
(3) Do you know how to share photos on the Internet?
(4) The bird's song makes him happy.
(5) At first, Sophie thought Nicholas honest.
(6) We found Alita: Battle Angel very interesting.
02 you should(또는 can) solve
03 (1) me full　(2) how to cook
04 (1) Do you know how to grow this flower?
(2) Tell me how many cookies to buy.
(3) They couldn't decide which way to take.
(4) My poor grade made my mom disappointed.
(5) We thought him stupid.
(6) This fan will keep you cool this summer.

05 (1) Do you know how to make triangle gimbap?

 (2) I can't decide what to write about.

 (3) I am not sure where to put the key.

 (4) Tell me which book to read next. 등 어법에 맞게 쓰면 정답

06 (1) interesting　(2) warm　(3) kind　(4) alone

07 (1) what I should eat

 (2) Which dress she should buy

08 (1) her happy　(2) made me excited

01 (1) draw의 목적어로 a triangle이 나와 있으므로 how 정도로 바꾸는 것이 적절하다. (2) '의문사+to부정사' 또는 '의문사+주어+should 동사원형'이 적절하다. (3) 'why+to부정사'는 사용하지 않는다. (4) 형용사 보어가 적절하다. (5) 동사 thought의 목적격 보어로 형용사가 적절하다. (6) Alita: Battle Angel이 우리를 재미있게 하는' 것이므로 interesting이 적절하다.

02 '의문사+to부정사' = '의문사+주어+should+동사원형'

03 (1) makes 동사로 '주어+동사+목적어+목적격 보어'의 형식을 이용한다.

 (2) 훌륭한 요리사라는 대답으로 보아 'how to cook ramyeon(라면을 요리하는 법)'이 적절하다.

04 (1) '의문사+to부정사'가 know의 목적어가 되도록 쓴다. (2) '의문부사+형용사+명사+to부정사' 형태로 사용되었다. (3) '의문형용사+명사+to부정사' 형태로 사용되었다. (4) make 동사를 이용하여 '주어+동사+목적어+목적격 보어'의 형식으로 쓴다. 엄마가 실망하는 것이므로 disappointed로 써야 한다. (5), (6) 동사 think와 keep을 이용하여 '주어+동사+목적어+목적격 보어(형용사)'의 형식으로 쓴다.

05 '의문사+to부정사'는 문장 속에서 주어, 목적어, 보어 역할을 하는 명사구로 사용되어 '~해야 할지, ~하는 것이 좋을지'라는 뜻을 나타낸다.

06 목적격 보어로 형용사를 쓰며 부사를 쓰지 않도록 주의해야 한다.

07 '의문사+to부정사'는 '의문사+주어+should/can+동사원형'으로 바꾸어 쓸 수 있다. 또한 의문사가 의문형용사로 쓰여 to부정사와의 사이에 명사가 올 수 있다.

08 (1), (2) 선물을 받고 행복을 느꼈고, 소식을 듣고 신나게 됐으므로 동사 make를 이용하여 행복하게 만들고 신나게 만들었다고 '주어+동사+목적어+목적격보어'의 형식으로 쓴다.

교과서
Reading

📎 확인문제　p.28

1 T　2 F　3 T　4 F　5 T　6 F

📎 확인문제　p.29

1 T　2 F　3 T　4 F　5 T　6 F

교과서 확인학습 A　p.30~31

01 Spirits
02 There lived
03 controlled
04 was in charge of
05 took care of
06 worked together
07 to make the room better
08 Take, away, pointy
09 waters them
10 Take, away, roll and break
11 exercises with it
12 tidy, make a mess
13 looked at
14 without us
15 all by myself
16 get some rest
17 in control
18 square
19 looked around
20 Much
21 picked up, to hang, on
22 hold my clothes
23 went to water
24 must be
25 picked up, to exercise
26 how to spin
27 to take out
28 have to
29 hurried out of
30 rushed over to
31 what to do
32 all the new square things
33 one another, realized
34 great, the others, once again

교과서 확인학습 B　p.32~33

1 Three Shape Spirits

2 There lived three shape spirits in Mike's room.

3 Square controlled the table, the bookshelf, and the window.

4 Triangle was in charge of the hangers and the plants.

5 Circle took care of the round things.

6 They worked together to make a nice room for Mike.

7 One day Square decided to make the room better and shouted at the other spirits.

8 "Take these plants away, or their pointy leaves will hurt someone!" he said to Triangle.

9 "But Mike waters them every day," said Triangle.

10 "Take this hula hoop away, or it will roll and break something!" he said to Circle.

11 "But Mike exercises with it every day," said Circle.

12 "I try to make this room tidy, but you two always make a mess," he complained.

13 Triangle and Circle looked at each other.

14 "So you think you can do it without us?" Triangle asked Square.

15 "Sure. I can make this room better all by myself," replied Square.

16 "Great! Then we can get some rest," Circle said to Square.

17 Triangle and Circle went out and Square was now in control.

18 He made the hangers, plants, and all the round things square.

19 Then he looked around and smiled.

20 "Much better!"

21 When Mike came home from school, he picked up a square hanger to hang his jacket on.

22 "What? This will not hold my clothes."

23 He went to water the plants and saw their square leaves.

24 "Poor things. … They must be sick."

25 He picked up the square hula hoop to exercise.

26 "Hmm … I don't know how to spin this."

27 He went to take out his bike and looked at the square wheels.

28 "Well, I can't ride this. I'll just have to walk."

29 Then he hurried out of the house.

30 When the other spirits came back, Square rushed over to them.

31 "Mike doesn't like his room. I don't know what to do," he said.

32 They looked at the hangers, the plants, and all the new square things.

33 Then they looked at one another, and Square realized his problem.

34 "Let's make this room great again," he said to the others, and the three spirits worked together once again.

시험대비 실력평가
p.34~37

01 ③　　　　02 three shape spirits / Square, Triangle, and Circle　　03 ②, ⑤
04 (A) the other　(B) tidy　(C) without　　05 ②, ④
06 ③　　　　07 He made the hangers, plants, and all the round things square. 08 ②, ⑤　　09 ④
10 I don't know what to do 또는 I don't know what I should do　　11 greatly → great　　12 ③
13 ②　　14 ①　　　　15 Square thought that he could make the room better all by himself without Triangle and Circle.　　16 ②　　　　17 ②

18 ③　　　　19 Triangle and Circle　　20 ④
21 I can make this room better all by myself
22 (A) used　(B) what　(C) happy
23 It made her excited.

01 ⓐ와 ③번은 책임, 담당, be in charge of: ~을 담당하다, ① (상품이나 서비스에 대한) 요금, ② 돌격[공격]하다, ④ 충전하다, ⑤ (요금, 값을) 청구하다

02 '세 도형 요정'을 가리킨다.

03 ① 사공이 많으면 배가 산으로 올라간다(어떤 일에 관여하는 사람이 너무 많으면 일을 망친다는 뜻). ② 백지장도 맞들면 낫다[한 사람이 하는 것보다는 두 사람이 하는 것이 낫다]. ③ 제때의 바늘 한번이 아홉 바느질을 던다(문제를 즉각 처리하면 일이 훨씬 수월해진다). ④ 아무리 안 좋은 상황에서도 한 가지 긍정적인 측면은 있다. ⑤ 백지장도 맞들면 낫다.

04 (A) 세 도형 요정들 중에서 Square가 '나머지' 요정들에게 소리치는 것이므로 the other가 적절하다. another+단수명사, (B) 난 이 방을 '정돈'하려고 애쓴다고 해야 하므로 tidy가 적절하다. tidy: 잘 정돈된, messy: 지저분한, (C) 우리 '없이' 다 할 수 있다고 생각하느냐고 해야 하므로 without이 적절하다.

05 ⓐ와 ①, ③, ⑤는 명사적 용법, ② 형용사적 용법, ④ 부사적 용법

06 'Circle'이 아니라 'Square'가 말했다.

07 square를 목적격보어로 써서, 5형식 문장을 만드는 것이 적절하다.

08 ⓑ와 ②, ⑤번은 '(틀림없이) …일 것이다[…임에 틀림없다]', 나머지는 모두 '…해야 한다(의무)', reception: (호텔 등의) 접수처, 프런트, garage: 차고,

09 사각형 잎사귀들을 가진 식물들이 몇 개 있었는지는 대답할 수 없다. ① Square was. ② He made them in the shape of a square. ③ He went to water the plants. ⑤ As he couldn't ride the bike because of the square wheels.

10 의문사+to부정사 = 의문사+주어+should

11 목적격보어 자리에 부사를 쓸 수 없으므로, 형용사 great으로 고치는 것이 적절하다.

12 위 글은 인격화한 동식물이나 기타 사물을 주인공으로 하여 그들의 행동 속에 풍자와 교훈의 뜻을 나타내는 이야기인 '우화'이다. ① (책·연극·영화 등에 대한) 논평[비평], 감상문, ② (신문·잡지의) 글, 기사, ④ 전설, ⑤ 시

13 ②는 'these plants'를 가리키고, 나머지는 모두 'Triangle and Circle'을 가리킨다.

14 ⓐ shout at: ~에게 소리치다, ⓑ with it: 그것을 가지고, 그걸로

15 Square는 Triangle과 Circle 없이 완전히 혼자서 방을 더 낫게 만들 수 있다고 생각했다.

16 ② 뭘 해야 할지 놀라서 '걱정스러워'하다가 다른 요정들과 다

시 한 번 함께 일하게 되어 '희망에 차고 기대하게' 되었다고 하는 것이 적절하다. worried: 걱정하는, hopeful: 희망에 찬, 기대하는, ① excited: 신이 난, disappointed: 실망한, ③ confident: 확신하는, ④ satisfied: 만족하는, depressed: 우울한, ⑤ upset: 속상한

17 세 요정들 중에서 Square를 제외한 나머지 두 요정을 가리키므로 the others가 적절하다. ① 다른 사람들[것들], ③ 또 하나(의) (셋 이상 중에서 두 번째를 가리킬 때 사용), ④ 몇몇, 몇 개[가지/사람], ⑤ (둘 중의) 다른 하나

18 ③ 방에 새로 사각형이 된 물건들이 몇 개 있는지는 알 수 없다. ① He rushed over to them. ② No, he doesn't. ④ No, he didn't. ⑤ To make the room great again.

19 Triangle과 Circle을 가리킨다.

20 "난 이 방을 정돈하려고 애쓰지만, 너희 둘은 항상 엉망으로 만들어."라고 '불평했다'고 하는 것이 적절하다. ① 칭찬했다, ② 요구했다, ③ 허락했다, ⑤ 방해했다

21 'better'를 보충하면 된다.

22 (A) '낡은' 청바지라고 해야 하므로 used가 적절하다. using: 사용하는, (B) 그걸 들 때 '뭘' 입어야 할지라고 해야 하므로 what이 적절하다. (C) 목적격보어 자리에 부사를 쓸 수 없고 형용사를 써야 하므로 happy가 적절하다.

23 엄마가 '들뜨게 될' 것이므로 excited로 바꾸는 것이 적절하다.

서술형 시험대비 p.38~39

01 (A) shape (B) controlled (C) in
02 He[It] controlled the table, the bookshelf, and the window.
03 for 04 (A) clothes (B) must (C) have to
05 자신의 옷을 걸고 있지 못할 것이라고 생각했다. / 불쌍하다고 생각하며, 병든 것이 틀림없다고 생각했다.
06 Square가 훌라후프를 사각형으로 만들었기 때문이다.
07 (1) 옷걸이를 사각형으로 바꾸었다.
 (2) 식물의 잎사귀들을 사각형으로 바꾸었다.
08 I should
09 (1) 사각형 훌라후프를 어떻게 돌리는지 몰라서 운동을 못하게 되었다.
 (2) 자전거의 바퀴가 사각형이 되어서 자전거를 탈 수 없게 되었다.
10 (1) If you don't take this hula hoop away, it will roll and break something!
 (2) Unless you take this hula hoop away, it will roll and break something!
11 with → without

01 (A) 명사 뒤에 명사가 나올 경우 앞의 명사는 형용사적 성질을 지니므로 복수형을 만들 수 없고 뒤의 명사에 ~(e)s를 붙

여야 하므로 shape가 적절하다. (B) control–controlled–controlled, (C) in charge of: …를 담당하여

02 Square는 '탁자', '책장', 그리고 '창문'을 담당했다.

03 make는 간접목적어를 직접목적어 뒤로 보낼 때 for를 붙인다.

04 (A) '옷'을 걸고 있지 못할 것이라고 해야 하므로 clothes가 적절하다. cloths: (특정 용도나 어떤 종류의) 천 (조각); 식탁보, 행주, 걸레, clothes: 옷, 의복, (B) 그들은 병든 것이 '틀림없다'고 해야 하므로 must가 적절하다. '추측'을 나타내는 must는 have to로 바꿔 쓸 수 없다. (C) 조동사를 두 개 겹쳐 쓸 수 없으므로 will 다음에 must를 have to로 쓰는 것이 적절하다.

05 Mike가 학교에서 집으로 왔을 때 보인 반응들을 쓰면 된다.

06 Mike는 '사각형 훌라후프'를 집어들고, "흠… 이걸 어떻게 돌리는지 모르겠어."라고 말했다.

08 I don't know how I can spin this.도 가능하다.

09 (1) Mike가 운동을 하기 위해 사각형 훌라후프를 집어 들었지만, "어떻게 돌리는지 모르겠어."라고 했다. (2) 자전거를 꺼내러 가서 사각형 바퀴들을 보고, "난 이걸 탈 수 없어. 그냥 걸어가야 할 것 같아."라고 했다.

10 명령문, or ~ = 'If you don't'나 'Unless you'를 앞에 쓰고 or를 생략하면 된다.

11 네가 우리 '없이' 다 할 수 있다고 생각하는 거냐고 하는 것이 적절하므로, with를 without으로 고쳐야 한다.

영역별 핵심문제 p.41~45

01 finally	02 ⑤	03 ②	04 ②
05 ④	06 ③	07 ④	08 ⑤
09 how to	10 ④	11 ⑤	12 ②
13 ①	14 ⑤	15 ②	
16 which to eat		17 (1) how (2) to sit	
(3) how (4) I should (5) special (6) found			
18 the all round things → all the round things / how to do → what to do			
19 ③	20 ②	21 tidy	22 or
23 alone	24 ①	25 ⑤	
26 (A) riding (B) Square		27 ④	
28 like his room			

01 유의어 관계이다. 서두르다 : 마지막으로

02 'how to divide'로 '어떻게 나누는지'를 나타내고, 두 번째 빈칸에는 '~하는 게 어때?'라는 의견을 제안하는 의미로 'How about ~?'을 사용한다.

03 어느 날 Square는 방을 더 낫게 만들기로 결심했고 나머지 요정들에게 소리쳤다. "이 식물들을 치워, 그렇지 않으면 그것들의 끝이 뾰족한 잎사귀들이 누군가를 다치게 할 거야!" 그가 Triangle에게 말했다.

04 '더 작은 부분으로 분리되다'는 의미로 divide(나누다)가 적절

7

하다. '나는 이 케이크를 네 개의 같은 조각으로 어떻게 나눌 수 있는지 알고 있다.'

05 '전에 알지 못하거나 알아차리지 못한 것을 서서히 이해하기 시작하다'는 의미로 **realize**가 적절하다

06 ③ **by myself**는 '혼자서'의 의미다, '저절로'는 **of itself**를 사용한다.

07 (A)는 첫 번째 그림처럼 3개의 똑같은 사각형으로 나눈다. (B)는 Ben이 '이것을 4개의 똑같은 조각으로 나누는 방법을 아니?' 라고 물었기 때문에 나머지 3개의 L 모양을 볼 수 있다는 말이 적절하다.

08 만드는 방법을 열거할 때 'First ~, Then ~, Finally, ~'의 순서로 쓴다.

09 두 대화의 빈칸은 '~하는 방법'을 묻고 있으므로 'how to+동사원형'이 적절하다.

10 'First ~, Then ~, Finally, ~'는 어떤 일을 열거할 때 사용하는 표현이다.

11 B의 대답으로 보아 샌드위치를 만드는 방법을 물어보는 것이 가장 자연스럽다.

12 '종이 비행기를 만드는 방법을 아니?'라는 물음에 어울리는 답은 ②번이다. 나머지 보기는 종이 비행기를 만드는 방법과 무관한 문장이다.

13 첫 문장에서는 형용사를 목적격 보어로 받을 수 있는 동사가 나와야 한다. want, order, ask, force 등은 목적격 보어로 보통 to부정사가 나온다. 두 번째 문장에서는 a square가 divide의 목적어로 나와 있으므로 where나 how가 적절하며 'why+to부정사'는 쓰이지 않는다.

14 ⑤ He wants to know when to begin the project. 또는 He wants to know when he should begin the project. 가 되어야 한다.

15 ① Let's make her happy. ③ The thick clothes keep me warm. ④ Jogging early in the morning makes me healthy. ⑤ Rick painted his house green. ② friendly는 명사 friend에 -ly를 붙여 형용사가 된 단어이다.

16 which to eat: 어느 것을 먹어야 할지

17 (1) the center of the biggest circle in a triangle이 목적어로 나와 있으므로 how가 적절하다. (2) '의문사+to부정사'가 적절하다. (3) why는 '의문사+to부정사'로 쓰이지 않는다. (4) '의문사+to부정사'나 '의문사+주어+should+동사원형'이 적절하다. (5) 목적격 보어로 형용사가 나와야 한다. (6) 목적격 보어로 형용사를 받을 수 있는 동사는 find이다.

18 'all the+형용사+명사'의 어순이 되어야 하며, do의 목적어가 없으므로 how가 아니라 what이 적절하다.

19 ⓐ와 ①, ②, ④는 부사적 용법, ③ 형용사적 용법, ⑤ 명사적 용법

20 ② Square는 탁자, '책장', 그리고 창문을 담당했다.

21 '정돈된 그리고 조직적인 방식으로 배열된', tidy: 깔끔한, 잘 정돈된

22 명령문 ..., or ~: …해라. 그렇지 않으면 ~할 것이다.

23 by oneself = alone: 혼자

24 ⓐ be in control: ~을 관리[제어]하고 있다, ⓑ 형용사적 용법의 to부정사에 의해 수식을 받는 명사(a square hanger)가 전치사 on의 목적어에 해당한다. hang something on a hanger: 옷걸이에 ~을 걸다

25 ⑤ this는 his bike를 가리킨다. the square wheels는 복수이기 때문에, 'them'으로 받아야 한다.

26 'Square'가 물건들을 사각형으로 만들었기 때문에 Mike는 재킷을 걸기, 훌라후프를 돌리기, 그리고 자전거 '타기'와 같은 일들을 할 수 없었다.

27 ⓐ와 ④번: 때를 나타내는 접속사(…할 때), 나머지는 다 의문부사(언제)

28 Square가 옷걸이들과 식물들을 사각형으로 만들어서 Mike가 '자신의 방을 좋아하지 않는 것'을 가리킨다.

단원별 예상문제
p.46~49

01 divide　　02 (A) First, cut off　(B) Finally[Lastly], wrap, up　　03 ④　　04 ③
05 The dog will kill the chicken.　　06 ④
07 ②　　08 ④　　09 ③　　10 ③
11 ④　　12 how to bake　　13 ③
14 (1) where I should fish　(2) how to get
(3) whom to look　(4) which apple I should choose
15 ③, ⑤　　16 Circle did.　　17 ⑤
18 ④　　19 ②　　20 ①
21 when to put them on　　22 ④

01 반의어 관계이다. 완전한 : 불완전한 = 결합하다 : 나누다

02 (A) 순서를 나열할 때 '먼저'는 First를 사용한다. cut off: '~을 자르다' (B) 순서의 마지막을 말할 때는 Finally[Lastly]를 사용하고, '~을 싸다'는 말은 wrap up이다.

03 (A) 누군가를 다치게 할 수 있다고 했기 때문에 잎이 뾰족한 pointy가 적절하고, (B) 훌라후프가 굴러가서 무언가를 부순다는 의미로 roll이 적절하다. (C) 너희 둘은 항상 엉망으로 만든다고 말하는 것으로 보아 불평한다는 것을 알 수 있다.

04 '몸의 윗부분을 덮는 짧은 코트'는 재킷이 적절하다.

05 쌀을 가지고 먼저 강을 건너게 되면 개와 닭만 남게 되어 개가 닭을 죽이게 될 것이다.

06 소년이 답을 언제 알고 있었는지는 대화에 언급되어 있지 않다.

07 김 위에 밥을 얹고 싸서 삼각형으로 만드는 것으로 보아 '삼각김밥'이 적절하다.

08 대화에서 언급된 wrap은 재료인 '포장지'가 아니라 동사로 '싸다'는 뜻으로 사용이 되었다.

09 ③번의 라면을 끓이는 방법을 묻는 말에 대한 답으로 빵을 이용한 샌드위치를 만드는 설명은 적절하지 않다.

10 '~와 마주하다, 직면하다'는 뜻은 face가 적절하다.

11 ④ The boy found the ants very strong. 목적격 보어로 형용사를 쓴다는 것에 유의한다. ⑤ 내 말 오해하지 마.

12 좋아한다는 대답으로 보아 'how to bake cookies'가 적절하다.

13 ③은 4형식으로 쓰였고 주어진 문장과 나머지는 모두 목적어와 목적격 보어가 있는 5형식이다.

14 '의문사+to부정사'는 '의문사+주어+should/can+동사원형'으로 바꿔 쓸 수 있다.

15 ⓐ와 ①, ②, ④: 이야기를 시작할 때 존재를 나타내는 문장에서 뜻이 없이 형식적 주어로 쓰인다. be동사와 주로 쓰이지만, 'come, live, happen' 등과도 쓰인다. ③과 ⑤: 거기에[에서], 그곳에[에서]

16 'Circle'이 둥근 것들을 돌보았다. did는 took care of the round things를 받은 대동사이다.

17 Square는 옷걸이들과 식물들과 모든 둥근 물건들을 '사각형'으로 만들었다.

18 ④는 의문사와 함께 쓰이는 명사적 용법이고, 나머지는 다 부사적 용법(목적)이다.

19 ② 사각형 옷걸이가 자신의 옷을 '걸고 있지 못할' 것이라고 생각했다.

20 ⓐ와 ①번은 [재료를 나타내어] …에서, …으로, ② …의 안에서 밖으로, ③ [원인·동기를 나타내어] …에서, … 때문에, ④ [기원·출처를 나타내어] …에서, …부터, ⑤ …의 범위 밖에, …이 미치지 못하는 곳에

21 대명사 them을 put과 on 사이에 쓰는 것이 적절하다.

22 삼각형 선글라스를 써야 할 때는 알 수 없고, 단지 내 어린 여동생은 언제 그걸 써야 할지 안다고만 되어 있다. ① 글쓴이, ② 종이 박스와 비닐봉지, ③ 글쓴이의 어린 여동생, ⑤ 행복하다.

서술형 실전문제 p.50~51

01 how to divide this into four equal pieces

02 First, stand with your back to the wind. Then, hold it up until it catches the wind. Finally, let the line out.

03 (A) Do you know how to divide this cake into four equal pieces?
 (B) How about dividing it this way?

04 (1) Do you know how to make three more triangles with three more pencils?
 (2) Let me know where to grow these flowers.
 (3) Can you tell me when to start?
 (4) The small black circles made it perfect.
 (5) It made me full at lunch time.
 (6) My father believes me honest.

05 or 06 (A) to make (B) pointy (C) waters

07 it will roll and break something

08 (1) 훌라후프를 사각형으로 바꾸었다.
 (2) 자전거의 바퀴들을 사각형으로 바꾸었다.

09 hung → couldn't hang / rode → couldn't ride

10 Square가 자전거 바퀴들을 사각형으로 만들었기 때문이다.

01 'how to 동사원형'을 이용하여 문장을 쓴다. 대화의 마지막 B의 말에서 다른 3개의 L 모양을 볼 수 있다고 했으므로 4개의 조각을 만드는 방법을 묻는 말이 적절하다.

02 어떤 일의 절차를 말할 때는 'First …, Then …, Finally, …' 순으로 나열한다. 연을 날리기 위해 먼저 해야 할 일은 바람에 등을 지고 서서, 그 다음 연이 바람을 탈 때까지 잡고 있다가 마지막으로 줄을 놓아 주는 것이 알맞은 순서다.

03 (A) 'how to+동사원형'과 'divide A into B' 구문을 이용하여 문장을 완성한다. (B) '~하는 게 어때?'라는 표현으로 How about 뒤에 동명사(-ing)를 사용하여 문장을 완성한다.

04 (1)~(3) '의문사+to부정사'는 문장 속에서 주어, 목적어, 보어 역할을 하는 명사구로 사용된다. (4)~(6) '주어+동사+목적어+목적격 보어'의 형식을 이용한다. 이때 보어 자리에는 부사가 아니라 형용사를 사용한다는 것에 주의한다.

05 명령문 ~, or … = ~해라, 그렇지 않으면 …

06 (A) decide는 to부정사를 목적어로 취하므로 to make가 적절하다. (B) '끝이 뾰족한' 잎사귀들이라고 해야 하므로 pointy가 적절하다. pointy: 끝이 뾰족한(pointed), pointing: 가리키는, (C) 동사로 쓰였으므로 waters가 적절하다. water: (화초 등에) 물을 주다

07 Circle이 훌라후프를 치우지 않으면 '굴러가서 뭔가를 부술 것이기 때문이다.'

09 Mike가 학교에서 집으로 왔을 때, 그는 옷걸이에 '옷을 걸 수 없었고', 그리고 자전거를 '탈 수 없었다.'

10 Mike는 사각형 자전거 바퀴들을 보고, "음, 난 이걸 탈 수 없어. 그냥 걸어가야 할 것 같아."라고 말했다.

창의사고력 서술형 문제 p.52

[모범답안]

01 (1) A: Do you know how to share a photo?
 B: Sure. First, press and hold a photo. Then, choose "Share." Finally, choose an SNS.
 (2) A: Do you know how to make potato salad?
 B: Sure. First, boil the potatoes. Then, cut them into pieces. Finally, put some sauce on them.

9

(3) A: Do you know how to make sandwiches?

B: Sure. First, put an egg on bread. Then, add some vegetables. Finally, put bread on top.

02 (1) Show me how to take care of the cow.

(2) I can't decide what to eat.

(3) Please tell me when to go.

(4) Let's decide where to put it.

(5) Let me know whom to meet.

03 (A) out of (B) when (C) excited (D) happy

단원별 모의고사

p.53~56

01 ③	02 select	03 ①	04 same
05 ⑤	06 ③	07 how to draw	
08 ②	09 ④	10 ①	11 ③

12 (A) First (B) into (C) on 13 me excited 14 ①, ⑤ 15 ⑤ 16 ②

17 (1) Do you know how to make triangle sunglasses?

(2) When to finish the works was an important issue.

(3) Tell me whom to meet. 또는 Tell me whom I should meet.

(4) The news made them sad.

(5) We found him honest.

18 Triangle was (in charge of the plants). 19 ②, ⑤

20 ② 21 and → or

22 (A) saw (B) to exercise (C) how 23 ③

01 ③번의 excited는 '흥분한'의 뜻으로 feeling relaxed(편안한)는 적절하지 않다. feeling very happy and enthusiastic(매우 행복하고 열광적으로 느끼는)으로 고쳐야 한다.

02 유의어 관계이다. 점 = 고르다, 선택하다

03 '특히 빠르게 계속 돌다'라는 의미로 spin(회전하다)이 적절하다.

04 케이크를 4개의 같은(equal) 조각으로 나누는 법을 묻고 있으므로 B의 대답에는 같은 크기와 모양이 된다는 말이 적절하다. 그래서 same이 와야 한다.

05 (A) in charge of: ~을 담당하여 (B) one another: 서로

06 G가 Let me see.라고 잠깐 생각을 하고 '연필을 반으로 부러뜨려도 돼?'라고 말하는 것으로 보아 답을 찾지 못해 문제가 어렵다는 것을 짐작할 수 있다.

07 B의 대답으로 보아 A는 도형으로 물고기를 그리는 방법을 물어보고 있음을 알 수 있다.

08 at a time: 한 번에, one by one: 하나씩

09 소녀는 개와 쌀과 닭을 함께 배에 태워서 갈 수 없다.

10 이 퍼즐은 4개의 같은 조각으로 나누는 것이다. G의 마지막 말에서 마지막으로, 'L 자 모양의 안쪽 모서리에 있는 3개의 작은

사각형에 색칠해'라고 했기 때문에 ①이 적절하다.

11 ③ '이 퍼즐을 푸는 방법을 아니?'라는 말에 '그것은 언제니?'라고 답하는 것은 어색하다.

12 순서를 열거할 때 (A)에는 First가 적절하다. (B) cut A into B: A를 B로 자르다 (C) put A on B: A를 B에 얹다[놓다]

13 makes 동사로 '주어+동사+목적어+목적격 보어'의 형식을 이용한다. 내가 신이 나게 되는 것이므로 excited로 써야 함에 주의한다.

14 it이라는 목적어가 있으므로 what은 적절하지 않으며 'why+to부정사'는 사용하지 않는다.

15 '동사+목적어+목적격 보어(형용사)'로 쓸 수 있는 동사는 keep이다.

16 ② I taught him how he could read English. 또는 I taught him how to read English.

17 (1) '의문사+to부정사'가 적절하며 triangle sunglasses라는 목적어가 있으므로 what은 어울리지 않는다. (2) '의문사+to부정사'가 주어로 쓰이면 단수 취급한다. (3) '의문사+to부정사'나 '의문사+주어+should+동사원형'이 적절하다. (4) 목적격 보어로 형용사가 나와야 한다. (5) 목적어로 목적격 him이 적절하며 목적격 보어로 형용사가 나와야 한다.

18 'Triangle'이 식물들을 담당했다.

19 @와 ②, ⑤: ~을 돌보다, ① take after: ~을 닮다, ③ look like: ~처럼 보이다, ④ call for: ~을 요구하다

20 ② it은 hula hoop를 가리키고, 나머지는 다 Square를 가리킨다.

21 "이 훌라후프를 치워, 그렇지 않으면 굴러가서 뭔가를 부술 거야!"라고 해야 하므로 or로 고치는 것이 적절하다. 명령문, or ~= ~해라, 그렇지 않으면 / 명령문, and ~= ~해라, 그러면

22 (A) '사각형 잎사귀들을 보았다'고 해야 하므로 went와 병렬 구문을 이루도록 saw라고 하는 것이 적절하다. (B) '운동을 하기 위해' 사각형 훌라후프를 집어 들었다고 해야 하므로 to exercise가 적절하다. (C) 이걸 '어떻게' 돌리는지 모르겠다고 해야 하므로 how가 적절하다.

23 ③ 만족스러워[흡족해] 하는, Square는 물건들을 사각형으로 만든 다음 주위를 둘러보고 미소 지으며 "훨씬 좋군!"이라고 말했다. ① 지루한, ② 실망한, ④ 부끄러운, ⑤ 긴장한, 초조한

empty: 비어 있는

05 (1) 면, 양털, 비단 또는 나일론과 같은 물질을 짬으로써 만들어진 천 (2) 입이나 손을 닦기 위해 사용하는 정사각형의 천이나 종이 (3) 폐기물을 다시 사용할 수 있도록 바꾸다 (4) 소수의 사람들만이 알고 있고 다른 사람들에게는 말하지 않는 어떤 것

Love the Earth

시험대비 실력평가　　　　　　　　p.60

01 ④　　　　　02 instead　　03 ⑤
04 in the middle of　　　05 ②　　　　06 ③
07 ④　　　　　08 ①

01 아이스크림 가게에서 한 가지 맛을 고르는 것은 어렵다.

02 너는 탄산음료 대신 많은 물을 마셔야 한다. / 다른 어떤 것이 사용되거나 발생했을 때 어떤 것이 사용되지 않거나 발생하지 않음을 말할 때 사용되는

03 'reduce'는 '줄이다, 축소하다'는 의미이고, '재사용하다'는 'reuse'이다.

04 '~의 한가운데'는 'in the middle of'를 사용한다.

05 '사람들이 버리는 가치 없는 어떤 것'은 trash(쓰레기)가 적절하다.

06 '많은 노력을 요구하는 새롭고 어려운 일'은 challenge(도전)이다.

07 '사실, 우리는 뻥튀기를 접시로 사용해서, 그것들을 먹고 아무것도 남기지 않을 수 있었죠.'

08 • 우리에게 쓰레기를 줄이기 위한 간단한 조언을 하나만 해 주세요. • 여러분은 학급 생일 파티를 열었지만, 쓰레기가 많이 나오지 않았어요.

서술형 시험대비　　　　　　　　　p.61

01 spotless　　02 (1) wrapping, recycled　(2) reusable
(3) machines　(4) powered　03 natural
04 (1) bin　(2) challenge　(3) cotton　(4) empty
05 (1) cloth, 천, 옷감　(2) napkin, 냅킨　(3) recycle, 재활용하다　(4) secret, 비결, 비밀

01 대화의 마지막에 'really clean(정말로 깨끗한)'이라고 했기 때문에 빈칸에는 'spotless(티끌 하나 없는)'가 적절하다.

02 (1) wrapping paper: 포장지, 재활용된다는 수동의 의미로 be동사 뒤에 과거분사 recycled가 적절하다. (2) 명사 water bottle을 수식하는 형용사 reusable이 적절하다. (3) 'many+복수 명사'로 machines가 맞다. (4) 동력을 공급받는다는 수동의 의미로 is 뒤에 과거분사 powered가 적절하다.

03 '음식이나 음료에 화학 물질이 첨가되지 않아서 건강하다고 여겨지는'의 의미를 지니는 'natural'이 적절하다.

04 (1) bin: (쓰레기) 통 (2) challenge: 도전 (3) cotton: 면 (4)

교과서 Conversation

핵심 Check　　　　　　　　　　p.62~63

1 ②　　　　　2 ③

교과서 대화문 익히기

Check(√) True or False　　　　p.64

1 T　2 T　3 F　4 T　5 T

교과서 확인학습　　　　　　　p.66~67

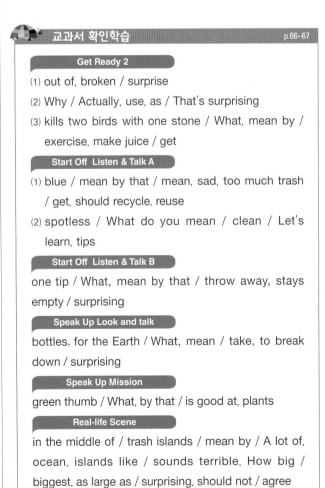

Get Ready 2
(1) out of, broken / surprise
(2) Why / Actually, use, as / That's surprising
(3) kills two birds with one stone / What, mean by / exercise, make juice / get

Start Off Listen & Talk A
(1) blue / mean by that / mean, sad, too much trash / get, should recycle, reuse
(2) spotless / What do you mean / clean / Let's learn, tips

Start Off Listen & Talk B
one tip / What, mean by that / throw away, stays empty / surprising

Speak Up Look and talk
bottles, for the Earth / What, mean / take, to break down / surprising

Speak Up Mission
green thumb / What, by that / is good at, plants

Real-life Scene
in the middle of / trash islands / mean by / A lot of, ocean, islands like / sounds terrible, How big / biggest, as large as / surprising, should not / agree

Fun Time

skateboard / surprising

big fish / What, mean / important

Express Yourself

(1) energy tree / mean / produces, is used, street lamp

(2) called / is called / special / powered

Learning Diary Listen & Speak

spotless / one tip / bin / What do you mean by that / throw away, stay empty / pleasure

 시험대비 기본평가 p.68

01 ④ 02 ① 03 What do you mean by that? 04 (A) → (C) → (B)

01 ④번의 No wonder you're upset.은 '네가 화내는 것이 당연해.'의 뜻이다.

02 상대방이 한 말에 대해 추가 설명을 요청할 때 쓰는 표현으로 '그게 무슨 뜻이에요?'라는 의미로 'What do you mean by that?'과 같은 의미의 'Can you tell me what it means?'를 사용한다.

03 의문사 what을 시작으로 일반동사 mean을 의문문을 만들고, 마지막에 by that을 쓴다. 여기서 that은 상대방이 말한 내용을 언급하는 대명사이고 by that은 '그 말로써, 그것으로'라는 뜻이다.

04 (A) 컵을 왜 먹고 있는지 묻자 → (C) 컵이 쿠키라고 설명하고 난 다음, 쿠키를 컵으로 사용하고 나서 먹는다는 부연 설명을 한다. → 마지막으로 놀랍다는 반응을 하는 (B)가 오는 것이 자연스럽다.

 시험대비 실력평가 p.69~70

01 ③ 02 ⑤ 03 They take 450 years to break down. 04 ④ 05 ②
06 tip 07 ④ 08 ③ 09 ⑤
10 ② 11 ③ 12 ②

01 B의 마지막 말에서 '운동도 하고 주스도 만든다.'고 했으므로 '일석이조'라는 표현이 적절하다.

02 'What do you mean by that?'은 상대방이 한 말에 대해 추가 설명을 요청할 때 쓰는 표현이다.

03 주어인 '그것들이'는 Plastic bottles를 가리키므로 대명사 they로 문장을 시작하고 '~하는 데 시간이 걸리다'는 표현은 'take+시간+to 부정사' 구문을 이용한다.

04 '깨끗한 쓰레기통 프로젝트를 하고 있어.'라는 말에 대해 추가 설명을 요구하는 표현이 적절하다. ②는 놀라움을 표현하는 말이다.

05 쓰레기를 버리지 않아서 쓰레기통이 비어 있다는 말에 놀라움을 나타내는 표현이 자연스럽다.

06 '유용한 충고'라는 의미로 '조언, 비결'의 뜻을 가진 tip이 적절하다.

07 그들이 얼마나 많은 쓰레기를 버리는지는 대화에서 언급되어 있지 않다.

08 많은 플라스틱 쓰레기가 바다에 흘러들어가서 쓰레기 섬이 된다는 말 다음에 '끔찍하다'는 표현이 오는 것이 적절하다. great를 terrible로 바꾸어야 한다.

09 A가 그는 정말 중요한 사람이라는 뜻이라고 설명하는 것으로 보아 의미를 묻는 질문이 오는 것이 적절하다.

10 친환경 버스는 쓰레기로부터 동력을 공급받는다는 대답으로 보아 친환경 버스의 특별한 점을 물어보는 것이 자연스럽다.

11 ③의 A는 '오늘 우울해.'라는 표현이다. B가 '그렇다면 무슨 색을 좋아하니?'라고 묻는 것은 어색하다.

12 G의 마지막 말에서 '그녀의 교실이 정말로 깨끗해.'라고 했기 때문에 spotless(티끌하나 없는)가 적절하다.

 서술형 시험대비 p.71

01 What do you mean by that?

02 The biggest one is about 14 times as large as South Korea.

03 don't throw away trash, so our trash can stay empty

04 That's surprising!

05 kills two birds with one stone

01 상대방이 한 말에 대해 추가 설명을 요청할 때 쓰는 표현은 'What do you mean by ~?'이다.

02 '~의 몇 배'는 '배수사(14 times)+as+원급(large)+as' 구문을 사용한다.

03 주어진 그림에서 'Make No Trash'와 쓰레기를 버리는 것이 금지되어 있는 것을 이용하여 영작한다.

04 당신이 무언가에 매우 놀랄 때 무엇이라 말하는가?

05 빈칸에 들어갈 표현에 대해 '무슨 뜻이니?'라고 G가 묻고 있다. B의 마지막 말에서 운동을 하면서 주스도 만든다고 했으므로 '일거양득'을 의미하는 표현이 적절하다.

[교과서]
Grammar

핵심 Check p.72~73

1 (1) a few (2) a little (3) a little

2 (1) was built (2) to (3) with

01 ⑤ 02 ②

03 (1) was broken (2) was written (3) a few (4) little

04 (1) a few → a little (2) washes → is washed

01 동사를 'be+pp'로 바꾸고 수동태 문장의 주어 자리에는 능동태 문장의 목적어가 오고, by 다음에는 능동태 문장의 주어를 목적격으로 쓴다.

02 뒤에 셀 수 있는 명사의 복수형 tips가 나오고 있으므로 a few가 적절하다. 내용상 few(거의 없는)는 적절하지 않다.

03 (1) 수동태는 'be+pp'의 형태이다. (2) 책 이름은 단수로 취급하며 과거에 쓰여진 것이므로 과거동사로 쓴다. (3) 뒤에 복수 명사가 나오고 긍정의 내용이므로 a few가 적절하다. (4) 뒤에 단수 명사가 나오고 부정의 내용이므로 little이 적절하다.

04 (1) 뒤에 단수 명사가 나오고 긍정의 내용이므로 a little이 적절하다. (2) 차가 세차되는 것이므로 수동태가 적절하다.

01 ④ 02 ⑤ 03 ③ 04 ①

05 ② 06 (1) to (2) for (3) of 07 ①

08 ① 09 ② 10 ⑤ 11 ②

12 a little 13 is caught / are made / is interested in / is covered with

14 (1) She was invited to the party.

(2) Used paper is recycled by many people.

(3) He was made to return early by his boss.

(4) A little energy is produced this way.

(5) Few people live to be one hundred years old.

15 was given (to)

16 (1) The air is cleaned by the green tower.

(2) A little bread is needed to make sandwiches by me.

(3) By whom was the picture *The Starry Night* drawn?

(4) Some food was cooked for John by Ms. Brown.

(5) Susan was seen talking on the phone with her friend by us.

(6) Their exam result can be shown to the students by teachers.

17 (1) was taken → took (2) wrote → was written by

(3) a little → a few

01 This book이 쓰여지는 것이므로 수동태가 적절하다.

02 minutes라는 복수 명사가 뒤에 나왔으므로 a little이 아니라 a few가 적절하다. ③번의 경우는 a little이 '약간의'라는 뜻으로

쓰인 것이 아니라 '하나의 작은'이라는 뜻으로 쓰인 것이다.

03 목적격보어가 원형부정사인 경우, 수동태 문장에서는 to부정사로 바뀐다.

04 ② Everyone liked her cute napkins. ③ There are a few people in the hall. ④ The flowers will be bought for her by Murphy. ⑤ I'll be there in a few days.

05 4형식의 직접목적어를 주어로 하는 수동태에서 choose는 간접목적어 앞에 for를 쓰는 동사이다.

06 직접목적어를 주어로 한 수동태에서 간접목적어 앞에 (1) tell은 전치사 to를, (2) make는 전치사 for를, (3) ask는 전치사 of를 쓴다.

07 (a) little+단수 명사. 문맥상 부정의 내용이 되어야 하므로 little이 적절하다.

08 'A dress sent to me was bought at the shop by Melanie.'는 옷을 Melanie가 샀다는 의미(누가 보냈는지는 모름)이고 'A dress bought at the shop was sent to me by Melanie.'는 옷을 Melanie가 보냈다(누가 샀는지는 모름)는 의미이다.

09 'a few+복수 명사: 긍정', 'few+복수 명사: 부정' 내용상 긍정의 의미가 적절하다. a deal of(= much)+단수 명사

10 throw away는 구동사로 하나의 단어처럼 취급하여 be thrown away로 나타낸다. away나 by를 빠뜨리지 않도록 주의한다.

11 be pleased with: ~로 기뻐하다 be filled with: ~로 가득 차다

12 뒤에 단수 명사 coffee가 나오고 약간 남아 있으므로 a little이 적절하다.

13 벌레가 잡히고 스마트폰이 만들어지는 것이므로 수동태가 적절하다. be interested in: ~에 흥미가 있다, be covered with: ~로 덮여 있다

14 (1), (2), (4) 파티에 초대되고, 종이가 재활용되고, 에너지가 생산되는 것이므로 수동태가 적절하다. (3) 목적격 보어 자리에는 동사원형이 쓰이지만 수동태 문장에서는 to부정사 형태로 바뀌어야 한다. (4) a little+단수 명사: 긍정, little+단수 명사: 부정 (5) a few+복수 명사: 긍정, few+복수 명사: 부정

15 직접목적어를 주어로 한 수동태에서 give는 간접목적어 앞에 전치사 to를 쓴다. 이때 인칭대명사 앞에 오는 to는 생략할 수 있다.

16 (1), (2) 동사를 'be+pp'로 바꾸고 수동태 문장의 주어 자리에는 능동태 문장의 목적어가 오고, by 다음에는 능동태 문장의 주어를 목적격으로 쓴다. (3) 수동태를 의문문 형태로 만들 때는 주어와 be동사의 위치를 바꾼다. by whom은 의문사로 취급하여 문장의 맨 앞에 써야 한다. (4) 직접목적어를 주어로 한 수동태에서 cook은 간접목적어 앞에 전치사 for를 쓴다. 또한 cook은 간접목적어를 주어로 수동태를 만들지 않는다. (5) 시제가 saw로 과거형이므로 was seen으로 쓰고, 목적격보어 talking

은 그대로 써준다. (6) 조동사가 있는 문장의 수동태는 '조동사
+be+p.p.' 형식을 갖는다.

17 (1) take place는 수동태로 쓰이지 않는다. (2) Hamlet이 쓰
여지는 것이므로 수동태가 적절하다. (3) (a) few+복수 명사,
(a) little+단수 명사

01 (1) Some books were given to Brian by Jane. **또는**
 Brian was given some books by Jane.

 (2) They will make this movie next month.

 (3) A dress was made for her daughter by Midori.

 (4) Hope was never completely given up by her.

 (5) By whom was the World Wide Web invented in
 1991?

02 (1) few (2) little (3) a few (4) a little

03 (1) One simple tip for reducing trash was given (to)
 us by them. **또는** They gave us one simple tip
 for reducing trash.

 (2) Today, this house is used by travelers.

 (3) The wooden table is made of wood.

 (4) Emily was never seen to sing in public by us.

 (5) When a child, a storybook was read (to) me
 every night by my mom.

 (6) A ring with an expensive stone will be sent to
 Kate.

04 Few

05 (1) A lot of trees are cut down to make paper.

 (2) Stars are not seen on a rainy night.

 (3) Street lights were turned on as it was getting
 dark.

 (4) The same question was asked of her.

 (5) She was made to write a letter to you by them.

 (6) Everybody was surprised at the news.

06 (1) a little → a few (2) few → little

 (3) Little → Few (4) a little → little

07 (1) Some chocolates were given (to) me by
 Matilda yesterday. I was given some
 chocolates by Matilda yesterday.

 (2) A beautiful hair band was chosen for her friend
 by Jenny.

 (3) The way to the bus stop was asked of me by
 the stranger.

08 A few

09 a little people → a few people

 a little cans → a few cans

 a little bottles → a few bottles

 few water → little water

01 (1) 수동태는 'be+pp'의 형태이다. (2) 미래 시제의 수동태는
'will be+과거분사'이다. (3) make는 직접목적어를 주어로 하
는 수동태만 가능하며 간접목적어 앞에 for를 써야 한다. (4)
give up은 구동사로 하나의 단어처럼 취급하여 be given up으
로 나타낸다. up이나 by를 빠뜨리지 않도록 주의한다. (5) 의문
사 who가 by whom으로 바뀌어 문두에 쓰이는 것에 주의한다.

02 a few+복수 명사: 긍정, few+복수 명사: 부정, a little+단수
명사: 긍정, little+단수 명사: 부정

03 (1) one simple tip을 주어로 하면 수동태가, They를 주어로
하면 능동태가 적절하다. (2) 집이 무엇을 사용하는 것이 아니므
로 진행형이 아닌 수동태가 적절하다. (3) be made of: ~로 만
들어지다(물리적 변화), be made from: ~로 만들어지다(화학
적 변화) (4) 목적격보어가 원형부정사인 경우, 수동태 문장에
서는 to부정사로 바뀐다. (5) read는 직접목적어를 주어로 하는
수동태만 가능하다. (6) sent은 직접목적어를 주어로 한 수동태
에서는 간접목적어 앞에 to를 쓴다.

04 거의 모든 학생이 성공하지 못했다는 것이므로 Few가 적절하
다.

05 (1) 수동태는 '주어+be동사+동사의 과거분사(+by+행위자)'의
형식이다. (2) 수동태의 부정은 'be+not+과거분사'이다. (3)
turn on을 하나의 단위처럼 생각해서 'be turned on'으로 써야
한다. (4) ask는 직접목적어를 주어로 한 수동태에서는 간접목
적어 앞에 전치사 of를 써야 한다. (5) 목적격 보어 자리에 동사
원형이 쓰이면 수동태 문장에서는 to부정사 형태로 바뀌어야 한
다. (6) be surprised at: ~에 놀라다

06 a few+복수 명사: 긍정, few+복수 명사: 부정, a little+단수 명
사: 긍정, little+단수 명사: 부정 (4)에는 내용상 부정의 말이 적절
하다.

07 직접목적어를 주어로 한 수동태에서 간접목적어 앞에 (1) give
는 전치사 to를, (2) choose는 for를, (3) ask는 of를 쓴다.

08 뒤에 복수 명사 pencils가 나오고 긍정의 내용이므로 a few가
적절하다.

09 (a) few+복수 명사, (a) little+단수 명사

교과서
Reading

확인문제 p.80

1 T 2 F 3 F 4 T

확인문제 p.81

1 T 2 F 3 F 4 T 5 T 6 F

01 Challenge
02 No Trash Challenge
03 Grade 2 Class 3
04 a few tips / living green
05 Wrapping Paper
06 didn't produce
07 your secrets
08 agreed not to wrap / is not easily recycled
09 such as, not, at all
10 Largest
11 chose the largest size
12 less packaging, less trash
13 Eat
14 how, serve
15 on plates
16 You know what
17 even the plates
18 ate the plates
19 by that
20 as plates, leave nothing behind
21 get it
22 quite
23 Bring
24 What about
25 didn't use
26 Instead, brought, from, took them back
27 Cloth
28 make less trash
29 cloth napkins
30 are not good for
31 where did you get
32 were made by
33 cut up
34 her cute napkins
35 Leave, Behind
36 one simple tip
37 Don't leave
38 Food waste
39 see
40 ate everything

1 No Trash Challenge

2 We all had a "No Trash Challenge" day last month.

3 The winner was Grade 2 Class 3.

4 Let's read the interview and learn a few tips for living green.

5 Do Not Use Wrapping Paper

6 Reporter: You threw a class birthday party, but didn't produce a lot of trash.

7 What were your secrets?

8 Minsu: First, we agreed not to wrap our gifts, because some wrapping paper is not easily recycled.

9 So we brought gifts such as teddy bears, key rings, and hairpins that were not wrapped at all.

10 Buy the Largest Size

11 Jieun: Also, we chose the largest size when we bought ice cream and cookies for the party.

12 Larger sizes use less packaging and make less trash.

13 Eat the Plates

14 Reporter: And how did you serve the ice cream?

15 Junha: We served it on plates.

16 You know what?

17 We ate even the plates after we used them.

18 Reporter: You ate the plates?

19 What do you mean by that?

20 Junha: Actually, we used popped rice cakes as plates, so we could eat them and leave nothing behind!

21 Reporter: Ah, I get it.

22 That's quite interesting.

23 Bring Your Own Things

24 Reporter: What about cups and spoons?

25 Minsu: We didn't use paper cups or plastic spoons.

26 Instead, we brought our own cups and spoons from home and then took them back.

27 Use Cloth Napkins

28 Reporter: What else did you do to make less trash?

29 Jieun: We used cloth napkins.

30 You know, paper napkins are not good for your skin.

31 Reporter: But where did you get the cloth napkins?

32 Jieun: They were made by Minji.

33 She cut up her old cotton shirt to make some for us.

34 Everyone liked her cute napkins.

35 Leave No Food Behind

36 Reporter: Please give us one simple tip for reducing trash.

37 Junha: Don't leave any food on your plate.

38 Food waste really is a big problem.

39 But see?

40 We ate everything, even our plates, ha-ha.

01 Grade 2 Class 3
02 ②, ④
03 ②
04 (A) Larger (B) popped (C) quite
05 ③
06 ①
07 ③
08 ①
09 ②
10 ②
11 ③
12 ④
13 Leave
14 reducing
15 (A) food (B) plates
16 is powered
17 친환경 버스가 쓰레기로부터 동력을 공급받는 것
18 few → little
19 ④
20 ②

15

21 ⑤　　　　22 How about

23 took back them → took them back

24 their own cups and spoons

25 presented / serve food / food waste / store rain water / save

26 (A) 식당에서 음식을 작은 접시에 제공하는 것
　　(B) 모든 집에서 빗물을 탱크에 저장하는 것

01 grade: 학년, 등급, 성적

02 ⓑ와 ②, ④: 동명사, ④ (목적이나 용도를 나타내는 동명사), living room: 거실, ① 형용사(현존하는, 당대의), ③, ⑤: 현재분사

03 인터뷰를 읽고, 친환경적으로 살기 위한 몇 가지 비결을 배우자고 했으므로, '친환경적으로 살기 위한 비결에 관한 인터뷰'가 이어진다고 하는 것이 적절하다.

04 (A) 크기가 '더 크면' 포장을 더 적게 사용하고 쓰레기를 더 적게 배출한다고 해야 하므로 Larger가 적절하다. (B) '튀겨진'이라고 해야 하므로 popped가 적절하다. popped rice cake: 뻥튀기, (C) '꽤' 흥미롭다고 해야 하므로 quite가 적절하다. quiet: 조용한

05 ⓐ와 ③번: (자격·기능 등이) ~로(서), ① [원인·이유] ~이므로, ② [양태·상태] ~ 하는 대로, ④ [때] ~하고 있을 때, ⑤ ~와 같은 정도로, (as ... as ~에서, 앞의 as는 지시부사, 뒤의 as는 접속사)

06 ① I know.: 이미 알고 있어요. ⓑ와 나머지: 알겠어요. (이제야) 이해가 되는군요.

07 give[have, throw, host] a party: 파티를 열다

08 ④ 부사적 용법, ⓑ와 나머지: 명사적 용법

09 민수네 반은 학급 생일 파티를 열었지만, 쓰레기가 많이 '나오지 않았다.'

10 연결되는 두 문장은 대비되는 내용을 나타내고 있으므로 instead가 가장 적절하다. ① 그러므로, ③ 비슷하게, ④ 즉, 다시 말해, ⑤ 게다가

11 old cotton shirt는 '천 냅킨'이 아니라 천 냅킨의 '재료'이다.

12 천 냅킨 제작에 걸린 시간은 알 수 없다. ① 종이 냅킨이 피부에 안 좋고, 천 냅킨 사용이 쓰레기를 더 줄이기 때문이다. ② 민지 ③ 민지의 낡은 면 셔츠, ⑤ 모두가 좋아했다.

13 접시에 음식을 남기지 말라고 했기 때문에, 제목으로는 음식을 '남기지' 마라가 적절하다.

14 전치사 다음에 동명사로 쓰는 것이 적절하다.

15 준하의 반 친구들은 접시에 '음식'을 남기지 않음으로써 쓰레기를 줄였다. 그들은 접시를 먹음으로써 심지어 '접시'조차 남기지 않았다.

16 Trash powers the green bus.를 수동태로 고치는 것이 적절하다.

17 앞 문장의 내용을 가리킨다.

18 energy는 셀 수 없는 명사이므로, little로 수식하는 것이 적절하다.

19 빈칸 ⓐ에 들어갈 말로는 재미있거나 놀라운 의견·소식 등을 말하려 할 때 쓰는 말인 You know what?(그거 알아?) 등을 쓰는 것이 적절하다. You know what? = Guess what! = I'll tell you what. = You know something?: (대화를 시작할 때) 아세요?, 있잖아요.

20 주어진 문장의 that에 주목한다. ②번 앞 문장의 내용을 받고 있으므로 ②번이 적절하다.

21 쿠키를 먹은 뒤 쿠키 봉투를 어떻게 재활용했는지는 대답할 수 없다 ① They chose the largest size. ② Because larger sizes use less packaging and make less trash. ③ They served it on plates. ④ They were made of popped rice cakes.

22 What about ~? = How about ~?: ~은 어떻습니까?

23 '동사+부사'로 이루어진 이어동사에서 목적어가 인칭대명사인 경우, 목적어를 부사 앞에 써야 한다.

24 민수의 친구들은 일회용의 종이컵이나 플라스틱 숟가락 대신 그들 자신의 컵과 숟가락을 사용했다.

25 ⓑ와 ⓒ: 식당에서 일하는 사람들인 they를 주어로 해서 고치는 것이 적절하다. ⓓ와 ⓔ: 집에 있는 일반 사람들인 people을 주어로 해서 고치는 것이 적절하다.

26 각각 앞 문장의 내용을 가리킨다.

🦉 서술형 시험대비　　　　p.90~91

01 green　　　02 (A) a few　(B) recycled　(C) were

03 wrapping paper, recycled　　　04 behind

05 more, more　　　06 Did you eat the plates?

07 Minji made them.

08 (1) in order to make　(2) so as to make　(3) in order that, could[might]　(4) so that, could[might]

09 (A) old cotton shirt　(B) skin

10 Why / How[What] about / Shall

11 we agreed not to wrap our gifts

12 (A) trash　(B) wrapped

01 live an eco-friendly life: 친환경적인 삶을 살다, live green: 친환경적으로 살다

02 (A) 뒤에 복수명사 'tips'가 나오므로 a few가 적절하다. a little+셀 수 없는 단수명사, (B) 몇몇 포장지가 쉽게 '재활용되지' 않기 때문이라고 해야 하므로 recycled가 적절하다. (C) 선행사(gifts such as teddy bears, key rings, and hairpins)가 복수이므로 were가 적절하다.

03 쉽게 '재활용되지' 않는 '몇몇 포장지'가 있기 때문이다.

04 leave ~ behind: ~을 뒤에 남기다, ~을 놓아 둔 채 잊고 오다

05 크기가 더 작으면 포장을 더 '많이' 사용하고 쓰레기를 더 '많이'

배출하기 때문이다.

06 You ate the plates?: '네가 접시를 먹었다고?'의 의미로, 평서문에 의문 부호를 붙이고 끝을 올려 말함으로써 상대방의 말을 되묻는 표현이 된다.

07 Minji를 주어로 해서 고치는 것이 적절하다.

08 in order to 동사형 = so as to 동사원형 = in order that 주어 can[may] = so that 주어 can[may]: ~하기 위하여(목적)

09 종이 냅킨은 '피부'에 안 좋기 때문에, 민지는 반 친구들을 위해 자신의 '낡은 면 셔츠'를 잘라 몇 개의 천 냅킨을 만들었다.

10 Let's 원형. = Why don't we 원형? = How[What] about ~ing? = Shall we 원형?: ~하는 게 어때?

11 'not'을 보충하면 된다.

12 비록 민수의 학급이 학급 생일 파티를 열었지만, 전혀 '포장되어 있지' 않은 선물을 가져왔기 때문에 '쓰레기'가 많이 나오지 않았다.

영역별 핵심문제 p.93~97

01 cultural	02 ⑤	03 ③	04 ②
05 ④	06 ②	07 ④	08 ⑤

09 What is the meaning of that? **10** ③

11 ②	12 ④	13 ②

14 (1) was given a box by the boy
 (2) were not wrapped at all

15 ④	16 ③	17 ②	18 ⑤

19 (1) I don't even know what happened to Jim.
 (2) A new smartphone was bought for Tom by his mom.
 (3) He was made to feel sick by the smell of the trash.
 (4) The dog is called Cutie by my dad.
 (5) He has little patience.
 (6) I need a few eggs to make some sandwiches.

20 ①	21 ④	22 ②, ⑤	23 ①
24 ④	25 ①, ⑤	26 ⑤	27 ①, ④

28 (1) **종이컵이나 플라스틱 숟가락을 사용하는 대신에, 자신의 컵과 숟가락을 집에서 가져온 후, 다시 가져갔다.**
 (2) **종이 냅킨 대신 천 냅킨을 사용했다.**

29 ①, ②, ④ **30** plates / plates

01 명사형에 '-al'을 붙여 형용사를 만드는 단어이다.

02 • 생일 파티를 열었지만 많은 쓰레기를 배출하지 않았다.
 • 접시에 음식을 남기지 마라. 음식물 쓰레기는 정말 큰 문제이다.

03 규모나 수에서 더 적게 만들다

04 • 나는 2주 동안 끔찍한 감기에 걸렸다. • 너의 어머니를 위한

선물을 붉은 리본으로 포장하는 것은 어때?

05 우리는 종이컵이나 플라스틱 숟가락을 사용하지 않았습니다. 대신에, 우리 컵과 숟가락을 집에서 가져온 후, 다시 가져갔습니다. take back: ~을 다시 가져가다

06 'reusable'은 '재사용할 수 있는'이다.

07 망가진 우산으로 가방을 만들었다는 말에 놀라움을 표현하는 말이 적절하다.

08 (D) 유리병이 지구에 큰 문제라는 화제를 제시하고 → (B) 무슨 의미인지 추가적인 설명을 요구하고 → (A) 추가적인 설명을 함 → (C) 마지막으로 놀라움을 표현

09 'What do you mean by that?'과 같은 의미로 사용되는 표현이다.

10 우리가 쓰레기를 너무 많이 버린다는 말에 재활용과 재사용을 더 많이 해야겠다는 말이 자연스럽다.

11 '깨끗한 교실을 위한 한 가지 비결이 뭐니?'라는 물음에 '깨끗한 쓰레기통 프로젝트'가 자연스럽다.

12 '캔이 지구에 큰 문젯거리다'는 말에 대한 추가적인 설명으로 적절한 것은 '분해되는 데 200년이 걸린다.'이다.

13 A의 마지막 말에 '그는 매우 열심히 일한다'라고 했으므로 ②가 적절하다.

14 능동태의 목적어가 주어 자리에 있으므로 수동태로 쓴다.

15 ① Each small plate has a little food on it. ② Let's read the interview and learn a few tips for living green. ③ I was made to leave the city by Jim. ⑤ My car was fixed by him last week.

16 첫 문장은 뒤에 oranges가 나오고 주스를 만들려면 오렌지가 있어야 하므로 a few, 두 번째 문장은 by로 보아 수동태로 쓰인 was broken이 적절하다.

17 These boxes will be sent to Ralph tomorrow by his brother. 상자는 보내지는 것이므로 수동태가 적절하다.

18 ⑤번은 뒤에 복수 명사가 이어지므로 a few가 적절하지만 나머지는 모두 단수 명사가 이어지므로 a little이 적절하다.

19 (1) happen은 자동사이므로 수동태로 쓰이지 않는다. (2) 직접 목적어를 주어로 한 수동태에서 buy는 간접목적어 앞에 for를 쓴다. (3) 목적격보어가 원형부정사인 경우, 수동태 문장에서는 to부정사로 바뀐다. (4) 목적어와 목적격 보어 자리에 모두 명사가 오더라도 목적어만 수동태의 주어 자리에 올 수 있다. (5), (6) a few+복수 명사: 긍정, few+복수 명사: 부정, a little+단수 명사: 긍정, little+단수 명사: 부정

20 be satisfied with: ~에 만족하다 / 나머지는 전치사 by를 쓴다.

21 몇몇 포장지가 쉽게 재활용되지 않기 때문에 전혀 포장되어 있지 않은 선물을 가져왔다는 내용의 글이므로, 제목으로는 '포장지를 사용하지 마라'가 적절하다.

22 주격 관계대명사 'that'이나 'which'가 적절하다.

23 not ~ at all = not ~ in the least: 조금도 (~ 아니다), ② 마

침내, ③ 거의 ~ 아니다, ④ 좀처럼[거의] ~ 않는, ⑤ 적어도
[최소한]

24 ④는 'ice cream and cookies'가 아니라 'popped rice cakes' 또는 'plates'를 지칭한다.

25 ② needless to say: 말할 필요도 없이 ③ on the contrary: 그와는 반대로 ④ at last: 마침내

26 준하네 반은 사용한 후에 접시를 '씻은' 것이 아니라 접시까지도 '먹었다.'

27 ⓐ와 ①, ④: 부사적 용법, ② 형용사적 용법, ③, ⑤ 명사적 용법

28 'Bring Your Own Things'와 'Use Cloth Napkins'의 내용을 쓰는 것이 적절하다.

29 ① trash: 주로 종이나 판지 등과 같은 물기 없는 쓰레기를 말한다. ② garbage: 음식물 찌꺼기나 다른 물기 있는 쓰레기를 가리키는 경향이 있다. ③ 재, ④ 영국 영어에서 더 이상 원하지 않거나 필요 없어서 버리는 쓰레기를 가리킬 때 보통 쓰이는 단어, ⑤ 재활용제품

30 우리는 '접시' 위의 음식뿐만 아니라 '접시'도 먹었다.

단원별 예상문제 · p.98~101

01 save
02 (A) wrap, recycled (B) plates
03 ④
04 ③
05 It is about 14 times as large as South Korea.
06 ④
07 ④
08 ③
09 is powered
10 ④
11 ③
12 ②
13 ①
14 (1) a few, a little (2) few (3) little
15 (1) I need a little ketchup.
 (2) I know a few students in the class.
 (3) Old books and magazines are collected in the recycling bin.
16 ②
17 ③
18 because it was not easy to wrap them → because some wrapping paper is not easily recycled 또는 to wrap them → to recycle some wrapping paper
19 ⑤
20 ④
21 (A) plates
 (B) nothing
22 ③
23 should[must] not
24 to make
25 (A) of (B) a little (C) a few

01 물을 절약하기 위해 수도꼭지를 잠가라.

02 (A) '재활용되다'는 수동태로 과거분사 recycled가 적절하다. wrap: 포장하다 (B) 복수 대명사 them을 사용하고 있기 때문에 접시는 복수 명사 plates가 적절하다.

03 식물을 잘 기른다는 표현으로 'have a green thumb'을 사용한다.

04 불만족스럽고 어려움을 야기하는 상황

05 가장 큰 쓰레기 섬은 얼마나 큰가?

06 한국이 플라스틱 제품을 가장 많이 사용한다는 내용은 언급되어 있지 않다.

07 ④는 '그것은 기진맥진하게 해!'라는 의미다.

08 '민지네 반은 티끌 하나 없어.'라는 말에 '끔찍하구나!'라는 대답은 어색하다.

09 '동력을 공급받다'는 표현은 수동태로 'be powered'를 사용한다.

10 The old lady was taken care of by one of the nurses. take care of가 하나의 단위처럼 쓰여서 'was taken care of by'의 형태로 써야 한다.

11 뒤에 셀 수 있는 명사의 복수형 blocks가 나오고 있으므로 a few가 적절하다.

12 Susan was heard to open the window by me. 목적격보어가 원형부정사인 경우, 수동태 문장에서는 to부정사로 바뀐다.

13 뒤에 are로 보아 복수 명사로 쓰인 deer이므로 단수 명사 앞에 오는 much는 들어갈 수 없다.

14 a few+복수 명사: 긍정, few+복수 명사: 부정, a little+단수 명사: 긍정, little+단수 명사: 부정

15 (1), (2) a few+복수 명사: 긍정, few+복수 명사: 부정, a little+단수 명사: 긍정, little+단수 명사: 부정 (3) 수거되는 것이므로 수동태가 적절하다. 특히 누가 그 동작을 했는지 중요하지 않거나 잘 모를 때 수동태 문장으로 표현한다.

16 a lot of = lots of = plenty of: (수와 양이) 많은, a great[good] deal of: (양이) 많은

17 ③, ④번: 현재분사(동작의 진행을 나타냄), ⓑ와 나머지: 동명사(목적이나 용도를 나타냄)

18 민수네 반은 '몇몇 포장지가 쉽게 재활용되지 않기' 때문에 전혀 포장되어 있지 않은 선물을 가져왔다.

19 ⓐ on plates: 접시에 담아, ⓑ by: [수단·방법·원인·작용·매개 따위] ~에 의해서, What do you mean by that?: 그게 무슨 뜻이죠?

20 ⓒ와 ④번: ~을 뒤에 남기다, ① 떠나다[출발하다], ② (정기 또는 특별 사유에 의한) 휴가(명사), ③ (어떤 상태, 장소 등에) 계속 있게 만들다[그대로 두다], ⑤ (관리, 처리 등을) 맡기다

21 준하네 반은 아이스크림을 나누어 줄 때 보통의 '접시' 대신에 뻥튀기를 사용했기 때문에, 먹기를 끝마쳤을 때 아무것도 남지 않았다.

22 우리는 접시까지도 모두 다 '먹었다'고 하는 것이 적절하다.

23 부정명령문은 You should[must] not을 사용하여 고치는 것이 적절하다.

24 take+시간+to부정사: ~하는 데 시간이 … 걸리다

25 (A) 오래된 양말로 손 인형을 만든 것이므로, 물리적 변화가 일어날 때 사용하는 of가 적절하다. be made of: 물리적 변화, be made from: 화학적 변화, (B) 뒤에 단수 명사가 나오므로 a little이 적절하다. (C) 뒤에 복수 명사가 나오므로 a few가 적절하다.

01 They take 450 years to break down.

02 in the middle of, a lot of plastic trash, 14 times as large as, not to use

03 (1) Is wrapping paper easily recycled (by you)?

 (2) My shoes were taken away by a dog.

 (3) I was told this story by an old lady. This story was told (to) me by an old lady.

 (4) People[They/We] use the energy tree as a street lamp.

 (5) People[They/We] made this tower out of plastic water bottles.

04 (1) How was the ice cream served?

 (2) I am called Princess by my dad.

 (3) They made few mistakes.

 (4) It took only a little time to make this.

05 pieces

06 So we brought gifts such as teddy bears, key rings, and hairpins that were not wrapped at all.

07 because some wrapping paper is not easily recycled

08 more packaging → less packaging, more trash → less trash

09 (A) how (B) nothing (C) interesting

10 (A) plates (B) ate

01 '~하는 데 시간이 … 걸리다'는 표현은 'take+시간+to부정사' 구문을 이용한다.

02 바다 한가운데 있는 쓰레기 섬에 관해 이야기하고 있다. 쓰레기 섬은 많은 플라스틱 쓰레기로 이루어져 있다. 가장 큰 섬은 남한의 약 14배 정도다. 학생들은 플라스틱 제품을 사용하지 않기로 결심한다.

03 (1) 의문문의 수동태는 능동태의 의문문을 평서문으로 바꾼 후 이것을 수동태로 고치고, 다시 의문문으로 바꾸면 쉽다. (2) away나 by를 빠뜨리면 안 되는 것에 주의한다. (3) 4형식 문장의 수동태는 간접목적어와 직접목적어 각각을 주어로 하는 수동태가 가능하며 직접목적어를 주어로 한 수동태에서 tell 동사는 간접목적어 앞에 전치사 to를 쓴다. (4), (5) 일반인이 주어인 능동태 문장의 수동태에서는 흔히 'by+목적격'이 생략된다. 특히 누가 그 동작을 했는지 중요하지 않거나 잘 모를 때, 수동태 문장으로 표현한다.

04 (1) the ice cream이 주어이므로 수동태가 적절하다. (2) My dad calls me Princess.를 수동태로 바꾼 문장이다. 목적어와 목적격 보어 자리에 모두 명사가 오더라도 목적어만 수동태의 주어 자리에 올 수 있다. (3), (4) a few+복수 명사: 긍정, few+복수 명사: 부정, a little+단수 명사: 긍정, little+단수 명사: 부정

05 dvice는 a piece of로 셀 수 있다. a few tips = a few pieces of advice

06 쓰레기가 많이 나오지 않은 비결은 '전혀 포장되어 있지 않은 곰 인형, 열쇠고리, 머리핀과 같은 선물을 가지고 온 것'을 가리킨다.

07 수동태로 쓰는 것이 적절하다.

08 크기가 더 크면 포장을 '더 적게' 사용하고 쓰레기를 '더 적게' 배출한다고 하는 것이 적절하다.

09 (A) 아이스크림은 '어떻게' 나누어 주었나요?라고 해야 하므로 how가 적절하다. (B) 뻥튀기를 접시로 사용해서, 그것들을 먹고 '아무것도 남기지 않을' 수 있었다고 해야 하므로 nothing이 적절하다. (C) 감정을 나타내는 동사는 감정을 유발할 때 현재분사를 쓰는 것이 적절하다.

10 준하네 반은 뻥튀기를 '접시'로 사용해서, 아이스크림과 함께 그것들을 '먹고' 쓰레기를 남기지 않았다.

|모범답안|

01 (1) A: Jieun has a heart of gold. B: What do you mean by that? A: She is a really kind person. B: I get it.

 (2) A: My brother is on cloud nine. B: What do you mean by that? A: He is really happy. B: I get it.

 (3) A: Junha is an early bird. B: What do you mean by that? A: He gets up early in the morning. B: I get it.

02 (1) Pyramids were built a long time ago.

 (2) The song, *Boy with Luv*, was sung by BTS.

 (3) The light was turned off by my sister.

 (4) Wine is made from grapes.

03 (A) a hand puppet (B) my old sock (C) only a little time (D) a used paper shopping bag (E) the holes

01 ⑤ 02 ② 03 ①

04 recycle, reuse 05 ③

06 ⓐ What a surprise! ⓑ What do you mean by that? 07 ④ 08 ④ 09 ⑤

10 ① 11 ③ 12 They take 4,000 years to break down. 13 makes of → is made of, a few → a little, a little → a few

14 ④ 15 ③ 16 ②

17 (1) Rain water is stored in the tanks.

 (2) A little energy is produced this way.

19 such as = like: ~와 같은

20 ⓑ와 ③, ④: 관계대명사(뒤에 불완전한 문장이 나옴), ①, ②, ⑤: 접속사(뒤에 완전한 문장이 나옴)

01 ⑤번은 napkin에 대한 영어 설명이다. wrapping paper는 'special paper that is used for wrapping presents'이다.

02 'can't see the forest for the trees'는 '전체 상황을 보지 못하다'라는 의미다.

03 제품을 포장하기 위해 사용되는 상자, 병, 플라스틱 등: packaging(포장, 포장재)

04 접두사 're-'는 'again(다시)'의 의미를 가지고 있다. 재활용하고 재사용해야 한다는 의미이다.

05 (A) 숟가락이 쌀로 만들어졌기 때문에 100% 천연제품이다. (B) 이 친환경 숟가락을 사용하여 플라스틱 쓰레기를 줄일 수 있습니다. (C) 숟가락들을 씻을 필요가 없기 때문에 물도 절약할 수 있습니다.

06 ⓐ: what을 이용하여 놀라움을 표현할 때 명사 surprise를 사용한다. ⓑ: 추가 설명을 요구하는 표현은 'What do you mean by ~?'이다.

07 민지의 교실이 spotless하다는 것은 매우 깨끗하다는 것을 의미한다.

08 플라스틱으로 만들어진 쓰레기 섬의 심각성에 대해 대화를 하고 있다. 플라스틱 제품을 사용하지 말자는 내용이 가장 자연스럽다.

09 '~의 몇 배'라는 표현은 '배수사+as+원급+as'이다. larger를 large로 고쳐야 한다.

10 중요한 사람이란 의미로 'a big fish'가 적절하다.

11 에너지 나무가 태양으로부터 에너지를 생산하고 밤에는 가로등으로 사용된다는 말에 놀라움을 나타내는 표현이 적절하다.

12 '~하는 데 … 시간이 걸리다'는 'take+시간+to부정사' 구문을 이용한다.

13 hand puppet이 만들어지는 것이므로 수동태가 적절하다. (a) few+복수 명사, (a) little+단수 명사

14 일반 사람이 주어인 능동태를 수동태로 바꿀 때 'by+일반 사람'은 생략 가능하다.

15 첫 번째 문장에서는 뒤에 food라는 단수 명사가 나오며 문맥상 긍정의 의미가 어울리므로 a little이 적절하다. 두 번째 문장에서는 음식이 제공되는 것이므로 수동태가 적절하다.

16 ②번은 과거 동사로 쓰였고 나머지는 과거분사로 수동태를 만들고 있다. solar panel: 태양 전지판

17 (1) 빗물이 저장되는 것이므로 수동태 (2) 약간의 에너지이므로 A little energy로 쓰고 생산되는 것이므로 수동태

18 (A) agree는 to부정사를 목적어로 취한다. (B) wrapping paper: 포장지, (C) 수동태로 써야 하므로 과거분사로 쓰는 것이 적절하다.

A Step Inside the Culture

시험대비 실력평가 p.112

01 ③	02 popular	03 ⑤	04 for free
05 ④	06 ②	07 character	
08 practice			

01 여러분은 자신의 느낌을 어떻게 표현하는가? 노래를 부르거나 춤을 추는가?

02 • 요즈음에는 손 글씨를 통해 감정을 표현하는 것이 인기다. <영영풀이> 대부분의 사람들이 좋아하는

03 'tale'은 '이야기'이고, '꼬리'는 'tail'이다.

04 '무료로'는 'for free'이다.

05 '누군가나 어떤 것을 그룹의 일부로 만들다'는 의미로 '포함하다'는 'include'가 적절하다.

06 '더 낮은 장소나 위치에'의 의미로 '… 아래에'라는 'below'가 적절하다.

07 '글자, 문자', '캐릭터, 역', '성격'의 의미를 가지는 단어는 character이다. • '한글은 한자보다 배우기에 훨씬 더 쉽다.' • '한국에서는, 초록색 공룡 둘리가 사랑 받는 캐릭터다.' •'관대함은 한국인의 성격의 일부이다.'

08 'practice'는 동사로 '연습하다'와 명사로 '연습'의 뜻을 갖는다. • 모든 캘리그래피 작가들은 자신의 독특한 스타일을 만들어 내기 위해 열심히 연습해야 했다. • 처음에는 손으로 글씨를 잘 쓰기가 쉽지 않지만, 연습하면 완벽해진다.

서술형 시험대비 p.113

01 (p)erformance 02 (a)utumn

03 (1) examples, below (2) difference (3) artistic touch (4) imagine, monster

04 (1) fantasy, 판타지, 환상 (2) monster, 괴물
 (3) dynasty, 왕조

05 (1) widely (2) lightning (3) to express
 (4) different, works, found

01 B의 '고마워. 너는 우쿨렐레 연주하는 것에 관심이 있니?'라는 대답으로 보아 A는 공연을 즐겼다는 말이 적절하다.

02 '여름과 겨울 사이의 계절'은 '가을(autumn)'이다.

04 (1) 당신이 상상하는 즐겁고, 신나고, 특이한 경험이 당신에게 일어나는 것 (2) 크고 무서운 상상의 동물 (3) 모두 같은 가문에 속한 한 나라의 일련의 통치자들

05 (1) '쓰이고 있다'는 동사를 수식하는 부사 'widely'가 적절하다. (2) light를 '번개' lightning으로 바꾸어 준다. (3) 진주어 역할을 하는 부정사 to express가 적절하다. (4) 동사 differ를 명사 'kind'를 수식하는 형용사 different로, many kinds of 뒤에 복수 명사 works를, find는 be동사와 함께 수동태를 만들어 과거분사 found로 쓴다.

Conversation

핵심 Check p.114~115

1 ⑤ 2 ④

교과서 대화문 익히기

Check(√) True or False p.116

1 T 2 F 3 T 4 F 5 T

교과서 확인학습 p.118~119

Get Ready 2

(1) enjoy listening, dance to / Great

(2) interested in cooking / sometimes, for

(3) Are you interested, Actually, calligraphy / Excellent

Start Off Listen & Talk A

(1) Good job, holding, How creative / in taking pictures / taking, for free / good for

(2) Good, expresses, feeling, autumn / Are, interested / taking / that

Start Off Listen & Talk B

did, awesome / made of / Are, interested in / How long, take to make / It took

Speak Up Look and talk

enjoyed, performance, a good job / interested, playing the / Can you

Speak Up Mission

interested, horror / am, I'm not, interested in, detective

Real-life Scene

practicing calligraphy / writing, looks fun / interested, calligraphy / What, think / looks like, dancing, open / got, means / did, job, try / Why not

시험대비 기본평가 p.120

01 ④　　　　02 ①　　　　03 I think you did a good job!　　04 (B) → (C) → (D) → (A)

01 한글에 관심이 있다고 대답하고 있기 때문에 한글을 배우고 싶다는 말이 자연스럽다.

02 ①의 '판소리에 관심이 있니?'라는 물음이 자연스럽다. Nancy의 마지막 말에 '판소리를 배우고 싶어.'라고 했기 때문에 ②의 물음은 자연스럽지 못하다.

03 자신의 생각을 표현하면서 상대방을 칭찬하는 말로, I think로 문장을 시작한다. '잘했다'는 표현은 'you did a good job'이다.

04 (B) 공연 즐거웠다는 말과 함께 잘했다는 칭찬을 하고 → (C) 칭찬의 말에 대해 고맙다는 답이 오고, 태권도에 관심 있는가의 물음에 → (D) 긍정의 답을 하고, 가르쳐 줄 수 있는지 묻고 → (A) 마지막으로 가르쳐 주겠다는 답이 오면 된다.

시험대비 실력평가 p.121~122

01 ③　　　　02 ⑤

03 Are you interested in riding a bike?

04 ②　　　05 ④　　　06 awesome　07 ④

08 ④　　　09 ③　　　10 ①　　　11 ①

12 ②　　　13 ②

01 '…에 맞춰 춤추다'는 'dance to'를 사용한다.

02 나머지는 모두 상대방을 칭찬하는 말이고, ⑤는 '나도 K-pop에 빠져 있어.'라는 뜻이다.

03 관심을 묻는 표현은 'be interested in'을 이용하고, in은 전치사이기 때문에 뒤에 riding(동명사)을 사용해야 한다.

04 B가 G의 작품을 보고 '유리로 만들었니?'라고 묻는 말에 G가 B에게 '유리 공예에 관심이 있니?'라고 묻는 말이 자연스럽다.

05 G의 마지막 말에 '한 달 걸렸어.'라고 했기 때문에 (B)에는 얼마나 걸렸는지 기간을 묻는 말이 적절하다.

06 '대단한 존경심과 걱정, 두려움을 느낄 정도로 매우 인상적이거나 심각하거나 어려운', '매우 좋은, 훌륭한'의 의미를 가지는 단어는 awesome이다.

07 캘리그래피를 쓰기 시작하는 것이 쉬운지는 언급되어 있지 않다.

08 '…처럼 보이다'는 표현은 'look+형용사'나 'look like+명사'를 사용한다. look 뒤에 명사 'a person'이 있으므로 전치사 like가 필요하다.

09 G의 대답이 Yes, I am.이기 때문에 Be동사 의문문으로 시작하고 그림에 관심이 있는지 묻는 의문문이 적절하다.

10 빈칸 다음에 B가 '그렇다면 무엇에 관심이 있니?'라고 묻고 있으므로 G는 한복에 관심이 없다는 것을 알 수 있다.

11 ①: '사진을 찍는 데 관심이 있니?'라는 말에 '잘했어'라고 답하는 것은 어색하다.

12 '동물에 관심이 있니?'라는 물음에 Yes로 답하고 있기 때문에 빈칸에는 '동물을 돌보는 것을 잘해.'라는 말이 적절하다.

13 주어진 문장은 '식물은 어때?'라는 뜻으로 '식물에도 관심이 있니?'라고 묻는 말의 앞인 ②가 적절하다.

서술형 시험대비 p.123

01 Are you interested in calligraphy?

02 This Korean word means "dance."

03 What do you think?

04 (A) interested in taking selfies

　　(B) I'm interested in cooking.

05 How long did it take to make it?

01 상대방이 관심이 있는지 묻는 표현은 'be interested in'을 이용하여 의문문을 만든다.

03 What do you think?가 '어떻게 생각해?'라는 표현이다.

04 B가 'No, I'm not.'으로 답한 것으로 보아 주어진 그림에서 take selfies는 관심이 없기 때문에 (A)는 셀피 찍는 데 관심이 있는지 묻는 것이 적절하다. (B)는 요리에 관심이 있기 때문에 I am interested in cooking.이 오는 것이 자연스럽다.

05 시간을 묻는 표현은 'How long ~?'으로 문장을 시작하고, '시간이 걸리다'라는 동사는 'take'를 사용한다. 그리고 비인칭 주어 it과 glass art를 가리키는 대명사 it을 사용한다.

교과서

Grammar

핵심 Check p.124~125

1 (1) learning　(2) ringing

2 (1) is it important to　(2) It, to learn

01 ③

02 (1) kick → kicking (2) the playing the piano man
→ the man playing the piano
(3) stars shining → shining stars
(4) live → to live (5) That → It (6) to not → not to

03 (1) The girls singing on the street are my students.
(2) It is a good idea to provide various programs.
(3) Look at the sleeping baby.

01 it을 가주어로 하고 to부정사를 진주어로 이용할 수 있는 ③번이 적절하다.

02 (1) 현재분사가 뒤에서 the boy를 수식하도록 하는 것이 적절하다. (2) 현재분사가 목적어나 어구를 수반할 때에는 명사 뒤에 와서 앞의 명사를 수식한다. (3) 현재분사가 단독으로 쓰일 때는 명사 앞에 와서 명사를 수식한다. (4) 진주어로 to부정사가 적절하다. (5) 가주어로는 That이 아니라 It을 쓴다. (6) to부정사의 부정은 to부정사 앞에 not[never]을 써서 'not[never]+to V'로 나타낸다.

03 (1) '거리에서 노래를 부르고 있는'이 '소녀들'을 수식하도록 현재분사의 후치 수식을 이용한다. (2) 가주어 it을 추가하여 to부정사를 진주어로 하여 영작한다. (3) '자고 있는'이 '아기'를 수식하도록 현재분사를 이용한다. 목적어나 다른 어구를 수반하고 있지 않으므로 명사 앞에 와서 명사를 수식하도록 한다.

01 ④ **02** ③ **03** ② **04** ①

05 ⑤ **06** (1) carrying (2) written (3) sleeping cat (4) to listen (5) It **07** ④ **08** ②

09 ③ **10** It is important to learn a foreign language. **11** ⑤ **12** ① **13** ①

14 (1) For me to do this work would be really stupid.
또는 It would be really stupid for me to do this work.
(2) It is easy to solve the puzzle.
(3) It was amazing to see such an old house there.
(4) There was a girl eating ice cream.
(5) A boy carrying a box got on the bus.
(6) Last week I read *Harry Potter* written by JK Rowling.

15 (1) beginning (2) dancing (3) frightened
(4) taken **16** ④ **17** ③ **18** ②, ⑤

01 The baby sleeping in the bed is really cute. 현재분사가 목적어나 부사구를 수반할 때에는 명사 뒤에 와서 앞의 명사를 수식한다.

02 ① It is common knowledge that swimming is a good exercise. ② It's kind of you to ask me some questions. ④ It's good to own your own business. ⑤ It's necessary to say no.

03 현재분사가 뒤에서 앞의 명사를 수식하도록 한다. It이 나와 있으므로 It을 가주어로 하고 빈칸에는 진주어로 이용할 수 있는 to부정사가 적절하다.

04 가주어로 It이 적절하다.

05 ⑤번은 동명사이고 나머지는 다 현재분사이다.

06 (1) 현재분사가 뒤에서 앞의 명사를 수식하도록 한다. (2) e-mail이 쓰여지는 것이므로 과거분사가 적절하다. (3) 현재분사가 단독으로 쓰일 때는 명사 앞에 와서 명사를 수식한다. (4) 진주어로 to부정사가 적절하다. (5) 가주어로 It이 적절하다.

07 ① The person running fastest in our class is Angie. ② Look at the men singing pansori. ③ His dream is helping[to help] the poor. ⑤ The boy is washing the dog.

08 ②번은 비인칭 주어(날씨)이지만 나머지는 모두 가주어로 쓰인 It이다.

09 현재분사가 뒤에서 명사를 수식하는 경우, 명사와 현재분사 사이에 '관계대명사+be동사'가 생략되어 있다고 볼 수 있다.

10 '외국어를 배우는 것(to learn a foreign language)'을 진주어로 하고 가주어 It을 이용하여 'It ~ to …' 형식으로 쓴다.

11 두 문장을 관계대명사로 한 문장으로 만든 후 '주격 관계대명사+be동사'를 생략하면 ⑤번과 같은 문장이 된다.

12 가주어로 it을 쓰고 진주어로 to부정사를 쓰는 것이 적절하다.

13 ① 축구를 하는 것이므로 '수동, 완료'의 의미로 쓰이는 과거분사가 아니라 '능동, 진행'을 나타내는 현재분사를 쓰는 것이 적절하다.

14 (1) For me가 의미상의 주어로 나와 있으므로 to do가 주어가 되도록 하거나 가주어 it을 사용하고 진주어로 to do를 쓴다. (2) 가주어로는 that이 아니라 it을 쓴다. (3) 진주어로 to부정사를 쓴다. (4) 분사가 목적어나 부사를 수반할 때에는 명사 뒤에 와서 앞의 명사를 수식한다. (5) 박스를 나르는 것이므로 현재분사가 적절하다. (6) *Harry Potter*라는 책이 JK Rowling에 의해 쓰여진 것이므로 과거분사가 적절하다.

15 (1), (2) 분사가 목적어나 부사구를 수반할 때에는 명사 뒤에 와서 앞의 명사를 수식한다. (3) 뉴스에 놀라는 것이므로 과거분사가 적절하다. (4) 사진이 찍히는 것이므로 과거분사가 적절하다.

16 '태권도를 배우고 있는 여자아이'이므로 현재분사를 이용하여 뒤에서 명사를 수식하도록 해야 한다.

17 '가주어(It) ~ 진주어(to부정사: to eat fast food often) …' 구문으로 쓰는 것이 적절하다.

18 ② 문장에 쓰인 형용사가 사람의 성향, 성격을 나타내는 말일 때는 to부정사의 의미상의 주어로 'of+목적격'을 쓴다. ⑤ 현재분사가 목적어나 어구를 수반할 때에는 명사 뒤에 와서 앞의 명사를 수식한다.

01 (1) Jack gave his wife a necklace made of pearls.

 (2) Who is the man cutting the beef sandwiches with a knife?

 (3) It is awesome to find a good book.

 (4) It is easy to start writing calligraphy.

 (5) Is it dangerous to look at the sun directly?

02 • (1) To kick a jegi is interesting.

 (2) It is interesting to kick a *jegi*.

 • (1) To do paragliding looks dangerous.

 (2) It looks dangerous to do paragliding.

03 (1) enjoying, It, to do (2) playing, It, to play

04 (1) The business woman running a big company is Sophie.

 (2) The bridge built long time ago is a connection to the past.

05 (1) It is silly to meet trouble halfway.

 (2) It was great to get your e-mail this morning.

 (3) It is safe to wear a helmet while riding a bike.

 (4) It was difficult for the police to calm down the angry crowd.

 (5) It is quite true that blood is thicker than water.

06 (1) The two girls wearing *hanbok* are my friends.

 (2) The man had the roof of his house painted blue.

 (3) It is interesting to talk about the past.

 (4) It's lucky for you to have a kind neighbor.

07 (1) sending → sent (2) played → playing

 (3) two laughing out loud people → two people laughing out loud

 (4) Buy → To buy[Buying], 또는 전체 문장 → It is not so hard to buy a ticket at the subway station.

 (5) This → It

 (6) for her eats → for her to eat

08 (1) for me to write letters in English

 (2) for her to watch the horror movie

01 (1) 목걸이가 진주로 만들어진 것이므로 과거분사로 쓴다. (2) 칼로 샌드위치를 자르는 것이므로 현재분사로 쓴다. (3)~(5) '가주어(It) ~ 진주어(to부정사) …' 구문을 이용한다.

02 to부정사가 문장의 주어로 쓰일 때 주어 자리에 가주어 it을 두고 to부정사 부분(진주어)을 문장 뒤로 보낸다.

03 현재분사의 '후치 수식'을 이용하고 '가주어(It) ~ 진주어(to부정사) …' 구문을 이용하여 쓴다.

04 분사가 목적어나 부사구를 수반할 때에는 명사 뒤에 와서 앞의 명사를 수식한다. 이때 명사와 분사 사이에 '관계대명사+be동사'가 생략되어 있다고 볼 수 있다.

05 (1) (1) 문장의 주어로 쓰인 to부정사를 뒤로 보내고 대신 주어 자리에 가주어 it을 쓴다. (5) 주어로 쓰인 that절의 경우에도 긴 that절을 뒤로 보내고 주어 자리에 가주어 it을 쓴다. (4)번의 경우 For the police는 to부정사의 의미상의 주어이다.

06 (1) 분사의 '후치 수식'을 이용한다. (2) 파랗게 칠해지는 것이므로 과거분사를 쓴다. (3), (4) '가주어(it) ~ 진주어(to부정사) …' 구문을 이용한다. (4) 당신이 운이 좋은 것이므로 의미상의 주어 for you를 써 주어야 한다.

07 (1) email이 보내지는 것이므로 과거분사가 적절하다. (2) 소년들이 축구를 하는 것이므로 현재분사가 적절하다. (3) 분사가 목적어나 부사구를 수반할 때에는 명사 뒤에 와서 앞의 명사를 수식한다. (4) to부정사나 동명사를 주어로 하거나 전체 문장을 '가주어(it) ~ 진주어(to부정사) …' 구문으로 고쳐 쓴다. (5) 가주어로 it을 쓰는 것이 적절하다. (6) for her가 to eat의 의미상의 주어가 되도록 고쳐야 한다.

08 (1) '영어로 편지를 쓰는 데 어려움이 있다'는 것을 '영어로 편지를 쓰는 것은 어렵다'는 문장으로, (2) Watching을 to watch로 바꾸고 for her를 to watch의 의미상의 주어로 하는 '가주어(it) ~ 진주어(to부정사) …' 구문을 이용하여 쓴다.

교과서
Reading

확인문제 p.132

1 T 2 F 3 F 4 T

확인문제 p.133

1 T 2 F 3 T 4 F 5 T 6 F

교과서 확인학습 A p.134~135

01 Write 02 How, feelings

03 sing, dance 04 draw a picture

05 Nowadays, through handwriting

06 works of art

07 includes an image 08 a season of fruit

09 Korean word, Chinese character

10 looks like, walking

11 express the feeling, through 12 calligraphy

13 not new 14 can be found

15 from, below 16 tell the difference

17 was created by 18 were painted with

19 in the late 1400s 20 was written with

21 Different writing tools, different styles

22 practice hard, unique styles 23 is widely used

24 designers' artistic touches

25 are some examples 26 the title

27 How 28 sharp teeth, ugly

29 How about

30 lightning, wizard hats 31 Anyone, writing

32 by hand, practice makes perfect

33 Keep trying, part, everyday 34 with your feelings

35 build up

1 Write Your Feelings

2 How do you express your feelings?

3 Do you sing or dance?

4 Do you write a poem or draw a picture?

5 Nowadays, it is popular to express feelings through handwriting.

6 Let's look at some works of art.

7 In the work of art on the right, the word includes an image of a delicious fruit, *hongsi*.

8 It shows that autumn is a season of fruit.

9 The work of art on the left shows a Korean word and a Chinese character.

10 It looks like a happy woman walking down a road with autumn leaves.

11 Both of these works express the feeling of autumn through beautiful handwriting.

12 This kind of art is called calligraphy.

13 Calligraphy is not new.

14 Many different kinds of calligraphy works from long ago can be found all around the world.

15 Look at the two examples from Korea and the UK below.

16 Can you tell the difference?

17 The left one was created by Chusa in the period of the Joseon Dynasty.

18 The characters were painted with a soft brush.

19 The right one, *The Canterbury Tales*, was created by Chaucer in England in the late 1400s.

20 It was written with a pen.

21 Different writing tools led to different styles of calligraphy.

22 Of course, all calligraphers had to practice hard to make their unique styles.

23 Today calligraphy is widely used around us.

24 You can find designers' artistic touches on movie posters, book covers, music CDs, and clothes.

25 Below are some examples.

26 Look at the title on the movie poster.

27 How do you feel?

28 Can you imagine the monster's big mouth, sharp teeth, and ugly, long tail?

29 How about the title on the fantasy novel?

30 Do you see Harry's lightning and the wizard hats?

31 Anyone can start writing calligraphy.

32 It's not easy to write by hand well at first, but practice makes perfect.

33 Keep trying and make it part of your everyday life.

34 Write with your feelings on birthday cards, bookmarks, or gifts.

35 Soon you will build up your own world of calligraphy.

01 ② 02 ②, ④ 03 ④ 04 ①

05 some examples are → are some examples

06 ②, ⑤ 07 ②

08 interesting → interested

09 (A) Chusa (B) Joseon Dynasty (C) soft brush

10 Different writing tools led to different styles of calligraphy. 11 ③ 12 ②, ⑤

13 writing calligraphy 또는 calligraphy

14 with your feelings 15 before / Before

16 We use *yuts* and *mals*.

17 (A) board (B) to play (C) interested

18 ③ 19 a soft brush, a pen 20 ③

21 ⑤ 22 ② 23 looks → looks like

24 ① 25 ②, ⑤ / ①, ③, ④

01 단어가 홍시의 '이미지'를 포함하고 있다고 하는 것이 적절하다. ① 현장, 장면, ③ 상상력, 상상, ④ 수치, 인물, 사람, 모습, ⑤ 경치

02 ⓑ와 ①, ③, ⑤: 앞의 명사를 뒤에서 수식하는 현재분사의 후치 수식, ②, ④: 동명사

03 ④ '그림'이 아니라 아름다운 '손 글씨'를 통해 가을의 느낌을 표현하고 있다.

04 ⓐ와 ①: (명사) 손길, 솜씨, (마무리) 손질, ② 마음을 움직이다, 감동시키다, ③ (명사) 만지기, 건드리기, ④ ~에 (손·손가락 등으로) 대다, 건드리다, ⑤ (음식물 따위에) 손을 대다, 먹다, 마시다

05 부사 'below'가 맨 앞에 왔기 때문에 '부사+동사(+대명사가 아닌) 주어'의 어순으로 도치시키는 것이 적절하다.

06 ②와 ⑤는 '영화 포스터의 제목'이 아니라 '공상 소설의 제목'에서 볼 수 있다.

07 ② 위 글은 '홍보 전단'이다. PR: 홍보(public relations), leaflet: (광고나 선전용) 전단, ① 요약, 개요, ③ (책·연극·영

화 등에 대한) 논평[비평], 감상문, ④ (신문·잡지의) 글, 기사, ⑤ 수필

08 사람의 감정을 나타내므로 과거분사로 고치는 것이 적절하다.

09 그것은 오래전의 캘리그래피 작품들의 한 예이다. 그것은 '조선 왕조' 시대에 '추사'가 '부드러운 붓'으로 그 글자들을 그려서 창작하였다.

10 lead to: ~로 이끌다, ~로 이어지다

11 '줄거리'는 알 수 없다. ① Chaucer, ② 영국, ④ 1400년대 후반, ⑤ 펜

12 ② That이 아니라 가주어 It을 쓰는 것이 적절하다. ⑤ by hand: (기계가 아닌) 사람 손으로, by the hand: 손을 잡고

13 '캘리그래피를 쓰는 것' 또는 '캘리그래피'를 가리킨다.

14 전치사 'with'를 사용하는 것이 적절하다.

15 Soon = It will not be long before = Before long: 곧

16 우리는 윷놀이를 하기 위해 '윷'과 '말'을 사용한다.

17 (A) 전통적인 '말판' 놀이라고 해야 하므로 board가 적절하다. board: 널빤지, (게임) 판, broad: 넓은, (B) 그것을 '하기 위해'라고 해야 하므로 to부정사의 부사적 용법(목적)을 나타내는 to play가 적절하다. (C) 감정을 나타내는 동사는 수식받는 명사가 감정을 느끼게 되는 경우에 과거분사를 써야 하므로 interested가 적절하다.

18 주어진 문장의 the difference에 주목한다. ③번 다음부터 '차이'가 설명되기 시작하므로 ③번이 적절하다.

19 '부드러운 붓'과 '펜'을 가리킨다.

20 이 글은 캘리그래피는 새로운 것이 아니고 오래전의 다양한 종류의 많은 캘리그래피 작품들이 세계 곳곳에서 발견되고 있다는 것을 다루고 있는 글이다.

21 (A) on the right[left]: 오른[왼]쪽의, (B) through: [수단·매체] ~을 통하여

22 ⓐ와 ③, ⑤번: 가주어, ① 그것(앞에 이미 언급되었거나 현재 이야기되고 있는 사물·동물을 가리킴), ② 가목적어, ④ 비인칭 주어(거리)

23 look+형용사: ~하게 보이다, look like+명사: ~처럼 보이다

24 이 글은 한국 문화 체험을 '홍보하는' 글이다. ① promote: 홍보하다, ② 비교하다, ③ (설문) 조사하다, ④ 알리다, 발표하다, ⑤ 연락을 주고받다, 의사소통을 하다

25 ⓐ와 ②, ⑤: 현재분사, ⓑ와 ①, ③, ④: 동명사

서술형 시험대비
p.142~143

01 (1) 노래를 부른다. (2) 춤을 춘다. (3) 시를 쓴다.
　 (4) 그림을 그린다. (5) 손 글씨를 통해 감정을 표현한다.

02 It looks like a happy woman walking down a road with autumn leaves.

03 (A) handwriting (B) calligraphy

04 be found

05 (1) Chusa's work (2) brush
　 (3) *The Canterbury Tales* (4) pen

06 fourteen hundreds

07 They had to practice hard.

08 artistic touches

09 (A) movie poster (B) fantasy novel

10 (A) How (B) includes (C) handwriting

11 (A) fruit (B) autumn (C) happy

12 We call this kind of art calligraphy.

01 첫 단락의 내용을 쓰는 것이 적절하다.

02 look like: ~처럼 보이다, 현재분사 walking이 이끄는 어구 전체가 뒤에서 앞의 명사 woman을 수식하는 것이 적절하다.

03 요즈음에는 '손 글씨'를 통해 감정을 표현하는 것이 인기이고, 이런 종류의 예술을 '캘리그래피'라고 부른다.

04 조동사가 포함된 수동태는 '조동사+be동사의 원형+과거분사'이다.

05 (1) 추사의 작품, (2) 붓, (3) 캔터베리 이야기, (4) 펜

06 1400s: 1400년대

07 모든 캘리그래피 작가들은 자신의 독특한 스타일을 만들어 내기 위해 열심히 연습해야 했다.

08 캘리그래피를 사용한 영화 포스터, 책 표지, 음악 CD, 그리고 의류들의 몇 가지 예들이고, 여러분은 그것들에서 디자이너들의 '예술적인 손길'을 발견할 수 있다.

09 캘리그래피 제목을 포함하고 있는 두 가지 상업적인 제품이 있다. 하나는 '영화 포스터'의 제목이고 다른 하나는 '공상 소설'의 제목이다.

10 (A) 느낌을 '어떻게' 표현하는가라고 해야 하므로 How가 적절하다. (B) 홍시의 이미지를 '포함하고 있다'고 해야 하므로 includes가 적절하다. exclude: 제외[배제]하다, (C) 아름다운 '손 글씨'를 통해 가을의 느낌을 표현한다고 해야 하므로 handwriting이 적절하다. drawing: 그림, 소묘, 데생

12 We나 They 등 일반인을 주어로 하여 능동태로 고치는 것이 적절하다.

영역별 핵심문제
p.145~149

01 (e)xcellent　　　02 ③　　　03 ⑤
04 ②　　05 ④　　06 ③
07 Look at the two men learning *pansori*. 08 ④
09 Do you have an interest in learning *Hangeul*?
10 ⑤　　11 ②　　12 ③　　13 ①
14 ⑤　　15 ③　　16 ④　　17 ④
18 ⑤
19 (1) Kate climbed the mountain covered with snow.
　 (2) When are you going to fix the broken window?
　 (3) Mariko looked at her daughter playing in the park.
　 (4) It is dangerous to ride a bike without a helmet.
　 (5) It was very wise of Laura to learn how to speak Chinese.

20 calligraphy 21 traditional culture → feeling 22 ①, ⑤ 23 ④ 24 ③
25 ② 26 ② 27 ③
28 (A) Anyone (B) by hand (C) Soon
29 Keep trying and make it part of your everyday life.

01 반의어 관계다. 포함하다 : 제외하다 = 형편없는 : 훌륭한
02 • 그림을 잘 그리기 위해서는 예술적 기교가 필요하다. • 가을이 오면, 나뭇잎들은 색이 변한다. • 그 여행은 루브르 박물관 방문을 포함했다.
03 다른 어떤 것 또는 누구와도 같지 않은
04 • 외국어를 배우는 것은 쉽지 않다. • 이 편지에 쓰여 있는 그의 필체(손 글씨)를 알아볼 수 없다.
05 ⓐ는 마트료시카 인형은 그것을 열면, 더 작은 인형들이 계속해서 나온다는 의미가 적절하므로 'keep -ing'가 오고, ⓑ는 각각의 인형 안에 더 작은 인형이 있기 때문에 inside가 적절하다.
06 'sharp'는 '날카로운'의 뜻이다.
07 '~을 봐'라는 명령문으로 동사원형으로 문장을 시작한다. 그리고 현재분사구인 learning pansori가 명사 men을 뒤에서 수식하는 구조다.
08 (D) 공연을 즐겼다는 말과 함께 상대방을 칭찬하고 → (A) 칭찬에 대해 감사의 답을 하고, 탈춤에 관심이 있는지 묻는다 → (B) 긍정의 답과 함께 가르쳐 줄 수 있는지 묻고 → 마지막으로 (C)의 승낙의 답이 오는 것이 자연스럽다.
09 일반동사 have를 이용한 의문문 'Do you have ~?'로 문장을 시작한다. 'an interest'는 명사로 have의 목적어 역할을 한다.
10 '이것이 나의 작품이야.'라고 한 말에 대해 칭찬하는 말이 오는 것이 자연스럽다.
11 쇼핑을 가는 데 관심이 있냐는 말에 부정의 답을 하고 있으므로 빈칸에는 관심 있는 다른 것을 언급하는 것이 자연스럽다.
12 예술 전시회에서 물을 수 있는 질문으로 ③이 가장 적절하다.
13 it을 가주어로 하고 의미상의 주어로 for students가 있으므로 to부정사를 진주어로 쓰는 것이 적절하다.
14 ⑤번은 동명사이지만 나머지는 모두 현재분사이다.
15 ③에는 사람의 성격이나 성질을 나타내는 형용사(foolish)가 왔으므로 의미상의 주어 앞에 of가 들어가야 한다. 나머지는 모두 for가 들어간다.
16 ④번은 인칭대명사로 쓰인 It이지만 나머지는 모두 가주어 It이다. 인칭대명사는 '그것'이라고 해석하지만 가주어는 해석하지 않는다.
17 in this town이라는 부사구를 수반하고 있으므로 현재분사가 뒤에서 앞의 명사 Everyone을 수식하도록 한다.
18 for me라는 의미상의 주어가 나왔으므로 to부정사를 진주어로 쓰는 것이 적절하다.
19 (1) 눈으로 덮인 것이므로 과거분사를 쓴다. (2) 창문이 깨진 것이므로 과거분사를 쓴다. (3) 놀고 있는 것이므로 현재분사를 쓴다. (4) to가 있으므로 '가주어(It) ~ 진주어(to부정사) …' 구문

을 이용하여 영작한다. (5) wise라는 사람의 성질을 나타내는 형용사가 나왔으므로 의미상의 주어로 'of+목적격'을 써야 한다.
20 calligraphy: 캘리그래피, 서도, 서예, 붓이나 특별한 펜을 사용하여 아름다운 손 글씨를 만드는 예술
21 본문에서 언급된 두 예술 작품은 아름다운 손 글씨를 통해 가을의 '전통 문화'가 아니라 '느낌'을 표현한다.
22 ⓐ와 ①, ⑤: 명사적 용법, ②: 형용사적 용법, ③, ④부사적 용법
23 부드러운 붓과 펜이라는 '각기 다른 필기구'가 각기 다른 캘리그래피의 스타일을 이끌었다고 하는 것이 적절하다. ① subject: (그림·사진 등의) 대상[소재]
24 tell the difference = distinguish: (차이를) 분간하다, 구별하다 ① 다르다, ② (~해야 한다고) 고집하다[주장하다], ④ (크기·모양 등에서) 서로[각기] 다르다, ⑤ (~하도록) 설득하다
25 왼쪽 작품은 '1400년대 후반'이 아니라 '조선 왕조 시대'에 창작되었다. 참고로 추사(秋史) 김정희(金正喜, 1786~1856)는 조선 후기의 문인이자 추사체를 만들어낸 명필가이며 실학자이다.
26 주어진 문장의 some examples에 주목한다. ②번 앞 문장의 예들에 해당하므로 ②번이 적절하다.
27 ③ 디자이너들이 캘리그래피 제목에 예술적인 손길을 어떻게 더하는지는 대답할 수 없다. ① Yes. ② It is used in movie posters, book covers, music CDs, and clothes. ④ We can imagine the monster's big mouth, sharp teeth, and ugly, long tail. ⑤ We see Harry's lightning and the wizard hats.
28 (A) '누구든지'라고 해야 하므로 Anyone이 적절하다. 긍정문의 any: 어떤 ~이라도, (B) '손으로' 글씨를 잘 쓰는 것이라고 해야 하므로 by hand가 적절하다. by hand: (기계가 아닌) 사람 손으로, on a keyboard: 키보드로, (C) '곧'이라고 해야 하므로 Soon이 적절하다. before long = soon: 곧, long before: 훨씬 이전에, 오래 전에
29 'everyday'를 보충하면 된다.

단원별 예상문제 p.150~153

01 tools 02 (A) period (B) title 03 ④
04 ③ 05 She is practicing calligraphy.
06 ⑤ 07 ④ 08 ② 09 ④
10 ③ 11 ③ 12 ③ 13 ④
14 It is important to stay healthy. 15 ②
16 ④ 17 ① 18 one
19 dynasty 20 ⑤ 21 ③
22 (A) artistic (B) tail (C) lightning
23 (1) Harry의 번개 (2) 마술사 모자 24 ②
25 easy → not easy 또는 difficult

01 망치와 톱은 목수의 도구이다. hammers and saws가 복수 명사이기 때문에 복수형 tools가 적절하다.
02 (A) period: 시대 (B) title: 제목

03 B의 마지막 질문 'How long did it take to make it?'은 '그 거 만드는 데 시간이 얼마나 걸렸니?'라는 뜻이므로 빈칸에는 걸 린 시간이 오는 것이 자연스럽다.

04 상상의 사건이나 사람에 관한 이야기

05 미나는 캘리그래피를 연습하고 있다.

06 위 대화는 캘리그래피 작품에 대해 이야기하면서 James가 미 나의 작품을 칭찬하고 자신도 한 번 해볼 수 있는지 묻고 미나가 한 번 그려 보라고 하는 내용으로 ⑤의 '캘리그래피와 함께 즐겁 게'가 적절하다.

07 미나의 작품은 두 팔을 벌리고 춤을 추는 사람처럼 보인다고 했 으므로 실제로 춤추는 사람을 그린 것은 아니다.

08 B의 대답이 '그것이 먹고 싶어.'라고 했으므로 ②가 적절하다.

09 ④는 '무엇에 관심이 있니?'라는 의미로 'Yes / No'로 답할 수 없는 의문문이다.

10 ③번 A가 '책을 읽는 것을 좋아하니?'라는 말에 '응, 그래. 책을 읽는 것은 지겨워!'라는 대답은 어색하다.

11 ⓐ It is fun to read books. ⓒ This calligraphy shows a tree growing in a pot. ⓔ Who was the man playing the piano on the stage? ⓗ It is a lot of fun to dance talchum.

12 ③번은 동명사이고 나머지는 모두 현재분사이다.

13 ① It is important to keep your teeth clean. ② It was boring to wait for her. ③ It was impossible to estimate the flood damage this year. ⑤ It is nice of you to help that old man.

14 '가주어(It) ~ 진주어(to부정사) …' 구문을 이용한다.

15 주어진 문장의 It에 주목한다. ②번 앞 문장의 the word를 받고 있으므로 ②번이 적절하다.

16 ⓐ와 ④: 문자, ① 성격, 기질, ② 특징, ③ (책·영화 등의) 등장 인물, ⑤ 인격

17 느낌을 표현하는 가장 좋은 방법이 무엇인지는 대답할 수 없다. ② It includes an image of a delicious fruit, hongsi. ③ It shows a Korean word and a Chinese character. ④ It looks like a happy woman walking down a road with autumn leaves. ⑤ It is called calligraphy.

18 one은 앞에 이미 언급했거나 상대방이 알고 있는 사람이나 사물 을 가리킬 때 명사의 반복을 피하기 위해 씀.

19 dynasty: 왕조, (동일 가문이 다스리는) 시대, 동일 가문에 속 하는 한 나라의 일련의 통치자들

20 '시를 인용한 이유'는 알 수 없다. 참고: 추사 김정희의 묵란도 '山上蘭花'는 추사가 난을 치고 화제(畵題)로 중국 청나라 판 교(板橋) 정섭(鄭燮)의 시를 쓴 작품이다. ① 추사, ② 한국, ③ 조선 왕조 시대, ④ 부드러운 붓

21 우리 주변에서 널리 쓰이고 있는 캘리그래피의 예들에 관한 글 이므로, 제목으로는 ③번이 적절하다.

22 (A) 디자이너들의 '예술적인' 손길이라고 해야 하므로 artistic 이 적절하다. artistic: 예술의, awkward: 어색한, (B) 괴물의 긴 '꼬리'라고 해야 하므로 tail이 적절하다. tale: 이야기, 소설, (C) Harry의 '번개'라고 해야 하므로 lightning이 적절하다.

lightening: lighten(가볍게 해주다[덜어 주다])의 현재분사 [동명사] 형태

23 공상 소설의 제목에서 'Harry의 번개'와 '마술사 모자'를 볼 수 있다.

24 처음부터 손으로 글씨를 잘 쓰기는 쉽지 않지만, '연습하면 완벽 해진다'고 하는 것이 적절하다. ① 신중하게 행동하라.(돌다리도 두드려 보고 건너라.) ③ 두 사람의 지혜는 한 사람의 지혜보다 낫다.(백지장도 맞들면 낫다.) ④ 해가 있을 때 건초를 만들어 라.(기회를 놓치지 마라.) ⑤ 서두르면 일을 그르친다.

25 처음부터 손으로 글씨를 잘 쓰기는 '쉽지 않다'고 해야 하므로 not easy 또는 difficult로 고치는 것이 적절하다.

서술형 실전문제
p.154~155

01 Are you interested in taking pictures?
02 How long did it take to make it?
03 calligraphy, practicing, brush, dance, good, writing
04 (1) for Dick to be sent to hospital because of his illness
 (2) for her to eat lots of vegetables
05 She bought a smartphone made in Korea.
06 it is popular to express feelings through handwriting.
07 (A) feeling (B) Korean word
 (C) Chinese character
08 (A) handwriting (B) feelings
09 (A) new (B) hard (C) unique
10 Chusa created the left one in the period of the Joseon Dynasty.
11 (A) Chaucer (B) a pen

01 'be interested in'을 사용하고, 전치사 in 뒤에 동사 'take'를 동명사 'taking'으로 바꾸어 쓴다.

02 '~하는 데 시간이 걸리다'라는 표현은 'take+시간+to부정사' 구 문을 이용한다.

03 미나와 James는 미나의 캘리그래피 작품에 대해 이야기 중이 다. 미나는 붓으로 캘리그래피를 연습하고 있다. 그녀는 "춤"을 의미하는 한국어를 쓰고 있다. James는 미나가 잘 했다고 생각 한다. 그는 캘리그래피를 써보려고 한다.

04 '~해야 한다'는 의미를 가주어 it을 이용하여 '~할 필요가 있다' 라고 쓰려면 진주어로 to부정사를 이용한다. 이때 의미상의 주 어를 빠뜨리지 않도록 주의한다.

05 분사가 명사 뒤에서 명사를 꾸며줄 때, 분사 앞에는 '주격 관계 대명사+be동사'가 생략되었다고 볼 수 있다.

06 to부정사가 진주어 역할을 하도록 영작하는 것이 적절하다.

07 그것은 가을의 '느낌'을 표현하는 캘리그래피이고, '한글 단어'와 '한자'를 보여 주고 있다. 그것은 단풍잎이 깔린 길을 따라 걷고 있는 행복한 여인처럼 보인다.

08 캘리그래피는 '감정'을 표현할 수 있는 '손 글씨'이다.

09 (A) 오래 전의 다양한 종류의 많은 캘리그래피 작품들이 세계 곳곳에서 발견되고 있다고 했으므로 캘리그래피는 '새로운' 것이 아니라고 하는 것이 적절하다. (B) '열심히' 연습해야 했다고 해야 하므로 hard가 적절하다. hardly: 거의 ~ 아니다, (C) 자신의 '독특한' 스타일을 만들어 내기 위해라고 해야 하므로 unique가 적절하다. common: 흔한, 공통의, 보통의

10 Chusa를 주어로 해서 고치는 것이 적절하다.

11 1400년대 후반 영국에서 'Chaucer'가 그것을 창작했다. Chaucer는 '펜'으로 그것을 썼다.

창의사고력 서술형 문제
p.156

|모범답안|

01 (1) A: Are you interested in going shopping?
　　B: Yes, I am. I go shopping very often. / No, I'm not. I'm interested in riding a bike.
　(2) A: Are you interested in cooking?
　　B: Yes, I am. I cook very often. / No, I'm not. I'm interested in collecting figures.

02 (1) It is not easy to learn English.
　(2) It is exciting to play yunnori
　(3) It is important to keep promises.
　(4) It is interesting to study history.
　(5) It's dangerous to swim in this river.
　(6) It's awesome to see his art collection.

03 (A) kicking　(B) traditional Korean game
　(C) one of our feet　(D) exciting

단원별 모의고사
p.157~160

01 ①　　02 led to　　03 ③

04 (A) interested　(B) taking　　05 ④

06 ⑤　　07 ⓐ You did a good job　ⓑ Are you interested in glass art　08 ③　　09 ④

10 ①　　11 ⑤　　12 It looks like a person dancing with open arms.　　13 sitting

14 (1) It is easy to use knives and forks.
　(2) It is important to read books.

15 (1) said → saying　(2) That's → It's

16 ②　　17 ③　　18 ⑤

19 (A) image　(B) autumn

20 ⓐ Chaucer created the right one, *The Canterbury Tales*, in England in the late 1400s.
　ⓑ Chaucer wrote it with a pen.

21 ①, ③　　22 ③　　23 Today calligraphy is widely used around us.　　24 ⑤

01 ①번은 'widely'에 대한 영어 설명이다. 'wildly'에 대한 영어 설명은 'in an uncontrolled or extreme way'로 '난폭하게, 미친 듯이'의 뜻이다.

02 '…을 이끌다'는 'lead to …'를 사용하고 과거시제이므로 'led to'가 적절하다.

03 특별한 펜이나 붓으로 만들어지는 아름다운 글씨

04 (A) 관심이 있는지 묻는 말로 be동사와 함께 사용되는 interested가 적절하다. (B)는 전치사 at 뒤에서 '~을 돌보다'는 의미로 'taking care of ~'가 적절하다.

05 '위의 예술 작품은 한글 단어와 한자를 보여 주고 있다. 그것은 마치 단풍잎이 깔린 길을 따라 걷고 있는 행복한 여인처럼 보인다.'

06 한글에 관심이 있느냐는 물음에. 배우고 싶다고 했으므로 관심이 있다는 긍정의 답이 적절하다.

07 ⓐ 칭찬을 할 때 'did a good job'을 이용한다. ⓑ be동사로 관심을 묻는 표현은 'Are you interested in ~?'을 사용한다.

08 '어떻게 생각하니?'라는 뜻으로 캘리그래피를 쓰고 나서 상대방의 의견을 묻는 말이기 때문에 ③이 적절하다.

09 '내가 해 봐도 되니?'라는 James의 말에 미나가 '이 붓을 잡아.'라고 말한 것으로 보아 승낙한 것을 알 수 있다.

10 '마음에 드니?'라는 물음에 'Sure.'라고 답했으므로 빈칸에는 미술 숙제에 대한 긍정의 말이나 칭찬의 말이 오는 것이 적절하다.

11 한복에 관심이 있느냐는 물음에 별로라고 말하고 있으므로 그렇다면 무엇에 관심이 있는지 물어보는 것이 자연스럽다.

12 '~처럼 보이다'는 'look like+명사'를 사용하고 '춤추고 있는'은 앞의 명사 a person을 수식하는 현재분사 dancing으로 바꾸어 준다. 'with open arms'는 '두 팔을 벌리고'의 의미다.

13 현재분사가 목적어나 부사구를 수반할 때에는 명사 뒤에 와서 앞의 명사를 수식한다.

14 (1) It을 가주어로 하고 to use를 진주어로 쓴다. to use의 목적어로 knives and forks를 쓴다. (2) It을 가주어로 하고 to부정사를 진주어로 쓴다.

15 (1) say는 '~라고 쓰여지다'라는 의미로 sign이 알려주고 있는 것이므로 현재분사가 적절하다. (2) 가주어로는 it을 사용한다.

16 It is not wise of you to put all your eggs in one basket.

17 이 글은 '손 글씨로 감정을 표현하는 것'에 관한 글이다.

18 ⓐ와 ⑤: 작품, ① (어떤 직장에서) 일하다, ② (기계 장치 등이) 작동되다, ③ 공장, 제작소, ④ (약 따위가) 작용하다

19 그것은 맛있는 과일인 홍시의 '이미지'를 포함하고 있는 캘리그래피이고, '가을'이 결실의 계절임을 보여 준다.

20 둘 다 Chaucer를 주어로 해서 고치는 것이 적절하다.

21 lead to: ~로 이끌다, ~로 이어지다, ⓒ와 ②, ④, ⑤: ~을 야기하다, 가져오다, ① ~로부터 생기다, ~이 원인이다, ③ ~이 생기다, 일어나다

22 ⓓ와 ②, ③, ⑤: 부사적 용법, ①: 명사적 용법, ④: 형용사적 용법

23 수동태로 쓰는 것이 적절하다.

24 ⑤ 공상 소설의 제목은 우리 주변에서 쓰이고 있는 '그림'이 아니라 '캘리그래피'의 좋은 예이다.

Lesson 8

Design for All

일반적인 높이보다 더 작은 (3) 어떤 상황이나 주제에 관한 개인적인 의견이나 믿음 (4) 어떤 것의 한쪽 편에서 반대편으로 가로질러 가다

시험대비 실력평가 p.164

01 ④ 02 universal 03 by herself 04 ⑤
05 ② 06 ② 07 switch
08 (f)ountain

01 그녀가 잘 보거나 들을 수 없고, 지팡이가 없이는 잘 걸을 수 없는 것으로 미루어 보아 빈칸에는 '어려움'이 적절하다.
02 • 그녀의 유니버설 디자인 아이디어의 한 가지 예는 저상 버스이다. <영영풀이> 세상의 모든 사람과 관련된.
03 '혼자서'는 'by oneself'를 사용한다. 주어가 'she'이기 때문에 재귀대명사는 herself로 바꾸어 준다.
04 'difficult'는 '어려운'의 뜻이다. '다른'은 'different'이다.
05 '노인들이나 부상당한 사람들이 걷기 위해 사용하는 길고 가는 나무로 된 막대'
06 '(…보다) 더 낮은 장소나 위치에'의 의미로 '… 아래에'라는 'below'가 적절하다.
07 'switch'는 명사로 '스위치', 동사로 '교대하다, 바꾸다'라는 의미로 사용된다. • 그것을 끄려면 어느 스위치를 눌러야 하나요? • 내가 다음 주말에 근무를 할 수가 없는데 당신이 나와 좀 바꿔줄 수 있나요?
08 '분수'는 'fountain'이다.

서술형 시험대비 p.165

01 (j)ourney 02 (1) crowded (2) tired of
 (3) uncomfortable 03 (f)lat
04 (1) view (2) tight (3) example, wheelchair,
 without (4) During, company
05 (1) product, 제품 (2) low, 낮은 (3) view, 관점,
 견해 (4) cross, 건너다

01 글의 마지막에 1982년에 여행(trip)을 끝마쳤다고 했으므로 1979년에 여행(journey)을 시작한 것을 알 수 있다.
02 (1) 동사 'crowd(가득 메우다)'를 명사 'buses'를 수식하는 형용사 'crowded'로 바꾸어야 한다. (2) 동사 'tire'를 형용사 'tired'로 고친다. (3) 주어진 단어 'comfortable'은 '편안한'의 뜻이므로 반의어인 'uncomfortable'로 고친다.
03 '다른 부분보다 더 높거나 더 낮은 부분을 가지지 않은' 즉, '평평한'의 뜻을 가진 'flat'이 적절하다.
05 (1) 팔기 위해 만들어지거나 재배되는 것 (2) 높이가 작은 또는

교과서 Conversation

핵심 Check p.166~167

1 ⑤ 2 ④ 3 thinking, planning

교과서 대화문 익히기

Check(√) True or False p.168

1 T 2 F 3 T 4 F 5 T

교과서 확인학습 p.170~171

Get Ready 2
(1) not happy about, fountain, too high / m planning to put / good idea
(2) don't like, in wheelchairs, get in / thinking of building, with, steps
(3) happy, get on, easily / planning to hang

Start Off Listen & Talk A
(1) not happy about / wrong / reach, I'm thinking of, another
(2) happy about, who / any / thinking, adding / good idea

Start Off Listen & draw
I'm not happy about / What's wrong with / the same, who, blind to colors / How about putting / walking, standing

Speak Up Look and talk
I'm not happy about, too low / thinking of putting

Speak Up Mission
not happy about, bookshelf / any ideas / thinking of putting

Speak Up Real-life Scene
doing / thinking, ways / wrong / turn on, by herself, too high / happy about, either, about that / thinking, step box, below / change, bigger one / turn on, easily

(1) I'm not happy about, too low, too hard / I'm thinking of buying, What, think / Looks great, so long, grows taller

(2) not happy about, handles, easy to use / How about

(3) I'm thinking of / doesn't have to

not happy, light switch / wrong / too small / any ideas / I'm thinking of changing, with, turn on

시험대비 기본평가　　　　　　　　　p.172

01 ⑤　　　02 ②　　　03 I'm not happy about the shirt.　04 (C) → (D) → (B) → (A)

01 몇몇 아이들에게 너무 높다고 했기 때문에 음수대가 마음에 들지 않는다는 말이 적절하다.

02 빈칸 뒤에 동명사 'building'이 있기 때문에 전치사 of가 있는 ②가 적절하다. 나머지 표현도 의도를 나타내는 말이지만 모두 동사원형이 뒤에 온다.

03 "I'm not happy about ..."은 '나는 …이 마음에 들지 않는다.'라는 의미로, 만족스럽지 못한 것에 대해 불평하는 표현이다.

04 (C) 책꽂이가 마음에 들지 않는다는 말이 오고 → (D) 나도 그렇게 생각한다는 동의의 말과 함께 어떤 아이디어가 있는지 묻고 → (B) '나는 …을 할까 생각 중이다'라는 뜻으로, 의도나 계획을 나타내는 말을 하고 → (A) 좋은 생각이라고 동의하는 말이 오는 것이 자연스럽다.

시험대비 실력평가　　　　　　　　p.173~174

01 ⑤　　　02 ②　　　03 What's wrong with it?
04 ③　　　05 ④　　　06 ⑤
07 She doesn't have to hold it with her fingers.
08 ④　　　09 That'll help her turn[to trun] on the light easily.　10 ①　　11 ③　　12 ③
13 I want to complain about the shirt.

01 대화의 내용상 그녀에 만족하지 못한다는 의미가 적절하다. ⑤는 불평하지 않는다는 의미다.

02 'I'm planning to …'는 의도나 계획을 나타낼 때 쓰는 표현이다.

03 '무슨 일이야?' 또는 '뭐가 문제니?'의 의미로 'the button'을 가리키는 인칭대명사 'it'을 사용한 'What's wrong with it?'이 적절하다.

04 색깔을 못 보는 사람들(색맹인 사람들)에게 교통 신호등이 똑같아 보이는 것이 문제여서 각 불빛에 그림을 넣자고 제안하고 있다. 'different'를 'the same'으로 바꾸어야 한다.

05 ④는 '너는 왜 각 불빛에 그림을 넣고 있니?'라는 뜻이다.

06 '할머니께서 국을 쉽게 드실 수 있도록 도움이 된다.'고 했으므로 이 숟가락을 살 거라는 의도를 말하는 표현이 적절하다.

07 have to를 이용하여 '…할 필요가 없다'는 뜻을 나타낼 때는 'don't have to'를 사용한다.

08 G의 마지막 말에서 '더 큰 것으로 바꿀 생각이야.'라고 말하고 있으므로 스위치가 너무 작다는 것을 알 수 있다.

09 'help+목적어+동사원형/to부정사' 형태로 사용된다.

10 ①의 'be happy with ...'는 '…이 마음에 들다'라는 뜻이다. A의 '나는 이 전등이 마음에 들어.'라는 말에 B가 '왜? 뭐가 문제니?'라고 말하는 것은 어색하다.

11 "I'm not happy about ..."은 '나는 …이 마음에 들지 않는다'라는 의미로, 만족스럽지 못한 것에 대해 불평하는 표현이다.

12 셔츠가 마음에 들지 않는다고 했기 때문에 빈칸에는 셔츠가 가지고 있는 문제점이 언급되는 것이 자연스럽다.

13 불평하는 표현으로 'I want to complain about ...'을 사용한다.

서술형 시험대비　　　　　　　　　　p.175

01 (1) I'm not happy about
　　(2) I'm thinking of decorating
02 I don't like the lights.
03 I'm not happy about it, either.
04 She can't turn on the light by herself.
05 He will change the switch to a bigger one.

01 (1)번은 happy를 이용해 사물함에 대한 불평을 나타내는 표현을 (2)는 'think of'를 이용하여 앞으로의 계획이나 의도를 말하는 표현을 사용한다. 전치사 of 뒤에 동명사를 사용해야 한다.

02 'I don't like ...'를 이용해서 불평을 표현한다.

03 'happy'를 이용하여 불평하는 표현은 'I'm not happy about ...'이다. 부정문에서 동의를 하는 '또한, 역시'는 'either'를 사용한다.

04 '…을 켜다'는 'turn on'을 사용하고 '…할 수 없다'는 부정의 의미로 can't turn on을 쓴다. '혼자서'는 재귀대명사를 이용하면 'by herself'가 적절하다.

05 아빠의 마지막 말에서 'I'll change the switch to a bigger one'이라고 했다.

Grammar

핵심 Check　　　　　　　　　　　p.176~177

1 (1) so　(2) that　(3) too
2 (1) clean　(2) to do　(3) to quit

01 (1) to wash → wash (2) swimming → swim

 (3) very → so (4) so → too

02 (1) draw (2) thrown (3) to drop

 (4) win(또는 to win)

03 ②

04 He hid himself so that no one could find him.

01 (1), (2) 사역동사의 목적어와 목적격보어의 관계가 능동일 경우 목적격보어로 원형부정사를 쓰는 것이 적절하다. (3) 'so+형용사[부사]+that+주어+동사'의 형태로 '매우 ~해서 …하다'라는 의미를 나타낸다. (4) so+형용사/부사+that+주어+can't … = too ~ to …

02 (1) 사역동사의 목적격보어는 목적어와의 관계가 능동일 경우 원형부정사가 쓰인다. (2) 사역동사의 목적격보어는 목적어와의 관계가 수동일 경우 과거분사가 쓰인다. (3) get이 '~하게 하다'라는 사역동사의 뜻으로 쓰일 때에는 목적격보어로 to부정사를 쓴다. (4) help는 목적격보어로 동사원형이나 to부정사가 나오며 뜻의 차이는 없다.

03 'so+형용사[부사]+that+주어+can't …'의 형태로 '너무 ~해서 …할 수 없다'

04 'so that+주어+동사' 구문으로 쓴다. 'so that+주어+동사'는 목적을 나타내어 '~하기 위해서' 혹은 '~하도록'이라는 의미로 쓰인다.

01 ⑤ 02 ④, ⑤ 03 ①

04 You speak so fast that I can't get you. 05 ③

06 (1) do (2) watch (3) painted (4) help (5) that

 (6) so (7) too (8) smart enough 07 ③

08 tall so that → so tall that 09 ③, ④

10 ③, ⑤ 11 ① 12 ②, ④ 13 ⑤

14 (1) The window is so heavy that I can't open it.

 (2) My brother's chair is too low for him to sit on comfortably.

 (3) These walls are thick enough to shut out outside sounds.

 (4) I finished my homework, so Mom let me watch TV.

 (5) The P.E. teacher had the boy bring the ball.

15 (1) repairing → to repair (2) to wear → wear

 (3) too strong → strong enough

16 ③ 17 ④

18 (1) so heavy that I can't move it

 (2) because it is very heavy

01 목적어와의 관계가 능동이므로 사역동사의 목적격보어로 원형부정사가 적절하고 원인과 결과를 나타내는 'so+형용사[부사]+that+주어+can't …' 구문이 적절하다.

02 help는 준사역동사로 목적어와 목적격보어의 관계가 능동일 경우 목적격보어로 원형부정사 또는 to부정사를 받는다.

03 '너무 ~해서 …할 수 없다'는 결과를 나타내는 'so+형용사[부사]+that+주어+can't …' 구문이 적절하다.

04 '너무 ~해서 …할 수 없다'는 의미의 'so+형용사[부사]+that+주어+can't …' 구문이 적절하다.

05 목적어와의 관계가 능동이므로 사역동사 have의 목적격보어로 원형부정사가 적절하다.

06 (1) 사역동사 have의 목적격보어로 원형부정사가 적절하다. (2) 사역동사 let의 목적격보어로 원형부정사가 적절하다. (3) 의자가 칠해지는 것이므로 목적격보어로 수동의 의미를 갖는 과거분사가 적절하다. (4) help는 준사역동사로 목적격보어로 원형부정사 또는 to부정사를 받는다. (5), (6) 'so+형용사[부사]+that+주어+can't …' 구문이다. (7) 'so+형용사[부사]+that+주어+can't ~'는 'too+형용사[부사]+to 동사원형'으로 바꿔 쓸 수 있다. (8) 'so+형용사[부사]+that+주어+can …'은 '형용사[부사]+enough+to 동사원형'으로 바꿔 쓸 수 있다.

07 물이 무엇을 끓이는 것이 아니라 주어가 물이 끓도록 하는 것이므로 사역동사 have의 목적격보어로 과거분사 boiled를 쓰는 것이 적절하다.

08 'so+형용사[부사]+that+주어+동사'는 원인과 결과를 나타내지만 'so that+주어+동사'는 목적을 나타낸다.

09 목적어와의 관계가 능동이므로 사역동사 help의 목적격보어로 원형부정사 혹은 to부정사가 적절하다.

10 'so+형용사[부사]+that+주어+can …'은 '형용사[부사]+enough+to 동사원형'으로 바꿔 쓸 수 있다.

11 want는 목적격보어로 to부정사가 나와야 한다.

12 ① Emily had her daughters take care of her dogs. ③ This rock is so heavy that I can't lift it. ⑤ It was such a nice concert that the $15 for the ticket seemed cheap.

13 (A) 사역동사의 목적어와 목적격보어의 관계가 능동이므로 원형부정사가 적절하다. (B) 동사 get의 목적어와 목적격보어의 관계가 능동이므로 to부정사가 적절하다. (C) 사역동사의 목적어와 목적격보어의 관계가 수동이므로 과거분사가 적절하다.

14 (1) 'so+형용사[부사]+that+주어+can[can't] …' 구문으로 영작한다. (2)~(3) 'so+형용사[부사]+that+주어+can …' = '형용사[부사]+enough+to 동사원형', 'so+형용사[부사]+that+주어+can't …' = 'too+형용사[부사]+to …' (4), (5) 사역동사의 목적격보어로 원형부정사를 이용한다.

15 (1) 목적어와의 관계가 능동이므로 get의 목적격보어로 to부

정사가 적절하다. (2) 사역동사의 목적격보어로 원형부정사가 적절하다. (3) 내용상 '너무 ~해서 …할 수 있다'는 '형용사[부사]+enough+to 동사원형' 구문이 적절하다.

16 'so ... that ~'은 so 뒤의 형용사나 부사가 원인을 나타내며, 접속사 that 뒤에는 그에 따른 결과를 나타낸다.

17 주어진 문장과 ④번의 make는 사역동사로 그 쓰임이 같다.

18 too ... to ~ = so ... that 주어 can't ~. 이때 to부정사 앞에 for 목적격으로 쓰인 것은 to부정사의 의미상의 주어로 that 이하의 절로 바꿀 때는 주격으로 바뀌어야 하며, to부정사로 썼을 때 생략된 동사의 목적어는 써 주어야 한다.

서술형 시험대비
p.182~183

01 (1) They made the students wear school uniforms.

(2) She doesn't let her kids watch TV late at night.

(3) I had my puppy get me the ball.

(4) My sister asked me to have her computer repaired.

(5) I helped my cousin bake[to bake] some cookies.

(6) He got his sister to help him with his homework.

02 Patricia had Benjamin repair her broken computer.

03 (1) My brother is too young to understand the words.

(2) Sam was smart enough to understand what the scientist said.

(3) This coffee is too hot for me to drink.

(4) The bookshelf is low enough for my little brother to reach.

04 (1) carry (2) repaired (3) to wait (4) do[to do]

05 (1) The storm was so strong that we couldn't go out.

(2) I was so tired that I didn't go there.

(3) The bus is so noisy that I can't hear the music.

(4) The fog was so thick that driving became really dangerous.

06 The button is so high that people in wheelchairs can't reach it.

07 (1) Eve allowed him to use her pen.

(2) She made Dan follow her advice.

08 because[as, since] the button is very high /
so high that the boy can't push it /
too high for the boy to push

09 take

01 (1)~(3) 사역동사의 목적어와 목적격보어의 관계가 능동이므로 목적격보어로 원형부정사가 적절하다. (4) 사역동사의 목적어와 목적격보어의 관계가 수동이므로 과거분사가 적절하다. (5) help는 목적격보어로 동사원형이나 to부정사가 나온다. (6) get이 '~하게 하다'라는 사역동사의 뜻으로 쓰일 때 목적격보어로 to부정사를 쓴다.

02 사역동사의 목적어와 목적격보어의 관계가 능동일 경우 목적격보어로 원형부정사를 쓴다.

03 (1) so ~ that 주어 can't ... = too ~ to ... (2) so ~ that 주어 can ... = ~ enough to ... (3), (4) 'so ~ that can[can't] ...' 구문에서 주절의 주어와 that 절의 주어가 서로 다를 경우 'too ~ to ...'나 '~ enough to ...'로 바꿔 쓸 때 'for+목적격'으로 의미상의 주어를 나타낸다. drink와 reach의 목적어가 문장의 주어와 같으므로 목적어를 쓰지 않음에 주의한다.

04 (1) 사역동사의 목적어와 목적격보어의 관계가 능동이므로 목적격보어로 원형부정사가 적절하다 (2) 목적어와 목적격보어의 관계가 수동이므로 목적격보어로 과거분사가 적절하다. (3) get은 사역동사의 의미로 쓰일 수 있지만 목적격보어로 to부정사가 나온다. (4) help는 준사역동사로 목적격보어로 원형부정사 또는 to부정사가 나온다.

05 (1), (3) 'so+형용사[부사]+that+주어+can't ...'의 형태로 '너무 ~해서 …할 수 없다'라는 의미를 나타낸다. (2), (4) 'so+형용사[부사]+that+주어+동사'의 형태로 '매우 ~해서 …하다'라는 의미를 나타낸다. so 뒤의 형용사[부사]는 원인을, that 뒤에 나오는 내용은 그에 따른 결과를 나타낸다.

06 '너무 ~해서 …할 수 없다'라는 의미를 나타내는 'so+형용사[부사]+that+주어+can't …' 구문을 이용한다.

07 사역동사 have, let, make는 목적격보어로 동사원형을 취한다. get, allow, force는 목적격보어로 to부정사를 취한다.

08 'so+형용사[부사]+that+주어+(can't) …' 구문은 기본적으로 '원인과 결과'를 나타낸다.

09 사역동사 let의 목적어와 목적격보어의 관계가 능동이므로 목적격보어로 원형부정사가 적절하다.

교과서
Reading

확인문제
p.184

1 T 2 F 3 F 4 T

확인문제
p.185

1 T 2 T 3 F 4 F 5 F 6 T

01 Universal Design
02 started a journey
03 looked over 80
04 couldn't see or hear
05 without a stick
06 With all these difficulties
07 with her weak hands
08 found herself in danger
09 very difficult for her, more than
10 what made her do
11 a 26-year-old designer
12 During the 1970's
13 How about designing
14 for those people
15 became tired of
16 Finally, to understand their difficulties
17 For this, uncomfortable, thick glasses
18 so, that, couldn't, without a stick
19 so, that, couldn't, with them
20 to make her hearing bad
21 During, go through
22 From, safely, easily
23 universal design, design for all
24 One example, buses
25 no steps, such a low floor, in a wheelchair, without any help
26 more comfortably
27 following Patricia's way
28 like, live better lives
29 from their point of view
30 next, a better place for everybody

1 Patricia Moore – Mother of Universal Design
2 In 1979, a woman started a journey to cities in the U.S. and Canada.
3 She looked over 80.
4 She couldn't see or hear well.
5 She couldn't walk well without a stick.
6 With all these difficulties, the woman had to climb stairs in subway stations and get on crowded buses.
7 She had to open heavy doors and use can openers with her weak hands.
8 Sometimes she got hurt or found herself in danger.
9 Every moment was very difficult for her, but she visited more than 115 cities and ended her trip in 1982.
10 Who was the woman and what made her do all this?
11 She was Patricia Moore, a 26-year-old designer.
12 During the 1970's, she worked for a big design company.
13 She often asked at meetings, "How about designing for old or weak people?"

14 The other designers always answered, "We don't design for those people."
15 She became tired of the same cold answer.
16 Finally, she decided to become one of "those people" and travel around many cities to understand their difficulties better.
17 For this, she put on her grandmother's clothes, uncomfortable shoes, and thick glasses.
18 The shoes were so uncomfortable that she couldn't walk well without a stick.
19 The glasses were so thick that she couldn't see well with them.
20 She also put lots of cotton in her ears to make her hearing bad.
21 During her journey, Patricia felt the difficulties old people go through.
22 From this experience, she designed products anybody could use safely and easily.
23 This was the beginning of "universal design," or "design for all."
24 One example of her universal design ideas is low-floor buses.
25 They have no steps and have such a low floor that even a person in a wheelchair can use them without any help.
26 Of course, this helps other people get on the bus more comfortably, too.
27 Today more and more designers are following Patricia's way.
28 Products like big flat light switches, doors with easy handles, and phones with touch buttons are helping people live better lives.
29 Look around you, feel the difficulties of people who are older or weaker, and try to find solutions from their point of view.
30 You could be the next Patricia Moore and make the world a better place for everybody.

01 (A) 26-year-old (B) The other (C) them
02 ②
03 We don't design for those people.
04 ③
05 difficulties
06 ②
07 (A) journey 또는 trip (B) 115 cities
08 ①, ④
09 (A) safely and easily (B) such (C) comfortably
10 low-floor buses
11 ②, ⑤
12 ⓐ such as ⓑ viewpoint

13 여러분의 주위를 둘러보고, 더 나이 들거나 더 약한
 사람들의 어려움을 느껴 보고, 그들의 관점에서 해결책을
 찾으려고 노력해야 한다.

14 ④ 15 too, for, to

16 세탁기 문이 너무 높아서 남동생이 그 안에 옷을 쉽게 넣을
 수 없다. / 이 세탁기는 옆문을 가지고 있어서 남동생이
 옷을 더 쉽게 넣을 수 있도록 도와줄 것이다.

17 ⓓ 18 over 19 ⑤ 20 ②

21 experience

22 she designed products anybody could use safely
 and easily

23 ① 24 ②, ③ 25 the glasses

26 easily 27 special legs

28 too high, to use

01 (A) 수사가 명사를 수식할 때는 단수로 써야 하므로 26-year-
 old가 적절하다. (B) Patricia Moore를 제외한 '다른' 디자
 이너들을 지칭하는 것이므로 The other가 적절하다. (C) 'The
 glasses'를 가리키므로 them이 적절하다.

02 ②We: The other designers, 나머지는 다 '나이 들거나 약
 한 사람들'을 지칭한다.

03 '우리는 그런 사람들을 위해 디자인하지 않습니다.'를 가리킨다.

04 이 글은 Patricia가 나이 들거나 약한 사람들의 어려움을 더 잘
 이해하기 위해 스스로 늙어 보이도록 분장을 하고 여행을 하는
 내용의 글이므로, 제목으로는 'Patricia는 나이든 사람들을 직
 접 이해하려고 노력했다'가 적절하다. in person: 직접[몸소],
 ④ for one's age: 나이에 비해서는, 그 나이로는

05 'difficult'의 명사형을 써야 하고, these가 있기 때문에 복수 형
 태로 쓰는 것이 적절하다.

06 ② rarely: 드물게, 좀처럼 ~하지 않는, 나머지는 다 '가끔'

07 1979년에, 한 여성이 미국과 캐나다의 도시로 '여행'을 시작했
 고, '115개 이상'의 도시를 방문한 뒤 1982년에 그녀는 여행을
 끝마쳤다.

08 help+목적어+원형부정사 또는 to부정사

09 (A) 동사 use를 수식하므로 부사인 'safely and easily'가 적
 절하다. (B) 'such+a+형용사+명사'이므로 such가 적절하다.
 (C) 동사 get을 수식하므로 부사인 comfortably가 적절하다.

10 '저상 버스'를 가리킨다.

11 선행사인 people을 수식하는 주격 관계대명사 who나 that이
 적절하다.

12 ⓐ like = such as: ~와 같은, ⓑ point of view =
 viewpoint: 관점[시각]

13 바로 앞 문장의 내용을 쓰는 것이 적절하다.

14 앞에 나오는 내용과 상반되는 내용이 뒤에 이어지므로
 However가 가장 적절하다. ① 그러므로, ② 예를 들어, ③ 게
 다가, ⑤ 즉, 다시 말해

15 so+형용사/부사+that+주어+can't ... = too ~ to ...

16 세탁기 문에 관한 단점과 개선된 점을 쓰는 것이 적절하다.

17 ⓓ 'for', 나머지는 다 'in'이 적절하다.

18 more than = over: ~ 이상

19 모든 순간이 그녀에게 매우 어려웠으나, 그녀는 1982년에 여행
 을 '끝마쳤다'.

20 (A) From this experience: 이 경험으로부터, (B) in a
 wheelchair: 휠체어를 탄

21 go through = experience: 겪다

22 긍정문의 any: '어떤 ~이라도'

23 ①번 다음 문장의 this에 주목한다. 주어진 문장의 내용을 받고
 있으므로 ①번이 적절하다.

24 ②, ③ so+형용사/부사+that+주어+can't ... = too ~ to ... =
 very ~, so+주어+can't ..., ① such 뒤에는 명사가 있어야 한
 다. ④ so ~ that can ... = ~ enough to, ⑤ in order that ...
 couldn't ~: ~하지 않기 위해서

25 '안경'을 가리킨다.

26 easily = with ease, 전치사+추상명사 = 부사

27 '특별한 다리'를 가지고 있는 책상을 가리킨다.

28 집에 있는 책상은 '너무 높아서' 그 여동생은 그것을 쉽게 '사용'
 할 수 없다.

서술형 시험대비 p.194~195

01 (A) looked (B) crowded (C) herself

02 ⓐ nineteen seventy-nine ⓓ one hundred (and)
 fifteen ⓔ nineteen eighty-two

03 ⓑ with → without ⓒ Without → With

04 (1) 그녀는 자신의 할머니 옷을 입고, 불편한 신발을 신고,
 두꺼운 안경을 썼다.
 (2) 그녀는 또한 그녀의 청력을 나쁘게 하려고 귀에 많은
 솜을 넣었다.

05 too / for / to

06 (A) old or weak (B) those people

07 use them → use 08 comfortably

09 (1) 크고 평평한 조명 스위치 (2) 편한 손잡이를 가진
 문 (3) 터치 버튼을 가진 전화기

10 living → live[to live] 11 older / weaker

12 safely 13 very / so

01 (A) look+형용사, look like+명사: ~처럼 보이다, 80은 형용
 사(기수사)이므로 looked가 적절하다. (B) '붐비는' 버스라고
 해야 하므로 crowded가 적절하다. crowded: 붐비는, 복잡한,
 crowding: 가득 메우는, 밀려오는, 떼 지어 모이는, (C) 주어와
 목적어가 같을 때는 재귀대명사를 써야 하므로 herself가 적절하
 다.

02 @와 @: 연도는 두 자리씩 끊어 읽는다. 21에서 99까지는 십 단위와 단 단위 사이에 hyphen(-)을 붙인다. @: hundred 다음에는 and를 넣어 읽는데, 생략도 가능하다.

03 ⓑ 지팡이 '없이'는 잘 걸을 수 없었다고 하는 것이 적절하다. ⓒ 이 모든 어려움을 '가진 채'라고 하는 것이 적절하다.

04 뒤에 이어지는 내용을 쓰는 것이 적절하다.

05 so+형용사/부사+that+주어+can't ... = too ~ to ..., for her: to부정사의 의미상의 주어

06 Patricia는 '그들'(나이 들거나 약한 사람들) 중의 하나가 되어 많은 도시를 여행함으로써 '나이 들거나 약한 사람들'의 어려움을 더 잘 이해하려고 노력했다.

07 use 다음의 them은 선행사인 products를 수식하는 목적격 관계대명사 that[which]으로 바꾼 다음 생략하는 것이므로, 또 them을 쓰는 것은 부적절하다.

08 부사형이 되어야 한다.

09 (1) big flat light switches, (2) doors with easy handles, (3) phones with touch buttons

10 help+목적어+원형부정사 또는 to부정사

11 their는 people who are older or weaker를 가리킨다.

12 in safety = safely: 안전하게, 전치사+추상명사 = 부사

13 so+형용사/부사+that+주어+can't ... = very ~, so+주어+can't ...

영역별 핵심문제 p.197~201

01 tight 02 ③ 03 ④ 04 ②

05 jumps rope 06 ①

07 There are some people who can't see.

08 ④ 09 ③ 10 ⑤ 11 ③

12 ④ 13 ⑤ 14 help, open

15 (1) This question is so difficult that I can't solve it.

 (2) The big panel was so light that it floated on the water.

 (3) He held her by the sleeve so tightly that she couldn't ran away.

 (4) The bus is so noisy that I can't hear the music.

 (5) He took a taxi so that he wouldn't be late.

16 ③ 17 ③ 18 taken 19 ③

20 ④ 21 ④

22 (A) During (B) anybody (C) is

23 Patricia felt the difficulties that[which] old people go through. 24 ②

25 (1) 그녀는 잘 보거나 잘 들을 수 없었다.

 (2) 그녀는 지팡이 없이는 잘 걸을 수 없었다.

26 used → use 27 ①, ④ 28 ②, ③

29 ⑤ 30 ② 31 ④

01 반의어 관계. 편안한 : 불편한 = 느슨한 : 꽉 조이는

02 여러분의 주위를 둘러보고, 더 나이 들거나 더 약한 사람들의 어려움을 느껴 보고, 그들의 관점에서 해결책을 찾으려고 노력해 봐라.

03 많은 사람들 또는 너무 많은 사람들이 있는

04 • 나는 숙제를 거의 끝마쳤다. 'almost'는 부사로 동사를 수식한다. 'most'는 형용사로 명사를 수식한다. • 그 개는 맹인 남자를 돕는다. 의미상 'old'도 가능하다. • 길을 건널 때는 조심해라. 'across'는 전치사로 '~을 가로질러'의 뜻이다.

05 '줄넘기를 하다'는 'jump rope'이고, 주어가 3인칭 단수이므로 jumps를 사용한다.

06 product'는 '제품'이고, '생산적인'은 'productive'이다.

07 '…가 있다'는 'There is[are] ...'를 사용한다. 주어가 복수 명사인 'some people'이므로 'There are some people'로 문장을 시작한다. '볼 수 없는'은 people을 수식하는 역할을 하므로 관계대명사 who를 이용한 문장을 사용해서, people뒤에 'who can't see'를 쓴다..

08 (C) 전등에 대한 불평에 대해 → (B) 이유와 무엇이 문제인지 묻는다 → (A) 문제점을 언급하자 → (D) 알겠다고 말하며 대안을 제시한다.

09 'What do you think?'는 '어떻게 생각하니?'의 뜻으로 상대방의 의견을 물어보는 표현이다. G의 대답 'Looks great' 앞에 오는 것이 자연스럽다.

10 '…할까 생각 중이야'라는 미래 계획이나 의도를 나타내는 말이 적절하다.

11 부정문에서 '또한, 역시'는 too 대신 either를 사용한다.

12 ④ step box(디딤대)에 무슨 문제가 있는지는 알 수 없다. ⑤번은 '누가 더 큰 스위치에 대한 아이디어를 생각해 냈는가?'라는 뜻이다.

13 ⑤ I was so thirsty that I drank a bottle of water.

14 주어진 문장을 영어로 옮기면 'It'll help my grandma open the door more comfortably.'이다.

15 (1), (3), (4) too ~ to ... = so+형용사[부사]+that+주어 +can't ... = very ~, so+주어+can't ... = 주어+can't ..., because+주어+동사+very ~ (2) ~ enough to ... = so+형용사[부사]+that+주어+can ... (5) 'so that+주어+동사'는 목적을 나타내어 '~하기 위해서' 혹은 '~하도록'이라는 의미로 쓰인다. 'so ~ that ...'과 혼동하지 않도록 유의한다.

16 사역동사의 목적격보어로 수동의 의미가 필요하므로 과거분사가 적절하다.

17 'so+형용사[부사]+that+주어+can't ...'의 형태로 '너무 ~해서 …할 수 없다'는 뜻을 나타낼 수 있다.

18 사역동사의 목적격보어로 '병원으로 데려가지는' 수동의 의미가 필요하므로 과거분사가 적절하다.

19 첫 문장에서 get이 '~하게 하다'라는 사역동사의 뜻으로 쓰일 때 목적격 보어로 to부정사를 쓴다. 두 번째 문장에서 help는 준사

역동사로 목적어와 목적격보어의 관계가 능동일 경우 목적격보어로 원형부정사 또는 to부정사를 쓴다.

20 ① He is tall enough to touch the ceiling. ② She ran fast so that nobody could catch up with her. ③ Ron asked me to have his computer repaired. ⑤ I'll have him copy all the files for the meeting.

21 ⓒ Sarah always lets me use her laptop computer. ⓓ It'll help my grandma (to) eat food more comfortably. ⓖ Charlotte did her best to have the project finished on time.

22 (A) during+기간을 나타내는 명사, for+숫자, (B) '누구나'라고 해야 하므로 anybody가 적절하다. 긍정문의 any: 어떤 ~이라도, (C) 주어가 'One example'이므로 is가 적절하다.

23 old 앞에 목적격 관계대명사 which[that]가 생략되어 있다.

24 주어진 문장의 This에 주목한다. ②번 앞 문장의 내용을 받고 있으므로 ②번이 적절하다.

25 앞 문단에서 찾아 쓰는 것이 적절하다.

26 had to에 걸리는 것이므로, 동사원형으로 고치는 것이 적절하다.

27 tired of = sick of = bored with: ~에 싫증 난, ②와 ⑤: tired with[from]: ~으로 피곤한 , ③ worn out: (특히 힘든 노동·운동으로) 매우 지친, 닳아서 못 쓰게 된

28 ⓑ는 '동사(make)+목적어(her hearing)+목적격보어(bad)'의 5형식 문장의 어순이다. ②, ③: 5형식, ① 4형식, ④ make = go(1형식), ⑤ 한 재산 벌다(3형식)

29 그녀는 청력을 나쁘게 하려고 일부러 귀에 많은 솜을 넣었다.

30 ⓐ와 ①, ②, ④: 명사적 용법, ③ 부사적 용법, ⑤ 형용사적 용법

31 이 글은 '주위를 둘러보고, 더 나이 들거나 더 약한 사람들의 어려움을 느껴 보고, 그들의 관점에서 해결책을 찾으려고 노력하라'는 내용의 글이므로, 제목으로는 '다른 사람들의 관점에서 해결책을 찾으라'가 적절하다.

단원별 예상문제
p.202~205

01 stick	02 (A) flat (B) handle	03 ③	
04 ⑤	05 ②	06 ④	07 ④
08 ③	09 ⑤		

10 I'm thinking of adding Braille on the sign.

11 She was so kind that she told me the way to the station.

12 very → so / riding → (to) ride **13** ①, ⑤

14 ③, ④ **15** ② **16** ①, ③, ④ / ②, ⑤

17 They have no steps and have such a low floor

18 ③

19 (A) universal design (B) design for all

20 ③ **21** trip **22** (A) difficulties
(B) 115 cities **23** ⓐ flat ⓑ handles ⓒ touch
24 your → their

01 그녀는 지팡이가 없이는 잘 걸을 수 없었다.

02 (A) flat: 평평한 (B) handle: 손잡이

03 빈칸 다음의 말에서 '아이들과 휠체어를 탄 사람들이 닿을 수 없다'고 했으므로 버튼이 너무 높다는 말이 적절하다.

04 소유물을 보관할 수 있고 일정 기간 동안 남겨둘 수 있는 금속으로 만들어진 종종 큰 벽장

05 '나도 그것이 마음에 안 들어.'라고 앞에 말한 내용에 대해 동의하는 표현으로 (②)가 적절하다.

06 여동생 Miso를 위해 스위치 아래에 디딤대를 놓고, 할머니를 위해 스위치를 더 큰 것으로 교체할 것이라는 말로 미루어 보아 제목은 '가족을 위한 좋은 아이디어'가 적절하다.

07 할머니가 혼자서 스위치를 켤 수 없는지는 대화에서 언급되어 있지 않다.

08 G의 마지막 말에 '그건 할머니가 쉽게 전등을 켤 수 있도록 도와줄 거야.'라는 말로 보아 스위치가 마음에 들지 않는다는 것을 알 수 있다.

09 G의 두 번째 말에서 그것이 너무 작다고 했기 때문에 문제점에 대한 해결책으로 더 큰 것으로 바꾸는 것이 적절하다.

10 표지판이 마음에 들지 않는 이유가 볼 수 없는 사람들이 있기 때문이라고 했다. 이 문제에 대한 해결책으로는 표지판에 점자를 추가하는 것이 적절하다.

11 'so+형용사[부사]+that+주어+동사'의 형태로 '매우 ~해서 … 하다'라는 의미를 나타낸다..

12 help는 목적격보어로 동사원형이나 to부정사가 나온다.

13 ② Ms. Han made her son go to bed immediately. ③ It gave him such a shock that he couldn't say a word. ④ I am so tired that I can't walk any more.

14 ① I'm too tired to go there. ② The man is so rich that he can buy the big house. 또는 The man is rich enough to buy the big house. ⑤ Mom made me clean my room.

15 사역동사(made)+목적어+원형부정사

16 ⓑ와 ①, ③, ④: 명사적 용법, ⓒ와 ②, ⑤: 부사적 용법

17 such+a+형용사+명사

18 이 글은 '유니버설 디자인'에 관한 글이다.

19 Patricia는 그녀가 직접 겪은 경험으로부터 '유니버설 디자인'을 만들었고, 저상 버스의 사례에서 볼 수 있듯이 그것은 '모두를 위한 디자인'이 될 수 있었다. in person: 직접[몸소]

20 주어진 문장의 all these difficulties에 주목한다. ③번 앞 문장의 내용들을 받고 있으므로 ③번이 적절하다.

21 journey = trip: 여행

22 비록 많은 '어려움'이 있었지만, 그 여성은 미국과 캐나다에 있는

'115개' 이상의 '도시'를 방문하였으며 1982년에 여행을 끝마쳤다.

23 ⓐ 크고 '평평한' 전등 스위치, ⓑ 편한 '손잡이'를 가진 문, ⓒ '터치' 버튼을 가진 전화기

24 '너의' 관점이 아니라 '그들의' 관점에서 해결책을 찾으려고 노력해야 한다.

서술형 실전문제
p.206~207

01 The traffic lights look the same to some people who are blind to colors.

02 I'm not happy about, too low / I'm thinking of / comfortably

03 by herself, high, a step box below, change, bigger, more easily

04 (1) Mom made me throw away the trash.
(2) The teacher made the students do homework.
(3) Anna made her daughter come home early at night.

05 (1) Betty was too busy to come to the party.
(2) This food is delicious enough for me to eat all.
(3) This problem is easy enough to solve.

06 (1) This ice cream is too cold for me to eat.
(2) It rained too hard for us to play soccer.

07 why 08 (1) What (2) Why (3) Shall

09 the, the

10 나이 든 사람들이 겪는 어려움에 대해 Patricia가 그녀의 여행 동안 겪었던 경험

11 low-floor buses 12 so

01 주어는 'The traffic lights'로 시작하고 'look the same to ...'(…에게 똑같이 보이다)를 주어 뒤에 위치시킨다. 관계대명사 who를 이용하여 'some people'을 수식하는 절을 만든다. 'be blind to …'는 '…을 못보다'라는 의미이다.

03 스위치가 너무 높기 때문에 미소는 혼자 전등을 켤 수가 없다. 그래서 그녀의 오빠는 스위치 아래에 디딤대를 놓기로 결심한다. 아빠도 스위치를 더 큰 것으로 바꿀 것이다. 미소와 할머니는 더 쉽게 전등을 켤 수 있을 것이다.

04 사역동사 make의 목적격보어로 동사원형이 적절하다.

05 'so+형용사[부사]+that+주어+can't ...' = 'too+형용사[부사]+to 동사원형', 'so+형용사[부사]+that+주어+can ...' = '형용사[부사]+enough+to 동사원형' 주절의 주어와 that절의 주어가 다를 경우 의미상의 주어(for+목적격)를 빠뜨리지 않도록 주의한다. 의미상의 주어가 for anyone과 같이 일반인일 경우 생략할 수 있다. 또한 that절의 목적어와 문장의 주어가 같을 경우 to부정사의 목적어를 쓰지 않는 것에 주의한다.

06 so+형용사[부사]+that+주어+can't ... = too ~ to ...

07 무엇이 그녀로 하여금 이 모든 것을 하게 만들었을까?(물주구문) = 그녀는 '왜' 이 모든 것을 했을까?

08 How about ~ing? = What about ~ing? = Why don't we 동사원형? = Shall we 동사원형? = Let's 동사원형.: ~하는 게 어때? 지금의 경우, Let's 동사원형은 마침표를 찍어야 하므로 ⓑ 대신 쓰기에 부적절하다.

09 the+형용사 = 복수 보통명사

10 첫 문장의 내용을 가리킨다.

11 '저상 버스'가 '유니버설 디자인'의 예에 해당한다.

12 so+형용사, such+a+형용사+명사

창의사고력 서술형 문제
p.208

|모범답안|

01 A: I'm not happy about the locker. It's too old.
B: I think so, too. Do you have any ideas?
A: I'm thinking of decorating its door.
B: That's a good idea.

02 (1) Amy made her brother fix her computer.
(2) She let her daughter go to the K-pop concert.
(3) The baby cried so loudly that I covered my ears.
(4) He spoke so fast that I could not understand him.

03 (A) so (B) that (C) can't (D) special legs

단원별 모의고사
p.209~212

01 ② 02 point of view 03 ④

04 (A) thinking (B) doesn't have to hold 05 ⑤

06 ① 07 I intend to put some pads on it.

08 ④ 09 I'm not happy about it, either.

10 ③ 11 ③

12 I'm thinking of changing it with a bigger one.

13 (1) The noise was so loud that I couldn't sleep.
(2) The steps are so high that I can't get on the bus.

14 ① 15 (1) it → 삭제 (2) to carry → carry

16 (A) better lives (B) solutions 17 their

18 저상 버스는 계단이 없고 낮은 바닥을 가지고 있어서 휠체어를 탄 사람도 아무 도움 없이 이용할 수 있는 것

19 ⑤ 20 ②, ③

21 ⓑ with → without ⓒ without → with

22 ① 23 her → herself

01 ②번은 'switch'에 대한 영어 설명이다. 'pad'는 'a piece of soft, thick cloth or rubber, used to protect a part of the body, give shape to something'(신체의 일부를 보호하고, 어떤 것에 모양을 부여하기 위해 사용되는 부드럽고 두꺼운 천이나 고무 조각)

02 point of view: 관점

03 사람들이 타고 내릴 수 있도록 버스나 기차가 멈춰서는 건물이나 장소

04 (A) '…할까 생각 중이다'는 계획을 말하는 표현으로 'I'm thinking of …'를 사용한다. (B)는 그림에 'Don't hold it. Just wear it'이라고 적혀 있는 걸로 보아 '손가락으로 그것을 잡을 필요가 없다'는 'doesn't have to'가 적절하다.

05 불만을 나타내는 표현이 아닌 것은 ⑤번으로 '이 장소에 대해 불평하고 싶지 않다'는 뜻이다.

06 버튼이 너무 높다고 말하고 있으므로 아이들이나 휠체어를 탄 사람들이 버튼에 닿을 수 없다는 'reach'가 적절하다.

07 책상이 너무 낮다는 불만에 어울리는 해결책으로 그 위에 몇 장의 패드를 놓는다는 말이 자연스럽다. 'intend to+동사원형'을 이용한다.

08 스위치가 너무 높다는 불만의 말에 대해 알맞은 해결책으로 '스위치 아래에 디딤대를 둘 생각이야.'라는 ④가 적절하다.

09 '나도 그렇다'는 의미로 부정문에서는 'either'를 사용한다.

10 G가 계단이 높다고 불만을 말하고 있고, B가 계단이 없는 새로운 길을 만들까 생각 중이라는 말로 보아 ③이 적절하다.

11 표지판에 점자(Braille)를 추가할까 생각 중이라고 말하는 것은 볼 수 없는 사람들에 대한 해결책이다.

12 '나는 …할까 생각 중이다'는 "I'm thinking of …"로 문장을 시작하고 전치사 of 뒤에는 동명사 changing을 사용한다. 'change A with B'는 'A를 B로 바꾸다'라는 의미이다.

13 'so+형용사[부사]+that+주어+can't …' 구문을 이용하여 원인과 결과를 나타낸다.

14 사역동사의 목적어와 목적격보어가 능동의 관계에 있을 경우 목적격보어로 원형 부정사를 쓴다.

15 (1) 'so+형용사[부사]+that+주어+can't …' 구문을 'too+형용사[부사]+to 동사원형' 구문으로 바꿀 때, that절 내의 동사의 목적어와 문장의 주어가 같으면 목적어를 쓰지 않는 것이 적절하다. (2) 사역동사의 목적어와 목적격보어가 능동의 관계에 있을 경우 목적격보어로 원형부정사를 쓴다.

16 그것은 더 나이 들거나 더 약한 사람들의 어려움을 느껴 보고, 그들의 관점에서 '해결책'을 찾으려고 노력함으로써 사람들이 '더 나은 삶'을 살도록 도와주는 방법이다.

17 put oneself in another's shoes: 상대편의 처지나 입장에서 생각하다(역지사지)

18 앞 문장의 내용을 가리킨다.

19 저상 버스는 다른 사람들도 버스를 '더 편안하게 탈 수 있도록' 도와준다.

20 ⓐ와 나머지들: 마침내, ② 실제로, 정말로, ③ 특히

21 ⓑ 지팡이가 '없이'는 잘 걸을 수 없었다고 하는 것이 적절하다. ⓒ 안경을 '쓰고'는 잘 볼 수 없었다고 하는 것이 적절하다.

22 get on: (버스 따위에) 오르다 / be difficult for: ~에게 어렵다

23 목적어가 주어 자신이므로 재귀대명사를 써야 한다.

Teens' Magazine

Reading 교과서

확인문제 p.216

1 T 2 T

확인문제 p.217

1 F 2 T 3 F

확인문제 p.218

1 F 2 T

확인문제 p.219

1 T 2 F 3 T

교과서 확인학습 A p.220~223

01 Teens'	02 in Shapes
03 Like	04 like, because
05 Snowman	06 outside
07 go out, play	08 have to
09 to snow, be cold	10 on days like these
11 a second, the most wonderful	
12 cover myself up, hide here	13 Looking Back
14 art	15 yours
16 UNTIL, OVER	17 slow walker
18 little things	19 Follow
20 My Bike	
21 take, To any place, home, enjoy riding	
22 Giving	23 there
24 here	25 umbrella
26 Between	27 Selfies
28 Though	29 robots
30 cute	31 a big cake
32 made him happy	33 Have you ever seen

34 What, Life	35 moment
36 take tests	37 have nothing
38 before, after	39 sleepy
40 after, rings	41 lovely time
42 lunch	43 favorite
44 last class	45 during break time
46 myself	47 awesome
48 than before	49 finishes earlier
50 because, rains, snows	51 for dessert
52 same class	53 most difficult
54 trash	55 Studying
56 Making a presentation	57 on time
59 Places, Village	60 Traditional
61 something delicious	62 make, full
63 choose, add, to	64 Youth
65 in the middle of	66 such as
67 take a break	69 near
70 after, because	71 to enjoy
72 Have Fun	73 Shape
74 cut, into, from	75 Five Lines
76 in such a way	77 Eating
78 are thrown away	79 breaks down into
80 go, fish	81 Up to
82 Let's	83 universal design
84 winners' works	85 come close
86 pull, away	87 need to
88 save lots of water	89 between
90 up, down easily	91 get some rest
92 special	93 together, for
94 LAUGH	95 Jokes
96 hopeful	97 full of
98 How, friendly	100 Why
101 To get	

교과서 확인학습 B p.224~227

1 Teens' Magazine

2 Works of Art in Shapes

3 Like a Circle

4 I love you like a circle because a circle never ends.

5 Snowman

6 It's cold outside.

7 I don't want to go out and play.

8 But Mom says I have to.

9 It's starting to snow and I'm going to be cold.

10 I don't like playing outside on days like these.

11 But wait a second, I have the most wonderful idea!

12 I'll cover myself up with snow and I'll hide here!

13 Looking Back with Your Handwriting

14 Life is art.

15 Live yours in COLOR.

16 IT ISN'T OVER UNTIL IT'S OVER.

17 I am a slow walker, but I never walk back.

18 I love the little things you do.

19 Follow your dream.

20 My Bike

21 Two wheels take me / To any place / To school / Back home / To the mountain / To the river / I love my bike / I enjoy riding it every day

22 Giving Tree

23 Out there – wet

24 In here – dry

25 Pretty big umbrella

26 Between me and the sky.

27 Selfies of This Year

28 Though we lost the game, we had a lot of fun.

29 Look at the robots we made.

30 Aren't they cute?

31 We made a big cake for Mr. Han.

32 It made him happy.

33 Have you ever seen a handsome Peter Pan like me?

34 What Do You Think of Your School Life?

35 The most uncomfortable moment

36 1. When I take tests

37 2. When I am really hungry and have nothing to eat

38 3. When I change clothes before and after P.E. class

39 4. others: When I am sleepy in class

40 When the teacher doesn't finish classes after the bell rings

41 The most lovely time

42 1. lunch time

43 2. class with my favorite teacher

44 3. the last class on Friday

45 4. others: when I am sleeping during break time

46 when I see myself in the mirror

47 The most awesome news

48 1. I got better grades than before

49 2. School finishes earlier today

50 3. I don't go to school because it rains or snows a lot

51 4. others: We eat delicious sweets for dessert

52 My best friend and I are in the same class

53 The most difficult work to do

54 1. Washing trash cans

55 2. Studying

56 3. Making a presentation in front of friends

57 4. others: Being on time every day

58 Group work

59 Places We Love in Our Village

60 Daehan Traditional Market

61 If you want to eat something delicious, visit Daehan Market.

62 You can buy "*yeopjeon*" and use it to make your lunch box full.

63 You can choose many kinds of food and add them to your lunch box.

64 Saebom Youth Center

65 This is Saebom Youth Center in the middle of our town.

66 We like this place because we can learn many things, such as dance and music.

67 We can also play board games and take a break here.

68 Mr. Kim's Bakery

69 This is a small bakery near the school.

70 We like to go there after school because we're always hungry!

71 It is good to enjoy delicious bread with friends.

72 Let's Have Fun with Puzzles!

73 Shape Puzzles

74 If you cut the shape A into two same pieces, you can then make all the other shapes(B, C, D, E, F, G) from those two pieces.

75 Ten Balls in Five Lines

76 Place 10 balls in 5 lines in such a way that each line has exactly 4 balls on it.

77 You Are Eating Plastic Spoons!

78 1. A lot of plastic spoons are thrown away every year.

79 2. Most plastic breaks down into smaller pieces in the ocean.

80 3. Very small pieces of plastic go into fish.

81 4. If you eat the fish, you eat the plastic, too. Up to 11,000 pieces each year!

82 Let's Make a Dream School!

83 We had a universal design contest for our school last month.

84 Here are the winners' works.

85 1. When your hands come close, water comes out.

86 When you pull your hands away, the water stops.

87 You don't need to turn or touch any parts.

88 We can save lots of water with this. — by O Juyeon(1–3)

89 2. This is our school park between two buildings.

90 Anybody can go up and down easily here.

91 Also we can sit and get some rest here. — by Gim Jimin(3-5)

92 3. These are special desks and chairs for the classroom.

93 For group activities, you can get them together and make a wonderful group table for three, four, or five students. — by Choi Yumi(2–1)

94 LET'S LAUGH

95 Funny Earth Day Jokes Ha! Ha! Ha!

96 Why are recycle bins hopeful?

97 Because they're full of cans.

98 How can you tell the ocean is friendly?

99 It waves.

100 Why did the sun go to school?

101 To get brighter.

서술형 실전문제 p.228~229

01 Though[Although]

02 (1) such as (2) are thrown away (3) friendly

03 (1) wheel, 바퀴 (2) circle, 원 (3) grade, 성적
(4) bread, 빵

04 (1) works (2) special

05 (1) I'll cover myself up with snow and I'll hide here!
(2) A cloth doll was made for her daughter by her.
(3) When did you go to Seoul?

06 (1) Though he is young, he has much gray hair.
(2) It is good to have friends.

07 like 08 go out and play

09 I'll cover myself up with snow and I'll hide here!

10 People throw away a lot of plastic spoons every year. 또는 People throw a lot of plastic spoons away every year.

11 but also 12 eleven thousand

13 깡통, 할 수 있다 14 일렁이다, 손을 흔들다

15 더 밝은, 더 똑똑한

01 양보의 부사절 though[although]가 적절하다. (1) 우리는 경기에서 졌지만, 아주 즐거웠다. (2) Anne은 Tim이 자신을 자

주 짜증스럽게 했는데도 그를 좋아했다.

02 (1) 춤과 음악 같은 많은 것을 배울 수 있어서 우리는 이곳을 좋아한다. (2) 해마다 많은 플라스틱 숟가락이 버려진다. throw away는 '버리다'는 뜻으로 숟가락이 버려지는 수동의 의미이기 때문에 be thrown away로 수동태가 적절하다. (3) 바다가 다정하다는 것을 어떻게 알 수 있는가? '다정한'의 의미로 명사 friend에 ly를 사용해서 형용사로 바꾸어 준다.

03 (1) 중심에서 막대기에 연결되어 차량 또는 기계 부품을 이동시키기 위해 사용되는 원형 물체 (2) 고정된 중심점으로부터 항상 동일한 거리인 점들의 연속된 곡선 (3) 누군가의 일이나 수행이 얼마나 좋은지 보여주는 숫자나 글자 (4) 밀가루, 물 및 보통 효모로 만들어지고 함께 섞어서 구워진 음식

05 (1) '동사+대명사 목적어+부사'의 어순이다. (2) make는 직접 목적어를 주어로 한 수동태만 가능하다. (3) when으로 시작하는 의문문이므로 현재완료 시제를 쓸 수 없다.

07 (A) don't like playing: 놀고 싶지 않다 (B) days like these: 이런 날

08 '내가 노는 것'이 생략되어 있다.

09 '눈으로 몸을 덮고 여기에 숨는 것'을 가리킨다.

10 People을 주어로 해서 고치는 것이 적절하다.

11 여러분이 물고기를 먹을 때, 물고기'뿐만 아니라' 그 물고기가 먹었던 아주 작은 플라스틱 조각들'도' 먹게 되기 때문이다.

12 'eleven thousands'처럼, 복수 형태로 쓰지 않도록 조심해야 한다.

13 재활용 통은 '깡통[할 수 있다]'으로 가득 차 있기 때문에 희망적이다.

14 바다가 '일렁이기[손을 흔들기]' 때문에 다정하다는 것을 알 수 있다.

15 태양은 '더 밝아지기[똑똑해지기]' 위해서 학교에 간다.

단원별 예상문제 p.230~234

01 ③ 02 like 03 ③

04 (1) breaks down (2) Up to (3) lots of

05 (1) cut, into, shapes (2) take, to

06 ① 07 ④ 08 up 09 ③

10 ② 11 so we like this place

12 (1) We had a universal design contest for our school last month.
(2) It is good to enjoy delicious bread with friends.

13 ⓐ ②, ⑤ ⓑ ①, ③, ④ 14 눈이 오는 날

15 me → myself 16 ④

17 that[which] 18 ② 19 ②

20 your life[lives] 21 ②, ④, ⑤

22 (A) last (B) during (C) myself 23 ⑤

24 ① 25 ⓐ yoopjeon ⓑ many kinds of food

26 ①, ⑤ 27 *yeopjeon* 28 time, ourselves
29 the robots (we made) 30 happily → happy
31 (A) awesome (B) dessert (C) the same
32 because of
33 school finishes earlier than usual → they got better grades than before 또는 the most wonderful → the second most wonderful
34 ② 35 like 36 ④

01 ③번은 'wave'에 대한 설명이다. 'shake hands'는 'to greet each other or say goodbye by briefly joining hands and moving them slightly up and down(짧게 손을 맞잡고 가볍게 아래위로 손을 움직임으로써 인사하거나 작별인사하다)'

02 유의어 관계다. 정확하게 : ~와 같은

03 '1. 시험을 칠 때 2. 정말 배가 고픈데 먹을 것이 없을 때 3. 체육 시간 전후에 옷을 갈아입을 때'는 모두 '불편한' 순간이다.

04 (1) break down: 분해되다 (2) up to: ~까지 (3) lots of: 많은

05 • cut A into B: A를 B로 자르다. 'all the other+복수 명사' 형태로 shapes가 맞다. • take A to B: A를 B로 데려 가다

06 '식사 끝에 먹는 단 음식'으로 '후식'이 맞다.

07 모두 반의어 관계이고, ④번은 '졸리는'의 뜻을 가진 유의어 관계다.

08 • cover A up with B: B로 A를 덮다 • up and down 위아래로

09 ① a such way → such a way ② is the ocean → the ocean is ④ either → too ⑤ little → lot[few]

10 ②번은 비인칭 주어이고 나머지는 모두 가주어이다.

11 '결과+because절(이유)' = '이유+so절(결과)'

12 (1) last month라는 과거를 나타내는 부사구가 있으므로 현재완료 시제를 쓸 수 없다. (2) 가주어로 That이 아니라 It이 적절하다.

13 ⓐ와 ②, ⑤: 현재분사, ⓑ와 ①, ③, ④: 동명사

14 '눈이 오는 날'을 의미한다.

15 주어와 목적어가 같으므로 재귀대명사로 고치는 것이 적절하다.

16 우리는 게임에 '졌지만', 아주 즐거웠다라고 해야 하므로, Though(비록 …이긴 하지만)가 적절하다.

17 목적격 관계대명사 that[which]이 생략되어 있다.

18 ⓒ와 ①, ④번: 경험 용법, ② 결과 용법, ③ 완료 용법, ⑤ 계속 용법

19 ⓐ 손 글씨 ② 캘리그래피: 붓이나 특별한 펜을 사용하여 아름다운 손 글씨를 만드는 예술, ① (컴퓨터 자료를 출력한) 인쇄(물), ③ 광고, ④ 생산물, 상품, ⑤ (물품·책 등의) 목록, 카탈로그

20 '너의 삶'을 가리킨다.는 entire와 같은 의미이다.

21 ⓒ와 ②, ④, ⑤: (형상·규모가) 작은(opp. big, large), ⓒ '작은' 일들, ① [추상명사·물질명사와 함께] (a little+명사) 《긍정적으로》 조금은 있는(some), 다소간의, 어느 정도의, ③ a little: 《긍정적으로》 조금은, 조금

22 (A) '마지막' 수업이라고 해야 하므로 last가 적절하다. last: 마지막의, latest: 최근의 (B) '쉬는 시간에'라고 해야 하므로 during이 적절하다. 'during+기간을 나타내는 명사', 'for+숫자' (C) 주어와 목적어가 같으므로 myself가 적절하다.

23 위 글은 'survey(설문조사)'이다. ① (책·연극·영화 등에 대한) 논평[비평], 감상문, ② 요약, 개요, ③ 수필, ④ (신문·잡지의) 글, 기사

24 ③ 학생들은 '쉬는 시간에 잠잘 때'보다 '점심 먹는 것'을 더 좋아한다.

25 ⓐ 엽전, ⓒ '많은 종류의 음식'을 가리킨다.

26 ⓑ와 ②, ③, ④는 부사적 용법, ① 명사적 용법, ⑤ 형용사적 용법

27 대한 전통 시장에서 여러분의 점심 도시락을 가득 채우고 싶다면, '엽전'을 쓸 수 있다.

28 have a lot of fun = have a good[great] time = enjoy oneself: 재미있게 놀다, 즐겁게 보내다

29 '우리가 만든 로봇들'을 가리킨다.

30 목적격보어 자리에 부사를 쓸 수 없으므로 형용사로 바꾸는 것이 적절하다.

31 (A) 가장 '멋진' 뉴스라고 해야 하므로 awesome이 적절하다. awesome: 기막히게 좋은, 굉장한, awful: 끔찍한, 지독한 (B) '후식'으로 맞있는 단것을 먹는다고 해야 하므로 dessert가 적절하다. dessert: 후식, desert: 사막 (C) '같은' 반이 되었다고 해야 하므로 'the same'이 적절하다.

32 because+주어+동사, because of+명사구

33 학생들에게는 '전보다 좋은 성적을 받았다'는 뉴스가 가장 멋진 뉴스이다.

34 이 글은 장소를 소개하는 글이므로, 제목으로는 '우리 마을에서 우리가 좋아하는 곳들'이 적절하다.

35 such as = like: ~와 같은

36 '하이킹을 갈 수 있다.'는 말은 언급되어 있지 않다.

교과서 파헤치기

Lesson 5

01 원
02 모양, 모습
03 구르다
04 흥분된
05 끓이다
06 끝이 뾰족한
07 공유하다
08 누르다
09 책꽂이
10 완벽한
11 운동하다
12 풀다, 해결하다
13 서두르다
14 비닐봉지
15 나누다
16 고르다, 선택하다
17 막대기, 나뭇가지
18 옷걸이
19 혼잡, 혼란
20 둥근
21 삼각형
22 어려운
23 불평하다
24 사각형
25 통제하다, 조절하다
26 다치게 하다
26 소리치다, 외치다
28 영혼, 요정
29 돌리다, 회전시키다
30 깨닫다, 알아차리다
31 마지막으로
32 물을 주다
33 서두르다, 돌진하다
34 잘 정돈된, 단정한, 깔끔한
35 서로
36 감싸다, 포장하다
37 ~을 치우다
38 ~을 담당하여
39 자기 혼자서
40 A를 B로 나누다
41 담당하고 있는, 통제 중인
42 A를 조각으로 자르다
43 반대편

01 boil
02 control
03 hurt
04 shape
05 face
06 finally
07 choose
08 stick
09 complain
10 hanger
11 triangle
12 solve
13 shout
14 pointy
15 carry
16 share
17 roll
18 bookshelf
19 perfect
20 round
21 tidy
22 divide
23 hurry
24 spin
25 spirit
26 reply
27 mess
28 realize
29 water
30 rush
31 without
32 puzzle
33 square
34 move
35 divide A into B
36 one by one
37 pick up ~
38 take away
39 put A on B
40 wrap up
41 in charge of ~
42 one another
43 by oneself

1 pointy, 끝이 뾰족한　2 spirit, 요정　3 roll, 구르다
4 perfect, 완벽한　5 excited, 흥분한　6 decide, 결정하다
7 mess, 혼란, 혼잡　8 complain, 불평하다
9 reply, 대답하다　10 hold, 잡고 있다, 시행하다

11 ruch, 서두르다, 돌진하다　12 hula hoop, 훌라후프
13 control, 조절하다, 통제하다
14 realize, 깨닫다, 알아차리다　15 hanger, 옷걸이
16 wheel, 바퀴

Get Ready 2

(1) can't stand alone, how to solve / Put, on, bottom
(2) how to divide, into, equal pieces / Let, see, dividing, the same size, shape
(3) doesn't move, how to move / Put wheels

Start Off Listen & Talk A

1 how to make three squares, with three moves / First, move this stick /
2 with, how to make / too difficult for, Can, break, in half / you can't

Start Off Listen & Talk B

how to divide, into, pieces / First, divide, into, equal, Then, divide, into, Finally / other, around

Speak Up Look and talk.

how to draw / First, Then, Finally, in the square

Speak Up Mission

how to make / show you how

Real-life Scene

how to solve / take, across, the river, only carries, at a time / take, to, other side one by one / without, eat the rice / First, Then, come back with / Finally

Express Yourself A

1 how to make / cut off, used jeans
2 looks great / how to make / First, Then, dried, Finally, wrap it up, make a triangle
3 how to fly / has to face, Hold, up

Learning Diary Check Yourself

how to draw, with shapes / First, triangle, Then, dots, Finally, small circles / draw, myself

Get Ready 2

(1) G: This bookshelf can't stand alone. Do you know how to solve this problem?
　　B: Put some legs on the bottom.
(2) G: Do you know how to divide this cake into four equal pieces?
　　B: Let me see. … How about dividing it this way? Then the pieces will be the same size and shape.

(3) G: This car doesn't move. Do you know how to move it?

B: Sure. Put wheels under the car.

1 G: These twelve sticks make four squares. Do you know how to make three squares of the same size with three moves?

B: Sure. First, move this stick here.

2 B: Here's a triangle with three pencils. Do you know how to make three more triangles with three more pencils?

G: Let me see. ··· It's too difficult for me. Can I break the pencils in half?

B: No, you can't.

B: Do you know how to divide this into four equal pieces?

G: Sure. First, divide it into three equal squares. Then, divide each square into four smaller squares. Finally, color three small squares in the inside corner of the L.

B: Oh, I can see three other L shapes around it! You're great!

A: Do you know how to draw a fish with shapes?

B: Sure. First, draw a large square. Then, draw a triangle. Finally, draw a small circle in the square.

A: Do you know how to make paper airplanes?

B: Sure. I'll show you how.

B: Do you know how to solve this puzzle?

G: What is it?

B: You must take a dog, a chicken, and a bag of rice across the river. The boat only carries you and one of the things at a time.

G: That's easy. I can take them to the other side one by one.

B: But without you, the dog will kill the chicken, and the chicken will eat the rice.

G: Let me see. ... First, take the chicken and come back. Then, take the rice and come back with the chicken.

B: And?

G: After that, take the dog and come back. Finally, take the chicken.

B: You're great!

1 B: Do you know how to make this?

G: Sure. First, cut off the leg from used jeans.

2 B: This looks great.

G I think so, too. Do you know how to make it?

B: It's easy. First, put some rice on *gim*. Then, add some dried fish and hot peppers. Finally, wrap it up and make a triangle.

3 B: Do you know how to fly this?

G: Yes. I'll show you how. It has to face the wind. Hold it up like this.

W: Excuse me. Do you know how to draw a mouse with shapes?

M: Sure. First, draw a large triangle. Then, draw two dots and 6 lines. Finally, draw two small circles.

W: Thanks. I'll draw it myself now.

01 Shape, Spirits

02 There lived, spirits

03 controlled, bookshelf, window

04 charge, hangers, plants

05 took care, round

06 worked together, for

07 decided, better, shouted

08 Take, away, pointy

09 waters, every day

10 Take, away, roll, break

11 exercises with, every

12 tidy, mess, complained 13 looked at, other

14 think, without, asked

15 better, by myself 16 get, rest, said

17 went out, in control

18 hangers, round, square

19 looked around, smiled 20 Much better

21 picked up, hang, on 22 hold, clothes

23 went, water, leaves 24 Poor, must be

25 picked up, to exercise 26 how to spin

27 take out, looked at 28 ride, have to

29 hurried out of

30 other, back, over

31 doesn't, what to do

32 hangers, all, square

33 one another, realized

34 great, others, once again

45

01 Shape, Spirits

02 There lived, shape spirits

03 controlled, bookshelf

04 was in charge of

05 took care of, round things

06 worked together to make

07 to make the room better, shouted at

08 Take, away, pointy leaves

09 waters them every day

10 Take, away, roll and break

11 exercises with it

12 try to, tidy, make a mess, complained

13 looked at each other 14 without us

15 make, better all by myself 16 get some rest

17 went out, in control 18 made, square

19 looked around, smiled 20 Much better

21 came home, picked up, to hang, on

22 hold my clothes 23 went to water

24 must be 25 picked up, to exercise

26 how to spin 27 to take out, looked at

28 can't ride, have to 29 hurried out of

30 other, came back, rushed over to

31 what to do

32 looked at, all the new square things

33 one another, realized

34 great, the others, once again

1 세 도형 요정들

2 Mike의 방에는 세 도형 요정이 살았다.

3 Square는 탁자, 책장, 그리고 창문을 담당했다.

4 Triangle은 옷걸이들과 식물들을 담당했다.

5 Circle은 둥근 것들을 돌보았다.

6 그들은 Mike에게 좋은 방을 만들어 주기 위해서 함께 일했다.

7 어느 날 Square는 방을 더 낫게 만들기로 결심하고 나머지 요정들에게 소리쳤다.

8 "이 식물들을 치워, 그렇지 않으면 그것들의 끝이 뾰족한 잎사귀들이 누군가를 다치게 할 거야!" 그가 Triangle에게 말했다.

9 "하지만 Mike가 매일 그들에게 물을 주는데." Triangle이 말했다.

10 "이 훌라후프를 치워, 그렇지 않으면 굴러가서 뭔가를 부술 거야!" 그가 Circle에게 말했다.

11 "하지만 Mike는 매일 그걸로 운동을 하는데." Circle이 말했다.

12 "난 이 방을 정돈하려고 애쓰지만, 너희 둘은 항상 엉망으로 만들어." 그가 불평했다.

13 Triangle과 Circle이 서로를 쳐다보았다.

14 "그래서 네 생각에는 네가 우리 없이 다 할 수 있다는 거야?" Triangle이 Square에게 물었다.

15 "물론이지. 난 완전히 혼자서 이 방을 더 낫게 만들 수 있어." Square가 대답했다.

16 "잘됐네! 그럼 우린 쉴 수 있겠어." Circle이 Square에게 말했다.

17 Triangle과 Circle이 밖으로 나갔고 이제 Square가 모든 것을 담당했다.

18 그는 옷걸이들과 식물들과 모든 둥근 물건들을 사각형으로 만들었다.

19 그리고 나서 그는 주위를 둘러보고 미소 지었다.

20 "훨씬 좋군!"

21 Mike가 학교에서 집으로 왔을 때, 그는 재킷을 걸기 위해 사각형 옷걸이 하나를 집었다.

22 "뭐야? 이것은 내 옷을 걸고 있지 못할 거야."

23 그는 식물에 물을 주러 가서 그것들의 사각형 잎사귀들을 보았다.

24 "불쌍한 것들… 그들은 병든 것이 틀림없어."

25 그는 운동을 하기 위해 사각형 훌라후프를 집어 들었다.

26 "흠… 이걸 어떻게 돌리는지 모르겠어."

27 그는 자전거를 꺼내러 가서 사각형 바퀴들을 보았다.

28 "음, 난 이걸 탈 수 없어. 그냥 걸어가야 할 것 같아."

29 그리고 나서 그는 서둘러 집을 나섰다.

30 다른 요정들이 돌아왔을 때, Square는 그들에게 달려갔다.

31 "Mike는 그의 방을 좋아하지 않아. 난 뭘 해야 할지 모르겠어." 그가 말했다.

32 그들은 옷걸이들, 식물들, 그리고 모든 새로 사각형이 된 물건들을 바라보았다.

33 그리고 나서 그들은 서로를 바라보았고, Square는 자신의 문제를 깨달았다.

34 "이 방을 다시 멋지게 만들자." 그가 나머지 요정들에게 말했고, 세 요정들은 다시 한 번 함께 일했다.

1 Three Shape Spirits

2 There lived three shape spirits in Mike's room.

3 Square controlled the table, the bookshelf, and the window.

4 Triangle was in charge of the hangers and the plants.

5 Circle took care of the round things.

6 They worked together to make a nice room for Mike.

7 One day Square decided to make the room better and shouted at the other spirits.

8 "Take these plants away, or their pointy leaves will hurt someone!" he said to Triangle.

9 "But Mike waters them every day," said Triangle.

10 "Take this hula hoop away, or it will roll and break something!" he said to Circle.

11 "But Mike exercises with it every day," said Circle.

12 "I try to make this room tidy, but you two always make a mess," he complained.

13 Triangle and Circle looked at each other.

14 "So you think you can do it without us?" Triangle asked Square.

15 "Sure. I can make this room better all by myself," replied Square.

16 "Great! Then we can get some rest," Circle said to Square.

17 Triangle and Circle went out and Square was now in control.

18 He made the hangers, plants, and all the round things square.

19 Then he looked around and smiled.

20 "Much better!"

21 When Mike came home from school, he picked up a square hanger to hang his jacket on.

22 "What? This will not hold my clothes."

23 He went to water the plants and saw their square leaves.

24 "Poor things. ... They must be sick."

25 He picked up the square hula hoop to exercise.

26 "Hmm ... I don't know how to spin this."

27 He went to take out his bike and looked at the square wheels.

28 "Well, I can't ride this. I'll just have to walk."

29 Then he hurried out of the house.

30 When the other spirits came back, Square rushed over to them.

31 "Mike doesn't like his room. I don't know what to do," he said.

32 They looked at the hangers, the plants, and all the new square things.

33 Then they looked at one another, and Square realized his problem.

34 "Let's make this room great again," he said to the others, and the three spirits worked together once again.

Your Turn

1. how to cook / First, Then, Finally, more minutes
2. how to make / boil, cut, into, put, on
3. how to make sandwiches / put, on bread, add, put, on top

Express Yourself

1. Square
2. out of used jeans
3. what to wear with
4. made, excited, made, happy

Link to the World

1. taught, at, when
2. call, father, math
3. how to draw, three sides, same length
4. how to find, the biggest circle
5. One day, an easier way to study
6. royal road to learning

Your Turn

1. A: Do you know how to cook *ramyeon*?
 B: Sure. First, boil some water. Then, put the *ramyeon* and dried soup mix. Finally, boil for 4 more minutes.

2. A: Do you know how to make potato salad?
 B: Sure. First, boil the potatoes. Then, cut them into pieces. Finally, put some sauce on them.

3. A: Do you know how to make sandwiches?
 B: Sure. First, put an egg on bread. Then, add some vegetables. Finally, put bread on top.

Express Yourself

1. Square for Mom
2. I made a square bag out of used jeans.
3. My mom knew what to wear with it.
4. It made her excited. That made me happy.

Link to the World

1. Euclid taught math at the Library of Alexandria when Ptolemy 1 was the king of Egypt.
2. People call him "the father of math."
3. He showed how to draw a triangle that has three sides of the same length.
4. He also showed how to find the center of the biggest circle in a triangle.
5. One day, Ptolemy 1 asked, "Is there an easier way to study math?"
6. Euclid replied, "There is no royal road to learning."

13 secret, 비결, 비밀 14 instead, 대신에

15 napkin, 냅킨 16 cloth, 천, 옷감

단어 TEST Step 1 p.21

01 포장, 포장지 02 도전 03 비결, 비밀

04 비어 있는 05 제공하다, 나누어 주다

06 티끌 하나 없는 07 선택하다 08 사실, 실제로

09 천, 옷감 10 재사용하다 11 재사용할 수 있는

12 줄이다, 축소하다 13 일어나다, 발생하다

14 포장지 15 대신에 16 엄지손가락

17 포장하다 18 접시 19 모으다, 수집하다

20 쓰레기 21 제품, 상품 22 끔찍한

23 저장하다 24 절약하다, 아끼다

25 자연의, 가공하지 않은 26 재활용하다

27 단순한 28 음식 쓰레기 29 무명, 면

30 (쓰레기) 통 31 피부 32 믹서기, 분쇄기

33 기계 34 언어 35 ~에 좋다

36 버리다 37 매우 바쁜 38 ~의 한가운데

39 중요한 사람 40 ~의 몇 배 41 매우 행복하다

42 원예에 재능이 있다 43 매우 친절하다

단어 TEST Step 2 p.22

01 packaging 02 store 03 challenge

04 skin 05 empty 06 natural

07 reuse 08 save 09 food waste

10 happen 11 collect 12 serve

13 island 14 reusable 15 spotless

16 item 17 choose 18 special

19 terrible 20 thumb 21 actually

22 reduce 23 bin 24 wrap

25 language 26 machine 27 simple

28 instead 29 ocean 30 trash

31 product 32 recycle 33 cotton

34 secret 35 cut up 36 in the middle of

37 throw a party 38 be good for 39 throw away

40 be powered 41 as busy as a bee

42 take 목적어 back 43 배수사 as 원급 as

단어 TEST Step 3 p.23

1 tip, 조언 2 skin, 피부 3 agree, 동의하다

4 reduce, 줄이다 5 thumb, 엄지손가락

6 challenge, 도전 7 wrapping paper, 포장지

8 leave, 남기다 9 trash, 쓰레기 10 cotton, 무명, 면

11 wrap, 포장하나 12 recycle, 새활봉하나

대화문 TEST Step 1 p.24~25

Get Ready 2

(1) beautiful / out of, broken / surprise

(2) Why, eating / Actually, use, as / That's surprising

(3) kills two birds with one stone / What, mean by / exercise, make juice / get

Start Off Listen & Talk A

(1) feel blue / mean by that / mean, sad, too much trash / get, should recycle, reuse

(2) spotless / What do you mean / clean / Let's learn, tips

Start Off Listen & Talk B

one tip, clean / clean / What, mean by that / throw away trash, stays empty / surprising, tell me more / problem

Speak Up Look and talk

bottles, for the Earth / What, mean by / take, to break down / surprising

Speak Up Mission

green thumb / What, by that / is good at, plants / get

Real-life Scene

in the middle of / trash islands / mean by / A lot of, ocean, becomes big islands like / sounds terrible, How big / biggest, as large as / surprising, should not / agree

Fun Time

skateboard, every day / surprising

big fish / What, mean by that / important

Express Yourself

(1) energy tree / mean / produces, is used, street lamp / surprising

(2) is, called / is called / special / powered by trash / surprising

Learning Diary Listen & Speak

spotless / one tip / clean bin / What do you mean by that / throw away, stay empty / Thanks for / pleasure

대화문 TEST Step 2 p.26~27

Get Ready 2

(1) B: This shopping bag is so beautiful.

 G. Thank you. We made it out of a broken umbrella.

B: What a surprise !

(2) B: Why are you eating a cup?

G: Actually , this cup is a cookie. I can use it as a cup and then eat it.

B: That's surprising!

(3) B: This bike blender kills two birds with one stone.

G: What do you mean by that?

B: When you ride this bike, you exercise and make juice .

G: Oh, I get it.

Start Off Listen & Talk A

(1) G: I feel blue today.

B: What do you mean by that ?

G: I mean I feel sad . We make too much trash.

B: Ah, I get it now. We should recycle and reuse more.

(2) G: Minji's classroom is spotless.

B: What do you mean by that?

G: Her classroom is really clean. Look.

B: You're right. Let's learn some good tips from her.

Start Off Listen & Talk B

B: Hey, Minji. What is one tip for a clean classroom?

G: Well, we're doing a clean bin project today.

B: What do you mean by that?

G: We don't throw away trash , so our trash can stays empty.

B: That's surprising! Please tell me more about it.

G: Sure. No problem .

Speak Up Look and talk

B: Plastic bottles are a big problem for the Earth.

G: What do you mean by that?

B: They take 450 years to break down.

G: That's surprising!

Speak Up Mission

A: My mom has a green thumb.

B: What do you mean by that?

A: She is good at growing plants.

B: I get it.

Real-life Scene

G: What are those in the middle of the ocean?

B: They are trash islands .

G: Trash islands? What do you mean by that?

B: A lot of plastic trash goes into the ocean and becomes big islands like those.

G: That sounds terrible ! How big are those islands?

B: The biggest one is about 14 times as large as South Korea.

G: That's surprising! I think we should not use plastic products.

B: I agree .

Fun Time

A: I skateboard to school every day.

B: That's surprising! A: Minsu is a big fish.

B: What do you mean by that?

A: I mean, he is an important person.

B: Ah, I get it.

Express Yourself

(1) B: This is the energy tree.

G: What do you mean by that?

B: It produces energy from the sun. And it is used as a street lamp at night.

G: That's surprising!

(2) B: What is this bus called?

G: It is called the green bus.

B: What is special about it?

G: The green bus is powered by trash.

B: That's surprising!

Learning Diary Listen & Speak

B: Hey, Minji. Your classroom is spotless.

G: Thank you.

B: What's one tip for a clean classroom?

G: Well, we're doing a clean bin project this week.

B: What do you mean by that?

G: We don't throw away trash, so our trash can stay empty.

B: Ah, I get it now. Thanks for your tip.

G: My pleasure .

본문 TEST Step 1 p.28~29

01 No, Challenge

02 had, Trash, last

03 winter, Grade, Class

04 Let's, few tips, green

05 Do, Wrapping Paper

06 threw, produce, trash

07 your secrets

08 agreed, wrap, because, recycled

09 brought, as, wrapped, all

10 Buy, Largest

11 chose, largest, bought

12 less packaging, trash

13 Eat, Plates

14 how, serve

15 seved, on plates

16 know what

17 even, after, used

18 ate, plates

19 mean by that

20 as plates, leave, behind

21 get it

22 quite interesting

23 Bring, Own

24 What about 25 didn't use, plastic

26 Instead, brought, took, back

27 Use Cloth 28 else, less trash

29 used cloth 30 good for, skin

31 where, get, cloth 32 were made by

33 cut up, make 34 Everyone, her cute

35 Leave, Behind

36 simple tip, reducing trash

37 Don't leave, plate 38 Food waste, big

39 But see

40 ate everything, even

01 Trash Challenge 02 No Trash Challenge

03 Grade 2 Class 3

04 Let's read, a few tips, living green

05 Do Not, Wrapping Paper

06 threw, didn't produce, lot 07 your secrets

08 agreed not to wrap, because, is not easily recycled

09 such as, not wrapped at all

10 Buy, Largest

11 chose the largest size, bought

12 less packaging, less trash 13 Eat, Plates

14 how, serve 15 served, on plates

16 You know what

17 even the plates, used

18 ate the plates 19 mean by that

20 popped, as plates, leave nothing behind

21 get it 22 quite interesting

23 Bring, Own 24 What about

25 didn't use

26 Instead, brought, from, took them back

27 Cloth 28 make less trash

29 used cloth napkins

30 are not good for your skin

31 where did you get 32 were made by

33 cut up

34 Everyone, her cute napkins

35 Leave, Behind

36 one simple tip, reducing trash

37 Don't leave, plate 38 Food waste

39 see 40 ate everything, even

1 쓰레기를 없애기 위한 도전

2 우리는 모두 지난달에 '쓰레기를 없애기 위한 도전'의 날을 가졌습니다.

3 우승자는 2학년 3반이었습니다.

4 인터뷰를 읽고, 친환경적으로 살기 위한 몇 가지 비결을 배웁시다.

5 포장지를 사용하지 마라

6 기자: 여러분은 학급 생일 파티를 열었지만, 쓰레기가 많이 나오지 않았어요.

7 비결이 무엇입니까?

8 민수: 우선, 우리는 몇몇 포장지가 쉽게 재활용되지 않기 때문에 선물을 포장하지 않는 것에 동의했습니다.

9 그래서 우리는 전혀 포장되어 있지 않은 곰 인형, 열쇠고리, 머리핀과 같은 선물을 가져왔습니다.

10 가장 큰 크기를 사라

11 지은: 또한, 우리는 파티를 위한 아이스크림과 쿠키를 살 때, 가장 큰 크기를 골랐습니다.

12 크기가 더 크면 포장을 더 적게 사용하고 쓰레기를 더 적게 배출하거든요.

13 접시를 먹어라

14 기자: 그리고 아이스크림은 어떻게 나누어 주었나요?

15 준하: 우리는 접시에 그것을 나누어 주었습니다.

16 아세요?

17 우리는 사용한 후에 접시까지도 먹었어요.

18 기자: 접시를 먹었다고요?

19 그게 무슨 뜻이죠?

20 준하: 사실, 우리는 뻥튀기를 접시로 사용해서, 그것들을 먹고 아무것도 남기지 않을 수 있었죠.

21 기자: 아, 알겠어요.

22 그거 꽤 흥미롭군요.

23 여러분 자신의 물건을 가져와라

24 기자: 컵과 숟가락은 어떻게 했나요?

25 민수: 우리는 종이컵이나 플라스틱 숟가락을 사용하지 않았습니다.

26 대신에, 우리 컵과 숟가락을 집에서 가져온 후, 다시 가져갔습니다.

27 천 냅킨을 사용해라

28 기자: 쓰레기를 더 줄이기 위해 그 외에 무엇을 했나요?

29 지은: 우리는 천 냅킨을 사용했어요.

30 아시다시피, 종이 냅킨은 여러분의 피부에 안 좋아요.

31 기자: 하지만 천 냅킨을 어디서 구했나요?

32 지은: 그것들은 민지가 만들었어요.

33 그녀가 우리에게 몇 개를 만들어 주기 위해 자신의 낡은 면 셔츠를 잘랐어요.

34 그녀의 귀여운 냅킨을 모두가 좋아했어요.

35 음식을 남기지 마라

36 기자: 우리에게 쓰레기를 줄이기 위한 간단한 조언을 하나만 해

주세요.

37 준하: 접시에 음식을 남기지 마세요.

38 음식 쓰레기는 정말 큰 문제입니다.

39 하지만 아시죠?

40 우리는 모두 다 먹었죠, 접시까지도요, 하하.

본문 TEST Step 4·Step 5 p.34~37

1 No Trash Challenge

2 We all had a "No Trash Challenge" day last month.

3 The winner was Grade 2 Class 3.

4 Let's read the interview and learn a few tips for living green.

5 Do Not Use Wrapping Paper

6 Reporter: You threw a class birthday party, but didn't produce a lot of trash.

7 What were your secrets?

8 Minsu: First, we agreed not to wrap our gifts, because some wrapping paper is not easily recycled.

9 So we brought gifts such as teddy bears, key rings, and hairpins that were not wrapped at all.

10 Buy the Largest Size

11 Jieun: Also, we chose the largest size when we bought ice cream and cookies for the party.

12 Larger sizes use less packaging and make less trash.

13 Eat the Plates

14 Reporter: And how did you serve the ice cream?

15 Junha: We served it on plates.

16 You know what?

17 We ate even the plates after we used them.

18 Reporter: You ate the plates?

19 What do you mean by that?

20 Junha: Actually, we used popped rice cakes as plates, so we could eat them and leave nothing behind!

21 Reporter: Ah, I get it.

22 That's quite interesting.

23 Bring Your Own Things

24 Reporter: What about cups and spoons?

25 Minsu: We didn't use paper cups or plastic spoons.

26 Instead, we brought our own cups and spoons from home and then took them back.

27 Use Cloth Napkins

28 Reporter: What else did you do to make less trash?

29 Jieun: We used cloth napkins.

30 You know, paper napkins are not good for your skin.

31 Reporter: But where did you get the cloth napkins?

32 Jieun: They were made by Minji.

33 She cut up her old cotton shirt to make some for us.

34 Everyone liked her cute napkins.

35 Leave No Food Behind

36 Reporter: Please give us one simple tip for reducing trash.

37 Junha: Don't leave any food on your plate.

38 Food waste really is a big problem.

39 But see?

40 We ate everything, even our plates, ha-ha.

구석구석지문 TEST Step 1 p.38

Project Do it yourself

1. is made of
2. a little time to make
3. Let's make a few, puppet show
4. is made out of, used
5. shines beautifully through

Express Yourself C

1. Green, Ideas
2. were presented by
3. is served on small plates
4. Food waste, reduced
5. rain water is stored
6. Water is saved

Link to The World

1. That, Can Eat
2. can eat these spoons
3. were made out of
4. natural
5. use, green, reduce, trash
6. can save, because, don't have to

구석구석지문 TEST Step 2 p.39

Project Do it yourself

1. This is a hand puppet. It is made of my old sock.
2. It took only a little time to make this.
3. Let's make a few more sock puppets and have a wonderful puppet show together.

4. This is a paper bag lamp. It is made out of a used paper shopping bag.

5. Light shines beautifully through the holes.

Express Yourself C

1. Green City Ideas

2. So many ideas were presented by the Earth Savers Club.

3. In the restaurants, food is served on small plates.

4. Food waste is reduced this way.

5. At every house, rain water is stored in the tanks.

6. Water is saved this way.

Link to The World

1. Spoons That You Can Eat

2. You can eat these spoons .

3. They were made out of rice.

4v They are 100% natural .

5. We can use these green spoons and reduce plastic trash .

6. We also can save water because we don't have to wash these spoons.

단어 TEST Step 1 p.40

01 멋있는, 대단한, 굉장한		02 ~의 아래에
03 고전의	04 실제로, 사실	05 예, 사례
06 계절	07 독특한, 특별한	08 널리
09 훌륭한, 뛰어난	10 차이	11 표현하다
12 판타지, 환상, 공상	13 포함하다	14 왕조, 왕가
15 마법사	16 이야기	17 탐정; 탐정의
18 공예	19 (사람, 동물의) 상, 모형	
20 예술의, 예술적인	21 공연	22 시
23 외국의	24 창의적인	25 인기 있는
26 괴물	27 둘 다	28 완벽한
29 도구, 수단	30 상상하다	31 손 글씨, 필적
32 번개	33 모으다	34 날카로운
35 ~로 만들어지다	36 ~로 이끌다, ~로 이어지다	
37 만들다	38 ~처럼 보이다	39 수업을 듣다
40 ~하는 데 시간이 걸리다		41 무료로
42 ~에 맞춰 춤추다	43 처음에	

단어 TEST Step 2 p.41

01 below	02 detective	03 craft
04 actually	05 perfect	06 character
07 performance	08 fantasy	09 creative
10 awesome	11 handwriting	12 hold
13 excellent	14 figure	15 poem
16 dynasty	17 difference	18 artistic
19 tale	20 horror	21 widely
22 popular	23 tail	24 foreign
25 learn	26 lightning	27 example
28 between	29 collect	30 monster
31 wizard	32 sharp	33 express
34 unique	35 dance to	36 at first
37 build up	38 for free	39 be interested in
40 lead to	41 be made of	42 take a class
43 look like+명사		

단어 TEST Step 3 p.42

1 artistic, 예술의 2 below, ~의 아래에 3 unique, 독특한
4 wizard, 마법사 5 dynasty, 왕조 6 express, 표현하다
7 include, 포함하다 8 lightning, 번개
9 nowadays, 요즈음에는, 오늘날 10 autumn, 가을
11 popular, 인기 있는 12 tale, 이야기 13 season, 계절

대화문 TEST Step 1
p.43~44

Get Ready 2

(1) enjoy listening, dance to / Great

(2) Are, interested in cooking / sometimes, for

(3) Are you interested in learning, Actually, calligraphy class, work / Excellent

Start Off Listen & Talk A

(1) Good job, holding, How creative / interested in taking pictures / taking, online class for free / good for

(2) Good, expresses, feeling, autumn / Are, interested / taking, on weekends / didn't that

Start Off Listen & Talk B

did, job, awesome / made of / Are, interested in glass art / How long, take to make / It took

Speak Up Look and talk

enjoyed, performance, a good job / interested, playing the / Can you / problem

Speak Up Mission

interested in watching horror / am, I'm not, interested in reading detective

Real-life Scene

are, doing / practicing calligraphy / writing, looks fun / interested, calligraphy / What, think / looks like, dancing, open / got, means / did, job, try / Why not, brush

Your Turn

writing something / art homework / did, good

Express Yourself

(1) learning / interested in / join, learn

(2) interested in / Not / what, interested / interested, traditional, awesome

(3) Look at, learning / interested / sound, want to learn

Learning Diary Listen & Speak

interested / good at taking care of / How about, interested, too / can't grow

대화문 TEST Step 2
p.45~46

Get Ready 2

(1) B: Do you like K-pop?

G: Yes. I enjoy listening to SJ's songs. I can dance to his songs.

B: Great!

(2) B: Are you interested in cooking Korean dishes?

W: Yes. I sometimes cook bulgogi for my family and they love it.

(3) B: Are you interested in learning *Hangeul*?

G: Yes. Actually, I'm learning it in my calligraphy class. Look! This is my work.

B: Excellent!

Start Off Listen & Talk A

(1) B: Good job! Someone is holding a cloud? How creative!

G: Thank you. Are you interested in taking pictures?

B: Yes, I am. Actually, I'm taking an online class for free.

G: Oh, good for you.

(2) G: Good work! I think your painting expresses the feeling of autumn well.

B: Thank you. Are you interested in painting?

G: Yes, I am. I started taking a class on weekends.

B: Oh, I didn't know that.

Start Off Listen & Talk B

B: You did a good job! It's awesome.

G: Thanks.

B: What is it made of? Glass?

G: Yes, it is. Are you interested in glass art?

B: Yes, very much. How long did it take to make it?

G: It took one month.

Speak Up Look and talk

B: I enjoyed your performance. You did a good job.

G: Thank you. Are you interested in playing the ukulele?

B: Sure. Can you teach me?

G: No problem.

Speak Up Mission

A: Are you interested in watching horror movies?

B: Yes, I am. I watch horror movies very often. / No, I'm not. I'm interested in reading detective stories.

Real-life Scene

James: What are you doing, Mina?

Mina: I'm practicing calligraphy.

James: You're writing with a brush. It looks fun.

Mina: Are you interested in calligraphy?

James: Yes, very much.

Mina: Look at this! I just wrote it. What do you think?

James: It looks like a person dancing with open arms.

Mina: You got it. This Korean word means "dance."

James: You did a good job! Can I try it?

Mina: Why not? Take this brush.

Your Turn

A: You're writing something. What's this?

B: It's my art homework. Do you like it?

A: Sure. I think you did a good job!

Express Yourself

(1) B: Look! Two girls are learning Hangeul.

 G: Are you interested in *Hangeul*, Kevin?

 B: Yes, very much. I want to join them and learn it.

(2) B: Julie, are you interested in *hanbok*?

 G: Not really.

 B: Then, what are you interested in?

 G: Well, I'm interested in taekwondo. It is a traditional Korean sport. It's awesome.

(3) G: Look at the two men learning *pansori*.

 B: Are you interested in pansori, Nancy?

 G: Sure. I like the sound of it. I want to learn it.

Learning Diary Listen & Speak

B: Minji, are you interested in animals?

G: Yes, I am. I'm good at taking care of them.

B: How about plants? Are you interested in them, too?

G: No, I'm not. I can't grow them well.

본문 TEST Step 1 p.47~48

01 Write, Feelings A
02 How, express, feelings
03 sing, dance 04 write, poem, draw
05 Nowadays, express, through
06 at, works, art
07 includes, image, delicious
08 autumn, season, fruit
09 work, word, Chinese character
10 looks like, walking down
11 Both, express, feeling, through
12 kind, called calligraphy
13 not new
14 kinds, works, be found
15 at, examples, below 16 tell, difference
17 created by, period
18 painted with, brush
19 created by, in, late 20 was written with
21 Different, tools, styles
22 Of, practice hard, unique
23 widely used around
24 artistic touches, clothes

본문 TEST Step 2 p.49~50

01 Write, Feelings
02 How, express. feelings
03 sing, dance
04 poem, draw a picture
05 Nowadays, popular, through handwriting
06 Let's look at, works of art
07 work of art, includes an image
08 a season of fruit
09 Korean word, Chinese character
10 looks like, walking, autumn leaves
11 express the feeling, through beautiful handwriting
12 called calligraphy 13 not new
14 can be found, around the world
15 examples from, below 16 tell the difference
17 was created by, period 18 were painted with
19 was created by, in the late 1400s
20 was written with
21 Different writing tools, different styles
22 Of course, practice hard, unique styles
23 is widely used around
24 designers' artistic touches, clothes
25 are some examples 26 the title
27 How, feel
28 sharp teeth, ugly, long tail
29 How about, fantasy novel
30 lightning, wizard hats
31 Anyone, writing calligraphy
32 to write by hand, practice makes perfect
33 Keep trying, part, everyday
34 with your feelings, bookmarks, gifts
35 build up

25 Below, examples 26 at, title, poster
27 How, feel
28 imagine, sharp, ugly, tail
29 How about, fantasy
30 lightning, wizard hats 31 Anyone, writing
32 by hand, practice, perfect
33 Keep trying, part, everyday
34 with, feelings, gifts 35 build up, own

1 여러분의 느낌을 써라

2 여러분은 자신의 느낌을 어떻게 표현하는가?

3 노래를 부르거나 춤을 추는가?

4 시를 쓰거나 그림을 그리는가?

5 요즘에는 손 글씨를 통해 감정을 표현하는 것이 인기다.

6 몇몇 작품을 살펴보자.

7 오른쪽 예술 작품에서는 단어가 맛있는 과일인 홍시의 이미지를 포함하고 있다.

8 그것은 가을이 결실의 계절임을 보여 준다.

9 왼쪽에 있는 예술 작품은 한글 단어와 한자를 보여 주고 있다.

10 그것은 마치 단풍잎이 깔린 길을 따라 걷고 있는 행복한 여인처럼 보인다.

11 이 두 작품은 아름다운 손 글씨를 통해 가을의 느낌을 표현한다.

12 이런 종류의 예술은 '캘리그래피'라고 불린다.

13 캘리그래피는 새로운 것이 아니다.

14 오래전의 다양한 종류의 많은 캘리그래피 작품들이 세계 곳곳에서 발견되고 있다.

15 아래에 있는 한국과 영국의 두 사례를 보라.

16 여러분은 그 차이를 구별할 수 있는가?

17 왼쪽 작품은 조선 왕조 시대에 추사에 의해 창작되었다.

18 그 글자들은 부드러운 붓으로 그려졌다.

19 오른쪽의 '캔터베리 이야기'는 1400년대 후반 영국에서 Chaucer에 의해 창작되었다.

20 그것은 펜으로 쓰였다.

21 각기 다른 필기구가 각기 다른 캘리그래피의 스타일을 이끌었다.

22 물론, 모든 캘리그래피 작가들은 자신의 독특한 스타일을 만들어 내기 위해 열심히 연습해야 했다.

23 캘리그래피는 요즘 우리 주변에서 널리 쓰이고 있다.

24 여러분은 영화 포스터, 책 표지, 음악 CD, 그리고 의류에서 디자이너들의 예술적인 손길을 발견할 수 있다.

25 아래에 몇 가지 예가 있다.

26 영화 포스터의 제목을 보라.

27 어떤 느낌이 드는가?

28 괴물의 커다란 입, 날카로운 이빨, 그리고 추하고 긴 꼬리를 상상할 수 있는가?

29 공상 소설의 제목은 어떠한가?

30 Harry의 번개와 마술사 모자가 보이는가?

31 누구든지 캘리그래피를 쓰기 시작할 수 있다.

32 처음부터 손으로 글씨를 잘 쓰기는 쉽지 않지만, 연습하면 완벽해진다.

33 계속해서 노력하고 자신의 일상의 한 부분이 되게 하라.

34 생일 카드, 책갈피, 또는 선물에 느낌을 담아 써 보라.

35 곧 자신만의 캘리그래피 세계를 만들게 될 것이다.

1 Write Your Feelings

2 How do you express your feelings?

3 Do you sing or dance?

4 Do you write a poem or draw a picture?

5 Nowadays, it is popular to express feelings through handwriting.

6 Let's look at some works of art.

7 In the work of art on the right, the word includes an image of a delicious fruit, *hongsi*.

8 It shows that autumn is a season of fruit.

9 The work of art on the left shows a Korean word and a Chinese character.

10 It looks like a happy woman walking down a road with autumn leaves.

11 Both of these works express the feeling of autumn through beautiful handwriting.

12 This kind of art is called calligraphy.

13 Calligraphy is not new.

14 Many different kinds of calligraphy works from long ago can be found all around the world.

15 Look at the two examples from Korea and the UK below.

16 Can you tell the difference?

17 The left one was created by Chusa in the period of the Joseon Dynasty.

18 The characters were painted with a soft brush.

19 The right one, *The Canterbury Tales*, was created by Chaucer in England in the late 1400s.

20 It was written with a pen.

21 Different writing tools led to different styles of calligraphy.

22 Of course, all calligraphers had to practice hard to make their unique styles.

23 Today calligraphy is widely used around us.

24 You can find designers' artistic touches on movie posters, book covers, music CDs, and clothes.

25 Below are some examples.

26 Look at the title on the movie poster.

27 How do you feel?

28 Can you imagine the monster's big mouth, sharp teeth, and ugly, long tail?

29 How about the title on the fantasy novel?

30 Do you see Harry's lightning and the wizard hats?

31 Anyone can start writing calligraphy.

32 It's not easy to write by hand well at first, but practice makes perfect.

33 Keep trying and make it part of your everyday life.

34 Write with your feelings on birthday cards, bookmarks, or gifts.

35 Soon you will build up your own world of calligraphy.

After You Read B

1. Korean characters
2. laughing out loud
3. characters mean
4. growing in a pot

Express Yourself C

1. Look at, learning[doing]
2. traditional Korean, wear, to do
3. It, to learn
4. Are, interested
5. come, try
6. Look at, playing
7. traditional Korea, to play
8. It, to play
9. Are, interested
10. come, try

Link to the World

1. Russian dolls, is called
2. When, keep coming
3. It, to see, inside each doll
4. The first set, with six children
5. many new styles, are created, loved

After You Read B

1. These Korean characters mean "Let's laugh."
2. This calligraphy shows two people laughing out loud .
3. These Korean characters mean "tree."
4. This calligraphy shows a tree growing in a pot .

Express Yourself C

1. Look at the two girls learning[doing] *taekwondo*.
2. Taekwondo is a traditional Korean sport, and we wear dobok to do it.
3. It is exciting to learn *taekwondo*.
4. Are you interested?
5. Please come and try.
6. Look at the two boys playing *yunnori*.

7. *Yunnori* is a traditional Korean board game, and we use yuts and mals to play it.
8. It is exciting to play *yunnori*.
9. Are you interested?
10. Please come and try.

Link to the World

1. This is a set of Russian dolls . It is called matryoshka.
2. When you open it, smaller dolls keep coming out of it.
3. It is interesting to see a smaller doll inside each doll.
4. The first set of matryoshka dolls was a mother doll with six children.
5. Today, many new styles of matryoshkas are created and loved by many people.

단어 TEST Step 1

p.59

01 책꽂이	02 또 하나의, 또 다른	
03 불편한	04 더러운	05 보편적인
06 눈이 먼	07 솜	08 꽉 조이는, 딱 붙는
09 청력	10 해결책	11 결심하다
12 쉽게	13 장식하다	14 더하다, 추가하다
15 어려움	16 자리, 좌석	17 마침내
18 거의	19 분수, 원천	20 손잡이
21 상품, 제품	22 낮은	23 붐비는
24 매달다, 걸다	25 여행, 여정	26 회사
27 욕조	28 순간	29 사물함
30 두꺼운	31 견해, 관점	32 교통
33 평평한	34 목욕	35 ~을 겪다
36 ~을 입다	37 조심하다	38 혼자서
39 위험에 처한	40 ~에 지친, ~에 싫증 난	
41 너무 ~해서 …할 수 없다		42 ~에 들어가다
43 점점 더 많은		

단어 TEST Step 2

p.60

01 almost	02 hang	03 dirty
04 stick	05 solution	06 cushion
07 decide	08 hearing	09 decorate
10 difficulty	11 easily	12 flat
13 bath	14 bathtub	15 fountain
16 handle	17 journey	18 cross
19 crowded	20 way	21 blind
22 bookshelf	23 locker	24 view
25 uncomfortable	26 low	27 thick
28 product	29 seat	30 company
31 tight	32 universal	33 traffic
34 another	35 get on	36 in danger
37 by oneself	38 more and more	
39 go through	40 put on	41 tired of
42 be thinking of	43 watch out	

단어 TEST Step 3

p.61

1 blind, 눈이 먼　2 crowded, 붐비는
3 below, ~의 아래에　4 solution, 해결책
5 cross, 건너다　6 stick, 지팡이　7 flat, 평평한
8 handle, 손잡이　9 journey, 여행, 여정
10 low, 낮은　11 product, 제품

12 uncomfortable, 불편한　13 view, 관점. 견해
14 decorate, 장식하다　15 company, 회사
16 locker, 사물함

대화문 TEST Step 1

p.62~63

Get Ready 2

(1) not happy about, fountain, too high / m planning to put lower / good idea
(2) don't like, in wheelchairs, get in / thinking of building, with, steps
(3) happy, in wheelchairs, get on, easily / planning to hang, safer seat

Start Off Listen & Talk A

(1) not happy about / wrong with / reach, I'm thinking of, another
(2) happy about, There are, who / any / thinking, adding Braille / good idea

Start Off Listen & draw

I'm not happy about / What's wrong with / traffic lights, the same, who, blind to colors / How about putting / walking, standing

Speak Up Look and talk

I'm not happy about, too low / thinking of putting

Speak Up Mission

not happy about, bookshelf / too, any ideas / thinking of putting another bookshelf / good idea

Speak Up Real-life Scene

are, doing / thinking, ways, help / wrong / turn on, by herself, too high / happy about, either, about that / thinking of putting, step box, below / change, bigger one / turn on, more easily

Express Yourself A

(1) I'm not happy about, too low, too hard / I'm thinking of buying, What, think / Looks great, for so long, after, grows taller
(2) not happy about, handles, easy to use / How about, easily
(3) I'm thinking of, help, eat / doesn't have to

Learning Diary Check Yourself

not happy, light switch / wrong / too small / any ideas / I'm thinking of changing, with, bigger, turn on

Get Ready 2

(1) B: I'm not happy about this fountain. It's too high for some kids.

G: Well, I'm planning to put lower fountains together with it.

B: That's a good idea.

(2) G: I don't like the high steps here. People in wheelchairs can't get in.

B: Right. I'm thinking of building a new way with no steps.

(3) G: I'm not happy about this swing. People in wheelchairs can't get on it easily.

B: Right. I'm planning to hang a bigger and safer seat for them.

G: Good idea.

Start Off Listen & Talk A

(1) G: I'm not happy about the button.

B: Why? What's wrong with it?

G: It's too high. Children or people in wheelchairs can't reach it. I'm thinking of putting another switch for them.

(2) G: I'm not happy about the sign. There are some people who can't see.

B: Right. Do you have any ideas?

G: Well, I'm thinking of adding Braille on the sign.

B: That's a good idea.

Start Off Listen & draw

B: I'm not happy about the lights.

G: What's wrong with them?

B: The traffic lights look the same to some people who are blind to colors.

G: Oh, I see. How about putting an image on each light?

B: A walking man on the green light and a standing man on the red light? Good idea!

Speak Up Look and talk

B: I'm not happy about the desk. It's too low.

G: Right. I'm thinking of putting some pads on it.

B: Good idea.

Speak Up Mission

A: I'm not happy about the bookshelf. It's too small.

B: I think so, too. Do you have any ideas?

A: I'm thinking of putting another bookshelf on it.

B: That's a good idea.

Speak Up Real-life Scene

Dad: What are you doing here?

Son: I'm thinking of ways to help Miso.

Dad: What's wrong?

Son: She can't turn on the light by herself. This switch is too high for her.

Dad: That's right. I'm not happy about it, either. Do you have any good ideas about that?

Son: I'm thinking of putting a step box here below the switch.

Dad: Good idea. And I'll change the switch to a bigger one.

Son: Great. Grandma will like it, too. She can turn on the light more easily.

Express Yourself A

(1) G: I'm not happy about my brother's chair. It's too low and too hard.

B: Right. I'm thinking of buying this one. What do you think?

G: Looks great. I think he can use it for so long, even after he grows taller.

(2) B: I'm not happy about the door handles in my house. They are not easy to use for my grandma.

G: How about this one? She will pull it and open the door easily.

B: That's good.

(3) G: I'm thinking of buying this spoon. It will help my grandma eat soup easily.

B: Right. She doesn't have to hold it with her fingers.

Learning Diary Check Yourself

G: I'm not happy about this light switch.

B: Why? What's wrong?

G: It's too small. Grandma can't use it easily.

B: Do you have any ideas?

G: I'm thinking of changing it with a bigger one. That'll help her turn on the light easily.

B: Good idea.

01 Mother, Universal Design

02 woman, journey, cities

03 looked over 04 couldn't see, hear

05 walk, without, stick

06 With, difficulties, climb, crowded

07 heavy, with, weak 08 got, found, in danger

09 moment, difficult, than, trip

10 Who, what, do

11 a 26-year-old designer

12 During, worked, company

13 meetings, designing, weak

14 other, design, those 15 became tired, same

16 Finally, around, understand, difficulties

17 clothes, uncomfortable, thick glasses

18 so, that, couldn't, without

19 thick, couldn't, with 20 put, of, make hearing

21 During, felt, go through

22 From, products, safely, easily

23 beginning, universal design

24 example, universal, low-floor

25 steps, such, without, help

26 course, other, get, comfortably

27 more, following, way 28 flat, easy, touch lives

29 around, weaker, point, view

30 next, better place, everybody

본문 TEST Step 2 p.68~69

01 Universal Design

02 started a journey to cities

03 looked over 80 04 couldn't see or hear

05 couldn't walk, without a stick

06 With all these difficulties, get on crowded

07 heavy doors, with her weak hands

08 found herself in danger

09 very difficult for her, more than

10 what made her do 11 a 26-year-old designer

12 During the 1970's, worked for

13 How about designing, weak people

14 for those people

15 became tired of, cold answer

16 Finally, to understand their difficulties

17 For this, put on, uncomfortable, thick glasses

18 so, that, couldn't, without a stick

19 so, that, couldn't, with them

20 lots of cotton, to make her hearing bad

21 During, felt, difficulties, go through

22 From this experience, safely, easily

23 beginning, universal design, design for all

24 One example, low-floor , buses

25 no steps, such a low floor, in a wheelchair,
 without any help

26 helps, get on, more comfortably

27 following Patricia's way

28 like, with, with, live better lives

29 Look around, from their point of view

30 next, a better place for everybody

본문 TEST Step 3 p.70~71

1 Patricia Moore – 유니버설 디자인의 어머니

2 1979년에, 한 여성이 미국과 캐나다의 도시로 여행을 시작했다.

3 그녀는 80세가 넘어 보였다.

4 그녀는 잘 보거나 잘 들을 수 없었다.

5 그녀는 지팡이 없이는 잘 걸을 수 없었다.

6 이 모든 어려움을 가진 채, 그 여성은 지하철역에서 계단을 올라가거나 붐비는 버스에 올라타야 했다.

7 그녀는 무거운 문을 열거나 그녀의 약한 손으로 깡통 따개를 사용해야 했다.

8 때때로 그녀는 다치거나 위험에 처하기도 했다.

9 모든 순간이 그녀에게 매우 어려웠으나, 그녀는 115개 이상의 도시를 방문하였으며 1982년에 여행을 끝마쳤다.

10 그 여성은 누구였고 무엇이 그녀로 하여금 이 모든 것을 하게 만들었을까?

11 그녀는 26살의 디자이너인 Patricia Moore였다.

12 1970년대 동안, 그녀는 큰 디자인 회사에서 일했다.

13 그녀는 종종 회의에서 물었다. "나이 들거나 약한 사람들을 위해 디자인하는 게 어떨까요?"

14 다른 디자이너들은 항상 대답했다. "우리는 그런 사람들을 위해 디자인하지 않습니다."

15 그녀는 똑같은 냉담한 대답에 지쳤다.

16 마침내, 그녀는 '그런 사람들' 중의 하나가 되어 그들의 어려움을 더 잘 이해하기 위해 많은 도시를 여행하기로 결심했다.

17 이를 위해, 그녀는 자신의 할머니 옷을 입고, 불편한 신발을 신고, 두꺼운 안경을 썼다.

18 신발은 너무 불편해서 그녀는 지팡이가 없이는 잘 걸을 수 없었다.

19 안경은 너무 두꺼워서 그녀는 안경을 쓰고는 잘 볼 수 없었다.

20 그녀는 또한 그녀의 청력을 나쁘게 하려고 귀에 많은 솜을 넣었다.

21 여행 동안, Patricia는 나이 든 사람들이 겪는 어려움을 느꼈다.

22 이 경험으로부터, 그녀는 누구나 안전하고 쉽게 사용할 수 있는 제품들을 고안했다.

23 이것이 '유니버설 디자인' 또는 '모두를 위한 디자인'의 시작이었다.

24 그녀의 유니버설 디자인 아이디어의 한 가지 예는 저상 버스이다.

25 그것은 계단이 없고 낮은 바닥을 가지고 있어서 휠체어를 탄 사람조차 아무 도움 없이 이용할 수 있다.

26 물론, 이것은 다른 사람들도 버스를 더 편안하게 탈 수 있도록 도와준다.

27 오늘날 점점 더 많은 디자이너가 Patricia의 방식을 따르고 있다.

28 크고 평평한 조명 스위치, 편한 손잡이를 가진 문, 터치 버튼을 가진 전화기와 같은 제품들은 사람들이 더 나은 삶을 살도록

29 여러분의 주위를 둘러보고, 더 나이 들거나 더 약한 사람들의 어려움을 느껴 보고, 그들의 관점에서 해결책을 찾으려 고 노력해 봐라.

도와주고 있다.

29 여러분의 주위를 둘러보고, 더 나이 들거나 더 약한 사람들의 어려움을 느껴 보고, 그들의 관점에서 해결책을 찾으려 고 노력해 봐라.

30 여러분은 다음의 Patricia Moore가 되어 세상을 모두에게 더 나은 곳으로 만들 수 있을 것이다.

본문 TEST Step 4~Step 5 p.72~75

1 Patricia Moore – Mother of Universal Design

2 In 1979, a woman started a journey to cities in the U.S. and Canada.

3 She looked over 80.

4 She couldn't see or hear well.

5 She couldn't walk well without a stick.

6 With all these difficulties, the woman had to climb stairs in subway stations and get on crowded buses.

7 She had to open heavy doors and use can openers with her weak hands.

8 Sometimes she got hurt or found herself in danger.

9 Every moment was very difficult for her, but she visited more than 115 cities and ended her trip in 1982.

10 Who was the woman and what made her do all this?

11 She was Patricia Moore, a 26-year-old designer.

12 During the 1970's, she worked for a big design company.

13 She often asked at meetings, "How about designing for old or weak people?"

14 The other designers always answered, "We don't design for those people."

15 She became tired of the same cold answer.

16 Finally, she decided to become one of "those people" and travel around many cities to understand their difficulties better.

17 For this, she put on her grandmother's clothes, uncomfortable shoes, and thick glasses.

18 The shoes were so uncomfortable that she couldn't walk well without a stick.

19 The glasses were so thick that she couldn't see well with them.

20 She also put lots of cotton in her ears to make her hearing bad.

21 During her journey, Patricia felt the difficulties old people go through.

22 From this experience, she designed products anybody could use safely and easily.

23 This was the beginning of "universal design," or "design for all."

24 One example of her universal design ideas is low-floor buses.

25 They have no steps and have such a low floor that even a person in a wheelchair can use them without any help.

26 Of course, this helps other people get on the bus more comfortably, too.

27 Today more and more designers are following Patricia's way.

28 Products like big flat light switches, doors with easy handles, and phones with touch buttons are helping people live better lives.

29 Look around you, feel the difficulties of people who are older or weaker, and try to find solutions from their point of view.

30 You could be the next Patricia Moore and make the world a better place for everybody.

구석구석지문 TEST Step 1 p.76

Express Yourself C1

1. washing machine, so, that, can't put, easily
2. However, side door
3. help, put, more easily

Project Step 3

1. so dangerous that, couldn't
2. to change, like
3. help, ride, safely

Link to the World

1. was born to
2. worked hard, became rich
3. were dying of, because of
4. spent almost all, saved
5. let her take a trip

구석구석지문 TEST Step 2 p.77

Express Yourself C1

1. The washing machine door in my house is so high that my little brother can't put clothes easily into it.
2. However, this machine has a side door.
3. It'll help my brother put clothes in more easily.

1. The hole cover was so dangerous that I couldn't ride my bike on it.
2. So I want to change the cover like this.
3. The new cover will help people ride a bike safely.

Link to the World

1. Kim Mandeok was born to a poor family in Jeju.
2. She worked hard and became rich.
3. In 1794, lots of people in Jeju were dying of hunger because of bad weather.
4. She spent almost all she had and saved a lot of people.
5. King Jeongjo let her take a trip to Mountain Geumgang.

Lesson S

단어 TEST Step 1 p.78

01 활동	02 느린	03 승자
04 맛있는	05 초, 짧은 시간, 두 번째	
06 바퀴	07 젊음, 청춘	08 정확하게
09 끝나다, 끝내다	10 쉬는 시간	11 밝은, 똑똑한
12 단것, 단 음식	13 친근한, 다정한	14 비록 ~일지라도
15 옷	16 특별한	17 성적
18 손 글씨	19 희망적인	20 쓰레기 통
21 파도치다, 손을 흔들다		22 밖에
23 젖은	24 고르다	25 바다, 대양
26 가까이; 닫다	27 장소; 놓다, 두다	28 절약하다
29 결코 ~하지 않다	30 갈아입다, 바꾸다	31 동그라미, 원
32 귀여운	33 거울	34 체육 수업
35 A를 B로 자르다	36 잠깐만	37 B로 A를 덮다
38 ~할 필요가 없다	39 위아래로	40 휴식을 취하다
41 ~와 같은	42 A를 B에 더하다	43 ~로 가득 차다

단어 TEST Step 2 p.79

01 slow	02 most	03 never
04 activity	05 circle	06 finish
07 friendly	08 close	09 outside
10 save	11 delicious	12 wet
13 shape	14 change	15 grade
16 handwriting	17 hopeful	18 second
19 break time	20 winner	21 choose
22 exactly	23 ocean	24 bright
25 trash can	26 special	27 P.E. class
28 place	29 wheel	30 clothes
31 though	32 wave	33 sweet
34 youth	35 take a break	36 up to
37 don't need to	38 cut A into B	39 walk back
40 add A to B	41 cover A up with B	
42 be full of	43 wait a second	

단어 TEST Step 3 p.80

1 sweet, 단것 2 friendly, 친절한 3 bread, 빵
4 choose, 고르다 5 ocean, 바다, 대양
6 handwriting, 손 글씨 7 wet, 젖은 8 save, 절약하다
9 winner, 승자 10 grade, 성적 11 wave, 손을 흔들다
12 youth, 젊음 13 place, 장소 14 mirror, 거울
15 circle, 원 16 wheel, 바퀴

01 Teens' Magazine

02 Works, Art, Shapes

03 Like, Circle

04 like, because, ends

06 cold outside 07 want, out, play

08 says, have to

09 starting, going, cold 10 outside, days like

11 wait, second, most 12 cover, up, hide

13 Looking Back with 14 Life, art

15 Live yours 16 UNTIL, OVER

17 slow, never, back 18 little things, do

19 Follow, dream 20 My Bike

21 take, place, Back, riding

22 Giving Tree 23 Out, wet

24 In, dry 25 Pretty big

26 Between, and 27 Selfies, Year

28 Though, lost, lot 29 Look at, made

30 Aren't, cute 31 made, big, for

32 made him happy 33 Have, seen, like

34 What, Think, Life 35 most, moment

36 take tests

37 When, hungry, nothing

38 change, before, class

39 When, sleepy , class

40 When, classes, rings 41 lovely time

42 lunch time 43 class with, favorite

44 last class

45 when, during break

46 when, myself, mirror 47 most awesome

48 got, grades, before 49 finishes earlier

50 because it, lot 51 delicious, for

52 best, in, same 53 most difficult, do

54 Washing, cans

56 Making, presentation, front

57 on, every 58 Group work

59 Places, Love, Village 60 Traditional Market

61 something delicious, visit

62 buy, use, make, full

63 choose, add, to 64 Youth Center

65 middle of, town

66 because, learn, such as 67 play, take, break

68 Mr, Bakery 69 small bakery near

70 after, because, hungry 71 It, to, with

72 Let's Have Fun 73 Shape Puzzles

74 cut, into, shapes, from 75 Balls, Lines

76 such, way, exactly

77 Eating Plastic Spoons 78 lot, thrown away

79 breaks down, pieces 80 pieces, go, into

81 If, too, to, each 82 Let's Make

83 universal, contest, last 84 winners' works

85 come close, out 86 pull, away, stops

87 need, turn, touch 88 save lots, with

89 our, between, buildings 90 Anybody, up, easily

91 can, get, rest

92 special, chairs, classroom

93 activities, together, wonderful

94 LET'S LAUGH 95 Funny, Jokes

96 recycle, hopeful 97 Because, full of

98 How, tell, friendly 99 It waves

100 Why, sun, to 101 get brighter

01 Teens' Magazine 02 Works, in Shapes

03 Like, Circle

04 like, because, never ends

05 Snowman 06 cold outside

07 go out, play 08 have to

09 to snow, going to be cold 10 on days like these

11 wait a second, the most wonderful

12 cover myself up, hide here

13 Looking Back with, Handwriting 14 Life, art

15 yours 16 UNTIL, OVER

17 slow walker, walk back 18 little things

19 Follow 20 My Bike

21 take, To any place, home, enjoy riding, every day

22 Giving 23 there, wet

24 here, dry 25 umbrella

26 Between, and 27 Selfies, This

28 Though, lost, lot 29 Look at, robots

30 Aren't cute 31 a big cake

32 made him happy

33 Have you ever seen

34 What, Think of, Life

35 uncomfortable moment

36 take tests 37 have nothing

38 change, before, after 39 sleepy in class

40 after, rings 41 most lovely time

42 lunch 43 class, favorite

44 last class

45 sleeping during break time

46 myself, mirror 47 most awesome

48 better grades than before 49 finishes earlier

50 because, rains, snows

51 delicious, for dessert

52 in the same class　53 most difficult, to do

54 trash cans　55 Studying

56 Making a presentation, front

57 on time　58 Group work

59 Places, Village　60 Traditional Market

61 something delicious　62 to make, full

63 choose, kind of, add, to　64 Youth Center

65 in the middle of　66 because, such as

67 take a break　68 Bakery

69 near

70 after, because, always hungry

71 It, to enjoy　72 Let's Have Fun

73 Shape Puzzles

74 cut, into, other shapes, from

75 Five Lines

76 in such a way, each line　77 Are Eating

78 are thrown away　79 breaks down into

80 go into fish, pieces　81 Up to, each year

82 Let's Make　83 universal design

84 winners' works　85 come close, out

86 pull, away　87 don't need to

88 save lots of water　89 between, buildings

90 up, down easily　91 get some rest

92 special, for

93 group activities, together, for

94 LET'S LAUGH　95 Jokes

96 Why, recycle, hopeful　97 Because, full of

98 How, tell, friendly　99 waves

100 Why　101 To get

본문 TEST Step 3　p.91~94

1 십대들의 잡지

2 모양으로 표현된 예술 작품

3 동그라미처럼

4 나는 동그라미처럼 너를 사랑해. 왜냐하면 동그라미는 절대 끝나지 않기에.

5 눈사람

6 바깥은 추워.

7 나는 밖으로 나가 놀고 싶지 않네.

8 하지만 엄마는 그래야 한다고 하시네.

9 눈이 오기 시작하고 나는 추워질 거야.

10 나는 이런 날에는 나가서 놀고 싶지 않아.

11 하지만 잠깐만, 나는 최고로 멋진 생각이 났어!

12 나는 눈으로 내 몸을 완전히 덮고 여기에 숨어야지!

13 손 글씨로 돌아보기

14 인생은 예술이다.

15 다양한 색깔로 살아라.

16 끝날 때까지 끝난 게 아니다.

17 나는 느리게 걷는 사람이지만 절대 물러서지는 않는다.

18 나는 네가 하는 작은 일들을 사랑해.

19 네 꿈을 좇으라.

20 나의 자전거

21 바퀴 두 개가 나를 데려가네 / 어느 곳으로든지 / 학교로 / 다시 집으로 / 산으로 / 강으로 / 나는 내 자전거가 아주　좋아 / 나는 그걸 매일 즐겨 타네

22 아낌없이 주는 나무

23 저곳 바깥은 – 젖어 있고

24 이곳 안쪽은 – 말라 있네

25 엄청 큰 우산이네

26 나와 하늘 사이에 있는

27 올해의 셀피들

28 우리는 게임에 졌지만, 아주 즐거웠다.

29 우리가 만든 로봇들을 봐.

30 귀엽지 않니?

31 우리는 한 씨 할아버지께 드릴 큰 케이크를 만들었다.

32 그것은 할아버지를 행복하게 해 주었다.

33 나처럼 잘생긴 피터 팬을 본 적이 있니?

34 학교생활에 대해 어떻게 생각하니?

35 가장 불편한 순간

36 1. 시험을 칠 때

37 2. 정말 배가 고픈데 먹을 것이 없을 때

38 3. 체육 시간 전후에 옷을 갈아입을 때

39 4. 기타: 수업 중에 졸릴 때

40 종이 울렸는데 선생님이 수업을 끝내지 않을 때

41 가장 사랑스러운 시간

42 1. 점심시간

43 2. 가장 좋아하는 선생님의 수업 시간

44 3. 금요일의 마지막 수업 시간

45 4. 기타: 쉬는 시간에 잠잘 때

46 거울 속의 나를 볼 때

47 가장 멋진 뉴스

48 1. 전보다 좋은 성적을 받았다

49 2. 오늘 수업이 일찍 끝난다

50 3. 비나 눈이 많이 와서 학교에 가지 않는다

51 4. 기타: 후식으로 맛있는 단것을 먹는다

52 가장 친한 친구와 내가 같은 반이 되었다

53 가장 하기 힘든 일

54 1. 쓰레기통 씻기

55 2. 공부하기

56 3. 친구들 앞에서 발표하기

57 4. 기타: 매일 제시간에 등교하기

58 모둠 활동

59 우리 마을에서 우리가 좋아하는 곳

60 대한 전통 시장

61 맛있는 것이 먹고 싶으면, 대한 시장을 방문하세요.

62 엽전을 사면 여러분의 점심 도시락을 가득 채우는 데 그걸 쓸 수 있어요.

63 많은 종류의 음식을 골라서 점심 도시락에 담을 수 있답니다.

64 새봄 청소년 센터

65 이곳은 우리 마을 한가운데에 있는 새봄 청소년 센터입니다.

66 춤과 음악 같은 많은 것을 배울 수 있어서 우리는 이곳을 좋아한답니다.

67 우리는 또한 이곳에서 보드게임도 하고 휴식도 취할 수 있어요.

68 김 씨네 빵집

69 이곳은 학교 근처의 작은 빵집입니다.

70 우리는 항상 배가 고파서 방과 후에 거기에 가는 것을 좋아해요!

71 친구들과 맛있는 빵을 즐기는 것이 좋아요.

72 퍼즐로 즐거운 시간을 보내자!

73 도형 퍼즐

74 A를 똑같은 두 개의 조각으로 자르면, 그 두 조각으로 다른 모든 형태(B, C, D, E, F, G)를 만들 수 있다.

75 5개의 선에 놓인 10개의 공

76 각각의 선 위에 정확하게 4개의 공이 놓이도록 10개의 공을 5개의 선에 놓아라.

77 너는 플라스틱 숟가락을 먹고 있다!

78 1. 해마다 많은 플라스틱 숟가락이 버려진다.

79 2. 대부분의 플라스틱 숟가락은 바닷속에서 더 작은 조각으로 부서진다.

80 3. 아주 작은 플라스틱 조각들이 물고기의 몸속으로 들어간다.

81 4. 여러분이 그 물고기를 먹으면 여러분도 플라스틱을 먹게 되는 것이다. 해마다 11,000개의 조각까지!

82 꿈의 학교를 만들어 보자!

83 지난달에 우리는 우리 학교를 위한 유니버설 디자인 경시대회를 열었습니다.

84 여기 우승자들의 작품이 있습니다.

85 1. 손을 가까이 가져가면 물이 나옵니다.

86 손을 멀리 떨어뜨리면 물이 멈춥니다.

87 어떤 부분도 돌리거나 만질 필요가 없습니다.

88 우리는 이것으로 많은 물을 절약할 수 있답니다. — 오주연(1–3)

89 2. 이것은 두 개의 건물 사이에 있는 학교 정원입니다.

90 여기서는 누구라도 쉽게 위아래로 이동할 수 있습니다.

91 또한, 우리는 이곳에 앉아 휴식을 취할 수 있습니다. — 김지민 (3–5)

92 3. 교실용의 특별한 책상과 의자가 있습니다.

93 모둠 활동을 하기 위해 그것들을 함께 모아 3명, 4명, 또는 5명이 활동할 훌륭한 모둠 책상을 만들 수 있습니다. — 최유미 (2–1)

94 웃읍시다

95 재미있는 지구의 날 농담들 하! 하! 하!

96 재활용 통은 왜 희망적인가?

97 왜냐하면 '깡통[할 수 있다]'으로 가득 차 있기 때문이지.

98 바다가 다정하다는 것을 어떻게 알 수 있는가?

99 그것이 일렁이기[손을 흔들기] 때문이지.

100 태양은 왜 학교에 가는가?

101 더 밝아지기[똑똑해지기] 위해서지.

1 Teens' Magazine

2 Works of Art in Shapes

3 Like a Circle

4 I love you like a circle because a circle never ends.

5 Snowman

6 It's cold outside.

7 I don't want to go out and play.

8 But Mom says I have to.

9 It's starting to snow and I'm going to be cold.

10 I don't like playing outside on days like these.

11 But wait a second, I have the most wonderful idea!

12 I'll cover myself up with snow and I'll hide here!

13 Looking Back with Your Handwriting

14 Life is art.

15 Live yours in COLOR.

16 IT ISN'T OVER UNTIL IT'S OVER.

17 I am a slow walker, but I never walk back.

18 I love the little things you do.

19 Follow your dream.

20 My Bike

21 Two wheels take me / To any place / To school / Back home / To the mountain / To the river / I love my bike / I enjoy riding it every day

22 Giving Tree

23 Out there – wet

24 In here – dry

25 Pretty big umbrella

26 Between me and the sky.

27 Selfies of This Year

28 Though we lost the game, we had a lot of fun.

29 Look at the robots we made.

30 Aren't they cute?

31 We made a big cake for Mr. Han.

32 It made him happy.

33 Have you ever seen a handsome Peter Pan like me?

34 What Do You Think of Your School Life?

35 The most uncomfortable moment

36 1. When I take tests

37 2. When I am really hungry and have nothing to eat

38 3. When I change clothes before and after P.E. class

39 4. others: When I am sleepy in class

40 When the teacher doesn't finish classes after the bell rings

41 The most lovely time

42 1. lunch time

43 2. class with my favorite teacher

44 3. the last class on Friday

45 4. others: when I am sleeping during break time

46 when I see myself in the mirror

47 The most awesome news

48 1. I got better grades than before

49 2. School finishes earlier today

50 3. I don't go to school because it rains or snows a lot

51 4. others: We eat delicious sweets for dessert

52 My best friend and I are in the same class

53 The most difficult work to do

54 1. Washing trash cans

55 2. Studying

56 3. Making a presentation in front of friends

57 4. others: Being on time every day

58 Group work

59 Places We Love in Our Village

60 Daehan Traditional Market

61 If you want to eat something delicious, visit Daehan Market.

62 You can buy "*yeopjeon*" and use it to make your lunch box full.

63 You can choose many kinds of food and add them to your lunch box.

64 Saebom Youth Center

65 This is Saebom Youth Center in the middle of our town.

66 We like this place because we can learn many things, such as dance and music.

67 We can also play board games and take a break here.

68 Mr. Kim's Bakery

69 This is a small bakery near the school.

70 We like to go there after school because we're always hungry!

71 It is good to enjoy delicious bread with friends.

72 Let's Have Fun with Puzzles!

73 Shape Puzzles

73 Shape Puzzles

74 If you cut the shape A into two same pieces, you can then make all the other shapes(B, C, D, E, F, G) from those two pieces.

75 Ten Balls in Five Lines

76 Place 10 balls in 5 lines in such a way that each line has exactly 4 balls on it.

77 You Are Eating Plastic Spoons!

78 1. A lot of plastic spoons are thrown away every year.

79 2. Most plastic breaks down into smaller pieces in the ocean.

80 3. Very small pieces of plastic go into fish.

81 4. If you eat the fish, you eat the plastic, too. Up to 11,000 pieces each year!

82 Let's Make a Dream School!

83 We had a universal design contest for our school last month.

84 Here are the winners' works.

85 1. When your hands come close, water comes out.

86 When you pull your hands away, the water stops.

87 You don't need to turn or touch any parts.

88 We can save lots of water with this. — by O Juyeon(1–3)

89 2. This is our school park between two buildings.

90 Anybody can go up and down easily here.

91 Also we can sit and get some rest here. — by Gim Jimin(3-5)

92 3. These are special desks and chairs for the classroom.

93 For group activities, you can get them together and make a wonderful group table for three, four, or five students. — by Choi Yumi(2–1)

94 LET'S LAUGH

95 Funny Earth Day Jokes Ha! Ha! Ha!

96 Why are recycle bins hopeful?

97 Because they're full of cans.

98 How can you tell the ocean is friendly?

99 It waves.

100 Why did the sun go to school?

101 To get brighter.

MEMO

MEMO

적중 100 + 특별부록

Plan B

우리학교
최신기출

천재 · 정사열 교과서를 배우는

학교 시험문제 분석 · 모음 · 해설집

전국단위 학교 시험문제 수집 및 분석
출제 빈도가 높은 문제 위주로 선별
문제 풀이에 필요한 상세한 해설

중2-2
영어

천재 · 정사열

2학년 영어 2학기 중간고사(5과) 1회

문항수 : 선택형(23문항) 서술형(7문항) 20 . . .

◎ 선택형 문항의 답안은 컴퓨터용 수정 싸인펜을 사용하여 OMR 답안지에 바르게 표기하시오.
◎ 서술형 문제는 답을 답안지에 반드시 검정 볼펜으로 쓰시오.
◎ 총 30문항 100점 만점입니다. 문항별 배점은 각 문항에 표시되어 있습니다.

[서울 관악구 ○○중]

01 다음 중 단어의 관계가 <u>다른</u> 하나는? (2점)

① vegetable : onion
② animal : mouse
③ square : circle
④ body : thumb
⑤ shape : triangle

[경기 ○○중]

02 다음 중 밑줄 친 단어의 의미가 같은 것은? (4점)

① He was absent from work. He <u>must</u> be sick.
　You <u>must</u> follow his directions.
② This bookshelf can't <u>stand</u> alone.
　They took a firm <u>stand</u> against the attack.
③ He <u>waters</u> the plants in his garden every day.
　The boy fell into the <u>water</u>.
④ <u>Hang</u> your coat up on the hook.
　I should <u>hang</u> the laundry to dry up on the rooftop.
⑤ The kite has to <u>face</u> the wind to fly well.
　He washed his <u>face</u> with cold water to wake up.

[서울 성동구 ○○중]

03 다음 중 짝지어진 대화가 가장 <u>어색한</u> 것은? (3점)

① A: This bookshelf can't stand alone. Do you know how to solve this problem?
　B: Sure. What is it?
② A: This car doesn't move. Do you know how to move it?
　B: Sure. Put wheels under the car.
③ A: Do you know how to divide this cake into 4 equal pieces?
　B: How about dividing it this way?
④ A: These twelve sticks make 4 squares. Do you know how to make 3 squares of the same size with three moves?
　B: Sure. First, move this stick here.
⑤ A: Here's a triangle with 3 pencils. Do you know how to make 3 more triangles with 3 more pencils?
　B: Let me see... It's too difficult for me.

[경남 ○○중]

04 다음 글의 (A), (B)에서 어법상 <u>어색한</u> 부분을 바르게 고쳐 문장을 다시 쓰시오. (4점)

> "(A)<u>I try to making this room tidy</u>, but you two always make a mess," he complained. (B)<u>Triangle and Circle looked at one other</u>. "So you think you can do it without us?" Triangle asked Square.

→ (A)＿＿＿＿＿＿＿＿＿＿＿＿＿＿
　(B)＿＿＿＿＿＿＿＿＿＿＿＿＿＿

05 다음 빈칸에 들어갈 수 <u>없는</u> 것은? (3점)

> The book makes me _____.

① sad ② angry

③ happily ④ excited

⑤ sleepy

06 위 대화의 밑줄 친 (가)를 조건에 맞게 영작하시오. (4점)

> **조건**
> • '의문사 + to부정사'를 사용할 것.
> • 8단어의 완전한 한 문장으로 쓸 것.

→ _____

07 위 대화의 (A)~(E) 중 다음 문장이 들어가기에 가장 알맞은 곳은? (3점)

> Then, take the rice and come back with the chicken.

① (A) ② (B) ③ (C)

④ (D) ⑤ (E)

[6~9] 다음 대화를 읽고 물음에 답하시오.

B: (가)이 퍼즐을 어떻게 푸는지 아니?
G: What is it?
B: You must take a dog, a chicken, and a bag of rice across the river. The boat only carries you and one of the things at a time.
G: That's easy. I can take them to the other side one by one.
B: But without you, the dog will kill the chicken, and the chicken will eat the rice.
G: (A) Let me see... (B) First, take the chicken and come back. (C)
B: And? (D)
G: (나)_____. (E)
B: You're great!

08 위 대화의 빈칸 (나)에 들어갈 말로 적절한 것은? (4점)

① Take the dog with the chicken. Finally, take the rice.

② Take the dog with the rice. Finally, take the chicken.

③ After that, take the dog and come back. Finally, take the chicken.

④ After that, take the dog and come back. Finally, take the rice.

⑤ After that, take the chicken with the dog. Finally, take the rice.

09 위 대화의 내용과 일치하는 것은?　(4점)

① The boat can carry a chicken and a bag of rice at the same time.

② If the girl takes the rice first, the chicken will be killed by the dog.

③ The girl and the dog must be taken to the other side of the river first.

④ On the way back from the other side of the river, the girl can not carry anything.

⑤ The speakers are talking about why a dog, a chicken, and a bag of rice must be taken across the river.

10 대화가 자연스럽게 이어지도록 (ㄱ)~(ㄹ)을 바르게 배열한 것은?　(2점)

Jimin: Do you know how to make sandwiches?

Chris:

(ㄱ) Add some vegetables.

(ㄴ) Sure.

(ㄷ) Put bread on top.

(ㄹ) Put an egg on bread.

Jimin: Thank you.

① (ㄱ) - (ㄴ) - (ㄷ) - (ㄹ)

② (ㄴ) - (ㄷ) - (ㄹ) - (ㄱ)

③ (ㄴ) - (ㄹ) - (ㄱ) - (ㄷ)

④ (ㄷ) - (ㄴ) - (ㄱ) - (ㄹ)

⑤ (ㄷ) - (ㄱ) - (ㄹ) - (ㄴ)

11 자연스러운 대화가 되도록 ⓐ와 ⓑ에 들어갈 문장을 고르면?　(4점)

A: Do you know how to cook *ramyeon*?
B: Yes, I do. First, boil some water. Then, ⓐ_____. Finally, ⓑ_____.

① ⓐ put the noodle and dried soup mix
ⓑ boil for 4 more minutes

② ⓐ boil the potatoes
ⓑ cut them into pieces

③ ⓐ put an egg on bread
ⓑ add some vegetables

④ ⓐ put the noodle and dried soup mix
ⓑ boil the tomatoes

⑤ ⓐ put bread on top
ⓑ boil for 4 more minutes

12 다음 중 어법상 옳은 문장은?　(3점)

① We think he honest.

② Mom made Ann angry.

③ I found the movie interest.

④ Mom kept the rice bowl warmly.

⑤ The contest made me nervously.

[13~14] 다음 대화를 읽고 물음에 답하시오.

The boy: Do you know how to solve this puzzle?
The girl: What is it?
The boy: You must take a dog, a chicken, and a bag of rice across the river. The boat only carries you and one of the things at a time.
The girl: That's easy. I can take them to the other side one by one.
The boy: But without you, the dog will kill the chicken, and the chicken will eat the rice.
The girl: Let me see.... First, take the chicken and come back. Then, take the rice and come back with the chicken.
The boy: And?
The girl: After that, take the dog and come back. Finally, take the chicken.
The boy: You're great!

14 What's the problem if the girl takes the rice first? (2점)

① The chicken will die.

② The dog will eat the rice.

③ The dog will kill the chicken.

④ The chicken will eat the dog.

⑤ The chicken will eat the rice.

[15~16] 다음 글을 읽고 물음에 답하시오.

Euclid taught math at the Library of Alexandria when Ptolemy I was the king of Egypt. People call him "the father of math." He showed how to draw a triangle that has three sides of the (A)[same / different] length. He also showed (B)[how / what] to find the center of the (C)[biggest / smallest] circle in a triangle. One day, Ptolemy I asked, "Is there an easier way to study math?" Euclid replied, "ⓐ_____"

13 다음 중 위 대화의 내용과 일치하지 <u>않는</u> 것은? (4점)

① The girl could solve the puzzle.

② Only one animal can take the boat with you at a time.

③ The puzzle is how to take the animals one by one to the other side of the river.

④ The problem is that the dog can kill the chicken and eat the rice.

⑤ The girl says she can take the boat with the chicken to come back.

15 위 글의 괄호 (A), (B), (C) 안에 들어갈 말을 바르게 연결한 것은? (4점)

	(A)	(B)	(C)
①	same	how	biggest
②	same	how	smallest
③	same	what	biggest
④	different	how	smallest
⑤	different	what	biggest

16 위 글의 ⓐ에 들어갈 가장 적절한 말은? (3점)

① Blood is thicker than water.

② There is no royal road to learning.

③ A sound mind is in a sound body.

④ You win some, you lose some.

⑤ Actions speak louder than words.

18 (A)의 우리말을 7단어로 영작하시오. (4점)

> 그 세 가지 모양들은 다시 한 번 협력했다.
>
> = _____

[19~24] 다음 글을 읽고 물음에 답하시오.

> Triangle and Circle went out and Square was now in control. He made the ⓐhangers, the plants, and all the round things square. Then he looked around and smiled. "(가)_____ better!(훨씬 좋군!)"
>
> When Mike came home from school, he picked up a ⓑsquare hanger to hang his jacket on.
>
> "What? This will not hold my clothes."
>
> He went to ⓒwater the plants and saw their square leaves.
>
> "Poor things.... They must be sick."
>
> He picked up the square hula hoop to ⓓexercise.
>
> "Hmm ... (A)나는 이것을 어떻게 돌려야 할지 모르겠어."
>
> He went to take out his bike and looked at the square wheels.
>
> "Well, I can't ⓔride this. I'll just have to walk." Then he hurried out of the house.

[17~18] 다음 글을 읽고 물음에 답하시오.

> When the other shapes came back, Square ⓐ_____ over to them.
>
> "Mike doesn't like his room. I don't know what to do," he said.
>
> They looked at the hangers, the plants, and all the new square things. Then they looked at one another, and Square ⓑ_____ his problem.
>
> "Let's ⓒ_____ this room great again," he said to the others. (A)그 세 가지 모양들은 다시 한 번 협력했다.

17 다음 중 ⓐ~ⓒ에 들어갈 알맞은 말은? (3점)

	ⓐ	ⓑ	ⓒ
①	rushed	realized	make
②	rushed	realized	take
③	rushed	realize	make
④	came	realized	take
⑤	comes	realized	make

19 위 글의 밑줄 친 ⓐ~ⓔ의 의미와 <u>다르게 쓰인 것</u>은? (3점)

① ⓐ I use the <u>hangers</u> for my pants and dresses.

② ⓑ She bought a <u>square</u> picture frame.

③ ⓒ I want to drink a glass of <u>water</u>.

④ ⓓ I <u>exercise</u> two times a week at the park.

⑤ ⓔ She is able to <u>ride</u> the bicycle.

20 위 글의 빈칸 (가)를 괄호 안의 우리말과 같도록 할 때 가장 알맞은 말은? (3점)

① Very ② Many

③ Much ④ So

⑤ A lot of

21 위 글의 내용과 일치하지 <u>않는</u> 것은? (4점)

① Mike hurried out of the house.

② Mike saw all square items in his room.

③ Mike doesn't know how to spin the round hula hoop.

④ Mike picked up a square hanger to hang on his jacket.

⑤ Mike thinks that he can't ride the bike with square wheels.

22 물건의 모양이 바뀌면서 Mike가 느낀 불편함에 관해 <u>잘못</u> 설명한 것은? (4점)

① Mike can't spin the square hula hoop.

② Mike thinks the square leaves look sick.

③ The square hanger can't hold the clothes.

④ Mike can exercise with the new hula hoop.

⑤ Mike can't ride the bike because of the square wheels.

23 Mike가 그의 재킷을 옷걸이에 걸 수 없었던 이유를 우리말로 쓰시오. (4점)

→ _____

24 위 글의 밑줄 친 (A)의 우리말을 영어로 쓰시오. (3점)

→ _____

[25~30] 다음 글을 읽고 물음에 답하시오.

ⓐThere lived three shape spirits in Mike's room. Square controlled the table, the bookshelf, and the window. Triangle was in charge of the hangers and the plants. Circle took care of the round things. They worked together ⓑto make a nice room for Mike.

One day Square decided to make the room better and shouted at (A)the other spirits.

"Take these plants away, (가)_____ their pointy leaves will hurt someone!" he said to Triangle. "But Mike waters ⓒthem every day," said Triangle.

"Take this hula hoop away, (가)_____ it will roll and break something!" he said to Circle.

"But Mike exercises with ⓓthem every day," said Circle.

"(B)나는 이 방을 깔끔하게 하려고 노력한다, but you two always make a mess," he complained.

Triangle and Circle looked at ⓔeach other.

"So you think you can do it without us?" Triangle asked Square.

"Sure. I can make this room better all by myself," replied Square.

"Great! Then we can get some rest," Circle said to Square.

Triangle and Circle went out and Square was now in control. He made the hangers, plants, and all the round things square. Then he looked around and smiled. "Much better!"

[충북 ○○중]

25 위 글을 읽고 답할 수 <u>없는</u> 것은? (3점)

① Who controlled the window?

② Who is the owner of the room?

③ What was Circle in charge of?

④ What does Mike water every day?

⑤ Why does Square want to rest?

[충북 ○○중]

26 위 글의 마지막에 Square가 느낀 감정은? (3점)

① unpleasant

② bored

③ careful

④ nervous

⑤ satisfied

[충북 ○○중]

27 위 글의 빈칸 (가)에 공통으로 들어갈 단어는? (3점)

① and ② so ③ or

④ but ⑤ then

[충북 ○○중]

28 위 글의 ⓐ~ⓔ 중 어법상 <u>어색한</u> 것의 개수는? (4점)

① 1개 ② 2개 ③ 3개

④ 4개 ⑤ 5개

[충북 ○○중]

29 위 글의 밑줄 친 (A)가 가리키는 것들을 영어로 쓰시오. (3점)

→ _____, _____

[충북 ○○중]

30 위 글의 밑줄 친 (B)의 우리말을 아래의 단어들을 배열하여 영작하시오. (3점)

make / I / tidy / room / to / try / this

→ _____

2학년 영어 2학기 중간고사(5과) 2회

문항수 : 선택형(26문항) 서술형(4문항) 20 . . .

◎ 선택형 문항의 답안은 컴퓨터용 수정 싸인펜을 사용
 하여 OMR 답안지에 바르게 표기하시오.
◎ 서술형 문제는 답을 답안지에 반드시 검정 볼펜으
 로 쓰시오.
◎ 총 30문항 100점 만점입니다. 문항별 배점은 각
 문항에 표시되어 있습니다.

[광주 ○○중]

01 다음 중 밑줄 친 표현이 문맥상 어색한 것은? (3점)

① The man is waiting to <u>across</u> the street.

② I <u>took</u> it <u>back</u> home to use it again.

③ I got failed. I <u>feel blue</u> today.

④ You can order <u>products</u> online.

⑤ <u>Throw away</u> all the round things.

[부산 ○○중]

02 다음 문장의 빈칸에 가장 적절한 것은? (3점)

Please _____ this cake into eight pieces.

① boil

② rush

③ divide

④ decide

⑤ control

[울산 ○○중]

03 다음 중 어법상 옳은 문장은? (3점)

① At first we thought him silly.

② I was gave a box by the boy.

③ I can find a little people around.

④ Nick told me how open the box.

⑤ Can you tell me which to bus take?

[서울 관악구 ○○중]

04 다음 중 B의 대답으로 어색한 문장을 고르면? (2점)

A: This bookshelf can't stand alone. Do you
 know how to solve this problem?
B: _____

① No, I can't.

② Oh, let me see.

③ Sure, I'll show you how.

④ Well, how about this way?

⑤ Yes. Put some legs on the bottom.

[충북 ○○중]

05 다음 문장의 빈칸에 들어갈 표현으로 적절한 것은? (3점)

I don't know how to ride a bicycle.
= I don't know how _____ should ride
 a bicycle.

① it ② I ③ he

④ they ⑤ she

[서울 관악구 ○○중]

06 다음 중 어법상 바른 것은? (3점)

① I found the movie interest.

② I will have a few ice cream.

③ This box keeps the soup hotly.

④ Tickets are sold at the box office.

⑤ This book was wrote by Harper Lee.

A: Mina, do you know how to solve this puzzle?
B: What is it, Junsu?
A: You must take a dog, a chicken, and a bag of rice across the river. The boat only carries you and one of the things at a time.
B: (가)그건 쉬워. I can take them to the other side (나)하나씩.
A: But without you, the dog will kill the chicken, and the chicken will eat the rice.
B: Let me see.... First, take the ⓐ_____ and come back. Then, take the ⓑ_____ and come back with the ⓐ_____.
A: And?
B: After that, take the ⓒ_____ and come back, Finally, take the ⓐ_____.
A: You are great.

*A: Junsu, B: Mina

[서울 성북구 ○○중]

08 (가)의 우리말을 영어로 쓰시오. (3점)

→ _____

[서울 송파구 ○○중]

09 위 대화의 내용과 일치하는 것을 모두 고르면? (4점)

① Mina knows how to solve the puzzle.
② The boat can carry all the things at a time.
③ They are talking about how difficult the puzzle is.
④ Mina can take the chicken and the rice at a time.
⑤ If Mina takes the rice first, the dog will eat the chicken.

[서울 송파구 ○○중]

07 위 대화의 흐름상 ⓐ~ⓒ에 들어갈 알맞은 말은? (4점)

	ⓐ	ⓑ	ⓒ
①	rice	dog	chicken
②	rice	chicken	dog
③	dog	rice	chicken
④	chicken	rice	dog
⑤	dog	rice	chicken

[서울 성북구 ○○중]

10 위 대화의 우리말 (나)의 표현으로 알맞은 것은? (3점)

① one to one
② one of one
③ one and one
④ one by one
⑤ one with one

11 다음 대화의 빈칸에 들어갈 말로 가장 알맞은 것은? (3점)

A: Do you know _____?
B: Sure. First draw a large square. Then, draw a triangle. Finally, draw a small circle in the square.

① how to draw shapes
② how to make a square
③ what to draw with shapes
④ how to draw a fish with shapes
⑤ how I should draw a mouse with shapes

12 〈보기〉에서 어법상 옳은 문장만을 있는 대로 고른 것은? (4점)

보기
(A) Can you tell me what to open this?
(B) Let's decide which place to visit first.
(C) Mike will can do his homework by himself.
(D) Tom is much more careful than his brother.
(E) Listening to music always makes us comfortable.

① (A), (C)
② (B), (D)
③ (A), (E)
④ (B), (C), (D)
⑤ (B), (D), (E)

13 다음 물음에 답하시오. (5점)

(1) 주어진 〈조건〉에 맞게 같은 뜻이 되도록 바꾸어 쓰시오.

조건
• 「의문사+to부정사」 구문을 이용할 것.

I don't know what I should say to him.

→ _____

(2) 주어진 〈조건〉에 맞게 의미가 통하도록 빈칸을 완성하시오.

조건
• 어휘 decide, to, can, invite를 모두 활용할 것.
• I를 포함하여 6단어로 쓸 것.

→ Tomorrow is my birthday. I'm going to have a party. I have so many friends. I_____. Please give me some tips.

Euclid taught math at the Library of Alexandria when Ptolemy I was the king of Egypt. People call him "the father of math." He showed how to draw a triangle that has three sides of the same length. He also showed (가)_____ the center of the biggest circle in a triangle. One day, Ptolemy I asked, "Is there an easier way to study math?" Euclid replied, "(나)_____."

[경기 ○○중]

14 위 글의 빈칸 (가)에 가장 알맞은 것은? (3점)

① how to find

② what to draw

③ what to teach

④ how to divide

⑤ how to make

[인천 ○○중]

16 위 글의 내용과 일치하지 <u>않는</u> 것은? (4점)

① Euclid is called 'the father of math' by people.

② Euclid taught math when Ptolemy I controlled Egypt.

③ Euclid was taught math at the Library of Alexandria.

④ Euclid thought that there is no easier way to study math.

⑤ Euclid showed the way we can find the center of the biggest circle in a triangle.

[17~20] 다음 글을 읽고, 물음에 답하시오.

(가)There lived three shape spirits in Mike's room: Square, Triangle, and Circle. (A) Square ⓐ_____ the table, the bookshelf, and the window. (B) Triangle ⓑ_____ the hangers and the plants. (C) Circle ⓒ_____ the hula hoops and the bike wheels. (D) The three spirits worked together to make a nice room for Mike. (E)

[인천 ○○중]

15 위 글의 빈칸 (나)에 들어갈 가장 적절한 말은? (4점)

① Habit is second nature.

② Actions speak louder than words.

③ You can't judge a book by its cover.

④ You win some, you lose more.

⑤ There is no royal road to learning.

[경기 ○○중]

17 위 글의 (A)~(E) 중 다음 문장이 들어갈 위치로 가장 적절한 곳은? (3점)

They were round in shape and good for spinning or rolling.

① (A)　　　② (B)　　　③ (C)

④ (D)　　　⑤ (E)

18 위 글의 밑줄 친 (가)<u>There</u>와 쓰임이 같은 것은? (3점)

① <u>There</u> she stopped.

② They will meet you <u>there</u>.

③ Put the cake <u>there</u> in the box.

④ Go <u>there</u> and give them some help.

⑤ <u>There</u> is some milk in the refrigerator.

19 빈칸 ⓐ~ⓒ에 모두 들어갈 수 있는 단어는? (4점)

① controlled

② changed

③ took over

④ brought

⑤ made out of

20 위 글을 읽고 주어진 물음에 우리말로 대답하시오. (4점)

(1) What did Square control?

→ _____

(2) Why did they work together?

→ _____

(가)_____ Mike came home from school, he picked up a square hanger to hang his jacket on. "What? This will not hold my clothes."

He went to water the plants and saw their square leaves.

"Poor things.... ⓐThey must be sick."

He picked up the square hula hoop to exercise.

"Hmm... I don't know (나)[to / this / how / spin]."

He went to take out his bike and looked at the square wheels.

"Well, ⓑI can't ride this. I'll just have to walk." Then he hurried out of the house.

(가)_____ the other spirits came back, Square rushed over to them.

"ⓒMike likes his room much. I don't know what to do," he said.

They looked at the hangers, the plants, and all the new square things. Then they looked at one another, and ⓓSquare realized his problem.

"Let's make this room great again," he said to the others, and ⓔthe three spirits worked together once again.

21 위 글의 ⓐ~ⓔ 중 글의 흐름과 맞지 <u>않는</u> 것은? (4점)

① ⓐ ② ⓑ ③ ⓒ

④ ⓓ ⑤ ⓔ

22 위 글의 빈칸 (가)에 공통으로 들어갈 단어는? (2점)

① That　　　　　② Who

③ Where　　　　④ When

⑤ What

23 위 글의 (나)의 밑줄 친 부분을 어법에 맞게 배열하시오. (3점)

→ _____

24 글의 내용으로 보아 Mike의 심경으로 가장 알맞은 것은? (4점)

① 행복한

② 외로운

③ 감사한

④ 편안한

⑤ 불편한

[25~30] 다음 글을 읽고 물음에 답하시오.

One day Square decided to make the room better and shouted at the other spirits.

"Take these plants away, (가)_____ their pointy leaves will hurt someone!" he said to Triangle.

"But Mike waters ⓐthem every day," said Triangle.

"Take this hula hoop away, (나)_____ ⓑit will roll and break something!" he said to Circle.

"But Mike exercises with it every day," said Circle.

"I try to make this room tidy, but you two always make a mess," ⓒhe complained.

Triangle and Circle looked at each other. "So you think you can do ⓓit without ⓔus?" Triangle asked Square.

"Sure. I can make this room better all by myself," replied Square.

"Great! Then we can get some rest," Circle said to Square.

25 빈칸 (가), (나)에 공통으로 들어갈 말로 가장 적절한 것은? (2점)

① or

② and

③ so

④ then

⑤ but

26 위 글의 밑줄 친 ⓐ~ⓔ가 지칭하는 대상으로 옳지 <u>않은</u> 것은?

(3점)

① ⓐ - plants

② ⓑ - hula hoop

③ ⓒ - Square

④ ⓓ - making this room mess

⑤ ⓔ - Triangle and Circle

27 위 글에서 'Square'의 성격으로 가장 적절한 것은? (4점)

① friendly

② humorous

③ considerate

④ warm-hearted

⑤ self-righteous

28 What did Square decide to do? (3점)

① Square decided to make the room better.

② Square decided to make the room messy.

③ Square decided to make the hula hoop clean.

④ Square decided to make the Circle and Triangle angry.

⑤ Square decided to make the room better with Mike.

29 위 글을 읽고, 다음 문장을 다른 문장으로 바꿀 때, 같은 의미를 지닌 문장은? (3점)

> Take these plants away, or their pointy leaves will hurt someone!

① If you don't hurt someone, you take these plants away!

② If you take these plants away, their pointy leaves will hurt someone!

③ If their pointy leaves hurt someone, you will not take these plants away!

④ If you don't take these plants away, their pointy leaves will hurt someone!

⑤ If you take these plants away, their pointy leaves will be hurt someone!

30 위 글의 내용과 가장 일치하지 <u>않는</u> 것은? (4점)

① Mike는 매일 식물에 물을 준다.

② Triangle은 방을 정돈하려고 노력하였다.

③ Square는 혼자서 방을 더 좋게 만들 수 있다고 말했다.

④ Circle은 Mike가 매일 훌라후프로 운동을 한다고 말했다.

⑤ Square는 Triangle과 Circle이 방을 엉망으로 만든다고 불평했다.

◎ 선택형 문항의 답안은 컴퓨터용 수정 싸인펜을 사용하여 OMR 답안지에 바르게 표기하시오.
◎ 서술형 문제는 답을 답안지에 반드시 검정 볼펜으로 쓰시오.
◎ 총 30문항 100점 만점입니다. 문항별 배점은 각 문항에 표시되어 있습니다.

[광주 ○○중]

01 What does it mean to "feel blue"? (3점)

① It means to feel like a color.
② It means to feel cool.
③ It means to feel sick.
④ It means to feel sad.
⑤ It means to feel excited.

[대전 둔산중 기출]

02 다음 짝지어진 단어의 관계가 〈보기〉와 <u>다른</u> 것은? (2점)

> 보기
>
> clean - dirty

① high - low
② full - empty
③ healthy - sick
④ safe - dangerous
⑤ natural - spotless

[경기 ○○중]

03 다음 중 어법상 옳은 것은? (4점)

① Pluto is discovered in 1930 by *Clyde Tombaugh*.
② An expensive necklace was bought for me by Jason.
③ Three balls of different colors is hidden under the tree.
④ A tall man was appeared from behind the door.
⑤ The building is under construction and it will finish next month.

[충북 ○○중]

04 다음 대화의 내용에 등장한 Jingyu에 대한 설명으로 알맞은 것은? (3점)

A: I think Jingyu is a really kind person.
B: Why do you think so?
A: Yesterday, I watched Jingyu helping his friend who had a broken leg.
B: You're right. He is good at helping teachers at school, too.

① Jingyu feels blue.
② Jingyu is an early bird.
③ Jingyu has a green thumb.
④ Jingyu has a heart of gold.
⑤ Jingyu is always on cloud nine.

[대전 ○○중]

05 다음 빈칸에 들어갈 말로 알맞은 것은? (4점)

A: Sam is on cloud nine.
B: What do you mean by that?
A: _____
B: I get it.

① He feels so sad.
② He is really happy.
③ He is a really kind person.
④ He is good at growing plants.
⑤ The weather is very nice today.

[6~8] 다음 대화를 읽고 물음에 답하시오.

B: Hey, Yuna. What is one tip for a clean classroom?
G: Well, we're doing a clean bin project today.
B: (A)그게 무슨 뜻이야?
G: We don't throw away trash, so our trash can stay empty.
B: That's surprising! Please tell me more about it.
G: Sure. No problem.

*B: Bart G: Yuna

06 위 대화와 관련하여 Yuna의 학급 표어로 가장 적절한 것은?

(3점)

① Tidy Up Desks
② Make No Trash
③ Be Quiet in Class
④ Be on Time
⑤ Don't Eat Food in the Classroom

08 위 대화의 내용과 일치하지 <u>않는</u> 것은? (4점)

① Bart wants to learn a good tip for a clean classroom from Yuna.
② A clean bin project is the key to Yuna's clean classroom.
③ For a clean classroom, Yuna's classmates don't throw away trash.
④ By doing a clean bin project, Yuna's classmates can keep their trash bin empty.
⑤ Bart will let Yuna know about the project when he meets her.

[9~13] 다음 대화를 읽고 물음에 답하시오.

A: What are those in the middle of the ocean?
B: They are trash islands.
A: Trash islands? (가)<u>What do you mean by that?</u>
B: A lot of plastic trash goes into the ocean and becomes big islands like those.
A: That sounds terrible! How big are those islands?
B: (A)<u>가장 큰 것은 대략 남한의 14배 만큼 커.</u>
A: That's (나)_____! I think we should not use plastic products.
B: I agree.

*A: Mina, B: Jiho

07 위 대화의 밑줄 친 (A)를 전치사 "by"를 이용하여 바르게 영작하시오.

(4점)

→ _____

09 밑줄 친 (가)와 바꾸어 쓸 수 있는 것은? (3점)

① Let me explain.
② I don't like the idea
③ Why do you think so?
④ Do you understand it?
⑤ Could you explain it?

12 위 대화의 내용과 일치하는 것을 2개 고르면? (3점)

① The islands are made of lots of trash.
② Jiho and Mina are going to the island.
③ Jiho and Mina are not going to use plastic products.
④ The islands are in the center of the continent.
⑤ The biggest island is forty times larger than South Korea.

10 위 대화의 빈칸 (나)에 알맞지 <u>않은</u> 것은? (4점)

① terrible
② shocking
③ precious
④ surprising
⑤ unbelievable

13 (A)의 우리말을 영어로 쓰시오. (5점)

→ _____

14 빈칸 ⓐ, ⓑ에 들어갈 말로 알맞게 짝지어진 것은? (4점)

A: What do you need to make sandwiches?
B: I need ⓐ_____ ketchup and ⓑ_____ tomatoes.

	ⓐ	ⓑ
①	a little	a few
②	a few	a little
③	few	little
④	a few	a few
⑤	a little	little

11 위 대화 후 앞으로 A와 B가 할 행동으로 가장 알맞은 것은? (2점)

① 매일 꾸준히 운동한다.
② 세계의 여러 섬을 여행한다.
③ 음식물 쓰레기를 재활용한다.
④ 플라스틱 일회용품을 쓰지 않는다.
⑤ 종이컵 대신 플라스틱 컵을 사용한다.

15 다음 ⓐ~ⓔ 중 어법이 맞는 것끼리 짝지어진 것은? (3점)

> ⓐ The glass was broken by Amy.
> ⓑ Tickets are sold at the box office.
> ⓒ Ray was written a letter in English.
> ⓓ Some books were given Brian by Ms. Lucy.
> ⓔ These cup bottles was made out of recycled paper.

① ⓐ, ⓑ

② ⓑ, ⓒ

③ ⓐ, ⓒ, ⓓ

④ ⓑ, ⓒ, ⓓ

⑤ ⓒ, ⓓ, ⓔ

16 다음 빈칸에 들어갈 가장 알맞은 문장은? (4점)

> A: This bike blender kills two birds with one stone.
> B: What do you mean by that?
> A: _____
> B: Oh, I get it.

① You can kill two birds with this bike.

② When you ride this bike with one stone, two birds will follow you.

③ This bike blender will make delicious juice for you.

④ With this bike, you can become strong enough to kill two birds with one stone.

⑤ This bike will make juice for you and also make you stronger.

17 Who has a good tip for the environment? (3점)

① Jiho: I carry paper cups to school.

② Yumi: When I give gifts to my friend, I use lots of wrapping paper.

③ Hana: I buy the smallest size when I buy ice cream.

④ Giho: I use my own cups and spoons instead of paper cups or plastic spoons.

⑤ Miso: When I brush my teeth, I turn on the tap.

[18~19] 다음 글을 읽고 물음에 답하시오.

> **Leave No Food Behind**
>
> Reporter: Please give us one simple tip for reducing trash.
> Junha: ⓐDon't leave any food on your plate. ⓑA lot of trees are cut down to make paper. ⓒFood waste really is a big problem. ⓓBut see? ⓔWe ate everything even our plates, ha-ha.

18 위 글의 밑줄 친 ⓐ~ⓔ 중 글의 흐름상 어색한 문장은? (3점)

① ⓐ　　② ⓑ　　③ ⓒ

④ ⓓ　　⑤ ⓔ

19 위 글을 읽고 주어진 지시에 답하시오. (4점)

(1) Junha가 Reporter에게 어떤 조언을 했는지 우리말로 쓰시오.

→ _____

(2) 그 조언을 실천하기 위해서 Junha가 어떻게 했는지 우리말로 쓰시오.

→ _____

20 위 글의 빈칸 (A)에 들어갈 말로 가장 적절한 것은? (3점)

① Use cloth napkins.
② Don't wrap your gifts for a party.
③ Use paper cups and plastic plates.
④ Leave no food behind on your plate.
⑤ Choose the largest size when you buy ice cream.

[20~22] 다음 글을 읽고, 물음에 답하시오.

> Reporter: Do you usually bring some cups and spoons when you go camping?
> Minsu: We didn't use paper cups or plastic spoons. Instead, we brought our own cups and spoons from home and then took them back.
> Reporter: What else did you do ⓐto make less trash?
> Jieun: We used cloth napkins. You know, paper napkins are not good for your skin.
> Reporter: But where did you get the cloth napkins?
> Jieun: They ⓑwere made by Minji. She cut up her old cotton shirt ⓒto make some for us. Her cute napkins ⓓwas liked by everyone.
> Reporter: Finally, please give us one simple and useful tip ⓔfor reducing trash.
> Jieun: (A)_____. Food waste really is a big problem. But see? We ate everything, even our plates, ha-ha.

21 위 글의 밑줄 친 ⓐ~ⓔ 중 어법상 어색한 것은? (2점)

① ⓐ ② ⓑ ③ ⓒ
④ ⓓ ⑤ ⓔ

22 위 대화를 읽고 대답할 수 없는 질문은? (4점)

① What did they use instead of paper cups and plastic spoons?
② What did they use instead of paper napkins?
③ Why did they use cloth napkins?
④ How can we recycle used napkins?
⑤ Who made the cloth napkins?

Reporter: And how did you serve the ice cream to make less trash?

Junha: My classmates and I served it on plates. You know what? We ate even the plates after we used them.

Reporter: You ate the plates? What do you mean by that?

Junha: Actually, we used popped rice cakes as plates, so we could eat them and leave nothing behind!

Reporter: I get it. That's quite interesting. What about cups and spoons?

Junha: We didn't use paper cups or plastic spoons. (가)_____, we brought our own cups and spoons from home and then took ⓐthem back.

[경기 ○○중]

24 위 글을 요약할 때, 빈칸 (A)와 (B)에 들어갈 말로 가장 적절한 것은? (4점)

Junha and his classmates have made less trash by (A)_____ the plates after using them and (B)_____ back their own cups and spoons they brought from home.

(A)	(B)
① eating	bringing
② serving	taking
③ recycling	making
④ serving	bringing
⑤ eating	taking

[경기 ○○중]

23 위 글의 밑줄 친 ⓐ가 가리키는 대상으로 가장 적절한 것은? (3점)

① the ice cream

② the plates

③ popped rice cakes

④ paper cups

⑤ our own cups and spoons

[경기 ○○중]

25 빈칸 (가)에 들어갈 알맞은 것은? (3점)

① Actually

② Instead

③ First

④ Also

⑤ Finally

[26~30] 다음 글을 읽고 물음에 답하시오.

We all had a "No Trash Challenge" day last month. The winner was Grade 2 Class 3. Let's read the interview and learn a few ⓐtips for living green.

(A)_____

Reporter: You ⓑthrew a class birthday party, but didn't (가)_____ a lot of trash. What were your ⓒsecrets?

Minsu: First, (나)우리는 선물을 포장하지 않기로 동의했어, because some wrapping paper is not easily ⓓrecycled. So we brought gifts such as teddy bears, key rings, new socks and hairpins that were not ⓔ wrapped at all.

26 빈칸 (가)에 들어갈 말의 영영 풀이로 맞는 것은? (4점)

① to have the same opinion

② to make or create something

③ to make smaller in size or number

④ something worthless that you throw away

⑤ something that is made and sold in large quantities

27 위 글의 흐름상, 밑줄 친 ⓐ~ⓔ의 의미로 적절하지 <u>않은</u> 것은? (2점)

① ⓐ 유용한 정보, 조언

② ⓑ (노력을) 쏟다

③ ⓒ 비밀, 비결

④ ⓓ (폐기물, 중고품 등을) 재활용하다

⑤ ⓔ (선물, 상품 등을) 포장하다

28 위 글을 제대로 이해하지 <u>못한</u> 사람은? (3점)

① 호날두: 지난달에 학급 생일잔치가 있었어.

② 벤제마: 리포터가 쓰레기를 줄이는 비결을 물어보고 있어.

③ 라모스: 어떤 포장지는 재활용하기가 쉽지 않아.

④ 크로스: 친구들이 포장하지 않은 생일 선물들을 들고 왔어.

⑤ 이스코: 이어질 글에 쓰레기를 줄이는 비법이 더 소개될 것 같아.

29 위 글의 (나)의 우리말을 영어로 쓰시오. (7 단어) (3점)

→ _____

30 위 글의 빈칸 (A)에 들어갈 제목으로 가장 적절한 것은? (4점)

① Eat the Plates

② Buy the Largest Size

③ Leave No Food Behind

④ Bring Your Own Things

⑤ Do not Use Wrapping Paper

◎ 선택형 문항의 답안은 컴퓨터용 수정 싸인펜을 사용하여 OMR 답안지에 바르게 표기하시오.
◎ 서술형 문제는 답을 답안지에 반드시 검정 볼펜으로 쓰시오.
◎ 총 31문항 100점 만점입니다. 문항별 배점은 각 문항에 표시되어 있습니다.

[광주 ○○중]

01 What does it mean to "have a heart of gold"? (4점)

① It means to be really happy.

② It means to get up early in the morning.

③ It means to be good at growing plants.

④ It means to be rich and wealthy.

⑤ It means to be a really kind person.

[서울 송파구 ○○중]

02 다음 중 영영 풀이가 알맞지 <u>않은</u> 것은? (2점)

① plate: a flat, round dish

② tip: a useful piece of advice

③ agree: to have the different opinion

④ reduce: to make smaller in size or number

⑤ trash: something worthless that you throw away

[서울 성동구 ○○중]

03 다음 문장과 같은 의미로 쓰인 것은? (3점)

> My mom has a green thumb.

① My mom is really happy.

② My mom works very hard.

③ My mom is a really kind person.

④ My mom is good at growing plants.

⑤ My mom gets up early in the morning.

[서울 구로구 ○○중]

04 각 표현과 그 의미가 바르게 연결되지 <u>않은</u> 것은? (3점)

① My father feels blue today.

= He feels sad today.

② My sister is an early bird.

= She gets up early in the morning.

③ Tina is on cloud nine.

= She is really happy.

④ My mom has a green thumb.

= She is good at growing plants.

⑤ This bike kills two birds with one stone.

= This bike uses two birds as one stone.

[경기 ○○중]

05 다음 대화의 빈칸에 들어갈 말로 <u>어색한</u> 것은? (3점)

> A: Junsu is an early bird.
> B: _____
> A: He is an early riser.
> B: I get it.

① What is that exactly?

② Tell me more about it.

③ What do you mean by that?

④ Do you understand what I mean?

⑤ Can you give more of an explanation?

[6~7] 다음 대화를 읽고 물음에 답하시오.

A: Hey, Minji. What is one tip for a clean classroom?
B: Well, we're doing a clean bin project today.
A: What is that exactly?
B: We don't throw away trash, so our trash can stay empty.
A: That's surprising! Please tell me more about it.
B: Sure. No problem.

[서울 성동구 ○○중]

06 위 대화를 요약하여 다시 쓸 때, 빈칸에 들어갈 알맞은 말을 11 단어의 완전한 영어 문장으로 쓰시오. (4점)

Minji and her classmates are doing a clean bin project. It means that _____.

[8~11] 다음 대화를 읽고 물음에 답하시오.

G: What are those in the middle of the ocean?
B: They are trash islands.
G: Trash islands? (가)_____
B: A lot of plastic trash goes into the ocean and becomes big islands like those.
G: That sounds terrible! How big are those islands?
B: The biggest one is about 14 times as large as South Korea.
G: (나)너무 놀라워! I think we should not use plastic products.

[서울 성북구 ○○중]

08 위 대화의 (가)에 들어갈 말로 <u>어색한</u> 것은? (3점)

① I'm not sure I understand.
② Tell me more.
③ I don't understand.
④ What do you mean?
⑤ Anything else?

[서울 구로구 ○○중]

07 위 대화를 읽고 민지의 학급 포스터 문구로 가장 적절한 것을 고르면? (3점)

① Tidy Up Desks
② Make No Trash
③ Reuse the Trash Can
④ Put Trash into the Bin
⑤ Keep the Classroom Empty

[충북 ○○중]

09 위 대화를 통해 알 수 있는 사실은? (4점)

① Trash islands are made of food waste.
② Using plastic products should be reduced.
③ Trash islands are in the middle of the land.
④ Every trash island is bigger than South Korea.
⑤ The biggest trash island is smaller than South Korea.

10 위 대화의 (나)의 영어 표현으로 적절하지 <u>않은</u> 것은? (2점)

① Believable!

② What a surprise!

③ I'm so surprised!

④ That's surprising!

⑤ I can't believe it!

12 두 사람의 대화로 가장 자연스러운 것은? (3점)

① A: I feel blue today.

B: What does that mean?

A: I mean I feel happy.

② A: Minji's classroom is spotless.

B: You're right. Her classroom is very dirty.

③ A: James is as nice as pie.

B: I agree with you. He is always kind and friendly to everyone.

④ A: My son is a couch potato.

B: I'm happy to hear that. He is an early bird.

⑤ A: What is a clean bin project?

B: We don't throw away trash, so our trash can stay full.

11 위 대화를 읽고 대답할 수 <u>없는</u> 질문을 <u>모두</u> 고르시오. (4점)

① Where are trash islands?

② What are they talking about?

③ How big is the biggest trash island?

④ What kinds of plastic products do they use?

⑤ Are there any trash islands in South Korea?

13 다음 밑줄 친 부분이 어법상 <u>어색한</u> 것을 고르시오. (2점)

① Paper <u>is using</u> for books and magazines.

② We <u>will make</u> the box out of this used paper.

③ A lot of trees <u>are cut down</u> to make paper.

④ Used paper <u>is recycled</u> by many people now.

⑤ Many soldiers <u>will be killed</u> if war breaks out.

14 밑줄 친 부분의 쓰임이 바른 것을 <u>2개</u> 고르면?　(3점)

① They made <u>few</u> mistakes.

② The woman paid <u>little</u> attention to us.

③ <u>A little</u> students bring their own cups.

④ They have <u>a few</u> interest in this topic.

⑤ Give me <u>a little</u> ideas about this project.

16 다음 대화를 자연스럽게 배열한 것은?　(3점)

ⓐ That's surprising.
ⓑ What does that mean?
ⓒ They take 450 years to break down.
ⓓ Plastic bottles are a big problem for the Earth.

① ⓐ - ⓑ - ⓒ - ⓓ

② ⓓ - ⓐ - ⓒ - ⓑ

③ ⓒ - ⓐ - ⓓ - ⓑ

④ ⓓ - ⓑ - ⓒ - ⓐ

⑤ ⓒ - ⓑ - ⓓ - ⓐ

15 다음 중 수동태로 바꾼 문장이 <u>어색한</u> 것은?　(4점)

① The mayor told everybody in the city big news.
　→ Everybody in the city was told big news by the mayor.

② The salesperson offered me a special discount.
　→ A special discount was offered to me by the salesperson.

③ Jason sells the store owners antique furniture.
　→ The store owners are sold antique furniture by Jason.

④ Kevin sent her the surprising present.
　→ The surprising present was sent to her by Kevin.

⑤ Tina gave me a cute watch.
　→ A cute watch was given to me by Tina.

17 다음 중 어법상 <u>틀린</u> 것은?　(4점)

① The TV was repaired by my uncle.

② Four languages are spoken in this country.

③ Aluminum is widely used in aircraft construction.

④ The girl was seemed nervous when she was in the car.

⑤ Organic cotton was grown in 20 countries worldwide.

18 다음 중 밑줄 친 부분의 쓰임이 <u>어색한</u> 것은?　(3점)

① I will have <u>a little</u> ice cream.

② Andy has <u>few</u> toys in his toy box.

③ He has <u>little</u> interest in this project.

④ She went out <u>a little</u> minutes ago.

⑤ We've got <u>a few</u> ideas for the title.

19 다음 대화의 빈칸에 가장 알맞은 말은?　(4점)

> A: How big are those islands?
> B: The biggest one is about 14 times
> _____ South Korea.

① as little as

② so small as

③ as many as

④ so much as

⑤ as large as

[20~25] 다음 글을 읽고 물음에 답하시오.

Bring Your Own Things

Reporter: What about cups and spoons?

Minsu: We didn't use paper cups or plastic spoons. ⓐ<u>Instead, we brought our own cups and spoons from home and then took back them.</u>

(가)_____

Reporter: ⓑ<u>What else did you done to make less trash?</u>

Jieun: We used cloth napkins. You know, paper napkins are not good for your skin.

Reporter: But where did you get the cloth napkins?

Jieun: (A)그것들은 민지에 의해 만들어졌다. ⓒ<u>She cutted up her old cotton shirt to make some for us.</u> Everyone liked her cute napkins.

Leave No Food Behind

Reporter: ⓓ<u>Please give us one simple tip for reduce trash.</u>

Junha: ⓔ<u>Don't leave many food on your plate.</u> Food waste really is a big problem. But see? We ate everything, even our plates, ha-ha.

20 What did they do to reduce food waste? (3점)

① They used paper napkins.

② They chose the food they liked.

③ They cooked food by themselves.

④ They brought food from their home.

⑤ They ate everything and didn't leave any food.

22 위 글의 ⓐ~ⓔ의 문장을 각각 어법에 맞게 고친 것은? (4점)

① Instead, we were brought our own cups and spoons from home and then took back them.

② What else did you done to making less trash?

③ She cutted up her old cotton shirt to make us some.

④ Please give us one simple tip for reducing trash.

⑤ Don't leave few food on your plate.

23 위 글의 내용과 일치하지 <u>않는</u> 것은? (3점)

① Minsu는 종이컵을 사용하지 않았다.

② Minsu는 집에서 숟가락을 가져와서 사용했다.

③ Junha는 음식물 쓰레기를 줄이라고 조언했다.

④ Jieun은 종이 냅킨이 피부에 좋지 않다고 생각한다.

⑤ 친구들은 Minji가 만든 천 냅킨에 대해 불평했다.

21 위 글에서 언급되지 <u>않은</u> 것은? (3점)

① Minsu brought his own cup.

② Paper napkins are not good for your skin.

③ Jieun's classmates liked the cloth napkins.

④ Everyone in Jieun's class brought their old cotton shirts.

⑤ Junha thinks that food waste really is a big problem.

24 [보기]의 단어를 <u>모두</u> 사용하여 (A)의 우리말과 같은 뜻이 되도록 영작하시오. (2점)

---보기---
by / Minji / were / they / made

→ _____

25 위 글의 (가)에 들어갈 문단의 제목으로 가장 알맞은 것은?

(3점)

① Leave No Food Behind

② Bring Your Own Things

③ Buy the Largest Size

④ Use Cloth Napkins

⑤ Do Not Use Wrapping Paper

Eat the Plates

Reporter: And how did you serve ⓐthe ice cream?

Junha: We served it on ⓑplates. You know what? We ate even the plates after we used ⓒthem.

Reporter: You ate the plates? What do you mean by that?

Junha: Actually, we used ⓓpopped rice cakes as plates, so we could eat ⓔthem and leave nothing behind!

Reporter: Ah, I get it. That's quite interesting.

26 Junha의 학급 생일잔치에 관한 위 글의 내용과 일치하지 <u>않는</u> 것은?

(3점)

① 그들은 뻥튀기를 먹었다.

② 그들은 사용한 접시를 먹었다.

③ 그들은 뻥튀기를 접시로 사용했다.

④ 그들은 아이스크림과 뻥튀기를 조금씩 남겼다.

⑤ 그들은 접시 위에 아이스크림을 올려놓고 먹었다.

[26~30] 다음 글을 읽고 물음에 답하시오.

We all had a "No Trash Challenge" day last month. The winner was Grade 2 Class 3. Let's read the interview and learn a few tips for living green.

Do Not Use Wrapping Paper

Reporter: You threw a class birthday party, but didn't produce a lot of trash. What were your secrets?

Minsu: First, we agreed not to wrap our gifts, because some wrapping paper is not easily recycled. So we brought gifts such as teddy bears, key rings, and hairpins (A)_____ (B)_____ (C)_____ (D)_____ (E)_____.

Buy the Largest Size

Jieun: Also, we chose the largest size when we bought ice cream and cookies for the party. (가) <u>더 큰 사이즈는 더 적은 포장을 사용하고 쓰레기를 덜 만들어.</u>

27 위 글의 (가)의 우리말을 영어로 쓰시오.

(4점)

→ _____

28 위 글의 내용상 ⓐ~ⓔ 중 가리키는 것이 <u>다른</u> 하나는? (3점)

① ⓐ ② ⓑ ③ ⓒ

④ ⓓ ⑤ ⓔ

29 위 글의 (A)~(E)를 〈보기〉의 어구들을 이용하여 어법에 맞게 배열하였을 때 (B)와 (D)에 들어갈 말이 알맞게 짝지어진 것은? (3점)

> 보기
>
> at all, wrapped, were, that, not

 (B) (D)

① that not

② that wrapped

③ were at all

④ were wrapped

⑤ wrapped not

30 Why did Minsu and his classmates agree not to wrap their gifts? (3점)

① They were not good at wrapping gifts.

② Wrapping paper is usually very expensive.

③ Wrapping paper can be recycled very easily.

④ People can't recycle some wrapping paper easily.

⑤ The gifts were large, so it was hard to wrap them.

31 주어진 영어 문장(1)과 우리말(2)을 조건에 맞게 수동태 문장으로 쓰시오. (5점)

(1) He gave me a cute doll.

= _____

> 조건
>
> • "I"를 포함하는 문장으로 쓰시오.

(2) 그는 어젯밤에 병원으로 실려갔다.

= _____ last night.

> 조건
>
> • "take"를 활용해서 영어 문장을 완성하시오.

2학년 영어 2학기 기말고사(7과) 1회

문항수 : 선택형(25문항) 서술형(5문항) | 20 . . .

◎ 선택형 문항의 답안은 컴퓨터용 수정 싸인펜을 사용
하여 OMR 답안지에 바르게 표기하시오.
◎ 서술형 문제는 답을 답안지에 반드시 검정 볼펜으
로 쓰시오.
◎ 총 30문항 100점 만점입니다. 문항별 배점은 각
문항에 표시되어 있습니다.

[광주 ○○중]

01 다음 중 뜻풀이가 올바르지 <u>않은</u> 것은? (3점)

① fantasy: a pleasant, exciting, or unusual
experience that you imagine is happening to
you

② tool: a piece of equipment, usually one you
hold in your hand, that is designed to do a
particular type of work

③ monster: the rear end of the body of an
animal

④ universal: related to everyone in the world

⑤ reach: to move your arm, hand toward
something that you are trying to touch or
pick up

[경기 ○○중]

02 다음 중 밑줄 친 부분의 의미가 <u>어색한</u> 것은? (3점)

① <u>Both</u> twins are very healthy now. (둘 다)

② The temperature was ten <u>below</u> zero. (아래에)

③ The dog barked and wagged its <u>tail</u>. (꼬리)

④ Every person has a <u>unique</u> fingerprint. (독특
한)

⑤ The tour <u>included</u> a visit to the Louvre
Museum. (배제했다)

[광주 ○○중]

03 다음 빈칸에 들어갈 말을 〈보기〉에서 골라 알맞은 형태로 바꿔
전체 문장을 답안지에 옮겨 적으시오. (4점)

> **보기**
>
> take, ring, sit, contain

→ The school sent me a brochure _____
the information I needed.

[광주 ○○중]

04 다음 대화 중 <u>어색한</u> 것은? (2점)

① A: Good job! Someone is holding a cloud?
How creative!
B: Thank you.

② A: Are you interested in glass art?
B: Yes, I am. I'm interested in sports.

③ A: How long did it take to make it?
B: It took one month.

④ A: I started taking yoga classes on weekends.
B: Oh, I didn't know that.

⑤ A: Are you interested in dancing *talchum*?
B: Sure. Can you teach me?

05 대화에서 언급되고 있는 작품에 대한 설명으로 올바르지 <u>않은</u> 것은? (3점)

> Chris: You did a good job! It's awesome.
> Jenny: Thanks.
> Chris: What is it made of? Glass?
> Jenny: Yes, it is. I'm going to name this work 'waves'.
> Chris: That's a great idea! How long did it take to make it?
> Jenny: It took one month.

① The title of the work is going to be 'waves'.

② It is made of glass.

③ It took one month to make it.

④ Chris made it by himself.

⑤ Chris thinks Jenny's work is great.

07 위 글의 (A)~(C)에 들어갈 말로 알맞은 것은? (2점)

	(A)	(B)	(C)
①	First	Next	Finally
②	Then	First	Finally
③	First	Finally	Next
④	Then	Next	Finally
⑤	First	Finally	Then

08 주어진 조건을 잘 보고 영작하시오. (4점)

> 조건
> • [한국어를 배우고 있는 두 남자를 봐.]를 7단어로 영작하시오.
> • learn의 현재분사를 사용하시오.

→ _____

[6~7] 다음 글을 읽고 물음에 답하시오.

> Teacher: Today we'll make ice cream. Which flavor do you want to make? How about strawberry? (A)_____, mix two cups of milk, two cups of heavy cream, and half a cup of sugar. (B)_____, cut five strawberries into small pieces. (C)_____, mix everything together and put it in the freezer. It's easy to make, isn't it? ⓐ[you, don't, home, making, try, why, it ,at]?

06 위 글의 밑줄 친 ⓐ의 단어를 배열하여 문장을 완성하시오. (3점)

→ _____

09 다음 대화의 순서가 가장 자연스러운 것은? (3점)

> ⓐ Thank you. Are you interested in painting?
> ⓑ Good work! I think your painting expresses the feeling of autumn well.
> ⓒ Yes, I am. I started taking a class on weekends.
> ⓓ Oh, I didn't know that.

① ⓐ-ⓑ-ⓒ-ⓓ ② ⓐ-ⓑ-ⓓ-ⓒ

③ ⓑ-ⓐ-ⓒ-ⓓ ④ ⓑ-ⓐ-ⓓ-ⓒ

⑤ ⓒ-ⓐ-ⓓ-ⓑ

[10~11] 다음 대화를 읽고 물음에 답하시오.

(A) Sure. Can you teach me?
(B) Thank you. Are you interested in play the ukulele?
(C) I enjoyed your performance. You did a good job.
(D) No problem.

[충북 ○○중]

10 위 대화를 흐름에 맞게 배열한 것은? (3점)

① (A) - (B) - (C) - (D)
② (B) - (D) - (C) - (A)
③ (B) - (A) - (D) - (C)
④ (C) - (B) - (A) - (D)
⑤ (C) - (A) - (B) - (D)

[충북 ○○중]

11 위 대화에서 문법이 어색한 문장을 찾아 고친 후, 그 문장 전체를 다시 쓰시오. (4점)

→ _____

[12~14] 다음 대화를 읽고 물음에 답하시오.

B: What are you doing, Mina?
G: ⓐI'm practicing calligraphy.
B: ⓑI'm writing with a brush. It looks fun.
G: ⓒAre you interested in calligraphy?
B: Yes, very much.
G: Look at this! I just wrote it. ⓓWhy do you think?
B: It looks like a person dancing with open arms.
G: ____(A)____ This Korean word means "dance."
B: ____(B)____ Can I try it?
G: ____(C)____ ⓔTake this brush.
 * B: Boy, G: Mina

[서울 성동구 ○○중]

12 ⓐ~ⓔ 중에서 대화의 흐름상 적절치 않은 것을 2개 고르면? (3점)

① ⓐ ② ⓑ ③ ⓒ
④ ⓓ ⑤ ⓔ

[서울 송파구 ○○중]

13 위 대화의 빈칸 (A)~(C)에 들어갈 말로 알맞은 것은? (4점)

	(A)	(B)	(C)
①	Good job!	You got it.	Sure!
②	What's up?	That's a good idea.	Why?
③	You got it.	No problem.	Of course.
④	You got it.	You did a good job!	Why not?
⑤	Not really.	That's right!	Why not?

[서울 송파구 ○○중]

14 위 대화의 내용과 일치하지 않는 것은? (4점)

① 소년은 캘리그래피에 관심이 많다.
② Mina는 '춤'을 뜻하는 영어 단어를 썼다.
③ Mina는 붓으로 글자를 쓰고 있다.
④ 소년은 캘리그래피를 써 보고 싶어 한다.
⑤ Mina가 쓴 글자는 춤추는 사람처럼 보인다.

15 밑줄 친 단어 중 어법상 쓰임이 <u>다른</u> 하나는? (4점)

① The <u>running</u> boy is my nephew.

② Nancy likes the man <u>wearing</u> a green shirt.

③ The dog <u>barking</u> at a stranger is Susan's dog.

④ Who is the girl <u>playing</u> the piano on the stage?

⑤ Susan likes <u>collecting</u> precious things like old coins.

16 Which is right for (A)? (4점)

① is not considered as art

② can be seen in many places

③ is hard to find all around the world

④ can be written well without practice

⑤ is not related to the commercial products

17 위 글의 밑줄 친 ⓐ~ⓔ 중에서 전체 흐름과 관계<u>없는</u> 문장은? (3점)

① ⓐ ② ⓑ ③ ⓒ

④ ⓓ ⑤ ⓔ

[16~22] 다음 글을 읽고 물음에 답하시오.

Today calligraphy (A)_____. ⓐYou can find designers' artistic touches on movie posters, book covers, music CDs, and clothes. ⓑBelow are some examples. ⓒNo one uses calligraphy works today. ⓓLook at the title on the movie poster. ⓔHow do you feel? Can you imagine the monster's big mouth, sharp teeth, and ugly, long tail? How about the title on the fantasy novel? Do you see Harry's lightning and the wizard hats?

Anyone can start writing calligraphy. (가)It's not easy to write by hand well at first, but (나)자꾸 연습하면 아주 잘하게 된다. Keep trying and make it part of your everyday life. Write with your feelings on birthday cards, bookmarks, or gifts. Soon you will (B)_____ your own world of calligraphy.

18 밑줄 친 (가)It과 그 쓰임이 <u>다른</u> 하나는? (3점)

① <u>It</u> is exciting to play *yunnori*.

② <u>It</u> is the best tool in this store.

③ <u>It</u> is awesome to find a good book.

④ <u>It</u> is important to learn a foreign language.

⑤ <u>It</u> is popular to express feelings through handwriting.

19 위 글에서 캘리그래피가 사용되는 곳이 <u>아닌</u> 것은? (3점)

① 모자 ② 옷

③ 책표지 ④ 음악 CD

⑤ 영화 포스터

20 위 글의 제목으로 가장 적절한 것은? (3점)

① Artist, Painting the World!
② A Step Inside the Adventure
③ Stop and Listen to the Music!
④ Welcome to the Magical World!
⑤ Calligraphy in Our Everyday Lives

21 위 글의 빈칸 (B)에 들어갈 말로 가장 적절한 것은? (4점)

① turn up ② push up
③ build up ④ jump up
⑤ put up with

22 위 글의 (나)의 우리말을 영어로 쓰시오. (세 단어로 이루어진 영어 속담) (3점)

→ _____

[23~26] 다음 글을 읽고 물음에 답하시오.

How do you express your feelings? Do you sing or dance? Do you write a poem or draw a picture? Nowadays, it is popular (가)[express / to express] feelings through handwriting. Let's look at some works of art.

(A) It looks like a happy woman (나)[walk / walking] down a road with autumn leaves. Both of these works express the feeling of autumn through beautiful handwriting. This kind of art (다)[calls / is called] calligraphy.

(B) It shows that autumn is a season of fruit. The work of art on the left shows a Korean word and a Chinese character.

(C) In the work of art on the right, the word includes an image of a delicious fruit, *hongsi*.

23 위 글의 흐름상 (A)~(C)의 순서로 가장 적절한 것은? (4점)

① (A)-(C)-(B) ② (B)-(A)-(C)
③ (B)-(C)-(A) ④ (C)-(A)-(B)
⑤ (C)-(B)-(A)

24 위 글의 주제로 가장 적절한 것은? (3점)

① the benefits of taking a walk
② the introduction of calligraphy
③ the history of Chinese characters
④ the importance of expressing our feelings
⑤ the difference between Korean and Chinese

25 위 글의 괄호 (가)~(다) 안에서 어법상 맞는 단어로 가장 적절한 것은? (4점)

	(가)	(나)	(다)
①	express	walk	calls
②	express	walking	is called
③	to express	walking	is called
④	to express	walking	calls
⑤	to express	walk	is called

26 위 글의 내용과 일치하지 <u>않는</u> 것은? (4점)

① *Hongsi* season is the fall.

② The word on the left looks like a human.

③ There are many ways to express feelings.

④ The calligraphy on the right has an image of a fruit.

⑤ Both works have a Korean word and a Chinese character.

28 위 글의 (A)가 가리키는 것은? (3점)

① The left one

② The Canterbury Tales

③ Joseon Dynasty

④ Calligrapher

⑤ England

29 위 글의 (B)to make와 용법이 같은 것은? (3점)

① He went to Paris <u>to study</u> art.

② <u>To walk</u> is good for your health.

③ She wants <u>to buy</u> a pink sweater.

④ There is no water <u>to drink</u> here.

⑤ My hobby is <u>to play</u> soccer.

[27~30] 다음 글을 읽고 물음에 답하시오.

Calligraphy is not ⓐ<u>new</u>. Many different kinds of calligraphy works from long ago can be found all around the world. Look at the two ⓑ<u>examples</u> from Korea and the UK below. Can you tell the ⓒ <u>difference</u>? The left one was created by Chusa in the period of the Joseon Dynasty. The characters were painted with a soft brush. The right one, *The Canterbury Tales*, was created by Chaucer in England in the late 1400s. (A)<u>It</u> was written with a pen. ⓓ<u>Same</u> writing tools led to different styles of calligraphy. Of course, all calligraphers had to ⓔ <u>practice</u> hard (B)<u>to make</u> their unique styles.

27 위 글의 밑줄 친 ⓐ~ⓔ 중에서 문맥상 낱말의 쓰임이 적절하지 <u>않은</u> 것은? (3점)

① ⓐ ② ⓑ ③ ⓒ

④ ⓓ ⑤ ⓔ

30 위 글의 요지로 가장 적절한 것은? (4점)

① We need to practice to write calligraphy well.

② The soft brush is the best tool for the calligraphy.

③ *The Canterbury Tales* is the first novel in the world.

④ Chusa used many kinds of writing tools to paint the characters well.

⑤ Calligraphy has a long history and it is found all around the world.

◎ 선택형 문항의 답안은 컴퓨터용 수정 싸인펜을 사용하여 OMR 답안지에 바르게 표기하시오.
◎ 서술형 문제는 답을 답안지에 반드시 검정 볼펜으로 쓰시오.
◎ 총 30문항 100점 만점입니다. 문항별 배점은 각 문항에 표시되어 있습니다.

[부산 ○○중]

01 다음 짝지어진 단어의 관계가 [보기]와 다른 것은? (2점)

> **보기**
>
> high - low

① clean – dirty
② weak – strong
③ solve – solution
④ cheap – expensive
⑤ get on – get off

[광주 ○○중]

02 다음 중 밑줄 친 부분의 의미가 문맥상 바르지 않은 것은? (3점)

① I occasionally visit my uncle in the country. (가끔)
② Both Janet and Amy are intelligent. (둘 다)
③ The express train started from Paris on time. (특정한)
④ People usually judge you by the company you keep. (친구)
⑤ The earth is round, not flat. (평평한)

[광주 ○○중]

03 다음 중 밑줄 친 부분의 쓰임이 나머지와 다른 것은? (3점)

① It is fun to go camping.
② It is an easy game to play.
③ It is dangerous to swim in this river.
④ It is wrong to tell a lie.
⑤ It is difficult to learn a foreign language.

[부산 ○○중]

04 다음 대화의 내용에서 Minji가 관심 있어 하는 것은? (3점)

> Mike: Minji, are you interested in animals?
> Minji: Yes, I am. I'm good at taking care of them.
> Mike: How about plants? Are you interested in them, too?
> Minji: No, I'm not. I can't grow them well.

① movie ② plants
③ sports ④ music
⑤ animals

[전남 ○○중]

05 Which sentence has the SAME MEANING? (2점)

> Are you interested in drawing pictures?

① Can you draw well?
② Do you like pictures?
③ Do you draw pictures often?
④ Do you like drawing pictures?
⑤ Maybe you will draw a picture.

07 위 대화의 내용과 일치하지 <u>않는</u> 것은? (4점)

① James wants to try calligraphy with a pen.
② The Korean word Mina wrote means "dance."
③ Mina is writing something with a brush.
④ James has lots of interests in calligraphy.
⑤ Mina wrote the word that looked like a person dancing with open arms.

[6~8] 다음 대화를 읽고 물음에 답하시오.

James: What are you doing, Mina?
Mina: I'm practicing calligraphy.
James: You're writing with a brush. It looks fun.
Mina: (A)_____
James: Yes, very much.
Mina: Look at this! I just wrote it. (B)_____

James: It looks like a person dancing with open arms.
Mina: You got it. This Korean word means "dance."
James: (C)_____ Can I try it?
Mina: (D)_____ Take this brush.

08 위 대화를 읽고 대답할 수 <u>없는</u> 것은? (3점)

① What is Mina doing?
② What is Mina writing with?
③ Does Mina write calligraphy well?
④ Does James want to try calligraphy?
⑤ How often does Mina practice calligraphy?

06 위 대화의 (A)~(D)에 들어갈 표현으로 알맞게 짝지어진 것은? (4점)

ⓐ You can say that again!
ⓑ What do you think?
ⓒ Why do you think so?
ⓓ Why not?
ⓔ Are you interested in calligraphy?
ⓕ Well done!
ⓖ You know what?
ⓗ Do you have any ideas about writing books?

(A)　(B)　(C)　(D)
① ⓑ　ⓒ　ⓕ　ⓐ
② ⓔ　ⓑ　ⓕ　ⓓ
③ ⓔ　ⓒ　ⓓ　ⓑ
④ ⓔ　ⓑ　ⓐ　ⓗ
⑤ ⓗ　ⓖ　ⓕ　ⓐ

09 다음 분사가 사용된 문장 중 알맞은 것으로만 짝지어진 것은? (4점)

ⓐ This is the radio that needs to be fixing.
ⓑ The book writing by Jane is worth reading.
ⓒ I walked on the fallen leaves.
ⓓ Do you know the lady wearing a red coat?
ⓔ Peaceful expression of slept baby made her happy.

① ⓑ, ⓒ, ⓓ ② ⓐ, ⓑ
③ ⓐ, ⓒ, ⓓ ④ ⓒ, ⓓ
⑤ ⓒ, ⓓ, ⓔ

10 다음 그림과 일치하지 <u>않는</u> 것은?　(3점)

[경기 ○○중]

① The man who is playing the piano is Jake.

② The man drinking milk at the table is Tom.

③ The woman singing beside the piano is Cathy.

④ The man who is making the sandwiches is Mike.

⑤ The woman sitting between Tom and Mike is Natalie.

[서울 관악구 ○○중]

11 다음 대화의 빈칸 (A)에 들어갈 가장 알맞은 문장은?　(4점)

> A: Hey, are you interested in *hanbok*?
> B: _____
> A: Then, what are you interested in?
> B: Well, I'm interested in *taekwondo*. It is a traditional Korean sport.

① It looks fun.

② Why not?

③ No thanks.

④ Not really.

⑤ Thank you so much.

[12~13] 다음 대화를 읽고 물음에 답하시오.

> Lee:　You did a good job! This work is awesome.
> Grace: Thanks.
> Lee:　(A)_____ Glass?
> Grace: Yes, it is. Are you interested in glass art?
> Lee:　Yes, very much. How long did it take to make it?
> Grace: It took one month.

[서울 성동구 ○○중]

12 다음 중 빈칸 (A)에 들어갈 알맞은 말은?　(3점)

① What is it made of?

② How do you make it?

③ How is it made?

④ What should I make it with?

⑤ What are you make of?

[서울 성동구 ○○중]

13 위 대화를 읽고 답할 수 있는 질문이 <u>아닌</u> 것은?　(3점)

① What is the title?

② Whose work is it?

③ Who made the work?

④ Is Lee interested in glass art?

⑤ How long did it take to make the work?

14 다음 중 밑줄 친 단어의 쓰임이 <u>다른</u> 하나는?　　(3점)

① Look at that <u>sleeping</u> baby.

② The girl <u>singing</u> well is my friend.

③ Do you know the man <u>talking</u> to Jake?

④ My English teacher likes <u>playing</u> pop songs.

⑤ The person <u>living</u> in a foreign country is a foreigner.

16 다음 질문에 영어 문장으로 답하시오.　　(4점)

Q: Why did Ms. Jan Coveney become interested in Korean *hanji* craft?

→ It is because _____.

[15~16] 다음 글을 읽고 물음에 답하시오.

Welcome to the Korean Culture Festival in Melbourne, Australia. Ms. Jan Coveney is showing people her ____ⓐ____ of art. She is Australian. When she was in Korea, she was interested in Korean *hanji* paper craft.

She ____ⓑ____ with *hanji* paper craft for about twenty years. She teaches many people how to make *hanji* paper craft. "I think Korean art is wonderful."

15 위 글의 빈칸 ⓐ, ⓑ에 들어갈 알맞은 말은?　　(3점)

	ⓐ	ⓑ
①	work	worked
②	worked	worked
③	works	has worked
④	worked	has worked
⑤	works	have worked

[17~21] 다음 글을 읽고 물음에 답하시오.

Calligraphy is not new. ⓐ<u>Many different kinds of calligraphy works from long ago can be found all around the world.</u> Look at the two examples from Korea and the UK below. Can you tell the difference? ⓑ<u>The left one was created by Chusa in the period of the Joseon Dynasty.</u> ⓒ<u>The characters were painted with a soft brush.</u>

ⓓ<u>The right one, *The Canterbury Tales*, was created by Chaucer in England in the late 1400s.</u> ⓔ<u>It was wrote with a pen.</u> Different (A)_____ such as a brush or a pen led to different styles of calligraphy. Of course, all calligraphers had to practice hard to make their unique styles.

17 위 글의 ⓐ~ⓔ 중 어법상 바르지 <u>않은</u> 것은?　　(3점)

① ⓐ　　　② ⓑ　　　③ ⓒ

④ ⓓ　　　⑤ ⓔ

18 문맥상 빈칸 (A)에 들어갈 말로 가장 적절한 것은? (4점)

① places

② letters

③ cultures

④ periods

⑤ instruments

19 위 글의 내용과 일치하지 <u>않는</u> 것은? (3점)

① The two calligraphy works were created with different tools.

② People in the past also enjoyed calligraphy.

③ Different writing tools eventually lead to the same styles of calligraphy.

④ Calligraphers have to practice hard to develop their own styles.

⑤ The right calligraphy work was created in the UK in the late 1400s.

20 위 글에 나온 단어의 설명이 <u>아닌</u> 것은? (4점)

① a story about imaginary events

② to train regularly so that you can improve your skill

③ a length of time during which a series of events takes place

④ a period of time when a particular family ruled a country or area

⑤ a strong feeling of shock and fear

21 위 글을 제대로 이해하지 <u>못한</u> 사람은? (3점)

① 펭수: 추사는 조선 시대 사람이다.

② 수지: 캘리그래피는 옛날에도 있었다.

③ 원영: 붓으로 쓰여진 캘리그래피도 있다.

④ 보검: 캘리그래피 작품을 소개하고 있다.

⑤ 은우: 다음은 미국 작품이 소개될 것이다.

[22~25] 다음 글을 읽고 물음에 답하시오.

Nowadays, calligraphy is (A)[wide / widely] used around us. You can find designers' artistic touches on movie posters, book covers, music CDs, and clothes. Below (B)[is / are] some examples. Look at the title on the movie poster. How do you feel? Can you imagine the monster's big mouth, sharp teeth, and ugly, long tail? What about the title on the fantasy novel? Do you see Harry's lightning and the wizard hats?

Anyone can start to write calligraphy. ⓐ<u>손으로 잘 쓰는 것은 쉽지 않다</u> at first, but practice makes perfect. Keep (C)[to try / trying] and make it part of your everyday life. Write with your feelings on birthday cards, bookmarks, or gifts. Soon you will make your own world of calligraphy.

22 위 글의 괄호 (A)~(C)에 들어갈 말을 바르게 연결한 것은?

(4점)

(A)	(B)	(C)
① wide	is	to try
② wide	are	trying
③ widely	is	to try
④ widely	are	to try
⑤ widely	are	trying

23 위 글의 내용과 일치하지 <u>않는</u> 것은? (4점)

① The title on the fantasy novel brings to mind a monster.

② These days we can find calligraphic works of art in various fields.

③ The title on the movie poster has an image of an imaginary animal.

④ You can imagine the wizard hats from the calligraphy used on the book cover.

⑤ Designers' artistic touches can be found from works of art such as movie posters, book covers, music CDs, and clothes.

24 위 글의 ⓐ를 〈조건〉에 맞게 영작하시오. (5점)

> **조건**
> • 'by, well'을 모두 이용할 것.
> • 'It ~ to부정사' 구문을 이용할 것.

→ _____

25 위 글을 읽고 우리 주변에서 찾아볼 수 있는 캘리그래피 작품이 <u>아닌</u> 것은? (3점)

① 영화 포스터

② 책표지

③ 음악 CD

④ 의류

⑤ 책갈피

[26~30] 다음 글을 읽고 물음에 답하시오.

(A) How do you express your feelings? Do you sing or dance? Do you write a poem or draw a picture? Nowadays, ⓐit is popular to express feelings through handwriting. (B)

In the work of art on the right, the word includes an image of a delicious fruit, *hongsi*. It shows that autumn is a season of fruit. (C) The work of art on the left shows a Korean word and a Chinese character. It looks like a happy woman ⓑ <u>walking</u> down a road with autumn leaves. (D) Both of these works express the feeling of autumn through beautiful handwriting. This kind of art is called calligraphy. (E)

26 위 글에서 다음 문장이 들어갈 곳으로 알맞은 것은? (3점)

> Let's look at some works of art.

① (A)　　② (B)　　③ (C)

④ (D)　　⑤ (E)

27 위 글의 밑줄 친 ⓐ와 쓰임이 같은 것은? (3점)

① <u>It</u> is the newest jacket in the store.

② <u>It</u> is dark in this room.

③ What day is <u>it</u> today?

④ I saw *Frozen ll* yesterday. <u>It</u> was exciting.

⑤ <u>It</u> is important to study foreign languages.

29 위 글의 ⓑ와 쓰임이 <u>다른</u> 문장을 <u>두 개</u> 고르면? (3점)

① Look at the <u>sleeping</u> baby.

② <u>Sleeping</u> is important.

③ He is swimming at the <u>swimming</u> pool.

④ There was a <u>shocking</u> story in the newspaper.

⑤ I was awakened by a <u>ringing</u> bell.

28 What is popular when you express your feelings nowadays? (3점)

① Singing

② Dancing

③ Handwriting

④ Drawing a picture

⑤ Writing a poem

30 위 글의 내용과 일치하지 <u>않는</u> 것은? (4점)

① *Hongsi* is a fruit.

② There is an image of *hongsi* on the right work.

③ The left work is written only in Korean.

④ Both works express the feeling of autumn.

⑤ We can see a walking woman on the left work.

◎ 선택형 문항의 답안은 컴퓨터용 수정 싸인펜을 사용
하여 OMR 답안지에 바르게 표기하시오.
◎ 서술형 문제는 답을 답안지에 반드시 검정 볼펜으
로 쓰시오.
◎ 총 30문항 100점 만점입니다. 문항별 배점은 각
문항에 표시되어 있습니다.

[경기 ○○중]

01 다음 영어 설명에 알맞은 것은?　　　(2점)

> an electrical device which you use to turn
> the device on or off

① switch　　　② locker
③ craft　　　④ pad
⑤ lightning

[전남 ○○중]

02 다음 빈칸에 올 수 없는 것은?　　　(3점)

> Mina _____ me study English.

① let　　　② wanted
③ made　　　④ had
⑤ helped

[광주 ○○중]

03 우리말을 〈조건〉에 맞게 영작하시오.　　　(4점)

> **조건**
> 1. 'smart, any questions'를 이용할 것.
> 2. 'so ... that ~ can'을 활용할 것.
> 3. 한글 해석 : 그는 너무 똑똑해서 그는 어떤 질
> 　문에도 답변할 수 있다.

→ _____

[경기 ○○중]

04 다음 문장 중 어법상 <u>어색한</u> 것을 고르시오.　　　(3점)

① Ms. Choi had the girls jump rope.
② Let me check the list in advance.
③ His stories always make me laugh loudly.
④ The window is so heavy that I can't open it.
⑤ Tom told Jerry play the piano in the concert.

[서울 성북구 ○○중]

05 그림에 맞게 빈칸에 알맞은 문장은?　　　(2점)

> A: I'm not happy about this place.
> B: Why? What's wrong?
> A: _____

① The desk is too low.
② The line is too long.
③ The music is too loud.
④ There is too much trash.
⑤ There are not enough chairs here.

Dad: What are you doing here?
Son: I'm thinking of ways to help Miso.
Dad: What's wrong?
Son: She can't turn on the light by herself. This switch is too high for her.
Dad: That's right. I'm not (A)_____ it, either. Do you have any good ideas about that?
Son: I'm thinking of putting a step box here below the switch.
Dad: Good idea. And I'll change the switch to a bigger one.
Son: Great. Grandma will like it, too. She can turn on the light more easily.

[인천 ○○중]

06 위 대화의 빈칸 (A)에 들어갈 말로 가장 알맞은 것은? (3점)

① ashamed of
② worried about
③ satisfied with
④ concerned about
⑤ astonished at

[부산 ○○중]

07 위 대화를 읽고 답할 수 <u>없는</u> 질문은? (4점)

① What will Dad do for Miso?
② What will Son do to help Miso?
③ Will Grandma like the new switch?
④ Can Miso turn on the light by herself?
⑤ What will Grandma do to help Miso?

[인천 ○○중]

08 위 대화의 상황을 다음과 같이 요약할 때, ⓐ~ⓔ 중 어휘의 쓰임이 올바른 것은? (3점)

Miso can't turn on the light by herself because the switch is too ⓐlow for her. To help her, her brother is ⓑplanning to put a step box ⓒabove the switch. Dad will change the switch to a ⓓsmaller one. Then, Miso and Grandma will be able to ⓔput the light on more easily.

① ⓐ ② ⓑ ③ ⓒ
④ ⓓ ⑤ ⓔ

[서울 성동구 ○○중]

09 다음 중 위 대화의 내용과 일치하는 것은? (3점)

① Miso can turn on the light easily.
② There is a big switch in the room.
③ The switch is low enough for Miso.
④ Dad will change the switch to a bigger one.
⑤ Son is going to put a step box for his grandma.

[서울 중구 ○○중]

10 다음 글을 읽고 괄호 안의 우리말을 영작하시오. (4점)

The hole cover was so dangerous that I couldn't ride my bike on it. So I want to change the cover like this. (<u>그 새로운 덮개는 사람들이 자전거를 안전하게 타도록 도와줄 것이다.</u>)

→ _____

[11~14] 다음 대화를 읽고 물음에 답하시오.

A: ⓐShe can't turn on the light by herself. ⓑThis switch is too high for her.
B: ⓒThat's right. ⓓI'm happy about it, too. ⓔDo you have any good ideas about that?
A: (가)나는 여기 스위치 아래에 디딤대를 놓을까 생각 중이야.
B: Good idea. And I'll change the switch (A)_____ a bigger one.
A: Great. Grandma will like it, too. She can turn on the light more easily.

11 위 대화의 밑줄 친 ⓐ~ⓔ 중 흐름상 어색한 것은? (3점)

① ⓐ　　　　② ⓑ　　　　③ ⓒ
④ ⓓ　　　　⑤ ⓔ

12 위 대화의 빈칸 (A)에 들어갈 말로 알맞은 것은? (3점)

① in　　　　② of　　　　③ to
④ on　　　　⑤ off

13 What will Grandma like about the new switch? (4점)

① color　　　　② height
③ place　　　　④ size
⑤ weight

14 위 대화의 우리말 (가)를 영어로 쓰시오. (11 단어) (4점)

→ _____

[15~19] 다음 글을 읽고 물음에 답하시오.

In 1979, a woman started a journey to cities in the U.S. and Canada. She looked over 80. She couldn't see or hear well. She couldn't walk well without a stick. With all these difficulties, the woman had to climb stairs in subway stations and get on crowded buses. ⓐSometimes she got hurt or found her in danger. Every moment was very difficult for her, (가)_____ she visited more than 115 cities and ended her trip in 1982. ⓑWho was the woman and why did she do all this? She was Patricia Moore, a 26-year-old designer.

During the 1970's, she worked for a big design company. She often asked at meetings, "Why don't you design for old or weak people?" The other designers always answered, "We don't design for those people." ⓒShe was tired of the same cold answer. Finally, she decided to become one of "those people" and travel around many cities to understand their difficulties better. For this, she put on her grandmother's clothes, uncomfortable shoes, and thick glasses. ⓓThe shoes were too uncomfortable for her walk well without a stick. She couldn't see well with (나)them. ⓔShe made her hearing badly by putting lots of cotton in her ears.

15 위 글의 밑줄 친 ⓐ~ⓔ 중, 어법상 맞는 것을 있는 대로 고른 것은? (4점)

① ⓐ, ⓑ
② ⓑ, ⓒ
③ ⓐ, ⓓ, ⓔ
④ ⓑ, ⓒ, ⓓ
⑤ ⓑ, ⓒ, ⓓ, ⓔ

16 위 글에 대한 내용과 일치하는 것은? (4점)

① Patricia had a long journey all around the world.
② Patricia felt happy with her old clothes and shoes.
③ The other designers in Patricia's company worked for old people.
④ Patricia tried to find the difficulties of old or weak people.
⑤ Patricia wanted to find a better place for old or weak people.

17 위 글의 내용으로 알 수 <u>없는</u> 사실은? (3점)

① 여행의 목적
② 여행 장소
③ 여행 기간
④ 여행의 어려움
⑤ 여행 장소의 수

18 위 글의 빈칸 (가)에 들어갈 어휘로 알맞은 것은? (3점)

① because
② so
③ and
④ or
⑤ but

19 위 글의 밑줄 친 (나)them이 가리키는 것을 찾아 쓰시오. (4점)

→ _____

20 다음 두 문장이 같은 뜻이 되도록 문장을 완성하시오. (4점)

> The P.E. teacher said to the boy. "Bring the ball."

= The P.E. teacher had _____.

[21~25] 다음 글을 읽고 물음에 답하시오.

(가)_____ the 1970's, Patricia Moore, ⓐa 26-years-old designer, worked for a big design company. She ⓑwas often asked at meetings. "ⓒHow about designing for old or weak people?" The other designers always answered, "We don't design for those people."

She became tried of the same cold answer. Finally, she decided to become one of "(A)those people" and travel around many cities to understand their difficulties better. For this, she put on her grandmother's clothes, uncomfortable shoes, and thick glasses. (B)She couldn't walk well without a stick because the shoes were so uncomfortable. The glasses she was wearing were very thick and she ⓓcouldn't see well with them. She also put lots of cotton in her ears to make her ⓔhearing bad.

23 Patricia Moore에 관한 글을 읽고 대답할 수 있는 질문은?

(4점)

① What cities did she travel around?

② How long did she work for the company?

③ Where did she buy a stick?

④ How good was her eyesight without glasses?

⑤ What was the other designers' reaction to her suggestion?

24 위 글의 밑줄 친 (A)가 가리키는 것을 찾아 쓰시오. (3점)

→ _____

21 위 글의 빈칸 (가)에 적절한 것은? (3점)

① For

② While

③ During

④ Where

⑤ Around

25 위 글의 밑줄 친 (B)와 같은 의미를 가진 문장은? (3점)

① The shoes were so uncomfortable that can't walk well without a stick.

② The shoes were very uncomfortable that she couldn't walk well without it.

③ The shoes was so uncomfortable that she couldn't walk well without a stick.

④ The shoes were so uncomfortable that she couldn't walk well without a stick.

⑤ The shoes was so uncomfortable that she couldn't walk well without them.

22 밑줄 친 ⓐ~ⓔ 중 내용의 흐름 및 문법상 올바르게 사용된 것을 **모두** 고른 것은? (4점)

① ⓐ, ⓑ ② ⓐ, ⓓ

③ ⓑ, ⓒ ④ ⓒ, ⓔ

⑤ ⓒ, ⓓ, ⓔ

[26~30] 다음 글을 읽고 물음에 답하시오.

During her journey, Patricia felt the difficulties old people ⓐgo through. From this experience, she designed products anybody could use safely and easily. This was the ⓑbeginning of "universal design," or "design for (가)_____."

One example of her universal design ideas is (A)_____ buses. They have no ⓒsteps and have such a (A)_____ that even a person in a wheelchair can use them without any ⓓhelp. Of course, this helps other people ⓔget on the bus more comfortably, too.

26 위 글의 밑줄 친 ⓐ~ⓔ의 의미로 올바르지 <u>않은</u> 것은? (3점)

① ⓐ: ~를 통해서 가다
② ⓑ: 시작
③ ⓒ: 계단
④ ⓓ: 도움
⑤ ⓔ: ~에 타다

27 위 글의 (A)에 들어갈 버스의 유형으로 알맞은 것은? (3점)

① tourist
② express
③ low-floor
④ eco-friendly
⑤ double-decker

28 위 글에서 찾을 수 있는 정보는? (3점)

① 휠체어의 종류와 그 가격
② Patricia가 고안한 제품의 특징
③ 한국의 universal design의 종류
④ Patricia가 여행한 국가와 그 도시
⑤ Patricia가 여행에서 만난 사람들의 이름

29 위 글의 흐름상 빈칸 (가)에 가장 적절한 것은? (3점)

① me
② her
③ all
④ past
⑤ teaching

30 Which is the best title of the text? (4점)

① Feeling the Difficulties of Old People
② How to Write an Essay After a Journey
③ Distinctive Feature of Low-floor Bus
④ The Beginning of Universal Design and Its Example
⑤ The Importance of Designing Wheelchairs Safely and Easily

◎ 선택형 문항의 답안은 컴퓨터용 수정 싸인펜을 사용하여 OMR 답안지에 바르게 표기하시오.
◎ 서술형 문제는 답을 답안지에 반드시 검정 볼펜으로 쓰시오.
◎ 총 30문항 100점 만점입니다. 문항별 배점은 각 문항에 표시되어 있습니다.

[경기 기출]

01 다음 빈칸 (a), (b)에 들어갈 말로 알맞게 짝지어진 것은? (3점)

• Ten years is not a short ___(a)___ .
• He turned the ___(b)___ and opened the door.

	(a)	(b)
①	monster	fountain
②	tail	bathtub
③	season	switch
④	period	handle
⑤	mess	swing

[전남 ○○중]

02 Which sentence has the SAME MEANING? (2점)

I'm thinking of making some cookies.

① I like cookies.
② I want to eat some cookies.
③ I intend to make some cookies.
④ I wish I could make some cookies.
⑤ I think you should make some cookies.

[광주 ○○중]

03 〈조건〉에 맞게 문장을 완성해 보시오. (4점)

조건
• 'too … to ~' 구문을 활용할 것.
• (a), (b) 문장과 같은 의미의 문장으로 만들 것.

(a) My brother is very young, so he can't understand the words.
(b) My brother is so young that he can't understand the words.

→ _____

[서울 성동구 ○○중]

04 다음 중 빈칸에 알맞은 말은? (2점)

A: _____ the cell phone.
B: What's wrong with it?
A: It's too old.

① I like
② I'm into
③ I don't expect
④ I'm satisfied with
⑤ I'm not happy about

[광주 ○○중]

05 Choose the right solution that solves the problem. (4점)

Chowon: I'm not happy about the sign. There are some people who can't see.
Bomin: Right. Do you have any ideas?
Chowon: Well, I'm thinking of _____ .
Bomin: That's a good idea.

① adding Braille on the sign
② putting some pads on it
③ decorating its cover
④ putting a "watch out" sign below it
⑤ hanging a wiper on it

Dad: What are you doing here?
Son: I'm thinking of ⓐways to help Miso.
Dad: What's wrong?
Son: She can't turn on the light by herself. This switch is ⓑtoo high for her.
Dad: That's right. I'm ⓒhappy about it, either. Do you have any good ideas about that for your sister?
Son: (A)_____ a step box here ⓓbelow the switch.
Dad: Good idea. And I'll change the switch to a ⓔbigger one.
Son: Great. Grandma will like it, too. She can turn on the light more easily.

[경기 ○○중]

06 문맥상 빈칸 (A)에 들어갈 말로 적절하지 <u>않은</u> 것은? (3점)

① I intend to put
② I'm going to put
③ I'm planning to put
④ I'm thinking of putting
⑤ I'm not happy about putting

[광주 ○○중]

07 What will Son do to help Miso? (3점)

① He will turn on the light for Miso.
② He will change the switch to a bigger one.
③ He will change the old switch into a new one.
④ He will put a step box below the switch.
⑤ He will put a cushion below the switch.

[부산 ○○중]

08 위 대화의 밑줄 친 ⓐ~ⓔ 중 내용 흐름상 <u>어색한</u> 것은? (3점)

① ⓐ ② ⓑ ③ ⓒ
④ ⓓ ⑤ ⓔ

[경기 ○○중]

09 대화의 내용과 일치하도록 빈칸 (A)~(C)에 알맞은 한 단어씩을 넣으시오. (단, (C)는 주어진 철자로 시작할 것) (5점)

Dad and Son are talking about ideas for their family. Miso can't turn on the light by herself because the switch is too (A)_____ for her. So, her (B)_____ decides to put a step box below the switch. Dad also will change the (C)s_____ of the switch because a bigger one will be better for both Miso and Grandma.

(A) _____ (B) _____ (C) s_____

[전남 ○○중]

10 위 대화를 읽고 대화한 내용 중 <u>잘못된</u> 것을 고르시오. (3점)

① A: Can Miso turn on the light alone?
　 B: No, she can't.
② A: Is Dad happy with the switch?
　 B: No, he isn't.
③ A: What will the boy do to help Miso?
　 B: He will put a step box below the switch.
④ A: What will Dad do for Miso and Grandma?
　 B: He will change the switch to a pretty one.
⑤ A: Will Grandma like the new switch?
　 B: Yes, she will.

11 다음 중 두 문장의 뜻이 같은 것은? (3점)

① I'm very tired. So I can't walk any more.
 = I am so tired that I can walk any more.

② The window is too heavy for me to open.
 = The window is so heavy that I can't open it.

③ I can't eat the soup because it is too hot.
 = The soup is so hot that I can eat it.

④ The button is very high. He can't push the button.
 = The button is high so that he can push it.

⑤ The shoes were comfortable enough for her to walk well.
 = The shoes were so comfortable that she couldn't walk well.

13 다음 대화와 조건을 잘 보고 문장을 완성하시오. (3점)

A: Mom, can I watch TV?
B: Did you finish your homework?
A: Yes, Mom.
B: Then, you can watch TV.

조건
• I finished my homework, so Mom let _____.의 빈칸 부분을 완성하시오.

→ Mom let _____.

14 다음 두 문장의 의미가 같도록 빈칸에 알맞은 말을 반드시 3단어로 쓰시오. (5점)

(1) He is so rich that he can buy the car.
= He is _____ _____ _____ buy the car.

(2) I am so young that I can't watch the movie.
= I am _____ _____ _____ watch the movie.

12 다음 문장 중 어법상 어색한 것을 고르시오. (3점)

① Mom had Lucy cook dinner for her family.
② It was so cold that I can't ride a bike.
③ It is not difficult to learn to dance.
④ His hobby is collecting old coins.
⑤ Look at that sleeping dog.

15 다음 중 어법상 옳지 않은 것은? (3점)

① I was too sleepy to study more.
② Mike is so shocked that he can't say a word.
③ The cake was too sweet that he can't eat it.
④ Mom was too sick to cook dinner for her family.
⑤ It was so cold that I couldn't ride a bike.

In 1979, a woman started a journey to cities in the U.S. and Canada. She looked ⓐover 80. She couldn't see or hear well. She couldn't walk well without (A)_____. ⓑWithout all these difficulties, the woman had to climb stairs in subway stations and get (B)_____ crowded buses. She had to open heavy doors and use can openers ⓒwith her weak hands. Sometimes she got hurt or found ⓓherself in danger. Every moment ⓔwas very difficult for her, but she visited more than 115 cities and ended her trip in 1982.

[광주 ○○중]

16 위 글의 ⓐ~ⓔ 중 문맥상 어색한 것은? (3점)

① ⓐ ② ⓑ ③ ⓒ

④ ⓓ ⑤ ⓔ

[부산 ○○중]

17 위 글 (A)에 들어갈 단어의 영영 풀이로 알맞은 것은? (3점)

① a long, thin wooden pole that especially old or injured people use to walk

② a building or place where buses or trains stop so that people can get on or off

③ a person's opinion or belief about a situation or subject

④ a button or key that controls the light or machine

⑤ an organization that makes money by producing or selling goods or services

[광주 ○○중]

18 위 글의 a woman과 관련하여 일치하지 <u>않는</u> 것은? (3점)

① 80세가 넘어 보였다.

② 지팡이 없이 잘 걸을 수 있었다.

③ 115개 이상의 도시를 방문했다.

④ 잘 보거나 잘 들을 수 없었다.

⑤ 미국과 캐나다에 있는 도시로 여행을 시작했다.

[경기 ○○중]

19 Which CANNOT be answered? (4점)

① When did the woman end her trip?

② How many cities did the woman visit?

③ When did the woman start a journey?

④ Why did the woman decide to travel around many cities?

⑤ What kinds of physical difficulties did the woman seem to have?

[광주 ○○중]

20 위 글의 빈칸 (B)에 가장 적절한 것은? (2점)

① on ② of

③ by ④ for

⑤ from

[21~25] 다음 글을 읽고 물음에 답하시오.

During her journey, ⓐPatricia felt the difficulties which old people go through. From (가)this experience, she designed products anybody could use safely and easily. This was the beginning of "universal design," or "design for all."

ⓑOne example of her universal design ideas are low-floor buses. They have no steps and have (A)_____ a low floor that even a person in a wheelchair can use them (B)_____ any help. Of course, ⓒthis helps other people to get on the bus more comfortably, too.

ⓓToday more and more designers are following Patricia's way. (C)_____, products like big flat light switches, doors with easy handles, and phones with touch buttons (나)_____. Look around you, ⓔfeel the difficulties of people that are older or weaker, and try to find solutions from their point of view. You could be the next Patricia Moore and make the world a better place for everybody.

[충북 ○○중]

21 위 글의 밑줄 친 ⓐ~ⓔ 중에서 문법적으로 어색한 것은? (3점)

① ⓐ ② ⓑ ③ ⓒ

④ ⓓ ⑤ ⓔ

[경기 ○○중]

22 위 글의 내용상 빈칸 (A)~(C)에 들어갈 단어가 바르게 짝지어 진 것은? (4점)

	(A)	(B)	(C)
①	so	with	However
②	so	without	For example
③	such	without	For example
④	such	without	However
⑤	such	with	Instead

[부산 ○○중]

23 위 글 (가)this experience가 가리키는 것을 본문에서 찾아 우리말로 쓰시오. (4점)

→ _____

[충북 ○○중]

24 위 글을 쓴 목적으로 가장 알맞은 것은? (3점)

① To introduce some information

② To make an appointment

③ To give tips for being famous

④ To say thanks to readers

⑤ To explain the reason

[경기 ○○중]

25 위 글의 문장 내 빈칸 부분 (나)를 아래의 〈번역〉과 〈보기〉에 제시된 단어를 참고하여 영작하시오. (4점)

번역

크고 평평한 조명 스위치, 편한 손잡이를 가진 문, 터치 버튼을 가진 전화기와 같은 제품들은 사람들이 더 나은 삶을 살도록 도와주고 있다.

보기

be / better / live / people / help

조건

1. 〈보기〉의 단어 중 일부는 중복 사용할 것.
2. 새로운 단어를 첨가하지 말 것.
3. 필요하다면 단어의 형태를 변형할 것.

→ _____

[26~30] 다음 글을 읽고 물음에 답하시오.

Who was the woman and (A)[do / all / what / this / made / her]? She was ⓐPatricia Moore, a 26-year-old designer. During the 1970's, she worked for a big design company. She often asked at meetings, "How about designing for old or weak people?" The other designers always answered, "We don't design for those people."

She became tired of the same cold answer. Finally, she decided to become one of "those people" and travel around many cities to understand their difficulties better. For this, she put on her grandmother's clothes, uncomfortable shoes, and thick glasses. (가)The shoes were so uncomfortable that she couldn't walk well without a stick. ⓑThe glasses were too thick for her to see well with them. She also put lots of cotton in her ears to make her hearing bad.

28 위 글의 밑줄 친 ⓑ문장을 같은 의미가 되도록 다음 조건에 맞게 바꿔 쓰시오. (4점)

조건
• so, that을 사용할 것.

→ _____

29 위 글의 밑줄 친 (가)의 문장을 'too ~ +의미상 주어+to ...' 구문을 활용하여 고치시오. (5점)

→ _____

26 위 글의 괄호 (A)에 주어진 단어를 바르게 배열하여 문장을 완성할 때 세 번째 오는 단어는? (3점)

① all ② do
③ this ④ her
⑤ made

27 위 글의 밑줄 친 ⓐPatricia Moore에 관하여 위의 주어진 본문을 바탕으로 바르게 설명한 것은? (3점)

① She has designed for old and weak people.
② The other designers always disagreed with her idea.
③ She owned a design company in the 1970's.
④ She got dressed to look like a young lady.
⑤ She prepared old clothes and shoes for her grandma.

30 위 글을 읽고 대화를 나눌 때 자연스럽지 않은 대화는? (3점)

① A: Where did Patricia Moore work during the 1970's?
B: She worked at a big design company.
② A: What did she do to make her hearing bad?
B: She put lots of cotton in her ears.
③ A: What did she often suggest at meetings?
B: She often suggested designing for old or weak people.
④ A: How did other designers react to her suggestion?
B: They put on her grandmother's clothes, uncomfortable shoes, and thick glasses.
⑤ A: Why did she decide to travel around many cities?
B: To understand the difficulties of old or weak people better.

Lesson 5 (중간) 1회

01 ③ 02 ④ 03 ①

04 (A) I try to make this room tidy.

 (B) Triangle and Circle looked at each other.

05 ③ 06 Do you know how to solve this puzzle? 07 ③

08 ③ 09 ② 10 ③ 11 ① 12 ② 13 ④ 14 ③ 15 ①

16 ② 17 ①

18 The three shapes worked together once again. 19 ③

20 ③ 21 ③ 22 ④

23 사각형의 옷걸이는 옷을 걸고 있을 수 없기 때문이다.

24 I don't know how to spin this. 25 ⑤ 26 ⑤ 27 ③

28 ① 29 Triangle, Circle

30 I try to make this room tidy.

01 ③ square : circle은 각각 '정사각형'과 '원형'이라는 뜻을 갖는 단어들이다. 나머지는 모두 오른쪽 단어가 왼쪽 단어에 포함되는 관계이다.

02 ① must: ~임에 틀림 없다; ~해야 한다

② stand: 서 있다; 입장, 태도

③ water: 물을 주다; 물

⑤ face: 마주하다; 얼굴

03 "이 책장은 혼자서 서 있을 수 없어. 이 문제를 어떻게 해결해야 하는지 알고 있니?"라는 A의 질문에 대해 "물론. 그게 뭐니?"라는 B의 대답은 흐름상 자연스럽지 않다.

04 (A) try to+동사원형: ~하려고 노력하다

(B) each other(=one another): 서로

05 make는 목적격 보어로 동사원형 또는 형용사, 현재분사/과거 분사 등을 취할 수 있다. ③ 부사 happily는 사역동사 make의 목적격 보어로 쓰일 수 없다.

06 상대방이 어떤 일을 할 수 있는지를 물어볼 때 "Do you know how to …?"라고 표현할 수 있다.

07 "그 다음, 쌀을 옮기고 닭과 돌아오는 거야."라는 문장이 들어가기에 가장 적절한 곳은 퍼즐을 푸는 방법을 설명하면서 우선 닭을 첫 번째로 옮긴 다음 두 번째로 쌀을 옮기라고 말하고 있는 (C)이다.

08 위 대화에서는 퍼즐을 푸는 방법을 설명하고 있다. 우선 닭을 첫 번째로 옮긴 다음 두 번째로 쌀을 옮기고, 다시 닭을 데리고 온 다음, 그 후에 개를 옮기고 마지막으로 닭을 옮기는 방식이 가장 적절하다.

09 위 대화에 따르면, 닭과 개만 남게 되면 개가 닭을 죽일 것이라고 언급되어 있다.

10 Chris가 지민이에게 샌드위치 만드는 방법을 설명해 주고 있다. Chris가 샌드위치 만드는 방법을 안다고 대답하고(ㄴ), 빵 위에 우선 달걀을 올리고(ㄹ) 채소도 추가한 다음(ㄱ), 빵을 맨 위에 올려놓는 순서(ㄷ)가 흐름상 가장 자연스럽다.

11 위 대화에서는 라면을 끓이는 방법에 대해서 설명하고 있다. 따라서 ⓐ에는 put the noodle and dried soup mix가, ⓑ에는 boil for 4 more minutes가 들어가는 것이 적절하다.

12 ① he → him / ③ interest → interesting / ④ warmly → warm / ⑤ nervously → nervous로 고쳐야 어법상 적절한 문장이 된다.

13 위 대화에 따르면, 이 퍼즐을 푸는 데 문제점은 개가 닭과 남게 되면 닭을 죽일 수도 있다는 것과 또 다른 문제점은 닭이 쌀을 먹어버리는 것이다.

14 위 대화에 따르면, 이 퍼즐을 푸는 데 문제점은 개가 닭과 남게 되면 닭을 죽일 수도 있다는 것("the dog will kill the chicken")이다.

15 (A) same 동일한 (B) how to+동사원형 ~하는 방법

(C) biggest 가장 큰

16 왕 Ptolemy는 Euclid에게 수학을 배우는 더 쉬운 방법이 있냐고 물어 보았다. 흐름상 빈칸에 들어갈 말로 가장 적절한 것은 ② There is no royal road to learning.(배움에 왕도는 없다.)이다.

17 ⓐ rush over ~에게 달려가다

ⓑ realize 깨닫다

ⓒ make 만들다

18 work together 같이 일하다, 협력하다

once again 다시 한 번

19 ⓒwater는 '물을 주다'라는 뜻으로, ③ water는 '물'이라는 뜻으로 사용되었다.

20 비교급을 강조할 때는 비교급 앞에 much, still, even, far, a lot 등의 부사를 쓰며 '(...보다) 훨씬 더 ~한'이라는 의미를 갖는다. very는 원급의 형용사(또는 부사)를 수식하며, 비교급은 수식하지 않는다.

21 Mike는 동그란 홀라후프가 아니라 네모로 변한 홀라후프를 돌릴 수 없다고 말했다.

22 Mike는 동그란 홀라후프가 아니라 네모로 변한 홀라후프를 돌릴 수 없다고 말했다.

23 Mike는 "What? This will not hold my clothes."라고 언급했다.

24 '의문사+to부정사' 중 'how+to부정사'는 '어떻게 …할지'라는 의미를 갖는다.

25 ⑤ Why does Square want to rest?(왜 네모는 휴식을 취하고 싶어하는가?)에 대해서는 언급되어 있지 않다.

26 위 글에 따르면, 네모는 원형과 삼각형 영혼을 내보내고 혼자서 모

든 물건들을 네모로 만든 다음 만족해하고 있다.

27 '명령문, or ~.'는 '…해라, 그렇지 않으면 ~일 것이다.'라고 해석된다.

28 ⓓ는 훌라후프를 가리키기 때문에 ⓓthem을 it으로 고쳐야 어법상 적절한 문장이 된다.

29 네모 이외의 원형과 삼각형이라는 다른 요정들을 가리킨다.

30 try to+동사원형: ~하려고 노력하다 / tidy 정돈된

Lesson 5 (중간)

```
01 ①  02 ③  03 ①  04 ①  05 ②  06 ④  07 ④
08 That's easy.       09 ①, ⑤       10 ④  11 ④  12 ⑤
13 (1) I don't know what to say to him.
   (2) I can't decide who to invite.
14 ①  15 ⑤  16 ③  17 ④  18 ⑤  19 ①
20 (1) Square는 탁자, 책장, 그리고 창문을 관리했다.
   (2) 그들은 Mike에게 좋은 방을 만들어 주기 위해서 함께 일했
      다.
21 ③  22 ④  23 how to spin this   24 ⑤  25 ①  26 ④
27 ⑤  28 ①  29 ④  30 ②
```

01 across는 cross(건너다)로 고치는 것이 문맥상 자연스럽다.

02 문맥상 ③ divide(나누다, 분배하다)가 들어가는 것이 가장 자연스럽다.

03 ② was gave → was given / ③ a little → a few / ④ how open → how to open / ⑤ which to bus take → which bus to take로 고쳐야 어법상 적절한 문장이 된다.

04 A가 "Do you know how to solve this problem?"(이 문제를 해결하는 방법을 아니?)라고 물었으므로 B가 "No, I can't."라고 대답하는 것은 적절하지 않다.

05 '의문사+to부정사'는 '의문사+주어+should(can)+동사원형'으로 바꿔 쓸 수 있다. 이때 전체 문장의 주어가 무엇이냐에 따라 간접의문문의 주어가 결정된다.

06 ① interest → interesting / ② a few → a little / ③ hotly → hot / ⑤ was wrote → was written으로 고쳐야 어법상 적절한 문장이 된다.

07 위 대화의 흐름상, ⓐ에는 chicken, ⓑ에는 rice, ⓒ에는 dog가 들어가는 것이 적절하다.

08 easy 쉬운

09 위 대화에 따르면, 미나는 진수가 풀지 못한 퍼즐을 풀고 있다. 또한 개와 닭 둘만 남겨지면 개가 닭을 죽일 것이라고 언급되어 있다.

10 one by one 하나씩

11 '의문사+to부정사' 중 'how+to부정사'는 '어떻게 …할지'라는

의미를 지니며 문장에서는 주로 목적어로 쓰인다.

12 (A) what → how / (C) will can do → will be able to do로 고쳐야 어법상 적절한 문장이 된다.

13 '의문사+to부정사'는 'what/when/where/how/who(m)+to부정사'의 형태로 쓰이며, 각각 '무엇을/언제/어디에서/어떻게/누구와 …할지'라는 의미를 갖는다. 'why+to부정사'는 거의 쓰이지 않는다.

14 글의 문맥상 ① how to find(찾는 방법)이 들어가는 것이 적절하다.

15 왕 Ptolemy는 Euclid에게 수학을 배우는 더 쉬운 방법이 있냐고 물어 보았다. 흐름상 빈칸에 들어갈 말로 가장 적절한 것은 ⑤ There is no royal road to learning.(배움에 왕도는 없다.)이다.

16 위 글에서 Euclid가 수학을 알렉산드리아 도서관에서 배웠다는 언급은 없다.

17 '그것들은 동그란 모양이었고, 회전시키거나 굴리기에 좋았다.'라는 문장이 들어가기에 가장 적절한 곳은 훌라후프를 설명하는 곳인 (D)이다.

18 (가)There는 '~이 있다'라는 존재의 유무를 나타낼 때 쓰이는 부사로 ⑤와 쓰임이 같다.

19 글의 문맥상 ⓐ~ⓒ 모두에는 ① controlled(통제했다, 제어했다)가 들어가는 것이 가장 자연스럽다.

20 위 글에 따르면, 네모는 네모난 모양의 물건들을 관리했으며, 그들은 모두 Mike에게 좋은 방을 만들어 주기 위해 협력했다.

21 글의 흐름상 Mike가 네모가 바꾼 방을 좋아하지 않았고 따라서 네모는 실망스러워했다. 따라서 ⓒMike likes his room much.는 Mike doesn't like his room much.로 바꾸는 것이 적절하다.

22 빈칸 (가)에는 접속사 When이 들어가는 것이 가장 자연스럽다.

23 「의문사+to부정사」는 문장에서 주로 목적어로 쓰인다.
how to+동사원형 ~: ~하는 방법

24 물건들이 사각형으로 바뀌었으므로 불편했을 것이다.

25 '명령문, or ~.'는 '…해라, 그렇지 않으면 ~일 것이다.'라고 해석된다. 이때 or 대신 and를 쓰게 되면, '…해라, 그러면 ~일 것이다.'라고 해석한다.

26 ⓓ는 방을 더 낮게 만드는 것을 의미한다.

27 위 글에서 네모는 원형과 세모 없이 자기 혼자서도 Mike의 방을 더 낮게 만들 수 있다고 생각하고 있다. 따라서 네모의 성격으로 가장 적절한 것은 ⑤ self-righteous(독선적인)이다.

28 위 글에 따르면, 네모는 Mike의 방을 더 낮게 만들기로 결심했다.

29 '명령문, or ~.'는 '…해라, 그렇지 않으면 ~일 것이다.'라고 해석된다. 따라서 if 가정법 문장으로 바꿀 경우엔 ④ If you don't take these plants away, their pointy leaves will hurt someone!(만약 네가 이 식물들을 버리지 않으면, 그 뾰족한 잎들이 누군가를 다치게 할 거야!)로 바꿀 수 있다.

30 방을 정돈하려고 노력한 것은 Square이다.

Lesson 6 (중간)

01 ④ **02** ⑤ **03** ② **04** ④ **05** ② **06** ②

07 What do you mean by that? **08** ⑤ **09** ⑤ **10** ③

11 ④ **12** ①, ③

13 The biggest one is about 14 times as large as South Korea.

14 ① **15** ① **16** ⑤ **17** ④ **18** ②

19 (1) 접시에 음식을 남기지 않는 것.
(2) 그는 접시 위의 음식뿐만 아니라 접시까지도 먹었다.

20 ④ **21** ④ **22** ④ **23** ⑤ **24** ⑤ **25** ② **26** ② **27** ②

28 ① **29** we agreed not to wrap our gifts **30** ⑤

01 feel blue는 '우울함을 느끼다'라는 뜻의 관용적 표현이다.

02 <보기>의 단어들은 반의어 관계이다. ⑤ natural - spotless는 각각 '자연스러운'-'결점이 없는'이라는 뜻을 가진 단어들이다.

03 ① is → was / ③ is → are / ④ was appeared → appeared / ⑤ finish → be finished로 고쳐야 어법상 적절한 문장이 된다.

04 A는 진규에 대해 그는 정말 친절한 사람("I think Jingyu is a really kind person")이라고 말했다. 따라서 ④ Jingyu has a heart of gold.가 가장 적절하다.

05 on cloud nine은 '매우 행복한'이라는 뜻의 관용적 표현이다. 따라서 ② He is really happy.이 정답이다.

06 위 대화에서는 교실을 깨끗하게 만들기 위한 '깨끗한 쓰레기통 프로젝트'에 대해서 이야기하고 있다. 따라서 Yuna의 학급 표어로 가장 적절한 것은 ② Make No Trash(쓰레기를 만들지 말자.)이다.

07 "What do you mean by ~?"는 상대방이 한 말에 대해 추가 설명을 요청할 때 쓰는 표현이다.

08 '깨끗한 쓰레기통 프로젝트'에 대해서 유나가 Bart에게 말해 주고 있다.

09 "What do you mean by ~?"는 상대방이 한 말에 대해 추가 설명을 요청할 때 쓰는 표현이다. 따라서 이와 바꿔 쓸 수 있는 표현은 ⑤ Could you explain it?이다.

10 위 대화에서는 바다에 생긴 쓰레기로 만들어진 섬에 대해서 이야기하고 있다. 따라서 빈칸에 들어갈 말로 적절하지 않은 것은 ③ precious(귀중한)이다.

11 바다에 생긴 쓰레기로 만들어진 섬에 대해서 이야기한 후, A는 우리가 플라스틱 제품을 사용해서는 안 된다고 생각해("I think we should not use plastic products.")라고 말했다.

12 위 대화에 따르면, 쓰레기로 만들어진 섬이 많이 존재하며, 지호와 미나는 플라스틱 제품을 쓰지 않기로 했다.

13 '배수사+as+형용사/부사의 원급+as'를 써서 ' …만큼 ~한/하게'라고 영작할 수 있다.

14 ketchup은 셀 수 없는 명사, tomatoes는 셀 수 있는 명사이다. 따라서 ① a little - a few가 들어가는 것이 가장 적절하다.

15 ⓒ was written → wrote / ⓓ Brian → to Brian / ⓔ was → were로 고쳐야 어법상 적절한 문장이 된다.

16 B가 A의 말에 대해 무슨 말이냐고 물어 보았으므로 A가 할 말로 가장 적절한 것은 일석이조를 설명하고 있는 ⑤ This bike will make juice for you and also make you stronger.(이 자전거는 쥬스를 만들어 주고 또한 당신을 건강하게 만든다.)이다.

17 환경에 대한 좋은 비결을 갖고 있는 사람으로 적절한 사람은 종이컵이나 플라스틱 숟가락 대신 자신의 컵과 숟가락을 사용한다.는 지호이다.

18 위 글에서는 음식물 쓰레기를 줄이기 위해 음식을 남겨서는 안 된다고 이야기하고 있다. 따라서 ⓑA lot of trees are cut down to make paper.(종이를 만들기 위해 많은 나무가 잘리고 있다.)라는 문장은 글의 흐름상 어색하다.

19 위 글에 따르면, 준하는 리포터에게 접시에 담은 음식을 남기지 말라고 조언했다. 또한 준하는 음식물 쓰레기를 줄이기 위해 음식뿐만 아니라 접시까지 먹었다고 한다.

20 위 글에 따르면, 리포터는 음식물 쓰레기를 줄일 수 있는 정보를 달라고 했다. 따라서 지은이가 할 말로 가장 적절한 것은 ④ Leave no food behind on your plate.(접시 위의 음식을 남기지 말라.)이다.

21 주어가 Her cute napkins라는 복수형이기 때문에 ⓓwas liked는 were liked로 바꾸는 것이 어법상 적절하다.

22 ④ How can we recycle used napkins?(우리는 어떻게 사용한 냅킨을 재활용할 수 있는가?)에 대해서는 위 글에서 언급되어 있지 않다.

23 인칭대명사 ⓐthem은 복수 명사를 가리킨다. 따라서 위 글에서는 ⑤ our own cups and spoons를 가리킨다.

24 위 글에 따르면, 준하와 같은 반 친구들은 접시를 사용한 다음 그 접시를 먹고, 집에서 가져온 컵과 숟가락을 다시 집으로 가져감으로써 쓰레기를 덜 만들었다. 따라서 (A)와 (B)에는 각각 eating과 taking이 들어가는 것이 적절하다.

25 위 글에서는 종이컵과 플라스틱 숟가락을 쓰는 대신 집에서 가져온 컵과 숟가락을 쓴다고 언급했다. 따라서 빈칸에 들어갈 말로 가장 적절한 것은 ② Instead(대신에)이다.

26 (가)에 들어갈 단어로 가장 적절한 것은 produce이다.

27 ⓑthrow는 '(파티를) 열다'라는 뜻으로 사용되었다.

28 학급 생일잔치가 언제 열렸는지에 대해서는 언급된 바 없다.

29 agree not to ~: ~하지 않기로 동의하다

30 위 글에서는 학급 생일잔치를 열었지만 포장지를 쓰지 않고 선물을

가져왔다고 한다. 따라서 빈칸에 들어갈 말로 가장 적절한 것은 ⑤ Do not Use Wrapping Paper(포장지 사용하지 말기)이다.

Lesson 6 (중간)

> **01** ⑤ **02** ③ **03** ④ **04** ⑤ **05** ④
> **06** they don't throw away trash, so their trash can stay empty
> **07** ② **08** ⑤ **09** ② **10** ① **11** ④, ⑤ **12** ③ **13** ①
> **14** ①, ② **15** ③ **16** ④ **17** ④ **18** ④ **19** ⑤ **20** ⑤
> **21** ④ **22** ④ **23** ⑤ **24** They were made by Minji. **25** ④
> **26** ④
> **27** Larger sizes use less packaging and make less trash.
> **28** ① **29** ④ **30** ④
> **31** (1) I was given a cute doll by him.
> (2) He was taken to the hospital

01 have a heart of gold는 '친절한 사람이다'라는 뜻의 관용적 표현이다.

02 agree는 '동의하다'라는 뜻을 가진 단어이다.

03 has a green thumb은 '식물을 잘 기르다'라는 뜻의 관용적 표현이다.

04 kill two birds with one stone은 '일석이조'라는 뜻의 관용적 표현이다.

05 B의 말에 대한 A의 대답으로 미루어 볼 때, 빈칸에 들어갈 말로 가장 적절한 것은 상대방이 한 말에 대해 추가 설명을 요청할 때 쓰는 표현이 알맞다.

06 위 대화에 따르면, '깨끗한 쓰레기통 프로젝트'는 쓰레기를 버리지 않음으로써 쓰레기통은 빈 상태로 깨끗하게 유지하는 것을 의미한다.

07 위 대화에서 민지의 학급은 쓰레기를 버리지 않는 '깨끗한 쓰레기통 프로젝트'를 통해 교실을 깨끗하게 유지하고 있다. 따라서 학급 포스터 문구로 가장 적절한 것은 ② Make No Trash(쓰레기를 만들지 말자)이다.

08 위 대화에서 G의 말에 대한 B의 대답으로 미루어 볼 때, 빈칸에 들어갈 말로 적절하지 않은 것은 ⑤ Anything else?(또 다른 건 없어?)이다.

09 위 대화에 따르면, 쓰레기가 바다로 흘러가 거대한 쓰레기 섬을 만들었다고 한다. 따라서 화자들은 플라스틱 제품을 쓰지 말자고 이야기하고 있으므로, ② Using plastic products should be reduced.(플라스틱 제품을 사용하는 것은 감소되어야 한다.)가 가장 적절하다.

10 "너무 놀라워!"라는 의미의 문장은 "Unbelievable!", "What a surprise!", "I can't believe it!" 등으로 영작할 수 있다.

11 ④ What kinds of plastic products do they use?(그들은 어떤 종류의 플라스틱 제품을 사용하는가?)와 ⑤ Are there any trash islands in South Korea?(남한에는 쓰레기 섬이 존재하는가?)에 대해서는 위 대화에서 언급된 바 없다.

12 "James는 매우 친절해."라는 A의 말에 대해 "나도 동의해. 그는 항상 모두에게 친절하고 다정해."라는 B의 대답은 흐름상 가장 자연스럽다.

13 ① is using → is used로 고쳐야 어법상 적절한 문장이 된다.

14 ③ A little → A few / ④ a few → a little / ⑤ a little → a few로 고쳐야 어법상 적절한 문장이 된다.

15 Jason sells the store owners antique furniture.를 수동태 문장으로 영작하면 목적어인 antique furniture가 주어 자리로 와서 Antique furniture is sold to the store owners by Jason. 이 되는 것이 적절하다.

16 A가 플라스틱 병이 지구의 큰 문제라고 말하자(ⓓ), B는 그게 무슨 뜻이냐고 묻는다(ⓑ). A는 플라스틱이 분해되는 데 450년이 걸린다고 대답하고(ⓒ) B가 놀랍다고 반응(ⓐ)하는 순서로 이어지는 것이 흐름상 가장 자연스럽다.

17 ④ was seemed → seemed로 고쳐야 어법상 적절한 문장이 된다.

18 ④ a little → a few로 고쳐야 어법상 적절한 문장이 된다.

19 '~보다 14배 큰'이라는 표현은 '14 times as large as'라고 쓸 수 있다.

20 마지막 문단에 따르면, 학생들은 음식물 쓰레기를 줄이기 위해서 접시 위의 음식을 남기지 않았고 접시까지 먹었다고 한다.

21 지은이네 반 학생들이 오래된 면으로 된 셔츠를 가져 왔는지에 대해서는 언급된 바 없다.

22 ⓓPlease give us one simple tip for reduce trash.를 Please give us one simple tip for reducing trash.로 고치면 어법상 적절한 문장이 된다.

23 민지가 만든 천 냅킨에 대해 친구들은 좋아했다고 언급했다.

24 "그것들은 민지에 의해 만들어졌다."라는 수동태 문장은 'They were made by Minji.'라고 쓸 수 있다.

25 두 번째 문단에서는 환경을 위해 종이 냅킨을 쓰는 대신 천으로 만든 냅킨을 대신 썼다고 이야기하고 있다. 따라서 문단의 제목으로 가장 적절한 것은 ④ Use Cloth Napkins(천으로 된 냅킨을 사용하기)이다.

26 마지막 문단의 준하의 말에 따르면, 학생들은 접시 위에 있는 음식들을 다 먹어 남기지 않았다고 한다.

27 larger 더 큰 / less 덜

28 ⓐthe ice cream은 아이스크림을 가리키는 반면, 나머지는 모두 the plates(접시들)를 가리킨다.

29 주어진 단어들을 배열하면, 'that were not wrapped at all'이

된다.

30 민수와 학급 친구들이 선물을 포장하지 않기로 한 이유는 몇몇 포장지들이 쉽게 재활용하기 힘들기 때문이라고 민수가 언급했다.

31 (1) 동사 give가 쓰인 능동태 문장을 수동태 문장으로 바꿀 경우 어떤 목적어가 주어 자리에 오느냐에 따라 문장 구조가 변한다. 간접 목적어(~에게)가 주어가 될 경우, 'be+given+직접 목적어(~을/를)+by 명사'의 형식이 된다. 반면 직접 목적어가 주어가 될 경우, 'be+given+to 간접 목적어+by 명사'의 형식이 된다.

(2) 능동태 문장을 수동태 문장으로 바꿀 때, 수동태 문장의 주어 자리에는 능동태 문장의 목적어가 오고, by 다음에는 능동태 문장의 주어를 쓴다. 수동태는 현재, 과거, 미래 시제로 쓸 수 있고, 'be동사+동사의 과거분사'에서 be동사로 시제를 표현한다.

Lesson 7 (기말) · 1회

> **01** ③ **02** ⑤
> **03** The school sent me a brochure containing the information I needed.
> **04** ② **05** ④ **06** Why don't you try making it at home?
> **07** ① **08** Look at the two men learning Korean. **09** ③
> **10** ④ **11** Are you interested in playing the ukulele?
> **12** ②,④ **13** ④ **14** ② **15** ⑤ **16** ② **17** ③ **18** ②
> **19** ① **20** ⑤ **21** ③ **22** Practice makes perfect **23** ⑤
> **24** ② **25** ③ **26** ⑤ **27** ④ **28** ② **29** ① **30** ⑤

01 monster는 '괴물'이라는 뜻을 가진 단어이다.

02 include는 '포함하다', '포함시키다'라는 뜻을 가진 단어이다.

03 빈칸에는 '관계대명사+be동사'가 생략되고 현재분사 containing (포함하다)이 들어가는 것이 어법상 적절하다.

04 유리 공예에 관심이 있느냐는 A의 질문에 대해 "응. 난 스포츠에 관심 있어."라는 B의 대답은 흐름상 자연스럽지 않다.

05 위 대화에 따르면, Chris가 직접 작품을 만든 것이 아니라 Jenny가 직접 만든 것이다.

06 "Why don't you ~?"는 "~하는 게 어떠니?"라는 뜻으로 상대방에게 무언가를 권유할 때 쓸 수 있는 표현이다.

07 위 글에서는 선생님이 아이스크림 만드는 법에 대해 순서대로 설명하고 있다. 따라서 빈칸에 들어갈 말로 가장 적절한 것은 순서대로 First, Next, Finally이다.

08 the two men을 수식하는 현재분사인 learning을 써서 Look at the two men learning Korean.이라고 영작할 수 있다.

09 A가 "좋은 작품이다! 내 생각엔 너의 그림은 가을 느낌을 잘 표현하고 있는 것 같아."라고 말하자, B는 고맙다고 대답하면서 A에게 그림에 관심이 있냐고 묻는다. A는 그렇다고 대답하고 주말에 수

업을 듣는다고 말한다. 이에 B는 "그건 몰랐네."라고 대답하는 순서로 이어지는 것이 대화의 흐름상 가장 적절하다.

10 A가 B의 공연에 대해 좋았다고 이야기하자 B는 고맙다고 대답하면서 우쿨렐레 연주하는 것에 관심이 있냐고 묻는다. A는 그렇다고 대답하면서 우쿨렐레를 가르쳐 줄 수 있는지 묻고, 이에 B가 그렇다고 대답하는 순서로 이어지는 것이 대화의 흐름상 가장 적절하다.

11 전치사 in 뒤에는 동명사 playing이라고 쓰는 것이 어법상 적절하다.

12 ⓑI'm writing with a brush.→ You're writing with a brush. / ⓓWhy do you think?→ What do you think?로 고쳐야 흐름상 적절한 문장이 된다.

13 (A)You got it. "바로 그거야." / (B) You did a good job! "너 잘 했다!" / (C) Why not? "왜 안 되겠어?"

14 위 대화에 따르면, 미나는 춤을 뜻하는 한국어 단어를 썼다.

15 ⑤collecting은 동명사로 문장에서 목적어 역할을 한다. 나머지 ~ing 형은 모두 현재분사로 명사를 수식하는 역할을 한다.

16 문맥상 (A)에는 오늘날에 캘리그래피가 우리 주변에서 많이 쓰이고 있다는 내용이 들어가야 적절하다. 따라서 ② can be seen in many places가 정답이다.

17 ⓒNo one uses calligraphy works today.라는 문장은 오늘날 캘리그래피가 우리 주변에서 많이 쓰인다는 글의 요지와는 무관하다.

18 (가)It은 진주어 to부정사구를 대신하는 가주어 it이다. ②It은 인칭대명사로 '그것'을 가리킨다.

19 위 글에서 캘리그래피가 사용되는 곳으로 movie posters, book covers, music CDs, and clothes을 예로 들었다.

20 위 글에서는 캘리그래피가 우리 주변에서 많이 쓰이고 있다고 이야기하고 있다. 따라서 위 글의 제목으로 가장 적절한 것은 ⑤ Calligraphy in Our Everyday Lives이다.

21 build up ~을 만들다, ~을 창조하다

22 Practice makes perfect.: "연습이 완벽을 만든다."라는 뜻으로 자꾸 연습하면 잘하게 된다는 것을 의미한다.

23 첫 문단에서 글씨를 통해 감정을 표현하는 것은 요즘 인기 있다고 이야기 하고 몇몇 작품을 살펴보자고 한다, (C)에서 오른쪽에 있는 예술 작품에서 단어가 홍시의 이미지를 포함하고 있다고 설명한다. 이어서 (B)에서 It은 hongsi를 가리키며 왼쪽 작품에 대해 이야기한다, 이어서 (A)에서는 왼쪽 작품에 대한 추가 설명과 두 작품 모두 아름다운 글씨를 통해 가을의 느낌을 표현하고 있다고 이어지는 것이 글의 흐름상 가장 적절하다.

24 위 글에서는 캘리그래피를 소개하고 예술 작품을 예로 들어 그것이 무엇인지에 대해서 설명하고 있다.

25 (가) to express: 가주어 It-진주어 to 구문의 진주어 / (나) walking: a happy woman을 수식하는 현재분사 / (다) is

called: 주어가 This kind of art이므로 수동형 동사인 is called 가 들어가는 것이 어법상 적절하다.

26 위 글에서 예시로 든 두 예술 작품 모두 한국어와 한자를 썼다고는 언급되어 있지 않다.

27 ⓓSame writing tools led to different styles of calligraphy.는 Different writing tools led to different styles of calligraphy.로 고치는 것이 글의 흐름상 적절하다.

28 (A)It는 인칭대명사로, 앞서 언급된 단수 명사인 ② The Canterbury Tales를 가리킨다.

29 (B)to make는 to부정사의 부사적 용법으로 사용되었다. 따라서 이와 쓰임이 같은 것은 ① He went to Paris to study art.(그는 예술을 공부하기 위해 파리에 갔다.)이다.

30 위 글에서는 캘리그래피가 오래 전부터 사용되어 왔고, 전 세계 곳 곳에서 발견할 수 있다고 이야기하고 있다.

Lesson 7 (기말) 2회

01 <보기>의 주어진 단어들은 반의어 관계의 단어들이다. 이와 관계 가 같지 않은 것은 ③ solve(해결하다) - solution(해결책)이다.

02 ③ express는 '특정한'이라는 뜻이 아니라 '급행의'라는 뜻으로 사용되었다.

03 ② It는 인칭대명사로 '그것'이라고 해석된다. 나머지는 모두 진주 어 to부정사 구를 대신하는 가주어 It이다.

04 위 대화에서 민지는 동물에 관심 있다고("Yes, I am. I'm good at taking care of them.") 말했다.

05 "Are you interested in ~?"은 "~에 관심이 있니?"라는 뜻으로 상대방의 관심사를 묻는 표현이다. 이와 같은 표현으로는 ④ "Do you like to부정사[동명사] ~?"를 쓸 수 있다.

06 (A) James가 미나의 캘리그래피를 보고 재밌어 보인다고 말했으 므로 이에 대한 미나의 질문은 ⓔ Are you interested in calligraphy?이 적절하다. / (B) 미나가 자신이 쓴 캘리그래피를 보여주고 있으므로 ⓑ What do you think?가 들어가는 것이 적 절하다. / (C) 미나가 자신이 쓴 글씨를 보여주자, James가 ⓕ Well done!이라고 반응하는 것이 흐름상 적절하다. / (D) James가 자신도 써 봐도 되냐고 물어봤으므로 미나가 ⓓ Why not?이라고 반응하는 것이 흐름상 적절하다.

07 위 대화에 따르면, James는 캘리그래피를 해 보고 싶어 하지만 펜 으로 써보고 싶어한다는 내용은 언급되어 있지 않다.

08 ⑤ How often does Mina practice calligraphy?(미나는 얼 마나 자주 캘리그래피를 연습하는가?)에 대해서는 위 대화에서 언 급된 바 없다.

09 ⓐ fixing → fixed / ⓑ writing → written / ⓔ slept → sleeping으로 고쳐야 어법상 적절한 문장이 된다.

10 Mike는 그림에서 식탁에 앉아 샌드위치를 먹고 있다.

11 A는 한복에 관심 있냐고 물었고 B의 대답을 들은 후, "그럼 무엇 에 관심이 있니?"라고 다시 묻는다. 따라서 빈칸에 들어갈 말로 가 장 적절한 것은 ④ Not really.(별로.)이다.

12 대화의 흐름상 ① What is it made of?(그건 무엇으로 만들어졌 니?)가 들어가는 것이 가장 자연스럽다.

13 ① What is the title?(제목은 무엇인가?)에 대해서는 위 대화에 서 언급된 바 없다.

14 ④ playing은 동명사로 문장에서 목적어 역할을 한다. 나머지 -ing 형은 모두 현재분사로 명사를 수식하는 역할을 한다.

15 ⓐ works 작품들 / ⓑ has worked (과거의 어느 시점부터 현재 까지) 작업해 왔다

16 위 글에 따르면, Jan Coveney가 한지 공예에 관심을 갖게 된 이 유는 한국의 예술이 아주 멋지다고 생각했기 때문이다.

17 ⓔIt was wrote with a pen.은 It was written with a pen.으 로 고치는 것이 어법상 적절하다.

18 빈칸 뒤에 such as a brush or a pen이라고 예시를 들었다. 따라서 빈칸에 들어갈 말로 가장 적절한 것은 ⑤ instruments(도구)이다.

19 위 글에 따르면, 다른 글쓰기 도구의 사용은 다른 캘리그래피 스타 일로 이어졌다고 언급되어 있다.

20 a strong feeling of shock and fear(강한 충격과 두려움의 감 정)이라는 뜻을 가진 단어는 위 글에서 언급된 바 없다.

21 위 글에서 다음에는 미국 작품이 소개될 것이라고 언급된 바 없다.

22 (A) widely: 널리, 광범위하게
(B) some examples가 주어이므로 are가 들어가는 것이 적절하 다.
(C) keep -ing: 계속해서 ~하다

23 위 글에서 판타지 소설의 제목이 괴물을 상기시킨다는 내용은 언급 되어 있지 않다.

24 to부정사(구)가 주어로 쓰일 경우, 대부분 주어 자리에 형식상의 주어(가주어) 'it'을 쓰고 원래 주어(진주어)인 to부정사(구)는 문 장의 끝으로 보낸다.

25 우리 주변에서 캘리그래피를 찾아 볼 수 있는 곳으로는 movie posters, book covers, music CDs, and clothes 등을 예시로 들었다.

26 '몇몇 예술 작품을 살펴 보자.'라는 문장이 들어가기에 가장 적절

한 곳은 감정을 표현하는 예술 작품을 예로 들고 있는 곳 앞인 (B)
이다.

27 ⓐit은 진주어인 to부정사구를 대신하는 가주어 it이다. 이와 쓰임이 같은 것은 ⑤ It is important to study foreign languages.(외국어를 배우는 것은 중요하다.)이다.

28 요즘 감정을 표현할 때 쓰이는 것으로 인기 있는 것은 ③ Handwriting(손글씨)이다.

29 ⓑwalking은 명사 a happy woman을 수식하는 현재분사이다. 이와 쓰임이 다른 것은 ② Sleeping(동명사)과 ③ swimming(동명사)이다.

30 왼쪽에 있는 작품은 한글 단어와 한자를 보여 주고 있다고 했다.

Lesson 8 (기말) 〔1회〕

> **01** ① **02** ②
> **03** He is so smart that he can answer any questions.　**04** ⑤
> **05** ③　**06** ③　**07** ⑤　**08** ②　**09** ④
> **10** The new cover will help people (to) ride bicycles safely.
> **11** ④　**12** ③　**13** ④
> **14** I'm thinking of putting a step box here below the switch.
> **15** ②　**16** ④　**17** ①　**18** ⑤　**19** thick glasses
> **20** the boy bring the ball　　**21** ③　**22** ⑤　**23** ⑤
> **24** old or weak people **25** ④　**26** ①　**27** ③　**28** ②　**29** ③
> **30** ④

01 '기계를 켜거나 끄기 위해 사용하는 전기 장치'라는 영영 풀이가 의미하는 것은 ① switch(스위치)이다.

02 목적격보어로 동사원형을 취하는 동사는 let, make, have, help 등이 있다.

03 'so+형용사[부사]+that+주어+동사' 구문은 '매우 …해서 ~하다'라는 의미이며 원인과 그에 따른 결과를 서술할 때 쓰인다.

04 ⑤ play → to play로 고쳐야 어법상 적절한 문장이 된다.

05 위 그림에 따르면, 소리가 너무 시끄러워서 A가 이에 대해 불만을 표현하고 있다. 따라서 빈칸에 들어갈 말로 가장 적절한 것은 ③ The music is too loud.(음악이 너무 시끄럽다.)이다.

06 대화의 흐름상, 전기 스위치의 위치가 높아 미소가 혼자서는 불을 켜고 끌 수 없다는 걸 들고 아버지 또한 그것이 불만스럽다고 말하는 것이 가장 자연스럽다.

07 ⑤ What will Grandma do to help Miso?(할머니는 미소를 돕기 위해 무엇을 할 것인가?)에 대해서는 위 대화에서 언급되어 있지 않다.

08 ⓐlow → high / ⓒabove → below / ⓓsmaller → bigger / ⓔput → turn으로 고쳐야 어법상 적절한 문장이 된다.

09 위 대화에 따르면, 아버지는 미소와 할머니를 위해 스위치를 더 큰 것으로 바꾼다고("And I'll change the switch to a bigger one.") 말했다.

10 준사역동사 help는 목적보어로 동사원형 또는 to부정사를 취한다.

11 ⓓI'm happy about it, too.를 I'm not happy about it, either.로 고쳐야 흐름상 적절한 문장이 된다.

12 change A to B: A를 B로 바꾸다

13 위 대화에서 A는 스위치를 더 큰 것으로 바꾸면 할머니가 좋아하실 것이라고 말했다.

14 'I'm thinking of -ing'는 '~할까 생각 중이다'라는 뜻으로 의도나 계획을 나타낼 때 쓰는 표현이다.

15 ⓐ her in danger → herself in danger / ⓓ walk well without a stick → to walk well without a stick / ⓔ made her hearing badly → made her hearing bad로 고쳐야 어법상 적절한 문장이 된다.

16 위 글에 따르면, 패트리샤는 노약자들이 겪는 어려움을 직접 경험해 보려고 했다.

17 위 글에 따르면, 여행의 목적에 대해서는 언급된 바 없다.

18 여행의 모든 순간이 그녀에게는 매우 힘들었지만 그녀는 115개의 도시를 방문했다고 한다. 따라서 빈칸에 들어갈 말로 가장 적절한 것은 ⑤ but(그러나)이다.

19 인칭대명사 them은 thick glasses(두꺼운 안경)을 가리킨다.

20 사역동사 let, make, have는 목적보어로 동사원형을 취한다.

21 During+시간: ~ 동안에

22 ⓐ a 26-years-old designer → a 26-year-old designer ⓑ was often asked → often asked로 고쳐야 어법상 적절한 문장이 된다.

23 ⑤ What was the other designers' reaction to her suggestion?(패트리샤의 제안에 대한 다른 디자이너들의 반응은 무엇이었나?)는 안 된다고 차갑게 대답했다고 언급되어 있다.

24 (A)는 old or weak people(노약자들)을 가리킨다.

25 (C)는 '신발이 너무 불편해서 지팡이 없이는 잘 걷지 못했다'는 의미의 문장이다. 따라서 이와 같은 의미의 문장은 ④ The shoes were so uncomfortable that she couldn't walk well without a stick.이다.

26 ⓐgo through는 '~을 겪다'라는 뜻으로 사용되었다.

27 모두를 위한 디자인의 예시로 든 버스는 ③ low-floor bus (저상 버스)이다.

28 위 글에 따르면, 패트리샤 무어가 고안한 "모두를 위한 디자인"의 특징은 누구나 쉽고 안전하게 쓸 수 있는 것이라고 한다.

29 패트리샤 무어가 고안한 "모두를 위한 디자인"의 특징은 누구나 쉽고 안전하게 쓸 수 있는 것이다. 따라서 빈칸에는 all(모두)가 들어가는 것이 적절하다.

30 위 글에서는 누구나 쉽고 안전하게 쓸 수 있는 제품을 고안해 낸 패트리샤 무어와 그녀의 "모두를 위한 디자인"에 대해서 설명하고 있다. 따라서 위 글의 제목으로 가장 적절한 것은 ④ The Beginning of Universal Design and Its Example(보편적인 디자인과 그 예시)이다.

Lesson 8 (기말) 2회

01 ④ 02 ③
03 My brother is too young to understand the words. 04 ⑤
05 ① 06 ⑤ 07 ④ 08 ③
09 (A) high (B) brother (C) size 10 ④ 11 ② 12 ②
13 me watch TV 14 (1) rich enough to (2) too young to
15 ③ 16 ② 17 ① 18 ② 19 ④ 20 ① 21 ② 22 ③
23 여행에서 나이든 사람들이 겪는 어려움을 느껴 본 것 24 ①
25 are helping people (to) live better lives 26 ④ 27 ②
28 The glasses were so thick that she couldn't see well with them.
29 The shoes were too uncomfortable for her to walk well without a stick.
30 ④

01 (a) period: 기간 / (b) handle: 손잡이

02 'I'm thinking of -ing'는 '나는 ~할까 생각 중이다'라는 뜻으로 의도나 계획을 나타낼 때 쓰는 표현이다.

03 'so ~ that 주어+can't' 구문은 '너무 ~해서 …할 수 없다'라는 의미로 'too ~ to+동사원형' 구문으로 바꿔 쓸 수 있다.

04 A의 말에 대한 B의 반응이 "그것에 무슨 문제가 있니?"라는 말이었다. 따라서 빈칸에 들어갈 말로 가장 적절한 것은 불만에 대해서 표현하고 있는 ⑤ I'm not happy about이다.

05 'I'm thinking of -ing'는 '나는 ~할까 생각 중이다'라는 뜻으로 의도나 계획을 나타낼 때 쓰는 표현이다. 따라서 위 대화의 흐름상 빈칸에는 ① adding Braille on the sign(표지판 위에 점자를 추가하는 것)이 들어가는 것이 가장 적절하다.

06 위 대화에서는 스위치가 너무 높아 전등을 켜고 끌 수 없는 미소를 돕기 위해 스위치 아래에 스텝 박스를 놓는 것을 고려 중이라는 내용이 들어가는 것이 가장 적절하다.

07 위 대화의 후반부에, 아들은 미소가 높이 위치한 전기 스위치에 닿을 수 있도록 스텝 박스를 스위치 아래 놓아둘 것("I'm thinking of putting a step box here below the switch.")이라고 말했다.

08 ⓒhappy는 unhappy로 고치는 것이 문맥상 자연스럽다.

09 (A) high: 높은 (B) brother: 오빠 (C) size: 크기

10 아버지는 미소와 할머니를 위해 무엇을 할 것이냐는 A의 질문에

대해 "더 예쁜 것으로 스위치를 바꿀 것이다"라는 B의 대답은 위 대화의 내용상 적절하지 않다.

11 'so ~ that 주어+can't[couldn't]' 구문은 '너무 ~해서 …할 수 없다[없었다]'라는 의미로 'too ~ to+동사원형' 구문으로 바꿔 쓸 수 있다.

12 ② can't → couldn't로 고쳐야 어법상 적절한 문장이 된다.

13 사역동사 let, make, have는 목적격보어로 동사원형을 취한다.

14 (1) rich enough to+동사원형: ~할 만큼 부자인
(2) too young to+동사원형: 너무 어려서 ~할 수 없는

15 ③ too sweet that he can't → so sweet that he couldn't로 고쳐야 어법상 적절한 문장이 된다.

16 ⓑWithout은 With로 고쳐야 문맥상 적절한 문장이 된다.

17 (A)에 들어갈 단어는 a stick(지팡이)이다.

18 위 글에 따르면, 지팡이가 없이는 잘 걸을 수 없었다고 언급되어 있다.

19 ④ Why did the woman decide to travel around many cities?(그 여자는 왜 많은 도시들을 여행하기로 결정하였는가?)에 대해서는 위 글에서 언급되어 있지 않다.

20 get on: ~에 타다

21 ⓑOne example of her universal design ideas are low-floor buses.는 One example of her universal design ideas is low-floor buses.로 고쳐야 어법상 적절한 문장이 된다.

22 (A) such a[an] 형용사+명사+that+주어+동사 ~: 아주 ~해서 …할 수 있다
(B) without: ~ 없이
(C) for example: 예를 들어

23 '이 경험'은 앞서 언급 되어 있듯이, 여행에서 패트리샤가 느낀 노약자들이 겪는 어려움을 의미한다.

24 위 글에서는 패트리샤 무어라는 디자이너와 그녀의 경험을 통해 "모두를 위한 디자인"에 대해서 설명하고 있다.

25 준사역동사 help는 목적보어로 동사원형 또는 to부정사를 취한다.

26 주어진 단어를 의미에 맞게 배열하면 what made her do all this?가 된다.

27 위 글에 따르면, 다른 디자이너들은 패트리샤의 노약자를 위한 디자인에 대한 제안을 거절했다고 한다.

28 'too ~ to+동사원형' 구문은 '너무 ~해서 …할 수 없다'라는 의미로 'so~ that 주어+can't[couldn't]'로 바꿔 쓸 수 있다.

29 'so ~ that 주어+can't[couldn't]' 구문은 '너무 ~해서 …할 수 없다[없었다]'라는 의미로 'too ~ to+동사원형' 구문로 바꿔 쓸 수 있다.

30 다른 디자이너들은 패트리샤의 제안에 어떻게 반응했냐는 A의 질문에 대해 "그들은 할머니의 옷을 입고 불편한 신발을 신고 두꺼운 안경을 썼어."라는 B의 대답은 본문의 내용으로 미루어 볼 때 자연스럽지 않다.

값 6,000원

적중 **100** + 특별부록

Plan B

우리학교
최신기출

천재 · 정사열 교과서를 배우는

학교 시험문제 분석 · 모음 · 해설집

전국단위 학교 시험문제 수집 및 분석
출제 빈도가 높은 문제 위주로 선별
문제 풀이에 필요한 상세한 해설

중2-2
영어

천재 · 정사열

값 6,000원